Time Out
Istanbul

Penguin Books

PENGUIN BOOKS

Published by the Penguin Group
Penguin Books Ltd, 27 Wrights Lane, London W8 5TZ, England
Penguin Books USA Inc., 375 Hudson Street, New York, New York 10014, USA
Penguin Books Australia Ltd, Ringwood, Victoria, Australia
Penguin Books Canada Ltd, 10 Alcorn Avenue, Toronto, Ontario, Canada M4V 3B2
Penguin Books (NZ) Ltd, 182-190 Wairau Road, Auckland 10, New Zealand

Penguin Books Ltd, Registered Offices: Harmondsworth, Middlesex, England

First edition 2001
10 9 8 7 6 5 4 3 2 1

Copyright © Time Out Group Ltd, 2001
All rights reserved

Colour reprographics by Westside Digital Media, 9 Bridle Lane, London W1
and Precise Litho, 34-35 Great Sutton Street, London EC1
Printed and bound by Cayfosa-Quebecor, Ctra. de Caldes, Km 3 08 130 Sta, Perpètua de Mogoda, Barcelona, Spain

Edited and designed by
Time Out Guides Limited
Universal House
251 Tottenham Court Road
London W1T 7AB
Tel + 44 (0) 20 7813 3000
Fax + 44 (0) 20 7813 6001
Email guides@timeout.com
www.timeout.com

Editorial

Editor Andrew Humphreys
Consultant editor Ken Dakan
Researcher Yeşim Erdem Holland
Copy Editing Desmond McGrath
Proofreader Lisa Osborne
Indexer Julie Hurrell

Editorial Director Peter Fiennes
Series Editor Ruth Jarvis
Managing Editor Dave Rimmer
Deputy Series Editor Jonathan Cox
Editorial Assistant Jenny Noden

Design

Art Director John Oakey
Art Editor Mandy Martin
Senior Designer Scott Moore
Designers Benjamin de Lotz, Lucy Grant
Scanning/Imaging Dan Conway
Picture Editor Kerri Miles
Deputy Picture Editor Olivia Duncan-Jones
Picture Researcher Cecile Borra
Ad Make-up Glen Impey

Advertising

Group Advertisement Director Lesley Gill
Sales Director Mark Phillips
Advertisement Sales (Istanbul) Ajans Medya
Advertising Assistant Catherine Shepherd

Administration

Publisher Tony Elliott
Managing Director Mike Hardwick
Financial Director Kevin Ellis
Marketing Director Christine Cort
General Manager Nichola Coulthard
Production Manager Mark Lamond
Production Controller Samantha Furniss
Accountant Sarah Bostock

Features in this guide were written and researched by:
Introduction Andrew Humphreys. **History** Andrew Humphreys, David O'Byrne (*Atta Turk!, Swords of misrule, The emperor's new nose* David O'Byrne; *At the drop of a hat, Turkish delights* Jeremy Seal). **Istanbul Today** Lucy Wood (*UEFA yes, EU no* Ben Holland). **Istanbul for Women** Lucy Wood (*Decoding the headscarf* Laurie Udesky). **Architecture** Andrew Humphreys, David O'Byrne (*Keeping up with the domes's* Andrew Humphreys; *The height of bad taste* Jon Gorvett). **Accommodation** Dominic Whiting (*Bed, board & legends* Andrew Humphreys). **Sightseeing introduction** Andrew Humphreys. **Sultanahmet** Jon Gorvett (*Harem-scarem* Andrew Humphreys). **The Bazaar Quarter** Jon Gorvett (*Bullets over Beyazıt* Jon Gorvett). **Eminönü & the Golden Horn** Jon Gorvett (*The extravagant express* Andrew Humphreys). **Beyoğlu** David O'Byrne (*Flying the flag* David O'Byrne; *The other Istanbul* Ken Dakan). **Karaköy to Beşiktaş** David O'Byrne (*A right old madam* Ken Dakan). **Ortaköy to Rumeli Hisarı** Dominic Whiting. **The Asian Shore** David O'Byrne. **Museums** Jon Gorvett. **Restaurants** Roni Askey-Doran, Ken Dakan, Jon Gorvett, Justin Huggler, Pelin Turgut, Laurie Udesky, Dominic Whiting (*Çiçek Pasajı & Nevizade, Dessert storm, The offal truth* Laurie Udesky). **Cafés & Bars** Roni Askey-Doran, Ken Dakan, Andrew Humphreys, Lucy Wood (*Hava nargile* Yeşim Erdem Holland). **Shops & Services** Heather Brown, Ken Dakan, Yeşim Erdem Holland (*Mall contents, Shopping the bazaar, Sweet stuff, The rug trade, What is 'Turkish' fashion?* Ken Dakan). **Istanbul by Season** Nicolas Monceau (*Chefs' special, Slippery people* Laurie Udesky). **Children** Amy Chaple. **Film** Nicolas Monceau (*Midnight Express keeps on running* Jon Gorvett; *Shooting more than films* Lucy Wood). **Galleries** Heather Brown. **Gay & Lesbian** Roni Askey-Doran, Ken Dakan (*Sex-change star shows the way* Ken Dakan). **Hamams** Sirpil Karacan. **Music: Rock, World & Jazz** Roni Askey-Doran, James Snow (*Good gyrations* Ken Dakan). **Music: Turkish** Bob Cohen, Brenna MacCrimmon (*Buying an instrument* Bob Cohen; *Hava Nagila again* Brenna MacCrimmon; *Sultans of kitsch* Ken Dakan). **Nightlife** Daniel Shabdukarimov (*Baywatch on the Bosphorus* Ken Dakan). **Performing Arts** Nicolas Monceau (*Karagöz* Nicolas Monceau). **Sport & Fitness** Ken Dakan, Ben Holland (*Welcome to Hell!* Ben Holland). **Getting Started** Dominic Whiting. **Upper Bosphorus** Jon Gorvett. **The Princes' Islands** Jon Gorvett. **Edirne** Jon Gorvett. **The Marmara Islands** Dominic Whiting. **Bursa** Dominic Whiting. **Iznik & Termal** Jon Gorvett. **Çanakkale & Gallipoli** Bill Sellars. **Assos & Troy** Dominic Whiting. **Directory** Ken Dakan, Jon Gorvett, Andrew Humphreys (*The Traffic Monster, Waiting for the big one* Jon Gorvett; *Bored, or just having regular sex?* Ben Holland).

The Editor would like to thank the following: Sophie Blacksell, Chris Bohn, Kevin Ebbutt, Will Fulford-Jones, Yeşim Erdem Holland, Nilay Keskin, Lesley McCave, Pierre Monceau and Pozitif Productions. Extra-special thanks to Ken Dakan and Lucy Wood.

Maps by JS Graphics, 17 Beadles Lane, Old Oxted, Surrey RH8 9JG. Digital data supplied by Apa Publications GmbH & Co. Verlag KG (Singapore branch).

Photography by Hadley Kincade except: page 6, 10, 15, 21, 73 AKG; page 19 The Kobal Collection; page 20 The Advertising Archives; page 201 Associated Press; page 231 Empics; page 245 Robert Harding; page 246 Turkish Information Office; page 249, 250 Istanbul Tourist Office; page 251 Robert Harding Picture Library; page 253 James Davis Worldwide Photographic Library; page 256 Ersin Alok; page 258 Explore Turkey.com; page 259 Eye Ubiquitous; page 261, 263 Trip; page 264 Britstock-IFA.
The following photographs were supplied by the featured establishments pages 178, 179, 183, 192, 211, 224, 226, 229.

Contents

Introduction

Check in your preconceptions at the door. PKK bombings, bonkers football fans, earthquakes, Islam and döner kebabs. In terms of bad press, Istanbul often seems to rank somewhere below Baghdad. But while all of these things are unarguably a part of Istanbul, they're just the smallest part of a much bigger, more appealing picture.

Think imperial mosques silhouetted against deep blue moonlit skies; glittery golden shop fronts in dimly lit bazaars; outdoor seafood dining on waterfront piazzas. All clichés too, perhaps, but all present and, clichés or not, all wonderfully Istanbul experiences.

British Designer of the Year Hussein Chalayan rates the Turkish capital as his favourite European city. The 'New York of the Middle East', is how he describes it. Sure, his Turkish roots might prejudice his opinions but he has solid reasons for loving the place. Venue of choice for Chalayan when in town is a ruined old British prison lovingly retored by a local architect and run as a restaurant serving Caucasian home-cooking. It's the perfect example of what, at this exact moment in time, makes Istanbul so great:

a fusion of tradition and internationalism, served up with panache.

Right now, the city is full of such ventures, particularly when it comes to cafés and bars. In our opinion, Istanbul trumps many Western cities in its diversity of venues and 'anything goes' attitude. Bounce round Beyoğlu from rooftop terrace to cellar dive to chic wine bar to the smokers' paradise of the nargile cafe. And keep on going because there's no such thing as closing time.

Youthful despite its great age, Istanbul is a mass of contradictions. The root of all this is that the city is still coming to terms with itself. Like its unique geography, straddling Europe and Asia, its inhabitants are in the process of forging an identity, one that is split between two poles, East and West. But what Istanbul is increasingly coming to realise is that it need not commit itself one way or the other. The Turks are discovering that there is such a thing as a viable third way, neither wholly East nor wholly West, but just cosmopolitan, cultivated Istanbul. Straddling two worlds and proudly offering the best of both.

ABOUT TIME OUT GUIDES

This is the first edition of the *Time Out Istanbul Guide*, one of an expanding series of *Time Out* guides produced by the people behind London and New York's successful listings magazine. Our team of writers and researchers, residents of Istanbul and experts in their fields, have plumbed the deepest cellar bars and peered from the highest minaret tops to compile this guide, certainly the most comprehensive collection of listings, reviews and informed comment yet to be published on the Turkish capital. It provides all the most up-to-date information you'll need to explore Istanbul or read up on its background, whether you're a local or a first-time visitor.

THE LOWDOWN ON THE LISTINGS

Above all, we've tried to make this book as useful as possible. Addresses, telephone numbers, websites, transport information, opening times, admission prices and credit card details are all included in our listings, where relevant. And, as far as possible, we've given details of facilities, services and events, all checked and correct as we went to press. However, owners and managers can change

their arrangements at any time. Before you go out of your way, we'd advise you to telephone and check opening times, ticket prices and other particulars.

While every effort has been made to ensure the accuracy of the information contained in this guide, the publishers cannot accept responsibility for any errors it may contain.

PRICES AND PAYMENT

The prices we've supplied should be treated as guidelines, not gospel. Fluctuating exchange rates as well as rampant inflation can cause charges, in shops and restaurants particularly, to change rapidly. Inflation is also the reason that we quote prices in US dollars throughout this book and not in Turkish Lira.

We have noted whether venues such as shops, hotels and restaurants accept credit cards or not, but have only listed the major cards – American Express (**AmEx**), Diners Club (**DC**),

There is an online version of this guide, as well as weekly events listings for more than 30 international cities, at http://www.timeout.com

MasterCard (**MC**) and Visa (**V**). Some businesses may accept other cards, a few may even take travellers' cheques.

For every restaurant we have given the price range for main courses as well as set menus where relevant. Accommodation prices take seasonal fluctuations into account.

If prices vary wildly from those we've quoted, ask whether there's a good reason. If not, go elsewhere. We aim to give the best and most up-to-date advice, so we always want to know if you've been badly treated or overcharged.

THE LIE OF THE LAND
Istanbul is nightmarish when it comes to finding your way around. Streets can have two or more names but quite often nobody seems to know what any of them are anyway. Postal codes are not used outside of the newer northern suburbs and even building numbers are frequently missing. Turkish addresses tend to be things like 'Across from the green mosque beside the old bridge'. But in almost all cases we have managed to provide a street name and number, and the name of the district. We have used the names of the main central districts (Sultanahmet, The Bazaar Quarter, Eminönü, Beyoğlu, The Asian Shore) as main divisions in our Sightseeing section and in chapters that are organised by area. Map references indicate the page and square on the street maps at the back of the book.

TELEPHONE NUMBERS
To phone Istanbul from outside Turkey, first dial the international code 00, then 90 (the code for Turkey) then either 212 (the city code for Istanbul's European shore) or 216 (the city code for Istanbul's Asian Shore), and finally the local

seven-digit number. Within Istanbul, if you are on the European side only dial the city code if you are phoning the Asian side and vice versa. We have included these codes in our listings.

ESSENTIAL INFORMATION
For all the practical information you might need for visiting the city, including visa and customs information, emergency telephone numbers and local transport, turn to the **Directory** chapter at the back of the guide. It starts on page 266.

MAPS
The map section at the back of this book includes useful orientation and overview maps of the country and city (starting on page 298; the street index begins on page 313).

LET US KNOW WHAT YOU THINK
We hope you enjoy the *Time Out Istanbul Guide*, and we'd like to know what you think of it. We welcome tips for places that you consider we should include in future editions and take note of your criticism of our choices. There's a reader's reply card at the back of this book for your feedback – or you can email us on istanbulguide@timeout.com.

WELCME

to an amazing network.

Turkish Airlines provides non-stop service to many destinations in 53 different countries over 4 continents. Flying in total to 78 international and 36 domestic destinations, we offer some of the best connections especially to the Middle, and the Far East regions.

In Context

History

First Byzantium, then Constantinople, now Istanbul; here history is writ large… and is often found wearing a hat.

Few cities have occupied the imagination as Istanbul has. Fought over throughout its history by armies from western Europe, the Middle East and Central Asia, in succession capital and centre of two of the greatest empires the world has seen, intriguing, perplexing and often frustrating, it still has the power to captivate as few other cities can.

> **'It's likely that the "clashing rocks" in the legend of the Argonauts were inspired by the Bosphorus Straits.'**

Most books will tell you that Istanbul's importance stems from being the only city in the world to bestride two continents, Europe and Asia. But in fact it's the other way round – the history of the area defined what we today know as the continents. The unique geography of the 35-kilometre (22-mile) Bosphorus Straits, with its steeply sloping shores running almost due north-

south, must have suggested to early seafarers that this indeed was where two worlds met.

The idea was already well established by the fifth century BC, when Herodotus was able to devote much of his *Histories* to the conflict between Greece and Persia, East and West, defining the 'them and us' attitude that still dominates relations between inhabitants of the two continents and leads every writer to suppose that Istanbul must be a bridge between the two.

BLIND BEGINNINGS

Despite its geographical advantages, prehistoric finds around Istanbul have been scarce, most likely due to the sheer intensity of occupation that has followed. Those that have been identified indicate that the area has been occupied since the first humans spread out of Africa. Neolithic sites from around 7000 BC have been found close to modern-day Kadıköy and Bronze Age remains dated to around 3200 BC have been unearthed in Sultanahmet, but these early chapters are still blank pages waiting to be written.

Around 1600 BC, seafaring Greeks had begun moving out of the Ionian peninsula, founding colonies around the Aegean and Mediterranean. By 750 BC they had passed through the Bosphorus and established settlements on the Black Sea coast of Anatolia and in the Caucasus. It's likely that the 'clashing rocks' episode from the legend of Jason and the Argonauts was inspired by the voyage up the Bosphorus Straits. The first Greek settlement in the area of what's now Istanbul was the colony of Chalcedon, founded around 675 BC in what is nowadays the Asian suburb of Kadıköy. According to Herodotus (the best source of the Classical sound bite), Chalcedon was dubbed 'the city of the blind', its founders having missed the clear geographical advantages of the opposite European shore.

'At the crossroads of Europe and Asia, it was destined to become a city of world importance.'

Within less than 20 years more clear-sighted parties had established themselves across the water on land now enclosed by the walls of Topkapı Palace. Roughly triangular, bounded on two sides by water, it was a natural fortress. To the north, the Golden Horn was a four-mile-long, half-mile-wide perfect deep-water harbour. The site offered access by sea to the Mediterranean, Africa and the Black Sea, and lay at the crossroads of mainland routes between Europe and Asia. It was destined to be a city of world importance. Its founding was attributed to a sailor by the name of Byzas, hence the name Byzantium.

Once it was established, others were quick to recognise the strategic importance of the new city and it was repeatedly taken by warring regional powers: first the Persians in 550 BC, then the Spartans, then the Athenians. The Byzantines quickly developed a skill for diplomacy and throughout the rest of the Classical period kept their predatory neighbours at bay through a series of shrewd alliances. When that failed, the city buckled down and dug in, successfully weathering sieges from the likes of King Philip of Macedon, who tested the walls and will of Byzantium for a whole year in 340-1 BC.

Good judgement ran out in AD 196 when, after three centuries of independence as part of the Roman province of Asia, the Byzantines backed the wrong side in an imperial power struggle. After a prolonged siege, the stern emperor Septimius Severus had Byzantium's walls torn down, the city put to the torch and a fair

proportion of the population put to death. Such a strategic location couldn't lie wasted for too long, and within a few years the emperor had rebuilt the city on a far grander scale with new temples, a colonnaded way and bigger, better walls enclosing an area almost twice the size of the previous city. For all its pomp, like earlier Greek Byzantium, nothing of Severus's city has survived.

NEW ROME, NEW ROME

By the end of the third century, the Roman empire had become too unwieldy to govern effectively from Rome and had been subdivided with part of the power shifted to Byzantium. The result was to create internal rivalries that ultimately could only be settled on the battlefield. In AD 324, Constantine, Emperor of the West, defeated Licinius, Emperor of the East, first in a naval battle on the Sea of Marmara, then on land on the Asian shore at a place called Chrysopolis, today's Üsküdar. With the empire reunited, Constantine set about changing the course of history, first by promoting Christianity as the official religion of the empire, then by shifting the capital from a jaded and cynical Rome to the upstart city on the Bosphorus. On 11 May 330, Constantine inaugurated his new seat of power as 'Nova Roma', a name by which the city has never been known since.

'Constantine plundered the empire for the tallest columns, the finest marble and an abundance of Christian relics.'

In Nova Roma, more popularly called Constantinople, the new uncontested emperor had a city hitherto uncorrupted by power that he could make over as he saw fit. He immediately embarked on a building programme, plundering the empire to bring in the tallest columns, the finest marble and an abundance of Christian relics, including the True Cross itself. He endowed the church of Haghia Eirene as the city's first Christian cathedral and commissioned a great palace, built adjacent to an extended hippodrome. To safeguard his capital, Constantine had new walls erected in an arc from close to what is now the Atatürk bridge over the Golden Horn looping south to present-day Koca Mustafa Paşa, enlarging the area of the city fourfold. Other than a burnt and badly aged column (*see page 77*) little physical evidence of Constantine's work survives, but he laid the foundations for an empire that was to endure for over 1,000 years.

First on your
"must see" list
in Turkey:

✿Garanti*24*

Cash Point

Emperor Constantine's **great palace** was built adjacent to an extended hippodrome.

The beginnings were not auspicious. On Constantine's death in 337, achievement and stability ended. His three sons quarrelled over the succession and the empire was divided between Eastern and Western emperors, who sometimes co-operated but more often fought. Fortunately, Constantinople was largely unaffected by the ensuing two centuries of turbulence, and was even enlarged by the construction of new city walls during the reign of Theodosius II (408-450), completed just in time to halt Attila's advancing

hordes. Rome was not so fortunate and was ripped apart by tribes of Goths and Vandals from the north. With no rival Constantinople was left to move towards a new era of greatness, reaching its apogee during the era of Justinian (527-565).

CROWD TROUBLE

Justinian's reign was marked by great confidence, which saw the empire extend itself round most of the Mediterranean coast, including the recapture of the lost dominion of

Italy from the 'barbarian hordes'. But a great deal of the glory belongs to the emperor's supporting cast. He was fortunate in having at his service a supremely competent general, Belisarius, who takes credit for all military successes. Similarly exceptional was Justinian's wife, Theodora, a former street entertainer and prostitute.

'The Greens and the Blues were a cross between political parties and football hooligans.'

Theodora is credited with saving her husband's skin when a revolt broke out among factions at the hippodrome. Known as the Greens and the Blues, these factions originated in trade guilds and were a cross between political parties and football hooligans. Normally rivals, the Greens (lower-class radicals) and the Blues (upper-class conservatives) united in 532 to protest the execution of some of their members. The subsequent uprising, buoyed on by chants of 'Nika, nika' ('Victory, victory') plunged the city into chaos. Justinian, bags packed and in the hall, was all for fleeing but Theodora persuaded him that it was 'better to die as an emperor than live as a fugitive'. In the event Belisarius, still only in his twenties, succeeded in trapping and massacring 30,000 rebels in the hippodrome, thereby restoring civil order.

Left presiding over a city of ruins soaked in its citizens' blood, Justinian needed to restore public faith. His answer was to embark on a grand programme of reconstruction, providing for the city spiritually (he endowed the city with more than 40 churches) and in a more temporal fashion – for example providing the city with immense water cisterns, one of which still draws appreciative gasps from visitors (**Yerebatan Sarayı**; *see page 74*). The crowning glory was a new cathedral, Sancta Sophia (now **Haghia Sophia**; *see page 69*). In the eyes of contemporary chronicler Procopious, 'God allowed the mob to commit this sacrilege knowing how great the beauty of this church would be'.

Although the death of Justinian was followed by a prolonged period of decline, largely resulting from internal rivalries (*see page 12* **The emperor's new nose**), Constantinople remained, as one Byzantine writer put it, 'the city of the world's desire'. There were plenty who

Justinian I, Byzantine emperor (527-65), during whose reign the empire was extended around the Mediterranean, recapturing Italy.

acted on those desires. Slavs (581), Avars (617), Persians and Avars (626), Arabs (669-79 and 717-18), Bulgars (813, 913 and 924), Russians (four times between 860 and 1043) and Pechenegs (1087) all marched on the city. Some armies were sufficiently daunted by the walls alone and quit before they'd even begun. Others persisted and laid siege. But all failed. Fortified defences were backed by the Byzantines' very skilled and well-equipped navy and more unconventional deterrents such as 'Greek Fire', a mysterious liquid fire that was sprayed with devastating effect.

TROUBLE WITH PICTURES

Trouble was also brewing internally on the theological front when the iconoclast Leo III became emperor in 726. Iconoclasts believed literally in the first commandment, which forbids the worshipping of 'graven images'. Their stance was a complete break with the Greek tradition of adorning churches with elaborate frescoes and mosaics, and the veneration of icons and the relics of martyred saints. Thus began a 'dark age' of almost 120 years, during which churches were stripped of their decoration and those who stayed faithful to icons (iconodules) were forced to flee to distant monasteries or to worship in secret at risk of denunciation and death. The feud over icons burned on until 845 and it wasn't until 867 that the first new mosaic was unveiled in Haghia Sophia – that of the Madonna and child, still *in situ* today.

'Basil II had 99 out of every 100 prisoners blinded. The remainder were left with one eye to lead their fellows home.'

Religious problems of a different kind surfaced during the Iconoclastic period when in 800 the Roman pope crowned the Frankish leader Charlemagne the first Emperor of the West for over 400 years. This was followed by emissaries to Constantinople proposing a marriage between Charlemagne and the then Byzantine empress Eirene. The aim was to re-unite the two halves of the later-Roman empire but the grandees of the Eastern church created by Constantine felt that they alone had the right to crown emperors. Unwilling to accept as supreme ruler an illiterate tribal leader unable to speak either Latin or Greek, they deposed Eirene shortly after the emissaries' arrival.

A restoration in Byzantine fortunes came during the reign of Basil II (976-1025) who succeeded not just in holding the fort but also

The emperor's new nose

While early Byzantine emperors had tended to die of natural causes or at least in battle, over the centuries the empire acquired a reputation for the brutal removal of unwanted heads of state. Seven-year-old Leo II was murdered by his father Zeno in 474 when the child was unfortunate enough to succeed his maternal grandfather Leo I. Zeno himself was reputedly buried alive seven years later. An army rebellion in 602 saw the centurion Phocas seize the crown, beheading the incumbent Maurice I and his five sons. Eight years later it was Phocas who lost his head. Byzantine bloodletting spawned a new vocabulary; in 641, dictionaries could add the word 'rhinometia', the removal of the nose, which was carried out on the emperor Heraclonas. Justinian II, deposed in 695, had both his nose cut off and his tongue slit. But Justinian had his revenge. With the help of an army of Bulgars he had himself re-appointed emperor. Well aware of the limitations of rhinometia as a preventative punishment, Justinian – now known as 'rhinokopia' (the man with no nose) – took no chances and had both usurpers beheaded. He continued his interrupted reign wearing an artificial nose of pure gold. That is until he was deposed once again and this time killed.

expanding the empire into Armenia and Georgia. A harsh though conscientious ruler, he is best known for meting out one of the most horrific punishments that Europe has ever seen: in 1014 after taking 15,000 Bulgars prisoner, he had 99 out of every 100 blinded. The remainder were left with one eye to lead their fellow soldiers home. When he saw the ruined army that returned to his capital, Bulgarian Tsar Samuel is said to have collapsed and died two days later.

Basil's most significant contribution to history came in 989 when he gave his 25-year-old sister Anna in marriage to Vladimir, Prince of Kiev, in return for the pagan prince's promise to convert to Orthodox Christianity. This Vladimir did, then founded the Russian church and converted his subjects *en masse* (earning himself a sainthood in the process).

FRYING PAN OR FIRE?

The death of Basil marked a turning point in Byzantine fortunes as they entered a period of terminal decline. This was signalled to all when, in 1071, a combination of incompetence and treachery led to the annihilation of a Byzantine army at Manzikert in eastern Anatolia. The victors were a new menace, the Selçuk Turks, who now flooded west across Asia Minor right up to the shores of the Sea of Marmara.

Meanwhile to the west, Europe had emerged from its dark ages to become a patchwork of states owing religious allegiance to the Pope in Rome. Both the West and Byzantium were nominally Christian, but theological differences coupled with the Western church's envy of its older and richer neighbour meant any common cause was superficial. In 1054, a dispute between papal officials and the Patriarch of Constantinople had resulted in mutual excommunications. Such animosity inaugurated the schism between the Roman and Orthodox churches that still exists today.

In its time of trouble, the empire fell into the hands of the scheming Ducas and Comneni families. They indulged their tastes for luxury, learning, and culture, making Constantinople perhaps the richest city in the world. Also the most decadent, as the dynasties indulged their penchant for intermarrying, intriguing, dethroning and murder. Where once Byzantine armies had conquered, the bloated and effete empire now relied on wealth and diplomacy. With the Selçuk Turks as the greater threat, Byzantium was forced to enlist the aid of Latin armies as paid mercenaries. The Latins were crusading to recapture the Holy Lands lost to the Turks, and, passing through Constantinople in 1097, they agreed to return to the emperor any formerly imperial territory that they might recapture. This was a promise they failed to keep. Instead the Crusaders set up their own Holy Land states. There followed 50 years of confused bruising between the Byzantine, Latin and Muslim armies, culminating in the Byzantines cutting Crusader supply lines and enabling the Selçuks to re-take lost territory.

Two or three relatively able emperors, notably John II (1118-43) and Manuel I (1143-80), applied clever diplomacy and judicious use of force to keep the empire intact and even extend its borders, but the good work was undone in 1185 with the accession of Isaac II. Isaac was totally incompetent and set the gains of the last 70 years in reverse. He was deposed by his brother Alexius III and imprisoned, but Isaac's son escaped and fled west where he offered enormous sums of money to the armies massing in Venice for the Fourth Crusade in exchange for helping his father and himself regain the imperial throne.

Justinian's crowning glory was the construction of the stunning **Haghia Sophia**.

Swords of misrule

Created in the early years of the Ottoman dynasty, the Janissaries were the sultan's shock troops, reputedly the first to breach the walls in the conquest of Constantinople. Initially they were entirely of Christian origin, boys who were forcibly converted to Islam and trained up into a crack and fiercely loyal fighting force. In times of peace they served to maintain order in the capital and other main cities, for which they were richly rewarded. But their privileged status meant that in later years they were also frequently the cause of disorder. Well-paid and pampered, there was no institution to control the imperial guard. *Quis custodiet ipsos custodes?* as the Romans would ask – 'Who guards the guardians?' In the case of the Janissaries the answer was, very definitely, no one.

When Süleyman the Magnificent died in 1566, at the height of imperial power, the Janissaries were strong enough to bring the capital to a standstill until they'd received the traditional 'accession bonus' paid by every new sultan to ensure his guards' loyalty – a dangerous tradition that meant the Janissaries had a vested in interest in changing sultans frequently. Later, as imperial power declined

during the 'rule of women', the soldiers had even less respect for the imperial offices and Istanbul became almost a battleground between the sultan and his guard. In 1622, worried at planned reforms, they deposed and brutally murdered 18-year-old sultan Osman II, cutting off his ear and presenting it to his mother, while between 1651 and 1783 they staged no fewer than 11 revolts. A favourite tactic was to put the city to fire, looting and raping in the ensuing panic.

Attempts to control them with the regular armed forces backfired. In 1807-8 the Janissaries provoked a full-scale civil war, slaughtering great numbers of the regular army, murdering Sultan Selim III and attempting to murder his successor, Mahmut II.

On gaining the throne Mahmut swore, 'Either the Janissaries will all be massacred or the cats will walk over the ruins of Constantinople.' Their end came in 1826 when yet another revolt was met by Mahmut's new Western-style army aided by a civilian population eager for revenge after decades of abuse. More than 5,000 Janissaries were killed and 6,000 sent into exile in several days of bloodletting that became known thereafter as 'the blessed event'.

With interest in a long and probably futile struggle in the Middle East never deep, the Latins needed little encouragement to accept.

'What the Crusaders couldn't strip away they destroyed, leaving the city in ruins.'

Threatened with the vastly superior force of the Crusaders, the Byzantines agreed to restore Isaac II to the throne. But Alexius III fled with the contents of the treasury and the crown jewels, leaving the reinstated emperor with no money to pay his mercenary allies. On 13 April 1204, the Crusaders stormed Constantinople. They sacked the city, stripping it of its treasures and relics and sending them back west; the four gilded bronze horses that now stand over the doorway of St Mark's cathedral in Venice came from Constantinople's hippodrome. What the Crusaders couldn't strip away they destroyed, leaving the city in ruins.

The victorious Latins then appointed one of their own, Baldwin of Flanders, as emperor and divided up the empire into a patchwork of fiefdoms and city states. Haghia Sophia

and many of the Orthodox churches were converted to the Latin rite, causing many of the priests and bishops to flee to Nicaea, one of three tiny Byzantine enclaves that endured (now Iznik; *see page 255*). As it was, the Latin state lasted until 1261 before the Byzantines were able to muster enough force to reclaim what remained of Constantinople.

OTTOMANS AT THE GATE

That the Byzantine state was able to survive for another 190 ineffectual years was down to the fact that the rival Selçuk empire had splintered into myriad warring *beyliks*, or fiefdoms. It was only a matter of time, though, before one *beylik* won out and by the first years of the 14th century a new power had emerged, the Osmanlı Turks, named after their first leader Osman, and better known to Westerners as the Ottomans. They captured Bursa (*see page 251*) from the Byzantines and made it their capital. During the reign of their first sultan, Orhan Gazi (1326-62), the Ottomans conquered most of western Asia Minor and advanced into Europe as far as Bulgaria, establishing a new capital at Adrianople, now Edirne (*see page 245*).

Constantinople had become a Byzantine island on an Ottoman sea. Inevitably the severely weakened, ruined and depopulated city was confronted with a Turkish army at its walls. This first occurred in 1394, and again in 1400, 1422 and 1442. Each time the attacks were repelled but this only forestalled the inevitable. Soon after becoming Ottoman sultan in 1452, Mehmet II constructed the fortress of Rumeli Hisarı on the European shore of the Bosphorus just north of the city. Fitted with cannons, it gave the Ottomans control of the straits and deprived Constantinople of vital grain supplies.

'The Ottoman besiegers poured into the city in their thousands.'

By April 1453, the Ottoman forces surrounding Constantinople numbered some 80,000; facing them were just 5,000 able-bodied men in a city whose population had fallen to less than 50,000. The Ottoman navy was anchored in the Sea of Marmara. It could not, however, gain access to the Golden Horn because of a great

Süleyman the Magnificent (1520-66).

chain that the Byzantines had stretched across its mouth from the castle of Galata across to modern-day Sirkeci. But one night, several weeks into the siege, in a truly audacious move, the Ottomans circumvented the boom by hauling 70 ships on rollers up over the ridge above Galata so that by morning they were in the Golden Horn and up against the city walls.

On 27 May, Mehmet invited the last Byzantine emperor, named Constantine, like the first, to surrender. He refused. The final assault was launched two days later. The defenders on the walls threw back waves of attackers, as they had many times before. This time, however, the besiegers forced an opening near the Golden Horn, and poured into the city in their thousands. By dawn it was all over, with an estimated 4,000 defenders lying dead. A contemporary account describes how 'blood flowed through the streets like rainwater after a sudden storm; corpses floated out to sea like melons on a canal'.

With the conquest of Constantinople, Mehmet, still only 21 years old, took the name 'Fatih', or Conqueror. He was apparently shocked at the ruined state of the once-great city and as he walked among the wrecked imperial palace, he is said to have recited lines from an old Persian poem: 'The spider spins the curtains in the palace of the Caesars, and the owl hoots its night call on the towers of Afrasiab.'

ISTANBUL, NOT CONSTANTINOPLE
Mehmet was intoxicated by the notion of Constantinople and its heritage as capital of Eastern and Western empires. It fitted his own imperial ambitions. Justinian's great cathedral, Haghia Sophia, was reconsecrated as a mosque and the Sultan attended prayer there the first Friday after the conquest. The Ottomans immediately set about repairing the damage sustained during the siege and the decay of preceding centuries. Defences were strengthened with a great seven-towered citadel at Yedikule where the land walls met the Sea of Marmara, and a palace was constructed on the site of what is now Istanbul University. Mehmet ordered craftsmen and artisans from the old capitals of Bursa and Edirne to move to his new city, which the Turks came to call Istanbul, said to come from the Turkish mispronunciation of the Greek *i stopol*, or 'to the city'. The sultan's viziers (ministers) were encouraged to build and endow the new capital with mosques, hamams and the beginnings of what would develop into the Grand Bazaar.

Efforts were made to repopulate the half-deserted city. Greeks, who had fled in the preceding years, were offered land and houses and temporary tax exemption. Craftsmen, merchants and those who would enhance the city's wealth were invited regardless of race or religion. At a time when 'heretics' were being burnt alive in Western Europe, the Ottoman regime granted all religions freedom of worship and the uncontested right to appoint their own religious leaders. Large numbers of Sephardic Jews expelled from Spain and Portugal took sanctuary in Istanbul, the only multinational, multi-faith capital in Europe.

On the Conqueror's death in 1481 a scuffle for succession was won by his elder son Beyazıt II, succeeded in turn by his son Selim I, known as 'the Grim' for his habit of having his grand viziers executed (inspiring the popular Ottoman curse, 'May you be a vizier of Selim!'). Although Selim's reign lasted only eight years, he presided over significant military victories, adding Syria and Egypt to the imperial portfolio. Further south, he saw off a Portuguese threat to Mecca and was rewarded with the keys to the Holy City, the sacred relics of the Prophet, and the title of Caliph, Champion of Islam. This made Istanbul not only the capital of one of the most powerful empires in the world, but, as it was still the home of the Orthodox Patriarchate, also the centre of two major religions.

'While heretics were being burnt alive in Western Europe, the Ottomans granted all religions freedom of worship.'

While Mehmet II made Istanbul the Ottoman capital, it was during the 46-year reign of Süleyman I (1520-66) that the city became a true imperial centre. Not without reason was Süleyman able to describe himself in his official correspondence as 'Sultan of Sultans, Sovereign of Sovereigns, Distributor of Crowns, the Shadow of God on Earth, Perfecter of the Perfect Number…' These days historians just settle for plain 'Süleyman the Magnificent'. By the time of his death he ruled an empire that covered the spread of North Africa, stretched east to India, and rolled from the Caucasus through Anatolia and the Balkans to Budapest and most of modern-day Hungary. Süleyman's armies reached the walls of Vienna in 1529, where they were finally turned back after an unsuccessful siege.

Key to Süleyman's military successes were the Janissaries, whose name comes from the Turkish *yeni ceri*, or 'new troops'. During the 16th century they were the most disciplined, well-armed and effective of all European armies, universally admired and feared. Later, though, their unchecked appetites for power and their lack of discipline would almost prove the empire's undoing (*see page 14* **Swords of misrule**).

Under Süleyman, Istanbul became synonymous with grandeur, the source of which was the imperial palace, Topkapı, founded by Mehmet the Conqueror, but gilded by the wealth, tributes and taxes from newly conquered territories. Severe and grave, Süleyman surprised all by falling under the spell of a slave girl, Haseki Hürrem, known universally as Roxelana due to her alleged Russian origins. So besotted was Süleyman that in the early 1530s he married Roxelana and dispensed with the company of all other women. In 1538, as a further expression of devotion, he commissioned a promising young architect, Mimar Sinan, to construct the Haseki Hürrem Mosque complex as a birthday present. This was Sinan's first major commission in Istanbul, launching a glorious career which was to span 50 years. During that time, he, more than any of the sultans or pashas, left his indelible mark on the city and indeed on most major cities of the Ottoman empire (*see page 38* **Keeping up with the domes's**).

THE RULE OF WOMEN

Süleyman should have been succeeded by his first son Mustafa, an able soldier and administrator, but Roxelana schemed against it. Mustafa was not her son. She succeeded in convincing the sultan that he was traitorous and Süleyman had him strangled. Selim, Roxelana's son, became heir apparent.

Such bloodletting to secure the imperial throne was not uncommon. Although the sultanate always remained in the family – every ruler of the Ottoman empire until its end was a descendant of Osman – the choice of which son or male relative would inherit the throne was left to 'the will of Allah'. More pragmatically, whichever of the sultan's sons happened to be in Istanbul, or got there first after the ruler's death, got the throne. Succession was a matter of life or death, for Mehmet the Conqueror had declared, 'For the welfare of the state, the one of my sons to whom Allah grants the sultanate may lawfully put his brothers to death.' They were strangled with a silken bowstring, preferably by deaf mutes who would not hear their cries. The beautiful and elaborate tombs built to house the families of butchered children scarcely hid the brutality of the deed. Thus when Süleyman died on campaign in Hungary, the grand vizier sent a secret messenger to the preferred heir, Selim, then maintained the fiction that the sultan was merely ill and issued orders in his name. Once Selim was secure in Istanbul the vizier announced the sultan's demise.

Good-time Turkey was born on 29 October 1923, when Mustafa Kemal **'Atatürk'** ('father of the Turks') was appointed president.

'Selim drowned in his bath, drunk, and Nurbanu had four of his five sons killed.'

Far from being grim, Selim II was known as Selim 'the Sot'. His rampant drunkenness rendered him useless as a ruler. The real power behind the throne was Nurbanu ('Princess Light'), one of Selim's wives, who used his drunkenness to take control of both the harem and the palace, marking the beginning of an 80-year period referred to as 'the rule of women'. It was an era that saw weak sultans manipulated by their wives and mothers, the valide sultana, between whom there were often struggles for power (*see page 73* **Harem scarem**).

Selim drowned in his bath, drunk, and Nurbanu had four of his five sons killed, leaving her own child Murat III to succeed as sultan. When Murat died in 1595, his wife Safiye in turn had 19 brothers of her son, Mehmet III, strangled.

With Mehmet's successor, Ahmet I, builder of the Sultanahmet (Blue) Mosque, the killing stopped, possibly out of fear of dynastic extinction. From Ahmet's time, male relatives of the sultan were instead confined to the Kafes, literally 'cage', a closed apartment deep inside Topkapı Palace. Here they were kept in complete isolation, apart from a few concubines who had been sterilised by the removal of their ovaries. Guards whose eardrums had been pierced and tongues slit served the prisoners.

Although slightly more humane than the earlier fratricidal practices the confinement did little for the captive's mental health. Numerous sultans died prematurely without leaving an heir and their siblings were uniquely unsuited to rule, having spent most of their adult lives incarcerated. In the last years of the empire the problem was to grow more acute as successive sultans had little or no experience of the outside world, or of government. Some emerged quite simply mad.

At the drop of a hat

Istanbul has seen some moments in her remarkable history but few more compellingly bizarre than those of 25 November 1925, when Mustafa Kemal Atatürk's ban on the fez came into force. The Ottoman national headgear was to give way by decree to modern Western hats that morning. Near the Dolmabahçe Palace, a bemused muezzin appeared on a minaret balcony to give the call to prayer in a bowler. Elsewhere, the city's more theatrical citizens tossed their fezzes into the Bosphorus or left them to be collected by charities and turned into slippers for the destitute. Articles appeared in the press on the right way to wear the new sartorial order – homburgs, panamas and flat caps.

Atatürk's wide-ranging revolution was intended to turn subjects of empire – Eastern, orthodox and Islamic – into citizens of the republic – Western, liberal and secular. But of all the sweeping reforms of the 1920s, the new leader regarded the abolition of the fez as of particular social significance. 'Gentlemen,' Atatürk explained in a 1927 speech, 'it was necessary to abolish the fez, which sat on the heads of our nation as an emblem of ignorance, negligence, fanaticism and hatred of progress and civilisation.'

Far from being a mere prop of music-hall comedians, the fez was the very badge of orthodox Turkish identity. It did not go quietly. Riots marked the abolition of the red hat whose tassel was said to symbolise the single hair by which devout Muslims were effortlessly raised to Paradise on their death. The unrest ended in executions. Caches of clandestine fezzes were uncovered. Special constables took to the streets and ordered citizens to remove their new hats in case fezzes lurked beneath them.

Nor was it the first time that headgear had been targeted to political ends. A century before, in the 1820s, Sultan Mahmut II had abolished the religious and reactionary turban for the fez; but by the 1920s, its 'modern' replacement looked equally dated and had become a symbol of similar reaction. Turkey's modernisers have long yearned for that ultimate measure of Westernisation, the bare head. But things go round; the turban is once again a common sight in Istanbul districts such as Fatih, heartland of the Islamic revival. And the battle between Turkey's secular and orthodox wings continues to be fought over the thorny issue of whether women should be allowed to wear headscarves in the universities (see page 78 **Bullets over Beyazıt**). The fez, meanwhile, is remembered in a street name deep in the Grand Bazaar – Fesçiler Caddesi, or 'Fez-makers' Street'. These days, the conical hat is sold to tourists, and some Istanbul hotel staff and ice-cream sellers continue to wear it. It has become a banal parody of its former, significant self. Just as Atatürk would have wished it.

The **Orient Express** brought tourists into Sirkeci Station for the first time in October 1883.

THE TURNING POINT

In 1683 the Ottomans failed in a second attempt to take Vienna. This marked the end of Ottoman military successes and expansions and the beginning of a series of reverses. Within three years they had lost Buda to the Austrians, and two years after that Belgrade. More defeats followed. Times had changed from the days when Süleyman the Magnificent was treated as a virtual god and all had to lower their eyes in his presence.

Pleasure-loving sultan Mehmet IV was accused of indifference to affairs of state and deposed by his vizier. His brother Süleyman was appointed instead, but, having spent 40 years in the Kafes, he refused to come out, believing that executioners were waiting. He had to be coaxed from hiding like a skittish kitten.

The problem lay not just with addled sultans. In the absence of a strong figurehead the Janissaries, once the sultan's finest troops, were now completely out of hand, threatening the sultan and killing ministers (*see page 14* **Swords of misrule**). Plagues were recurrent. In 1603 a fifth of the population was wiped out, in 1778 possibly a third. Such outbreaks had been eliminated in Europe by the early 1700s by the use of quarantines, but the fatalistic Turks accepted the epidemics as God's will.

Of the advances in science and technology that were revolutionising Western societies and economies in the 18th century, the Ottomans were not only ignorant but arrogantly dismissive. One Turkish dignitary visiting a scientific laboratory in Vienna in 1748 could describe all he had seen as 'toys' and 'Frankish trickery'.

When Selim III took the throne in 1789 his position was perilous; disobedient guards, recurrent plague, economic decline, military defeats, moribund culture and a restless populace heavily taxed and suffering under poor administration. But he was at least sufficiently aware to know that he had to do something to remedy the empire's ills.

He looked to the West for inspiration. He established a consultative council and Western architectural influences started to make themselves felt at the palaces. More crucially, he attempted to reform the army. For this the sultan earned the emnity of the Janissaries, who felt that their privileges were being threatened. They rose up in revolt, deposed Selim and murdered him.

> ### 'The fez was taken to heart by the city, worn by all as a symbol of modernism.'

The Janissaries were finally crushed in 1826 by sultan Mahmut II (1808-39), who had narrowly escaped from the palace with his life the day Selim had been killed. He went on to implement extensive and much-needed reforms, instigating what historian Philip Mansel calls 'revolution from above'. Local government was introduced to Istanbul for the first time, together with the city's first police and fire services. Quarantine and plague hospitals were established on his orders. He allowed the formation of limited companies and in 1828 brought an Italian conductor to train the imperial band to play Western music.

Mahmut appeared at public functions wearing western clothes and, most striking of all, banned the wearing of robes and turbans, except for the clergy, introducing the crimson-wool fez from Morocco. This was soon taken to heart by the city, worn by all as a symbol of modernism. More than just a hat, the fez became, in the words of nationalist writer Falih Rifki Atay, 'part of the Turkish soul' (*see page 18* **At the drop of a hat**). However Mahmut's addiction to all things Western led to his untimely death – allegedly from cirrhosis caused by a love of champagne.

Turkish delights

Turkey's metropolis has been attracting bad press ever since Martin Luther prayed to be delivered from 'the World, the Flesh, the Turk and the Devil' back in the 16th century. It was from Istanbul that the hordes of the 'terrible Turk' arrived at the gates of Vienna in 1529.

Istanbul's extensive contribution to European culture gives the lie to such prejudices. Take the Turkish bath. Over the ages, Istanbul took to the bathing habits of the Romans and made them its own before exporting the tradition to Europe, where it survives today in Budapest and elsewhere. It is the hamam, however, that reigns supreme among the many European bathing hybrids that it informed. It is to the sauna what the palace is to the shed, a ritual of sensuous, even brutal grandeur played out on a heated marble slab beneath an ancient domed ceiling, best enjoyed at the city's historic hamams, notably **Çemberlitaş** or **Cağaloğlu**, both near the Grand Bazaar. See page 202.

FRY'S feast from the fabulous East!

Here's your magic-carpet ride to romance! *Real* Turkish Delight now doubly delicious in a cream-smooth coating of Fry's MILK Chocolate. Have some TODAY.

4D

And it was from Istanbul that coffee was introduced into Europe, initially via Venice. The espresso can be said to owe its origins to Turkish coffee, served thick and strong in dainty china cups. Julia Pardoe, a visitor to Istanbul in the 19th century, greatly admired Turkish coffee and declared 'what a sad pity it is that we know nothing about the making of coffee in Europe'. Today, Turkish coffee is not no longer so ubiquitous in Istanbul; it has given way to tulip-shaped glasses of black tea and the relentless advance of Nescafé. But it remains widely available in the city's cake shops, notably along Istiklal Caddesi in Beyoğlu. You might even take it with a piece of *lokum* or Turkish delight, not the gelatinous purple stuff advertised by belly dancers in diaphanous veils, but a delicious sweet rolled in sugar and studded with nuts.

Or you could take that coffee with a croissant, the breakfast pastry supposedly inspired by the emblem on the sultan's flag. The tale is told in both

THE TANZIMAT ERA

Mahmut's successor, Abdül Mecit (1839-61), continued his father's reforming programme, resulting in what was to be a last blossoming of the Ottoman empire. Again according to Philip Mansel, 19th-century Istanbul 'owed its grandeur to its defiance of nationalism'. As in the city of Mehmet the Conqueror, race and religion were not supposed to be an issue. Greek, Armenian, Kurd, Circassian, Turk, Christian, Muslim and Jew were all said to be equal and to this end two great imperial decrees of 1839 and 1856 were issued, forming the basis for what was known as tanzimat or 'the reforms'.

The sultan further embraced the new era by moving out of Topkapı and into a new Western-style imperial palace at Dolmabahçe. But the real hub of the city was the bridge built

across the Golden Horn in 1845. The first to link the two sides of the water, it became the most popular of places, where a dozen or more races dressed like peacocks spent each evening promenading. Between palace and bridge, the largely non-Muslim, European districts of Galata and Pera (modern-day Beyoğlu), originally founded as Italian traders' enclaves in Byzantine times, were rapidly developing into a new commercial and entertainment district centred on the Grand Rue de Pera, location for an increasing number of theatres, cafés, bars and hotels. Istanbul was shifting its locus from south of the Golden Horn to north.

Mid-19th century the city began to receive its first proper 'tourists', drawn by the Oriental mystique of the capital of the Ottoman sultans. Almost immediately the sightseeing circuit *page 83* **The extravagant express**), which pulled into Sirkeci Station for the first time in October 1883.

Vienna and Budapest. During the Ottoman siege of Vienna (or Buda), the Turks are said to have begun tunnelling under the walls. A bright Hungarian (or Austrian) baker's boy heard them and raised the alarm. To commemorate this bright boy's initiative and alertness, bread dough was rolled into the shape of the Islamic crescent – or *croissant* in French. To this day you snack on a crescent-shaped Hungarian *kifli* or a curly Austrian *Kipferl*, while the French started baking them with flaky *feuilletage* pastry in the late 19th century. Something to ponder next time you're enjoying a 'Continental' breakfast.

experienced by visitors today was set. Mark Twain roadtested it in the late 1860s and wrote of it in *Innocents Abroad*. They dropped anchor in the Golden Horn and were rowed ashore to visit Haghia Sophia ('the rustiest old barn in Heathendom'), the Whirling Dervishes ('about as barbarous an exhibition as we have witnessed'), the Grand Bazaar ('a monstrous hive of little shops') and a hamam ('a malignant swindle'). He was, however, fascinated by the beggars on the Galata Bridge – the three-legged woman, the man with an eye in his cheek, the man with fingers on his elbow. 'Bismillah! The cripples of Europe are a delusion and a fraud. The truly gifted flourish only in the byways of Pera and Stamboul.' Had Twain been visiting just 15 years later his mood might have been improved by the opportunity to roll into Stamboul on the Orient Express (*see*

'A paranoid ruler, Sultan Abdül Hamit hid in constant fear of being bumped off and had several members of his family killed.'

Political reforms culminated in 1876 in the drafting of a constitution and the establishment the following year of the first Turkish parliament – albeit with very limited powers. But it was short-lived. A year later, despite their defeat by the Turks and allies in the Crimean War just 30 year earlier, the Russians again seized Ottoman lands in the Balkans and Caucasus. Called to account, Sultan Abdül Hamit responded by dissolving parliament and ruling by decree from his new labyrinthine palace at Yıldız. A paranoid ruler, he hid at Yıldız in constant fear of being bumped off and had several close members of his family and many ministers, generals and other court officials killed. British prime minister Gladstone called him the 'Great Assassin'. Turks called him 'Abdül the Damned'.

Reform had already progressed too far to allow this reversion to complete imperial rule. Small clandestine groups later known as 'Young Turks' kept up the pressure for change. Most were weeded out and crushed, but one, the Committee of Union & Progress, based in Salonika, succeeded in seizing control of the Ottoman army in Macedonia. By 1908 the CUP was powerful enough to send a telegram to the ageing despotic sultan demanding the restoration of the constitution and parliament. Faced with a rebellious revolutionary army marching on Constantinople, Abdül Hamit acceded to their demands.

Elections to the new parliament saw all but one of the seats won by the CUP, whose elected deputies included Arabs, Greeks, Jews, Armenians and Albanians. It took a pitched battle in Taksim Square to fight off the challenge of Islamic groups, but once that was won reforms were back on the agenda. What should then have been a period of rebirth and growth was instead one of chaos and turmoil as Europe saw the imminent demise of Ottoman rule as a chance to carve up what remained of its empire.

EMPIRE'S END
In 1911 Italy seized Rhodes and blockaded the Dardanelles. The following year the Balkan states launched their own offensive, which saw them take all Ottoman possessions in Europe and

Modern skyscrapers displace minarets as the main feature of Istanbul's skyline.

Bulgarian troops advance to within 40 kilometres (25 miles) of Istanbul. News that Russia, which had long coveted Istanbul and control of the Bosphorus Straits, had joined an alliance with Britain and France left Turkey with little option but to turn to Germany and the two signed a formal alliance. Despite a historic victory at Gallipoli, in which they stemmed the Allied invasion and forced a withdrawal, the country was on the losing side in World War I. In its aftermath they could do nothing but watch as the former Ottoman empire was divided up between European powers. The British and French took over the Arab lands, occupied Istanbul in 1919 and enthroned a puppet sultan there.

A Greek army occupied much of the remaining territory. Many in Greece had long aspired to the 'great idea' of retaking 'Constantinople' and making it the capital of a Greater Greece (an aim that today still underpins the ideology of the Greek far right). This had support in high places, including from British cabinet minister Lord Curzon, who, in the face of clear evidence to the contrary, claimed that Muslims were in the minority in Istanbul. Greece was permitted by the European powers to occupy parts of the Aegean coast and eastern Thrace. Turkish leaders in Istanbul seemed incapable of countering the threat and groups of disillusioned soldiers began slipping out of the city, banding together under the leadership of Mustafa Kemal, the young Turkish general who had masterminded resistance at Gallipoli. In 1919 Kemal led a revolt from the interior, formally declaring independence and forming a new government in

Ankara. 'Henceforth,' he declared, 'Istanbul does not control Anatolia, but Anatolia Istanbul.' In other words: 'Turkey for the Turks.'

> **'Lord Curzon, in the face of clear evidence to the contrary, claimed that Muslims were in the minority in Istanbul.'**

After two years of bitter fighting, the Turks succeeded in forcing the Greeks back to Izmir, which was all but destroyed in the final battle. It was a defining moment for the emergent Turkish state, which was now able to negotiate with the Allies on equal terms. In 1922 the sultanate was abolished and the reigning sultan reduced to little more than a ceremonial figurehead. In fear of his life, the last sultan, Vadettin, fled Istanbul for Italy, with his son accepting the throne. In July 1923 the new state was strong enough to win back some of the territory lost through the treaty of Lausanne, paving the way for a complete allied withdrawal from Istanbul three months later.

LET THE GOOD TIMES ROLL
A matter of days after re-occupying Istanbul, on 29 October 1923 Turkey adopted a new secular republican constitution, appointed Mustafa Kemal 'Atatürk' ('father of the Turks') as its president and fixed upon Ankara as its capital. It was a break with almost 1,600 years of tradition, which saw the replacement of one of the world's most fabulous cities by a small windswept hillside town that lacked almost every modern

amenity, but which was far enough from the new country's borders to make it secure from invasion. Within six months the 1,300-year-old tradition of the sultanate was completely abolished and the last members of the Ottoman dynasty sent into exile.

Bold, sweeping reforms followed. The European calendar was adopted, then the Swiss civil code and the Italian penal code – abolishing the role of religion in law. The fez – itself a fairly recent replacement for the turban – was banned in favour of western hats, women were granted equal rights to men, and language reforms replaced Arabic script with the Latin alphabet. Later, in 1935, all Turks were obliged to adopt surnames and lists of suggested ones were posted everywhere. The name Constantinople, still common in both official and popular usage, was banned because of its imperial associations. The post office would only accept 'Istanbul' as an address on letters. On a deeper level, Atatürk precipitated a change in national self-perception. Previously 'Turk' was a term applied to backward provincials, while the cultured and elite saw themselves as Ottoman. Now the slogan was 'How happy are they who call themselves Turks'. From being the most international of cities, Istanbul rapidly became the most nationalistic.

> **'Atatürk drank and gambled all night, napped for a while, then got up to conduct the country's affairs.'**

Although no longer the political powerhouse, Istanbul continued to prosper as the undisputed cultural and economic capital of the new republic. The Grand Bazaar remained the centre of commerce, while Pera – now renamed Beyoğlu – entered a wild and heady period buoyed by optimism and pro-Western reforms that allowed for previously unheard-of levels of freedom. Added to the cocktail were a couple of hundred thousand White Russian refugees fleeing the far more po-faced Soviet revolution, including the odd genuine aristocrat. The Russians were to dominate the cultural life of the district for decades, opening cafés, bars and restaurants, and even introducing Istanbul to the 'jazz age' via a black American, a Mr Thomas, who'd owned a famous bar in Tsarist Russia, but joined the exodus to the Bosphorus and there opened a dance hall.

As a leader Atatürk was the personification of good-time Turkey. A man of immense energy, he drank and gambled all night, napped for a couple of hours then got up to conduct the country's

The changing face of 21st-century Istanbul.

affairs. He may have moved the capital to Ankara, but his heart was in Istanbul.

Atatürk died in 1938. His casket was placed in the throne room of Dolmabahçe Palace, where hundreds of thousands came to view the body. Crowds at the palace grew so disorderly that riot police charged and a dozen people were trampled to death. He was succeeded by Ismet Inönü, who had masterminded the Turkish forces in the war against Greece, but Atatürk has hardly been allowed to die and his image is still all over Istanbul today (*see below* **Atta Turk!**).

EXPERIMENTS IN DEMOCRACY

At the outbreak of war in Europe, Turkey opted to remain neutral. Battle did go on in Istanbul, however, as the city became the espionage capital of World War II. No less than 17 different intelligence agencies operated there and half the population seemed to be making a living trading information. Packed with refugees from all over Europe, Istanbul was also something of a safe haven for Jews escaping the Nazis, and had been so all through the 1930s. Purges of Jewish intellectuals in Germany had coincided with a re-organisation of Istanbul University and by 1940 the institution employed some 120 Jewish exiles, many of them leaders in their respective fields.

Turkey finally entered the war on the Allied side in February 1945, by which time the German threat had been supplanted by that of the Soviet Union. Stalin, like the Tsars before him, wanted control of the Bosphorus. By 1947 the threat of Communist take-over in Greece and Turkey caused US president Harry Truman to launch his 'Truman Doctrine' heralding a new era of US involvement in international affairs. This saw Turkey admitted to Nato and the opening of US bases in the country.

At the same time, Turkey began to experiment with democracy. The foundation of the Democrat Party (DP) in 1946 should have heralded a new era, but the ruling Republican People's Party (CHP) won a huge majority in elections widely believed to have been rigged.

By 1950, though, the DP was trusted enough to win power and party leader Adnan Menderes became prime minister. With the help of an economic boom assisted by anti-Soviet-inspired US aid, Menderes was able to reshape Istanbul with mass imports of cars and trucks and a programme of road building implemented to accommodate them. Vast areas of old Istanbul were flattened to make away for the broad concrete strips of Vatan Caddesi, Millet Caddesi and Atatürk Bulvarı.

Atta Turk!

He's the centre of a personality cult that makes those of Lenin and Mao Tse Tung seem shy and retiring by comparison. What's more, he's dead and absolutely nobody is being forced to put up his posters, erect statues, parrot his slogans, buy the mug, the clock, the teapot, the T-shirt. But they all still do. More than 60 years after his death, the image of **Mustafa Kemal Atatürk** remains omnipresent, from the paper banknotes with their bewildering number of zeros, to newspaper mastheads, to profiles carved into hillsides. His name honours airports and stadiums, boulevards and bridges. Back in the 1920s it was seriously proposed that they rename Istanbul Gazi Mustafa Kemal. In 1999 a coordinated Internet voting campaign almost boosted Atatürk on to the front cover of *Time* magazine as the readers' choice of 'Man of the Century' until the ploy was scuppered by a Greek and Armenian counter-action.

Many Turks will privately admit that they find the iconography excessive but accept it as a necessary counter to the threat of anti-secular political Islam. Fervent 'Kemalists' (as proponents of Atatürk are known) often give the impression that the only thing standing

between Turkey and the plunge into Iranian-style Islamic revolution is the image of the 'Father of the Turks' and a few choice slogans daubed around.

What is beyond debate is Atatürk's status as one of the most influential political figures of the 20th century, not to say a military commander of true genius. His effect on the outcome of the allied landings at Gallipoli in World War I can best be summed up in the official British army history: 'Seldom in history can the exertions of a single divisional commander have exercised so profound an influence not only on the course of a battle but on the destiny of a nation.'

Kitsch and iconography aside, each year Atatürk is commemorated at 9.05am on 10 November – the anniversary of his death. Sirens blare out across the country signalling a minute's silence. People stand motionless and on the roads traffic pulls over and drivers get out to stand. It is a genuinely moving, not to say eerie experience, and one that speaks far more eloquently than the mini-industry of memorabilia. Still, we wouldn't say no to the franchising rights.

A worsening economic climate in the late 1950s saw the DP becoming more authoritarian. In 1960 Menderes tried to stifle the CHP, still led by the veteran Inönü, with the result that the military seized power, banned the DP and hanged Menderes and two of his senior ministers for treason. Democracy was reinstated, but the 1960s were marked by a rise in extremism, most notably on the far left, which organised mass demonstrations against the American military presence. With no party able to form a stable government, violence increased and the military again seized power in 1971.

The rubber ball of democracy bounced back once more, but there was still no real consensus on the way to move forward; Western-style free-market or semi-Soviet style command economy? Left-wing extremists took the struggle for revolution onto the streets, where they were met by far-right groups often working in tandem with the security forces. Weak coalitions came and went and achieved little, while political violence, exacerbated by economic hardship, increased to alarming levels. Istanbul's daily death toll was seldom below 20.

In September 1980, the army again took over, installing a government of technocrats and retired officers. A wave of terror resulted in over 100,000 arrests. In a startling attempt to break with the past, all political parties were closed and their leaders banned from active politics.

PEASANTS AND YOUTH

Although initially welcomed by Turks fed up with political violence, love for the authoritarian military regime soon palled. In 1983, the first free elections resulted in an overwhelming victory for the broad-based Motherland Party and its founder, former bureaucrat Turgut Özal. His popularity was helped in no small part by the fact that he was so unpopular with the generals. Faced with an economy that still closely resembled those of Eastern Europe, he implemented a series of rapid market-oriented reforms that helped attract investment, but also resulted in widespread corruption and sleaze. As the Turkish saying goes, 'He who holds the honeypot is going to lick his fingers.' Other reforms aimed at countering the appeal of the left eased controls on religious organisations and allowed for the setting up of hundreds of religious-instruction schools that within a decade would become breeding grounds for Islamist extremism.

Since the 1950s Istanbul had also been undergoing far-reaching demographic changes. Anti-Christian riots in 1955 had resulted in a massive exodus of the city's once significant Greek population. In their stead, the city began rapidly filling with migrants from the provinces.

To peasants from rural Anatolia, Istanbul was – and to some extent still is – El Dorado, a place of opportunity and riches. Settling on the city fringes in *gecekondu*, literally 'night settlements', a term used to describe squatter houses put up overnight without permission, these newcomers have swollen the population from three million in 1970 to over 10.5 million at the end of the century. Istanbul has become a collection of villages with parts of the city known by names such as 'little Gazientep' and 'little Sivas' after the Anatolian towns from which most of the residents originate.

Cheap labour from such shantytowns helped fuel the economic boom of the 1980s, although the spread of unplanned suburbs put unbearable strain on the city's infrastructure, clogging roads and polluting out-of-town reservoirs to leave some areas without water for weeks at a time.

By the early 1990s the old guard had returned to active politics, splitting the vote between six main parties. Elections in 1995 were indecisive, resulting eventually in an unpopular centre right-Islamist coalition. Fuelled by decades of hatred for the country's secular institutions, the Islamists set about wrecking what they couldn't control, in the process bringing the economy to the brink of collapse. A potential confrontation with the army was averted by defections from both coalition partners, which brought a more stable multi-party coalition.

THE FUTURE IS EUROPE

Elections in 1999 brought a surprising coalition of the far right, centre right and the left together under the leadership of veteran prime minister Bülent Ecevit. After eight months of what was reckoned to be the most successful Turkish government in decades and on the eve of the new millennium, Turkey was rewarded by being accepted as a candidate for EU membership, 36 years after it first applied. Unrelated but no less momentous was the success of Istanbul's top football team Galatasaray (*see page 232*) in winning the UEFA Cup, followed by the national team reaching the final eight of Euro 2000. Even without much-needed EU funds for redevelopment, Istanbul is in the throes of a transformation. A long-awaited metro system, promising relief from the worst of the traffic congestion, has finally opened, and plans are afoot for a tunnel under the Marmara to link the European and Asian rail lines. And while unchecked development continues to blight the skyline, reaction to the destruction of the city's heritage has started to become more vocal.

Although few believe that membership of the EU can solve all of Turkey's or Istanbul's problems, or bring continued success on the football field, a corner does seem to have been turned and the mood is very much one of hope.

Key events

Pre-history
7000 BC Neolithic fishing settlements at Kadıköy, Pendık and Yarımburgaz.
3200 BC Bronze Age settlement at Sarayburunu.
750 BC Greek sailors pass through the Bosphorus.

The Greek Colony
675 BC Greek colony of Chalcedon founded in what is now Kadıköy.
658 BC Greek colony of Byzantium founded.
546 BC Byzantium falls to Persians.
129 BC Creation of Roman province of Asia Minor; Byzantium keeps independence.
AD 73 Byzantium incorporated into Roman province of Bithynia.
196 Byzantium sacked by Roman Emperor Septimius Severus.
324 Constantine defeats co-emperor in battle, makes the city new capital of Roman empire.

From Eastern Rome to Byzantine Empire
326-330 Constantine christens the city 'New Rome'. Instead it becomes Constantinople.
413 Theodosius II constructs new city walls.
537 Emperor Justinian dedicates new cathedral of Haghia Sophia.
745-7 Plague wipes out one third of population.
976-1025 Reign of Basil II, longest reigning and most successful Byzantine emperor.
1071 Selçuk Turkish army conquers Anatolia.
1096 First Crusade reaches Constantinople, helps recapture lands lost to Selçuk Turks.
1147 Manuel I makes peace with Selçuks.
1204 Fourth Crusade sacks Constantinople.

Ottomans at the gate
1394-1442 Ottomans besiege Constantinople four times.
1453 Mehmet II conquers the city and declares it capital of the Ottoman empire.
1492 Spain's exiled Jewish population invited by Beyazıt II to settle in Istanbul.
1517 Selim the Grim captures Cairo and appoints himself Caliph of all Islam.
1520-66 Reign of Süleyman the Magnificent – empire reaches its zenith.

Decline of the empire
1566 Beginning of the 'rule of women'.
1622 Janissaries murder Osman II.
1651-1783 Janissaries revolt 11 more times.
1778 Plague wipes out one third of population.

1807-8 Janissaries wage civil war.
1813 Hundreds of thousands die of plague.
1826 Janissaries destroyed by Mahmut II.

From reform to repression and revolution
1839 Beginning of the 'Tanzminat' (reform) era.
1845 Galata bridge spans the Golden Horn.
1853 Dolmabahçe Palace completed.
1854 First Istanbul stock exchange opens.
1854-6 Crimean War and revolts against Ottoman rule in the Balkans.
1877 First Ottoman parliament.
1878 Russians sieze Balkans, Abdül Hamit closes parliament and rules by decree.
1883 Orient Express pulls into Istanbul.
1899 'Young Turk' groups formed in military.
1908 First elections. CUP emerges victorious.
1912 First Balkan war, Bulgarian troops threaten Istanbul.
1913 Second Balkan war.

The Great War
1914 Ottomans enter war on German side.
1918 Allied forces occupy Istanbul.
1919 Atatürk declares independent Turkey.
1920 Turkish parliament formed in Ankara.
1922 After two years fighting Turks force Greeks out of Iznik. Sultanate abolished.

The republic
1923 Allied occupation of Istanbul ends, Ankara declared capital of new republic.
1938 Atatürk dies.
1935-1941 Turkey provides safe haven for Jews fleeing German Reich.
1950 First democratically elected Turkish government.
1960 Prime Minister Adnan Menderes deposed in coup, hanged the following year.
1971 Instability in government and extremism prompts second army coup.
1980 Daily warring between left and right groups and inability to form stable government prompts third military coup. Over 100,000 arrested.
1983-present Growth of shanty towns on outskirts of Istanbul as migrants move in from rural areas.
17 August 1999 Earthquake devastates parts of Istanbul and north-west Turkey, killing 20,000.
December 1999 Turkey formally accepted as candidate for membership of EU.
May 2000 Galatasaray win the UEFA cup.

Istanbul Today

Tension between commerce and the Koran makes
a new world of the old city.

Traffic gridlock. The streets heave with
revellers in a blare of colour and sound. The
time: 1am and the night's still young. The place:
Taksim Square, Istanbul. Confused? Wasn't
Turkey about Shari'a, a second Iran? A muddle
of terrorism, human rights abuses, barbarity?
Midnight Express and all that? Yet while Tony
Blair's 'Cool Britannia' still debates the wisdom
of extending UK licensing laws beyond 11pm,
Istanbul is partying the nights away at a
proliferating range of venues. Under an
Islamic local government.

Of course, it hasn't always been so. When
the Islamic Welfare Party (later banned and
re-formed as the Virtue Party) first won the local
elections in 1994, its initial campaign of action
was heavy-handed. Tables and chairs were
whipped away from outside restaurants and
cafés selling alcohol; new alcohol licences
became almost impossible to come by; kebab
joints run by members of the bearded
brotherhood suddenly burgeoned; and for
the first time in the history of the republic,

public-sector employees were allowed to wear
headscarves to work. Mustafa Kemal Atatürk,
founder of the modern secular Turkish state,
would have turned in his grave. But the threat
was short-lived. Local traders and consumers
revolted, the municipality wised up to its best
interests, lowered its hard-sell Islamic profile
and became more accommodating. This made
possible the recent explosion of bars, cafés and
clubs in the city, particularly in Beyoğlu, where
ten years ago there were at most a couple of bars.
Today there are hundreds.

That's not to say there's no regulation. The
arrival of Sadettin Tantan (former chief of the
Istanbul drugs squad) as interior minister after
the April 1999 general election marked the
beginning of an uncompromising clean-up
campaign targeting drugs, corruption and the
mafia. In practical terms, this means that armies
of police periodically descend on vibrant venues
at their busiest hours to do spot drug checks, ID
checks (for under-age drinking), or to inspect the
impossibly bureaucratic paperwork routinely

foisted on proprietors. A recent victim of the clampdown was a chic high-society venue on the Golden Horn, owned by a former Istanbul mayor, which had been run for two years without an alcohol licence. The owner's bulging portfolio of connections failed to impress the relentless Tantan, who engineered a 007-style raid on the place while a corporate function was in mid-swing. Its doors are now firmly closed.

'On winter nights ten years ago, Istanbul resembled a horror-film set.'

CLEANING UP ITS ACT

While old habits die hard – particularly corrupt ones – the city does have a cleaner image these days. Literally as well, for which the municipality deserves credit. Major tree-planting campaigns – a million saplings went down in 1999 – landscaping projects and park openings in recent years give Istanbul serious garden city pretensions, within the next decade at least. Although not yet the lido it was promised to be by now, the Golden Horn is considerably less

odorous than it was – and is even an occasional playground for passing dolphins. Pavements are swept, trash is collected, public toilets are modern, hygienic and plentiful. Simit sellers have been given fancy uniforms and olde-worlde carts. The impression is of a city a whole lot cleaner than London or Paris.

Another important factor has been the advent of natural gas. On winter nights ten years ago, the city resembled a horror-film set, as pungent layers of yellow fog swirled around street lamps. Though the pollution may not have disappeared altogether, at least oxygen masks are no longer essential. Transport is also barely recognisable. Environment-friendly single- and double-deckers have infiltrated the exhaust-churning municipal fleet, plying mapped routes with pristine bus stops. There's a new, air-conditioned tram, running from the south side of the Golden Horn to the city walls. A long-touted metro, several years in the pipeline, finally opened in autumn 2000 and is expected to lighten the traffic load. A proposal for an underwater tunnel connecting the two continents was favoured recently over one for a third suspension bridge. No mean achievements in a relatively short period of time.

Istiklal Caddesı – the heart of modern, secular Istanbul.

Vakko department store –
Turkish take on
Western capitalism.

Change is happening at lightning speed.
It's also constant, reflecting a dynamic
community and its voracious appetite for
innovation. Witness the boom in mall culture,
mobile phones, Internet cafés, Viagra sales, the
new Manhattan skyline in the district of 4th
Levent and the snowballing foreign franchises.

TRADITION RULES

This may look like a sell-out to Western
capitalism, but it isn't. Or not entirely. Sure,
increased access to global media and foreign
travel opportunities have created a new
awareness of and appetite for the outside world,
but ask most Turks and you'll find there's an
unbreakable emotional bond to the *memleket*
(homeland) and, by association, to things
Turkish. Thus, a new Dunkin' Donuts sets up
on the main street in Beyoğlu, but almost right
beside it a good-looking, traditional Turkish
eaterie is about to open its doors. Custom and
tradition coexist with modernity. Respect for
them is deep-seated.

Religious holidays (*dini bayramlar*) are a
case in point. On these occasions, entire
extended families sling on their *bayram* best,
pile into a single car and troop off on family
visits. A typical visit begins with members of
the younger generation filing past a line-up of
seniors to kiss their hands, continues with a
substantial feast and probably ends with a trip

to the cemetery to visit those relatives no longer
above ground. During festivals such as Kurban
Bayramı (Feast of the Sacrifice), whole herds
of goats, sheep, bulls, camels – the bigger the
better – fall to the knife. Sacrificial offerings
are still considered expedient on occasions as
various as giving birth, opening a new factory
or laying the foundations of a house. More
practical is the custom of removing grubby
shoes outside the front door of any home, said
to originate from the times when tuberculosis –
and gobbing in the street – was rife. Cleanliness
is right up there with godliness anyway, and
in this case health, too.

'Family relations involve a delicate interplay of real and profound affection, expectation and obligation.'

Above all, tradition rules the family home,
defining the hierarchy and its inherent roles.
Father (*baba*) may wear the trousers, inasmuch as
his word is final and he's the family ambassador,
but it's mother (*anne*) who runs the household in
practice. Her role is considered sacred. Lower
down the pecking order, big brother (*abi*) can order
his younger siblings around to his heart's content,
but in return he bears responsibility for their
welfare and future. Relations involve a delicate
interplay of real and profound affection, expecta-
tion and obligation. But families are rock solid and
valued as such – necessarily so in the absence of
a welfare state, where they're the only safety and
support network. Both within the family and
without, the tradition of hospitality is legendary.
Guests, including complete strangers, Turkish or
foreign, are welcomed with such unquestioning
warmth and sincerity, it's humbling.

GOING TO THE DOGS?

Then again, there are those who'd argue that
Istanbul has gone to the dogs, that things are not
what they used to be. And maybe they have a
point. In 30 years, the population of the city has
swelled by some 30 times to around 15 million
and its boundaries have sprawled far beyond the
original seven hills. The dogs they refer to are
the mass of migrants from the east. During the
1970s whole villages in Anatolia emptied out
under the twin threats of terrorism and economic
bankruptcy. The result: Istanbul's urban
gentility was crowded out by rural rough-and-
readiness. But also local colour. Migrants from
the same part of the country flowed into
communes on the urban fringes, bringing their
customs, traditions, and lifestyle with them and
creating a string of villages within the city.
Maybe Istanbul today isn't like the old days

(where is?), but everyone coexists happily enough, whether migrant, native or part of the residual Greek, Armenian or Jewish minorities.

'During the 1999 earthquake, rescue teams and ordinary people were rallying in the thick of the destruction.'

Common to them all is a strong sense of enterprise and opportunism. Though the climate is changing as regulation creeps in, anyone with a few grams of initiative can do or sell more or less anything they like. And they do. In the early 1990s, everyone was opening foreign exchange bureaux. Then it was banks and bars. Today it's authentic Anatolian diners and mobile-phone outlets. And though the wealth gap is widening, even the poorest of the poor seem to have a secret stash under the mattress. People also share a remarkable sense of resilience and solidarity, qualities that were put severely to the test by the earthquake of August 1999. Before the government in Ankara

had even opened its mouth, civilian rescue teams and ordinary people from Istanbul were rallying in the thick of the destruction. One year on, it was again civil society that organised the heartfelt vigil to remember the dead and grieving.

People put the same brave face as before on repeated knocks to the tourism industry, a bastion of the local, and national, economy. If it's not the ghost of Oliver Stone's screenplay that's deterred foreign visitors, it's been the terrorism threat, the Hizbollah threat or the hooligan threat. But foreign perceptions of Istanbul can't be all bad: in the last few years, the city has picked up serious prestige points, especially in the cultural and entertainment field. The line-up at various recent festivals speaks for itself. Theo Angelopoulos were here, so were Youssef Chahine, the Buena Vista Social Club, Philip Glass, the RSC, Matthew Bourne's male swans, Kiri Te Kanawa, Lou Reed, Jimi Tenor, Stomp and Circus Oz (let's gloss over Jethro Tull and Julian Lloyd Webber) to name but a few.

Without too many people west of Edirne noticing it, Istanbul is rapidly gaining a changed and thoroughly modern face. Western perceptions will, *inşallah,* one day soon catch up.

UEFA yes, EU no

Istanbul is the only city in the world whose inhabitants have the option of living in Asia and working in Europe, or vice versa. Stand on the shores of the Bosphorus weekday mornings or evenings and you will see these inter-continental commuters, stuck in the heavy traffic above on the two great high-strung suspension bridges, or streaming on and off the ancient ferryboats. Their journey raises the kind of identity questions seldom pondered on the 8.13 from Guildford. Is Turkey part of Europe? Is Istanbul a European city?

There are lots of ways to approach these well-worn questions. One is to think of Europe in terms of overlapping circles. Istanbul and Turkey are part of some of these (such as the Council of Europe), but not of others (for example, the European Free Trade Area). Istanbul's football and basketball clubs compete for European trophies and Turkey usually does a damn sight better than Norway in the Eurovision Song Contest, but in other contexts the city is treated as part of the Middle East.

The most important of these institutional versions of Europe – the magic circle – is, of course, the European Union. When Turks talk about being part of Europe, they are often referring to membership of the EU, the holy grail

of Turkish foreign policy. When Turkey was officially accepted as a candidate for membership at the EU's Helsinki summit in December 1999, this goal suddenly appeared to be within reach, although it will take at least a decade for Turkey to meet all of the conditions.

But European identity is not a document issued by bureaucrats in Brussels. Istanbul has been part of the European drama for centuries. Today it is returning to its historic role as the economic hub of South-east Europe. For Europe's businesspeople, as for its scholars or football supporters, Istanbul is another stop on the European circuit. And Istanbul's educated classes have long been brought up to speak European languages, and to admire European art and culture – not as respectful outsiders, but from the inside. For these Turks, being European means being part of the modern world.

On the other hand, mass migration from central and eastern Turkey has transformed Istanbul in recent decades. Together with the departure of most of the Greek population, this has arguably left it less European than a century ago. Many of the newcomers come from a culture that is far more Middle Eastern than European. With each new arrival, the effort to fuse the two cultures begins anew.

Istanbul for Women

Between Muslim tradition and secular modernity, sisters are doing it for themselves.

'Everything we see in the world is the work of women.' The words – who'd have thought? – of Mustafa Kemal Atatürk, architect of the Turkish republic and womaniser extraordinaire. Besotted bedroom cant? No, the West-is-best leader translated words into action, so that by 1934 polygamy had been outlawed, women had the vote and there were 18 of them sitting in parliament. Women had it good. But that was then. What about now?

Take a stroll through Beyoğlu, the hip heart of Istanbul, or a Bosphorus tea garden, or even Ümraniye, one of the conservative shanty town suburbs, and you'll find little to substantiate the hackneyed 'little Iran' myth most of the West imagines is Turkey. What you will see is bared midriffs, tattoos, pierced anatomies and lycra mixing with muted raincoats and headscarves. Anything goes. And it all goes together. What may also surprise is the rarity of flowing black tents or *chadors*. Wearers, known by locals as 'kara fatma' ('cockroaches'), really are the exception and tend to stick together in their rare radical outposts.

So much for (modern) appearances. Women's place in politics, at least, has progressed ostensibly nowhere in 66 years: they are no better represented in government than in 1934. Not that there haven't been opportunities. In 1995, just two years after entering politics, a wizard economics professor, Tansu Çiller, was elected Turkey's first and only female prime minister. But just as women got excited about their prospects, the inimitable Mrs Çiller sold out to her ambition and fell in with the wrong crowd. Too soon there were allegations of corruption and the queen of gaffes was unable to save herself with diplomatic sweet talk.

The 1990s rise and fall of mayoress of Şişli, Gülay Atığ, was a similar story of wasted promise at local level. Impressed initially by her prowess, the Istanbul constituency soon smelled a rat or two, by which time she'd already eloped with the man behind her misdemeanours. While both failed spectacularly to advance the status of women, they did at least break the mould and prove the mettle of the fairer sex, if in a decidedly anti-heroic kind of way.

'One third of women in Turkey are functionally illiterate, compared with ten per cent of men.'

Equality may still be a long way off in other areas, but progress is in the right direction. In the world of business, women have made major inroads over the last decade, grabbing a growing number of board positions in large corporations. Women also number significantly among the traditionally male dominated professions of law and medicine. This, obviously, is a function of improved education opportunities. Women currently outnumber men at the university undergraduate level. But still, this belies an aching disparity in literacy rates between the genders. Around one third of women in Turkey are functionally illiterate, compared with a mere ten per cent of men.

THE CINDERELLA SYNDROME

At the social level, the story is – like so much about Turkey – complex and contradictory. Istanbul restaurants, cafés, bars and clubs are full of women: solo women, women with women, women with men. There are still some men-only bastions, typically the *kahvehane* (coffee-cum-gambling house) and *birahane* (drinking den), where heads turn and eyes do more than stare if female flesh crosses the threshold. But frankly, who'd want to go to these places anyway?

Women drink, women smoke, women gyrate on tables, women party till they drop. But the Cinderella syndrome is often not far away. Nights promising passion often end with an unromantic parting of ways to respective parental homes – by the appointed hour. Likewise, the late-teen tryst in secluded café corner often trips up over maternal intervention. The scene goes something like this. Mobile rings. And rings. Juliet grudgingly disengages from Romeo to answer. Yelling over the background music, Juliet swears to mother that she's at the language school and must get back to her English lesson. She switches off and takes up anxiously where she left off with pouting and by now reluctant Romeo.

None of this is, perhaps, surprising in a tradition-based and nominally Islamic society (Turkey is a secular state, but the population is 99 per cent Muslim) where gender roles die hard. Education helps define attitude, so that migrant families from the school-starved east tend to be more rigidly conservative in outlook. For girls, then, marriage is a must – the earlier the better and often arranged – with sheet inspections after the wedding night par for the course. Migrant areas are also manned with frighteningly efficient neighbourhood watch schemes, net curtains twitching every time somebody leaves or enters a building. This is also destined to change as second-generation migrants hit the education system and absorb urban values. But even among the educated classes, the road to equality can be a seriously uphill struggle pitched against mostly macho menfolk.

'Public molestation of a woman is considered ultimately shameful.'

For all that, women don't perhaps get as raw a deal as it seems. In spite of the hard labour involved, mothers are rewarded with almost sacred status in society. Sadly domestic violence is all too common – and all too often swallowed by victims for fear of creating worse problems. But again, there's cause for optimism with a law recently passed which enables victims to seek a restraining order against the perpetrator.

Outside the home, public molestation or abuse of a woman is considered ultimately shameful. So wandering hands in a crowded bus can result in the owner of the hands being practically lynched. This is one of the things that makes Istanbul an exceptionally safe city.

Matters are slightly different where foreign women are concerned. Female visitors to Istanbul can find themselves subject to unsolicited but basically non-threatening attention from local males, especially in the more heavily touristed areas like Sultanahmet. It's simple enough to see why; compared to Turkish women, Westerners are easy. In this respect the Turkish media also has a lot to answer for. Any press or TV coverage of the tourism industry is bound to feature a scantily clad fair-skinned blonde on a beach. Hence the simmering stares – possibly also disapproving glares – many foreign women encounter. Perceptions are changing with easier access to the international media and greater exposure to tourism. But not that fast. Dress demurely, learn to ignore.

And remember: nothing in Turkey is quite what it seems.

Decoding the headscarf

A woman in a tightly tied floral headscarf totters down the street in high heels. Between mincing steps, the seductive curve of a calf slips out from the lengthy slit in her ankle-length skirt. It's a common dress contradiction that the Turks call 'closed at the top and open at the bottom'. It's also not unusual to see a covered woman wandering arm in arm with a very much uncovered friend in mini-skirt and skimpy top.

To the uninitiated, covering the head may seem simply to express identification with Islam. In many ways it does but there are deeper subtleties involved – cultural as well as religious. The style of head-covering and the garb that goes with it can signify something as radical as a statement of solidarity with Islamic law in Iran, as compromising as a bow to family pressure, or as innocuous as a gesture to cultural tradition. The complex range of tacit messages is hardly surprising: Turkey sits uneasily astride east and west, embraces a myriad of cultures and has a mere 75-year history of secular government. Even now, teething troubles are to be expected.

As was the case in 1996, when the Welfare Party (now banned) became the first Islamists to be elected in the history of the republic. Islamic women students leapt on the bandwagon and have been campaigning ever since to break a ban on wearing headscarves at university – with such fierce determination that many thousands have been expelled (*see page 78* **Bullets over Beyazıt**).

Trivial though it may appear from the outside, the headscarf issue cuts to the heart of modern Turkish identity. It also raises the question of democracy – ironic, when it was Atatürk who imposed the ban on religious wear in public-sector institutions. Again, with the eruption of this issue in 1996, democratic principles tended to be thrown aside in the name of defending the secular order against a looming and sinister Islamic threat. A whole set of new regulations was introduced at universities to enforce the ban, such as making students carry photo IDs exposing their locks. Resourceful diehards crammed wigs over their headscarves.

In terms of style, women intent on making a political statement generally wear scarves that cover their heads, shoulders and necks. Drab colours are the order of the day and coordinate with similarly drab raincoats. The uniform is distinct from the easier style adopted by middle-aged migrants from the villages, who tie scarves, often of braided white muslin, loosely under the chin allowing the odd strand of hair to stray. Here the headscarf is less statement than habit. The rich and fashion-conscious, on the other hand, might opt for silk chic tied à la Katherine Hepburn – Armani meets Islam. At the opposite end of the spectrum, the flowing black tent çarşaf or 'sheet' is as radical, if for different reasons. Though allegiance to Islamic law is one interpretation of the dress code, pressure from male relatives may often provide another explanation.

Strange that a square of cloth so small could signify so much to so many.

Architecture

A thousand years' worth of extraordinary structures.
Shame about the skyscraper, though.

In Istanbul, architecture is history. Those looking for contemporary cutting-edge building design will have to go elsewhere. High-profile projects, especially those with big names attached, are the preserve of cities with resources to spare. Istanbul hasn't any. It's all the municipality can do to provide basic accommodation for the continued influx of settlers. Added to which, the business of shoring up a failing infrastructure – new transport systems, tunnels, bridges – and the need for quick-fix solutions leaves little opportunity for the promotion of a modern architectural culture.

This hasn't always been the case. Had *Architectural Digest* been around any time during the sixth to the 17th centuries, Istanbul's architects would have been front-cover material issue after issue. As the fabulously wealthy imperial capital of the Byzantines and then Ottomans, for the best part of a millennium and a half Istanbul was endowed with some of the most remarkable architecture the loaded treasury of an empire could buy. At the time

they were built, Justinian's Church of St Sophia (now the **Haghia Sophia**; *pictured above, and see page 69*) and Sinan's **Süleymaniye Mosque** (*see page 80*) were marvels of engineering and milestones in artistic development to rival anything created in Europe. Styles developed here were exported far and wide, south through the Levant to Egypt and west throughout Greece and the Balkans.

When the era of the great empires passed, Istanbul became an assimilator of architectural styles from elsewhere, all reworked with a particular Turkish twist. So while it's certainly no Brussels or Vienna, Istanbul does harbour a little-known legacy of art nouveau twists and fancies. No less interesting is the reaction to this referencing of Europe, which manifested itself in a new, no less eclectic, national architecture movement that briefly flourished following the birth of the Turkish Republic. So even if there isn't much to excite in glass and steel, Istanbul's legacy in stone is sufficiently rich and vast to offer ample compensation.

ARCHES, VAULTS AND DOMES

When in AD 330 Constantine began to build his new capital on the Bosphorus (*see page 7*), 'Nova Roma' was literally that, a new Rome constructed in the same style as the old one, but a thousand miles to the east. The change in location proved significant, as the proximity to Asia Minor and Syria resulted in an infusion of new ideas and methods. Very quickly the traditional Roman column-and-lintel way of building, inherited from the Greeks, gave way to a more fluid architecture based on arches, vaults and domes. Supplanting stone, the smaller and more malleable unit of the brick became the building material of choice.

Although Constantine's city boasted great secular structures, including fortified walls, forums, a hippodrome and an imperial palace (none of which survive in their original form), it's the churches he built that most came to symbolise the Byzantine style. Originally these took two distinctive forms: longitudinal basilicas, usually with three aisles, and 'centralised' churches, which were circular, square or octagonal. Through a merging of the two a characteristic Byzantine form emerged. Istanbul's oldest standing church, **St John of St Studius** (*see page 88*), was built in AD 463, a century and a quarter after Constantine's death. It's a basilica in that it has three aisles, but it's also nearly square in plan.

Development continued during the reign of the emperor Justinian (AD 527-565), possibly the greatest builder in the city's history. He was patron to four great churches: SS Sergius and Bacchus, now the **Küçük Haghia Sophia Mosque** (*see page 76*); the rebuilt **Haghia Eirene** (*see page 72*); the **Church of the Holy Apostles**, quarried for the **Fatih Mosque** (*see page 85*); and the great cathedral of **Haghia Sophia**. What distinguished these structures from all that had come before was the dome. Domes had indeed been built previously, but

never on this scale. With Haghia Sophia, Justinian's goal was to enclose the greatest space possible, creating a physical impression of the kingdom of God, one that was tended by the emperor. To achieve this he is said to have eschewed traditional builders and master craftsmen and instead employed the services of two mathematicians. Such was the impression created that the huge dome was described by Byzantine historian Procopius (a contemporary of Justinian) as 'appearing to be suspended from heaven by a golden chain'.

'For all its spatial grandeur Haghia Sophia is dull, dull, dull on the outside.'

Byzantine innovations elsewhere included the **city walls** (*see pages 88-90*) erected early in the fifth century by Theodosius II. These also made use of vaulting to support the floors in the 192 towers that punctuated their length. Vaults and domes underground rather than above ground were employed to create Constantinople's distinctive cisterns, of which there were more than 30 (*see page 74*).

Post-Justinian, the Byzantine empire was to continue for close to another 800 years, during which time architectural styles evolved further. No emperor ever tried to match Justinian's audacious cathedral. Instead, later structures tended to be more modest in size and more harmoniously proportioned. Decoration came to play a larger part. For all its spatial grandeur Haghia Sophia is dull, dull, dull on the outside, whereas surviving later churches such as **St Saviour in Chora** (Kariyer Mosque; *see page 90*) and the 12th-century **Church of the Pantocrator** (now the Zeyrek Mosque; *see page 85*) employ multiple domes, narthexes and apses executed in alternating bands of brick and roughly dressed stone. Glazed pottery set into the external walls forms friezes that echo interior mosaics and tiling, which flourished in the later Byzantine period following the miserable repressions of the Iconoclastic era (*see page 11*). These buildings are thoroughly charming and deserve much greater attention than the few visitors they generally receive.

DOMES AND MINARETS

Ottoman architecture is often presented as essentially a continuation of the Byzantine tradition, but that's an oversimplification. Established in the 14th century, it grew out of the development of a great many architectural influences all over Anatolia, most notably the Selçuks. But, like the Byzantines, especially those of the early era, the Ottomans shared a

Thoroughly charming: **St Saviour in Chora**.

predilection for centrally-planned structures topped by big domes. In that respect, Constantinople's Haghia Sophia was inspirational. More than that, it was a benchmark. A great challenge. Once the Ottomans had captured the city in 1453 the task of constructing a dome larger than Justinian's was to occupy imperial architects for more than a century. It was eventually achieved by a master-builder named Sinan (*see page 38* **Keeping up with the domes's**) during the reign of Sultan Süleyman the Magnificent, although the dome in question graced a mosque in **Edirne** (*see pages 245-8*), not the capital.

'Ottoman architects were perpetually questing to minimise the number of columns and supports.'

Islam also defined how Ottoman architecture would develop. An egalitarian religion with no hierarchical orders, no saints in need of side chapels, no use for obfuscating trappings like naves and apses, its mosques required nothing more than a single, large, open space with as little clutter as possible. A domed central chamber proved to be the best way of achieving this. Unlike at the Haghia Sophia with its heavy, very visible internal structure, Ottoman architects were perpetually questing to minimise the number of columns and supports needed. That's what all the half domes are about, extending the internal space while spreading the structural load. It's almost incidental that the external effect is so beautiful – a cascade of gracefully descending curves. Slender, pencil-pointed minarets, originally intended as platforms for the five daily calls to prayer, frame the composition, while surrounding courts keep the secular city at bay.

Mosques also served as a focal point for related institutions, such as schools (*medreses*), hospitals (*daruşşifas*), libraries (*kitaplıks*), mausoleums (*türbes*), public kitchens (*imarets*) and even public baths (*hamams*). There were also often buildings called *tekkes* to house dervishes (members of mystical fraternities) and other holy men. The entire complex was then called a *külliye*.

Istanbul's Ottoman architectural glory is the city's most photogenic asset, with a series of great mosques and *külliyes* dominating the skyline. Tragically, although the empire survived for almost half a millennium, building-wise it peaked as early as the 16th century and went nowhere from there. Even the much-admired **Sultanahmet Mosque** (*see page 75*), built across from Haghia Sophia in the 17th

century, is no more than a reprise of what Sinan had achieved a century earlier.

FRILLS AND LACE
As the Ottoman empire declined so European influence made itself felt. This was most definitely not a good thing. From the early 17th century to the mid-18th century much of Europe had undergone a flirtation with baroque (originally a term of abuse deriving from the Italian word barocco, meaning a contorted idea) and rococo (from the French rocaille, used to describe a certain type of shell and pebble decoration in the 16th century and with definite derogatory overtones). So to the Ottoman simplicity and clarity of function was wedded the decorative excesses and indulgences of these decadent and redundant imported stylings. The bastard offspring goes by the name of 'Turkish Baroque'. One of the earliest and most accessible examples is the **Nuruosmaniye Mosque** (*see page 79*) beside the Grand Bazaar, completed in 1755. Its large dome rests on four huge semicircular arches filled with long vertical windows that brighten the interior, but the absence of semi-domes makes the profile appear stumpy.

By the 19th century European styles were almost completely dominant, with the 'Turkish' dropping out of 'Turkish Baroque' altogether. Rather than mosques or religious institutions, the defining structures of the time are palaces. **Dolmabahçe** (*see page 99*), for example, is a good illustration of the changes taking place in Istanbul architecture at the time. It was the work of the Armenian Balyan family, who for almost a century were the most important and influential architects in the empire. The elders of the family got their knowledge of Western building styles from drawings and etchings brought by travellers and diplomats; younger sons were sent to study at the École des Beaux Arts in Paris. As a result Dolmabahçe is a showy mix of baroque and neo-classicism, with interiors designed by Sechan, who had also done the interiors of Garnier's grand Paris Opera House. Further palaces at **Çırağan** (*see page 100*) and **Beylerbeyi** (*see page 109*) are also the work of the Balyans. A younger Balyan is responsible for the dynasty's most appealing work, the **Mecidiye Mosque** (*see page 101*), built 1853-5 and still a muddle of competing influences, but with a superb waterside site, strangely improved by the backdrop of the high-tech Bosphorus suspension bridge.

It wasn't just foreign architectural influences making their way to Istanbul, but foreign architects too. Sir Charles Barry, who designed the Houses of Parliament in London, knocked up a neo-renaissance British embassy building (1845;

Keeping up with the domes's

If there was a poll to name the person who's made the single biggest contribution to Istanbul, in whatever way, odds are that name would be **Mimar Sinan**. He was chief of imperial architects under Süleyman I 'the Magnificent' and two successive sultans, and it's quite likely Süleyman would never have been considered quite so magnificent if wasn't for the legacy of Sinan.

Born around 1490 into a Christian family in central Turkey, Sinan was taken into the sultan's service as part of an annual levy of Christian boys. Trained as a military engineer, he served in seven of Süleyman's campaigns before being appointed chief imperial architect in 1538. He constructed his first mosque in Aleppo, Syria, that same year, and by the time he died exactly 50 years later he'd racked up an incredible 477 buildings, of which more than 100 were mosques. Pretty much single-handedly, Sinan wrote the stylebook for Ottoman architecture, in particular developing the typology of the great imperial mosque as a single main domed square surrounded by half domes and domed side aisles. This he exhibited to near perfection in his **Süleymaniye Mosque** (1560-75; pictured; see page 80), which set the pattern for mosque building for almost the next 200 years and continues to dominate the Istanbul skyline today.

As with earlier mosques, the plan follows that of Hagia Sophia, with a huge dome flanked by two semi-domes. Sinan's genius was to support the whole structure on four piers, avoiding the need for additional columns or arcading, creating one immense unified enclosed space. From the outside the profile is the most beautiful on the skyline, a confection of rippling semi-domes. The buildings of the surrounding complex are also beautifully proportioned.

Sinan's genius wasn't confined to huge imperial buildings. The **Sokollu Mehmet Paşa Mosque** (see page 76) demonstrates his ability to work in difficult, confined spaces, the sloping site proving no obstacle to designing one of the most beautiful of the city's smaller mosques.

However, according to his own writings, Sinan considered the Süleymaniye merely 'good workmanship', withholding his pride instead for his **Selimiye Mosque** in Edirne (see page 246):

'Architects of any importance in Christian countries consider themselves far superior to Muslims, because until now the latter haven't accomplished anything comparable to the dome of Haghia Sophia. Thanks to the All Powerful and the favour of the sultan, I have succeeded in building a dome for Sultan Selim's mosque that surpasses that of Haghia Sophia.'

Over 200 buildings credited to Sinan still stand, most in either Istanbul or Edirne. Apart from Süleymaniye and Sokollu Mehmet Paşa Mosque, the most prominent in Istanbul are the **Rüstem Paşa Mosque** (see page 83) and **Şehzade Mosque** (see page 84).

Botter House – cast-iron treasure.

now the consulate, *see page 273*) in what is now Beyoğlu. A German named Jachmund designed **Sirkeci Station** (*see page 266*), terminus of the Orient Express. The prolific Swiss-born Fossati brothers, for a time official architects to Czar Nicholas I, designed a handsome embassy (now consulate) for the Russians (1837; Istiklal Caddesi 443), another for the Dutch (1855; Istiklal Caddesi 393), and undertook a major restoration of Haghia Sophia in 1847-9. And an Italian, Raimondo D'Aronco, introduced Istanbul to art nouveau.

> **'At the turn of the century, Istanbul suburbs were as wealthy, influential and style conscious as any in Europe.'**

The existence of Istanbul's art nouveau heritage generally comes as a surprise. It is owed to the fact that at the turn of the century suburbs such as Galata and Pera (now Beyoğlu) were as wealthy, influential and style conscious as any in Europe. D'Aronco lived in the city between 1893 and 1909, serving ten years as chief of the imperial architects. Foremost among his existing buildings is the **Botter House** at Istiklal Caddesi 475-7. A seven-storey residence built for a Dutch couturier to the imperial court, it has a narrow frontage 'overgrown' with cast-iron flora. It would be a national treasure in any European capital, but here its interior was ripped out in the 1960s as part of a conversion to a bank and it now lies semi-derelict and decaying. D'Aronco's nearby and equally excellent **Laleli Fountain** (Laleli Çeşmesi) at the corner of Laleli Çeşme Sokak and Şair Ziya Paşa Caddesi beside the Galata Tower is happily in a better state of repair. Also worth a look are the same architect's **Şeyh Zafir Complex** (see page 100) on Yıldız Caddesi in Beşiktaş and the **Egyptian consulate** (*see page 102*) in Bebek.

BRUTAL BUT TURKISH

European style went out of fashion overnight in 1923 when the Turkish National Assembly declared the founding of the Republic. In keeping with the spirit of the times, there was a new popular building style, the First National Architectural Movement (FNAM), pioneered by Vedat Tek and Kemalettin Bey, a former student of Jachmund. FNAM was all about reinterpreting Turkey's classical Ottoman heritage using contemporary western building technology. Notable examples include Bey's **Hotel Merit Antique** at Ordu Caddesi 226 in Laleli, with its typically wavy Ottoman roofs and Islamic-styled arches executed in reinforced concrete, and an office building known as **4. Vakıf Hanı** at Hamidiye Caddesi 64-8 in Eminönü, with gratuitous frilly domes plonked at the corners of an otherwise dour block.

Flirtations with modernism occurred in the 1930s, but that always seemed more suited to Ankara, the country's recently created 'modern' capital. In Istanbul architects generally continued to prefer to reference the city's centuries of architectural heritage. Sedad Eldem may be Turkey's best known 20th-century architect, responsible for more than 100 buildings over a 50-year career. His work often straddled the line between slavish historicism and clever re-rendering. His **Taşlık Coffee House** (now the Şark restaurant in the Swissôtel complex, Maçka), is a 17th-century Bosphorus mansion (*yalı*) slightly adapted and rebuilt with modern

Vakıf Hanı: Ottoman style revisited.

The height of bad taste

The competition has been stiff, with several strong contenders going up in recent years, but now there is a clear winner, one on which almost every public voice is in agreement: the ugliest building in Istanbul is Gökkafes. The name means 'Skyscraper'. You can't miss it. Thirty floors topped by a red glasshouse. It's Canary Wharf's ugly kid sister, wearing a silly hat. But whereas Canary Wharf is well out of central London and in a suitably high-tech, high-rise setting, Gökkafes towers ten times higher than its elderly city centre neighbours. To add insult to injury, it rises from a swath of green parkland that was supposedly a protected area. But such terms have little meaning in Istanbul.

Back in the 1980s, then-president Turgut Özal ushered in an era of get-rich-quick politics. One nice little earner was to designate key areas as 'tourism zones', which meant that normal strictures concerning zoning laws and planning permits no longer applied. So the back door was opened for a booming trade in the construction of big hotels, off which Özal and cronies are rumoured to have done very nicely, thank you. Gökkafes, too, is part hotel. The parkland in which it's sited, which contains the Harbiye cultural complex, Beşiktaş Stadium and Democracy Park, was laid out by French architect Henri Prost in 1937 as a green area and given protected status, but since the 1980s it's become peppered with five-star monoliths.

Gökkafes has been greeted with protests and construction has on more than one occasion been halted. Locals were initially perhaps

encouraged by the example of the Park Hotel, a concrete blockhouse that was being raised on Inönü Caddesi, just east of Taksim Square. It was stopped by the voluble objections of local residents, crucially lent weight by a mayor up for re-election. But in the case of Gökkafes, building was resumed when the city governor (an unelected post) cunningly shifted the municipal boundaries so that the building was no longer any business of the stroppy Beyoğlu municipality and was instead part of Şişli, run by Motherland, the political party formerly headed by Özal.

A number of challenges to Gökkafes are awaiting a court hearing, but part of the building has already been leased to a large US hotel chain. Meanwhile the building's owners are happily suing the ass off anyone who stands in their way.

So, like it or not, the city has a new monument: Gökkafes, testimony to the fact that in Istanbul, there is little that money cannot buy.

---

materials. Sadly the Swiss Hotel has done some revisionism of its own and made disfiguring changes to Eldem's original design, making it unfair to judge the building on present evidence.

STRIPPED BRICKS AND SPILLED BEER
For the past 50 years, over-riding all style issues have been two factors: low cost and maximum return. The architectural result is a lot of badly poured concrete and anonymous off-the-peg foreign designs allowing for little creative local input. The cause of good architecture has also not been helped any by the lack of regulated urban planning (*see above* **The height of bad taste**).

One spot of hope, however, is the renovation and reuse of 19th-century buildings, especially in the downtown district of Beyoğlu.

One of the trendsetters was **Hayal Kahvesi** (*see page 207*) a bar on Büyükparmakkapı

Sokak. In 1992 investors took a derelict shop space and stripped it out, exposing the brick walls and French vaulted ceiling. A mezzanine floor was constructed over the street windows, allowing for more seating and a stage and bar.

'For months, queues jammed the narrow street outside Hayal Kahvesi.'

For months after Hayal Kahvesi opened, queues of eager scensters jammed the narrow street outside wanting a look in. Nowadays, the place is nothing special, but at the time it was a genuinely new phenomenon and, as such, can claim part of the credit for leading the charge that's made Beyoğlu the Soho of Istanbul.

Accommodation

Accommodation

Feature boxes

Accommodation

Breakfast surrounded by Sultanahmet minarets or stay within crawling distance of Beyoğlu's bars and clubs.

As a long-standing tourist mecca that's been accommodating curious Westerners since the middle of the 19th century, Istanbul is thick with hotels. At the same time, as a long-standing tourist mecca, a lot of the city's hotels are a bit on the well worn side of things. Even some of the high-end, five-star places have been around since the 1950s and are seriously showing their age. In some cases that age has been used to good effect. While there's no Schrager or Hempel here, Istanbul does have a nice semi-hip line in 'Ottoman' boutique hotels. Also known as 'special licence' hotels, these are old Ottoman-era houses imaginatively converted into some quite unique accommodation. Actually, in many cases it goes a lot further than mere conversion, as frequently the original building has been demolished and reconstructed entirely from scratch in concrete with old-style dressing applied on top. So guests get both nostalgia and all modern amenities.

The first of these Ottoman boutique places was **Ayasofya Pansiyonları** (*see page 47*), founded by the **Turkish Touring & Automobile Association** (*see page 270*), who funded the project with revenues accrued from issuing import documents to cars. Committed to the promotion of Turkish culture, the TTAA went on to open several similar hotels (as well as restaurants, handicraft centres and the **Istanbul Library**; *see page 276*), with the pick of the bunch being perhaps **Yeşil Ev** (*see page 47*). In the late 1990s, policy changes deprived the TTAA of import licence revenues and the organisation's money dried up, but other businesses and individuals have picked up the baton, such as American Ann Nevans at the **Empress Zoe** (*see page 49*).

LOCATION, LOCATION AND LOCATION

There are basically two choices: south of the Golden Horn or north of the Golden Horn. Whichever you choose, expect to spend plenty of time in taxis, as most visitors split their time about equally between the two areas. South of the Golden Horn means mosques, bazaars and all the tourist sights of Sultanahmet. This has traditionally been the centre for the city's budget and mid-range accommodation. Almost all the

Four Seasons – once the infamous Sultanahmet prison, now a top-class joint. See p46.

cheapest options are on and around Akbıyık Caddesi and Utangaç Sokak, two parallel streets east of Haghia Sophia, although increasingly the area is moving upmarket and now has one of the best deluxe options in the **Four Seasons**. It's also where you'll find all the Ottoman boutique places. Most hotels have rooftop breakfast terraces – it's hard to beat morning coffee surrounded by minarets and a glinting silvery Bosphorus in the background.

North of the Golden Horn is the business and entertainment district of Beyoğlu. There are plenty of backstreet mid-range places that put you right among the shopping, restaurants, bars and clubs. They lack the views or romance of the Sultanahmet hotels, but are just a short stagger home to bed at night. Most of the city's high-rise, high-end options are clustered around Harbiye, an area of green parkland just north of Taksim Square. As well as being close to Beyoğlu, it's conveniently situated for shopping trips to the fashionable areas of Nişantaşıand Teşvikiye. All the culture of old Istanbul is a ten-minute taxi ride away ($3-$4), downhill and across the Galata or Atatürk bridges, although at the wrong time of day – morning and evening rush hours for example – that can stretch to up to half an hour.

Staying over on the Asian Shore is a realistic option only if you have business over on that side or simply want to be alone – although even Greta Garbo preferred to stay on the European side: at the **Pera Palas**; *see page 62* **Bed, board & legends**).

RESERVATIONS
In line with basic economic principles of supply and demand, hotels don't come cheap in Istanbul. Competitively priced places book up quickly, particularly during the summer when they're choked with large tour groups, conventions and conferences. May to September, Christmas, New Year and national holidays (*see page 282*) are the busiest times. Beware also of major cultural events like the various major international film, theatre and music festivals (*see chapter* **By Season**). At such times definitely book ahead.

Plenty of hotels now take bookings by email and there are also a few useful Internet sites for bookings, notably www.istanbulhotels.com, which brings together about 80 of the city's hotels and offers discounts for online booking. Alternatively, www.istanbul.hotelguide.net provides basic information and links to local hotel websites.

If you arrive without a reservation there are several booking agents at Atatürk airport in the international arrivals hall (at the opposite end to the tourist information desk). They have an extensive list of mainly three- and four-star hotels and they don't take any commission from the customer.

The best Hotels

For murderous passions
Agatha Christie found inspiration at the **Pera Palas** and a British ambassador survived a bomb. See page 62 **Bed, board & legends**.

When money is no object
For the epitome of luxurious living check in to the **Çırağan Palace Hotel Kempinski**, regularly voted one of the world's best hotels. See page 55.

For Hemingway fans
He didn't much care for 'old Constan' but probably appreciated the fine little bar at the **Büyük Londra Hotel**. See page 61.

For bar crawlers
The perfect hotel for people who rarely go to bed, the **Hotel Residence** is at the centre of Beyoğlu's bar district. See page 61.

For high style on a low budget
Small but perfectly formed, the **Empress Zoe** is sheer affordable class. See page 49.

For wilfully wacky decor
Gypsy colours and circus-styling make the **Kybele Hotel** about as fun as board and lodgings get. See page 51.

For breakfast with a view
Minarets, domes and seascapes come as part of the package with **every hotel in Sultanahmet** except the Hotel St Sophia...

For an early morning alarm call
...as do crack of dawn wake-ups courtesy of the müezzin delivering the early morning call to prayer.

In all but a few of the high-end hotels room rates include tax (17 per cent) and breakfast. Prices quoted in this book are high-season rates, which normally apply from the end of May to the beginning of September, at Christmas and New Year, as well as during national holidays. Outside these times you can expect a discount of up to 30 per cent. Rates are particularly open to bargaining in the mid-range and budget categories, especially if you can pay cash in foreign currency. Most places happily accept dollars or sterling.

Listings in this guide are divided into the following categories: **Deluxe** (upwards of $250 a night for a double); **High-end** ($150-$250); **Mid-range** ($70-$150); **Budget** ($30-$70); and **Rock-bottom** (under $30).

Merit Antique – architecturally significant.

South of the Golden Horn

Deluxe

Four Seasons

Tevfikhane Sokak 1, Sultanahmet (0212 638 8200/ fax 638 8210/www.fourseasons.com). Tram Sultanahmet. **Rates** $290-$520 single; $320-$550 double; $700-$2,000 suite. Rates do not include tax (17%). **Credit** AmEx, DC, MC, V. **Map** p303 N10.
Always a fairly elite sort of place, for 66 years this building served as the infamous Sultanahmet Prison, whose inmates included some celebrated political prisoners. In 1986 it was renovated and reopened as one of the top hotels in town – *Midnight Express* gave way to pure Oriental fantasy. Underneath all the glamour the building's original function remains evident in wall-top watchtowers and a central court which takes little imagining to see stripped of its flowers and shrubbery as a prison yard. Cells have given way to 54 beautiful high-ceilinged rooms, a modest number ensuring intimacy and top-class service. There's an excellent gazebo restaurant; if you can't afford a room here it's at least worth stretching the plastic for lunch.
Hotel services *Air-conditioning. Babysitting. Bar. Business services. Concierge. Gym. Parking. Restaurant.* **Room services** *CD player. Mini-bar. Room service. Safe box. Telephone: 2 lines. TV: cable; VCR (latest film releases available at concierge). Voicemail.*

High-end

Armada

Ahırkapı Sokak 24, Çankurtaran, Sultanahmet (0212 638 1370/fax 518 5060/ www.armadahotel.com.tr). **Rates** $145 single; $175 double. **Credit** AmEx, MC, V. **Map** p303 O11.
Sandwiched between waterside Kennedy Caddesi and the suburban railway line in a middle-of-nowhere seeming sort of area, the Armada scores low on location, although it is only a ten-minute walk up the hill to sight-studded Sultanahmet. However, most rooms have fantastic uninterrupted Bosphorus views and, despite being a large, generic, modern hotel, the 120-room Armada has been sufficiently well designed to avoid typical four-star blandness. The lobby area is attractive with a terrapin pond and café, while the rooms, if not exceptional, are certainly very comfortable. If the budget doesn't stretch to the Four Seasons and the Yeşil Ev is packed, then of the very few high-end options south of the Bosphorus this is definitely one of the best.
Hotel services *Air-conditioning. Bar. Business services. Parking. Restaurant. Wheelchair access.* **Room services** *Mini-bar. Room service. Telephone. TV.*

Merit Antique

226 Ordu Caddesi, Laleli (0212 513 9300/fax 512 6390/www.meritantiquehotel.com.tr). Tram Laleli. **Rates** $160-$190 single; $200-$240 double. **Credit** AmEx, DC, MC, V. **Map** p302 H10.
Head and shoulders above everything else in this district of mostly mediocre, mid-range places, the architecturally significant Merit Antique (*see p39*) is frequented by a curious blend of holidaying Europeans and seriously besuited businessmen. Transformed in a 1986 facelift, the four original buildings are linked by an airy atrium in which several restaurants, including the only kosher venue in town, compete for space with an aviary of chattering birds and a glitzy water feature. Ostentation rather than style marks the decor but the comfortable rooms are more restrained. Despite the double glazing you'd be wise to think twice about a room overlooking the ceaseless traffic of Ordu Caddesi.
Hotel services *Air-conditioning. Bar. Business facilities. Gym. Parking. Restaurant. Swimming pool.* **Room services** *Mini-bar. Room service. Telephone. TV: cable.*

Polat Renaissance Istanbul Hotel

Sahil Caddesi, Yeşilyurt (0212 663 1700/ fax 663 1755/www.renaissancehotels.com). **Rates** $190-$215 single; $220-$245 double; $320-$420 suite. **Credit** AmEx, DC, MC, V.
The airport hotel of choice, the Polat Renaissance is just a five-minute taxi ride from the international terminal in the coastal suburb of Yeşilköy. A striking blue-glass skyscraper by the sea, it's ultra-modern and stylish with a soaring central atrium overlooked by balconies. At least half of the 390 rooms also have excellent views over the Sea of

Marmara. The full range of facilities includes a heated outdoor pool.
Hotel services *Air-conditioning. Bar. Business services. Gym. Handicapped-equipped rooms. No-smoking floors. Parking. Restaurant. Swimming pool.* **Room services** *Mini-bar. Room service. Telephone. TV: cable.*

Yeşil Ev

Kabasakal Caddesi 5, Sultanahmet (0212 517 6785/ fax 517 6780). Tram Sultanahmet. **Rates** $120 single; $160 double; $250 Pasha's room. **Credit** AmEx, MC, V. **Map** p303 N10.

Flagship of the TTAA's fleet of 'restored' Ottoman properties, this place, the 'Green House', enjoys an unrivalled location on a leafy cobbled street mid-way between Haghia Sophia and Sultanahmet Mosque. A stately wooden mansion painted green and white, it's like some grand country house. Stepping over the threshold is like entering the set of a 19th-century costume drama, with every room decked out with repro furniture, wood-panelled ceilings, creaky parquet flooring and artfully positioned antique rugs. It's all a bit like a stage set and very chintzy, but if yours is an Ottoman fantasy, then this is certainly the place to live it out. Room 31, the Pasha's Room, is distinguished by an en suite Turkish bath. Best of all is the well-kept shady garden, in summer the venue for a fine café (*see p142*) and a so-so restaurant. This place is hugely popular and with only 19 rooms advance booking is essential.
Hotel services *Cafe. Restaurant. Room service.* **Room services** *Mini-bar. Telephone.*

Mid-range

Hotel Ararat

Torun Sokak 3, Sultanahmet (0212 516 0411/fax 518 5241/hotelararat@turk.net). Tram Sultanahmet. **Rates** $45 Single; $55 double; $65 treble or room with view. **Credit** MC, V. **Map** p303 N11.

Noting the success of the Empress Zoe, the owners of the Ararat called in its architect Nicos Papadakis to have a go at their place. It opened early in 2000 and if the results aren't quite as inspired as the Zoe, the Ararat still breaks the mould with marbled walls and an effective orange-tinged colour scheme that works well with the dark stained-wood floors. Bedrooms have modern wooden four-posters for guests to loll in while getting an eyeful of the Sultanahmet Mosque over the road, which looms at the window threatening to muscle its way in. Breakfast area on the roof.
Hotel services *Bar.* **Room services** *Telephone.*

Ayasofya Pansiyonları

Soğukçeşme Sokak, Sultanahmet (0212 513 3660/ fax 513 3669/www.ayasofyapansiyonlari.com). Tram Gülhane. **Rates** $80-$90 single; $100-$120 double; $200 suite. **Credit** AmEx, MC, V. **Map** p303 N10.

This is the scheme that kicked off the whole Ottoman boutique hotel phenomenon. Constructed in the 1980s by the Turkish Touring & Automobile Association as pristine clones of buildings that once stood on the site, Ayasofya Pansiyonları is a row of pastel-painted clapboard-clad houses simply furnished in period-style. Between them they provide 57 single and double rooms and four three-bedroom suites. The setting is fantastic, a narrow sloping cobbled lane squeezed between the high walls of Topkapı Palace and the back of Haghia Sophia. Breakfast is served in the garden or gazebo of the Konut Evi, a four-storey annexe of the hotel at the end of the street. At night the whole thing is lamp-lit. Walt Disney couldn't do better.
Hotel services *Bar. Parking. Restaurant.* **Room services** *Telephone.*

Yeşil Ev – it ain't half Ottoman.

some like it
grand and enchanting...

It happens at the Hilton

Ayasofya Pansiyonları. *See p47.*

Citadel

32 Kennedy Caddesi, Ahırkapı (0212 516 2313/ fax 516 1384/www.citadelhotel.com). **Rates** $110 single; $140 double; $210 suite. **Credit** AmEx, DC, MC, V. **Map** p303 O11.

Occupying a renovated and strikingly pink three-storey mansion, this Best Western affiliate has 31 rooms and six suites decked out in Barbie colours and the only thing between you and the Sea of Marmara is – alas – six lanes of speeding traffic. Not far from the fish restaurants of Kumkapı, though, and the conservatory bar and decent restaurant lessen the feeling of isolation.

Hotel services *Air-conditioning. Bar. Restaurants (3). Garden.* **Room services** *Mini-bar. Telephone. TV.*

Empress Zoe

Adliye Sokak 10, off Akbıyık Caddesi, Sultanahmet (0212 518 2504/fax 518 5699/www.emzoe.com). *Tram Sultanahmet.* **Rates** $55 single; $75 double; $105-$120 suite. 10% discount for payment in cash. **Credit** MC, V. **Map** p303 O11.

Named after a racy Byzantine regent (*see p70*), the Empress Zoe is one of the best and quirkiest of the city's small hotels. Its sunken reception area incorporates parts of a 15th-century hamam with cold marble offset by warm sepia walls and deep red covers on the bench seating. Guests have to be nimble, as rooms can be reached only up a tight wrought-iron spiral staircase. In contrast to the gilt and frills of most other 'period' hotels, the Zoe's 19 small rooms are tastefully decorated in dark wood and richly coloured textiles, enlivened by small personal touches chosen by proprietress and former San Franciscan Ann Nevans. There's a small stone-garden for breakfast and a fine rooftop bar for a nightcap with a view. Class from top to bottom. Reservations are a must.

Hotel services *Bar.* **Room services** *Telephone.*

Ibrahim Paşa Hotel

Terzihane Sokak 5, Sultanahmet (0212 518 0394/ fax 518 4457/pasha@ibm.net). Tram Sultanahmet. **Rates** $70 single; $90 double; $150 suite. **Credit** AmEx, DC, MC, V. **Map** p303 M11.

A cream-painted three-storey stone townhouse tucked round the corner from the Museum of Turkish and Islamic Art (*see page 115*), this is an elegant little place that doesn't overplay the old Ottoman card. It's smart and bright with just enough judiciously placed rugs and bits of copperware to remind you that this is Istanbul. Of the 19 rooms, the nicest of the bunch are those on the front with large windows, even though the view is only of the blank wall of the museum opposite. There are plenty of minarets and domes on show from the rooftop terrace.

Hotel services *Bar. Parking.* **Room services** *Air-conditioning. Mini-bar. Room services. Telephone. TV.*

Kariye Hotel

Kariye Camii Sokak 18, Edirnekapı (0212 534 8414/ fax 521 6631). **Rates** $80 single; $110 double. **Credit** AmEx, MC, V. **Map** p304 D4.

Class from top to bottom: **Empress Zoe**, one of Istanbul's best and quirkiest small hotels.

Ibrahim Paşa Hotel – elegant. *See p49.*

From the same people that brought you the Ayasofya Pansiyonları and Yeşil Ev, this is yet another 19th-century Ottoman residence stripped down and dressed up by the Turkish Touring & Automobile Association and pressed into service as a hotel. Downstairs, the house restaurant, **Asıthane** (*see p132*), is renowned for its fine Ottoman cuisine. Next door is the **Church of St Saviour in Chora** (*see p90*), one of Istanbul's most essential sights. But the big snag is the location, right out by the old city walls and a good half-hour's bus ride from Sultanahmet or upwards of $6 in a cab. We can't think of a single plus to being out in this part of town, but if you had a reason to be around here, then this would be the place to stay. **Hotel services** *Bar. Parking. Restaurant.* **Room services** *Minibar. Telephone.*

Kybele Hotel

Yerebatan Caddesi 33-5, Sultanahmet (0212 511 7766/fax 513 4393/www.kybelehotel.com). Tram Sultanahmet. **Rates** $45 single; $75 double; $90 treble or suite. **Credit** MC, V. **Map** p303 N10.

Owners the Akbayrak brothers have a thing about vintage glass lamps, that much is obvious, as the interior is hung with 1,002 of them (so they say, we didn't count). The eccentricities continue, as every room is crammed with kilims, candlestands, empty bottles and other knick-knacks. Garish pink and green paint schemes heighten the sense of fun. It all makes sense when you learn that one of the brothers was formerly an antique dealer, while another spent three years with an Australian circus. The 16 bedrooms are smallish, particularly the singles, but they are comfortable enough and have beautiful en suite marble bathrooms. Breakfast is served in a courtyard as colourful as a Gypsy caravan. **Hotel services** *Bar. Cafe.* **Room services** *Air-conditioning. Mini-bar. Telephone.*

Orient Express Hotel

Hüdavendigar Caddesi 34, Sirkeci (0212 520 7161/ fax 526 8446/www.orientexpresshotel.com). Tram Sirkeci. **Rates** $70 single; $90 double; $120 treble. **Credit** AmEx, MC, V. **Map** p303 N9.

It's amazing what difference a matter of a few hundred metres can make, but rooms that would go for perhaps $120 in Sultanahmet go for about two-thirds of that just down the hill and round the corner in Sirkeci. You have to do without the Ottoman frills, but otherwise amenities are excellent and the rooms, 54 of them, are comfortable if on the small side. No mosques in view from the roof terrace; instead there's a fine panorama of the Golden Horn, glorious at night. **Hotel services** *Air-conditioning. Bar. Parking. Restaurant. Swimming pool.* **Room services** *Mini-bar. Telephone. TV.*

Hotel St Sophia

Alemdar Caddesi, Sultanahmet (0212 528 0973/ fax 511 5491/www.istanbulhotels.com/stsophia). Tram Gülhane. **Rates** $90 single; $140 double; $180 suite. **Credit** AmEx, DC, MC, V. **Map** p303 N10.

Right in the shadow of Haghia Sophia and across from the Yerebatan Sarayı, this hotel is another conversion job on a 19th-century Ottoman house. Extensive renovations have perhaps left it a bit over-polished and low on atmosphere, but it can't be faulted in the comfort stakes. Of the 27 rooms, all of them tastefully furnished and decorated in warm yellow tones, the suites on the top two floors have Jacuzzis and balconies that overlook Justinian's great cathedral. In the warmer months breakfast is served in a small and pleasant courtyard. A Best Western affiliate. **Hotel services** *Air-conditioning. Babysitting. Bar. Parking.* **Room services** *Mini-bar. Room service. Telephone. TV: cable.*

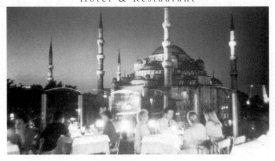

Ambassador - Ticarethane Sok.
~ $70/night.

Kybele Hotel – a thing about vintage glass lamps. *See p51.*

Hotel Turkoman

Asmalıçeşme Sokak 2, Sultanahmet (0212 516 2956/ fax 516 2957/www.turkomanhotel.com).
Tram Sultanahmet. **Rates** $70 single; $90 double.
Credit AmEx, MC, V. **Map** p303 M11.
Right on the Hippodrome and about opposite the Egyptian obelisk, the Turkoman's rooftop terrace affords perhaps the best views of the Sultanahmet Mosque – or, as the hotel itself more lyrically puts it, 'You will catch the exciting and amazing Blue Mosque almost with your hands'. Bright, unfussy rooms with brass bedsteads and parquet flooring also benefit from large windows, although in the summer months the mosque is hidden from the lower floors by foliage.
Hotel services *Cafe. Bar.* **Room services** *Mini-bar. Telephone.*

Hotel Yaşmak Sultan

Ebussuut Caddesi 18-20, Sirkeci (0212 528 1343/ fax 528 1348/www.yasmak.com). Tram Sirkeci.
Rates $90 single; $120 double; $120-$200 suite.
Credit AmEx, DC, MC, V. **Map** p303 N9.
Largish (84 rooms), modernish hotel with a canary yellow paint job and stripy red and white awnings. Rooms are smart and clean if uninspiring and the range of facilities is good. Location is also not bad, on a fairly quiet street about equidistant from Sultanahmet Square, the Bazaar Quarter and the Galata Bridge, none of which are more than ten minutes' walk away. In the basement is a fitness centre, sauna and hamam.
Hotel services *Air-conditioning. Babysitting. Bar. Business services. Gym. Handicapped facilities. Internet café. Parking. Restaurant.* **Room services** *Mini-bar. Hair-dryer. Room service. Telephone. TV.*

Budget

Alp Guesthouse

Adliye Sokak 4, off Akbıyık Caddesi, Sultanahmet (0212 517 9570/fax 518 5728/ www.alpguesthouse.com). Tram Sultanahmet. **Rates** $20-$30 single; $50-$60 double. 5% more if paying by credit card. **Credit** AmEx, MC, V. **Map** p303 O11.
A mock timber-framed house (as in 'Alpine') which dispenses with its theme inside making no attempt at disguising the concrete surfaces, just softening them a little with a few kilims. Odd, but not without some appeal, as attested by a wall covered by photographs and letters from happy customers. Bedrooms are simply furnished, those on the top floor with sea views going for a premium. Avoid the dingy basement quarters, especially in winter, when the boilers are fired up.
Hotel services *Left luggage.* **Room services** *Telephone.*

Berk Guesthouse

Kutlugün Sokak 27, Sultanahmet (0212 517 6561/ fax 517 7715/www.berkguesthouse.com). Tram Sultanahmet. **Rates** $35-$70 single; $45-$90 double.
No credit cards. Map p303 N11.

Orient Hostel – base camp for the backpacker scene. *See p55.*

A family-run guesthouse in a quiet street next to the Four Seasons Hotel. The original house was owned by Grandma Yeşim, but that was torn down and rebuilt as a hotel in the mid-1980s, which is now run by her grandchildren. In truth, for a place with such basic facilities the hotel is on the pricey side, and the extra $45 charged for 'deluxe' is outrageous. But plenty of people appreciate the family atmosphere and there's a whole bunch of regulars who check in year after year. There's a tiny walled garden where breakfast is served, as well as a roof terrace and lounge area.

Hotel services *Safe.* **Room services** *Air-conditioning (extra). Refrigerator (some rooms). Telephone.*

+ **Nomade Hotel**   *also Ambassadori*

15 Ticarethane Sokak, Sultanahmet (0212 511 1296/ fax 513 2404/hotelnomade@hotmail.com). Tram Sultanahmet. **Rates** $40 single; $50 double; $65 treble. **Credit** MC, V. **Map** p303 N10.

The comfortable kilim-hung reception is perfect for watching the bustling pedestrian traffic outside, while the cushion-strewn rooftop terrace is one of the most scenic in Istanbul. In between lie 15 elegantly homely rooms, with minimal mustard-hued decor, walnut furniture and ethnic bedspreads. French-educated twin sister proprietors Esra and Hamra ensure that standards remain high, and though there's no restaurant in the hotel, they also run the Rumeli Café bistro (*see p138*) just across the road. Plenty of other cafés, bars and restaurants in the vicinity, too.

Room services *Telephone.*

Hotel Şebnem

Adliye Sokak 1, off Akbıyk Caddesi, Sultanahmet (0212 517 6623/fax 638 1056/ www.sebnemhotel.com). Tram Sultanahmet. **Rates** $35 single; $50 double; $70 family room. **Credit** MC, V. **Map** p303 O11.

Of the countless small hotels filling the narrow streets to the east of Haghia Sophia this is one of the best. Tucked away on a quiet cul-de-sac, it's private and stylish, with more than a little thought given to the decor and general maintenance. Rooms are smallish but tasteful. Couples with kids might appreciate the family rooms with a double and two twin beds along with a refrigerator. An attractive roof terrace has views across the Sea of Marmara to the Princes' Islands.

Room services *Refrigerator in family rooms. Telephone.*

Side Hotel & Pension

Utangaç Sokak 20, Sultanahmet (0212 517 2282/ fax 517 6590/www.sidehotel.com). Tram Sultanahmet. **Rates** $10-$40 single; $25-$50 double. **Credit** V. **Map** p303 N11.

Clean and well looked-after by a genuinely friendly management who seem to get a kick out of having all these nice people come to stay with them. Most rooms, certainly those on the hotel side, have en suite bathrooms with modern plumbing, even shower cubicles in some cases – the Istanbul norm is just a showerhead flooding the bathroom. Rooms, however, vary greatly, so take a look at a few before deciding. Pension rooms are slightly more basic, the cheapest with shared bathroom. As is standard

with Sultanahmet hotels, there's a rooftop terrace where breakfast is served. Free tea in the foyer and a small book-exchange shelf.
Hotel services *Left luggage.* **Room services** *(hotel rooms only) Refrigerator. Telephone. TV.*

♨ Hotel Uyan

Utangaç Sokak 25, Sultanahmet (0212 516 4892/ fax 517 1582/www.uyanhotel.com). Tram Sultanahmet. **Rates** $30-$40 single; $40-$50 double. **Credit** MC, V. **Map** p303 N11.
Despite its stark, modern-looking exterior, the Uyan is in fact housed in a 75-year-old building that until fairly recently was a family residence. Rooms are simply furnished and airy, and a small bathroom has been added in the corner of each. Main selling point (and with so many similar places all competing for business, every hotel has to have its unique feature) is that the Uyan has the highest roof terrace. Guests can watch the nightly sound and light show at Sultanahmet Mosque without moving farther than a few feet from their rooms. During the day, the deck is private enough for sunbathing, as it's not overlooked by surrounding buildings.
Hotel services *Bar.* **Room services** *Telephone.*

Rock-bottom

Orient Hostel

Akbıyık Caddesi 13, Sultanahmet (0212 517 9493/ fax 518 3894/www.hostels.com/orienthostel). Tram Sultanahmet. **Rates** $7-9 dorm bed; $19-$45 single/double. **Credit** AmEx, MC, V. **Map** p303 N11.
For years now the Orient has been the mainstay of Istanbul's backpacker scene, base camp for a constant stream of the great unwashed and footloose tramping their way across Asia or down through the Middle East. Despite a clientele whose idea of adapting to local customs is to dispense with soap and other fascistic implements of personal hygiene, the place is kept commendably clean – even the much abused shower cubicles and toilets are serviceable. As well as a whole gamut of backpackerish services, including cheap Internet access and discounted airline tickets, the Orient has a lively social scene, including barbecues, belly-dancing and nargile nights down in the basement bar or up in the rooftop restaurant. There is also a women-only dormitory.
Hotel services *Bar. Internet access, Left luggage. Restaurant. Safe. Telephone & fax. Travel agency.*

Sultan Tourist Hostel

Terbıyık Sokak 3, off Akbıyık Caddesi, Sultanahmet (0212 516 9260/fax 517 1626/ www.feztravel.com/sultan). Tram Sultanahmet. **Rates** $7 dorm bed; $15 single; $18 double. **Credit** MC, V. **Map** p303 N11.
Also catering for the backpacking fraternity, the Sultan has a choice of double or single rooms or mixed-sex dormitories. Recently redecorated, all the accommodation is bright and airy, although

only a single shower/toilet on each floor is a major drawback. There's a restaurant up top, as well as a games room and computer centre.
Hotel services *Bar. Internet access. Laundry. Left luggage. Restaurant. Safe. Telephone & fax. Travel agency.*

Yücelt Interyouth Hostel

Caferiye Sokak 6/1, Sultanahmet (0212 513 6150/ fax 512 7628/www.yucelthostel.com). Tram Sultanahmet or Gülhane. **Rates** $6.50 dorm bed; $16 single; $19 double. **No credit cards. Map** p303 N10.
Before the Orient there was the Yücelt, the overlanders Istanbul hangout en route to the Maharishi in the 1960s and 1970s. Its location is incredible, on the cobbled lane that runs right by the side of Haghia Sophia, and must have added a fair bit of magic to many a stoned evening. Today it's more like a school camp, with 320 beds for eager travel virgins, bunked up in six-bed dorms. Some very basic singles and doubles are also available. Huge range of facilities of a youth club nature.
Hotel services *Bar. Internet access. Laundry. Left luggage. Restaurant. Satellite TV.*

North of the Golden Horn

Deluxe

Ceylan Inter-Continental

Asker Ocağı Caddesi 1, Taksim (0212 231 2121/ fax 231 2180/www.interconti.com). **Rates** $305-$375 single; $335-$375 double; $1,800-$4,000 suite. Rates do not include 17% tax. **Credit** AmEx, DC, MC, V. **Map** p307 P1.
Formerly the Sheraton, the Inter-Continental is an 18-floor Goliath and was until recently the highest hotel on the city skyline. (That dishonour may now fall to the monstrous Gökkafes if, as rumoured, part of it does go to one of the five-star chains. *See p40* **The height of bad taste**). The style is brash, the tone set by a horrendous golden staircase spiralling it's way up from the lobby area. A versions to the decor aside, the hotel is plenty comfortable, with full facilities that even run to a golf simulator to keep your swing in. Perhaps the pick of the dining offerings is the Safran (*see p135*) on the very top floor, which combines excellent Ottoman cuisine with unsurpassable views. Vertigo sufferers should stay well back from the windows in the Panorama Bar next door.
Hotel services *Air-conditioning. Bar. Business services. Concierge. Gym. Hamam. Handicapped suites. Parking. Restaurant. Swimming pool.* **Room services** *Mini-bar. Room service. Telephone. TV: cable.*

Çırağan Palace Hotel Kempinski

Çırağan Caddesi 84, Beşiktaş (0212 258 3377/fax 259 6687/www.ciraganpalace.com). **Rates** $300-$750 single/double; $750-$7,500 suite. Rates do not include 17% tax. **Credit** AmEx, MC, V.
This is the number one hotel in town, a modern annexe to a 19th-century palace on the Bosphorus.

The Kempinski was originally built in 1874 for Sultan Abdülaziz, an ill-fated ruler who disposed of himself with a pair of scissors in one of its chambers. In 1908 it became the seat of parliament but burnt down two years later. In the following decades the ruins were used as a football stadium and outdoor swimming pool. In 1986, following ambitious rebuilding and restoration, parts of the original complex, together with additional new buildings, became an extraordinarily luxurious 310-room hotel under the management of the German Kempinski chain. In fact, only 12 suites are in the palace, along with restaurants (including Laledan and Tuğra, *see p125 and p136*) and public rooms, worth a look for the bizarre decor, described by one journalist as 'post-Orientalist psychotropic'. All other rooms are in the annexe. If you're paying out this much cash, then make sure to choose rooms on the waterfront, not the park side, and hope that the weather's fine enough to make use of the stunning outdoor pool, which appears to flow into the Bosphorus. Armchair travellers should check out the excellent website.

Hotel services *Air-conditioning. Bars. Business services. Concierge. Data ports. Disabled access. Gym. Hamam. Parking. Restaurant. Swimming pool.* **Room services** *Mini-bar. Room service. Telephone. TV: cable.*

Hilton Istanbul

Cumhuriyet Caddesi, Harbiye (0212 315 6000/ fax 240 4165/www.hilton.com). **Rates** $295-$325 single; $325-$355 double; $700-$1,350 suite. Rates do not include 17% tax. **Credit** AmEx, DC, MC, V.

First of the modern high-rise blocks to brutalise the skyline north of the Golden Horn, providing sweeping views for its guests and an eyesore for everyone else. Given the price bracket, it's far from exceptional in terms of rooms, decor and facilities, although the parkland setting is a bonus, with its one-kilometre-long running track looping through 13 acres of gardens. Not all rooms have those premium Bosphorus panoramas, and this is reflected in the pricing. Back when this was about the only deluxe option in town, Ian Fleming stayed here in 1955 doing some groundwork for his novel *From Russia With Love*, which was published two years later.

Hotel services *Air-conditioning. Babysitting. Bar. Beauty salon. Business services. Concierge. Data port. Gym. Hamam. No-smoking floors. Parking. Restaurant. Swimming pool. Tennis courts. Wheelchair access.* **Room services** *Mini-bar. Room service. Telephone. TV: cable.*

Hyatt Regency Istanbul

Taşkışla Caddesi, Taksim (0212 225 7000/ fax 225 7007/www.istanbul.hyatt.com.tr). **Rates** $240-$285 single; $270-$315 double; $340-$850 suite. Rates do not include 17% tax. **Credit** AmEx, DC, MC, V. **Map** p307 P1.

A ten-minute walk north-east of Taksim Square, the Hyatt Regency has gone for an Ottoman kösk look, with architecture and interiors that attempt to suggest an imperial palace, using modern materials and a somewhat more restrained budget. While the

Çırağan Palace Hotel Kempinski – quite literally palatial. *See p55.*

Hyatt is to be commended for keeping the building low, views from the rooms can't compete with those at some of the other five-stars. It scores high on business facilities, with an information library and private offices for rent and a luxury apart-hotel with its own separate check-in and elevators. The faux art nouveau Polo Lounge is for members only, but Harry's Jazz Bar (*see p212*) is popular with the city's expat residents.

Hotel services *Air-conditioning. Bar. Beauty salon. Business services. Conference facilities. Hamam. Health club. Parking. Restaurant. Swimming pool. Tennis courts.* **Room services** *Data port. Mini-bar. Room service. Telephone. TV: cable.*

Marmara Hotel

Taksim Square, Taksim (0212 251 4696/fax 244 0509/www.themarmara.com.tr). **Rates** $230-$250 single; $260-$280 double; $380-$1,000 suite. **Credit** AmEx, DC, MC, V. **Map** p309 P2.

Situated at ground zero on Taksim Square, this is definitely the place if you've a preference for city hotels that place you right at the heart of things. Most of its 410 rooms have decent views. It's Turkish-owned (now with a sister establishment in

Manhattan) and maybe isn't quite as polished as some of the international competition, but it buzzes. The Brasserie (*see p143*) on the ground floor, with large picture windows overlooking the square, is an established meeting-place for the city's chic set, and the Aqua Lounge is usually packed with conspicuously busy suited types socialising between conferences. On the top floor, the Panorama Bar (*see p151*) offers excellent views.

Hotel services *Air-conditioning. Bar. Beauty salon. Business services. Concierge. Dry cleaning. Gym. Hamam. Laundry. Parking. Restaurant. Swimming pool.* **Room services** *Data port. Mini-bar. Room service. Telephone. TV: cable.*

Swissôtel Istanbul The Bosphorus

Bayıldım Caddesi 2, Maçka (0212 326 1100/ fax 326 1122/www.swissotel.com). **Rates** $250-$440 single; $280-$440 double; $500-$2,500 suite. Rates do not include 17% tax. **Credit** AmEx, DC, MC, V.

One of the less obtrusive of the hotel giants, the Swissôtel sits on the hillside above the Dolmabahçe Palace, addressing the Bosphorus. Despite its size (600 rooms), good management ensures that a personal element is kept to the fore with well thought-

Marmara Hotel – at the heart of things.

Richmond Hotel – the only place to stay on the whole of Istiklal Caddesi. *See p60.*

out touches like a big bowl of Swiss chocolates sitting at the check-in desk. Rooms are a decent size, exceptionally comfortable and packed with all the gimmickry a modern hotel can offer. Sports facilities are particularly good and the hotel has two of the best restaurants in town in La Corne d'Or (*see p125*) and Taşlık (*see p135*). Location is a problem, though; the hotel is a good 20-25 minute walk from Taksim Square and guests will find themselves reliant on taxis.
Hotel services *Air-conditioning. Babysitting. Bar. Beauty salon. Business services. Concierge. Gym. Hamam. No-smoking floors. Parking. Restaurant. Swimming pool. Wheelchair access.* **Room services** *Data port. Mini-bar. Room service. Telephone. TV: cable.*

High-end

Dilson Hotel

Sıraselviler Caddesi 49, Taksim (0212 252 9600/ fax 249 7077/www.dilson.com). **Rates** $120 single; $160 double; $250-$300 suite. **Credit** AmEx, DC, MC, V. **Map** p309 O2.
Not the greatest of hotels. The reception area is especially naff with its pseudo-Roman statuary and stage-set columns. However, matters do improve on the guest floors. Rooms on the front of the building, looking across at the Haghia Triada church, are at least bright and of a good size, if a little noisy. Otherwise it's over-priced and mediocre: you're paying for the very central location.
Hotel services *Air-conditioning. Parking. Restaurant.* **Room services** *Telephone. TV.*

Divan Hotel

Cumhuriyet Caddesi 2, Elmadağ (0212 231 4100/ fax 248 8527/www.divanoteli.com.tr). **Rates** $175 single; $210 double; $830 suite. **Credit** AmEx, DC, MC, V. **Map** p307 P1.
This quiet, Turkish-owned 169-room hotel benefits from a decent location just north of Taksim Square. It's slightly old-school in appearance – very 1970s (which in Istanbul generally means that it actually dates from the mid-1980s) – but well looked after. Rooms are large, but avoid those overlooking Cumhuriyet Caddesi, which is far too noisy to be silenced by mere double glazing.
Hotel services *Air-conditioning. Bar. Beauty salon. Business services. Concierge. Gym. Parking. Restaurant.* **Room services** *Mini-bar. Room service. Telephone. TV: cable.*

Dorint Park Plaza

Topçu Caddesi 23, Taksim (0212 254 5100/ fax 254 7160). **Rates** $165 single/double; $340-$490 suite. **Credit** AmEx, MC, V. **Map** p307 O1.
Part of a German chain, this smart, modish hotel on a quiet backstreet two ticks from Taksim Square is run with characteristic efficiency. A gleaming white exterior gives way to leather and wood panel inside. Rooms are tastefully done with excellent bathrooms. Very much a business hotel, slick and professional, not too exciting but solid. One for Audi drivers.
Hotel services *Air-conditioning. Bar. Business services. Gym. Parking. Restaurant. Swimming pool.* **Room services** *Mini-bar. Room service. Safe. Telephone. TV: cable.*

The Madison Hotel

Recep Paşa Caddesi 23, Taksim (0212 238 5460/fax 238 5151/www.themadisonhotel.com.tr). **Rates** $120 single; $160 double; $200 suite. **Credit** AmEx, MC, V. **Map** p307 P1.

North-west of Taksim Square, between Tarlabaşı Bulvarı and Cumhuriyet Caddesi are a series of parallel streets, quiet and almost residential in character, that are home to a handful of good mid-range hotels, including the Dorint Park Plaza (*see p59*) and this one. The Madison is a modern, four-star hotel with decent-sized rooms. Apart from an insipid colour scheme, there's little cause for complaint. Bathrooms are small but elegant, decked out in marble, and some thoughtful person has even put an extra telephone next to the toilet. The indoor pool-side bar is most pleasant.

Hotel services *Air-conditioning. Bar. Gym. Parking. Restaurant. Swimming pool.* **Room services** *Hamam. Mini-bar. Room service. Telephone. TV.*

Princess Hotel Ortaköy

Dereboyu Caddesi 36-8, Ortaköy (0212 227 6010/ fax 260 2148). **Rates** $140 single; $170 double; $190-$400 suite. **Credit** AmEx, DC, MC, V.

This hotel is far from the sights, and few people other than those doing business up in nearby Levent and Maslak choose to stay in Ortaköy, but if scurrying around all the mosques isn't on your agenda, then this is an option well worth considering. It's a modern hotel with generously sized rooms and a full complement of facilities. Most appealing is its proximity to the quayside area teeming with small crafts shops, bars and cafés, and the beautiful waterfront plaza and its fish restaurants. From here you have the option of avoiding the traffic that clogs Istanbul's roads by catching a Bosphorus ferry all the way down to the sightseeing district of Sultanahmet.

Hotel services *Air-conditioning. Bar. Business services. Concierge. Gym. Hamam. Parking. Restaurant. Swimming pool.* **Room services** *Mini-bar. Room service. Telephone. TV: cable.*

Richmond Hotel

Istiklal Caddesi 445, Tünel, Beyoğlu (0212 252 5460/fax 252 9707). **Rates** $160 single; $195 double. **Credit** AmEx, MC, V. **Map** p308 M4.

Amazingly, the Richmond is the only hotel on the whole mile-and-a-half length of Istiklal Caddesi. Why this should be so is baffling, as the street is perfect for hotels; scenically cobbled, lined with shops, cafés and bars, pedestrianised (so no noisy traffic), plenty of grand old apartment blocks ripe for conversion. Rather than go for a straight conversion, what the Richmond has done is rip out the old building while retaining the façade and dropping a brand spanking new structure in behind. If the interior isn't quite so clever, the hotel does have a good relaxed atmosphere and a friendly staff. There's the obligatory rooftop restaurant and a decent bar, but with such an excellent location chances are you won't be making much use of them.

Hotel services *Air-conditioning. Bar. Business services. Concierge. Parking. Restaurant.* **Room services** *Hair-dryer. Mini-bar. Room service. Telephone. TV: cable.*

Taksim Square Hotel

Sıraselviler Caddesi 15, Taksim (0212 292 6440/ fax 292 6449/www.taksimsquarehotel.com). **Rates** $150 single; $200 double. **Credit** AmEx, DC, MC, V. **Map** p309 P2.

Smart, modern – only around three years old – and bang in the centre of town, the Taksim Square is popular with visiting businessmen. Of the 87 rooms, 32 have a view across rooftops to the Bosphorus; in the rest, guests have to be content with watching the street life down on busy Sıraselviler and the diners on the rooftop terrace of the Burger King opposite.

Hotel services *Air-conditioning. Bar. Business services. Restaurant.* **Room services** *Mini-bar. Room service. Telephone. TV.*

Mid-range

Galata Residence

Bankalar Caddesi, Hacı Ali Sokak 27, Karaköy (0212 2924841/fax 244 2323/ www.galataresidence.com). **Rates** $117 single; $120 double. **Credit** MC, V. **Map** p306 M6.

An apartment hotel with history. The building formerly belonged to an important Levantine banking family, the Kamondos, who gave their name to the arty public staircase (*see p92*) that leads up to the residence from Voyvoda Caddesi, the old banking street of 19th-century Pera. It later served as a Jewish school. In recent times the solid brick building has been split into 16 comfortably furnished apartments, each of which sleeps four. Every unit is furnished in a homely sort of way, maybe a bit maiden-auntish, but certainly not objectionable, and each has its own fully equipped kitchen. There's a restaurant on the roof and a bare-brick vaulted cellar café. The location is a big plus, enough to walk over the bridge to Eminönü and the bazaar area and just down the hill from the Galata Tower and Beyoğlu. Discounted rates are available for extended stays.

Hotel services *Air-conditioning. Parking. Restaurant.* **Room services** *Hair-dryer. Kitchenette. Room service. Safe. Telephone. TV: cable.*

Galata Residence – comfortable apartments.

Büyük Londra Hotel – the place for dedicated nostalgia hunters.

Hotel Residence

Sadri Alışık Sokak 19, off Istiklal Caddesi, Beyoğlu (0212 252 7685/fax 243 0084/www.cantur.com.tr). **Rates** $80 single; $100 double; $200 suite. **Credit** AmEx, MC, V. **Map** 309 O3.

A bit difficult to find, tucked away up a narrow side street, but worth the effort of searching. The rooms, though small, are bright and very well-equipped. The location is great too, right among the bars and nightlife of Beyoğlu. Unlike many other places in the area, the Residence doesn't accept short-stay customers, so you won't be woken by things going bump, bump, bump in the night.

Hotel services *Air-conditioning. Bar. Restaurant.* **Room services** *Mini-bar. Room service. Telephone. TV.*

Villa Zurich

Akarsu Caddesi 44-6, Cihangir (0212 293 0604/ fax 249 0232/www.villazurich.com.tr). **Rates** $80 single; $120 double; $180 suite. **Credit** AmEx, MC, V. **Map** p307 O4.

Ten minutes' walk down Sıraselviler Caddesi from Taksim Square in the *yabancı* (foreigner) neighbourhood of Cihangir, the Villa Zurich is conveniently close to the centre but also pleasantly removed from all the fuss. Cihangir has a good local feel with small grocers, butchers and other essential businesses mixed in with the odd Western-style café or continental-style charcuterie catering for the area's high density of expats. The hotel is vaguely European in character, with restrained decor and 43 comfortable, well-equipped guestrooms. Breakfast is taken on the rooftop restaurant, which throughout the day serves from an odd menu of Japanese and Turkish food.

Hotel services *Air-conditioning. Babysitting. Bar. Restaurant. Parking.* **Room services** *Mini-bar. Room service. Telephone. TV.*

Budget

Hotel Avrupa

Topçu Caddesi 30, Talimhane, Taksim (0212 250 9420/fax 250 7399). **Rates** $22-$30 single; $30-$45 double. **No credit cards. Map** p307 O1.

In business since 1966, which makes it a relative old-timer round here, the Avrupa has recently been spruced up with a new paint job and some refurnishing. Brightly painted, unfussy rooms with small en suites are good value. There's a breakfast room, but no restaurant or bar – not really a problem so close to Taksim Square.

Room services *Telephone.*

Büyük Londra Hotel

Meşrutiyet Caddesi 117, Tepebaşı (0212 245 0670/ fax 245 0671). **Rates** $60 single; $80 double. **Credit** AmEx, MC, V. **Map** p308 M3.

Built around the same time as the nearby Pera Palas (*see p62* **Bed, board & legends**), the Büyük Londra hasn't aged half as well. Where the Palas is like some grand old sleep-in museum, the Londra is

Bed, board & legends

Built in 1892 as the last stop on the Orient Express, the **Pera Palas** is the most fadedly aristocratic of hotels. It was built by the same company that ran the famed Paris to Istanbul trains and in the early days pampered guests were carried on cushioned sedans from Sirkeci station to waiting hotel transport. Today, superseded in comfort and facilities by the modern sleek and efficient five-stars, the Palas is the preserve of a less exalted crowd than the statesmen, stars and spies that used to cross its lobby, site of one successful and one failed assassination attempt.

Up a short flight of steps, the hotel lift is at the centre of a sweeping staircase and has large ornate gates, a velvet bench and a bellboy in brocaded livery. Rooms are off long corridors and 27 of the 145 have brass plaques with the names of famous past guests: Sarah Bernhardt, Greta Garbo, Mata Hari, Alfred Hitchcock and Jackie Onassis. One just says 'Petroleum Billionaire' while another belongs to Yakup Kadri Karaosmanoğlu, apparently a 'Well Known Writer'. Slightly better-known writer Agatha Christie wrote part of *Murder on the Orient Express* while staying here. Room 404 is a mini-museum in her honour. A bigger draw, attracting bus-loads of local schoolkids, is Room 101, Atatürk's room, complete with original furniture, photos and such excellent presidential memorabilia as the Great Turk's driving goggles and panama hat.

Rooms are not particularly luxurious but compensate in charm and idiosyncracies with hardwood floors, brass beds and vast chrome-filled bathrooms. The Pera Patisserie is a fine little Viennese-style coffeeshop, while the Orient Express bar is the place to muse upon

the decline of servile porters, black-stocking glamour and lobby shoot-outs in the hotel industry of today.

Pera Palas

Meşrutiyet Caddesi 98, Tepebaşı, Beyoğlu (0212 251 4560/fax 251 4089). **Rates** $140 single; $220 double; $380 suite. **Credit** AmEx, DC, MC, V. **Map** p308 M4.
Hotel services *Bar. Concierge. Parking. Restaurant.* **Room services** *Mini-bar. Room service. Telephone. TV.*

a dusty, near-rundown old curiosity shop. Caged parrots peer dolefully out of the lounge windows. Portable coal burners, wind-up gramophones, valve radios and other ancient junk clutters up the corridors and rooms. Hemingway stayed here in 1922, sent by the *Toronto Daily Star* to cover the Turkish war of independence. Doubtless it was a little cleaner and better-run in those days. Unashamedly tatty, it's now a place for dedicated nostalgia hunters only, but it has its fans.
Hotel services *Bar.* **Room services** *Refrigerator. Telephone.*

Hotel Monopol

Meşrutiyet Caddesi 223, Tepebaşı, Beyoğlu (0212 251 7326/fax 251 7333). **Rates** $40 single; $60 double; $90 suite. **Credit** MC, V. **Map** p308 M4.

Close by the US consulate, the Monopol is the best of a row of otherwise samey mid-range hotels. Despite the early-1980s look of the decor, the hotel has been open for less than ten years. The 75 rooms with en suites are a good size and well-equipped. Management needs to tighten up though: *Time Out*'s photographer was checked into a room with an unemptied ashtray and filthy towels. Still, manager Adnan is friendly and speaks good English. European tour groups make up a fair chunk of the clientele.
Hotel services *Air-conditioning. Safe.* **Room services** *Mini-bar. Telephone. TV.*

Vardar Palace Hotel

Sıraselviler Caddesi 54, Taksim (0212 252 2888/ fax 252 1527/www.vardarhotel.com.tr). **Rates** $50 single; $60 double. **Credit** AmEx, MC, V. **Map** p307 O3.

Two minutes from Taksim Square, the Vardar occupies a drab-looking 19th-century building on Istanbul's sleaziest strip, where Sıraselviler narrows to canyon-like proportions and fills up at night with the backwash from metal bars and pimp joints. Inside, however, the hotel is bright and pleasant and a typical middling three-star. Rooms have good high ceilings, although any feeling of airiness is sabotaged by a too-dark colour scheme. Front-facing rooms can get noisy, especially around 2am. **Hotel services** *Air-conditioning. Bar. Laundry. Restaurant.* **Room services** *Mini-bar. Telephone. TV.*

Rock-bottom

Hotel Silviya

Asmalımescit Sokak 54, Tepebaşı (0212 292 7749). **Rates** $13 single; $22 double. **No credit cards.** **Map** p308 M4.

Owned and run by natives of Rize on the Black Sea coast, this is a new arrival on the Beyoğlu accommodation scene, tucked away just off Istiklal Caddesi. Asmalımecit is a good area to be in, recently revitalised with the opening of several art galleries and cafés. The hotel has 28 spotlessly clean rooms simply decked-out with brand new furniture and well-plumbed bathrooms. Beside the ground floor reception – so new that the pinewood panelling still smells of the forest – there's a small breakfast room and a kitchenette where you can fix yourself a snack. Rates are currently such a steal that they're bound to rise as more people get to know about the place. **Hotel services** *Restaurant.* **Room services** *Mini-bar. Telephone. TV.*

Hotel Yonca

Tarlabaşı Bulvarı, Toprak Lüle Sokak 5, Beyoğlu (0212 293 9391). **Rates** $10 single; $20 double. **No credit cards.** **Map** p308 N2.

On the south side (the preferred side) of Tarlabaşı Bulvarı, the Yonca is one of the better of a great many small, seedy-looking places in this bar-filled area of narrow backstreets south of Istiklal Caddesi. Rooms are nothing fancy but are reasonably clean– which is about as much as you can hope for at this price. **Hotel services** *Safe.* **Room services** *Telephone. TV.*

The Asian Shore

High-end

Bosphorus Pasha

Yalıboyu Caddesi 64, Beylerbeyi (0216 422 0003/ fax 422 0012/www.bosphoruspashahotel.com). **Rates** $275-$375 single; $330-$370 double; $750 suite. **Credit** AmEx, DC, MC, V.

A wedding-cake Bosphorus mansion, the Pasha is the city's most exclusive get-away. It is like staying at an English stately home, only this one faces one of the world's busiest waterways. There are just 14 rooms, all gilt furniture and heavy drapes and perhaps a little stuffy. To relax, just slip into the Jacuzzi (front rooms only) and soak up the view of ships gliding beneath the awesome Atatürk suspension bridge. The high-class Italian restaurant, Cicconi's, is worth a visit even if you can't afford to splash out on a room. **Hotel services** *Air-conditioning. Bar. Restaurant.* **Room services** *Telephone. TV.*

Mid-range

Hotel Eysan

Rıhtım Caddesi 26, Kadıköy (0216 346 2440/ fax 418 9582/www.hoteleysan.com). **Rates** $60 single; $80 double; $100 suite. **Credit** MC, V. **Map** p311 W6.

The four-star Eysan is the conspicuous yellow building east of the ferry landings on Kadıköy's bustling waterfront. Although a bit plain, the rooms are at least spacious and most have Bosphorus views. It offers good value, but then it is very hard to attract people to the idea of staying over on the Asian shore. **Hotel services** *Air-conditioning. Bar. Restaurant.* **Room services** *Mini-bar. Room service. TV.*

Budget

Kent Hotel

Serasker Caddesi 8, Kadıköy (0216 336 2453/ fax 449 1693). **Rates** $16 single; $32 double. **No credit cards. Map** p311 W7.

Not sure that the red carpet leading up to the hall to reception is enitrely appropriate – this is a budget hotel – but it's nice to have ambitions. The 24 rooms are clean and simple. Breakfast is served in a small dining area on the third floor and free mineral water is available from dispensers on each level. It's just a short walk from the ferry terminal and the surrounding streets are pleasantly busy with small shops and cafés. It's not exactly royal then, but perfectly acceptable. **Hotel services** *Free mineral water.* **Room services** *Telephone. TV.*

Camping

Ataköy Tatil Köyü

Rauf Orbay Caddesi, off Ataköy Tatil Köyü, Bakırköy (0212 559 6014/fax 560 0426). **Rates** $10 per tent (2-man); $2.50 extra for car. **No credit cards.**

On the Marmara coast about 15km (10miles) from the centre, this campsite is conveniently situated near Ataköy train station, from where there are regular trains into Sirkeci. The site is clean and has good facilities, including a tennis court, pool (summer only) and bar, although make sure you don't get a pitch too close to the noisy road.

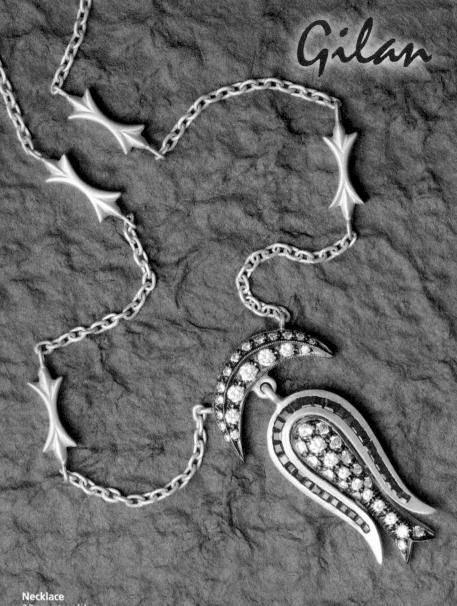

Gilan

Necklace
22 carat gold,
diamond, ruby

Anatolian Civilization Collection

Sightseeing

Introduction

Lose yourself in two continents, masses of mosques, a diversity of downtown districts, and the grandest bazaar of them all.

Istanbul is sightseeing heaven. You want churches. It's got 'em. Mosques? Istanbul has gorgeous mosques, maybe the world's finest. Palaces? In abundance. Bazaars? The biggest. And then there are the fortresses, city walls, underground cisterns, public baths, Whirling Dervish theatres, islands, parks, museums…

It wouldn't be an exaggeration to say that in its sheer volume of things to see, Istanbul rivals Rome, Paris or London.

But there's little logic to how it's all laid out. No grand masterplan. The topography doesn't help, involving numerous hills split between three land masses, two on the European side of

Neighbourhood watch

Sultanahmet

Mosques, palaces, museums and lots of hotels all centred on Sultanahmet Square and the Hippodrome. Cafés and restaurants charge a premium among all the stunning history.

Bazaar Quarter

Hard to say exactly where it starts or ends but the core of the bazaar lies in two districts, Çemberlitaş and Beyazıt, the latter home to Istanbul's main university.

Eminönü

Waterfront transport hub on the Golden Horn at the southern end of Galata Bridge. Includes the old mercantile districts of Sirkeci and hamam-rich Cağaloğlu.

Fatih, Fener & Balat

Conservative districts west of Atatürk Bulvarı, south of the Golden Horn, considered a bit beyond the pale by sophisticated Istanbulites but with a wealth of fascinating history and architecture.

City Walls

As far west as most visitors want to venture, the walls rule a line from the Golden Horn in the north to the Sea of Marmara in the south, passing through the working-class suburbs of Edirnekapı, Topkapı and Yedikule.

Beyoğlu

Ground zero for consumerism, nightlife, arts and entertainment. Beyoğlu is a blanket name for various small neighbourhoods including Galata, with its distinctive tower above the Golden Horn, Tünel at the south end of Istiklal Caddesi, Asmalımescit, Galatasaray and Taksim.

Karaköy

At the north end of the Galata Bridge, a formerly seedy port area with a ferry terminal and a small daily fish market.

Beşiktaş

A major transport hub, downhill and due east of Taksim Square. It possesses the most amazing public toilets (see page 282), as well as the **Dolmabahçe Palace** and a couple of major museums beside the Bosphorus.

Ortaköy

Southernmost of the 'Bosphorus villages' – suburbs on the European shore. Famed for its weekend craft market and with a pleasant waterfront piazza, though a bit too popular for its own good.

Arnavutköy

Where every Istanbulite would love to live given the cash. Full of gorgeous waterfront wooden mansions (yalıs). Plebs can soak up the ambience at a wealth of cafes and small restaurants.

Bebek

For our purposes Bebek, with neighbouring castle Rumeli Hisarı, marks Istanbul's northern city limit. A fine half day can be had by taking a bus or ferry up here then walking back via Arnavutköy to Ortaköy.

Kadıköy & Üsküdar

The two main centres on the Asian shore, neither of which is possessed of great monuments or other sightseeing musts, but they make up for it in character and plenty of quirky little corners.

the Bosphorus divided by the Golden Horn and one on the Asian Shore. There's no uptown or downtown or inner circle or any other convenient way to read the city. It's just a matter of learning the districts (*see page 66* **Neighbourhood watch**). Street patterns are irregular, generations of city planners seemingly almost phobic when it comes to straight lines and right angles. Buildings crowd and block sightlines, every now and again opening up to expose a view that takes you completely by surprise. In such a set-up there's no such thing as a wrong turn, only alternative routes.

THE HISTORIC HEART

Most of the sights that could properly be described as unmissable – either because you really ought to see them or simply because you couldn't avoid them if you tried – are in and around **Sultanahmet** and the **Bazaar Quarter**, which together constitute the city's historic heart. If this is your first time in Istanbul, then here's where you are going to be spending the greater part of your walking hours. Most hotels are around here too, but there's not much in the way of bars or restaurants, so at night locals tend to clear out and leave the place to visitors. The area occupies the highest part of a fat thumb of land that's wrapped around by the **Sea of Marmara** and the **Golden Horn**. Its spine is **Divan Yolu** along which the tram runs. With stops beside the main mosques, bazaars and markets, **the tram** (*see page 268*) is the best way to get around this side of town. It's air-conditioned too, a blessing in summer.

South of Divan Yolu there's little of interest. To the north, market streets slope precipitously down to **Eminönü** beside the Golden Horn. Here the tram terminates, over the road from some cattle-shed terminals for ferries up the Bosphorus and over to the Asian Shore. Also here are two bus stations; one north of the main road for buses to Taksim Square (46H), one to the south, beside the **Egyptian Market**, for services up the European shore of the Bosphorus to Bebek and beyond (22, 25E, 40).

The Golden Horn bisects European Istanbul, but the halves are linked centrally by two bridges, the Galata and, further west, the Atatürk. West of the Atatürk Bridge, still on the south side of the water, is a place where few visitors venture, a grouping of neighbourhoods with an overtly Islamic nature, including **Fatih**, **Fener** and **Balat**. Even further west is Eyüp, an area beyond the page limits of this book but possessed of the fine **Eyüp Sultan Mosque**, one of the most sacred Islamic sites outside of Mecca, Medina and Jerusalem.

The best Sightseeing

For a course in city history
From Byzantium to Istanbul, learn how the city got the way it is at the **Archaeology Museum**. See page 112.

For further enlightenment
Centrepiece of two empires, **Haghia Sophia** is the historical heart and soul of Istanbul. See pages 69-70.

For imperial excesses
Istanbul's premier sight, **Topkapı Palace**, has much to see but not necessarily a lot to like. See pages 70-74.

For imperial elegance
If architecture is frozen music then the **Süleymaniye Mosque** is one of the most spiritually uplifting pieces you'll ever hear. See page 80.

For the 'Oriental' experience
The Grand Bazaar is everything most people imagine Istanbul to be. Funny thing is, it's not staged for the tourists – it really is like that. See page 78.

For the unexpected
An experiment in existential street furniture, the **Kamondo Stairs** are so 'un-Istanbul' they made the cover of an Albert Camus book. See page 92.

For getting hot & bothered
Without a good sweat, scrape and pummel, your Istanbul experience is incomplete. Get it all at the **Cağaloğlu Hamam**. See page 204.

For cooling off
Get on the water. Either a ferry over to the Asian Shore or a boat up the Bosphorus to Bebek. See pages 101 and 105.

For photos to inspire envy
Circle the viewing galleries at **Galata Tower** and fall in love with the city. See page 91.

Mosque etiquette

At least half of Istanbul's major sights are mosques. Non-Muslims are welcome to visit any of them, but should steer clear of busy prayer times, of which noon – and especially Friday noon – is the main one. Note that prayer times vary throughout the year, so noon prayers don't take place exactly on the stroke of midday, but can fall anywhere between 11.30am and 1.30pm. The evening prayer is at sundown. Dress modestly: no shorts, short skirts or bare shoulders. This is especially vital for visits to mosques out of the tourist loop, such as places in conservative areas like Fatih, Fener and Balat. Shoes must be removed, although in some places cloth covers are provided to slip over your footwear. Photography is usually allowed, but don't point your camera at people at prayer.

PLACES TO PLAY

North of the Golden Horn is the city centre district of **Beyoğlu**, Istanbul's West End and the place to play once sightseeing is done. At its heart is **Istiklal Caddesi**, a broad pedestrianised European-style boulevard sprouting a tangle of narrow side streets filled with shops, cafés, bars, restaurants and clubs (*see map page 308-9*). Developed largely in the late 19th century, it's an area of great character and grandiose architecture, well worth exploring by day too.

At its north end, Istiklal Caddesi empties into **Taksim Square** – large and charmless, recommended only as a place to pick up a taxi. North are newer districts of **Harbiye**, **Şişli**, **Nişantaşı** and **Teşvikiye**, not 'sightworthy' enough to cover in this section, but possible visits for shopping, eats or entertainment. Further north still, **Etiler** and **Levent** are out where the money's at; dine or club up here and your bank manager is going to know about it.

All these areas are 'uphill'; downhill along the shores of the Bosphorus are a whole other string of small districts, often referred to as the **'Bosphorus villages'**. Places like **Ortaköy**, **Arnavutköy** and **Bebek** are picturesque clusters of attractive wooden villas with folksy shops and markets and open-air cafés and restaurants. There's not much in the way of major sights, but these neighbourhoods are definitely worth a wander. They are linked by several bus services or, better still, you can travel up here by ferry (mornings and evenings only; *see page 269*).

Ferry is also the way to go to get over to the **Asian Shore**. Visitors expecting some significant change in character to mark a hop of continents are going to be disappointed. Knives and forks aren't suddenly exchanged for chopsticks midway across the Bosphorus. Instead, the Asian Shore is a vast dormitory for Istanbulites who commute each day over to jobs west of the water. Not only is real estate cheaper here, but it's less crowded and more rural than densely urban European Istanbul. The character of the Asian shore is also heavily shaped by large numbers of immigrants from the Turkish provinces.

► For more on **getting around** Istanbul, see pages 267-70.
► For **boat trips** to the upper Bosphorus, see page 241.

Sultanahmet

Mosques and palaces, museums and minarets – Istanbul's oldest district basks in the splendour of two empires.

Map p303

Sultanahmet is the Istanbul of postcards. The 'Orient' of the Turkish Delight ad. It's a thumbnail of land surrounded by sea on three sides with a panoramic profile of spiky minarets and cascading domes. Surrounding the mosques are palaces, museums and assorted historical oddments, testament to a heritage that encompasses the birth, youthful exuberance, mature middle age and drooling dotage of not one but two great empires: the Byzantine empire and the Ottoman empire.

Haghia Sophia

Focal point for disgorging tour buses and feeding ground for taxis, Sultanahmet Square (*Ayasofya Meydanı*) is the obvious place to begin exploring. It acts as a forecourt for what was formerly the greatest church in Eastern Christendom, Sancta Sophia ('Divine Wisdom'), captured and reconsecrated as the chief mosque of the Ottoman empire. To the Turks it's Ayasofya, a phonetic rendering of the Greek **Haghia Sophia**, the name by which the building is more traditionally known.

Third on the site to bear the name, the church was dedicated on 26 December AD 537 by Emperor Justinian. He had come to power less than a century after the fall of Rome (*see pages 10-11*) and was eager to prove his capital a worthy successor to imperial glory. Approached by a grand colonnaded avenue beginning at the city gates, Justinian's cathedral towered over all else and was topped by the largest dome ever constructed – a record it held until the Romans reclaimed their pride just over a thousand years later with Michelangelo's dome for St Peter's. In the meantime, Justinian's dome took on almost fabled status. One often recounted story is that it was of such thin material that the hundreds of candles hung high within would cause it to glow at night like a great golden beacon, visible to ships far out on the Marmara Sea. More likely, the light shone from the 40 windows around its base, which during the day admitted streams of sunlight that were reflected by an interior covered in dazzling gold mosaics.

Adding to the wonder, the church served as a vast reliquary housing a pilgrim's delight of biblical treasures, including fragments of the

First church, then mosque: **Haghia Sophia**.

True Cross, the Virgin's veils, the lance that pierced Jesus's side, St Thomas's doubting finger, and an assortment of other saintly limbs, skulls and clippings.

All of this was lost in 1204 when adventurers and freebooters on Western Christendom's Fourth Crusade, raised to liberate Jerusalem and the Holy Lands, decided they would be equally content with a treasure-grabbing raid on the luxurious capital of their Eastern brethren (*see page 14*). At Haghia Sophia they ripped the place apart, carrying off everything they possibly could, and added insult to thievery by infamously placing a prostitute on the imperial throne.

MOSLEM MAKEOVER

Just short of a quarter century later, further destruction was threatened when in 1453 the Ottoman armies led by Mehmet breached the walls of Constantinople and put its Byzantine defenders to flight (*see page 15*). Those taking

Masses of mosaics in the **Haghia Sophia**.

refuge in the church were slaughtered, but the conquering sultan is supposed to have rounded on a looting soldier he found hacking at the marble floors and told him: 'The gold is thine, the building mine.' So Haghia Sophia was spared. But it was lost to Christianity; resounding to the chant 'There is no god but Allah and Mohammed is his Prophet,' the former church became a mosque.

To the domed central basilica were added four minarets from which to deliver the Muslim call to prayer – the construction of these was staggered and only two are matching. In 1317 a series of unsightly buttresses was deemed necessary when the church seemed in danger of collapse. These aside, what you see today is essentially the church as it was in Justinian's time.

At the death of the Ottoman empire, with plans afoot to partition Istanbul along national lines (*see page 22*), both the Greeks (on behalf of the Eastern Church) and the Italians (on behalf of the Western Church) lobbied for Haghia Sophia to be handed over to them, and in Britain a St Sophia Redemption Committee was formed. The Ottoman government posted soldiers in the mosque with machine guns to thwart any attempt at a Christian coup. An expedient solution was effected by the leaders of the new Turkish republic in 1934, who deconsecrated the building and declared it a museum. It's a move that still evokes controversy, with Islamists periodically calling for its restoration as a mosque. Comparing the pristine state of neighbouring historical mosques with the shabby peeling salmon-pink of Haghia Sophia, you have to wonder if the Islamists don't have a case.

At least the interior remains impressive, particularly the main chamber, roofed by its still fabulous dome, 30 metres (98 feet) in diameter. The other great feature is the mosaics. Plastered over by the Muslims, they were only revealed again during renovations in the mid 19th century. Some of the best decorate the inner and outer narthexes, the long, vaulted chambers just inside the main entrance. The non-figurative are the earliest, dating from the reign of Justinian. Other mosaics adorn the galleries, reached by a stone ramp at the northern end of the inner narthex.

At the east end of the south gallery, next to the apse, is a glimmering representation of Christ flanked by the famous 11th-century Empress Zoe, one of the few women to rule Byzantium, and her third husband Constantine IX. A virgin until the age of 50, Zoe married late. She obviously developed a taste for what she discovered, going through a succession of husbands and then lovers in the years left to her. On the mosaic in question, the heads and inscriptions show signs of being altered, possibly in an attempt to keep up with her active love life. En route to see Zoe, you pass a tomb set in the floor, burial place of Enrico Dandalo, Doge of Venice, one of the leaders of the Fourth Crusade, and the man held responsible for persuading the Latins to attack Constantinople. Following the Ottoman conquest of the city, it's said that his tomb was smashed open and his bones thrown to the dogs.

Haghia Sophia

Ayasofya Camii Müze
Sultanahmet Square (0212 522 1750). Tram Sultanahmet. **Open** 9.30am-4.30pm Tue-Sun; closed Mon. Gallery closes 30 mins earlier. **Admission** $6. **No credit cards. Map** p303 N10.

Topkapı Palace

Directly north of Haghia Sophia are the walls shielding the imperial enclave of **Topkapı Palace**. Part command centre for a massive military empire, part archetypal eastern pleasure dome, the palace was the hub of Ottoman power for more than three centuries, until it was superseded by the Dolmabahçe Palace in 1853. In terms of lavish decor and exquisite siting, it rivals Granada's Alhambra, and beats hands down almost anything else in Europe. At least half a day is needed to explore fully, but if pushed for time, highlights are the Harem, Imperial Treasury and the views from the fourth and innermost courtyard.

Entrance is via the **Imperial Gate** (*Bab-ı Hümayün*), which leads into the first of a series of four courts that become more private the deeper into the complex you penetrate. This first was a public court and housed a hospital and dormitories for the palace guards, hence the popular name,

Topkapı Palace

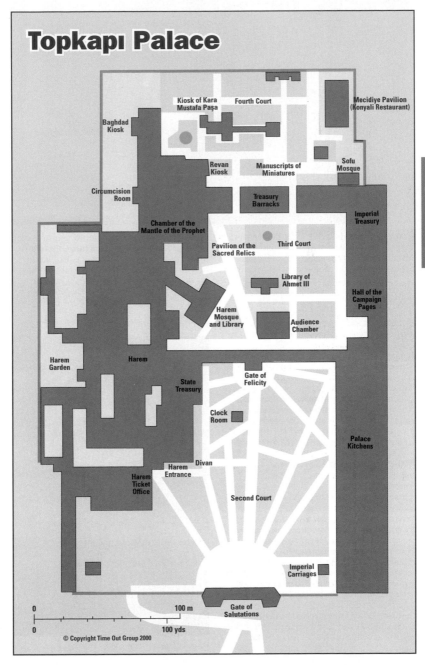

Kiosk of Kara Mustafa Paşa

Fourth Court

Mecidiye Pavilion (Konyali Restaurant)

Baghdad Kiosk

Revan Kiosk

Manuscripts of Miniatures

Sofu Mosque

Circumcision Room

Treasury Barracks

Imperial Treasury

Chamber of the Mantle of the Prophet

Pavilion of the Sacred Relics

Third Court

Library of Ahmet III

Hall of the Campaign Pages

Harem Mosque and Library

Audience Chamber

Harem Garden

Harem

State Treasury

Gate of Felicity

Clock Room

Palace Kitchens

Harem Entrance

Divan

Harem Ticket Office

Second Court

Imperial Carriages

0   100 m
0   100 yds

Gate of Salutations

© Copyright Time Out Group 2000

No running in the harem! **Topkapi Palace**.

Court of the Janissaries. Off to the left is **Haghia Irene** (*Aya Irini Kilisesi*), built by Justinian and thus a contemporary of Haghia Sophia, but it has the distinction of being the only pre-Ottoman conquest church in the city that was never turned into a mosque. It's closed most of the time, but serves as one of the most appealing concert venues during the **International Istanbul Music Festival** (*see page 180*) and as an exhibition space during the **International Istanbul Bienniale** (*see page 182*).

Down the hill to the left is the **Archaeological Museum** (*see page 112*), but the palace proper is entered through the Disneyesque gate ahead. Tickets are bought on the right, just before the gate, beside the **Executioner's Fountain**, where the chief axeman washed his blade after carrying out his grisly work. The heads of his victims were displayed on top of the truncated columns that stand either side of the fountain.

A semi-public space, the second court is where the business of running the empire was carried out. This is where the viziers of the imperial council sat in session in the Divan, overlooking gardens landscaped with cypresses, plane trees and rose bushes. Where once there would have been crowds of petitioners awaiting their turn for an audience, nowadays are queues lined up waiting to get in to the **Harem** (*see page 73* **Harem-scarem**), an introverted complex of around 300 brilliantly tiled chambers on several levels, connected by arcaded courts and fountain gardens. Entrance is limited to set numbers at set times, admitted as a group and led around by official guides. It's not the ideal way to see the place, locked in a crowd and herded around, but it's the only way, and the Harem is an unquestionable must-see. Tickets are sold separately, beside the Harem entrance.

Around from the Harem entrance, a low brick building topped by shallow domes is the former State Treasury, present home of an exhibition of arms and armour, interesting for the contrast between cumbersome, bludgeonly European swords and the lighter, more deadly-looking Ottoman model. Across the gardens, a long row of ventilation chimneys punctuates the roofline of the enormous **kitchens**, which catered for up

Haghia Irene – that's the church, by the way.

to 5,000 inhabitants of the palace. They now contain a collection of ceramics, glass and silverware, much of it originating from China and Japan and imported via Central Asia along the legendary Silk Route. The earliest pieces are Chinese Celadon, particularly valued by the sultans because it was supposed to change colour when brought into contact with poison.

All paths in the second court converge on the **Gate of Felicity** (*Bab-üs saadet*), which serves as the backdrop every year for a performance of Mozart's *Abduction From the Seraglio*, part of the **International Istanbul Music Festival** (*see page 180*). It also gives access to the third court. Within is the **Audience Chamber** (*Arz Odası*) which is where, until it was supplanted in the role by the Sublime Porte (*see page 82*), foreign ambassadors would present their credentials. Although the sultan would be present on such occasions, he would never deign to speak with a non-Turk and all conversation was conducted via the grand vizier.

Off to the right is the **Hall of the Campaign Pages** (*Seferli Koğuşu*), whose task it was to look after the royal wardrobe. They did an excellent job: there's a perfectly preserved 550-year-old,

Harem-scarem

From its inception in around 1540 until its dissolution in the early 20th century, the Topkapı harem was home, prison and entire world to almost four centuries of palace women. The only men allowed to enter were the sultan, princes and eunuch guards – *haram* is the Arabic word for 'forbidden'. Women had no problem getting in, but once admitted they were in for life. Most entered as slave girls presented to the sultan as gifts. It was forbidden to make slaves of Muslims so they were all Christians or Jews. Circassian girls from what is now Georgia and Armenia were favoured because of their fair skin, but even the best was still only valued at a fifth of the price of a good horse. They were converted to Islam, 'palace-trained', taught to sing, dance, play instruments and to give pleasure of a more physical kind.

But notions of the harem as a sensual hothouse are misplaced. It was more like one great ever-present headache. The fastest route to advancement was to catch the eye of the sultan or a prince. At any one time a dozen or so girls would be chosen as imperial handmaids and bedmates. Giving birth to the sultan's child ensured exalted status. If it was a boy there was even the chance he might one day become sultan and his mother *valide sultana*, 'mother of the sultan', most powerful woman in the land. With such high stakes, along with the sex came the violence as the women manoeuvred, plotted, poisoned and knifed their way up the harem hierarchy. A mother with the sultan's child was particularly vulnerable – Murat III (1574-95), for example, fathered 103 children, only one of which was ever going to make the throne.

All the while, harem girls also had to court the favour of the present *valide sultana*, responsible for selecting girls for the sultan, and avoid the attentions of the *kizlar ağasi*, the

The Turkish Bath by Jean Auguste Ingres.

chief black eunuch. A go-between for the sultan and his mother, privy to all palace secrets and at the same time surrounded by women who were trained to arouse while he himself was sexually incapable, the chief black eunuch tended to be a dangerous combination of corrupt, scheming and vindictive. He got his kicks stuffing girls in sacks, loading them into a boat and dumping them overboard into the Bosphorus. This on the instruction of the *valide sultana*, the Rosa Klebb of her day.

Alev Lytle Croutier sums it all up very nicely in her fine book *Harem: The World Behind the Veil*, describing it as a world of 'frightened women plotting with men who were not men against absolute rulers who kept their relatives immured for decades'. Far from being a palace of delights, the Topkapı Harem is more of a chamber of horrors.

red-and-gold silk kaftan worn by Mehmet II, conqueror of Constantinople. Things get even more glittery next door in the **Imperial Treasury** (*Hazine*). Many of the items here were made specifically for the palace by a team of court artisans that at its height numbered over 600, and quite a lot of what's displayed here has never left the confines of the inner courts. Not that too many people outside the sultan's circle would have much use for a diamond-encrusted set of chain mail or a Koran bound in jade. Items like the Topkapı dagger, its handle set with three eyeball-sized emeralds, one of which conceals a watch face, are breathtaking in their excesses, vulgarity and sheer bloody uselessness.

And so to the sublime. The fourth, and final, court is a garden with terraces stepping down towards Seraglio Point. Buildings are limited to a bunch of reasonably restrained pavilions, while the views over the Bosphorus are wonderful. As are the sea breezes on a sun-beaten summer's day. The very last building to be constructed within the palace, the **Mecidiye pavilion** (*Mecidiye Köşkü*), built in 1840, houses a restaurant and café with terrace seating worth angling for.

Topkapı Palace

Topkapı Sarayı
Soğukçeşme Sokak, Gülhane (0212 512 0480). **Open** 9am-5pm Mon, Wed-Sun; closed Tue. *Harem* 9.30am-4pm Mon, Wed-Sun; closed Tue. **Admission** $6. *Harem* $4. **No credit cards. Map** p303 O9.

Yerebatan Sarayı

Running downhill from Topkapı's Imperial Gate, **Soğukçeşme Sokak** is an amazing example of urban set design. Formerly a row of dilapidated old wooden buildings, in the 1980s the original street was demolished and recreated in concrete disguised under pastel-painted weatherboard panelling. Intended to evoke the atmosphere of Ottoman Istanbul, the 'old houses', which now look quite smart, are actually hotels and tourist restaurants. One contains the **Istanbul Library** (also known as the Çelik Gülersoy Foundation; *see page 276*).

A left turn uphill, across the tram tracks, and then to the first turn right, brings one to a lone, single-storey stone building that marks the entrance to the **Yerebatan Sarayı** (Sunken Palace), the grandest of several underground cisterns that riddle the foundations of this part of the city. Built by the Emperor Justinian at the same time as the Haghia Sophia, it was forgotten for centuries and only rediscovered by a Frenchman, Peter Gyllius, in 1545 when he saw that people in the neighbourhood got water by lowering buckets through holes in their basements. It's a tremendous engineering feat, with brick vaults supported on 336 columns spaced at four-metre intervals. Prior to restoration in 1987 the cistern could only be explored by boat (Bond rowed through in *From Russia With Love*; *see page 287*), but these days

Go soak your head at the **Yerebatan Sarayı**. *See p75.*

Sultanahmet Mosque, aka the Blue Mosque.

there are concrete walkways. Still, the subdued lighting and subterranean cool are welcome on hot days. Look for the two Medusa heads recycled from an even more ancient building and casually employed as column bases. There's a café down here and occasional concerts of classical Turkish and Western music are given; check with the ticket office for further details.

Scheduled to open some time in 2000 is the **Binbirdirek Cistern**, also known as the Cistern of a Thousand and One Columns (although there are only 224). Constructed in Constantine's time and restored by Justinian, it's the city's second largest cistern. It has been dormant for decades after providing space for a spinning mill, but is slated to open sometime as an underground craft market.

Binbirdirek Cistern
Binbirdirek Sarnıcı
Işık Sokak, off Divan Yolu Caddesi. Tram Sultanahmet. **Map** p303 M10.

Yerebatan Sarayı
Yerebatan Caddesi 13 (0212 522 1259). Tram Sultanahmet. **Open** *May-Oct* 9am-5.30pm daily. *Nov-Apr* 9am-4.30pm daily. **Admission** $4. **No credit cards. Map** p303 N10.

Sultanahmet Mosque

Seductively curvaceous and enhanced by a lovingly attended park in front, Sultanahmet Mosque is Islamic architecture at its sexiest. Commissioned by Sultan Ahmet I (1603-17) and built for him by Mehmet Ağa, a student of the great Sinan (*see page 38* **Keeping up with the domes's**) it was the last of Istanbul's magnificent imperial mosques, the final flourish before the rot set in. It provoked hostility at the time because of its six minarets – only the Prophet's mosque at Mecca had such a number. But it does make for a beautifully elegant silhouette, particularly gorgeous when floodlit at night.

By contrast, the interior is clumsy, marred by four immense pillars that seem disproportionately large for the fairly modest dome (compared to Haghia Sophia) that they support. Most surfaces are covered by a mismatch of Iznik tiles, whose predominant colour gives the place its popular name, the Blue Mosque. Part of the mosque complex, the Imperial Pavilion, now houses the **Vakıflar Carpet Museum** (*see page 116*), while in the north-east corner of the surrounding park is the *türbe* or **Tomb of Sultan Ahmet I**. This also contains the cenotaphs of his wife and three of

Egypt, Rome and Byzantium come together at the **Hippodrome**.

obelisk, removed from the Temple of Karnak at Thebes (now Luxor). It was originally carved around 1500 BC to commemorate the victories of Pharaoh Thutmosis III. By contrast, it stands on a base added in the fourth century AD showing the Byzantine emperor Theodosius enjoying a day at the races with his family.

Next to it is the bronze **Serpentine Column**, carried off from the Temple of Apollo at Delphi, where it commemorated a Greek victory over the Persians in 480 BC. When it was brought to the Byzantine capital by Constantine, its three entwined serpents all had heads; all were decapitated at some point in history. One detached head survives and is displayed in the Archaeological Museum (*see page 112*). A third monument is known as the **Column of Constantine**, a pockmarked and crumbling affair, once sheathed in gold-plated bronze, but stripped by the looting Fourth Crusaders.

Downhill from the south-west corner of the Hippodrome, the **Sokollu Mehmet Paşa Mosque** is another *tour de force* by Sinan (*see page 38* **Keeping up with the domes's**). It's one of his later buildings (constructed 1571-72), praised by architectural historians for the way it copes with an uneven, sloping site. If you can get inside (hang around and somebody will usually turn up with a key) you will see that the tiling is especially lovely, as are the painted calligraphic inscriptions, set among vivid floral motifs.

Almost directly south, downhill toward the sea, is the **Küçük Haghia Sophia Mosque**, the 'Little Haghia Sophia', so-called because of its resemblance to Justinian's great cathedral. In essence, it's a scaled-down version. Like its larger namesake, it was originally a church, Sts Sergius and Bacchus, after the patron saints of the Christianised Roman army. Also like its namesake, it's not much to look at from the outside but possesses a fine interior, including a frieze honouring Justinian and Theodora. As at the Sokollu Mehmet Paşa Mosque, it might be necessary to rustle up whoever has the key.

Following Küçük Ayasofya Caddesi back uphill leads past the **Mosaic Museum** (*see page 114*) and beyond that a small carpet and crafts complex with a sunken terrace café where you can smoke *nargile* (*see page 146* **Hava nargile.**

his sons, two of whom, Osman II and Murat IV, ruled in their turn, Ahmet being the sultan who abandoned the Ottoman practice of strangling other potential heirs on the succession of the favoured son.

Sultanahmet (Blue) Mosque
Sultanahmet Camii
At Meydanı Sokak 17 (0212 458 0776). Tram Sultanahmet. **Open** 9am-5pm daily. *Sound & light show* May-Sept just after dusk daily. **Admission** free. **Map** p303 N11.

The Hippodrome & south

On the north side of the courtyard of the Sultanahmet Mosque, a strip of over-touristed tea houses and souvenir shops fringes the **Hippodrome** (*At Meydanı*), formerly the focal point of Byzantine Constantinople. Originally laid out by the Roman emperor Septimius Severus during his rebuilding of the city (*see page 7*), it was later enlarged by Constantine to its present dimensions – the modern road exactly traces the old racing lanes. In addition to races, the space was used for court ceremonies, coronations and parades.

Now an elongated park circled by traffic, the Hippodrome retains an odd assortment of monuments standing on what was the *spina*, the raised area around which chariots would have thundered. Closest to the mosque is an **Egyptian**

Sokollu Mehmet Paşa Mosque
Sokollu Mehmet Paşa Camii
Şehit Mehmet Paşa Sokak 20-24. Tram Sultanahmet. **Open** 10am-dusk daily. **Admission** free. **Map** p303 M11.

Küçük Haghia Sophia Mosque
Küçük Ayasofya Camii
Küçük Ayasofya Caddesi. Tram Sultanahmet. **Open** prayer times only, daily. **Admission** free. **Map** p303 M12.

The Bazaar Quarter

A sprawling Oriental wonderland; the energy of the Grand Bazaar spills far beyond its walls.

Map p302
Forget the mall: Istanbul's bazaar is shopping at its rawest: a vast disordered sprawl of one million and one goods, all mixed together. No departments, no signs. In place of 'don't mind if you do' sales assistants are some of the most charming and ruthless traders in the Near East. You want a discount, a cut-price offer, then you're going to have to bargain for it. That goes for Turks as much as tourists, because what seems like an oriental wonderland to visitors is Saturday's shopping venue for the locals. Buying and selling aside, the area around the bazaar is packed with historical monuments and other sightseeing interludes.

Beyazıt Square

The place to start is the irregularly shaped Beyazıt Square, 100 metres (328 feet) west of the Beyazıt tram stop. Site of the Forum in Roman times, it regained importance when the early Ottomans built a palace here, the Eski Saray, which served as the pre-Topkapı seat of government. It burnt down in 1541. Nothing remains of the Roman era except for the **Burnt Column** (or Hooped Column; Çemberlitaş), one stop back on the tram, erected by Constantine to celebrate the city's dedication as new imperial capital in AD 330. The column was topped by a statue of the emperor, but this was destroyed in an 1106 hurricane. Its present sorry, blackened state results from one of the city's periodic fires. The iron hoops are structural reinforcements added in the fifth century.

Other significant Ottoman structures are still standing around the square. On the east side is the **Beyazıt Mosque**, built in 1501-6, the second great mosque complex to be founded in the city. The first, the **Fatih Mosque** (*see page 85*) was destroyed, making Beyazıt the oldest imperial mosque in town. It's still in use, usually full of market traders at prayer times.

Facing the mosque is the gigantic gate to **Istanbul University**, previously the Ottoman Ministry of War. In the 1960s and '70s, the university was a favourite battleground for both left and right, and is still a centre for political protest (*see page 78* **Bullets over Beyazıt**). As a result, the gardens behind the gate and Beyazıt Tower, a prominent city landmark, are off limits to all but university students.

Birds not bullets in **Beyazıt Square**.

To the left of the gate is a small *medrese*, part of the Beyazıt Mosque complex, now the **Calligraphy Museum** (*see page 112*). Still in a literary vein, to the left of the mosque's main entrance is the **Booksellers' Bazaar**, a courtyard and lane where the written word has been traded since early Ottoman times. Initially, printed books were considered a corrupting

European influence, so only hand-lettered manuscripts were sold until 1729, the year the first book in Turkish was published. Much of the trade now is in student textbooks and framed calligraphy for tourists. The booksellers' space is under threat from merchants pushing everything from Byzantine coins to used mobile phones.

Beyazıt Mosque

Beyazıt Camii
Beyazıt Square (0212 519 3644). Tram Beyazıt.
Open 10am-final prayer call daily. **Admission** free.
Map p302 K9.

Booksellers' Bazaar

Sahaflar Çarşısı
Sahaflar Çarşısı Sokak, Beyazıt. **Open** 8am-8pm daily.
Credit MC, V. **Map** p302 K10.

Grand Bazaar

Beyond the booksellers is the **Fesciler Gate** (*Fesciler Kapısı*) and the area once known as the *bitpazarı*, literally 'headlice bazaar', so named for the junk merchants that traded here. They're long gone, replaced by shops selling clothes and footwear. Step through the gate – one of 18 – to reach the Grand Bazaar (in Turkish, *Kapalı Çarşı*, or 'Covered Market'), a world apart, made up of a maze of interconnecting vaulted passages with its own banks, baths, mosques, cafés, restaurants (of which the best is probably the Havuzlu Lokanta), police station and post office. Not to mention some four thousand shops, all glittery and fairy lit in the absence of natural light.

Constantinople was always one of the world's most important trading centres, with extensive open markets in Byzantine times. The Ottomans ushered in a new economic era, with the city at the centre of an empire that stretched from the Arabian deserts almost to the European Alps. In 1461 Mehmet the Conqueror ordered the construction of a *bedesten*, a great lock-up with thick stone walls, massive iron gates and space for several dozen shops. This survives in modified form as the **Old Bedesten** (*İç Bedesten*), at the very heart of the bazaar. It remains a place where the most precious items are sold, including the best old silver and antiques. The **Sandal Bedesten** was added later, named after a fine Bursan silk and filled with textile traders. It now hosts a carpet auction at 1pm every Wednesday, well worth attending as an audience spectacle.

A network of streets grew up around these two original structures – whenever the economy was booming, the market would physically expand, only to be cut back by fires. Then, as the Ottoman empire declined after 300 years of wealth, so did the legendary splendour of the bazaar. In 1894 a devastating earthquake hit the bazaar particularly hard. It wasn't until the 1950s that it began to revive, as the republic found its economic footing.

Bullets over Beyazıt

Proximity to Istanbul University has regularly filled Beyazıt Square with a ready supply of student demonstrators, who, throughout the 1970s in particular, would just as happily trade automatic fire as essay plans. On one infamous occasion in 1975, a half-dozen leftist students were gunned down in the square by their neo-fascist classmates, the 'Grey Wolves'. Throughout the period leading up to the 1980 coup, there were violent clashes between left and right outside the university gates.

While the Grey Wolves have moved on, graduating to become mafia bosses and politicians (the Nationalist Action Party, second-largest component of the governing coalition, is full of them), a new generation of activists has taken their place. Since the late 1990s the inflammatory issue keeping the square abuzz has been headscarves. A long-standing ban on this Islamic headgear, as well as on Islamic-style beards for male students, was invoked in 1997, with offending individuals barred from the university. Cue showdowns on the square between students and police. While strangely reluctant to intervene in knife attacks on visiting football fans, the ranks of Robocop-geared warriors seem only too happy to deploy tear gas, water cannon and rubber-coated lead against 18-year-old headscarfed female medical students.

This may, however, be a thing of the past, as the police have recently instituted a number of schemes intended to bring out their caring, sharing side. Courses in classical music for riot cops were begun in 1998, the idea being that listening to Brahms might sooth the itch in trigger fingers. Meanwhile, city police stations are being repainted in friendly pinks and pastels. A little unfortunate, then, that inspections of several of the new stations by the Turkish Parliamentary Human Rights Committee in early 2000 uncovered various implements of torture in the cells. Station chiefs denied ever having seen them before.

A maze of interconnecting vaulted passages, the **Grand Bazaar** is a world apart.

Much of the current prosperity comes from gold (of which nearly 100 tons is sold in the bazaar each year), coachloads of 'black bag' shoppers from the former Soviet Union (so called because of their habit of filling bin sacks with cheap clothing) and tourism. But, among the sea of mantlepiece trinkets, nasty leather jackets, no-label jeans and hippie-wear, there are attractive quality goods to be had (*see page 167* **Shopping the Bazaar**). To take time out from the constant hard sell, head for the **Şark Kahvesi**, a fine old-style coffeehouse on the prominent Yağlıkçılar Caddesi.

If you can find your way out on the east side of the bazaar, you emerge into daylight beside the **Nuruosmaniye Mosque**, the first in the city executed in the style known as Turkish Baroque (*see page 37*). Istanbul historian John Freely describes the architecture as possessing a 'certain perverse genius'. That's debatable, but the plane-tree courtyard is lovely.

The bazaar extends much further than the limits of the covered area, spilling over into a crazed warren of narrow streets that zag and zig all the way down to Eminönü and the Golden Horn (*see pages 81-3*). A rule of thumb is that if

you're lost, just keep heading downhill. On the way you'll see the contemporary bazaar at its most frenetic. From the Nuruosmaniye follow **Mahmut Paşa Yokuşu** north. This principal market street given over to the rag-trade is lined with wholesalers knocking out 'Lacoste' T-shirts and 'Levi's' jeans in basement workshops. Along the way, great stone-arch gateways lead into numerous *hans*, medieval merchant hostels with storage rooms and accommodation around a central courtyard. Down Mahmut Paşa Yokuşu on the left is the **Kürkçü Han**, the oldest in the city, now in a sad state of disrepair.

The next left up Çakmakçılar Yokuşu brings you to the **Valide Han**, the grandest and most interesting of the lot. Through the first small courtyard is the main court, 55 metres (180 feet) square, surrounded by a double-tiered arcade whose cell-like chambers are still given over to commerce. A vaulted tunnel leads from the far corner to a third court, containing the remains of a Byzantine tower. It's possible to exit from here to Vasıf Çınar Caddesi, which you can follow west for 250 metres (720 feet) to the magnificent **Süleymaniye Mosque** (*see page 80*).

Reflection of Ottoman glory – the magnificent **Süleymaniye Mosque**.

Grand Bazaar

Kapalı Çarşı
Tram Beyazıt for Fesciler Gate or Çemberlitaş for Nuruosmaniye Gate. **Open** 8.30am-7pm Mon-Sat; closed Sun. **Map** p302 L9.

Nuruosmaniye Mosque

Nuruosmaniye Camii
Vezirhanı Caddesi, Beyazıt. Tram Çemberlitaş. **Open** 9am-final prayer call daily. **Admission** free. **Map** p302 L10.

Süleymaniye Mosque

The Süleymaniye is perhaps the city's most perfect Ottoman construction. Completed in 1557, it represents both the empire at its height under Süleyman the Magnificent and arguably the crowning achievement of architect **Mimar Sinan** (*see page 38* **Keeping up with the domes's**). It's built on Istanbul's highest hill, exploiting the topography to impress. The approach is along Prof Sıddık Sami Onar Caddesi, formerly known as 'Addicts Alley' because its cafés sold hashish to be smoked on the premises or taken away. No longer, although the area is still popular with students from the nearby university. The low-rise multi-domed buildings surrounding the mosque are part of its *külliye* (*see page 37*) and include a hospital, asylum, han, hamam and soup kitchen – the latter now the **Darüzziyafe** restaurant (*see page 137*).

The mosque itself is entered via gardens, then an arcaded courtyard, the columns of which are said to have come from the Byzantine royal box at the Hippodrome. Its interior is remarkable for the lightness of its soaring central prayer space, enhanced by some 200 windows. Decoration is minimal but effective, including stained glass added by Ibrahim the Mad and sparing use of Iznik tiles (which Sinan would later go a bundle on at the **Rüstem Pasha Mosque**, just down the hill; *see page 82*).

In a small walled garden behind the mosque are several *türbes* (tombs) including that of Süleyman, recently beautifully restored, adjacent to that of Haseki Hürrem, the sultan's influential wife, better known as Roxelana. Outside the compound wall, just to the north in a triangular site between two streets, is the **Tomb of Sinan**, with a stone carved bust of the master builder.

Süleymaniye Mosque

Süleymaniye Camii
Tiryakiler Çarşısı, off Prof Sıddık Sami Onar Caddesi, Süleymaniye (0212 514 0139). Tram Beyazıt or Eminönü. **Open** 9am-7pm daily. **Admission** free. **Map** p302 K8.

Tahtakale

From the Süleymaniye head downhill for Tahtakale, a market district renowned for dodgy electronic goods, bootleg CDs, cameras of unverifiable origin and a whole slew of other dubious merchandise. Would you really buy condoms that come in a packet with a photocopied label? Traders sell from wooden trays hung round their necks or from suitcases, easy to close up and run with when the market police make a raid. Tahtakale is also a good spot for cigar purchases: apparently genuine Cohiba/Havana stock at substantially reduced prices. It's a fun place to browse, and there are great bargains to be had, provided durability is not a priority.

Eminönü & the Golden Horn

With trains and boats and ancient markets, Eminönü is a bustling crossroads.

Still some fish on **Galata Bridge**. *See p82.*

Map p303

A former maritime gateway to the city, Eminönü remains a place of constant exchange – from the commuters that use its ferry terminals to the commerce that fills the backstreets. Its most prominent landmark is the imposing **New Mosque**, plagued by pigeons and constantly busy with worshippers. Begun in 1598, construction suffered a setback when the architect was executed for heresy, and it wasn't until 1663 that the mosque was finally completed. The fact that it is so obviously a working mosque tends to keep visitors at bay, but nobody objects to non-Muslims entering, providing they are suitably respectful (*see page 68* **Mosque etiquette**). Built after the classical period of Ottoman architecture, it is nonetheless a regal structure, and particularly uplifting seen floodlit from a taxi barrelling by after a night on the town.

On the landward side of the mosque is Istanbul's **pet market**, a harrowing experience for animal-lovers. South and west are the high brick walls of the enclosed **Egyptian Market**, also known as the Spice Bazaar. (It's a tenuous link, but it was as background fluff on a Turkish

TV game show that former Spice Girl Geri Haliwell got her first showbiz break.) The market was constructed as part of the New Mosque complex, and its revenues helped support the mosque's philanthropic institutions. The name comes from its ancient association with the arrival of the annual 'Cairo caravan' – ships bearing rice, coffee, incense and henna from Egypt. Nothing quite so useful is sold here nowadays. While its L-shaped vaulted corridor is undeniably pretty, its shops and stalls purvey a motley assortment of cheap perfumes, cheap gold and confectionary, admittedly including some of the best Turkish Delight in town. Most interesting of the stores are a handful of places pushing so-called aphrodisiacs, remnants of a once thriving herbal drugs and potions market, in which tradesmen doubled as doctors. A few such practitioners remain, plying their concoctions in older, poorer parts of the city.

One very good reason to pay a visit to the Egyptian Market is **Pandeli's** (*see page 133*), a famed Greek-run restaurant tucked upstairs just inside the northern market entrance. Immediately behind the market, opposite the

Serving up small-fry on the dockside.

angle of its corner, the **Mehmet Efendi Coffeeshop** is worth a look in for its excellent art deco staircase. The coffee's not bad either. Two blocks west, on the right-hand side is the **Rüstem Paşa Mosque**, raised above shops and workshops whose rents pay for its upkeep. It was built in 1561 by Sinan (*see page 38* **Keeping up with the domes's**) for a son-in-law and vizier to Süleyman I. Smaller in scale than Sinan's better-known masterworks, this place is noted for its overwhelming use of coloured tiles.

ON THE WATERFRONT
Between the markets and mosques and the water is one of the city's busiest roadways and the terminus from which trams start out for a journey up the hill to Sultanahmet, the Grand Bazaar and beyond. Mingling with the leaden smell of the traffic and the whiff of a dodgy sewage system is the far more pleasant aroma of deep-frying fish. This comes from a string of small boats moored at the dockside, cooking up their day's catch of small fry for sale in sandwiches to passers-by. Appetites are quickly lost at the sight of the scum and assorted crap floating on the water. The Golden Horn is filthy, a long-standing dump for the worst of the city's pollution.

Neither is the waterfront appeal helped by the fact that the current **Galata Bridge**, the vital link between the two sides of European Istanbul, is such an ugly structure. It replaces a famed earlier bridge, built in 1909-12 with a suspended lower level filled with fish restaurants and what was at one time Istanbul's only rock bar (Kemanci, since moved up to Taksim; *see page 208*). But the rock was out-heavied by the restaurants – the food critic of the daily

Cumhuriyet was shot dead by one proprietor after giving his place a bad review. The current bridge, a concrete ramp with four ugly steel towers at its centre (they're supposed to raise the bridge, but don't work) was built in the 1980s to accommodate the growing traffic. Its commercial spaces remain unlet.

The best that can be said of Eminönü's waterfront is that it is functional and operates fine if you're looking to catch a ferry across to the Asian Shore or join a cruise up the Bosphorus. Aesthetically, matters improve once you move into the backstreets, which contain some of the city's most intriguing 20th-century architecture, much of it executed in the First National style (*see page 39*); check out **4. Vakıf Hanı** (64 Hamidiye Caddesi), the **Central Post Office** (Şehin Şah Pehlevi Caddesi) or, for some attractive art nouveau detailing, the **Flora Han** (18 Şehin Şah Pehlevi Caddesi).

END OF THE LINE
Across Ankara Caddesi, along which the tram runs, closer down to the waterfront is **Sirkeci Station** (*Sirkeci Istasyonu; see page 266*), Europe's last train stop. On its completion in 1881, Sirkeci was the eastern terminus for trains from the European capitals, including the legendary Orient Express (*see page 83* **The extravagant express**). Disfigured by modern additions and conspicuously lacking in grandeur, (although there is a great 'period' barbershop), it's now a station for commuter trains packed with workers heading home to tower-block suburbs.

From the station, the main road climbs up into the district of Cağaloğlu, traditionally the centre of the country's newspaper industry, but, with the exception of *Cumhuriyet*, the press has recently moved en masse to flashier media plazas near the airport. The best reason to visit the area now is for a good sweat and pummelling at the **Cağaloğlu Hamam** (*see page 204*), one of the finest traditional bathhouses in Istanbul.

To the east, the district is bounded by the curve of Alemdar Caddesi, where just along from the Gülhane tram stop is the historic **Sublime Porte**, an ornate, monumental gateway with floppy rococo roofing. At one time it was the entrance to the palace and offices of the Grand Vizier, the administrator of the empire. Foreign ambassadors were accredited to the 'Sublime Porte', which became a synonym for the Ottoman government. The current gate dates from 1843 and is now the entrance to the city governorate.

Opposite, on a corner of the wall enclosing Gülhane Park, is the Alay Köşkü, an elaborate treehouse-like platform from where sultans would observe parades or, in the case of Ibrahim the Mad, take pot shots with a crossbow at

The extravagant express

Byword for glamour, the **Orient Express** existed in several versions on various routes, most famously Paris–Vienna–Budapest–Istanbul. Its maiden departure was 4 October 1883 from Gare de l'Est, Paris. Between the Western 'city of light' and the Eastern exoticism of its ultimate destination, the train passed through a patchwork of mercurial Balkan kingdoms, popularly associated with Gypsy musicians and titled aristocracy, and always tinged with the promise of war or revolution. Incidents such as bandits holding up the train and taking its passengers hostage in 1891, and the stranding of the train in a snowdrift for several days in 1929 only added to the legend.

Such episodes could be endured in the comfort of carpeted cabins with damask drapes and silk sheets for the fold-down beds, or in the saloon with leather armchairs and a bookcase evoking the atmosphere of a London gentleman's club. Meals were served in the Wagon Restaurant, beneath gas chandeliers of brass and crystal at tables set with Baccarat crystal, starched napery and monogrammed porcelain. The kind of passengers who could afford all this tended to be minor royals and dignitaries, diplomats, financiers, celebrated correspondents and stars of the stage – adding the perfect cast list to a perfect setting for writers like Agatha Christie and Graham Greene (see page 286).

The appearance of the Iron Curtain at the end of World War II signalled the end of this particular line. Sporadic current revivals have proved nothing more than sops to moneyed nostalgia buffs. In this age of Go, Easyjet and Ryanair, 81 hours 40 minutes and a second mortgage on the house just to get from Paris to Istanbul seems just a little bit extravagant. But then it always was.

Sightseeing

---

passing pedestrians. Formerly part of the lower grounds of the Topkapı Palace, **Gülhane Park** is a fairly sad place, with more concrete on the ground than grass. It contains the dire **Gülhane Zoo** and, for connoisseurs of lost causes, the **Tanzimat Museum**, which commemorates the 1839 liberalising reforms proclaimed from this very spot by Sultan Abdul Mecid and then roundly ignored by all (*see page 20*). The collection, exhibited in a small wooden hut, amounts to little more than a wall of portraits, a waxwork head and torso and some yellowing imperial decrees.

Exiting the park across the highway is **Seraglio Point**, a well-manicured grassy viewing point overlooking the confluence of the Golden Horn and Bosphorus as they flow together into the Sea of Marmara. If you can block out the traffic thundering along the coastal highway at your back, it's a restful place to sit a while before heading back west, where a walk of about five minutes returns you to waterfront Eminönü.

Rüstem Paşa Mosque – mini-Sinan. *See p82.*

New Mosque

Yeni Camii
Eminönü Meydani 8 (0212 527 8505). Tram Eminönü. **Open** 9am-dusk daily. **Admission** free. **Map** p303 M8.

Egyptian Market

Mısır Çarşısı
Yeni Cami Meydani (0212 513 6597). Tram Eminönü. **Open** 8am-7pm Mon-Sat; closed Sun. **Admission** free. **Credit** most shops take AmEx, DC, MC, V. **Map** p302 L8.

Mehmet Efendi Coffeeshop

Kurukahveci Mehmet Efendi
Tahmis Caddesi 66. (0212 511 4262). Tram Eminönü. **Open** 8.30am-6.45pm Mon-Sat; closed Sun. **Map** p302 L8.

Rüstem Paşa Mosque

Rüstem Paşa Camii
Hasırcılar Caddesi 90 (0212 526 7350). Tram Eminönü. **Open** 9am-dusk daily. **Admission** free. **Map** p302 L7.

Tanzimat Museum

Tanzimat Müzesi
Gülhane Park (0212 512 6384). Tram Gülhane. **Open** 9am-4.30pm Mon-Fri; closed Sat, Sun. **Admission** free. **Map** p303 O9.

Fatih, Fener & Balat

The most conservative Islamic neighbourhoods feature a strong Christian and Jewish heritage.

Map pp304-5

Between Sultanahmet and the city walls (*see page 88*), these three neighbourhoods are some of the most religiously conservative in Istanbul. Headscarves, *chadors* and the baggy *şalvar* trousers worn by devout men are much in evidence. But although currently an Islamic stronghold, a visit to these areas also provides a reminder that until as recently as the early 20th century, Christians and Jews made up some 40 per cent of the population. Visitors should dress modestly and avoid revealing clothing.

Fatih

The easiest way to visit Fatih is to take the tram west from Sultanahmet and hop off at the Üniversite or Laleli stop. Walk north to the **Şehzade Mosque**, the first great complex by Sinan (*see page 38* **Keeping up with the**

domes's), completed in 1548 and regarded by him as 'apprentice work'. It stands in the shadow of the mighty **Aqueduct of Valens**, supported on two rows of imposing arches. For a city often under siege, a reliable water supply was of supreme importance. Constructed by Roman emperor Valens in the late 4th century AD, the aqueduct continued to bring water from the lakes and streams north of the city to Istanbul's many cisterns until the late 19th century.

In the 1950s, as part of a major metropolitan road-building programme, Atatürk Bulvarı was ploughed through Fatih and routed under the aqueduct, creating a memorable entryway for any visitor approaching the city centre for the first time. On its north side is the attractive little Medrese of Gazanfer Ağa, now the **Cartoon Museum** (*see page 113*). Further north, passing by one of Istanbul's better examples of modern architecture, the **Social Insurance Building** by Sedad Eldem (*see page 39*) is what's now

Zeyrek Mosque was formerly the Byzantine **Church of the Pantocrator.** *See p85.*

Sightseeing

known as the Zeyrek Mosque (Zeyrek Camii).
In pre-Conquest times, however, it was the
Byzantine **Church of the Pantocrator**. Built
in the early 12th century for the wife of Emperor
John II Comnenus (1118-43), it became the
imperial residence during the Latin occupation
and a mosque after the conquest. Although in
a deplorable state of repair, the church retains
some splendid internal decoration, including
exquisitely carved door frames and marble
mosaic paving which, if you're lucky, one of
the caretakers will reveal by drawing back the
carpets and removing a section of the wooden
floor. The church was once the centre of a huge
monastery complex, fragments of which litter
the surrounding streets. The most interesting are
the *ayazma* (sacred spring) and carved marble
steps in the basement of the Zeyrek Türk Eğitim
Gönülleri Vakif, just opposite the mosque's
entrance. Overlooking Atatürk Caddesi and the
Golden Horn, part of the monastery structure
is open as the swish Zeyrekhane restaurant
and café, the garden of which contains various
archaeological fragments.

Back south of the aqueduct, Fevzi Paşa
Caddesi runs directly west to the city walls,
splitting Fatih in two. Around 200 metres along
and just off to the south at the bottom end of Kız
Taşı Caddesi, is the **Column of Marcian**
(Kız Taşı), a 5th-century column which once
supported a statue of Roman emperor Marcian.
Its name in Turkish stems from a myth attesting
to its power to identify true virgins – apparently
the column would sway whenever an 'impure'
woman walked by.

MOSQUE BAROQUE

To the north of Fevzi Paşa Caddesi, raised on an
embankment, is the **Fatih Mosque**, a vast 18th-
century baroque structure. It occupies the site of
the Church of the Holy Apostles, burial place of
most Byzantine emperors, Constantine included.
However, the church was already in ruins by the
time Mehmet II conquered Constantinople, and
he used it as a quarry for his own mosque, built
in 1470 to celebrate his victory ('fatih' means
'conqueror'). The building was in turn destroyed
by a 1766 earthquake. Now all that remains of
Mehmet's original structure is the courtyard
and parts of the main entrance. The tomb of the
Conqueror stands behind the prayer hall. To
this day, Fatih Mosque remains a popular place
for the pious, many even bringing picnics and
making a day of their visit.

On Wednesday the streets around the mosque
complex are filled with the vast **Çarşamba
street market**, a great spectacle as well as
a shopping experience (*see page 175*).

About a kilometre further along Fevzi Paşa
Caddesi are the remains of the 5th-century

Selim I Mosque – honouring Selim the Grim.

Roman **Cistern of Aetios**, now the Vefa
Stadium, home to second division football club
Karagümrükspor. The original walls of the
ancient reservoir are still clearly visible.

There's a larger reservoir of the same period,
the **Cistern of Aspar**, on Yavuz Selim Caddesi,
directly north of the Fatih Mosque along
Darüşşafaka Caddesi. This one now houses a
sports complex, and again the original retaining
walls are still visible.

Overlooking the cistern is the **Selim I
Mosque** (Yavuz Selim Camii), built to
commemorate sultan Selim the Grim, so
nicknamed for his habit of executing senior
officials on a whim. Notwithstanding the
barbaric reputation of its founder, the mosque
is one of the most beautiful in the city. Little
visited, it has a beautiful garden courtyard,
while the views from the terrace overlooking
the Golden Horn are breathtaking.

Through the warren of backstreets to the
west stands another well-preserved Byzantine
structure, the **Church of the Pammakaristos**,
known locally as Fethiye Camii. For more than
100 years following the Ottoman conquest, it
served as the home of the Greek Orthodox
Patriarchate, until it was appropriated for Islam
by Murat III in the late 16th century. A side
chapel contains some excellent mosaics, with
Christ Pantocrator ('the All-Powerful') at the
centre of a dome surrounded by solemn Old
Testament prophets. The chapel can only be
visited by application to the directorate office
in the grounds of Haghia Sophia (*see page 69*).

Şehzade Mosque

Şehzade Camii
Şehzadebaşı Caddesi. Tram Üniversite or Laleli.
Open 9am-dusk daily. **Admission** free.
Map p302 H8.

Church of the Pantocrator

Zeyrek Camii
Ibadethane Sokak, off Atatürk Bulvarı, Küçükpazar.
Open 9am-dusk daily. **Admission** free.
Map p302 H7.

Sightseeing

The remains of Byzantine emperor Constantine rest in peace under **Fatih Mosque**. *See p85.*

Fatih Mosque

Fatih Camii
Fevzi Paşa Caddesi, Fatih. **Open** 9am-dusk daily.
Admission free. **Map** p305 G7.

Selim I Mosque

Yavuz Selim Camii
Yavuz Selim Caddesi, Fatih. Bus 55T, 90, 99A.
Open 9am-dusk daily. **Admission** free.
Map p305 G5.

Church of the Pammakaristos

Fethiye Camii
Fethiye Caddesi, Fatih. Bus 90. **Open** 9am-dusk daily.
Admission free. **Map** p305 F4.

Fener & Balat

Until the early part of the last century Fener was
primarily Greek, while Balat was mainly Jewish.

The most picturesque approach to the two
districts is on foot from the Selim I Mosque,
heading downhill past the red-brick Fener
Greek School for Boys. A little below to the left
is the only Byzantine church still in Greek hands,
the **Church of Panaghia Mouchliotissa**.
It was built in the late 13th century to honour
Princess Maria, daughter of emperor Michael
VIII, who was sent as a bride to Hulagu, khan
of the Mongols. She returned after his death to
live out her days as a nun – hence the church's
alternative name, St Mary of the Mongols. Its
immunity from conversion was reputedly at the
request of one of Mehmet II's architects, a Greek,
and a decree issued by the Conqueror to this
effect is the church's proudest possession.

The streets around and below here boast
a great many beautiful 19th-century Greek
houses and more churches down along the

former sea walls, parts of which still remain.
Immediately to the north of the Panaghia church
stands the stretch of walls breached by the
Crusaders in 1204. East along Incebal Sokak
is the **Greek Orthodox Patriarchate**, an
unprepossessing walled compound that has
been the world centre of the Greek Orthodox
faith for the past 400 years. Entrance is through
a three-sided gate. The central section is welded
permanently closed in memory of Patriarch
Gregory V, who was hanged from it in 1821 as
punishment for the outbreak of the Greek War of
Independence. The main Patriarchal Church of
St George dates only from 1720. Architecturally
it's unremarkable except for the richness of the
internal decoration, particularly the silver altar
screen. Much of the rest of the site is made up of
modern offices built to replace those destroyed
in a fire in 1951.

Back west along Yıldırım Street stand some of
the finest old Greek residences in town, including
the Fener Mansions, which date from the 17th
and 18th centuries. Most of these buildings are in
a terrible state of repair. The only one presently
occupied serves as the Istanbul **Womens'
Library** (Kadın Kütüphanesi; *see page 283*). As
the first institution of its type in Turkey, it has
proven to be a great success, as has the building's
restoration, which includes seating in the form
of an amphitheatre outside.

Equally unique is the church of **St Stephen
of the Bulgars**, which is one of Turkey's only
examples of a neo-Gothic building. Erected in
1871, it is also exceptional for being constructed
entirely from prefabricated cast-iron sections,
cast in Vienna and brought to Istanbul by barge
down the Danube. Though it is an oddity in

Istanbul, cast-iron churches were in fact
something of a fashion in Europe at the time. It
was built for Istanbul's Bulgarian community
and is still used today by Macedonian Christians.
It stands in an attractive park.

THE JEWISH QUARTER

Inland from St Stephen, the streets take on a grid
pattern in what used to be Istanbul's main Jewish
district. The neighbourhood boasts the city's
oldest synagogue, the **Ahrida**, founded in the
15th century before the Ottoman conquest.
Although it was founded by Macedonians
from the town of Ohrid (of which 'Ahrida' is a
corruption), its congregation was later formed
from the Sephardic community that was booted
out of Spain during the inquisitions. Renovation
to celebrate the 500th anniversary of their arrival
in 1992 uncovered fragments of 16th-century
frescoes. The wooden dome, although restored in
17th-century baroque style, remains exquisitely
beautiful. The synagogue also boasts an unusual
boat-shaped platform thought to represent Noah's
Ark. It is still in use by the Sephardic community,
many of whom remain fluent in the medieval
Spanish dialect Ladino.

Just around the corner is one of the most
interesting churches in the city: the Armenian
Orthodox **Church of Surp Hireşdagabet** (Holy
Archangels). Originally a Byzantine church,
tentatively dated to the 13th century, it was
taken over by the Armenians in the early 17th
century and they retain possession today.
Although much of the building dates only from
1835, the side chapel and the *ayazma* (sacred
spring) below it are original Byzantine features.
The spring boasts some Greek inscriptions. Also
of interest are a pair of bronze doors bearing four
pictorial panels thought to date from the time of
the Latin conquest.

The church is still in use, yet its regular
congregation is composed almost exclusively
of headscarved Muslim women – many devout
Muslims take both Christian and Jewish rituals
very seriously as 'precursors' of Islam. A curious
tradition is associated with the church. Every 16
September, a miracle cure is reputedly bestowed
on one member of its congregation, and on this
day Muslims from all over Turkey, many with
birth defects or incurable illnesses, crowd the
church hoping to be the lucky recipient.

To the west, the land rises steeply up towards
the remains of the Blachernae Palace (*see page
90*) and fragmented sections of the city walls.
On the coast road are remains of the sea walls,
interrupted by the **Old Galata Bridge**. This has
been constructed using sections of a much-loved
1912 bridge which used to span the Golden Horn
in the same spot where the new Galata Bridge
now stands (*see page 82*).

In 1998, a Unesco- and EU-sponsored p
identified various different ways of restoi
and preserving some of the many historical
buildings scattered across this area. However,
although money has yet to be allocated to the
project, and the only tangible result so far has
been the boom in local property prices that
followed in the wake of speculators gambling
on the area's future renovation.

Church of Panghia Mouchliotissa

Kanli Kilise
Tevkii Caddesi, Fener. **Open** 10am-5pm daily.
Admission free. **Map** p305 G4.

Greek Patriarchate

Sadrazam Ali Paşa Caddesi, Fener. **Open** 9am-5pm
daily. **Map** p305 G4.

Church of St Stephen of the Bulgars

Mürsel Paşa Caddesi, Fener. **Open** 9am-6pm daily.
Admission free. **Map** p305 G3.

Ahrida Synagogue

Ahrida Sinagogu
Kürkçüçeşme Sokak 9, Balat. **Map** p305 F3.
Entrance is only by appointment with the Chief
Rabbinate (0212 243 5166).

Church of Surp Hireşdagabet

Kamiş Sokak, Balat. **Admission** free. **Map** p305 F3.
Open only for Thursday morning services.

Church of St Stephen of the Bulgars. *See p86.*

Sightseeing

The City Walls

Europe's most extensive medieval fortifications can still hold their own
after a millennium and a half.

Sightseeing

Constructed between AD 413 and 447 during
the reign of Theodosius II (408-450), the walls
of Constantinople are the largest remaining
Byzantine structure in modern-day Istanbul.
Up to the Ottoman conquest in 1453, they stood
for over 1,000 years against invading armies,
resisting siege on more than 20 occasions. This
secured the continuation of empire and had an
enormous effect on the history of Europe.

From the Sea of Marmara in the south, the
walls encompass the old city in a great arc,
stretching four miles (6.5 kilometres) to the shore
of the Golden Horn in the north. Coupled with
the sea walls that also ringed Constantinople,
they constituted Europe's most extensive set of
medieval fortifications.

A triumph of engineering, the land walls
comprise inner and outer ramparts with a
terrace in between. The outer wall is two metres
(seven feet) thick and around 8.5 metres (30 feet)
high with 96 towers overlooking the 20-metre

Golden Gate of **Yedikule Fortress**. See p89.

(70-feet) wide moat below. The five-metre
(16-feet) thick inner wall looms above at a height
of around 12 metres (40 feet), and sports a
further 96 fortified towers. In between runs a
walkway for defending soldiers.

Large stretches have been rebuilt in recent
years, drawing criticism from scholars for
inappropriate use of modern materials, but the
new sections are undeniably impressive.

WALL WALKING

There are several ways to get to the walls
depending on which bit you want to visit – see the
listings at the end of this chapter for details of
how to reach the various sights. It's possible to
walk the whole length, along both the inside and
outside and occasionally on top, although care
should be taken as some sections are deserted
save for vagrants. Best place to begin is down
on the Marmara coast at Yedikule. Take a bus
from Eminönü (80) or Taksim (80T) or for a more
scenic ride a suburban train from Sirkeci station
to Yedikule. The line passes under the ramparts
of Topkapı Palace and winds in and out of what
remains of the southern stretch of sea walls.

From Yedikule station there's a worthwhile
detour a couple of minutes' walk back east in the
form of the ruins of the **Church of St John of
Studius** – the oldest church in the city. Built in
AD 463, it was originally part of a monastery
complex that constituted one of the most
important spiritual centres of Eastern
Christendom. Until it was looted by the Fourth
Crusaders, the church supposedly held the most
sacred of relics, the head of John the Baptist.
Converted into a mosque in the late 15th century,
the building was abandoned after being badly
damaged in an 1894 earthquake. What remains
is in an advanced state of decay, but two marble
door frames open on to a nave and two aisles
separated by two rows of moss-covered columns.
Parts of the mosaic floor also survive.

The walls begin down on the Marmara
shore with the imposing **Marble Tower** on a
promontory by the sea. It served as an imperial
summer pavilion and also as a prison. A chute
is still visible through which the corpses of the
executed were dumped into the sea.

Back over the coast road is the near pristine
Gate of Christ, the first of 11 fortified gates in
the walls, and north beyond that, over the other

side of the railway line, **Yedikule Fortress**.
Impressively restored, the originally Byzantine
'castle of the seven towers' was remodelled by
the Ottomans. Its western face incorporates the
Golden Gate (now bricked up), a late Roman
triumphal arch erected by Theodosius I around
AD 390, predating the city walls. The fortress
was later used as a prison for foreign envoys and
saw many executions, including that of sultan
Osman II, dragged here by his own Janissaries
(*see page 14* **Swords of misrule**). Entrance is
through a door in the north-east wall; the
vertiginous battlements offer wonderful views.

FLYING FISH

From Yedikule to the Belgrade Gate (Belgrad
Kapı), formerly the main Byzantine military gate,
and onwards to the Silivri Gate it is possible to
walk on top of the walls or on the terrace below.
In the vicinity of the latter, just 500 metres
outside the walls, is the **Shrine of Zoodochus
Pege** ('life-giving spring'). Originally an ancient
sanctuary of Artemis, the first church was built
over the spring in the early Byzantine era.
Destroyed and rebuilt many times since, the
present structure dates only from 1833. The
shrine itself is a pool containing 'sacred' fish,
said to have leaped into the spring from a monk's
frying pan on hearing him say that a Turkish
invasion of Constantinople was as likely as
fish coming back to life. Outside, the courtyard
contains the tombs of several Greek patriarchs
and is paved with gravestones, many bearing
signs indicating the trade of the deceased. Some
are written in Karamanlı, the Turkish dialect
spoken by Anatolian Greeks, and others are
carved in Greek script.

The next gate along, the Mevlevihane, bears
several inscriptions including one in Latin
boasting how Constantine erected the final phase
of the walls in 'less than two months'. Further
north beyond Millet Caddesi stands Topkapı,
or Cannon Gate, so named because during the
final siege, the gate was besieged by the largest
cannon in the Turkish arsenal, measuring eight
metres (28 feet) long and capable of firing a
projectile up to a mile.

Close by is one of the lesser-known but
loveliest works by Sinan (*see page 38* **Keeping
up with the domes's**), the **Kara Ahmet
Paşa Mosque**. Dating from 1554 and built for
a vizier of Süleyman I, it boasts some beautiful
Iznik tiling.

North of Topkapı the walls descend into the
Lycus river valley, now a channel for the six lanes
of Vatan Caddesi. Lower than the surrounding
land, this stretch was particularly difficult to
defend. Indeed, it was here in 1453 that the
besieging Ottomans concentrated their attack
and finally broke through. More than 500 years

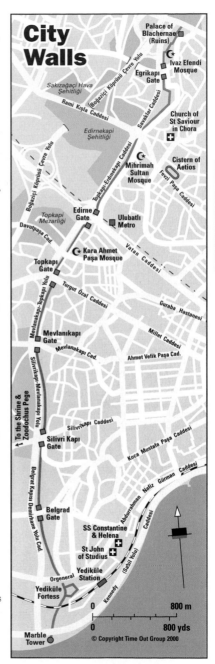

Sightseeing

later, the battlements in this section remain in the worst state of repair. Just within the walls is the similarly dilapidated district of Sulukule, since Byzantine times the Gypsy quarter of the city. Ramshackle wooden buildings press up against the ramparts, and it's one of the few parts of Istanbul where it's necessary to be cautious.

A little to the north, Mehmet the Conqueror made his triumphal entry into the city on the afternoon of the conquest through Edirnekapı, the Edirne gate. A plaque on the south side of the gate commemorates the event. Just inside stands the **Mihrimah Mosque**, commissioned by Süleyman the Magnificent for his daughter Mihrimah and built by – who else? – Sinan.

PICTURES ON WALLS

A short walk inland and to the north is one of Istanbul's truly outstanding sights. Yet it is often overlooked because it is so far out off the beaten track. The **Church of St Saviour in Chora** (also known as the Kariye Mosque) is second perhaps only to Haghia Sophia, making it one of the city's most dazzling Byzantine monuments. It was built in the late 11th century, but the mosaics and frescoes at the root of its fame were added when the church was remodelled in the 14th century.

These are arguably the most important surviving examples of Byzantine art anywhere in the world, unparalleled both in execution and state of preservation. Those in the narthexes depict the genealogy and life of Christ, and the life of the Virgin Mary. Elsewhere are scenes of the Day of Judgement, Heaven and Hell, and the Second Coming. Most spectacular of all is the Resurrection, which has Christ breaking the gates of hell beneath his feet and wrenching Adam and Eve from their tombs.

Ironically, this Christian art owes its state of preservation to the church's conversion to Islam in the early 16th century, when the frescoes and mosaics were covered over. They stayed concealed until their rediscovery in 1860. At the end of the street beside the church, the Kariye Hotel has a good restaurant, called the **Asithane** (*see page 132*), serving Ottoman cuisine.

As the city walls approach the Golden Horn, they terminate at the Byzantine **Blachernae Palace**. First constructed around AD 500, it was extended in the 11th and 12th centuries, by which time it had become the favoured imperial residence, covering the entire hilltop. Reports reaching the west of Blachernae's splendour probably inspired the crusaders to invade and sack the city. It's now mostly in ruins. The best preserved sections are the brick-and-marble three-storey façade known as the **Palace of the Porphyrogenitus**, and the five floors of tunnels and galleries below the Ahmet tea

Palace of the Porphyrogenitus – preserved.

garden, which were cleared of rubble in 1999 for a film shoot and are rather awesome in their medieval splendour. Entrance to the palace remains is from the Ahmet tea garden next to the Ivaz Efendi Mosque.

Blachernae Palace

Anemas Zindanları
Ivaz Ağa Caddesi, Ayvansaray. Bus 5T, 99A. **Open** 9am-7pm daily. **Admission** $1.50. **Map** p89.

Church of St John of Studius

Imrahor Camii
Imam Aşir Sokak, Yediküle. Bus 80, 80T/train from Sirkeci. **Map** p89.

Church of St Saviour in Chora

Kariye Camii
Kariye Camii Sokak, Edirnekapı (0212 631 9241). Bus 28, 86, 90. **Open** 9.30am-4.30pm daily. **Admission** $3. **Map** p89.

Kara Ahmet Paşa Mosque

Kara Ahmet Paşa Camii
Undeğirmeni Sokak, Fatma Sultan. Tram Topkapı. **Open** prayer times only. **Admission** free. **Map** p89.

Shrine of Zoodochus Pege

Balıklı Kilise
Seyit Nizam Caddesi 3, Silivrikapı (0212 582 3081). Tram Seyitnizam. **Open** 8am-4pm daily. **Admission** free.

Yedikule Fortress

Yedikule Müzesi
Yediküle Meydanı Sokak, Yediküle. Bus 80, 80T/ train from Sirkeci. **Open** 9.30am-4.30pm Mon,Tue, Thur-Sun; closed Wed. **Admission** $2. **Map** p89.

Beyoğlu

The city's downtown is both heart and soul of secular Istanbul.

Map p306-7

Istanbul's 'downtown', Beyoğlu is where the city comes to work, shop and play. A vast area with boundaries that are hard to define, for the purposes of this guide it's everything up the hill north of the Golden Horn as far as Taksim Square. The focus, however, is Istiklal Caddesi, the broad pedestrianised spine off which spread countless narrow vertebrae. Most of these streets are unsuitable for traffic and the only way to explore is by foot.

The origins of the name Beyoğlu are obscure but by the mid-19th century it was being used by Turks to refer to the area covering the port of Karaköy, Galata (just inland of Karaköy) and the Levantine suburb of Pera up the hill. Foreign-occupied areas since Byzantine times, these were trading colonies across the water from the walls of Constantinople proper, founded by merchants from Italian city states such as Genoa and Venice.

After the Ottoman conquest in the 15th century it was to Galata that the European powers sent their first ambassadors – who also doubled as heads of trading companies. As trade increased, Galata became crowded with seamen's bars and brothels, and the diplomats and merchants moved up the hill to the wooded slopes of Pera, a Greek word meaning 'beyond'.

By the 17th century, Galata/Pera was a substantial city in its own right with a multi-ethnic population known collectively as 'Levantines'. As well as the Italians, there were many other significant communities, as outlined by a Turkish chronicler of the time: 'The Greeks keep the taverns; most of the Armenians are merchants or money-changers; the Jews are the go-betweens in amorous intrigues and their youths are the worst of all the devotees of debauchery.'

It was during the 19th century that the area acquired its present character. Imported architectural trends, combined with increased use of iron and brick as building materials instead of the traditional wood, made it feasible to construct buildings that could survive the fires that regularly devastated the city.

After the republic, the area officially became known as Beyoğlu and blossomed with new cafés, restaurants, theatres and concert halls. Older residents still speak wistfully of never daring to go to Istiklal Caddesi without a collar

and tie. But World War II brought a discriminatory wealth tax which hit the Christian and Jewish minorities hard (Muslims were exempt) and after the war many chose to leave for Greece, America or Israel. Then, in the 1950s and '60s, political tensions caused most of the remaining Greek population to depart. In their place came a flood of poor migrants from Anatolia and Beyoğlu lost its cachet.

By the late 1980s, Istiklal Caddesi and the area around it was rundown, sleazy and even a little dangerous. That all began changing in late 1990 after the simple measure of closing the street to traffic and making it a pedestrian precinct. The subsequent transformation has been swift. Although no longer as chic as it once was (the money has moved north to Nişantaşı, Etiler and Levent), Beyoğlu has been reclaimed as the city's vibrant heart.

Galata

Echoing its mercantile origins, Galata remains almost completely commercial. There's even a row of ships chandlers still trading down along Yüzbaşı Sabahattin Evren Caddesi. Despite extensive development, a wealth of fascinating buildings still remain, some of them even dating back to Genoese times.

Central to the area's history and easily the most distinctive landmark north of the Golden Horn, the conical-capped **Galata Tower** was originally constructed in 1348. Named the Tower of Christ, it stood at the apex of fortified walls. After the Ottoman conquest it was used to house prisoners of war and was for a time an astronomical observatory. During the 19th century it was a fire-spotting station. In the 1960s it was restored and had a restaurant and nightclub added. Both are completely missable but it is worth paying to ascend to the 360-degree viewing gallery up top, offering some of the most spectacular views in the city.

Just downhill of the tower on Camekan Sokak, **Beyoğlu hospital** is a large building with a vaguely Gothic tower. It was built in 1904 as the British Seaman's Hospital, designed by Percy Adams, better known as architect of Senate House at London University.

The tower afforded clear sightlines to incoming ships, allowing them to signal ahead

Kamondo Steps – part staircase, part art.

news of disease, an important consideration in the days before ship-to-shore radio.

Just around the corner on Galata Kulesi Sokak stands the former British consular prison. The Ottomans allowed favoured nations to imprison their own nationals. The building has recently been put to imaginative new use as a café/restaurant, the **Eski Ingiliz Karakolu** (*see page 123*).

On the same street as the gaol is what was formerly the parish church of Galata's Maltese community, the Dominican **Church of St Peter and Paul**. It's a superb neo-classical affair built by the Swiss-born Fossati brothers (*see page 39*), dating from 1841 but containing a number of much older relics.

Further downhill on Kartçınar Sokak stand the remains of the palace of the Podesta, the Genoese governor who was sent out each year from the early 13th century, while opposite is the **Han of St Peter**, a French consular building and lodging house from 1771, also birthplace of the poet Andre Chenier. Both buildings are in sad state of repair.

The **Kamondo Steps** connecting Kartçınar Sokak with Voyvoda Caddesi are one of the city's finest bits of urban design. Part staircase, part sculpture, they were immortalised in the early 1960s in a famous photograph by Henri Cartier Bresson. They're named after the local Jewish banking family who paid for their construction.

From the 18th century on it was the Galata bankers who kept the declining Ottoman empire afloat, albeit at ruinous rates of interest. **Voyvoda Caddesi** was the banking centre and although the financial institutions have moved out, the street remains lined with imposing pieces of 19th-century grandeur. Most impressive is the Ottoman Bank building, slated to open as the museum of Beyoğlu in 2001.

ARABS AND JEWS

South of Voyvoda, **Perşembe Pazarı Sokak** also boasts some fine 18th-century merchants' houses, while 100 metres (320 feet) west on Fütühat Sokak stands the only remaining

Flying the flag

When Ankara became the Turkish capital in 1923, Istanbul was left with a vast heritage of fine diplomatic buildings. A legacy of the time when the Ottoman empire was, if not ruled, then certainly steered by a select group of a half dozen powerful European ambassadors, some of these buildings are virtual palaces. The former Prussian embassy on Gümüşsuyu Caddesi is a Teutonic monolith, while the former British Embassy, now consulate, at Meşrutiyet Caddesi 34 is a fine neo-renaissance affair.

Most beautiful are the Palais de France and Palazzo Venezia, originally the Venetian embassy. The latter, dating from the late 17th century, is faced by the former French courthouse, the pair fronting a small square (Çukur Bostanı) which looks more like Italy than Istanbul.

These and the other former embassies on Istiklal Caddesi now serve as consulates and are off limits to the public. One exception is the building opposite the Swedish consulate, now known as Narmanli Han (Istiklal Caddesi 390). This was constructed in the early 1800s as the Russian embassy, later converted into artists' ateliers and writers' lodgings and is now slated for a hotel development. It's an unusual structure that looks more like a fortress than a diplomatic palace – perhaps a reflection of Russian/Ottoman relations at the time.

But perhaps the foreign building in Beyoğlu which most reflects its parent country is the US consulate (Meşrutiyet Caddesi 104-108). Originally the house of a Genoese Merchant, and known as the 'Palazzio Corpi', it was won in a poker game by an American who donated the building to his government.

Galata Tower: conically capped. *See p91.*

Genoese church, now known as **Arap Mosque**.
Constructed between 1323 and 1337 and
dedicated to St Dominic and St Paul, it was the
largest of Constantinople's Latin churches. In the
early 16th century it was converted to a mosque
to serve the needs of Moorish exiles from Spain,
which is possibly the source of its current name,
'Arab mosque'. Despite extensive alterations, the
building is clearly that of a typical medieval
church with apses and belfry.

Further along on Yanıkkapı Sokak is the only
remaining gate from the Genoese walls, the
Burned Gate (Yanık Kapı), still bearing a
plaque with St George's cross, symbol of Genoa.

Galata's historic Jewish presence is
maintained at the **Neve Shalom Synagogue**.
Not particularly old (the oldest synagogues are in
Fatih), it is nevertheless the main centre of
worship for the city's surviving Jews. Since a
terrorist attack in 1986, access to it and Beyoğlu's
other four active synagogues is only possible
with permission of the Chief Rabbinate (0212 243
5166); visit in person with your passport at
Yemenci Sokak 23, near the US consulate.

Arap Mosque
Arap Camii
Fütühat Sokak, Galata. **Open** 9am to dusk daily.
Admission free. **Map** p306 L6.

Galata Tower
Galata Kulesi
Galata Square (0212 293 8183). **Open** 9am-7pm daily.
Admission $3. **Map** p308 M5.

Neve Shalom Synagogue
Büyük Hendek Caddesi 67, Galata (0212 244 1576).
Open by appointment only. **Map** p308 M5.

Tünel

Opened in 1876, the one-stop **funicular railway**
that runs from lower Galata up to southernmost
Istiklal Caddesi is, after London and New York,
the third-oldest passenger underground in the
world. In its heyday it carried as many as 40,000
people a day.

Tünel, the area around the upper station, is
currently in transition between shabby neglect
and arty affluence. Best example of this is the
proliferation of chic new cafés such as **KaVe** (*see
page 148*), occupying a 19th-century Italiante
passageway opposite the funicular.

Just round the corner on Galip Dede Caddesi is
the **Galata Mevlevihanesi**, a working dervish
lodge, which also goes by the name of the
Museum for Classical Literature. Home of the
Whirling Dervishes (*see page 218*), it's the only
institution of its kind in Istanbul open to the
public. A courtyard leads through to the
octagonal *tekke* (lodge), a restored version of the
1491 original. Here, on the last Sunday of the
month, the dervishes put on performances at
times advertised on hoardings outside.

At other times, the tekke can be visited to see
the dervish exhibits, including instruments and a
number of beautifully illuminated Korans and
Mesnevis, the poetic masterwork of the Mevlana,

World's third-oldest passenger underground – the one-stop **funicular railway**.

The other Istanbul

Beyoğlu has always been a neighbourhood apart, never quite fitting in with the rest of Istanbul. It is no longer, as it was during Ottoman times, a colony of ethnic minorities and Europeans, a piece of Europe in the heart of the Ottoman capital.

The Armenians, Greeks, Jews and Russians ceased dominating the cultural and commercial scene over half a century ago, although the churches, schools and grand buildings that they built still dot the district. Somehow though, Beyoğlu has never lost its status as the 'other' Istanbul. The district today is not so much what the English word 'cosmopolitan' implies (that is, international), as what the Turkish word 'kozmopolit' means: a mix of diverse peoples. The difference is that the peasants, biker babes, local roughs, club kids and bereted intellectuals that congregate in Beyoğlu are all Turkish.

Writers have struggled to define Beyoğlu. To Mithat Cemal Kuntay it was 'unconquered Istanbul', a 'coquette redolent of stale perspiration and old lavender'. Contemporary novelist Orhan Pamuk sees the area as Istanbul's 'hub of dreams', a place to 'pick up the scent of other lives'.

No other district elicits devotion and stirs passions like Beyoğlu. Nowhere else in the city would there be grassroots support for weekly panels on neighbourhood culture and history, or plans made for a museum exhibiting local documents and artefacts.

It was the Islamist Virtue Party that forced the issue of Beyoğlu's identity on to the national agenda. Former prime minister Necmettin Erbakan announced plans in the mid 1990s to erect a monumental mosque in Taksim. The proposal seemed reasonable enough. The dozens of churches and synagogues in the area have tiny and dwindling congregations, whereas Friday prayers at the handful of small mosques overflow into the streets. Opponents pointed out that Taksim was the symbol of secular Turkey. Proponents retorted that Taksim Square was currently dominated by Haghia Triada Greek Orthodox Church. The general, ill-defined sentiment was that a large mosque just wouldn't suit Beyoğlu.

Beyoğlu has become the focal point of arguments over Turkey's identity. The role of religion in a secular society, the form 'Westernisation' should take, the extent to which conservative attitudes can be changed and challenged. It represents a growing appreciation for the past and a vision of the future, Turkey's chance to refine and adapt to its own tastes the piece of Europe it first fostered, then inherited. What was once Istanbul's window on Europe has become Europe's window on what Turkey may one day become.

a 13th-century Persian poet who founded the Mevlevi dervish sect.

Also within the complex is the tomb of Galip Dede, the 17th-century Sufi poet after whom the street is named, and the Hamusan, or 'Silent House', a small cemetery filled with marker stones topped by dervish plant-pot hats.

Galata Mevlevihanesi

Galip Dede Caddesi 15, Tünel (0212 245 4141). **Open** 9.30am-4.30pm Mon, Wed-Sun; closed Tue. **Admission** $1.50. **Map** p308 M5.

Istiklal Caddesi

Originally known as Cadde-i Kebir (the high street), and later La Grande Rue De Pera, Istiklal Caddesi gained its present name – 'independence street' – in the wake of the founding of the republic. In character though, it remains completely pre-republican, graced with some wonderfully extravagant architecture. The **Botter House** at No.475-7 is an art

nouveau masterpiece by Raimondo D'Aronco (*see page 39*), built for Jean Botter, Sultan Abdül Hamit's tailor. His daughter offered to leave the building to the city council, but they refused to guarantee its preservation and since her death it has been falling into ever-worsening decay. A few doors up at No.401 the **Mudo Pera** has a similarly ornate art nouveau interior of highly polished wood.

The street's churches are more restrained, often hidden from the street – the result of a restriction forbidding non-Muslim buildings to appear on the city skyline, which held sway until the 19th century. Oldest is **St Mary Draperis** at No.429, a fairly humble building dating from 1789 that at one time served as the Austro-Hungarian embassy. This particular stretch of Istiklal is lined with former embassies (*see page 92* **Flying the flag**), some of the buildings still serving as consulates, others converted to new uses.

West of the main street is the small backstreet neighbourhood of **Asmalımescit**, home of the

Sightseeing

Busy new **Beyoğlu** buzzes night and day.

city's low-rent art scene, full of studios and small galleries, and a good locale for casual cafés and cheap eateries. Its western boundary is Meşrutiyet Caddesi, address of the famed **Pera Palas Hotel** (*see page 62* **Bed, board & legends**) with its Orient Express associations and celebrity-filled guest book.

Galatasaray

Hardly big enough to constitute a district, Galatasaray refers simply to the streets surrounding the old French **Galatasaray Lycée**, founded in 1868. The current building, which dates from 1907, includes the small **Galatasaray museum** (*see page 113*), dedicated to the top Istanbul football team, whose origins lie with the school.

The slight widening of Istiklal in front of the Lycée is known as **Galatasaray Square**. In recent years it's become the venue for regular political demonstrations, most notably by the 'Saturday Mothers', female relatives of the many political activists who have 'disappeared' over the past 20 years. Such demonstrations are illegal and the 'mothers' are usually met by bus-loads of armoured riot police.

Beyoğlu nightlife once revolved around the *meyhanes* (Turkish tavernas) of **Çiçek Pasajı** (Flower Passage; *see page 130*), formerly the Cité de Pera building, a combination shopping arcade and apartment block. Its heavily restored façade faces the school gates. These days it's the domain of tourists, a beautiful glass-roofed setting for an over-priced middling meal. Adjacent is the **Balık Pazarı** (Fish Market), still lined with shops fronted by great wooden trays of marine life on ice. Two passages to the left are filled with second-hand and antiquarian bookstores, and various other odd and interesting shops, while off to the right is **Nevizade Sokak** (*see page 130*), crammed full of pavement restaurants and the liveliest and loudest dining spot in town.

Çiçek Pasajı represents old Beyoğlu. The new Beyoğlu is focused on the stretch of Istiklal Caddesi stretching north of Galatasaray. Old fashioned meyhanes and the gentility of book stores and churches and period architecture give way to department stores, music megastores, multiplexes, Benetton and its ilk, and an ever-proliferating number of bars and cafés. This part of town is busier at 2am than it is at 2pm.

For those abroad in the daylight hours, history still lurks in the sidestreets. **Yeşilçam Sokak**, just north of Çiçek Pasajı, was formerly the home of Turkish cinema, lined with film company offices. They're gone but the **Emek** cinema (*see page 189*) remains, dating to the 1930s but part of the older Sempdoryan complex which fronts on to Istiklal Caddesi. This imposing neo-classical structure boasts an elaborate entrance lobby and in the last century was home to the Cercle d'Orient gentlemen's club. Unbelievably, the owners have recently been given permission to demolish the entire complex and replace it with an office and car park development. That's progress.

South of upper Istiklal Caddesi is the small backstreet district of **Çukurcuma**, full of jogging, twisting, narrow alleys that are home to the antique trade. Though tiny, it's a world away from the brash commerce of Istiklal.

Taksim

At its north end, Istiklal Caddesi empties into **Taksim Square**. The name comes from the stone reservoir (*taksim*) on the west side. Built in 1732 on the orders of Mahmut I the *taksim* was at the end of a series of canals and aqueducts that brought water down from the Belgrad Forest (*see page 242*).

Despite the picturesque associations, the square is one of the world's uglier public plazas. Big it may be, but it is completely lacking in grandeur – little more than a snarled transport hub with a small park attached. This is a place to pass through on the way to someplace else rather than a destination in itself.

But the square is regarded as the heart of modern Istanbul and symbol of the secular republic. So much so that in 1997, when Turkey's short lived Islamist government unveiled plans to build a huge mosque in an adjacent lot, they were forced to backtrack in the face of public disapproval (*see page 95* **The other Istanbul**).

Karaköy to Beşiktaş

Istanbul's waterfront districts are the haunts of sailors, sultans and whores.

Map p307

The districts that comprise the heart of modern Istanbul lie high up on the hill above the Bosphorus, but down at water level a chain of small historic neighbourhoods runs north from the Galata Bridge. First of these is Karaköy, which faces Eminönü across the Golden Horn. It's been a port area since Byzantine times when the north shore of the Horn was a separate settlement – the Genoese colony of Galata – distinct from Constantinople. In the late 19th century the quayside was crowded with taverns and cheap sailors' hostels but much of the maritime traffic has since moved out to Yenikapı and Karaköy has been cleaned up. It's now a photogenic waterfront strip with a daily fish market.

The area still boasts a number of monuments reflecting its grittier past. One street inland is the district's oldest building, the **Yeraltı Mosque**. Buried beneath a 19th-century wooden mansion, its interior boasts a forest of squat columns supporting low vaults, and was clearly never designed as a mosque. In fact, this is the remains

Plenty more in the sea: Karaköy's **fish market**.

of the Byzantine castle of Galata that once guarded the entrance to the Golden Horn. It was from here that a great chain was stretched across the waterway blocking access to enemy ships in times of siege. The upper part of the castle was probably demolished following the Ottoman conquest in 1453, and the remaining lower floor was converted into a mosque in 1757.

Further inland are a couple of curious churches. The Russian Orthodox **Church of St Andrea** on Balyoz Sokak, is on the top floor of what appears to be a 19th century apartment building but was actually built as a monastery. The monks have long gone and most of the building is rented out but the church has experienced a resurgence over the past decade thanks to increased numbers of Russians visiting the city since the collapse of the Soviet Union. Around the corner is the **Church of St Panagia** belonging to the tiny Turkish Orthodox sect, which broke away from the Greek church in the 1920s and whose mass is delivered in the Karamanli Turkish dialect.

The oldest church in Karaköy is the **Church of St Benoit** on Kemeraltı Caddesi, founded by the Genoese in the 14th century, although the earliest parts date from the 15th century when it belonged to the Benedictines. It's now part of a Catholic school and access is by application only (call 0212 244 1026 for information).

GUNS AND SMOKE

North along Kemeraltı the road is overlooked by a series of advertising hoardings depicting blondes wielding automatic pistols. Firearms were banned soon after the founding of the Republic but gun laws were liberalised in the late 1980s. Unsurprisingly, the result has been an increase in accidental shootings – not least during the celebrations accompanying weddings and footballing victories when guns are commonly fired off into the air (*see page 231* **Welcome to Hell**).

The gun shops are just a little further on the same street, lying appropriately enough in the shadow of the **Tophane**, the former Ottoman cannon foundry. There's been a foundry on this site since the days of Mehmet the Conqueror, although the current building with its distinctive row of ventilation towers dates only to 1803. Recently renovated, it's now used as an occasional arts and exhibition centre.

Opposite the Tophane are two mosques. The southernmost is the **Kılıç Ali Paşa Mosque**, commissioned by and named for an Ottoman naval commander and built by the famed architect Sinan (*see page 38* **Keeping up with the domes's**), who was by this time (1580) in his 90s. The design pays homage to Haghia Sophia and is similarly unimpressive from the outside but magnificent inside. There's some particularly beautiful Iznik tiling around the prayer niche.

Just over the road in the park is the **Nusretiye Mosque**, built in the late 1820s in the baroque style by Kikor Balyan, whose sons would later design the nearby Dolmabahçe Palace. It was commissioned by Sultan Mahmut II to commemorate his crushing of the Janissary corps (*see page 14* **Swords of misrule**). Behind the mosque is the city's current 24-hour hotspot, a row of cafés specialising in nargiles (*see page 146* **Hava nargile**).

From here the main road continues past the modern port and the **Mimar Sinan Fine Arts University**, occupying a building constructed in 1855 as twin palaces for Sultan Abdül Mecit's daughters. It also later saw service as a home of the Ottoman parliament. Further along is the **Molla Çelebi Mosque**, another Sinan masterpiece, constructed in 1566, and beyond

Karaköy's **nargile cafés** – smoking non-stop.

that the Kabataş ferry and seabus terminal. Yet another dome and minaret composition (the Dolmabahçe Mosque, constructed at the same time as Dolmabahçe Palace) stands opposite a valley carrying a road up to Taksim Square. Just up on the right is the Inönü Stadium, Istanbul's best football venue and home of **Beşiktaş** football club (*see page 232*). Towering over it is the monstrous high-rise development of dubious legality known as 'Gökkafes' (*see page 40* **The height of bad taste**).

Yeraltı Mosque

Yeraltı Camii
Kermankeş Caddesi, Karaköy. **Open** 9am-dusk daily. **Admission** free. **Map** p307 N6.

They're changing guards at **Dolmabahçe Palace,** evidence of imperial decline. *See p99.*

A right old madam

Matild Manukyan, an elderly Armenian businesswoman, is Turkey's dirty little secret. The mention of her name usually provokes a blush or a snicker, and she was held up in the mid-1990s as representing everything wrong with the country. Yet by rights, she ought to be considered something of a national heroine. Manukyan put the spotlight on the tax-evading ways of filthy rich businessmen when she was awarded a plaque by the Turkish president for being the country's highest tax-paying individual. She also triggered an investigation into links between the Mafia and state security officials when she survived a bomb attack that killed her chauffeur. But both of these achievements are overshadowed by her occupation as a 'mama', or madam. Although Manukyan has no hand in the daily running of her brothel in central Karaköy and points out that she was landed with the property by a bankrupt creditor, she has become the grandmotherly face of a phenomenon most Turks would rather not think about.

Prostitution in Turkey is rampant, but legal only at licensed, state-regulated brothels, of which Manukyan's *genelev* (literally 'public house') is one. The genelev isn't a house but a maze of narrow, cobbled alleyways lined with glass-front shops and enclosed by high walls. Visitors present their ID cards to police at the front gate, then amble through the alleys eyeing the merchandise, which ranges from young girls fresh out of the village to obese aunties in bras and slippers intent on their knitting.

Legalised prostitution faces virtually no public opposition, except from Islamists. Teens are regularly taken to the brothels by brothers and uncles for their sexual initiation. Fallen women are a common fixture in films, tabloids and even music videos. The prevalent view is that regulated prostitution is a necessary evil and an escape valve for randy bachelors. The government has responded to the few complaints by introducing legislation barring entry to students in school uniform and banning the construction of brothels within 200 metres of government offices, schools, places of worship and football fields.

The last measure, if strictly enforced, would mean the closure of the Karaköy brothel, which lies in a neighbourhood dense with mosques, civil servants and schoolkids. But the resourceful madam has alternative diversions in mind; she plans this year to open a small museum dedicated to her business achievements and displaying her plaque.

Sightseeing

Kılıç Ali Paşa Mosque
Kılıç Ali Paşa Camii
Necatibey Caddesi, Tophane (no phone). **Open** 9am-dusk daily. **Admission** free. **Map** p307 O5.

Tophane
Cannon Foundry
Necatibey Caddesi, Tophane (0212 252 1600). **Open** for exhibitions only. **Map** p307 O5.

Dolmabahçe

A celebration of just about everything that was awful about 19th-century European design, **Dolmabahçe Palace** is irrefutable evidence of an empire on its last legs. The outside is bad enough but it's trumped by the interior decoration, the work of a French opera designer, for which words like 'faux' and 'excess' seem inadequate. Highlights are the 36-metre-high throne room with its four-ton crystal chandelier (a gift from Queen Victoria), the alabaster baths and a 'crystal staircase' which wouldn't look out of place in Las Vegas. It was in Dolmabahçe in 1938 that Atatürk died, although his apartment is not on the tour itinerary (visitors are only allowed round the palace in guided groups).

Passing the palace, the road is flanked by impressive colonnades of plane trees. These were planted last century when the palace was constructed and though it almost certainly wasn't a consideration at the time, the choice of the plane was a good one given the tree's high tolerance to air pollution.

As the plane trees end, the road enters Beşiktaş, an unsightly concrete shopping and transport hub with a silvery statue of Atatürk for a centrepiece (*see page 17*). It wasn't always this way. The area was once a quiet suburb of dignified terraced houses and plush mansions. The last remaining terrace is on Spor Caddesi, built to house the staff of Dolmabahçe Palace, while the last of the mansions crumble up on Barbaros Bulvarı.

Despite having no real harbour, Beşiktaş can boast of strong nautical connections. Down on the waterfront is the **Naval Museum** (*see page 114*) and nearby the tomb and statue of Hayrettin Paşa, the Ottoman admiral known in the west as Barbarossa. The tomb is by the prolific Sinan, who also designed the **Sinan Paşa Mosque** over the road for still another Ottoman admiral.

Yıldız Park – former imperial pavilions.

Dolmabahçe Palace

Dolmabahçe Sarayı
Dolmabahçe Caddesi, Beşiktaş (0212 236 9600).
Open 9am-4pm Tue, Wed, Fri-Sun; closed Mon, Thur.
Closes one hour earlier Nov-Apr. **Admission** *Selamlık*
$8, *Harem* $8, *combined ticket* $12. **Map** p307 R2.

Yıldız

To the north-west of Beşiktaş are the extensive
grounds of **Yıldız Palace**, a sprawling complex
of buildings of which only the Yıldız Palace
Museum, and the Şehir Museum are open – and
the latter only sporadically. Most buildings date
from the late 19th century when Abül Hamit II
abandoned Dolmabahçe for fear of attack by
foreign warships.

The Yıldız Museum contains porcelain and
furniture from the palace and some of Abdül
Hamit's possessions, most poignantly the
carpentry set with which he passed his time after
being deposed in 1908. The Şehir museum has
18th-century engravings and paintings and a
collection of gifts given to successive mayors.

Back on Yıldız Caddesi is one of the most
striking monuments in the city, the **Şeyh Zafir
Complex**. Comprising a tomb, library and
fountain it commemorates an Islamic sheikh but
is designed in art nouveau style by Raimondo
D'Aronco (*see page 39*).

A little further along, a side road leads
off Yıldız Caddesi to the left into Yıldız Park,
formerly the palace grounds, now a pleasantly
overgrown hillside forest. There are several
former imperial pavilions including the Şale
Pavilion, a D'Aronco-designed building set in

private gardens at the top of the park, open to
the public as the **Yıldız Chalet Museum**.
You'll know when you're there thanks to a sign
advising that firearms are not to be taken any
further. Inside, the long, creaking wooden
corridors have a dark and musty quality, the
60 rooms furnished with the original ornate
furniture of the period, including Abdül Hamit's
bed. Visiting in winter darkness, it's possible
to imagine the approaching doom of empire, or
the creak of the floorboards as 'the sinister figure
of the sultan's astrologer, Abu al-Huda, crept
across the anteroom towards his master's
chamber,' as one 19th-century British diplomat
described the scene.

The obligatory tour takes you to the Grand
Salon, a massive court chamber, empty except
for a line of chairs around the edge which point
up the empty grandeur of the place. Outside in
the gardens, the peaceful phut-phut of sprinklers
in summer, or the looming darkness of winter
only add to the melancholia.

Also in the park is the **Imperial Porcelain
Factory**, which mass produces rather weedy
china but does so in another splendid building
designed by D'Aronco.

Across from the park entrance, between Yıldız
Caddesi and the Bosphorus is what's left of the
Çırağan Palace, the last of the Ottoman
imperial palaces, built for Abdül Aziz who died
there – probably murdered – in 1876 two years
after it was completed. In 1908 it was restored to
house the Ottoman parliament but it burnt down
in 1910 and remained a shell until it was rebuilt as
a hotel by the Kempinski chain (*see page 55*).
The tawdriness of the restoration has attracted
criticism but the view from the waterside terrace
is undeniably spectacular.

Imperial Porcelain Factory

Yıldız Parkı ici (0212 260 2370). **Open** 9am-noon,
1-4pm Mon-Fri; closed Sat, Sun. **Admission** $1.
No credit cards.

Şeyh Zafir Complex

Yıldız Caddesi, Beşiktaş. Closed to the public.

Yıldız Chalet Museum

Yıldız Şale Müzesi
*Palanga Caddesi, Yıldız Park, Beşiktaş (0212 259
4570).* **Open** 9.30am-5pm Tue, Wed, Fri-Sun; closed
Mon, Thur. Closes one hour earlier Nov-Apr.
Admission $1.50. **No credit cards.**

Yıldız Palace

Yıldız Sarayı
Yıldız Caddesi, Beşiktaş (0212 258 3080). **Open**
9.30am-4.30pm Tue-Sun; closed Mon. **Admission**
$3.50. **No credit cards.**

Yıldız Park

Çırağan Caddesi, Beşiktaş. **Open** 9am-10pm daily.
Admission free; cars $1.50. **No credit cards.**

Ortaköy to Rumeli Hisarı

Istanbul's village suburbs offer waterfront promenades, swanky nightclubs and an ancient fortress.

North of Beşiktaş (*see page 99*) the districts along the European shore of the Bosphorus become more strung out. Separated by long stretches of near empty coast road, Ortaköy, Arnavutköy and Bebek feel like small waterfront villages, although firmly part of metropolitan Istanbul.

Exploring them couldn't be simpler as several buses (25E from Eminönü, 40 from Taksim) run along the coast road. A far more relaxed way of travelling is to take one of the half-hourly ferry services from Eminönü stopping at Beşiktaş, Ortaköy and Bebek. Unfortunately these are commuter services and so only run in the mornings (around 8am to 10am) and evenings (around 5pm to 8pm). A good full day of it can be had by taking a bus or boat up to Bebek, exploring Rumeli Hisarı and then walking all the way back down to Ortaköy along the waterside promenade.

Ortaköy

Glancing at a map it is not really clear what Ortaköy, the 'Middle Village', is in the middle of. It has long been a thriving social and commercial centre for anyone wanting to escape the crush of the inner city. In the 17th century, Ottoman chronicler Evliya Çelebi noted with a hint of disdain, 'The place is full of infidels and Jews; there are two hundred shops, of which a great number are taverns.'

Evidence of the continued presence of non-Muslims in the neighbourhood is found on the main road where a **synagogue** (built 1913) and the Greek Orthodox church of **Haghia Phocas** (1872) hide behind gated courtyards. Ortaköy's most prominent monument, however, is the **Mecidiye Mosque**, set dramatically on a promontory jutting into the strait. Built for Sultan Abdül Mecit in 1854 by Nikoğos Balyan, the architect responsible for the excesses of the Dolmabahçe, it avoids the vulgarity of the palace, standing instead as one of the most attractive baroque buildings in the city.

Just to the south of the mosque, beside the ferry landing stage, the waterfront piazza **Ortaköy Square** (Iskele Meydanı) has been attractively renovated. Fringed with open-air cafés and restaurants, it's one of the city's most pleasant places to eat out on a midsummer evening (**Çinar Restaurant**; *see page 119*).

The tight nexus of streets inland from the square has been brutally gentrified in recent years, scrubbed up and filled with useless shops so that the area resembles something along the lines of London's Covent Garden. On Sunday it's the venue for a popular **craft market**.

North of the mosque, a masonry shell is all that remains of the **Küçük Esma Sultan Sarayı**, a palace built at the beginning of the 17th century and later occupied by the daughter of Abdül Hamit I. Married off to an important court official at the tender age of 14, the princess was widowed just ten years later. Flying in the face of tradition, she declined to remarry, dedicating herself instead to a hedonistic lifestyle that scandalised polite Istanbul society.

Nearby and besieged by traffic crawling around the one-way system are the twin leaded domes of a 16th-century hamam, yet another work by Mimar Sinan (*see page 38* **Keeping up with the domes's**). Recently restored by the management of the nearby **Princess Hotel Ortaköy** (*see page 60*), plans are afoot to open the building to the public as some sort of exhibition or cultural centre.

ON TO KURUÇEŞME

North of Ortaköy the road passes under the first bridge to cross the straits, the kilometre-long **Atatürk Bridge**, finished just in time for the Turkish Republic's 50th birthday celebrations in 1973. Beyond is a fairly dull stretch notable only for a string of exclusive nightspots where Istanbul high-society go to shake their stuff (*see page 222* **Baywatch on the Bosphorus**).

Likewise, Kuruçeşme, the next stretch of Bosphorus real estate, has little to detain anyone, despite its historical claims as the site of a church built by Constantine the Great and of the column on top of which sat Simeon the Stylite, a 5th-century saint, for 27 years. No trace remains of either.

Arnavutköy

Arnavutköy, 'the Albanian Village', is far more low-key than Ortaköy and has yet to be spoilt by an influx of venture capital. To the water, it presents an attractive face, with its picturesque terrace of 19th-century wooden *yalıs* (Bosphorus

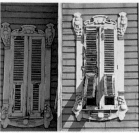

Arnavutköy – 19th-century *yalıs. See p101.*

mansions), although the traffic sweeping past them does detract.

In Ottoman times the local population was not Albanian, as the name would imply, but predominantly Greek and Armenian. It's overwhelmingly Turkish today but a small community of Greeks still lives around here and celebrates mass at the Orthodox **Church of Taxiarchs** in the backstreets. Next to the church is a small chapel containing a sacred spring, or *ayazma*, which is reached down a set of polished marble stairs.

The church sits at the centre of a grid of narrow streets spotted with down-to-earth eateries and local shops. Worth hunting out is **Deli Kızın Yeri** (*see page 173*), the 'Mad Girl's Place', a household and gift shop with unusual and unique stock, much of it made on the premises.

More than a few of the local businesses occupy great old wooden houses with lace-like trim, pulpit balconies and ridiculous amounts of ornamentation. The number of such buildings undergoing restoration increases almost weekly and Arnavutköy is rapidly taking on an almost fairytale appearance.

Supposedly enjoying official protection, this architectural heritage has ironically long been under threat from the government itself – plans for a third Bosphorus bridge threatened literally to rip apart the neighbourhood with great concrete supports. However, vociferous opposition from local residents and campaigners seems to have swayed officials towards a less contentious, but more expensive, tunnel project, although Arnavutköy's stay of execution has yet to be confirmed.

Bebek

Just north of Arnavutköy, a small white lighthouse marks Akıntı Burnu, a promontory jutting out into the straits which is named after the strong current that swirls and eddies past the shore. It's a favourite spot for local fishermen who not only cast out from the shore, but also

trawl from rickety wooden boats which battle against a flow so brisk that in days gone by sailing ships often had to be towed around the point by porters.

From Akıntı Burnu it's a ten-minute stroll along a broad promenade set low beside the water to the next waterside 'village', Bebek. Ranged around an arching bay backed by wooded hills, it occupies a hugely attractive spot and has been developed into an affluent, desirable suburb with the air of a Hampstead on the Bosphorus.

At the southern edge of Bebek, on the edge of a small waterfront park is one of the neighbourhood's more ostentatious buildings, a handsome white, wooden art nouveau mansion commissioned by the ruler of Egypt and still in service as the **Egyptian consulate**. It was designed by the prolific Italian architect, Raimondo D'Aronco (*see page 39*), who would likely be a bit aggrieved at the current tatty state of the place and the clusters of satellite dishes that mar its profile.

At the top end of the park is Bebek's tiny ferry station and an equally diminutive brown stone mosque dating from 1912. Next door, the **Bebek Café** is as basic as they come – sawdust on the floor, bare walls – but it's a pleasant, unaffected place for a coffee. Round the corner, the high street is a bit of a letdown, lined with modern buildings, including an overly prominent McDonald's, and choked by traffic. But take any of the streets heading uphill, away from the water, and almost immediately you're surrounded by greenery and wooden terraces. Head up Hamam Sokak opposite the park and after a few minute's walk there's another good place to take a break and get something to eat in the **Café de Pera**.

Back on the high street, among the shops selling silk ties and antiques, is **Meşhur Bebek Badem Ezmesi** (*see page 171* **Sweet stuff**) specialising in marzipan beautifully displayed in glass-fronted hardwood display cabinets.

NORTH OF BEBEK

On the heights north of Bebek, reached from the waterside road through a rather anonymous gateway, is the leafy campus of **Boğaziçi University**. Turkey's foremost institute of higher education, the university traces its origins back to 1863 when Cyrus Hamlin, an American missionary who rubbed shoulders with Florence Nightingale (*see page 108*), established a Christian college on the site. Called Robert College after its rich American benefactor, it first

It's all open-air in **Ortaköy Square**. *See p101.*

drew its student body solely from the Greek, Armenian and Jewish communities, although entry restrictions were later relaxed to admit Turkish students too. Robert College developed a reputation for excellence which has more or less survived its 1971 conversion to a mixed-sex state university. Its prestigious alumni include current prime minister Bülent Ecevit and sleaze-spattered former PM Tansu Çiller.

Back down by the waterline, the promenade winds north towards Rumeli Hisarı, about a ten- to 15-minute walk away. Before reaching the castle, a sign points up a steep road beside the **Kayalar Mezarlışı**, one of Istanbul's oldest Muslim cemeteries, to the **Aşıyan Museum** housed in the eyrie of celebrated poet Tevfik Fikret (1867-1915). It's an attractive wooden mansion and although the exhibits don't amount to much (the poet's possessions) the views from the upper-storey balconies are wonderful.

Aşıyan Museum

Aşıyan Müzesi
Aşıyan Yolu, Rumeli Hisarı (0212 263 6986). Bus 25E, 40. **Open** 9am-5pm Tue, Wed, Fri-Sun; closed Mon, Thur. **Admission** $2.

Rumeli Hisarı

Rounding the point to the north of Aşıyan brings you face-to-face with the imposing fortress of Rumeli Hisarı and below it the village suburb of the same name. Extending up the hill in the shadow of the second Bosphorus bridge, the village is a leafy, rarefied place, with only the background roar of traffic to impinge on the atmosphere of suburban bliss. Just before the small central square is a real oddity, **Edwards of Hisar**, an upper-crust tailor more suited to Savile Row than the middle Bosphorus. An atmospheric lunch possibility is Rumeli Hisarı's former ferry station, now an expensive fish restaurant. Alternatively, there's a line-up of simpler eateries nearer the castle, including the very decent **Kale Café**.

At a span of 1,090 metres (3,634 feet), the Fatih Bridge is among the longest suspension bridges in the world. Designed, like the Atatürk Suspension Bridge, by a British engineer, it was completed in 1988 but has a historic precedent: it spans the straits at the point where King Darius of Persia crossed via a pontoon bridge with his army in 512 BC.

THE FORTRESS

Consisting of three huge towers joined by crenellated defensive walls, the fortress was raised in a hurry as part of Mehmet II's masterplan to capture Constantinople. Facing the 14th-century castle of Anadolu Hisarı (already in Ottoman hands) across the Bosphorus'

Rumeli Hisarı – fortress for fantasies.

narrowest stretch, Rumeli Hisarı was designed to cut Byzantine maritime supply lines and isolate Constantinople from its allies. For this, it earned itself the nickname Boğazkesen, the 'Throat-Cutter'. The sultan took an active role in the castle's construction, planning its layout personally before entrusting his three chief ministers with the task of raising the main towers. Work was completed in August 1452, just four short months after commencing. Garrisoned by a troop of Janissaries and bristling with cannon, several of which can be seen lying below the walls, Rumeli Hisarı soon proved its effectiveness, sinking a foolhardy Venetian merchant vessel which attempted to run the blockade. The castle, however, was a victim of its own success. Having helped secure the Ottoman conquest of Constantinople, it lost its military importance and was downgraded to a prison.

The castle was restored by the government in 1953 and contemporary visitors can clamber around the walls, playing out childhood fantasies. An open-air theatre within the courtyard hosts musical events almost nightly through the summer (*see page 181*).

Rumeli Hisarı

Rumeli Hisarı Müzesi
Yahya Kemal Caddesi, Rumeli Hisarı. Bus 25E, 40. **Open** 9am-4.30pm Tue-Sun; closed Mon. **Admission** $2.

The Asian Shore

Istanbul's other continent is less hectic, more rural and lures Europe over to shop.

Seen on the map, Istanbul may appear to be split into two cities, one in Europe and one in Asia. But this has never been the reality. Historically 'the city' was always the area within the Byzantine walls, south of the Golden Horn, with even nearby neighbourhoods such as Beyoğlu regarded as separate entities. And even as late as the early 1980s, the Asian Shore was little more than a bunch of small disconnected villages. Today these have coalesced into a sprawl of dormitory suburbs for European Istanbul.

Though lacking the European city's richness, the Asian Shore does offer a pleasantly less hectic experience and enough of interest to sustain several visits. The two main urban centres of Üsküdar and Kadıköy offer shopping and markets with a regional slant, a laid-back café scene and a sprinkling of historic and architectural sights. North of Üsküdar, the settlements along the Asian Bosphorus still resemble the quiet fishing villages they so recently were.

Although two great suspension bridges now span the straits, the best way to get here is by boat. Between 6am and midnight ferries depart every 15 minutes from Eminönü (just west of Sirkeci station), Karaköy and Beşiktaş for both Üsküdar and Kadıköy. The crossing takes around 20 minutes.

AN EARLY START

While most of what's interesting dates from the past 100 years or so, the area's history predates that of the European shore. The oldest settlement in the Istanbul metropolitan area, Chalcedon, was discovered near Kadıköy and dates from neolithic times, much earlier than anything on the European side. The first Greek city was also founded at Kadıköy in 675 BC – 17 years before the founding of Byzantium.

But, separated by water from their more powerful European neighbour, the Asian settlements suffered badly over subsequent

Sahaf – five floors creaking with secondhand and antiquarian books. *See p106.*

Bağdat Caddesi – fashion-victim heaven and *nouveau-riche* cruise. *See p107.*

millennia, and the work of various invading armies explains the lack of any early remains.

Before the 19th century, only Üsküdar saw any significant development. That changed in 1852 when a steam ferry company, Şirket-i Hayriye (literally 'the good deeds company'), started plying its trade across the straits. Rich Levantines from Beyoğlu began constructing elaborate summer mansions along the shore to the south and east of Kadıköy.

For the first 50 years of the service, the ferries were all the product of British shipyards. In fact, trade between the Ottoman and British empires was at such a level that by the end of the 19th century the Kadıköy suburb of Moda was more or less an English colony.

Post-republic, most of the mansions were demolished and replaced with apartment buildings. They retained their mansion garden settings, though, something which gives the Asian Shore, especially between Kadıköy and Bostancı, a more spacious feel than the European side.

Kadıköy

No trace remains of the Greek or Byzantine settlements of Chalcedon, but modern Kadıköy does retain many hints of its 19th-century incarnation as an area largely settled by Greeks, Armenians and Europeans.

Arriving by ferry this isn't immediately apparent as the two most noticeable buildings, the Istanbul Municipal Theatre and Kadıköy Municipality, are in the unlovely style of the First National Architectural Movement (*see page 39*). But 50 metres (165 feet) further inland around the **Mustafa Iskele Mosque** is the old bazaar, an area of narrow streets lined with tiny two- and three-storey buildings, many dating from the last century. Some of the best food shopping in Istanbul is to be had here. At the top end of Yasa Sokak are delis stocking a huge range of regional Turkish produce, particularly cheeses and breads. **Esmer Ekmek** on Mühürdar Caddesi bakes on the premises in a wood-fired oven. Several shops specialise in Turkish pickles; the sour preservative liquid is considered a delicacy fit for drinking and is sold separately by the glass.

Further inland past two churches, one Armenian Catholic, one Greek, **Dumlupınar Sokak** boasts a number of cafés in 19th-century terraced houses. **Çinili Café** at No.10 is above a shop specialising in Turkish comic books while **Sahaf** at No.12 is a creaky, five-floor emporium of second-hand and antiquarian books, almost all of which are in Turkish, with a good musty café on an upper floor. Nearby **Cafer Ağa Medrese Sokak** is great for browsing junk, while **Dellalzade Sokak** is lined with shops selling proper antiques.

The whole area has a lively café and bar scene, the Asian Shore's rather downmarket answer to Beyoğlu, and has something of a student quarter feel. It's worth aiming to be here on a Tuesday for the **street market** (Salıpazarı; *see page 175*) filling the streets north of the bull statue, a local landmark on Söğütlüçeşme Caddesi, the main street. The market is an Istanbul institution with crowds drawn from all over the city by an abundance of fresh produce and cheap designer-label clothing.

South of the bull statue, on Bahariye Caddesi, is the **Sürreya Cinema** (*see page 190*), oldest picture house in town. Originally built by an Ottoman paşa as an opera house, its over-the-top neo-classical façade is a reminder that this area was once distinctly well-to-do.

Beyond the cinema, Kadıköy gives way to the posher suburb of **Moda**. A few minutes' walk south is the waterfront, a popular promenade with a tiny ferry terminal designed in late Ottoman revival style by Vedat Tek (*see page 39*), and recently nicely restored.

SOCCER AND SHOPPING

East of Kadıköy is Rüştü Saraçoğlu Stadium, home of **Fenerbahçe** football club (*see page 232*). Although currently eclipsed by Galatasaray, Fener has traditionally been one of Turkey's top three teams, its support

traditionally drawn from Istanbul's lower middle classes. Such is the fanaticism of supporters round here that the area is often referred to as 'The Republic of Fenerbahçe'.

Behind the stadium is **Bağdat Caddesi**, one of the city's best-known streets. For much of its immense length it's an unremarkable swathe of asphalt but passing through the plush suburb of Suadiye it metamorphoses into fashion-victim heaven. Lined with upmarket clothing and design stores, beauty clinics, pavement cafés and restaurants, it's the cruising strip of choice for *nouveau-riche* Istanbul.

Coastal Fenerbahçe, where Kalamış Caddesi runs past the yacht marina, is more picturesque. Opposite the marina are three fine examples of turn-of-the-century merchants' houses. At Kalamış Caddesi 79 is **Villa Mon Plaisir**, a spectacular wood and brick art-nouveau mansion. Although it's not open to the public, the façade includes beautiful tiled friezes depicting the seasons. Further along at No.87 and No.89 stand two wooden houses designed by Raimondo D'Aronco (*see page 39*) for Jean Botter (whose Beyoğlu residence was also designed by D'Aronco; *see page 95*). Both buildings are open to the public as bar-cafés.

By far the best restored mansion in the area is back inland at Erenköy on Sinan Ercan Caddesi. The **Reşat Paşa Konağı** is a superbly preserved example of a late-Ottoman wooden mansion complete with oil-painted ceiling panels. The house is open as a restaurant serving Ottoman fare to a period music accompaniment.

At the far southern end of Bağdat is **Bostancı**, an area with little of interest; the only reason to be here is to take a ferry to the Princes' Islands (*see pages 243-4*).

Haydarpaşa

Across the bay from Kadıköy stands the imposing edifice of **Haydarpaşa station**, looking like nothing so much as a Rhineland castle – unsurprising given that it was a gift from Kaiser Wilhelm of Germany and was designed by German architects. It's the terminus of the Anatolian railway system, the end of the line for trains from as far east as Aleppo in Syria. Adjacent to the station is the small but perfectly formed **Haydarpaşa ferry terminal**, another Ottoman revivalist design by Vedat Tek (*see page 39*).

The area north of Haydarpaşa is thinly developed, largely because it belongs to the military and to Marmara University. Each own one of the two imposing buildings that truly dominate the area.

The **Selimiye Barracks** were originally constructed in 1799 during the reign of Selim III

Seasons to be cheerful – **Villa Mon Plaisir**.

Sightseeing

as part of his plan to create a 'new army' to challenge the hegemony of the Janissaries. He was murdered for his efforts and his barracks burnt down. Thirty years later Sultan Mahmut II was more successful, defeating the Janissaries (*see page 14* **Swords of misrule**) and raising the present building.

During the Crimean War (1853-6) the barracks served as a hospital in the charge of **Florence Nightingale** (1820-1910). The rooms she occupied in the north-west corner tower are now a small museum containing some furniture of dubious authenticity, copies of some pamphlets she wrote on military nursing and, of course, a lamp. It's still very much a military base and so access to the museum is allowed by application only. Currently it's necessary to fax the names and nationalities of all visitors to 0216 333 1009 and await approval.

The other grand building is the former **Haydarpaşa High School**, now Marmara University medical faculty. It's the largest of the many commissions completed by Raimondo D'Aronco, this time working with French architect Alexandre Vallaury. Devoid of detail, the seaward façade with its large arched windows and stylised minarets is clearly designed to be viewed from a distance. The grand entrance on the landward side is the exact opposite, with a wealth of detail.

Close by the High School, just off Burhan Felek Caddesi, is the **British Crimean War Cemetery**, containing the graves of Crimean War and World War I dead, as well as of later British civilians. As far-flung corners of foreign fields go, it's rather pleasant, with neatly manicured lawns tended by the Commonwealth War Graves Commission. Access is through the gate lodge which is usually manned; otherwise call 0216 217 1010.

Largest of the area's cemeteries is the **Karaca Ahmet cemetery**, named after a warrior companion of the second Ottoman sultan Orhan. The cemetery is thought to have been founded as early as the mid-14th century and estimates put the number of interments at over a million, making it easily the largest boneyard in Turkey.

Selimiye Barracks

Selimiye Kışlası
Çeşme Kebir Caddesi, Üsküdar (0216 343 7310).
Bus 12, 12a, 13, 13b, 14 from Kadıköy.
Open by appointment only Mon-Fri; closed Sat, Sun.
Admission free.

Üsküdar

In contrast to lively Kadıköy, Üsküdar is conservative, populated largely by transplants from rural Anatolia. During the Muslim holy month of Ramazan, Üsküdar is the site of one of

Maiden's Tower, or is it Leander's? *See p109.*

the city's largest *iftar* (literally 'break-fast') tents, with masses of food donated by Islamic businesses. Licensed restaurants and bars are few and far between, although there's no shortage of supermarkets and food shops. The main point of interest for shoppers is the warren of antique shops on Büyük Hamam Sokak. Otherwise, the district's main attractions are its mosques. In Ottoman times, Üsküdar was a favourite place to build these because of a belief that the Asian side lay closer to Mecca.

The **Iskele Mosque** (1548) opposite the ferry terminal, and the **Şemsi Ahmet Paşa Mosque** (1580) down on the shore are both the work of Sinan (*see page 38* **Keeping up with the domes's**). The Şemsi is particularly attractive, on the Bosphorus waterfront and with nicely proportioned ancillary buildings. Inland on Şemsi Paşa Caddesi stands the earliest of Üsküdar's mosques, the **Mehmet Paşa Mosque**, built in 1471 for the then grand vizier. He was of Greek origin, which may explain the strong Byzantine influence in a design which incorporates a cylindrical drum under the dome. The **Yeni Valide Mosque** back on Uncular Caddesi also has a Greek connection. It was constructed for Sultan Ahmet III whose mother was born Greek, captured at age three, and grew up in the harem where she graduated from mistress to wife to mother of the sultan (*valide sultana*). The building is a late example of classical Ottoman style with an attractive façade but a disappointing interior.

LEANDER'S TOWER

On a small island off the southern shore of Üsküdar is a stubby white tower, diminutive but for some reason one of the city's best loved landmarks, endlessly recycled in graphics and logos. Although the island was occupied by a fortress in Byzantine times, the tower only dates from the last century. It has been used as a quarantine centre, a lighthouse, a customs control point and a hideout for the villainous Elektra in 1999's James Bond picture, *The World Is Not Enough.*

In Turkish it's known as Kız Kulesi, or **Maiden's Tower** – supposedly because a princess was once confined here after a prophet foretold that she would die from a snakebite. The fatal bite was duly delivered by a serpent which arrived in a basket of fruit. The same story is associated with numerous other castles around the coast. In English it's known as Leander's Tower, the name deriving from the Greek myth of Leander, who swam the Hellespont – again, absolutely nothing to do with this island. In late 2000, the tower was scheduled to open as a restaurant.

The Asian Bosphorus

The first township north of Üsküdar is **Kuzguncuk**, which as recently as the 1920s had a population almost entirely Greek, Armenian and Jewish. Some churches and synagogues remain, all dating from the 19th century. Of more interest are the quaint streets of old houses, notably Icadiye Caddesi, which has some fine old wooden Jewish houses.

Just beyond the first Bosphorus Bridge stands **Beylerbeyi Palace**, last of the great ugly Ottoman palaces. Facing north-west, it gets little direct sunlight and the place was intended as a summer annex to the main palace at **Dolmabahçe** (*see page 99*). Beylerbeyi didn't even have its own kitchens; food was brought over from the European shore by boat. After being deposed in 1908, Sultan Abdül Hamit II spent the last years of his life here.

Tours of the palace take 15 to 20 minutes and, apart from the main palace with its sumptuous furnishings, immense crystal chandeliers and over-the-top decoration, also take in some of the five adjoining pavilions. As with Dolmabahçe across the water, the whole place reeks of the strained decadence of declining Ottoman rule.

The village of **Beylerbeyi**, on the other hand, boasts a pretty harbour with tea gardens and a few pleasant restaurants. The nearby **Hamidievvel Mosque** is unusual in having a rose garden. At weekends, the area by the ferry jetty gets taken over by craft stalls.

North from here the landscape gets a whole lot greener. The 1990s saw property prices soar as rich refugees from the European shore began to move in. The most expensive properties are the *yalis*, the wooden shoreside mansions which hug the strip between the road and the sea. As they're mostly invisible behind high security walls and satellite dishes, you'll need to take a Bosphorus cruise to see their elaborate waterfront façades.

Çengelköy, the next town up, was effectively still a village until it featured in a long-running TV soap, *Süper Baba*, precipitating an influx of money and car showrooms. The harbour is still pleasant, though, and there are a couple of waterside fish restaurants offering good views.

Further north, on the shore at **Vaniköy**, stands the Kuleli Naval Officers' Training College, constructed in 1860 and still in use. A little further on, perched on the Kandilli hilltop, is the **Palace of Adile Sultan**, built as a girls' school, gutted by fire and currently undergoing restoration.

The wide valley to the north of Kandilli is split by two narrow rivers, Küçüksu and Göksu Deresi, together once known as the 'Sweet Waters of Asia'. These days, Küçüksu is little more than an open sewer, while Göksu Deresi to the north is crammed with weekend pleasure craft. In Ottoman times, the water meadows between the two were a popular picnic ground for the rich. Even Sultan Abdül Mecit got in on the act, erecting the modest **Küçüksu Palace** on the shore.

On the north bank of the Göksu stands the castle of **Anadolu Hısarı**, constructed by Sultan Beyazıt I around 1390 and extended by Mehmet II in 1452 when he was planning his final assault on Constantinople. Parts of the outer barbican have been demolished to allow the road to pass through, but the inner keep remains intact, although currently closed to the public.

Beylerbeyi Palace

Beylerbeyi Sarayı
Abdullah Ağa Caddesi, Üsküdar (0216 321 9320). Bus 15 from Üsküdar. **Open** 9.30am-4pm Tue, Wed, Fri-Sun; closed Mon, Thur. **Admission** $5.

Küçüksu Palace

Küçüksu Sarayı
Küçüksu Caddesi, Beykoz (0216 332 3303). Bus 15 from Üsküdar/101 from Beşiktaş. **Open** 9.30am-4pm Tue, Wed, Fri-Sun; closed Mon, Thur. **Admission** $5.

Sightseeing

RAHMİ M.KOÇ
M Ü Z E S İ
M U S E U M

If you would like to see
how a minting press works
or see replicas of Edison's
first electric light bulb
and phonograph or
how steam power is applied
at sea, on land and
on locomotives or
to examine model ships
and planes and to have fun,
we invite you to experience
this magnificent atmosphere.

OPENING TIMES
10:00 - 17:00 daily, except Monday

ADDRESS
Hasköy Cad. 27, Hasköy 80320
İstanbul-Turkey

+90-212-256 71 53
+90-212-256 71 54
+90-212-256 71 56 (fax)
e-mail: rmkmuseum@koc.com.tr
http://www.rmk-museum.org.tr

Museums

Istanbul's exhibits encompass the wealth of two millennia, from Ottoman artefacts to Atatürk's underwear.

The world-class
Archaeology Museum. *See p112.*

Istanbul's museums encompass a sweep of history and culture as wide and broad as that of the city itself. Mostly run by municipal and state authorities, there's a definite air of antiquity about these buildings, and we're not talking about the exhibits. The museums are largely mothballed institutions, in which the only interactive element is you handing over your money, and where the small armies of underworked employees have perfected the skill of sleeping with their eyes open. As a result, priceless antiquities regularly go walkies to resurface in the auction houses of London, Amsterdam and New York. Most recently a 15th-century Topkapı Koran was recovered in northern Cyprus in May 2000 after being lifted from the palace eight months earlier. A museum security video of the night of the break-in showed the guards snoring contentedly as the thieves rustled past, while the camera for the Koran room itself, along with the alarms, had been switched off to save electricity. Still, Istanbul has antiquity to spare, and there will always be plenty to see.

Principal among the museums are the old imperial palaces – **Topkapı** (*see page 70*) and **Dolmabahçe** (*see page 99*). After those, the most important collections are held at the **Archaeology Museum** and the **Museum of Turkish & Islamic Art**. Beyond that, the **Rahmi M Koç Museum** is fun and the others, well, a few of them do at least make up in quirkiness what they lack in quality.

Outside of the major museums, be prepared for exhibits labelled only in Turkish. Inquiries after English-speaking tour guides will likely bring hopeless, embarrassed shrugs from the museum attendants. Check around the entrance for printed foreign-language guides, which, as well as offering a pointer on what's inside, are often also great exercises in syntactic meltdown. Major museums have book and souvenir shops, but film shows and cultural programmes are well off the radar.

Opening hours vary, but, by and large, Monday is the day they all close. Tickets are sold on the door only, and students generally get half price admission on presentation of an ISIC card (*see page 280*). Photography is almost always permitted, provided you don't use a flash.

Archaeology Museum

Arkeoloji Müzesi
*Topkapı Sarayı, Sultanahmet (0212 520 7740). Tram
Gülhane.* **Open** 9am-4.30pm Tue-Sun; closed Mon.
Admission $4. **No credit cards. Map** p303 O9.

Arguably one of the best of its kind in the world, the
Archaeology Museum sits within the Topkapı
grounds, downhill from the first court (*see p70*). It
was founded in the mid-19th century to try and
staunch the flow of antiquities then being spirited
out of the country by foreign archaeologists and
collectors to fill the great museums of Europe.
Housed initially in what is now the **Tiled Pavilion**
(*see below*), the institution came of age in 1881
when Osman Hamdi Bey (1842-1910), Turkey's pre-
eminent archaeologist, was made director and
commissioned a new building, extended since on
three occasions to keep up with the burgeoning
number of items it has to house.

Greeting visitors is a grinning statue of Bes, a
demonic Cypriot demi-god of inexhaustible power
and strength, qualities required by anyone hoping
to get through even a fraction of the 20 galleries
within. Starting with the pre-Classical world, it
covers 5,000 years of history, with artefacts gath-
ered from all over Turkey and the Near East and
grouped thematically. Highlights include a collection of sixth to fourth-century BC sarcophagi from a
royal necropolis at Sidon, in modern Lebanon.
Their discovery in 1887 was the making of Hamdi
Bey, whose life and works are also the subject of a
small exhibition. Thought to have been made for a
line of Phoenician kings, they display an extraordinary development of funereal styles, from the
Ancient Egyptian to the Hellenistic. The finest is
known as the Alexander Sarcophagus (late fourth
century BC) because of the scenes of the
Macedonian general's victory at Issus (333 BC)
adorning its side panels.

Up on the first floor, 'Istanbul Through the Ages'
is the city's history presented through a few well-
labelled key pieces, including a serpent's head
lopped off the column in the **Hippodrome** (*see
p76*) and a section of the iron chain that stretched
across the Bosphorus to bar the way of invaders
(*see p15*). One great innovation is a small children's
area, complete with specially low cabinets and a
Wooden Horse.

Part of the museum complex, the **Tiled Pavilion**
(*Çinili Köşk*) dates back to 1472 and the reign of
Sultan Mehmet II, Ottoman conqueror of
Constantinople. It's built in a Persian style and was
an imperial viewing stand that overlooked a large
gaming field, now occupied by the main museum
building. Covered floor to ceiling in tilework, it acts
as a museum of ceramics. Just to the south, beside
the entrance to the complex, is the **Museum of
the Ancient Orient**, containing antiquities from
the Egyptian, Hittite and Mesopotamian cultures,
including some wonderful monumental glazed-
brick friezes from the main Ishtar Gate of sixth-
century Babylon.

Mustafa's monogram: **Atatürk Museum**.

Make a point of visiting the outside toilets for the
unintended display of eerily fascinating civil
defence posters urging responsible citizens to
contact the authorities immediately if they witness
the beginnings of a nuclear holocaust.

Atatürk Museum

Atatürk Müzesi
*Halaskargazi Caddesi 250, Şişli (0212 240 6319). Bus
46H.* **Open** 9am-4pm Mon-Wed, Fri, Sat; closed Thur,
Sun. **Admission** free.

In northern Şişli sits this icon of contemporary
Turkey, the candy pink Atatürk Museum. An old
Ottoman house in which Mustafa Kemal once
stayed, it now contains three floors of memorabilia
of the Great Man, from his astrakhan hat to his silk
underwear, via a wine-stained tablecloth on which
he bashed out the new Turkish alphabet over a picnic lunch in 1928. The top floor also has a collection
of propaganda paintings from the liberation war,
depicting scenes of Greek brutality with, in a couple
of instances, the flag of the perfidious British flut-
tering in the background. Marvel at how Greek soldiers of the period could ever have been taken
seriously advancing into battle with those fluffy
pom-poms on their shoes.

Calligraphy Museum

Vakıf Hat Sanatları Müzesi
*Beyazıt Square, Beyazıt (0212 527 5851/zcozsayiner@
hotmail.com). Tram Beyazıt.* **Open** 9am-noon, 1-4pm
Tue-Sat; closed Sun, Mon. **Admission** $1.50; $0.75
students. **No credit cards. Map** p302 K10.

Occupying an historic former *medrese* beside the
monumental university gate, this is a surprisingly
limited celebration of what was one of the principal
arts of the Ottoman empire. Forbidden to portray
humans or other living beings by their religion

(although this wasn't always strictly adhered to), Islamic artists developed alternative forms of virtuosity. Calligraphy was regarded as a particularly noble art because it was a way of beautifying the text of the Koran. But the sanctity of the text placed restrictions on the flourishes that could be added. Not so with the sultan's *tuğra*, or monogram, which incorporated his name, titles and patronymics in one highly stylised and elaborate motif. The forerunner of the modern trademark.

Despite next to non-existent labelling (all in Turkish) and the lugubrious attendants that trail visitors from exhibit to exhibit, there's a lot here that's worth seeing. The tile art is excellent and there are a number of brilliantly illuminated Korans from the 13th to 16th centuries. The museum also has a pleasant courtyard that features examples of stone-carved calligraphy.

Cartoon Museum

Karikatür ve Mizah Müzesi
Kavacılar Sokak 12, off Atatürk Bulvarı, Fatih (0212 521 1264). **Open** 10am-6pm daily. **Admission** free. **Map** p302 H8.

Set in a beautiful Ottoman *medrese*, part of the 17th-century Gazanfer Ağa Külliyesi, this is one of the city's more unusual, not to say educational, museums. Where instructors once lectured students in Islamic theory, they now give sketching lessons and host workshops on engraving and screen printing. The permanent collection, which includes

Unusual, educational – **Cartoon Museum**.

pieces dating back to the 1870s, illustrates the long-standing popularity of caricature and satire in Turkey, and the recurrence of certain themes, particularly the insidious impact of the West. It also brings home the alarming longevity of a number of figures on the Turkish political scene, including prime minister Bülent Ecevit, whose moustachioed visage appears lampooned on magazine covers from the 1960s, '70s, '80s and '90s. Temporary exhibits feature work by international as well as Turkish cartoonists and change regularly. There's also a humour library and an archive, which is viewable by appointment.

Galatasaray Museum

Galatasaray Lisesi, Istiklal Caddesi 263, Beyoğlu (0212 249 0297). **Open** 1-3pm Wed; closed Mon, Tue, Thur-Sun. **Admission** free. **Map** p308 N3.

Barely more than a trophy room, this is officially the museum of the Galatasaray School sports club, now more famous for its football team (*see p232*). Exhibits include photographs, memorabilia and numerous cases crammed with medals and trophies, though not the 1999-2000 UEFA Cup.

Military Museum

Askeri Müze ve Kültür Sitesi
Vali Konağı Caddesi, Harbiye (0212 233 2720). Bus 46H. **Open** 9am-5pm Wed-Sun; closed Mon, Tue. **Admission** $0.60. **No credit cards.**

The sheer size and wealth of this place says as much about the military's current clout in Turkey as it does about its history. For many years this was one of the few national museums to have any money spent on it, so the collection is nothing if not comprehensive. As a result, all but the most hardened of military enthusiasts are going to suffer serious battle fatigue well before the interminable procession of rooms and corridors comes to an end.

Definitely worth seeing are the campaign pavilions of the Ottoman sultans, gloriously colourful silk and cotton affairs with embroidered decoration. Pity the poor baggage mules who had to transport them, along with carpets and throne. Upstairs in the 20th-century section there's a decent display dealing with the 1915 Gallipoli campaign, plus a jumbled collection of War of Independence equipment and a bizarre set of furniture constructed out of bayonets and gun parts. Space is also given to Turkey's largely forgotten contribution to the UN forces in the Korean War. In the same vein, a section on Turkish participation in NATO and allied operations in Somalia, Bosnia and Kosovo is scheduled to open in late 2000.

The Military Museum is also the venue for performances by the Mehter Band, a modern-day incarnation of a marching band of Janissaries that traditionally accompanied the sultan into battle. Their bombastic music, with accompanying lyrics of heroism, actually had an impact on Europe, giving rise to the Spanish *a la turca* style and inspiring both Mozart (*Marcia Turca*) and Beethoven (*Opus 13*). It was through the Mehter

Sightseeing

Paving the way at the **Mosaic Museum.**

that the kettle drum (the Turkish *kös*) was introduced into Western orchestras. Abolished in 1826, the band was re-established in 1914 and performs every day that the museum is open between 3pm and 4pm.

Mimar Sinan University Museum of Fine Arts

Mimar Sinan Üniversitesi Istanbul Resim ve Heykel Müzesi
Barbaros Hayrettin Paşa Iskelesi Sokak,
off Beşiktaş Caddesi, Beşiktaş (0212 261 4298/
rector@msu.edu.tr). Bus 25E, 28, 40, 56.
Open 9.30am-4.30pm Wed-Sun; closed Mon, Tue.
Admission free. **No credit cards.**
Housed in one of the many former Ottoman palaces that line the waterfront in this part of town, the museum holds a permanent collection of Turkish art from the last 150 years, mainly by artists with connections to the Mimar Sinan university. The best known name is Osman Hamdi Bey, the one-time director of the Archaeology Museum (*see p112*) and also the first Turkish artist who dared make the human figure the main subject of a painting. There's also a library and archive.

Mosaic Museum

Büyüksaray Mozaik Müzesi
Arasta Çarşısı, Torun Sokak 103, Sultanahmet (0212 518 1205). Tram Sultanahmet. **Open** 9.30am-4.30pm Tue-Sun; closed Mon. **Admission** $1.50. **No credit cards. Map** p303 N11.
Behind the Sultanahmet Mosque and slightly downhill towards the Marmara is a small 17th-century shopping street, built to provide rental revenue to provide for the upkeep of the mosque. It's been converted into a tourist bazaar ('Hey mister, wanna buy a carpet?'), off which is a pre-fab hut sheltering a fantastic archaeological find.

Uncovered in the mid-1950s, it's an ornamental pavement belonging to the Byzantine Great Palace (which stood where the mosque is now), probably dating from the era of Justinian. It depicts some mythological and hunting scenes. Horses, stags, monkeys, dogs, fishermen and herdsmen demonstrate a pastoral idyll, although this is disturbingly skewed by bloody depictions of stags and lizards being eaten by winged unicorns. There are also smaller mosaics mounted on the walls.

Naval Museum

Deniz Müzesi
Barbaros Hayrettin Paşa Iskelesi Sokak,
off Beşiktaş Caddesi, Beşiktaş (0212 261 0130/
http://abone.superonline.com/navalmuseumturk/
index.htm). Bus 25E, 28, 40, 56. **Open** 9am-12.30pm, 1.30-5pm Wed-Sun; closed Mon, Tue. **Admission** $0.50. **No credit cards.**
This museum is housed in two buildings on the Bosphorus east of Dolmabahçe Palace, right next to the ferry terminal at Beşiktaş. In the larger is an extensive collection of model ships, ship figure-heads and oil paintings of various British and French battleships being blasted in the abortive Dardanelles campaign of World War I. Upstairs is a room of commemorative plaques to Turkish sailors killed on duty from 1319 to the Cyprus war of 1974, the battle flag of Barbarossa, the 16th-century Ottoman pirate/naval hero, and just about everything that wasn't nailed down on Atatürk's yacht, the *Savarona*, including a set of silver toothpicks.

More impressive is what's in the smaller building: a collection of Ottoman *caïques*. Elegant, bird-like barges of light wood and built for speed, these craft give a strong sense of the splendour of imperial city transport in the Ottoman golden age. At one time they were as symbolic of the city as the gondola of

Venice. Boats were used as much to get around as horse and carriage (a lesson lost on the present municipality). The sultans' caïques, displayed here, were rowed by Bostanci, an imperial naval unit who doubled as palace gardeners. The largest, a 1648 model, required some 144 Bostanci to power it along. They were apparently required to bark like dogs as they rowed so they wouldn't overhear the sultan's conversations.

Rahmi M Koç Industrial Museum

Rahmi M Koç Müzesi
Hasköy Caddesi 27, Hasköy (0212 256 7153/ www.rmkmuseum.org.tr). Bus 54T from Taksim. **Open** 10am-5pm Tue-Sun; closed Mon. **Admission** $1.50. **No credit cards**.
Though it's way out of the centre, up past the old Galata Bridge on the north side of the Golden Horn, this museum is worth a trek. Founded by the head of the Koç industrial group, one of Turkey's major players, it's crammed with the technologies and tomorrow's worlds of times past. From Ottoman astrolabes to giant clunky German telex machines, 19th-century trams to soda and slot machines. There's a room full of classic cars and bikes, from a Penny Farthing to a Harley-D. The collection even includes the forward section of a US air force B-24D Liberator bomber, *Hadley's Harem*, which was shot down in 1943 and recovered from the sea bed off Turkey's Mediterranean coast some 50 years later.

Plenty of the exhibits have moving parts, which can be manually activated by buttons or levers, and there's a walk-on ship's bridge with a wheel, sonar machines and alarm bells that can be operated with sound effects. Great fun. Try to visit on a Saturday when all the working models are in action. Everything is well labelled in both English and Turkish.

The building itself is also quite exceptional – an 18th-century foundry where anchors and chains were once cast for the city dockyards. It has an extremely good French bistro in the Café du Levant (*see p121*).

The Sabancı Collection

Atlı Köşk, Emirgan
www.sabanci.com.tr
Information is thin on the ground at present, but word is that in September 2001 the largest private collection of Ottoman art in the world as well as Turkish painting and sculpture is due to open to the public. Amassed by philanthropist industrialist Sakip Sabancı, it is to be displayed in the former family mansion up in Emirgan on the shores of the Bosphorus, beyond the second bridge. In recent years exhibitions drawn from this collection have been hung in the Met in New York, the Louvre in Paris and in Moscow. The opening in Istanbul is hugely anticipated. For updated information check the website or ask around at some of the local art galleries (*see p192*).

Museum of Turkish & Islamic Art

Türk ve Islam Eserleri Müzesi
Hippodrome, At Meydanı 46, Sultanahmet (0212 518 1805). Tram Sultanahmet. **Open** 9am-4.30pm Tue-Sun; closed Mon. **Admission** $4. **No credit cards**. **Map** p303 M11.

Ships ahoy! The piratical Barbarossa guards the entrance to the **Naval Museum**. *See p114.*

Sightseeing

Museum of Turkish & Islamic Art. *See p115.*

One of those museums where the building and its history overshadow the collection within. Overlooking the Hippodrome, the museum occupies the restored 16th-century palace of Ibrahim Paşa. A Greek convert to Islam, Ibrahim was the confidant of Süleyman I and in 1523 was appointed Grand Vizier. When his palace was completed the following year it was the grandest private residence in the Ottoman empire, rivalling any building of the Topkapı Palace. However, later, when Süleyman fell under the influence of the scheming Roxelana (*see p16*), the sultan was persuaded that Ibrahim had to go and he was strangled in his sleep. The palace was seized by the state and has variously been used as a school, a dormitory, a court, a barracks and a prison, before being restored as a museum.

The well planned collections housed in cool rooms around a central courtyard include carpets, manuscripts, miniatures, woodwork, metalwork and glasswork, ranging from the earliest period of Islam through to modern times, with a focus on Selçuk, Mamluk and Ottoman. Exhibits are presented chronologically and geographically, with explanations provided. On the ground floor, a gallery showcases modern Turkish and foreign artists, and there's an interesting ethnographic section, including a recreation of a *kara cadır* or 'black tent', the residence of choice for many of the nomadic Anatolian tribes who developed the art of the *kilim*. Upstairs, the Great Hall contains what's reckoned to be one of the finest collections of carpets in the world.

There's also an excellent café in a shaded courtyard with an adjacent covered terrace overlooking the Hippodrome.

Vakıflar Carpet Museum

Vakıflar Halı Müzesi
Sultanahmet Mosque, Sultanahmet (0212 518 1330).
Tram Sultanahmet. **Open** 9am-noon, 1-4pm Tue-Sat; closed Sun, Mon. **Admission** $1.50; $0.75 students. **No credit cards. Map** p303 N11.

In what was once the Imperial Pavilion of the Sultanahmet Mosque (*see p75*) complex, used by the sultan whenever he visited for services, is an extensive collection of carpets from all over Turkey and all periods of history. The setting is appropriate, considering that until quite recently most of these carpets and rugs lay inside living mosques, which is how they've come to be preserved. Presentation is sparse, and this is, frankly, all done much better at the **Museum of Turkish & Islamic Art** (*see p115*). For rug enthusiasts only.

For rug enthusiasts, carpets at the **Vakıflar Carpet Museum**. Magic!

Eat, Drink, Shop

Restaurants

And you thought it was all döner kebabs.

Anyone who doubts the central role of food in Turkish culture need only visit Topkapı Palace and take a look at the kitchens. They are vast. Or read down a list of types of food specialists hired to please the sultan's palate. It has been said that food was the demise of the Ottoman empire as successive sultans became too fond of their stomachs and lost all their appetite for war and conquest.

As the Ottomans once controlled the entire eastern Mediterranean basin, imperial chefs were able to raid the ingredients and cuisines of Greece, the Balkans, the Caucasus and the Levant for inspiration. A continual quest for imperial approval also played its role in the creative and sometimes enigmatic names of dishes such as 'the imam fainted' (an aubergine dish), 'lady's lips' (pastry in thick syrup), 'slit stomach' (aubergine stuffed with mince meat) and 'ladies' thighs' (battered, fried meatballs).

The 'indigenous' cuisine encountered in Istanbul today is simplified palace food that long ago made its way outside the imperial quarters and into common kitchens.

WHERE TO EAT
Istanbul eats in time with the rest of Europe; breakfast (*kahvaltı*) in the morning, lunch (*öğle yemeği*) around 1pm and dinner sometime after 6pm in the evening. While lunch tends to be taken on the run these days, often at cafeteria-type places known as *lokanta* (*see page 136* **Turkish fast food**), dinner is as much about social interaction as sustenance.

Meals tend to be long, drawn-out affairs where the food and drink are secondary to conversation and company. It's not uncommon to take a seat at 8pm and still be at the table long gone midnight.

One of the most pleasurable ways of Turkish dining is to feast on *meze* (hors d'oeuvre). At many restaurants a tray or cart is brought over from which choices are made and transferred to the table. Portions are small so you can order a great many and get to taste a wide variety of dishes in one sitting.

It's quite acceptable to just stick with meze, calling the waiter and his tray back to your table throughout the evening and never ordering any mains. Typical meze are salads, yogurt-based dishes, aubergine and other vegetable purées, chopped liver, vegetables stuffed with rice, white cheese, beans, anchovies, calamari and other seafoods. Best places for meze munching are

meyhanes (*see page 130*), the traditional folksy taverna-type restaurants. These are heavily concentrated in Beyoğlu, particularly around Nevizade Sokak (*see page 130* **Çiçek Pasajı & Nevizade**), and over in the fish-rich Kumkapı district; *see below*.

Another Istanbul dining experience is Ottoman (*see p132*). Various restaurants serve traditional 'palace' cuisine that can trace an ancestry back to the Topkapı kitchens. Most overtrade on the heritage angle when it comes to decor, but the food can be exceptional and some dishes are rarely found anywhere outside western Turkey.

As for kebabs, despite the high profile of the döner abroad, where the revolving spit of meat is a better known symbol of Turkey than its national flag, it is possible to stay in Istanbul and never touch a piece of grilled lamb once. Though that would be a shame. Avoid the streetside vendors and head for a *kebapçı* or *ocakbaşı*, places that specialise in charred flesh, to find out what a real kebab is all about; *see page 129*.

TIPPING AND RESERVATIONS
Tipping is expected. Ten per cent is generally sufficient. Sometimes it's already figured into the bill, so check. In high-end places tipping is expected in addition to the added service charge. Reservations are normally a must on Friday and Saturday evenings, but are not usually needed during the week.

Fish

Istanbul's extensive coastline means that fish features strongly on local menus. Traditionally, the place to head is **Kumkapı**, on the coast road south-west of Sultanahmet. Centred on Ördekli Bakkal Sokak, it's a cluster of small restaurants with pavement seating, typically frequented by large parties of Turks looking for a good night out. It's brash and loud and fun if you're in the mood, but the quality of the food isn't always great – it's the quantity of the alcohol that keeps the punters happy. For a superior fish experience head up to Yeniköy on the Bosphorus; *see page 240*.

Balıkçı Sabahattin
Seyit Hasan Koyu Sokak 50, Cankurtaran (0212 458 1824). Tram Sultanahmet. **Open** noon-midnight daily. **Complete dinner** $25. **Credit** MC, V. **Map** p303 N11.

Although it's just five minutes from Sultanahmet, few tourists find their way here. Instead, it's left to a discerning local clientele to make the most of the catch of the day, accompanied by a standard selection of meze. The food is just that little bit better than you generally get at Kumkapı and the location is secluded, on a small cobbled street in a largely residential district. Seating outside in summer.

Çınar Restaurant

Iskele Meydanı 42, Ortaköy (0212 261 5818). **Open** noon-2am daily. **Main courses** $6-$11. **Credit** AmEx, DC, MC, V.

A handful of almost identical restaurants line up on the west side of the waterfront square at Ortaköy. They are all fine places to pass an evening, with views of moonlight on the Bosphorus and a sociable atmosphere with banquet seating. There's no menu; meze with a seafood slant are presented on a tray for selection and if you're still hungry after that, another tray comes out with an artful presentation of different fish. Alcohol is served and entertainment comes in the form of fortune-telling Gypsies and street vendors peddling the most unbelievable tat.

Hanedan

Barbaros Meydanı, Çiğdem Sokak 27, Beşiktaş (0212 259 4017). **Open** noon-midnight daily. **Complete dinner** $28-$38. **Credit** AmEx, MC, V.

At street level a meat restaurant (it does beautiful roast lamb), but the two floors above serve some of the best seafood in Istanbul. A kitchen that is more ambitious than most goes beyond just frying and grilling and prepares fish in a variety of sauces. Meals here are complemented by superb views over the Bosphorus and of distant Sultanahmet; which are especially good if you manage to land a seat on the terrace.

Marina Balık Restaurant

Ferryboat dock, Kuruçeşme (0212 287 2653). **Open** noon-midnight daily. **Main courses** $6-$20. **Credit** MC, V.

What looks like a rustic shack in Kuruçeşme park is actually a fairly classy establishment with starched very white tablecloths and black-suited, fabulously efficient wait staff. House speciality is fish cooked in rock salt served with sautéed mushrooms, tomatoes and herbs. Recommended.

Rumeli Iskele

Yahya Kemal Caddesi 1, Rumeli Hisarı (0212 263 2997). **Open** noon-midnight daily. **Main courses** $38-$45. **Credit** AmEx, MC, V.

Traditional but elegant interior, although the seats to aim for are out on the wooden pier-like deck that looks across the straits to the hilltop castle of Anadolu Hisarı. The service is unobtrusive and efficient and the food, while holding few surprises (fresh seasonal fish standards and seafood meze), is reliably good. Not a restaurant to go out of the way to visit, but a solid option if in the area.

Eat, Drink, Shop

Changa – Charles Eames chairs below turn-of-the-century ceilings. *See p123.*

ONE OF İSTANBUL'S CLASSICAL PLACES:
SÜLEYMAN NAZİF

Süleyman Nazif, a bar-restaurant that is situated
in Nişantaşı during winter and in Yeniköy during
summer time has become for the last 10 years
one of the favourite places for people who live in İstanbul.

Süleyman Nazif's Nişantaşı and Yeniköy branches
are both serving a variety of foods,
starting from lunch time up till late at night.

Nişantaşı **Süleyman Nazif** will open its doors
in November and will be this winter too
the most trandy place of İstanbul.

With its cosy decoration, its wide variety of delicious foods
and drinks and with its warm hospitality,
Nişantaşı **Süleyman Nazif** will be once more
one of your favourite place to go
during the long winter nights.

Summer Place	Winter Place
Köybaşı Cad. No: 79	Vali Konağı Cad. No: 39/2
Yeniköy / İstanbul	Nişantaşı / İstanbul
Tel: +90.212.223 04 38	Tel: +90.212.225 22 43or44

The best Restaurants

Laledan
Fine views of the Bosphorus. See page 125.

Malta Köşkü
Palatial pavilion in the park. See page 133.

Pandeli
Old world feel, great grub. See page 133.

Vogue
Gives you a James Bond feel. See page 128.

Musa Ustam Ocakbaşı
Heaven for football fans. See page 129.

Eski Ingiliz Karakolu
Authentic prison food. See page 123.

Cumhuriyet Işkembe Salonu
Sobering 2am tripe soups. See page 129.

Changa
Pretend you're not in Turkey. See page 123.

International

Only recently has international cuisine moved out of a five-star setting and into the popular dining scene. It remains an upmarket option and, other than in its fast-food incarnation, one that the average Turk can't really afford.

C Fischer

Inönü Caddesi 51B, Gümüşsuyu, Taksim (0212 245 3375). **Open** noon-2am daily. **Main courses** $5-$9. **Credit** AmEx, MC, V. **Map** p307 Q2.
Founded by German immigrants, this restaurant now specialises in German, Austrian, Russian and Hungarian dishes, alongside Turkish staples. A weird combination, and one of the few restaurants anywhere in which you can follow stuffed vine leaves with goulash. Kitchen closes at 10pm.

Cafe du Levant

Rahmi M Koç Industrial Museum, Hasköy Caddesi 27, Hasköy (0212 235 6328). **Open** Sept-July 10am-2.30pm, 3-10.30pm Tue-Sun; closed Mon. *Aug* closed. **Main courses** *meat dishes* $11-$12; *fish dishes* $20-$22. **Credit** AmEx, DC, MC, V.
Excellent French cuisine served in a wonderfully decorated bistro, kitted out with 19th-century furniture from the neighbouring Industrial Museum (*see p115*). Recommended particularly for weekend lunches, when it gets crowded and reservations are advisable. Pricey, but worth splashing out on.

Eat, Drink, Shop

Mete Göktuğ (left), owner of **Eski Ingiliz Karakolu**, takes a gaol break. *See p131.*

Changa

Sıraselviler Caddesi 87/1, Taksim (0212 251 7064).
Open 12.30-3pm, 7pm-2am Mon-Sat; closed Sun.
Main courses lunch $15; dinner $25. **Credit** AmEx,
DC, MC, V. **Map** p309 O2.
Sleek, sophisticated and aware that it's too sexy for
its drab Taksim surroundings. Clever use of limited
space on three floors and plenty of original touches.
Scenesters settle into Charles Eames chairs below
turn-of-the-century ceilings and select from a fusion
menu created by bestselling cookbook author and
chef Peter Gordon. Attractive bar with a downtown
Manhattan feel. The place for Istanbulites to get a
glimpse of the city's dining future.

Chinese Unlimited

*Ahmet Fetgari Sokak 164/1, Teşvikiye (0212 240
3166).* **Open** noon-3pm, 7-10.30pm Mon-Sat; closed
Sun. **Main courses** $7-$14.
Stylish decor (unusually for an Istanbul Chinese
there's not a single Oriental lantern in sight) and
Hong Kong, Cantonese and Hunan cuisine, all pass-
ably well done and available for take out or home
delivery. The restaurant is popular with the yup-
piesque Nişantaşı crowd, meaning the occasional
wait for a table on Friday and Saturday nights. It's
in the street behind Teşvikiye mosque.

Cookbook

*Güzelbahçe Sokak 5/2, off Valikonağı Caddesi,
Nişantaşı (0212 219 1394).* **Open** noon-3.30pm Mon-
Sat; closed Sun. **Set menu** $18 (includes glass of
imported wine). **Credit** MC, V.
Began life as a cookery book store – and it still sells
books – but it now also offers a weekly-changing
lunch menu of world food all prepared following
recipes contained within the books on the shelves.

Downtown

Abdi İpekçi Caddesi 7/2, Nişantaşı (0212 224 3915).
Open noon-2am Mon-Sat; closed Sun. **Main courses**
$12-$20. **Credit** MC, V.
Trendy eaterie that's a favourite with Istanbul's hip
media crowd. Half-Norwegian co-owner Mehmet
loves experimenting with food and has put together
an eclectic menu of Continental European dishes
with hints of Scandinavia. Reservations are not
accepted but the stylish ultra-modern bar helps
pass the wait. Kitchen closes at 10pm.

Dubb Indian Restaurant

*İncili Çavuş Sokak 10, Sultanahmet (0212 513 7308).
Tram Sultanahmet.* **Open** noon-10.30pm Tue-Sun;
closed Mon. **Main courses** $8-$9. **Credit** AmEx, MC,
V. **Map** p303 N10.
The only authentic Indian in Istanbul. Housed in a
restored Ottoman building on three cosy saffron-
hued levels one street north of Divan Yolu. A dozen
well-prepared curries and other standards like tan-
dooris and biriyanis. In a city where international
cuisine typically equals pricey, dinner at Dubb is
surprisingly reasonable.

Eski Ingiliz Karakolu

*Galata Kulesi Sokak 61, Galata, Beyoğlu (0212 245
1861).* **Open** noon-11pm Tue-Sun; closed Mon. **Main
courses** $4-$6. **Credit** V. **Map** p306 M5.
Serves up Georgian food in a former British prison
in a historic Genoese quarter of a Turkish city.
Owner and architect Mete Göktuğ is one of a rare

Şarabi – cool, clean, smart and wildly international. *See p126.*

Eat, Drink, Shop

breed intent on preserving the architectural fabric of Galata, to which end he's converted this old gaol into a restaurant. In the name of authenticity, he has done nothing to pretty up the place, leaving the peeling paint on the walls, complete with prisoners' graffiti. It's atmospheric to say the least. The food is also exceptional.

Four Seasons

Istiklal Caddesi 509, Tünel, Beyoğlu (0212 293 3941). **Open** noon-3pm, 6-11pm Mon-Sat; closed Sun. **Main courses** $4-$14. **Credit** AmEx, DC, MC, V. **Map** p308 M4.

Not a particularly old restaurant (established 1974), it nevertheless aims to convey a sense of 'old Pera' – pre-republic multicultural Beyoğlu – through nostalgic decor, stiff service and a mainly French menu. Lots of meat in sauces. Good value ($5) set lunches Monday to Friday.

La Corne d'Or

Swissôtel Istanbul The Bosphorus, Bayıldım Caddesi 2, Maçka (0212 259 0101). **Open** 7pm-11.30pm Mon-Sat; closed Sun. **Main courses** $24. **Credit** AmEx, DC, MC, V.

Another contender for best French restaurant in town. The chef here is keen on experimentation: try his duck liver and *ceps* ravioli, an unexpected blend of French and Italian. For more traditional French fare, go for the fish soup. If you feel like giving the credit card a real workout then it's got to be the duck glazed with honey and coated in sherry sauce. Food is everything and conversation

is kept to a hushed murmur, although it's worth glancing up occasionally to take in the stunning views out over the Bosphorus.

Laledan

Çırağan Palace Hotel Kempinski, Çırağan Caddesi 84, Beşiktaş (0212 258 3377). **Open** 7am-11am, noon-3pm, 7pm-11pm daily. **Main courses** $15-$23. **Credit** AmEx, MC, V.

Of the two main Çırağan restaurants (the other one is Tuğra; *see p136*) this is definitely the better. It offers a choice of Italian or international menus and from them one dish is truly original and delicious: mushroom risotto in blueberry sauce. Also recommended is the rack of lamb with a mille feuille of potato and red bell pepper coulis. It has a magnificent summer terrace overlooking the old palace and the Bosphorus.

Le Cigare

Meşeli Sokak 3, 4th Levent (0212 279 8698). Metro Levent. **Open** Oct-May 7pm-3am daily. *June-Sept* closed. **Main courses** $20-$26. **Credit** AmEx, MC, V.

Straight out of a novel by F Scott Fitzgerald, set on two floors with a bar/club below and restaurant on top, this place simply oozes exclusivity and Old Money. The decor is a mixture of hardwood panelling and floors with plush leather chairs. Regulars have their own boxes which hold their favourite cigars. The extensive menu has a French emphasis and there's a selection of cigars, cognac and port wines. In summer it closes in Istanbul and moves south to the coastal resort of Bodrum.

Dessert storm

The ubiquitous *baklava*, the flaky pastry filled with nuts and laced with a sugary syrup, is Turkey's best known contribution to dessert culture. But apart from boxes of Turkish delight, few other sweets make it out of the country. That is the rest of the world's loss, as the country that gave rise to those treats has a variety of other imaginative ways to sweeten the palate.

Among the least exotic are *tavuk gogsu*, a milk pudding featuring vanilla with gum arabic and chicken breast, and *sutlac*, rice pudding with a carmelised coating baked on top.

Aşure, on the other hand, does not at first glance look like food fit for humans, let alone a favoured dessert. It's a pudding made up of gum arabic flavouring, rose water, cinnamon and at least 12 varieties of nuts and legumes, usually including chickpeas, almonds, hazelnuts, raisins and currants. It's not only tasty, it's good for you.

There are at least two different legends about aşure. According to one, as the passengers on

Noah's Ark prepared to disembark, they pooled the remains of the foodstuffs they had left, mixed it all together, and produced aşure.

The other has it that aşure originated among the Alevi, a reformist branch of Islam, and must include 12 different nuts and legumes to represent the 12 prophets of the Alevi. It's usually eaten after ramadan, which lasts 12 days.

In summer, it's common to see street vendors dressed in traditional Ottoman filigree vests, fez, sporting a fake curly moustache and touting a ladle full of gravity-defying ice-cream. This is Maras ice-cream (*Maras dondurma*), so thick that you'll be given a knife and fork to cut through it. The key to its consistency is that it's made from goat's milk and *sahlep*, a thickener derived from orchid root.

Maras ice cream was first developed in an ice-cream parlour in Kahramanmaras, south-eastern Turkey, where legend has it that one of its inventors went on to use the ice-cream to hang himself.

The offal truth

While many Turks celebrated when Turkey formally became a candidate for EU membership, others were in a panic about losing their much beloved *kokoreç*, one of the many preparations of innards that delight local palates, if not queasy foreigners.

The large intestines of sheep or lamb are skewered, grilled and then served up in bread, sometimes with onion and tomato, and sprinkled with thyme and cumin. Street vendors are likely to appear anywhere, and you can also find *kokoreç* at fast-food *bufes*.

The panic arose because *kokoreç* has become contraband in Greece as a result of EU regulations. The EU think it's unhealthy. Rumour has it that in Greece some street vendors still surreptitiously fire it up.

Most any organ touches a chord with Turks. You'll find kidney, heart, brain, tripe, spleen and liver dishes, some as grilled or fried hot starters or main courses at restaurants. Watch out, then, for *Arnavut ciğeri* (Albanian sautéed liver), *böbrek* (kidney), *koç yumurtası* (ram's testicles, often cooked in lemon and tomato sauce) and *kelle*, roasted sheep's head with the brain, eyes and tongue still *in situ*. The cheeks are said to be particularly tender. Lungs give a spongy, tender consistency to köfte from Tekirdag, an area in western Turkey.

Tripe is so popular in Turkey that it has restaurants entirely devoted to it, *işkembeçis*. After a night of imbibing, many Turks end up at the 24-hour iskembeci, where they lap up tripe soup, thought to be an antidote to a raging hangover. One such is Lale Işkembecisi, Istiklal Caddesi, 238, where you can slurp it up in the elegance of a 300-year-old, high-ceiling building with chandeliers. If you have the stomach for it.

Le Select

Manolya Sokak 21, Levent (0212 268 2120). Metro 1 Levent. **Open** noon-3pm, 7pm-1am daily. **Main courses** $11-$20. **Credit** AmEx, DC, MC, V.
Exudes an air of pristine English-style elegance while still maintaining a cosy atmosphere perfect for romantic dining. The menu is an eclectic mix of French and Italian. Reservations are a must as the restaurant is extremely popular with a mature crowd of regulars.

Manhattan Café

Güzelbahçe Sokak 8, Nişantaşı (0212 234 3379). **Open** 11.30am-10.30pm Mon-Sat; closed Sun. **Main courses** $6-$12. **Credit** MC, V.
Founded by brothers who served their apprenticeship running a Turkish restaurant in New York, this is a lively bistro with ceiling fans and banquettes. Like the stock at their gourmet shop (*see p169*) down the block, everything is imported, including a wide selection of wines and beers. Manhattan draws a young professional crowd both for lunches and after work to lounge at the long polished-wood bar.

Mezzaluna

Abdi İpekçi Caddesi 38/1, Maçka (0212 231 3142). **Open** noon-3pm, 7-11pm Mon-Sat. **Main courses** $10-$12. *Full menu* $23-$30 (3 courses and drinks). **Credit** AmEx, MC, V.
The place in Istanbul for a spot of power lunching. It is also renowned as the place to head for some fine Italian dining on classic pasta dishes or garlicky thin-crust pizzas accompanied by a bottle of decent Italian, French or Californian wine. There's some good tiramisu and heavenly crème brulée to finish dining and dealing.

Rejans

Emir Nevruz Sokak 17, Galatasaray, Beyoğlu (0212 244 1619). **Open** *mid Sept-May* noon-3pm, 7pm-midnight daily. *June-mid Sept* noon-3pm, 7pm-midnight Mon-Sat; closed Sun, **Main courses** $3-$9. **Credit** MC, V. **Map** p308 N3.
Founded by White Russians who had relocated to Istanbul in the wake of the Soviet revolution, Rejans was reputedly one of Atatürk's favourite restaurants. The food is no longer particularly grand or particularly Russian, but the place still has bags of charm. There's acres of polished wood, high ceilings, a musicians' gallery and an often drunk doorman to hang winter coats on hooks personalised with the names of long-dead customers. Forgo the rakı or beer and order lemon vodka.

Şarabi

İstiklal Caddesi 174, Beyoğlu (0212 244 4609). **Open** noon-1.30am daily. **Main courses** $5-$9. **Credit** AmEx, MC, V. **Map** p308 N3.
A smart wine bar-cum-eaterie with a cool, clean European look and three high arched windows looking on to Istiklal Caddesi. The menu is wildly international – around the world in a meal. Begin in Japan with a sashimi appetiser, on to northern Italy for mushroom ravioli in basil cream and wind up in France with mousse au chocolat. Menus change quarterly. The choice of wines is good and it's one of the few places that has any beers other than Efes, including Guinness. Service is grudging.

Sunset Grill & Bar

Yol Sokak 1, off Adnan Saygun Caddesi, Ulus Parkı, Ulus (0212 287 0357). Metro 1 Levent. **Open** noon-3pm, 7pm-2am daily. **Main courses** $10-$19. **Credit** AmEx, DC, MC, V.

T-Square – founded by two architects, well designed for an early evening meet. *See p128.*

Chill round the grill at **Musa Ustam Ocakbaşı**.
See p129.

Serves up modern Californian cuisine in a soft-hued venue north of the centre and high above the Bosphorus, commanding fantastic views. As well as imaginative meat and fish dishes, a sushi bar was added in 2000. But if you're going to splash out this much to dine, then make the most of it by going in warm weather on a clear night to sit in the verdant garden.

T-Square

Sıraselviler Caddesi 67/1, Taksim (0212 243 6969). **Open** 9am-midnight daily. **Main courses** $6-$12. **Credit** AmEx, MC, V. **Map** p309 O3.
This is a sleek, well-designed bar/café/restaurant founded by two young architects (and hence the name). It's good as an early evening meeting-drinking venue, and the food is normally excellent if you can cope with cheesy names such as 'Nacho-macho beans'. There's an expansive menu of mostly American and international dishes. It also has a good selection of breakfast fare, such as pancakes or vegetable and cheese omelettes. In summer, there's a pleasantly un-urban garden terrace. Be warned though, that T-Square's popularity can make for some painfully slow service.

Ulus 29

Yol Sokak 1, off Adnan Saygun Caddesi, Ulus Parkı, Ulus (0212 265 6181). Metro 1 Levent. **Open** noon-3pm, 7pm-1am daily. **Main courses** $8-$35. **Credit** AmEx, DC, MC, V.
Enter through a tunnel-like corridor with a flooring of old carpets and kilims and walls hung with blankets into what appears to be a giant tent. In summer pass through to the garden terrace for open-air dining with Bosphorus views. Cuisine is accomplished French, but most are here to be seen rather eat.

Vogue

A Blok 13th Floor, BJK Plaza, Süleyman Seba Caddesi, Beşiktaş (0212 227 2545). **Open** noon-3pm, 7pm-midnight Mon-Sat; 10am-4pm, 6pm-11pm Sun. **Main courses** $10-$30. **Credit** AmEx, MC, V.
The restaurant with the best view in town. It also has extremely chic white and chrome decor and was supposedly all set to star in the 1999 James Bond flick *The World Is Not Enough* until shooting in Istanbul was cancelled at the last minute. The fusion cuisine, an innovative blend of Turkish and continental, manages to hold its own. Service is excellent; reservations are essential.

Kebabs, köfte & offal

Meat is part of most Turkish meals, but not typically the centrepiece. It normally comes minced, stuffed in vegetables or pastry, or chopped and diced as one of many meze. Steaks, fillets and roasts don't feature in the Turkish kitchen. Instead, when Istanbulites want meat they head to dedicated meat restaurants such as the *kebapçı* (kebab seller), *köfteci* (specialising in spiced ground meat made into balls and grilled on a skewer), *ocakbaşı* (a restaurant with an open grill for skewered meat) or *işkembe* (tripe).

Ali Baba

1 Caddesi 92, Arnavutköy (no phone). **Open** 11am-11pm daily. **Main courses** $3-$5. **No credit cards**.
With a reputation out of proportion to its cramped premises, queues and/or table-sharing are the norm at this long-running backstreet eaterie. Devotees maintain that the köfte here is the best in town. It comes with white bean salad (*piyaz*), pide and nothing else. A local slant on fast food; eat and leave.

Cumhuriyet İşkembe Salonu

Duduodaları Sokak 25, Balık Pazarı, Beyoğlu (0212 292 7097). **Open** 7pm-5.30am. **Main courses** $1.50-$3.50. **No credit cards**. **Map** p308 N3.
A stagger away from the meyhanes of Nevizade Sokak, a small no-frills, fluorescent lighting and formica tripe soup shop (*see p126* **The offal truth**). Inebriated night owls swear by the powers of the *iskembe*, but, depending on how much of a skinful

you've had, why not go for the *paça*, chopped trotters in broth, or *baş*, roasted sheep's head served minus the skull but with eyeballs intact.

Develi

Samatya Balık Pazarı, Gümüşyüzük Sokak 7, Kocamustafapaşa (0212 529 0833). **Open** noon-midnight daily. **Main courses** $4-$6. *Set menu* $16-$20. **Credit** MC, V.
There's a little bit of travelling involved to get here (it's on the Marmara coast west of Kumkapı), but then there aren't too many places in town serving such excellent south-eastern Turkish cuisine. Starters include rarely encountered delicacies such as sharp and crumbly tulum cheese and walnut spread. Meat dishes include pistachio and minced lamb kebab, which has none of the fattiness found in less refined kebab shops, and *içli köfte* – meatballs with a cracked wheat and walnut batter and a hint of cinnamon. There's a no-smoking section and great sea views. Worth flagging down a taxi for. The set menu comprises three courses and unlimited drinks.

Musa Ustam Ocakbaşı

Küçükparmakkapı Sokak 14, Beyoğlu (0212 245 2932). **Open** noon-midnight daily. **Main courses** $4-$6. **Credit** AmEx, DC, MC, V. **Map** p309 O3.
Aim for a seat round the *ocak*, an open, glowing coal grill where the restaurant's *çöp şiş* – chunks of lamb on bamboo skewers – are grilled. These come on huge skewers and the trick is to wrap the thin papery bread round the meat, grip firmly and draw out the skewer, leaving a lamb sandwich. Care is required, as elbow space is at a premium – all three floors are

Eat, Drink, Shop

Degüstasyon – reliable TV dinners, prepared by a TV chef. *See p131*.

Çiçek Pasajı & Nevizade

In the 140-year-old **Çiçek Pasajı** (pictured; map p308 N3), or flower passage, you may find a sense of history and the place buzzing with conversation that echoes off the domed ceiling and from the numerous meyhanes and bars. Restaurant hawkers will attempt to lure you in with a flurry of different languages and gestures, a sure sign that the place is already over-touristed. Another is that the food in the passage is unremarkable and often overpriced.

To escape, go in further and turn right into the Balık Pazarı (fish bazaar). Your next right will be into **Nevizade Sokak**, the real heart of meyhane nightlife in Istanbul, where local artists, intellectuals, café politicians and romantic crooners come to ingest rakı, meze and fish, and recharge their creative batteries. Here a bottle of rakı can lead to fierce political debates, the mending of a soured friendship or a chorus of Turkish folk songs.

In warm weather, tables are set outside the historic wooden buildings, leaving a narrow passage where everyone is on the move. Gypsy clarinettists, violinists and drummers playing fasıl music roam from table to table in their efforts to charm an audience. Vendors sell all manner of kitsch and trinkets: bas-relief plastic pictures of Venice; miniature violins, lamps that light up and sing. Men with pink squawking duck puppets on one hand catch your eye in order to reveal a row of mounted prayer beads for sale on the other. Pot-bellied men pour shots of Chivas Regal and Johnny Walker, while children selling roses squeeze between waiters carrying platters of circassian chicken, octopus salad and other meze.

Unlike those in Çiçek Pasajı, the Nevizade meyhanes are generally quite good. **Boncuk** at number 19 offers Armenian specialities. **Imroz** at number 24 has splendid meze and seafood. Even in summer its rather unimpressive, fluorescent-lit multi-level interior is packed. Along Kamariye Sokak, **Saki** at number 19 has friendly service and lively clientele. The newer **Bade** next door at number 17 is the creation of five brothers from the Black Sea region. It offers a nice selection of of fish meze, fasıl music and a spacious multi-level interior with warm yellow walls and inlaid green and salmon floral tiles.

tightly packed most nights. Alcohol is served and the atmosphere gets boisterous. There's no better place in town to watch a live football match on TV.

Tarihi Selim Usta Sultanahmet Köftecisi

12 Divan Yolu, Sultanahmet (0212 513 1438). Tram Sultanahmet. **Open** 11am-11pm daily. **Main courses** $2.50. **No credit cards. Map** p303 N10.

Good eating options are thin on the ground in Sultanahmet, but this place has locals queuing out of the door. It serves only köfte, prepared over a great open-flame grill. Bread, green salad, *pilav* (rice) and *piyaz* (white-bean salad) are the only accompaniments. It's a formula that's been working for around 80 years and has spawned many imitators along this street, hence the label: 'Historical Sultan Ahmet Köfte Restaurant'.

Tike

Hacı Adil Caddesi 4, Aralık 1, 2 Levent (0212 281 8871). Metro 1 Levent. **Open** noon-3pm, 6pm-midnight Mon-Fri; noon-midnight Sat, Sun. **Main courses** $6. *Full dinner* $23. **Credit** AmEx, MC, V.

An upmarket take on the humble kebab joint. Despite uneven service from bow-tied waiters and charmless decor, Tike is packed even on weekdays with a casually chic, upwardly mobile clientele. The draw is marinated fatless lamb kebab, which is melt-in-your-mouth tender. Fill a thin pide bread full of it and garnish with the rocket, mint and parsley, or tomato and onion salad garnishes set on the table. Large garden terrace for summer dining.

Meyhanes

Traditionally associated with getting absolutely wrecked on rakı, the local anise-based alcohol, meyhanes are not the place for quiet romantic dining. Drinking and music are as much a part of the package as the food – reflected in the common practice of charging a set price that covers the meal, all drinks and entertainment. Favourites with the locals for birthdays and other ripping loose celebrations, meyhanes are definite good-time dining.

Asır

Kalyoncu Kulluğu Caddesi 94/1, off Tarlabaşı Bulvarı, Beyoğlu (0212 297 0557). **Open** noon-midnight daily. **Main courses** $11-$15. **Credit** MC, V. **Map** p308 N2.

No-frills basement venue on the fringes of one of central Istanbul's slightly rougher neighbourhoods. Unlike other meyhanes, popular for the music, this place is more famous for its meze, including an excellent *topik*, an Armenian purée of chicken, chickpea, cinnamon, currants and spices, and a fantastically good *ezme*, the ubiquitous dish of finely chopped tomato, hot pepper, onion and walnut. A serious drinking and smoking den.

Aynalı Meyhane

Tramvay Caddesi 104, Kuruçeşme (0212 265 9600).
Open 8pm-1.30am Mon-Sat; closed Sun. **Set menu**
$25. **No credit cards.**
Whitewashed walls, wooden floors and an oddment
of mirrors hung on the walls (aynalı means 'with
mirrors'). Simple but attractive with a menu rich in
unusual Aegean specialities, many vegetarian,
including *ısırgan otu* (nettles), *kayısılı kereviz* (celery
root with apricots), *cevizli karnıbahar* (cauliflower
and walnuts), and lamb flavoured with quinces. The
entertainment is a Gypsy band (9.30-11.30pm) with
a bitchy transvestite singer. Dance if you want to,
but take care not to upstage her or you risk a tongue
lashing. *See also p216.*

Degüstasyon

*Balık Pazarı, Sahne Sokak 41, Galatasaray, Beyoğlu
(0212 292 0667).* **Open** 11am-2am daily. **Set menu**
meat dishes $18; *fish* $25. **Credit** AmEx, DC, MC, V.
Map p308 N3.
Good, reliable Turkish cuisine, prepared by one of
Turkey's TV chefs at a modest place near the
bottom end of the Fish Market. It's a little less hectic
than Nevizade around the corner, but with some
seating in the passage for people-watching. There's
also a largish upstairs room with a terrace suitable
for groups. Service is friendly and there's *fasıl*
music on weekend nights after midnight. Popular
with the English-language teaching crowd.

Galata Restaurant

*Orhan Apaydın Sokak 11-13, Tünel, Beyoğlu (0212
293 1139).* **Open** 7.30pm-midnight Mon-Sat; closed
Sun. **Set menu** $16-$20. **Credit** MC, V. **Map** p308 M4.
Popular little place (reservations are a must at
weekends) in a restored historic building. The
warm, convivial atmosphere is enhanced by
nightly live music. Food is good if not exceptional
and, although it's a set meal, an array of meze are
presented from which to make a choice and there
are two alternative main dishes and desserts. *See
also p217.*

Ilhami'nin Yeri

Osmanzade Sokak 6, Ortaköy (0212 260 8080). **Open**
noon-1am daily. **Set menu** $15. **No credit cards.**
As Ortaköy has become increasingly gentrified its
meyhanes have disappeared; this is now the last
survivor. As if to make the case for its continued
existence, walls are bedecked with photos of
decades of happy diners. The food is better than
average with both fish and meat mains. In summer
there's an excellent upper floor terrace, perfect for
catching Bosphorus breezes on a balmy evening.
There's also *fasıl* music most nights, engendering
an animated atmosphere, not entirely matched by
the laidback waitering.

Kallavi 20

*Kallavi Sokak 20, off Istiklal Caddesi, Beyoğlu (0212
251 1010).* **Open** 7pm-2am Mon-Sat; closed Sun. **Set
menu** $21. **No credit cards. Map** 308 M3.
A strange arrangement of two dining rooms facing
each other across a narrow alley. In both the decor is
simple and uncluttered – all the better for shoving
tables aside later to create space to dance. The fixed
price for the set menu may seem high, but the food is
both excellent and endless, with course after varied
course. It also includes as much as wine or rakı as
you can drink. (Turks don't drink a huge amount, so
this isn't as rash an offer as it may seem.) Musicians
kick in around 9.30 to 10pm most nights. Much
singing and dancing generally ensues. Reservations
are a must. *See also p217.*

Özler

*Ibni Kemal Caddesi, Sirkeci (no telephone). Tram
Sirkeci.* **Open** 11am-midnight daily. **Main courses**
$4-$10. **No credit cards. Map** p303 N9.
Local workers and the occasional tourist from the
nearby hotels rub shoulders in this rough-and-
ready backstreet meyhane near Sirkeci station.
Meat, fish and kebabs are grilled on a large metal
range and on summer evenings tables choke the
narrow street. Things can get lively with the predominantly male moustachioed crowd when
there's a football match on TV, helped along by
generous quantities of rakı.

Refik

*Sofyalı Sokak 10-12, Asmalımescit, Beyoğlu (0212 243
2834).* **Open** noon-3pm, 6pm-midnight Mon-Fri; 6pm-
midnight Sat; closed Sun. **Full dinner** $20. **No credit
cards. Map** p308 M4.

Established in 1954, this is the quintessential back-street meyhane, and a great place to become immersed in meze culture and rakı. It's a famous leftist haunt with a devoted clientele of journalists and intellectuals presided over by gruff-voiced Refik Arslan, who still meets patrons at the door. Most of the regulars smoke and drink far more than they eat, but the restaurant is also known for its food. Many of the dishes come from the Black Sea region – fishy things – and choices are made from two glass-fronted refrigerators. Look and point. There's no music, as it would interfere with the intense conversation.

Yakup 2

Asmalımescit Sokak 35/37, Beyoğlu (0212 249 2925).
Open *Oct-May* noon-1.30am Mon-Sat; 6.30pm-1.30am Sun. *June-Sept* noon-1.30am Mon-Sat; closed Sun.
Main courses $4-$12. **Credit** AmEx, MC, V. **Map** p308 M4.

Owned by Yakup Arslan, brother of Refik (*see above*), this is a larger, more utilitarian-looking establishment, but draws a similar crowd. Again, it's very smoky and boozy, but the selection of mezes is vast and most are excellent. Forget mains, just take a table here and fill it with small plate after small plate of octopus salad, sautéed carrots in a yogurt garlic sauce, stuffed clams or Albanian-style liver. Generally has a great atmosphere.

Ottoman

Ottoman refers to the elaborate dishes that originated in the kitchens of the sultan's palace, mixing rice, fruit and vegetables with meat and the massive variety of fish that comes from Turkey's three surrounding seas. It's a broad cuisine and hard to define, but the common element is a decadent richness. Take, for example, *tavuk göğsü*, a delicate sweet pastry filled with a cream made from thinly shredded chicken breast, pulverised almonds and vanilla. This is a cuisine of excess.

Amedros

Hoca Rüstem Sokak 7, Sultanahmet (0212 522 8356).
Tram Sultanahmet. **Open** 10am-midnight daily.
Main courses $8-$12. **Credit** MC, V. **Map** p303 M10.

A European-style bistro in a side street just north of Divan Yolu that also does some interesting Ottoman dishes. House special, *testi kebabı*, is lamb roasted with vegetables in a sealed clay pot that is cracked open tableside. In summer, candle-lit tables are lined up out front; in winter the action retreats inside, where diners are warmed by a crackling fire.

Asithane

Kariye Hotel, Kariye Camii Sokak 18, Edirnekapı (0212 534 8414). **Open** noon-2pm, 7-11pm daily.
Main courses $8. **Credit** AmEx, DC, MC, V.
Map p304 D4.

Next to the Church of St Saviour in Chora (*see p90*) and housed in a 19th-century mansion restored as the Kariye Hotel (*see p49*), the Asithane gets four stars for its location alone, with an extra one added for the lovely summer terrace and rose garden. The menu changes regularly, but specialities are typically extravagant Ottoman offerings like *hünkar beğendi*, tender lamb on a purée of aubergine, fruit-and-meat stews, and some excellent desserts.

Feriye

Kabataş Kültür Merkezi, Çırağan Caddesi 124, Ortaköy (0212 227 2216). **Open** noon-3pm, 7-11pm daily. **Main courses** $16. **Credit** AmEx, DC, MC, V.

Vedat Başaran, co-owner and celebrity chef, has taken an obsession with Ottoman cooking to new heights, even going as far as to learn Arabic script so he could read old recipes in their original form. The result of his labours is a really mouth-watering menu featuring items which resemble traditional Turkish fare, but boast delicate touches that would be difficult to find elsewhere. Preparing the food is a labour of love, one dessert can take up to 18 hours to prepare. Feriye is spectacularly set in what used to be the Ottoman sultan's palatial grounds on the shores of the Bosphorus, where there are summer tables outside.

Hacı Abdullah

Sakızağacı Caddesi 17, off Istiklal Caddesi, Beyoğlu (0212 293 8561). **Open** 11am-10pm daily. **Main courses** $6. **Credit** AmEx, DC, V. **Map** p308 N3.

Lays claim to being the oldest restaurant in Istanbul – 110 years old – although the bright airiness and fresh painted walls lend the place an almost contemporary feel. Of the three rooms, by far the most pleasant is at the back, skylit with a glittering chandelier and pinkish tones. There is an English-language menu listing what is quite probably the choicest selection of ready-prepared Turkish/Ottoman dishes in town. It makes for a great lunch place. It is also renowned for its jarred preserved pickles and fruits, which make a very

colourful display in the front room, but they are somewhat bewilderingly described in the house brochure as 'the symbols of pooped politicians'.

Malta Köşkü

Yıldız Park, Beşiktaş (0212 258 9453). **Open** 9am-10pm Mon-Fri; 9am-noon, 1pm-9pm Sat, Sun. **Main courses** *buffet lunch or dinner* $13. **Credit** AmEx, MC, V.

It's not so much the food that counts in Malta Köşkü as the setting, an 1870 pavilion in Yıldız Park up on a hill to the right of the main entrance. Inside there is palatial decor, outside (during the spring and summer only) there's a terrace with an excellent view of the Bosphorus. The buffet lunch served at weekends is always popular. If there's no room, neighbouring Çadır Köşkü also does a buffet brunch on Sunday mornings from 10am to 1pm.

Pandeli

Mısır Çarşısı 1, Eminönü (0212 527 3909). **Open** noon-4pm Mon-Sat; closed Sun. **Main courses** $11. **Credit** MC, V. **Map** p302 L8.

Occupying a wonderful set of domed rooms above the entrance of the Egyptian Market (*see p81*) this place is very much the essence of genteel old Stamboul. Decorated throughout in blue-and-white tiling, it is worth a visit for the interior alone, but the food is also excellent, served by the grumpy waiters in white shirts. Though mainly known for its fish, particularly the sea bass, many prefer the lamb dishes. Try for a table in the front room with views out over the plaza to the Golden Horn. Note that it is open for lunch only.

Pandeli – very much the essence of genteel old Stamboul.

A semi-historic lunch option at **Kanaat Lokanta**. *See p138.*

Restaurants by area

Sultanahmet

Amedros (Ottoman p132); **Balıkçı Sabahattin** (Fish p118); **Develi** (Meat p129); **Dubb Indian Restaurant** (International p123); **Pudding Shop** (Turkish fast food p138); **Rami** (Ottoman p135); **Rumeli Café** (Turkish fast food p138); **Tarihi Selim Usta Sultanahmet Köftecisi** (Meat p130).

Eminönü

Konyalı (Turkish fast food p138); **Özler** (Meyhane p131); **Pandeli** (Ottoman p133).

Bazaar Quarter & west

Asithane (Ottoman p132); **Cennet** (Turkish fast food p136); **Darüzziyafe** (Turkish fast food p137).

Beyoğlu

Asır (Meyhane p130); **Badehane** (Vegetarian p138); **Degüstasyon** (Meyhane p131); **Ela** (Turkish fast food p137); **Eski Ingiliz Karakolu** (International p123); **Fıccın** (Turkish fast food p137); **C Fischer** (International p121); **Four Seasons** (International p125); **Galata Restaurant** (Meyhane p131); **Hacı Abdullah** (Ottoman p133); **Indian Restaurant** (Vegetarian p140); **Kallavi 20** (Meyhane p131); **Marko Paşa Şark Sofrası** (Turkish fast food p138); **Musa Ustam Ockbaşi** (Meat p129); **Nuh'un Ambarı** (Vegetarian p140); **Nature and Peace** (Vegetarian p140); **Parsifal** (Vegetarian p140); **Refik** (Meyhane p131); **Rejans** (International p126); **Safran** (Ottoman p135);

Şarabi (International p126); **Şemsiye** (Vegetarian p140); **Tadım** (Turkish fast food p138); **T-Square** (International p128); **Yakup 2** (Meyhane p132); **Zencefil** (Vegetarian p140).

Beşiktaş to Rumeli Hisarı

Ali Baba (Meat p129); **Aynalı Meyhane** (Meyhane see p131); **Çınar Restaurant** (Fish p119); **Feriye** (Ottoman p133); **Hanedan** (Fish p119); **Ilhami'nin Yeri** (Meyhane p131); **Laledan** (International p125); **Malta Köskü** (Ottoman p133); **Marina Balık Restaurant** (Fish p119); **Rumeli Iskele** (Fish p119); **Tuğra** (Ottoman p136); **Vogue** (International p128).

Maçka, Nişantaşı & Teşvikye

Chinese Unlimited (International p123); **Cookbook** (International p123); **Downtown** (International p123); **La Corne d'Or** (International p125); **Manhattan Café** (International p126); **Mezzaluna** (International p126); **Taşlık** (Ottoman p135).

Etiler & Levent

Le Cigare (International p125); **Le Select** (International p126); **Sunset Grill & Bar** (International p126); **Tike** (Meat p130); **Ulus 29** (International p128).

Asian Shore

Hercai (Vegetarian p138); **Kanaat Lokanta** (Turkish fast food p138).

Rami

6 Utangaç Sokak, Sultanahmet (0212 517 6593). Tram Sultanahmet. **Open** noon-midnight daily. **Main courses** $11. **Credit** MC, V. **Map** p303 N11.

Three-storey restaurant in a renovated Ottoman house. Sepia-toned nostalgia is big on the menu here, with an interior of antique furniture and old yellowing prints. Also gracing the walls are works by Uluer Rami, the Turkish impressionist after whom the restaurant is named. From the top-floor room (advance booking required) diners have front row seats for the post-dusk sound and light show at the Sultanahmet Mosque. The cuisine on offer is traditional Turkish.

Safran

Ceylan Inter-Continental, Asker Ocağı Caddesi 1, Taksim (0212 231 2121). **Open** 7-11pm daily. **Main courses** $9-$12. **Credit** AmEx, DC, MC, V. **Map** p307 P1.

The Safran provides proof that hotel restaurant food need not be bland and disappointing. On the top floor of the Ceylan (*see p55*) overlooking the Bosphorus, the restaurant serves a mixture of Turkish and harder-to-find Ottoman cuisine. These are dishes that require top-notch culinary skills and take hours to prepare. The result is a menu which boasts deliciously flavoured sauces and dishes with an unusual mixture of ingredients. The compulsory after-dinner Turkish coffee is enhanced by the restaurant's wide cigar selection.

Taşlık

Swissôtel Istanbul The Bosphorus, Bayıldım Caddesi 2, Maçka (0212 259 0101). **Open** 7pm-midnight Mon-Sat; closed Sun. **Main courses** $8-$11. **Credit** AmEx, DC, MC, V.

Serves up Turkish cuisine at its most refined, with a menu of intricately prepared, rarely seen dishes. Especially exotic are the delicately spiced fried prawns. The best main courses are those slowly cooked in the clay oven, such as *kuzu incik*, lamb with rosemary and tomato. Also recommended is *folyoda kaşarlı piliç*, a chicken stew with mild cheese melted over the top. The wine list is interesting, with little known wines from south-eastern Turkey, pricey but better than some more familiar Turkish labels.

Eat, Drink, Shop

Tuğra

Çırağan Palace Hotel Kempinski, Çırağan Caddesi 84, Beşiktaş (0212 258 3377). **Open** 7pm-midnight daily. **Main courses** $13-$23. **Credit** AmEx, DC, MC, V.

The food isn't as good as it should be, given that this is the city's top hotel (*see p55*), but the setting in a former palace harem overlooking the Bosphorus can't be faulted. The Ottoman-inspired menu is *à la carte*, but save space for desserts, as they tend to be the part of the meal that lives up to expectations.

Turkish fast food

A *lokanta* is the basic Turkish restaurant, the equivalent of the Western cafeteria. Food is usually *hazır yemek* (ready food) laid out in a bain-marie. No Turkish language skills are necessary; just look and point. Standard dishes include meat and vegetable stews, *çorba* (soup), rice, potato purées and salads. Core trade is often local shoppers and office workers and there's a rapid turnover, so you can be pretty sure that the food is fresh.

Cennet

90 Divan Yolu, Çemberlitaş (0212 513 1416). Tram Çemberlitaş. **Open** 8am-11pm daily. **Main courses** $2.50-$4. **No credit cards. Map** p303 M10.

Unashamedly touristy, with cushions strewn around low wooden tables and women in 'traditional' costume preparing food cross-legged at metal stoves. But if you can stand the manufactured atmosphere, it's as good a place as any to try

What's on the menu

Useful phrases

Can I see a menu?
Menüye bakabilir miyim?
Do you have a table for (number) people?
(Number) kişilik masanız var mı?
I want to book a table for (time) o'clock.
Saat (time) için bir masa ayırmak istiyorum.
I'll have (name of food).
Ben (name of food) istiyorum.
I'll have (name of food) without salt.
Ben tuzsuz (name of food) istiyorum.
I'll have (name of food) without oil.
Ben yagsiz (name of food) istiyorum.
I'm a vegetarian.
Et yemiyorum.
Can I have an ashtray?
Kültablası alabilir miyim?
Can I have the bill please?
Hesap, lütfen.

Basics

menu **menü**
cover **couver**, usually for bread and water
service charge **servis**
glass **bardak**
cup **fincan**
knife **bıçak**
fork **çatal**
spoon **kaşık**
napkin **peçete**
plate **tabak**
starter **meze**

Main courses

dessert **tatlı**
breakfast **kahvaltı**
lunch **öğle yemeği**
dinner **akşam yemeği**

Menu

baked **fırında pişmiş**
boiled **kaynamiş**
fried **kızarmiş**
grilled **ızgara**
roast **kavrulmuş**
water **su**
milk **süt**
fresh-squeezed orange juice **taze portakal suyu**
apple juice **elma suyu**
cherry juice **vişne suyu**
apricot juice **kayısı suyu**
peach juice **şeftali suyu**
red wine **kırmızı şarap**
white wine **beyaz şarap**
beer **bira**
tea **çay**
coffee **kahve**; Turkish coffee **Türk kahvesi**; without sugar **sade**; a little sugar **az şekerli**; medium sweet **orta şekerli**; sweet **şekerli**
bread **ekmek**; thin flat bread **pide** or **lavaş**
brown bread **kepekli ekmek**
rice **pilav**
bulgar **bulgur pilavi**
soup **çorba**
pasta **makarna**
fruit **meyve**
hardboiled/softboiled egg **katı yumurta/ rafadan yumurta**
beef **dana**
lamb **kuzu**
chicken **tavuk**
fish **balık**
spinach **ıspanak**
okra **bamya**
peas **bezelye**
peppers **biber**
tomatoes **domates**

solid Anatolian staples such as *gözleme*, filled filo-pastry pancakes, or *mantı*, small parcels of dough-wrapped meat, washed down with *ayran* (a watery yoghurt drink).

Darüzziyafe

Şifahane Sokak 6, Süleymaniye (0212 511 8414). Tram Üniversite. **Open** noon-11pm daily. **Average** $15. **Credit** AmEx, MC, V. **Map** p302 J8.

Almost half a millennium after Sinan designed the Süleymaniye Mosque (*see p80*), the kitchen is still in working order, cooking up meals for diners in the arched halls or, when the weather is particularly good, seated out in the courtyard under the branches of an ancient plane tree. The food is fairly unexceptional, but the location and the ambience are unique.

Ela

Jurnal Sokak 4, Tünel, Beyoğlu (no telephone). **Open** noon-11pm daily. **Main courses** $4-$10. **No credit cards.** **Map** p308 M4.

Serves a handful of dishes freshly prepared each morning. Nothing too ambitious, just typically good solid Turkish fare, such as stuffed vegetables served with rice and whole wheat bread. Patrons mostly lunching artists who have nearby studios.

Fıccın

Kallavi Sokak 13/1, Beyoğlu (0212 293 3786). **Open** Nov-May 11am-6pm Mon-Fri; 9am-5pm Sat; closed Sun. June-Oct 11am-6pm Mon-Fri; closed Sat, Sun. **Main courses** $1.50-$3. **No credit cards.** **Map** p308 M3.

A small lunchtime venue so successful that in recent years it has been expanded to occupy three

carrots **havuç**
onions **soğan**
spring onion **demet soğan**
potatoes **patates**
arrugula **roka**
zucchini squash **kabak**
aubergine **patlıcan**
cucumbers **salatalık**
white beans **kuru fasülye**
red beans **barbunya**
broad beans **bakla**
lentils **mercimek**
purslane **semizotu**
lettuce **marul**
banana **muz**
apples **elma**
oranges **portakal**
cherries **kiraz**
grapes **üzüm**
watermelon **karpuz**
honeydew melon **kavun**
hazelnuts **fındık**
walnuts **ceviz**
peanuts **fıstık**
pistachio nuts **şam fıstığı**
cheese **peynir**
yogurt **yoğurt**
garlic **sarımsak**
salt **tuz**
red/black/hot pepper **pul/kara/acı biber**
thyme **kekik**
mint **nane**
lemon **limon**
honey **bal**
mustard **hardal**
ketchup **ketçap**
ice-cream **dondurma**
cake **kek**

Some Turkish dishes

Zeytinyağli cold dishes with olive oil.
Imambayıldı aubergines cooked with onion and tomato and olive oil, served cold.
Kısır Turkish tabouleh salad with parsley, bulgar, lemon, tomato, onion, olive oil, pomegranate, mint.
Çoban salata shepherd's salad, tomatoes, cucumbers, hot peppers and onions with lemon and olive oil.
Mücver deep-fried patties made with grated courgette in a batter of egg and flour. Kind of like potato pancakes.
Karnıyarık baked aubergines stuffed with minced meat, onion, tomato spices.
Börek flaky savoury pastry with parsley and/or white cheese, minced meat, spinach, other vegetables.
Dolma vegetable such as cabbage, grape leaves, pepper or squash, served cold and stuffed with rice, pine nuts, currants and spices. Served hot, they're usually also stuffed with minced meat.
Çerkez tavuğu shredded chicken served cold in a walnut cream sauce.
Köfte usually meatballs, though some varieties come without meat, such as mercimek köftesi, fried lentil balls.
Kebap sliced, diced, chunks or minced meat cooked a variety of ways.
Lahmacun spiced minced meat on a thin crust pizza-like bread called pide.
Pirzola lamb chops.
Güveç casserole cooked in a clay pot that seals in the flavour and tenderises whatever is inside. A particularly tasty one is **Karides güveç**, shrimps cooked with onions in a peppery tomato sauce with melted cheese on top.

separate premises on the same street. Each has the same simple menu of tried and tested Turkish favourites such as *mercimek çorbası* (lentil soup), and *biber dolması* (stuffed peppers).

Kanaat Lokanta

Selmanı Pak Caddesi 25, Üsküdar (0216 333 3791). **Open** 7am-10.30pm daily. **Main courses** $3-$4. **No credit cards. Map** p310 X2.

Bustling, semi-historic place with courtly waiters. Despite being ready prepared, mains include some fairly ambitious fare, such as *elbasan tava*, large chunks of beef cooked with kaşar cheese, eggs and vegetables. A good lunch option when sightseeing in this part of town.

Konyalı

Mimar Kemalettin Caddesi 5, Sirkeci, Eminönü (0212 513 9610). **Open** 7am-9.30pm daily. **Main courses** $2.50-$4. **No credit cards. Map** p303 M8.

A city institution specialising in *börek*, pastry triangles stuffed with minced meat or any one of a dozen different kinds of cheese. There are standing-only counters to eat at, but most of the trade is takeaway. Photographic evidence would seem to suggest that both Haile Selassie and Benazir Bhutto are *börek* fans, although their snacks were consumed at the Konyalı's restaurant at Topkapı Palace, and not at this humble little place opposite Sirkeci station.

Marko Paşa Şark Sofrası

Sadri Alışık Sokak 8, Beyoğlu (0212 252 8080). **Open** 8am-midnight daily. **Main courses** $1-$4. **Credit** AmEx, MC, V. **Map** p309 O3.

Perennially popular lunchtime spot just off Istiklal Caddesi specialising in *gözleme*, filled filo-pastry pancakes. Popular fillings are any kind of cheese, particularly *çökelek*, a dry cottage cheese, mince meat (*kıymalı*), mashed potato (*patatesli*) or spinach (*ıspanaklı*). This is food traditionally associated with country markets where local women do the rolling, filling and grilling on the spot, which is why there's a girl in 'village' dress sitting in the window.

Pudding Shop

18 Divan Yolu, Sultanahmet (no phone). Tram Sultanahmet. **Open** 7am-11pm daily. **Main courses** $5-$8. **Credit** MC, V **Map** p303 N10.

Pushing your tray along the stainless steel counter, it's hard to believe that this is the place that fed a generation of travellers heading out on the hippy trail 30 years ago (and was immortalised in *Midnight Express*). Still run by the Çölpan family, it continues to serve cheap, basic and unthreatening Turkish fare to foreigners and is exceptional only as an historical footnote.

🐝 Rumeli Café

Ticarethane Sokak 8, off Divan Yolu, Sultanahmet (0212 512 0008). Tram Sultanahmet. **Open** 10am-2am daily. **Main courses** $5-$8. **Credit** AmEx, DC, MC, V. **Map** p303 M10.

A former printworks with an atmospheric interior of unclad brickwork and stained floorboards

turned into a café-restaurant by the owners of the Nomade Hotel (*see p54*) with the help of the architect who designed the Empress Zoe (*see p49*). Tables are put out on Ticarethane, a pedestrianised street running north off Divan Yolu, during summer, while in winter there's a crackling open fire inside. Food is traditional Turkish with a Greek/Mediterranean twist and is very good. One of the few places in Sultanahmet we can wholeheartedly recommend.

Tadım

Meşelik Sokak 36/1, Taksim (0212 252 0923). **Open** 7am-7pm Mon-Sat; closed Sun. **Main courses** $3-$5. **No credit cards. Map** p309 O2.

Basement *lokanta* with unappealing exterior disguising a cheerful, brightly coloured interior. Standard array of choices, including soups, stews, a few vegetarian options, as well as meat from the grill and desserts. A constant stream of delivery boys heading out the door with trays on their shoulder testify to the popularity of this place with workers in neighbouring offices.

Vegetarian

For piscivores and meat-eaters Istanbul is heaven, but until recently the idea of a meal without flesh was an utterly alien concept. Vegetarianism was viewed as some kind of mental disorder. Now a handful of vegetarian restaurants have opened, although some of these places don't feel entirely comfortable with the idea and keep a bit of meat on the menu just to be on the safe side. Some non-vegetarian places are also worth visiting for their meat-free dishes, including Ela (*see page 137*) on Jurnal Sokak in Tünel. Note that much of Turkey's produce is organic by default as many farmers can't afford expensive sprays and fertilisers.

Badehane

General Yazgan Sokak 5, Tünel (0212 249 0550). **Open** 11am-2am daily. **Main courses** $2.50-$4. **No credit cards. Map** p308 M4.

Lovingly prepared salads and stews, Turkish fare and a range of exotic culinary experiments. On Wednesdays a guest chef is invited to cook for a full house of eager diners. Often a group of musicians will show up and sing for their supper and the atmosphere is that of a private party.

Hercai

Dumlupınar Sokak 21, Kadıköy, Asian Shore (0216 414 2826). **Open** 10am-10pm daily. **Main courses** $1.50-$2.50. **No credit cards. Map** p311 W7.

Occupies an entire three-storey 19th-century house. Admire original cinema posters while dining on the likes of *imam bayıldı* ('the imam fainted'), a dish made from aubergines cooked gently in olive oil and served cold. The *mantı* (Turkish ravioli) and spinach quiche are also recommended. Good value, with great service and a peaceful atmosphere.

Eat, Drink, Shop

Some sing for their
supper at **Badehane**.
See p138.

Zencefil – ever-changing daily specials keep regulars coming back.

Indian Restaurant

Zambak Sokak 8, Beyoğlu (0212 292 3180). **Open**
noon-11pm Mon-Sat; closed Sun. **Main courses** $8-
$9. **Credit** MC, V. **Map** p309 O2.
Indian paraphernalia and a lingering aroma of burning incense. It was totally vegetarian, but Banu, the
owner, has succumbed to pressure from carnivores
and added chicken to her menu. Mulligatawny soup
is excellent, along with good samosas, tasty biriyanis and some tongue-numbing curries.

Nuh'un Ambarı

Yeni Çarşı Caddesi 54, Galatasaray (0212 292 9272).
Open noon-7.30pm Mon-Sat; closed Sun. **Main
courses** $2.50. **Credit** V. **Map** p308 N3.
Istanbul's first fully organic wholefood restaurant
does a roaring trade at lunchtime serving special
tofu salad and tasty herbed potatoes with glasses of
Turkish-produced soya milk and freshly squeezed
organic fruit juice. Home-baked breads are a speciality. Out front is a health-food shop (*see p170*).
Even the walls are built with hand-made mud
bricks. As right-on as it gets.

Nature and Peace

*Büyükparmakkapı Sokak 21/23, Beyoğlu (0212 252
8609).* **Open** 11am-11pm daily. **Main courses** $7-
$10. **Credit** AmEx, MC, V. **Map** p309 O3.
Bunches of dried herbs and vegetables scattered
around the walls create a warm country kitchen
ambience. Check out the blackboard specials before
you look at the menu. Good things to go for include
green lentil patties, the house salad and falafel. The
cheesecake is the best in Istanbul and the pumpkin
pie is also good when in season.

Parsifal

Kurabiye Sokak 13, Beyoğlu (0212 245 2588).
Open 11am-11pm daily. **Main courses** $4.
Credit AmEx, MC, V. **Map** p309 O2.
Veggie delights such as leek and soya burgers,
spinach pie and broccoli au gratin. Helped along
with a little French influence in decor and design, it
fills up quickly most nights, though a reservation is
rarely necessary. Try the mushroom soup and see
the blackboard for the daily special. Dessert of
choice is banana crêpes.

Şemsiye

Şehbender Sokak 18, Tünel (0212 292 2046).
Open 9am-10pm Mon-Sat; closed Sun.
Main courses $2.50-$4. **Credit** AmEx, MC, V.
Map p308 M4.
Traditional Turkish cuisine but without the meat.
Stuffed vine leaves and yoghurt sauce or sautéed
vegetables and rice. All food is home-made and the
service is impeccable.

Zencefil

Kurabiye Sokak 3, Beyoğlu (0212 244 4082).
Open 9.30am-10.30pm Mon-Sat; closed Sun.
Main courses $4. **No credit cards. **Map** p309 O2.
The house salad with soya beans and beetroot is
particularly outstanding, as are the vegetable
lasagna and the potatoes with mushrooms. Bread is
home-baked. The high quality and ever-changing
daily specials keep regulars coming back. Wine by
the carafe or home-made lemonade in summer. For
dessert the lemon pie is delicious. Food to linger
over; not the best place if in a hurry.

Cafés & Bars

Coffee slowly makes way for cocktails in Istanbul's thriving café culture.

The Turks must be wondering what's going on. Cappuccino, latte, frappé, decaf... What is all this? Lukewarm, fluffy, milky, watered-down travesties of the hard-edged bitter beverage that the Ottoman empire first introduced to Europe, and hence America, in the 17th century. But then coffee Turkish style is something of an acquired taste. 'Of all the unchristian beverages that ever passed my lips,' wrote Mark Twain, 'Turkish coffee is the worst. The cup is small, it is smeared with grounds; the coffee is black, thick, unsavoury of smell, and execrable in taste. The bottom of the cup has a muddy sediment in it half an inch deep. This goes down your throat, and portions of it lodge by the way, and produce a tickling aggravation that keeps you barking and coughing for an hour.' Maybe the poor Turks have been crying out all along for Aroma or Starbucks to come rescue them from gritty caffeine hell.

While the Western coffee chains have yet to arrive – and long may they keep their distance – the last decade has seen the continued demise of traditional coffeehouse culture in favour of a cornucopia of more cosmopolitan cafés keeping pace with all the new-fangled caffeine fads. For the modern Istanbulite, true Turkish coffee (Türk kahvesi) has been relegated to the status of a post-prandial sip.

As coffee-drinking habits have changed, so too have attitudes to alcohol. Turks may be Muslims but they've always enjoyed the alcoholic buzz. In times past, few Muslims would risk being accused of encouraging other Koran-fearing types to drink, so the sale of liquor was entrusted to Istanbul's Christian Greeks. They ran the city's *meyhanes* (tavernas), where meze provided excuses for round after round of rakı, the local aniseed spirit. Times change. Meyhanes are still a vital part of the scene but it's no longer necessary to excuse the booze with a plate of feta cheese and bread.

ISTANBUL GETS A LIFE

When a tentative first few Western-style bar-cafés opened for business in the 1990s they triggered a revolution in the city's social life: it suddenly got one. Ten years ago the option of going out to drink without having to dine simply did not exist. Now, a single sidestreet off Istiklal Caddesi can be crammed with so many continental cafés, dive bars, folk music

Top five — Bars

Bilsak Fifth Floor
Hamburg brothel bar chic combined with stunning views. See page 143.

Cambaz
Dancing on the tables and fold-up cinema seats. See page 145.

Kaktüs
Afternoons measured out in coffeespoons, evenings lost in beer. See page 148.

Pano
Decent house plonk and a vibrant taverna atmosphere. See page 151.

Tophane Nargile cafés
Istanbul's 24-hour smoking zone. See page 146 **Hava Nargile**.

joints, techno clubs and wine bars that if you attempted to have a drink in each one you'd pass out before you got halfway.

Youth lends the scene freshness. There is no such thing as an archetypal Istanbul venue. There are bars and there are cafés but most places blur the line between the two, serving coffee and food throughout the day, getting increasingly smoky and alcoholic as the evening wears on. When it comes to decor, anything goes. The Parisian Left Bank look is popular, best experienced at places like **Kaktüs** (*see page 148*), **Pia** (*see page 151*) and **Cadde-i Kebir** (*see page 145*), and there are wannabe sophisticates such as **Dulcinea** (*see page 146*) and **Serendip** (*see page 151*), but most places are true one-offs, reflections of the personalities, finances and other resources of whoever runs the place. **Eski Beyrut** (*see page 147*) is a student squat with beer, **Cambaz** (*see page 145*)

▶ For details of **music clubs and other venues**, see chapters **Music: Rock, World & Jazz** and **Music: Turkish**. For details of **late clubs** see chapter **Nightlife**. For **gay bars and clubs**, see chapter **Gay & Lesbian**.

is an ongoing house party, **Bilsak Fifth Floor** (co-owned by a film actress and a singer; *see page 143*) is cabaret. What these last three have in common, along with a great many other Istanbul bars and cafés, is a rough-edged and opportunist air, everybody trying their hand, chancing it. Of course, the flip side is a high fatality rate. Your favourite bar today may well be gone tomorrow. All the more reason to live it up now.

Apart from those listed here, other places that are possibles for a drink include jazz café **Gramofon** (*see page 212*), rock bars **Buddha** (*see page 210*), **Hayal Kahvesi** (*see page 207*) and **Kemanci** (*see page 208*), and pre-club venues **Cantina** (*see page 222*) and **Godet** (*see page 223*).

Sultanahmet

The strange case of Sultanahmet: a district packed with hotels, and hence also of tourists knackered after a hard day's sightseeing and hoping for a convivial place to slump and order a drink, and it's just not happening. Other than a row of over-priced cafés on the Hippodrome, the odd backpacker joint on Akbıyık Caddesi and the fall-back of the hotel lobby bar, there is little that could be held up as any sort of a nightlife scene. Instead, most visitors opt for jumping into a taxi and heading across the Golden Horn to Beyoğlu. That's the option we recommend. If for some reason you are tied to Sultanahmet for the evening, as well as the places below consider also giving your lungs a workout at one of the nargile cafés (*see page 146* **Hava Nargile**).

Cheers

Akbıyık Caddesi 20 (no phone). Tram Sultanahmet. **Open** 10-2am daily. Licensed. **No credit cards.** **Map** p303 N11.

Akbıyık is backpacker boulevard, lined with cut-rate travel agencies, hostels and last-ditch dining options. Bars are as transient as the clientele they serve and Cheers is just the latest name to be attached to this particular venue. But whatever the name, the place stays the same: small, cramped and crowded most nights with an international mêlée made giddy on loud rock, the cheapest beer in town and drinks specials. On the right night it feels like a student house party; on the wrong night you may find yourself reduced to trading tales of dormitories and dysentery with a Danish round-the-worlder.

Sultan Pub

Divan Yolu 2 (0212 528 1719). Tram Sultanahmet. **Open** 9-1am daily. Licensed. **Credit** AmEx, MC, V. **Map** p303 N10.

About the only streets in Sultanahmet offering any signs of life are tiny Seftalı Sokak, at the bottom end of Divan Yolu, and Ticarethane Sokak, one block back. On Seftalı two or three small bar/restaurants have tables on the street. One of them is a crowded little cellar dive with loud music, another is the Sultan, which proudly boasts to have been around since 1975 – a claim put in context by its location opposite the entrance to cisterns dating back 1,500 years. Not that the Sultan has much else going for it, but if you can snag a pavement seat with a view across the Hippodrome to Sultanahmet Mosque then there are worse places to nurse a beer.

Yeşil Ev Beer Garden

Kabasakal Caddesi 5 (0212 517 6785). Tram Sultanahmet. **Open** 8.30am-11pm daily. Licensed. **Credit** AmEx, MC, V. **Map** p303 N10.

A pretty garden filled with towering laurel, linden and horse chestnut trees belonging to the Yeşil Ev guesthouse (*see page 47*). It's a beautiful setting, quite unique for Istanbul, and easily the finest place for an early evening drink anywhere this side of the Golden Horn. In winter guests are sheltered in a large glasshouse-type structure with luxurious hanging gardens. Pricey but worth it.

Alkazar Café – nave-like space. *See p143.*

Beyoğlu

For most of its recent history Beyoğlu was a
rundown district of fading 19th-century
grandeur filled with dine-at-your-peril kebab
joints, coffeehouses and *paviyon* (bellydance
dives with illegal prostitution). It was only after
Hayal Kahvesi (*see page 207*) opened in 1992,
followed the next year by **Kaktüs** (*see page 148*),
that the area took off as the central nightlife
district it is today. A few of the sleazier joints have
been around forever and should still be given a
wide berth but they've been joined by a flood of
new bars and clubs burrowed into old spaces.

The greatest variety is found in the streets
that run off either side of Istiklal Caddesi up
at the Taksim end, with venues that meet
the needs of every tribe. Africans, goths,
rastas, the arty set, Anatolian immigrants,
intellectuals and football fans all congregate
here in an atmospheric mix, often sharing the
same bar space rather than clumping into
cliques. The spread of new hangouts is
bringing new life to areas that have been
dormant for decades. A short walk south, the
even narrower and more winding backstreets
of Çukurcuma, Asmalımescit and Tünel
harbour a quieter array of places, targeting
niche markets such as jazz fans, art aficionados
and lovers of Aegean singalongs.

35mm

Istiklal Caddesi 24/26, Beyoğlu (0212 243 5530).
Open 9.30am-midnight daily. Not licensed. **Credit**
MC, V. **Map** p309 O2.
First-floor house café of the AFM Fitaş cinema multiplex (*see p188*), done out in minimal black and
chrome decor with diner-style banquettes, counter
seating and unnecessary movie stills. The wide
floor-to-ceiling windows on two sides give you the
impression that you're sitting in a glass box. Seats
overlook the cinema foyer on one side, Istiklal
Caddesi on the other – views that typically provide
better entertainment than the bubblegum usually
screening next door. No booze, but coffee, various
teas, sandwiches, cakes and pastries.

Alkazar Café

Istiklal Caddesi 179, Beyoğlu (0212 249 7297). **Open**
9am-midnight Mon-Fri, 10am-midnight Sat, Sun.
Licensed. **Credit** MC, V. **Map** p308 N3.
Period 1940s-style café attached to the Alkazar cinema. Wonderful long dark-wood bar that cries out
for a tall, slim lady who knows how to hold a cigarette
and can teach you how to whistle. Lunch-time menu
is adventurous international and excellent, although
the cold stone, plain walls and nave-like central
space make for an uncomfortably ecclesiastical air
when empty. Better to visit in the evenings when the
place fills with early cinema-goers, young professionals and semi-intellectuals. Waiters have a good
sideline in touting tickets for sold-out screenings.

Bilsak Fifth Floor – committed barflies.

Baykuş

Bekar Sokak 22, Beyoğlu (0212 292 8844). **Open** 11-
2am daily. Licensed. **Credit** MC, V. **Map** p309 O2.
Push aside red velvet drapes to enter – a suitably
dramatic touch of the owner, theatre actress Ülkü
Duru. Inside varnished plank floors, turquoise banquettes, ochre walls, original art and light jazz on
the CD player add up to a sophisticated ambience
aimed at pleasing a theatre/publishing/performing
arts crowd. Also very popular with French types
from the cultural centre round the corner. The menu
has suitably highfalutin leanings and includes
items like carpaccio and fancy pastas. Hosts occasional party nights when all pretensions are cast
aside and the place really kicks loose.

Bilsak Fifth Floor

5th floor, Soğancı Sokak 7, off Sıraselviler Caddesi,
Cihangir (0212 293 3774). **Open** 5pm-2am Mon-Sat;
closed Sun. Licensed. **Credit** MC, V. **Map** p309 O3.
The Bilsak building is an anonymous apartment
block on a quiet backstreet in a residential part of
town. It is not the kind of place you find by chance
but plenty in the know beat a regular path here.
Ground floor is Bar Bahçe (*see page 197*), Istanbul's
best gay bar, while a ride up in the lift is the 'Fifth
Floor' haunt of artists, minor film types, up-and-
coming actresses and committed barflies. The food
here is excellent but we come for the leopardskin
sofas and thick red curtains, a bar that can cope
with cocktails and the views over a nightlit city that

glimmers like smouldering embers. It's a great 'last one of the night' stop-off, when long past the pumpkin hour there's often just you, the view and a barman who's never in too much of a hurry to call time.

The Brasserie

Marmara Hotel, Taksim Square, Taksim (0212 251 4696). **Open** 6.30am-11pm daily. Licensed. **Credit** AmEx, DC, MC, V. **Map** p309 P2.

Spacious room with great glass windows overlooking the square – not that it's much of a view – and which never feels crowded even though usually filled to capacity. It has bit of a démodé 1970s feel redolent of a department store cafeteria, but the constant chatter and clatter of crockery makes for a lively air. Favoured by ladies with poodles and shopping bags but no longer by journalists since a *Cumhuriyet* writer was assassinated by a bomb here in the mid-1990s. The bakery is one of the best for takeaway chocolate, croissants, cakes and pastries. Small outdoor terrace opens in fine weather.

Cadde-i-Kebir

Imam Adnan Sokak 7, Beyoğlu (0212 251 7113). **Open** 8-2am daily. Licensed. **Credit** AmEx, MC, V. **Map** p309 O2.

Laid-back continental-style bar-café owned by film-maker Reis Çelik, attracting a fairly mature casual crowd, and a decent place for lunch or coffee. It comes into its own in the warmer months when the front is opened out to the street. Don't like the barman's choice of music? Move up to the front and listen to the frenetic *halk müziği* booming from the café next door. On summer nights its roof terrace opens up on the building opposite (No.10), which is a pleasant place with trailing greenery that you can usually count on being less crowded than the terraces at Cambaz or Life next door.

Café Frappé

Bekar Sokak 21, Beyoğlu (0212 293 1524). **Open** 10am-midnight daily. Not licensed. **No credit cards**. **Map** p309 O2.

Intimate is the word. Up a creaky staircase, Frappé is a small room with four tables, bare wooden floorboards, a bright red vintage fridge and walls crowded with cherubs bearing bottles and swirling clouds in nicotine tones. In the late afternoon the place fills with high school kids sneaking crafty fags out of view of the adults and weaning themselves on to coffee with cold frappés. It scores highly for good strong filter coffee, delivered to the table in its glass beaker. Large selection of teas too, along with sandwiches, salads and desserts. Gay-friendly scene by night.

Cambaz

Hacı Ahmet Sokak 2, off Kurabiye Sokak, Beyoğlu (0212 243 5473). **Open** 2.30pm-2am daily. Licensed. **No credit cards**. **Map** p309 O2.

There's no sign on the door at street level (it's first on the right coming from Kurabiye), and when you push the door open, the hallway inside is dark and positively Dostoyevskian, while the helter-skelter staircase is plain scary. But one floor up Cambaz ('Trapeze Artist') is one of the most extrovert bars in town. Heavily patronised by colleagues of owner Rıza Sönmez, a young actor and aspiring producer, its decor is brash (film paraphernalia and cinema seats), the music is full-volume and the patrons are

The intimate **Café Frappé** – four tables, bare floorboards and good, strong filter coffee.

Hava nargile

A nargile is a waterpipe. A hookah. A 'hubbly-bubbly', if you must. It's been smoked in Turkey since the beginning of the 17th century, despite religious authorities periodically denouncing the practice and calling for it to be banned. Murat IV (1623-40) went as far as passing the death sentence on anyone caught having so much as a quick puff.

In the late 19th and early 20th century, nargile smoking was the fashionable high-society thing to do, particularly among women. That fad passed and in republican Istanbul the nargile was relegated to a pastime of the peasantry.

Why now in the 21st century it should suddenly be making a comeback is anybody's guess. But in the last couple of years a whole slew of cafés devoted to the waterpipe have opened, with more likely to follow. A few of these are aimed squarely at tourists but otherwise most custom comes from students.

Nargile tobacco is typically soaked in molasses or apple juice, giving it a slightly sweetened flavour, but you can get it straight and strong by asking for 'tömbeki'.

Nargile cafés serve tea and coffee but no alcohol. Prices are around $2 to $3 a pipe, and a smoke lasts a good hour or more. Contrary to popular misconception, hashish is not an option. Also no longer on the menu is the old Ottoman blend of opium, perfume and crushed pearls. Shame, but there you go.

The best place to sample a nargile is on the nameless pedestrian strip off Tophane Iskelesi behind the Nusretiye Mosque (map p307 O5). Until recently there was nothing but a row of small shops down here, but now it's lined with nothing but nargile cafés and at any given moment, day or night, there might be upwards of 300-400 people here, an extraordinary mix of students and couples and families, all belching forth great clouds of grey smoke. It's a fine place to wind down in the early hours after a night out in Beyoğlu. Otherwise, you might try one of the following:

Enjoyer Café

İncili Çavus Sokak 25, Sultanahmet (0212 512 8759). Tram Sultanahmet. **Open** *summer* 9am-2am daily; *winter* 9am-midnight daily. Not licensed. **No credit cards. Map** p303 N10.
Most touristed of the nargile cafés, lying on the pedestrianised street just north of Divan Yolu. Avoid the fruity tobaccos.

Meşale

Arasta Bazaar 45, Sultanahmet (0212 518 9562). Tram Sultanahmet. **Open** 24 hours daily. Not licensed. **No credit cards. Map** p303 N11.
A sunken café beside an arcade of tourist shops but quite pleasant late on when the shutters have come down and locals replace the visitors. Dervish dancing shows on Friday, Saturday and Sunday nights between 7pm and 10pm. In winter Meşale relocates to Mahmut Paşa Yokusu 13, off the Hippodrome.

Erenler Çay Bahçesi

Çorlulu Ali Paşa Medresesi, Yeniçeriler Caddesi 36/28, Beyazıt (0212 528 3785). Tram Beyazıt. **Open** *summer* 7am-3am daily; *winter* 7am-midnight daily. Not licensed. **No credit cards. Map** p302 L10.
Occupying the courtyard of an old Ottoman seminary, Erenler comprises a collection of low tables and benches under ivy-hung trellises. Beautiful. Despite the signs advertising 'Magic Waterpipe Garden' few tourists actually visit and instead it's filled with students from nearby Beyazıt University.

even louder. If you've ever wanted to stand on a tabletop and sing pop with young Turks you may well get your opportunity here. During summer the bar moves two storeys up to a roof terrace, which also gets jam-packed. Sönmez also has plans to open a separate venue, 'Kuklaci' (Puppeteer), on two floors of the same building.

Cep Art Café

Asmalımescit 41, Tünel (0212 292 0038). **Open** 8am-midnight daily. Licensed. **No credit cards. Map** p308 M4.
Beyoğlu's Asmalımescit district is becoming the Bohemian bit of town, the place where art and alcohol mix, and no more so than at this place. Behind a vivacious crimson exterior with potted plants and two small tables out front, Cep fills two floors of a late 19th-century house. Art on the walls is complemented by eccentric furnishings such as old card and sewing-machine tables, and shelves crammed with copper and tin pots. Sounds hoary and contrived, but it works. Other nice touches include backgammon boards and good home-cooking.

Dulcinea

Meşelik Sokak 20, Beyoğlu (0212 245 1071/ café@dulcinea.org). **Open** 10.30-2am daily. Licensed. **Credit** MC, V. **Map** p309 O2.
Upmarket place opposite the leafy graveyard of the Greek Haghia Triada church frequented by people

who like to dress in labels, talk loudly on cell phones and drop big bucks on Martinis. Spacious interior of blond wood, leather and tiled floor is the closest Istanbul gets to Conran. It's too haughty to encourage dropping in for coffee, but it does superb, surprisingly reasonably priced food from a menu divided into manic/classic/active sections with detailed descriptions including preparation time. Evenings it gets crowded with conspicuous consumers and takes on the character of a London City wine bar. There are resident DJs at the weekend (*see page 222*) and the basement hosts occasional dance workshops and acts as an art exhibition gallery.

Eski Beyrut

Imam Adnan Sokak 28/2, Beyoğlu (0212 293 4921). **Open** 11-2am daily. Licensed. **No credit cards.** **Map** p309 O2.

Student drinking dive concealed behind a yellow grilled door and up a steep flight of stairs. It serves very cheap drinks – about a dollar a beer – drawing overwhelmingly dense crowds at weekends, and is the place you're most likely to meet a pissed Turk or tight-fisted expats trying to make an English-teaching wage stretch to a memorably hedonistic weekend. Watch your step on the way down and try not to puke in the corridor.

Ferdane

Mis Sokak 22A, Beyoğlu (0212 245 4582). **Open** 10am-2am daily. Licensed. **No credit cards.** **Map** p309 O2.

It seems perverse that in an area where so many buildings are in a state of utter decay someone should go to the effort of applying distressed decor complete with artistically rendered cracks and fissures. Why not just leave the real ones exposed? Combined with the exposed brick and poor lighting, Ferdane feels like exactly what it is: an old coal cellar. A popular cellar, though, with a laid-back troglodyte crowd, a shaggy '60s vibe and home-made cherry wine. Difficult to spot, the entrance is down a short flight of steps beside the American Bar.

Gizli Bahçe

Nevizade Sokak 27, Beyoğlu (0212 249 2192). **Open** 1pm-2am daily. Licensed. **Credit** MC, V. **Map** p308 N3.

The name means 'Secret Garden' – appropriate given that you haven't a hope of finding this place unless you know what you're looking for. Locate the doorman, negotiate your way past him, up two flights of stairs and in through the sliding door. You've discovered Istanbul's 'lounge' scene. A chill-out area of old sofas, easy chairs and coffee tables leads through to an American bar – standing room only – with DJs playing trance, techno and funk. Off to the side is a bright greenhouse-like area with tables and chairs so if anyone wants to quit being so studiedly cool for a while they can sit and talk.

Istavrit Kültür Kulübü

Istiklal Caddesi 237, Beyoğlu (0212 292 8545). **Open** 9am-midnight daily. Not licensed. **Credit** MC, V. **Map** p308 N3.

The ground floor here is taken up by an alternative music and book store, the top floor is set to open as an Internet café, while the two floors between are taken up by a café that feels a bit like a student common room. Tacky decor comprising fake foliage and fake wooden beams, but this place is nonetheless hugely popular, despite having no licence, dispensing mugs of coffee and the kind of food your mother used to pack for lunch.

The James Joyce

Zambak Sokak 6, Beyoğlu (0212 244 0241/ www.irishpubjamesjoyce.com). **Open** 10-2am daily. Licensed. **Credit** MC, V. **Map** p309 O2.

Better than your usual overseas Irish kit pub, the James Joyce is more rock and less sham. Yeah, there's the usual clichéd Irish tat on the walls but what matters is that punters – a mix of worldly Turks and, on weekend nights, foreigners – are kept happy with a wide range of beers, Irish breakfast served all day and live music every night except Tuesday. It gets loud and crowded downstairs, especially when a band's on (\$8 cover charge) but there's a slightly quieter mezzanine level with more elbow room. Heavy singles scene: deliver your best lines at full volume.

Kaffeehaus

Tünel Square 4, Tünel (0212 245 4028/www. kaffeehaus-istanbul.com). **Open** *summer* 9am-9pm daily. Not licensed. **No credit cards.** **Map** p308 M4.

Kaktus – waiting for Godard? *See p148.*

Coffee or tea at **KaVe**, in a passage lit at dusk by candles and Victorian lamps.

Its plate-glass-and-steel modernist look leaves Kaffeehaus with a cold, harsh feel. But if you can snag a table beside the great glass frontage – upstairs or down – it offers prime people-ogling opportunities. The food is good; in the morning, try the minimalist *menemen*, a breakfast dish of eggs, cheese and pepper. It's also a good place to find out what's happening via the noticeboard and piles of flyers. There are plans for staging live music in the near future and the owners are also hopeful of securing an alcohol license, which would make this a good first stop for an evening spent bar-crawling up Istiklal Caddesi.

Kahvedan

Akarsu Caddesi 50, Cihangir (0212 292 4030). **Open** 9am-10pm Mon-Sat; 10am-3pm Sun. Not licensed. **Credit** AmEx, MC, V. **Map** p309 O4.
Tranquil neighbourhood café just ten minutes' walk from Taksim Square. De rigueur dark wood tables and chairs complemented by yellow walls, cut flowers, light jazz, excellent coffee and a menu heavy on salads, crepes and spaghetti. Young professionals and artists come for the occasional cello recital, homemade desserts, fine Sunday brunch and a chance to catch up with neighbours and friends.

Kaktüs

Imam Adnan Sokak 4, Beyoğlu (0212 249 5979). **Open** 9-2am Mon-Sat; 11-2am Sun. Licensed. **No credit cards. Map** p309 O2.
First of the new wave of café-bars when it opened in the early 1990s, Kaktüs has since spawned countless imitators. The dark-wood interior, wooden tables and chairs owe a great deal to the old-style French café and the patrons do their best to enhance the atmosphere by chainsmoking like troopers, sipping blonde beers and black coffee and looking as though they were auditioning for a role in a Godard film. Food is served throughout the day from a constantly changing short-order menu. Staff are cool but efficient and have great taste in music. It's the kind of place where you drop in for an early evening beer and end up staying all night.

Kay's

Güneşli Sokak 32, Cihangir (0212 249 5024). Open 10.30am-midnight Mon-Sat; closed Sun. **Credit** MC, V. **Map** p309 P3.
Former owner Kay has packed up and returned to Australia but she left much of herself behind. Kay's Australian bric-à-brac, train collection and photos of friends line the walls. Her bratwurst, liver with cherry sauce and home-made pudding remain on the menu. The upbeat reggae, pop and jazz tunes have not been updated. The regular crowd of expats at the bar may even be swapping stories about her. Popular with an international crowd, a devoted Turkish clientele and a place where families and single women are equally comfortable.

KaVe

Tünel Geçidi 10, Tünel (0212 251 4338). **Open** 8am-midnight daily. Not licensed. **Credit** AmEx, MC, V. **Map** p308 M4.

Pano Wine Bar. The crowd tends to stick with house wine. *See p151.*

Opposite the upper station of the Tünel funicular a
short 'passaje', an Italianate 19th-century arcade
of shops, has been enlivened by a surprising out-
burst of potted greenery. Benches and heavy
garden furniture among the bushes and shrubs
belong to the café, which also occupies three beautiful bare-brick rooms with flagged floors and big
arched windows. It's a great example of the reuse
of old buildings that's increasingly enlivening
Beyoğlu. As well as coffees and tea, KaVe has a
short menu of sandwiches, salads, hot entrées and
classic desserts. Visit at dusk when the passage is
lit by candles and Victorian lamps.

Köyu Kahve
Hayriye Sokak 5/2, Çukurcuma (0212 251 7714).
Open 10am-midnight Mon-Sat; closed Sun. Licensed.
No credit cards. Map p308 N3.
Atmospheric back-alley café with seating out front
on a picturesque, stepped street that leads down
from the Galatasaray Hamam. It's run by three
industrial/graphic designers and frequented by
local antiques dealers and a theatre crowd who
appreciate the attempt at an 'old Pera' feel, including the old Turkish tango constantly playing on the
ancient gramophone.

Life
Imam Adnan Sokak 12, Beyoğlu (0212 244 0486).
Open 10-4am daily. Licensed. **Credit** MC, V. **Map**
p309 O2.
Red leather and pop art on the ground and mezzanine floors provide a suitably vivacious setting for
a funk, techno and trance-fuelled crowd. There's a
definite pre-club vibe. But typical of Beyoğlu, step
into the lift and it's a different scene altogether. Go
up to the fifth floor and the average age of the punters jumps by some 20 years as an older crowd of
arty types and casually dressed professionals hang
out on a glass-enclosed roof terrace. At weekends
you may have to put up with cheesy synth duos but
they're worth enduring for the best views in
Beyoğlu. One of the few bars in the area with a door
policy, designed to keep out unaccompanied males.

Madrid
İpek Sokak 16, Beyoğlu (no phone). **Open** 2pm-2am
daily. Licensed. **No credit cards. Map** p309 O2.
Serious good-time drinking den on four levels.
There's a loose Spanish theme with the odd bit of
Andalusian tiling, some Goya prints and a signed
poster of Almodóvar's *All About My Mother* in the
basement, but otherwise the real attraction is cheap
beer and a lively mix of people knocking it back.
Beware the tight iron staircases, lethal if you've had
a few too many. The place is popular with the city's
English-language teaching crowd.

Mavi Café
Altıpatlar Sokak 18, Çukurcuma (0212 252 8710).
Open 9.30am-3pm daily. Licensed. **No credit cards.**
Map p309 O3.
Anyone who's visited the Aegean town of Bodrum
will recognise the source of inspiration for Mavi

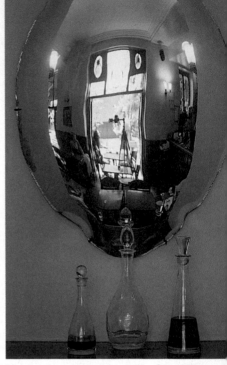

Pia: classic, uncluttered, creative. *See p151.*

Café, with its whitewashed walls, dark blue woodwork, fireplace, original art covering the walls and
guitar-led singalongs about summer loves and
Mediterranean nights. If this sounds a bit much,
escape to the tiny patio or less raucous second floor.
The crowd is mostly Turkish professionals and
French-language teachers.

My Moon
Bekar Sokak 18, Beyoğlu (0212 243 1108).
Open 9.30-2am Mon-Fri; 10.30-2am Sat, Sun.
Licensed. **Credit** MC, V. **Map** p309 O2.
Pale terracotta floor tiles and warm ochre walls
lend a vaguely Mediterranean feel to the long,
narrow room, maybe just a little too formal to be
completely convincing. Upstairs is more casual.
The European styling attracts a young moneyed
professional crowd and there's a good buzz most
nights of the week. The fairly standard menu
includes some original touches and their breakfasts
are particularly good.

Palyaço
Imam Adnan Sokak 30, Beyoğlu (0212 293 5761).
Open 1pm-2am daily. Licensed. **No credit cards.**
Map p309 O2.
Narrow ground-floor café-bar run by the same
young actor behind Cambaz. Like Cambaz it fills up

each evening with students and similar nosing for a big night out on a small budget. However, the volume is not quite as raucous and food is served (winter only) from a menu drawing from minority cuisines such as Jewish and Armenian. Palyaço means clown, hence the troupe of marionettes dangling from the ceiling.

Pano Wine Bar

Hamalbaşı Caddesi 26, Galatasaray (0212 292 6664). **Open** noon-2am daily. Licensed. **No credit cards.** **Map** p308 N3.

Modern take on a traditional Greek taverna, and inspiration for a wave of new wine bars currently mushrooming all over Beyoğlu. Patrons prop themselves up at long, thin high counters that ensure lots of body contact with strangers. Though more expensive imported stuff is available, the crowd tends to stick with the reasonably drinkable house wine, sold by the glass and bottle. Absolutely packed and rowdy most nights but worth visiting in the afternoon too for some excellent food, including a good cheese platter.

Panorama Bar

Marmara Hotel, Taksim Square, Taksim (0212 251 4696). **Open** 5pm-2am daily. Licensed. **Credit** AmEx, DC, MC, V. **Map** p309 P2.

Decor is that of a nondescript hotel lobby and drinks are wildly expensive ($8 a beer) but what you come here for is the view. The Panorama is on the 20th floor and has floor-to-ceiling windows taking in an almost unrivalled sweep of the city. Stand up there and go giddy at it all. You are Lex Luther, Superman cannot stop you this time and soon all this will be yours. Give it your maddest cackle.

Pia

Bekar Sokak 6, Beyoğlu (0212 252 7100). **Open** 9.30am-2am daily. Licensed. **Credit** MC, V. **Map** p309 O2.

Classic uncluttered look and a gallery-style upper floor give a sense of space when there isn't much at all. Ornate mirrors and a single George Grosz print set the tone. This is a favoured hang-out for writers, filmmakers and other low-key creative types. Exceptionally friendly staff take orders from an extensive menu served all day with dishes inspired in part by the wanderings of the café's owners. The food rarely disappoints and the daily specials are usually worth the gamble. Excellent coffee and cheesecake.

Refika

Müeyyet Sokak 11, Tünel (0212 245 5652). **Open** noon-5.30pm Tue-Fri; 11am-6pm Sat, Sun; closed Mon. Not licensed. **No credit cards.** **Map** p308 M4.

Istanbul's take on an artsy SoHo café courtesy of Defne Koryurek, petite owner, who lived and studied in the States for many years. It's not so much the look of the place – small, high-ceilinged, French-glazed façade, minimal decor – but what's on offer. The breakthrough idea (for Istanbul) of bottomless cups of Colombian coffee for one. Even

better are the weekend brunches with home-made pancakes and maple syrup and Eggs Benedict (winter only) cooked by Defne. People trek across town especially and, as the place has only half a dozen tables, it's not uncommon to queue. If you can't make it weekends, the weekday lunch menu is almost as good.

Sefahathane

Atlas Pasajı, Istiklal Caddesi 209, Beyoğlu (0212 251 2245). **Open** 10-2am daily. Licensed. **Credit** AmEx, MC, V. **Map** p308 N3.

Atlas Pasajı is the domain of the black-clad and angst-ridden, a shopping centre for secondhand threads, indy music and retro kitsch. Sefahathane is part way down, opposite the entrance to the Atlas cinema (*see p189*). It's narrow with white banquettes and big windows filled with harsh artificial lighting and neon, presenting an almost Edward Hopperish picture. By day the place does a lethargic trade in coffees for shoppers and cinema-goers but in the evenings it swells with Istanbul's pierced, tatooed and hair-dyed. Patrons spill into the *pasajı*, held together by trance and techno pulsing from within.

Serendip

Yeşilçam Sokak 28, Beyoğlu (0212 245 5048). **Open** noon-2am daily. Licensed. **Credit** AmEx, MC, V. **Map** p308 N3.

Myott – scene's elder statesman. *See p152.*

Although open year-round, Serendip comes into its own in winter as a warm, embracing place with a great open log fire. Walls of raw brick are draped in purple velvet, lighting is subdued, upholstery is fur (fake) and floors are terracotta tiled. It's totally seductive and absolutely the place to take a date. Bone up on city history before you go as the building is constructed over an ancient well and cisterns (exposed to view) and you want to be able to seduce with your erudition.

Şehbender Café

Şehbender Sokak 14, Asmalımecit (0212 292 7314). **Open** noon-midnight Mon-Sat; closed Sun. Not licensed. **No credit cards. Map** p308 M4.
Grotto-like basement café with bare-brick walls, kilims on tiled floors and an eclectic assortment of mismatched furniture, plus a tiny whitewashed yard at the back with a couple of small tables. It's run by the exuberant Esin, who comes from a well-known family of artists and performers and works hard to inject a little bit of showbiz panache. She draws an appreciative bunch of regulars, and lunchtime the place fills with Jewish accountants who work in the area. The café has no licence but a fair bit of under-the-counter dispensing goes on.

Tukan

Zambak Sokak 9, Beyoğlu (0212 292 9907). **Open** 10-2am daily. Licensed. **Credit** AmEx, DC, MC, V. **Map** p309 O2.
The name means toucan, but the only tropical touches are a painting of the bird and bright orange walls. The rest is cool, sleek and northern: low lighting, leather furniture, quiet jazz and blues. It's favoured by business types and young serious professionals, heads together at the American bar or one of 12 tables lining the long, unadorned room. Good place for an afternoon cappuccino and there's an international menu, heavy on vegetarian dishes.

Urban Café

Kartal Sokak 6/A, Galatasaray (0212 252 1325). **Open** 11-1am Mon-Fri; 11-2am Sat; 1.30-11pm Sun. Licensed. **Credit** MC, V. **Map** p308 N3.
From a street-level entrance, two tiers of seating step down to a sunken wine cellar, while stairs lead up to a small gallery. It's a strange arrangement, like a cutaway model, but one that creates lots of private spaces, softly lit, with soothing cornflower blue walls. Quiet jazz and plenty of tables mark it as a place for an older crowd, although the age range of patrons is well and truly mixed. Definitely more a place to meet with friends than somewhere to get to know strangers. The food is excellent, with the seafood fettucine highly recommended.

Vareli Wine Bar

Oteller Sokak 7/9, Tepebaşı (0212 292 5516). **Open** 11-3am daily. Licensed. **Credit** AmEx, MC, V. **Map** p308 M4.
Eschewing the put-on sophistication of the typical wine bar, Vareli goes for high camp. Flickering candles and storm lamps barely pierce the gloom, tables

are fashioned from huge barrels, and waiters swash and buckle in white pirate shirts and crimson hats. The house sound system plays opera. There's a decent selection of wines, although available only by the bottle, not by the glass. Food is also served.

Yağmur Cybercafé

Şehbender Sokak 18/2, Asmelımecit (0212 292 3020). **Open** 9am-11pm daily. Not licensed. **No credit cards. Map** p308 M4.
Most people come to this long-established Internet café for the computer access (*see p276*) but the lemon-hued walls, bare-wood floors, kilims and unobtrusive background music also make it a peaceful environment to sit back and pull out a book. A limited menu runs to one hot dish of the day, plus sandwiches, salads and cakes, but also a few items less common in this town, including waffles and good milkshakes.

Beşiktaş to Arnavutköy

The **North Shield** aside, Beşiktaş is not a place that figures much on anyone's social itinerary. Ortaköy on the other hand is the second best place to be after Beyoğlu. On the waterfront there's plenty of open-air café seating, busy every night through until the early hours. The back streets harbour more cafés as well as a number of small bars.

A couple of miles north, Arnavutköy has far fewer options but is still well worth an evening's exploring several venues in gorgeous wooden mansions overlooking the Bosphorus.

Coco Pazzo

1. Cadde 62, Arnavutköy (0212 265 2129). **Open** 7pm-2am daily. Licensed. **Credit** DC, MC, V.
One of few places that can entice committed Beyoğluphiles to venture down to the Bosphorus shore. Coco Pazzo's chic industrial frontage conceals a soft interior of low lighting, leather and burnished steel. Hip hop and funk set the mood but are kept low enough not to interfere with conversation. The food is excellent.

Myott

İskele Sokak 14, Ortaköy (0212 258 9317). **Open** 9am-5pm daily. Not licensed. **No credit cards.**
An elder statesman of the café scene, Myott has been a breakfast favourite for around a decade. It's about the only place outside the five-star hotels where you can start the day with muesli, fresh fruit and nuts. Get there soon after opening if you want to secure a table, otherwise be patient.

North Shield

Spor Caddesi 1/3, Akaretler, Beşiktaş (0212 259 3030). **Open** 11-1am Mon-Thur; 11-2am Fri, Sat; 5pm-1am Sun. Licensed. **Credit** MC, V.
Join affluent Turkish businessmen and moneyed foreigners in this replica 'English' pub. It's reasonably convincing, though the range of drinks is

The best Bars with a view

Four Seasons Sultanahmet
Rooftop garden bar so close to Haghia Sophia it feels like part of the furniture. See page 46.

Empress Zoe
Plenty of Sultanahmet hotels have roof terraces; this is one of the few with a bar. See page 49.

Armada Hotel
Ocean breezes overlooking the Sea of Marmara. See page 46.

Richmond Hotel
The only rooftop bar with views over Istanbul's main drag. See page 60.

Panorama Bar
Enclosed 20th-floor bar at the Marmara Hotel. See pages 58 and 151.

Ceylan Inter-Continental
Enclosed rooftop bar, a vertiginous 18 floors up. See page 55.

Bilsak Fifth Floor
Enclosed bar looking across Cihangir to the Bosphorus. See page 143.

Life
Rooftop just off Istiklal Caddesi. There's no view to speak of but there are blissfully cool breezes. See page 150.

Cambaz
Summer rooftop bar overlooking Tarlabaşl and the Golden Horn (pictured). See page 145.

disappointing and the prices frightening. Five branches in town, including one in the AFM Fitaş cinema complex (*see p188*) on Istiklal Caddesi.

Kadıköy

Nightspots on the Asian Shore are quieter than those on the European side; whether that's good or bad depends on your point of view. But for anyone staying in Beyoğlu or Sultanahmet having to get a ferry home at the end of the night (last sailing midnight) is a bit of a bind.

Café Antre
Miralay Nazım Sokak 10, Kadıköy (0216 338 3483). Open 10am-10pm daily. Not licensed. **Credit** MC, V. **Map** p311 W8.
Run and largely frequented by women, Antre has large windows letting in plenty of natural light and

has one floor set aside for non-smokers. Staff are extremely amiable and speak English.

Karga
Kadife Sokak 16, Bahariye (0216 449 1725). **Open** 11am-2am daily. Licensed. **No credit cards. Map** p311 W8
Three floors of wooden everything – floors, fittings, tables and chairs – give this place the feel of an old pirate ship. It's one of Kadıköy's most popular bars and heaves at weekends.

Mosquito Café
Arayıcıbaşı Sokak 4/2, Kadıköy (0216 418 5659). Open 9.30am-10pm daily. Not licensed. **Credit** AmEx, MC, V. **Map** p311 W7.
Quiet little place with a vaguely hippyish feel (the glass-topped tables have pressed dried flowers underneath). Favoured by students. It also does food and excellent cakes and desserts.

Shops & Services

Turks may now favour Western-style malls, but you can still hunt for handicrafts at the Bazaar or haggle for the perfect rug.

Eat, Drink, Shop

There are two main kinds of shopping experience: casual browsing, involving a great deal of wandering and haggling, in which the actual purchase is secondary to the search itself; and the more straightforward hunt for a particular item or items. Istanbul is definitely a place for the former. With extensive bazaars and street markets and hordes of one-off quirky stores hidden in back alleys, shopping is high adventure rather than high fashion. You can find designer wear, local, imported, knock-down, remaindered and pirate, but there's more fun to be had with the odd, unique and impractical: old jewellery, 'Ottoman' ceramics, carpets, sweets, musical instruments, calligraphy, a fez, baggy Turkish trousers. All the kind of stuff that you were never even aware existed, but once seen can't do without.

For specifics – useful items – the best bet is one of the malls (*see page 157* **Mall contents**) or a department store. These are also the places where there's the best chance of finding an English-speaking shop assistant.

Prices are not as cheap as might be expected. Certain locally produced items and handicrafts are a steal, but high quality clothing generally carries a higher price tag than abroad. Household appliances and furniture are considerably more expensive. Services, on the other hand, are a bargain if you're able to find a reputable shop and overcome the language barrier to explain exactly what you want done. Exceptions are laundry and any repairs requiring imported parts.

TAXES

Value-added tax (KDV) of 17 to 25 per cent is levied on goods and services. In theory, visitors are entitled to a refund on leaving the country on single purchases over $100 made in Turkish lira from shops displaying the tax-free sales sticker. Your passport has to be presented at the time of buying and you need to ask for a special invoice (*özel fatura*). The invoice is given to customs on departure and the refund posted on. This can take months and it's common for the refund never to arrive at all. Agreeing to forego a receipt can often get you a discount in small family-run shops, as it allows them to fiddle their taxes.

SHOPPING AREAS

Sultanahmet caters almost exclusively to tourists and has more than its fair share of tacky souvenir joints and irritatingly persistent carpet vendors.

Some of the handicraft places aren't bad, although prices are marked up. The shops become more interesting as you head west along Divan Yolu towards the area of the Grand Bazaar. The Bazaar has lost its lustre for locals, who prefer to spend their cash at Western-style malls, but it still offers unrivalled shopping for the curious and patient, and there are certainly things in it worth buying (*see page 167* **Shopping the Bazaar**).

Eminönü is downhill and downmarket. Full of small shops and street traders, it draws mainly local crowds looking for rock-bottom bargains, copycat goods and pirated music and software. Take a look along Mahmutpaşa Yokuğu, Hamidiye Caddesi and the streets that cross them. The tradition of entire streets specialising in the sale of particular items lives on in Tahtakale, the neighbourhood adjacent to Eminönü and just below the Grand Bazaar. This is the place for handmade wooden objects, from simple spoons to elaborate shelving, metal objects, including watering cans and barbecues, and brass lanterns and coffee grinders.

Beyoğlu is a shopping district in a more Western mould. The main drag, Istiklal Caddesi, mixes clothing shops with antique books, department stores, commercial galleries, music stores and Parisian-style passages, including Atlas Pasajı with its eclectic bunch of record stores, second-hand clothes shops and bric-à-brac. The bigger, more mainstream shops tend to be to the north end of Istiklal, the smaller, more individual places to the south.

The best window shopping is in Nişantaşı and Teşvikiye, two small neighbouring districts a mile or so north of Taksim Square. They're home to Istanbul's greatest concentration of international designer names, as well as to those Turkish boutiques able to hold their own against the mania for all things foreign. The other chi-chi shopping zone is on the Asian Shore; Bağdat Caddesi, a four-lane highway lined by labels, labels, labels. This is some of the city's hottest real estate, so the spending opportunities keep growing. Hip new cafés and restaurants have elbowed in among the retailers to help lure moneyed Istanbulites from the European side.

Back in European Istanbul, the once far-flung northern district of Etiler has moved a lot closer since the opening of the new metro. Shopping up

Çukurcuma – Istanbul's antiques alley.

here means either the **Akmerkez Mall** (*see page 157* **Mall contents**) or the **Ulus Market** (*see page 175*).

Antiques

Until recently Turks were in the habit of throwing out antique items and replacing them with manufactured goods. But old has become chic – and prices have rocketed. There is some wonderful stuff around, though. The place to hunt is Çukurcuma, a small backstreet neighbourhood in Beyoğlu behind the Galatasaray Lycée. Look for things like great old Anatolian trunks, traditionally painted as part of a bride's trousseau, or carved wooden panels and doors from old buildings.

There isn't a fixed market price for antiques. It's essential to bargain. Before pitching your price, find out first whether the piece is exportable: antiques can be taken out of the country; antiquities can not. Something a mere century old poses no problem, but a genuine 17th-century Iznik tile is a definite no-no. Not only will it be confiscated by customs, but you could end up in jail.

A9
Atiye Sokak 9, Teşvikiye (0212 241 5533). **Open** 9.30am-7pm Mon-Sat; closed Sun. **Credit** MC, V.
Specialises in antique objects from Anatolia,

including century-old hope chests, lamps, tiles, copper artefacts candelabras and handmade woollen pillows from Konya.

Antikarnas Istanbul
Faik Paşa Yokuşu 15, Çukurcuma (0212 251 5928). **Open** 9am-8pm Mon-Sat; closed Sun. **No credit cards. Map** p309 O3.
In a restored four-storey townhouse, this is a great place to browse among some 19th-century Ottoman landscape paintings, Selçuk ceramics and a museum's worth of genuine antiquities. But even if you could afford the prices (18th-century painted wooden ceiling: a snip at $160,000) most of the stock would not be allowed out of Turkey.

Kerim
Atiye Sokak 14, off Abdi Ipekçi Caddesi, Teşvikiye (0212 231 3717). **Open** *Mid June-mid Sept* 9.30am-7pm Mon-Fri; closed Sat, Sun. *Mid Sept-mid June* 9.30am-7pm Mon-Sat; closed Sun. **No credit cards.**
Among the designer stores of this fashionable shopping district, here are antiques as lifestyle accessories. High-quality stuff – mirrors, icons, paintings and silver – with price tags to prove it.

Old Bedesten
Grand Bazaar. Tram Beyazıt or Çemberlitaş. **Open** 9am-7pm Mon-Sat; closed Sun. **Map** p302 L9.
At the heart of the Grand Bazaar, 'İç Bedestan' is a cluster of stores, many of which specialise in religious icons, brought here by the suitcase load from the former Soviet Union. Also plenty of silver, old jewellery and fob watches with Arabic numerals.

Tombak II
Faik Paşa Yokuşu 34/A, Çukurcuma (0212 244 3681). **Open** 10am-7pm Mon-Sat; closed Sun. **No credit cards. Map** p309 O3.
Eccentric array of collectibles and curios, ranging from 100-year-old bars of soap and 1940s European razors in their original packaging for a dollar, to silver tea services and turn-of-the-century toys.

Yaman Antikhan
Faik Paşa Yokuşu 41, Çukurcuma (0212 249 5188) **Open** 10am-7pm Mon-Sat; closed Sun. **No credit cards. Map** p309 O3.
Seven floors, with antiques mainly on ground level. It's an upmarket selection imported mainly from the Far East and Europe, as well as a fine range of Anatolian fabrics, clothing, paintings and furniture.

Art supplies & stationery

Artists' materials are almost all imported from Europe, but shops tend to stock the cheaper student ranges, so better quality paints and materials can be hard to find.

Matisse Sanat Market
Kadıköy İş Merkezi 10/83, Neşet Ömer Sokak, Kadıköy (0216 338 5225). **Open** 9am-7.30pm Mon-Sat; closed Sun. **No credit cards. Map** p311 V7.

This well set-out shop with helpful staff in a passage in Kadıköy Market is easily the best art supplies shop in the city. Primed and unprimed Italian linen, stretchers, easels, papers in assorted weights, brushes and a wide selection of oils, acrylics and watercolours. Chances are if you can't find it here, then you're not going to find it at all.

Office 1 Superstore

Yeni Maçka Caddesi 59/1, Teşvikiye (0212 230 3670/delivery service 0800 211 6134). **Open** 9am-7.30pm Mon-Fri; 10am-6pm Sat; closed Sun. **Credit** MC, V.

Not too much in the way of art supplies, but has two well-stocked floors of general office supplies and will deliver.

Özen Kırtasiye

Sıraselviler Caddesi 66/A, Taksim (0212 244 3270). **Open** 8.30am-8.30pm Mon-Sat; 1-4pm Sun. **Credit** AmEx, MC, V. **Map** p309 O3.

In a tiny basement and marked only by a little sign saying 'fotokopi', this place is crammed with the widest range of artists' materials in Beyoğlu, including artist-quality paints, a good selection of brushes, paper and drawing materials.

Mall contents

Some 500 years after Mehmet the Conqueror presided over the building of Istanbul's first covered shopping centre, the Grand Bazaar, its second, Galleria, was opened in Bakırköy in 1988. After such a long wait, consumers went wild over the ice-skating rink, bowling alley, vast kiddie arcade 'Fame City', department store Printemps and the novelty of perusing the wares of 135 shops protected from the elements and free of hawkers.

When Akmerkez (pictured) opened several years later it had Istanbulites whole-heartedly embracing blue-collar American pastimes such as bowling and hanging out at the food court.

But while elsewhere this is Homer Simpson territory, the novelty value in Turkey ensures that Akmerkez is high class. Inflated prices, heavy security and its high-rent location conspire to keep out the riff-raff. So much so that it's common to spot celebrities on a shopping binge or taking in a movie.

Currently, there are plans for the construction of an astonishing 65 new shopping centres and hypermarkets. That and the completion of the new public transport network will make malls accessible for the masses in a way not seen since around the late 15th century.

Akmerkez

Nispetiye Caddesi, Etiler (0212 282 0170). Metro Levent. **Open** 10am-10pm daily.
Winner of several international design awards, but basically a well-maintained and planned mall unlikely to impress foreign visitors. In addition to 246 shops, also has a men's and women's hairdresser, tailoring services, travel agency, exchange bureau, supermarket and cinemas. Food court on top floor features international and Turkish versions of fast food.

Capitol

Mahir Iz Caddesi, Altunizade, Asian Shore (0216 391 1920). **Open** 10am-10pm daily.
Residents of the Asian side were delighted by the opening of this mall, but there's absolutely no reason for anyone else to be. Boasts a supermarket, cinema, shops and cafés.

Galleria

Sahil Yolu, Ataköy (0212 559 9560). **Open** 10am-10pm daily.
Following the bankruptcy of anchor stores Printemps and Fame City, Galleria has fallen on hard times. Currently run by a state bank, it's slated for privatisation and there's talk of instituting a general makeover aimed at luring more affluent shoppers.

Eat, Drink, Shop

Shopping by area

Sultanahmet

Altınbaş (Jewellery p166); **Arasta Bazaar** (Handicrafts p173); **Bosphorus** (Jewellery p166); **Bread and Water** (p168 The rug trade); **Cafer Ağa Medressi Applied Handicrafts Centre** (Handicrafts p173); **Dosim** (Handicrafts p173); **Istanbul Handicrafts Centre** (Handicrafts p173); **Ottoman Gallery** (p168 The rug trade); **Sırça Handicrafts Centre** (Handicrafts p174); **Sofa** (Handicrafts p174); **Teknik El Kırtasiye** (Art supplies & stationery p158); **Van Halıcılık** (p168 The rug trade).

Bazaar Quarter

Beyazıt Tekstil (Hats p165); **Lider Mücevherat** (Watch & jewellery repairs p176); **Old Bedesten** (Antiques p167); **Ortaasya ve Semertkan El Sanatlar** (p168 The rug trade); **Sofa** (p174 handicrafts).

Eminönü

Doğubank Işhanı (Household p174); **Golden Horn Handicrafts Centre** (Handicrafts p173); **Kurukahveci Mehmet Efendi** (Food & drink p169); **Nazik Optik** (Sunglasses p167); **Yalçın Express** (Photography p176).

Beyoğlu

ABC Kitabevi (Bookshops p158); **Ada Music** (Music p175); **Ali Muhiddin Hacı Bekir** (Handicrafts p172); **Antikarnas Istanbul** (Antiques p155); **Asri Turşucu** (Food p169); **Aznavur Pasajı** (Handicrafts p173); **Bubble** (Fashion p162); **Butik Katia** (Accessories p166); **Bünsa** (Health food p170); **Cihangir Erkek Kuaförü** (Barbers p172); **Denizler Kitapevi** (Antiquarian books p159); **Dünya Kitapevi** (Newsagents p158); **Galatasaray Başar Spor** (Sporting goods p176); **Gizem Ahahtar** (Keycutting & locksmiths p174); **Ilke** (Shoes p167); **Ipek** (Accessories p165); **Kod Music Shop** (Music p175); **La Cave** (Wine p171); **Librairie de Pera** (Antiquarian books p159); **Megavizyon** (Music p175); **Mudo** (Department stores p161); **Nuh'un Ambarı** (Health food p170); **Ottomania** (Antiquarian books p159); **Özen Kırtasiye** (Art supplies p157); **Pandora** (Bookshops p158); **Paşabahçe** (Household p174); **Pulp** (Fashion p165); **Raksotek** (Music p175); **Robinson Crusoe** (Bookshops & newsagents p159);

Teknik El Kırtasiye

Ankara Caddesi 123, Sirkeci (0212 527 2482). Tram Sirkeci. **Open** 9am-7pm Mon-Sat; closed Sun. **Credit** AmEx, MC, V. **Map** p303 M9.

Of several artists' suppliers and stationers on this street (just up from Sirkeci Station) this is the best.

Bookshops & newsagents

Istanbul is a fine place for books on Istanbul and Turkey, but otherwise English-language selections are limited. Most of the better bookshops are on or just off Istiklal Caddesi. For a good browse there's the **Booksellers' Bazaar** (Sahaflar Çarşısı; *see page 167*), off Beyazıt Square, where among the textbooks and Turkish literature, there are new and used English books. The **Museum of Turkish & Islamic Art** (*see page 115*) has a decent bookshop. The small newsagents on Taksim Square by the Marmara Hotel has a decent selection of world press.

ABC Kitabevi

Tünel Square 1, Beyoğlu (0212 293 5605). **Open** 9am-7pm Mon-Sat; closed Sun. **Credit** MC, V. **Map** p308 M4.
Small but varied collection of new if slightly battered books on sale at low prices. The odd selection includes children's fiction, computer manuals and a small shelf full of 'erotic' works.

Dünya Kitapevi

Istiklal Caddesi 469, Beyoğlu (0212 249 1006/ dunya.com.tr). **Open** 8am-8pm Mon-Sat; noon-6pm Sun. **Credit** MC, V. **Map** p308 M4.
The selection of English-language books is limited, but this shop is worth earmarking for the city's most extensive range of international magazines and newspapers. It has a café and reading area, with library-like atmosphere.
Branches: Kadıköy Iş Merkezi 10/137, Kadıköy (0216 347 7906); Narlıbahçe Sokak, Cağaloğlu (0212 513 5079).

Pandora

Büyükparmakkapı Sokak 3, Beyoğlu (0212 243 3503/243 3504/www.pandora.com.tr). **Open** 10am-8pm Mon-Thur; 10am-10pm Fri, Sat; 1pm-8pm Sun. **Credit** AmEx, MC, V. **Map** p309 O3.
Brilliant little place with helpful English-speaking staff. It has three floors, the top one totally devoted to English-language titles – fiction, poetry, art, local interest and a decent history section. Flyers and posters advertise what's on around town.

Remzi Kitabi

Akmerkez Mall, Nispetiye Caddesi, Etiler (0212 282 2575). Metro Levent. **Open** 10am-10pm daily. **Credit** AmEx, MC, V.
Popular bookshop with stacks of English-language publications.

Safi Dry Cleaning (Drycleaning p162); **Savoy** (Food p170); **Şık Çamaşır Yıkama** (Laundry p162); **Şimşek Video** (Video rental p176); **Simurg** (Bookshops p159); **Sportland** (Sporting goods p176); **Surreal Kılık** (Fashion p165); **Sütte** (Food p170); **Tombak II** (Antiques p155); **Vakko** (Department stores p162); **Yaman Antkhan** (Antiques p155).

Nişantaşı
Body Plus (Cosmetics p161); **Jet Set** (Shoe repairs p176); **Manhattan Gourmet Shop** (Food & drink p169); **Ottomania** (Household p174); **Yargıcı** (Fashion p165); **Zeki Triko** (Swimwear p167); **Urart** (Jewellery p166).

Teşvikiye
A9 (Antiques p155); **Çigan Butik** (Fashion p163); **Gorgeous** (Accessories p165); **Gönül Paksöy** (Fashion p165); **Kerim** (Antiques p155); **Office 1 Superstore** (Stationery p157).

Karaköy
Aidata (Computers p161); **Gün Şah** (Watch repairs p176); **Karaköy Pazarı** (Accessories p165).

Beşiktaş to Bebek
Deli Kızın Yeri (Handicrafts p173); **Diğer Lezzetler** (Food & drink p169); **Erol Fotoğrafçılık** (Photography p176); **Gizem Beauty Centre** (Hair & beauty p172); **Iznik Vakfı** (Handicrafts p173); **Kevser** (Handicrafts p173); **Meşhur Bebek Badem Ezmesi** (p171 **Sweet stuff**); **Ortaköy Market** (Handicrafts p174).

Asian Shore
Capitol (p157 **Mall contents**); **Ebristan Istanbul Ebru Evi** (Handicrafts p173); **Matisse Sanat Market** (Art supplies p155); **Salıpazarı** (Markets p175); **Zihni Music Center** (Music p175).

Etiler
Akmerkez Mall (p157 **Mall contents**); **Beymen** (Department stores p161); **Damat Tween** (Fashion p163); **Derimod** (Leather p166); **Derishow** (Leather p167); **MOS Kuaför** (Hair salon p172); **Remzi Kitabi** (Bookshops p158); **Sevil Parfümeri** (Cosmetics p161); **Shoe and Me** (Shoes p167); **Silk & Cashmere** (Fashion p165); **Ulus market** (Markets p175); **Ve Saire** (Vintage & second-hand p168).

Branches: Mayadrom Shopping Centre, Yıldırım Göker Caddesi, Akatlar (0212 284 5701); Rumeli Caddesi 44, Nişantaşı (0212 234 5475).

Robinson Crusoe
Istiklal Caddesi 389, Beyoğlu (0212 293 6968). **Open** 9am-9pm Mon-Sat; 10am-9pm Sun. **Credit** AmEx, DC, MC, V. **Map** p308 M4.
Good-looking place with many English-language titles including a small but strong stock of fiction and a selection of international music and art mags.

Simurg
Hasnun Galip Sokağı 2A, Beyoğlu (0212 292 2712/ simurgkitabevi@superonline.com). **Open** 9.30am-9.30pm Mon-Sat; 1-8pm Sun. **Credit** AmEx, MC, V. **Map** p309 O3.
Two shops side-by-side under the same ownership that stock a wide selection of new and used books and music. Go for the thrill of the unpredictable find – back issues of the *Literary Quarterly of the University of Oklahoma* or Petula Clark on vinyl.

Antiquarian books

Denizler Kitapevi
Istiklal Caddesi 395, Beyoğlu (0212 243 3174/ 249 8893). **Open** 10am-7.30 pm Mon-Sat; closed Sun. **Credit** MC, V. **Map** 308 M4.
Specialises in maritime subjects and maps, but also

has a collection of around 20,000 film posters, including some rare old stuff like an original *Gone With the Wind*, Turkish release. The 130-year-old shop premises used to house the Dutch Consulate.

Librairie de Pera
Galipdede Cadessi 22, Tünel (0212 252 3078/ www.LibrairieDePera.com.tr). **Open** 10.30am-7pm Mon.-Sat; closed Sun. **Credit** AmEx, V.
Map p308 M5.
Old and rare books, mostly to do with travel and Turkey, as well as maps and prints. If you have any particular wants, this is probably the place.

Ottomania
Sofyalı Sokak 30-32, off Istiklal Caddesi, Beyoğlu (0212 243 2157/eren@turk.net). **Open** 9am-6.30pm Mon-Sat; closed Sun. **Credit** AmEx, MC, V.
Map p308 M4.
Old maps, engravings and rare books. This is a second generation family-owned shop that also has a stall in the Sahaflar Çarşısı. Serious prices for serious collectors.

Second-hand

There are half a dozen shops jam-packed with second-hand books, many in English, in the Aslıhan Pasajı, just off the Balık Pazarı halfway down Istiklal Caddesi. The passage is open from

Eat, Drink, Shop

English reads: **Robinson Crusoe**. *See p159.*

8am-8pm Mon-Sat. Some shops also deal in vinyl, magazines and old postcards.

Computers

Computers cost up to 30 per cent more in Turkey than in Europe or the US, making it advisable to bring what you can from abroad. For spares or technical support, firms representing international companies are listed below. For listings without addresses, call and ask for the nearest distributor. All listed companies have staff with at least minimal English-language skills.

Aidata

Ada Han, Kemeraltı Caddesi 87, Karaköy (0212 249 8149/www.aidata.com.tr). **Open** 9am-7pm Mon-Fri; 10am-3pm Sat; closed Sun. **Credit** MC, V. **Map** p306 N5.
Computer sales, accessories, spare parts and repair service. Represents Aidata, but also sells Hewlett Packard, Macintosh and Compaq on order.

Arena Aş

0212 233 3070/www.arena.com.tr
Represents Compaq in Turkey.

Bilkom

0212 293 3940/www.bilkom.com.tr
Apple's Turkish distributor.

Boyut Aş

Talatpaşa Mahallesi Emirgazi Caddesi 2, Okmeydanı (0212 222 7885).
Leading IBM stockist. Call for further information.

Vatan

Cumhuriyet Caddesi 79, Elmadağ (0212 234 4800/ vatan@vatanbilgisayar.com). **Open** 9am-6pm Mon-Fri; 10am-3pm Sat; closed Sun. **Credit** AmEx, MC, V.
Computer sales, accessories, fax machines, spare parts, printers, internet packets and repair service. Represents Hewlett Packard and Acer.

Cosmetics

Foreign cosmetics are increasingly popular and such global brands as Nivea and Ponds are now produced under licence. For more exclusive brands, such as Estée Lauder and Clinique, there are shops specialising in perfume and cosmetics, but stiff import duties mean high prices.

You can also find cosmetics and perfumes at beauty salons, but it is still worth stocking up on duty-frees before you arrive.

Body Plus

Akkavak Sokak 21, Nişantaşı (0212 248 5839). **Open** 9.30am-7.30pm Mon-Sat; closed Sun. **Credit** AmEx, MC, V.
Cosmetics for sensitive skins and pregnant women. Brands include Dermologica Galenic and Lierac.

Sevil Parfümeri

Akmerkez Mall, Nispetiye Caddesi, Etiler (0212 282 0268/www.sevil.com.tr). Metro Levent. **Open** 10am-10pm daily. **Credit** AmEx, DC, MC, V.
Two branches, one at street level and the other on the upper level, both stocking all the big names.

Department stores

Beymen

Akmerkez Mall, Nispetiye Caddesi, Etiler (0212 282 0380). Metro Levent. **Open** 10am-10pm daily. **Credit** AmEx, MC, V.
Originally a men's clothing store, selling a range of tailored suits, top-quality dress shirts and ties, Beyman now also carries imported clothing and home accessories for the new breed of 'cool' male and execs and their PR mates.
Branches: Galleria, Sahil Yolu, Ataköy (0212 559 3250); Bağdat Caddesi, Suadiye, Asian Shore (0216 467 1845); Teşvikiye (0212 232 2240).

Mudo

Istiklal Caddesi 401, Beyoğlu (0212 251 8682). **Open** 10am-7.30pm Mon-Sat; closed Sun. **Credit** MC, V. **Map** p308 M4.
Turks unsure of how to set about decorating their homes tastefully, entrust themselves to this 'lifestyle concept' store. It has a full range of local and imported kitchen, bathroom, living-room and garden furnishings.

Eat, Drink, Shop

House tunes and repetitive shoes at the **Bubble** clubwear boutique.

Branches: Akmerkez Mall, Nispetiye Caddesi, Etiler (0212 282 0474); Rumeli Caddesi 58, Nişantaşı (0212 225 2941).

Vakko

Istiklal Caddesi, 123-5, Beyoğlu (0212 251 4092). **Open** 10am-7pm Mon-Sat; closed Sun. **Credit** AmEx, DC, MC, V. **Map** p309 O3.

Until the mid-1980s, Vakko was the authority on fashion in Turkey. Though since losing many of its customers to international labels, it has managed to maintain its own brand, carrying chiefly own-label clothing and accessories.

Branches: Akmerkez, Nispetiye Caddesi, Etiler (0212 282 0695); Bağdat Caddesi 422, Suadiye, Asian Shore (0216 467 4204).

Drycleaning & laundry

Coin-operated laundromats are non-existent and laundries are extremely scarce outside of Beyoğlu and neighbouring Cihangir (with its high foreign resident quotient). As a service mainly aimed at foreigners, laundry prices are high.

Safi Dry Cleaning

Bekar Sokak 24/A, off Istiklal Caddesi, Beyoğlu (0212 244 4068). **Open** 7am-7pm Mon-Sat; closed Sun. **No credit cards. Map** p309 O2.

Although there are plenty of dry-cleaners around, this is one of the most conveniently located, just south of Taksim Square. Next-day service at reasonable charges: trousers $3, shirts $1.50 and overcoats $8.

Şık Çamaşır Yıkama

Akarsu Yokuşu, Cihangir (0212 245 4375). **Open** 8.30am-8pm Mon-Sat; closed Sun. **No credit cards.** **Map** p309 O4.

Rates here are $1.50 per kilogram (2.2 lb), including folding. Ironing costs $1 per shirt, $1.25 for trousers, $2 per dress. Next-day service for no extra charge, but usually isn't next-day. Pick-up and delivery for area vaguely defined as 'nearby'.

Fashion

Since the textile sector boomed in the 1980s Turkey has become the world's second-largest exporter of fabrics. A few Turkish designers have even achieved international recognition (*see page 163* **What is 'Turkish' fashion?**). For all that, a trawl through the boutiques makes it clear that Istanbul is not exactly queuing up for its turn on the catwalks. Bright colours, wild patterns and unusual combinations are associated with village folk, not with bold fashion statements. Classic cuts, solid colours and irreproachable, if unimaginative, designs dominate.

Bubble

Süslü Saksı Sokak 12/1, Beyoğlu (0212 251 2165/www.bubble12.com). **Open** 10am-8pm Mon-Sat; closed Sun. **Credit** MC, V. **Map** p309 O2.

Clubwear boutique with a DJ spinning house in the back and a limited but impeccably selected range of clothing, shoes and accessories for men and women. Labels include LUC series, Skim.com and the creations of Arzu Kaprol, Bahar Korçan and

Hakan Yıldırım, innovative young designers who feel confident enough not to rely on well-worn Turkish motifs in a bid to gain attention overseas.

Çigan Butik

Milli Reaşürans Çarşısı 45, Teşvikiye (0212 246 0802). **Open** 10am-6.30pm Mon-Sat; closed Sun. **Credit** AmEx, MC, V.

Ethnic, handmade clothing in natural fibres from the Balkans and Central Asia and own-brand clothes in cotton, silk, linen and wool. In a fashion scene sadly lacking in originality and ideas, the colourful designs and unusual patterns found here are probably the closest thing you will find to a radical statement.

Damat Tween

Akmerkez Mall, Nispetiye Caddesi, Etiler (0212 282 0112/282 1736/www.tween.com.tr). Metro Levent. **Open** 10am-10pm daily. **Credit** AmEx, MC, V.

One of the local boys made good, Damat has branches in 12 countries, as well as throughout Turkey. Classic menswear, from sport to suits, but well ahead of the pack in terms of design and quality.

What is 'Turkish' fashion?

Turkish designers face the same challenges as their counterparts in any other country, plus a few more. International designers dominate in Istanbul, and the days of Turkish haute couture look numbered. One of the reasons for this is that tastes have evolved so rapidly. As recently as ten years ago, stylish was equated with ostentation: big hair, tulle, feather boas, chunky gold jewellery, satin gloves, bows and bangles. Today, even a famed arabesque singer such as Ebru Gündes chooses to appear in concert wearing the Versace dress made famous by Jennifer Lopez at the Grammy Awards.

International designers borrow heavily from ethnic influences, but Turkish fashion seems uncertain of how to borrow from its own history and culture. Menswear designers held a fashion show at the Dolmabahçe Palace featuring reproductions of Atatürk's favourite dressing gowns and frock coats. Fashion shows featuring reproductions of stylish 19th-century Ottoman clothing are also in vogue. But Turkey has yet to produce its own version of Vivenne Westwood, a designer able to take period costumes and transform them into cutting-edge high fashion.

The two Turkish designers with an international following – Rifat Ozbek and Hussein Chalayan – were both educated at London's St Martin's School of Art and both went on to be chosen British Designer of the Year. Ozbek refers to the 'sensuous' influence of Ottoman tile patterns, but also cites Indonesian ikat patterns and North American Indian beading as influences. Chalayan managed to enrage devout Muslims by designing Islamic headdresses for otherwise nude models (pictured) but, for all that, he's an international designer who draws on international sources of inspiration.

So what, exactly, is 'Turkish' fashion? The Association of Istanbul Textile and Garment

Exporters (ITKIB) rather belatedly realised that Turkish fashion will come of age only when a 'Made in Turkey' label carries a special cachet. The organisation's decision to sponsor Turkish designers got off to an auspicious start with Chalayan's show at London Fashion Week 2000. More recently, ITKIB sponsored another young Turkish designer, Vienna-based Atıl Kutoğlu, at New York Fashion Week. These sponsorship activities are part of a new co-ordinated approach by business and government to promote Turkey as a label. Fashion, along with sport, the arts, cultural events and tourism, is seen as a means to improve Turkey's overseas image.

INTERNATIONAL
HOSPITAL
ISTANBUL

International Hospital İstanbul, is situated on the Marmara seacoast about 5 minutes from Atat,rk Airport and 20 minutes from the urban center. Rendering round-the-clock medical services 365 days a year and incorporating Surgical, Coronary, Open Heart and Neonatal Intensive Care Units, International Hospital Istanbul is able to transport patients by Land, Sea and Air ambulances 24 hours a day. International Hospital is the leader in the private health sector in Turkey with its quality service, distinguished personnel, modern technology and institutional understanding.

Physicians with academic standing and international experience, nurses with superior skills, continually trained personnel proud of the services they render, working with team spirit, respect and love these are what constitute the basics of high quality service at the International Hospital.

International Hospital Istanbul has agreements with many foreign insurance companies ;

BUPA International
PPP Health Care
Blue Cross & Blue Shields
J.Van Breda & C International
International SOS (AEA company)
Denwa Assistance

As our name implies our mission has always been to provide our patients with internationally accepted quality medical care, and to assure that its national & international patients are pleased with health care services they receive.

İstanbul Caddesi No: 82. 34800, Yeşilköy - İstanbul / TURKEY
Tel: +90.212.663 30 00 (Pbx), Fax: +90.212.663 28 62
e-mail: info@internationalhospital.com.tr
www.internationalhospital.com.tr

Gönül Paksöy

Atiye Sokak 6/A, Teşvikiye (0212 261 9081). **Open**
1pm-7pm Mon; 10am-7pm Tue-Sun. **Credit** AmEx,
MC, V.

Mrs Paksöy claims that her shop is unique not only in
Turkey, but the world. Choice raw silk and antique
Ottoman fabrics up to 100 years old are cut to her
design, hand-dyed and sewn. Each creation is a one-
off. So maybe $150 for a silk blouse isn't that bad
after all. She also designs Ottoman-style slippers,
handbags and shoes, as well as interpreting classical
Ottoman jewellery. For men, there is a collection of
machine-made scarves, sweaters and ties at her
second shop across the road at Atiye Sokak 1/3.

Pulp

*Atlas Pasajı 42, off Istiklal Caddesi, Beyoğlu (0212 244
3420/www.pulp-on.com).* **Open** 9am-9.30pm daily.
Credit DC, MC, V. **Map** p308 N3.

One of Istanbul's few shops carrying affordable
urban and clubwear. Brands include Sabotage,
Freemen, Airwalk, Dickies, Futurewear and Vans.

Silk & Cashmere

*Akmerkez Mall, Nispetiye Caddesi, Etiler (0212 282
0235/www.cashmere.com.tr). Metro Levent.* **Open**
10am-10pm daily. **Credit** AmEx, MC, V.

Premium quality silk and pure cashmere fashions
and accessories for men and women. Best of all, due
to a joint venture with supplier Lufa of China, prices
are half those of other world labels. There's also a
duty-free shop at Atatürk airport.

Full-on 'Fantastique' fashion – **Surreal Kılık**.

Surreal Kılık

*Atlas Pasajı 8, off Istiklal Caddesi, Beyoğlu (0212 292
4333/www.sibelgokce.com.tr).* **Open** 11am-9pm daily.
No credit cards. Map p308 N3.

Big-name belly dancer Sibel Gökçe traded in her
tassels to open a clothing shop selling, as the carrier
bag puts it, 'High Tech, Vibes, Underground,
Kitsch, Fantastique' fashions and accessories for
women. Imports from Italy, Hong Kong and
Thailand, and one-offs by innovative Turkish
designers such as Ümit Ünal and Sibel herself.

Yargıcı

*Valikonağı Caddesi 30, Nişantaşı (0212 225 2952/
yargici@yargici.com.tr).* **Open** 9.30am-7-30pm; closed
Sun. **Credit** AmEx, DC, MC, V.

The Turkish Marks & Spencers; chain store with
nine branches stocking relatively reasonably
priced own-brand, good quality ladies' and men's
fashions, mainly sport and classic. Established in
1984 and one of few Turkish brands holding its own
against foreign competition.

Branches: Akmerkez Mall, Nispetiye Caddesi, Etiler
(0212 225 2952); Bağdat Caddesi 343, Erenköy (0216
350 2873).

Accessories

Gorgeous

*Reaşürans Çarşısı 54, off Teşvikiye Caddesi, Teşvikiye
(0212 233 6288).* **Open** 10am-8pm Mon-Sat; closed
Sun. **Credit** MC, V.

Stocks a colourful collection of handbags, hats,
belts and gloves for both day and evening wear. Its
extensive selection and range of oversize clothing
from size 16 upwards is the major draw.

İpek

*Istiklal Caddesi 230/7-8, Beyoğlu (0212 249 8207/ 293
7388).* **Open** 8.30am-7pm Mon-Sat; closed Sun.
Credit AmEx, MC, V. **Map** p308 N3.

Colourful silk and woollen scarves, ties and shawls
featuring Ottoman designs, some based on *tuğras*,
the calligraphic seals of Ottoman sultans. Good
prices, wide selection.

Karaköy Pazarı

Rıhtım Caddesi, 85, Karaköy (0212 245 1198). **Open**
8.30am-7pm Mon-Fri; 9.30am-5pm Sat; closed Sun.
Credit MC, V. **Map** p306 N6.

This shop under the multi-storey car park in
Karaköy stocks leather bags, luggage, belts and
purses. Prices are marked on the goods, but are
negotiable. Nothing awe-inspiring here, but good
quality Turkish leather is a find these days.

Hats

Beyazıt Tekstil

*Yağlıkçılar Caddesi 10, Grand Bazaar (0212 513
2393) Tram Beyazıt or Çemberlitaş.* **Open** 9am-
6.30pm Mon-Sat; closed Sun. **Credit** MC, V.
Map p302 L9.

Yargici – Turkey's answer to Marks & Sparks has branches all over town. *See p65.*

Wholesale fezzes plus Islamic headgear and paraphernalia, including worry beads, alcohol-free cologne and twigs from Mecca for brushing teeth.

Butik Katia

Danışman Geçidi 37, Galatasaray, Beyoğlu (0212 249 4605). **Open** *June-Sept* 10.30am-6pm Mon-Fri; closed Sat, Sun. *Oct-May* 10.30am-6pm Mon-Sat; closed Sun. **No credit cards. Map** p308 N3.

Opened by Madam Katia in the 1940s, this was where society ladies of Pera (now Beyoğlu) came for their hats, the styles of which kept pace with Paris fashions. Today her daughter carries on the family business, selling her own-brand creations to a moneyed clientele. Hats also available for rent.

Jewellery

Altınbaş

Divan Yolu 80/1, Sultanahmet (0212 520 5791). Tram Sultanahmet. **Open** 9am-6pm; closed Sun. **Credit** AmEx, DC, MC, V. **Map** p303 M10.

A high-class, gold and precious-stone jewellery store with unusual, elaborate and showy pieces, some incorporating traditional Ottoman designs.

Bosphorus

Divan Yolu 56/39, Sultanahmet (0212 512 3920). Tram Sultanahmet. **Open** 9am-11pm daily. **Credit** AmEx, MC, V. **Map** p303 M10.

Semi-precious stones set in silver using traditional Turkic designs. Many pieces are far from delicate,

but if you like to feel the weight of your jewellery, then you'll find these striking designs appealing.

Urart

Abdi İpekçi Caddesi 18/1, Nişantaşı (0212 246 7194) **Open** 9am-7pm Mon-Sat; closed Sun. **Credit** AmEx, DC, MC, V.

Sophisticated silver and gold jewellery which draws its inspiration from ancient Anatolian civilisations, from Hittite through to Byzantine. Pricey. **Branch:** Swissôtel, Bayıldım Caddesi 2, Maçka (0212 259 0231).

Leather

The Grand Bazaar is the place for bargain-basement jackets and coats, but quality can be shoddy and true bargains are rare. **Derishow** and **Derimod** (*deri* means leather) have slowly developed a reputation for quality. Prices are only slightly lower than what you'd expect in Europe, but both chains have frequent sales.

Derimod

Akmerkez Mall, Nispetiye Caddesi, Etiler (0212 282 0668). Metro Levent. **Open** 10am-10pm daily. **Credit** AmEx, MC, V.

Carries a larger range than Derishow and has more branches around the city. Also carries an extensive range of discount leather accessories. **Branches:** Büyükdere Caddesi 59, Maslak (0212 286 5103); Süreyya Paşa Mevkii 25/1, Maltepe (0216 383 4033).

Derishow

Akmerkez Mall, Nişpetiye Caddesi, Etiler (0212 282 0408). Metro Levent. **Open** 10am-10pm daily. **Credit** AmEx, DC, MC, V.

Conservative but stylish leather fashions for men and women.

Branches: Bağdat Caddesi 437, Suadiye, Asian Shore (0216 360 5179); Valikonağı Caddesi 85, Nişantaşı (0212 231 1510).

Sunglasses

Nazik Optik

Doğubank Iş Hanı 122, Sirkeci (0212 512 2097). Tram Sirkeci. **Open** 9am-7pm; closed Sun. **Credit** MC, V. **Map** p303 N8.

Leading brands such as Rayban. Also does repairs.

Swimwear

Zeki Triko

Akkavak Sokak 47/2, off Valikonağı Caddesi, Nişantaşı (0212 233 8279/www.zekitriko.com.tr). **Open** 9.30am-7.30pm Mon-Sat; closed Sun. **Credit** AmEx, DC, MC, V.

The most famous swimwear company in Turkey, they export worldwide. Also stock a range of bags, blouses, towels and beach shoes.

Shoes

Turkish women tend to have small feet and finding anything over size 39 (British size 6) can be tricky. **Hotiç**, which has branches around the city and in the Akmerkez Mall, sells up-to-the-minute styles at prices averaging $100 a pair, although tales of the shoes falling apart after a couple of months are not uncommon. Shoes are not a good buy in Istanbul.

Ilke

Istiklal Caddesi 376, Beyoğlu (0212 244 0007). **Open** 9am-9pm daily. **Credit** AmEx, DC, MC, V. **Map** p308 M4.

Three floors of mainly Turkish and Italian, moderately priced women's, men's and children's shoes.

Shoe and Me

Upper level, Akmerkez Mall, Nişpetiye Caddesi, Etiler (0212 282 0277). **Open** 10am-10pm daily. **Credit** AmEx, MC, V.

Shopping the Bazaar

The Grand Bazaar is, above all else, the scene of an invisible tug-of-war. Most tourists enter the market prepared to admire its historical and architectural details, but disinclined to peruse the thousands of shops that are the real reason for its existence. Shopkeepers, for their part, cajole and entreat in a dozen languages and are determined not to permit visitors to indulge in such a non-commercial activity as sightseeing.

A vicious cycle is in spin. The growth of suburbs, malls and automobiles have translated into fewer Turks shopping the Bazaar, making the merchants ever dependent on international visitors. Except for gold and silver jewellery, most of the shops catering to locals have been replaced by stalls aimed squarely at tourists, who are put off by the increasingly aggressive tactics of hawkers and cling more tightly than ever to their purses. While the Grand Bazaar remains one of the top items on any sightseeing agenda, its 65 streets have deteriorated into a kind of gauntlet, with lines of shopkeepers haranguing scurrying visitors often intent on little more than finding the nearest exit.

It's unfortunate. The Grand Bazaar not only has the most extensive collection of tourist-oriented goods, but many items on sale here won't be found elsewhere. This is the place for carpets, jewellery, backgammon sets, meerschaum pipes, copper, leather, silver objects, bric-à-brac, fabrics, fezzes, daggers, Turkish slippers, rose oil... the list goes on.

The only way to shop the Bazaar successfully is to ignore unwanted overtures and, if you have a particular item in mind, to head for the section specialising in what you're after. **Kalpakçılarbaşı** and **Kuyumcular** are mainly lined with gold and jewellery shops, **Keseciler Caddesi** has the greatest concentration of carpets, **Old Bedesten** is the place for expensive antiques and artefacts.

When entering the main entrance of the Bazaar from Yeniçeriler Caddesi, head to the extreme back right section for silver, the extreme left-hand area for leather and copper. For souvenirs in general, go straight down **Yağlıkçılar Sokak**, making forays into the alleys on your right. Continue along the same street to look over fabrics. It's best to allow plenty of time for comparison shopping and bargaining. Above all else, follow the golden rule: what is it worth to you?

For more information on shopping the Bazaar: **antiques** (*see page 155*); **carpets** (*see page 168*); **gold** (*see page 166*); prayer beads, fezzes and religious items (**Beyazıt Tekstil**; see page 165).

Eat, Drink, Shop

Upmarket shoes, mainly Italian.
Branch: Maçka Caddesi 24, Teşvikiye
(0212 225 0616).

Vintage & second-hand

The second-hand clothing market has yet to
catch on in Istanbul, but there are a few venues
mostly selling extremely expensive antique
costumes or stained, torn garments.

Ve Saire

*Akmerkez Mall, Nispetiye Caddesi, Etiler (0212 282
1071). Metro Levent.* **Open** 10.30am-7pm Mon;
10.30am-10pm Tue-Sun. **Credit** MC, V.
Buried deep on level three of the underground
parking garage, this place is a 'recycled' clothing
boutique, with a who's who of mainly women's
fashion labels. Most articles start at $50.

Food & drink

The choicest produce, best cuts of meat and
freshest baked goods can be found at your local
greengrocers, butchers and bakers. Most
neighbourhoods also have weekly street markets
with a wide range of produce, cheeses, olives,
spices and staples. Look for a *hamal*, a man with a
large wicker basket on his back, if you want to
negotiate home delivery for around $1. The
numerous stalls to the right of the **Egyptian
Market** (*see p81*) are worth exploring and shops
at the **Balık Pazarı** midway along Istiklal
Caddesi carry wonderful produce from quail eggs
to *crème fraiche*. For a wide selection of regional
produce from all over Turkey visit the various
delicatessans just inland of the ferry terminal at
Kadıköy on the Asian Shore.

The rug trade

Pity the poor carpet merchant, the used car
dealer of the Orient. Carpet buying has become
so associated with hassle, hustle and
hoodwinking that many a tourist trumpets a
return home without floor coverings as a
testament to their ability to hold on to
hard-earned cash and withstand being
badgered into purchases so obvious they must
be banal. Pity the poor, uninformed tourist.

Acquiring a carpet or kilim (flat-weave rug) can
be intimidating and requires both homework
and common sense. First, determine your price
range and get a realistic idea of what you can
afford. If you're interested in handmade
carpets made of natural fibres – and there's no
reason to buy anything else in Turkey – expect
to spend upwards of $300. Cushion covers
salvaged from high quality but damaged
carpets are a much cheaper alternative,
starting at about $10 for good quality pieces.
Dealers will humour you by allowing you to singe
a few threads of carpet, the much advised way
to distinguish synthetic fibres from natural. You
would be hard pressed to find anything other
than natural fibres, but be aware that vegetable
dyes were almost entirely replaced by chemical
dyes in Anatolia by the 1880s, and
re-introduced only recently to satisfy the
Western passion for all things natural. Don't
believe claims that a carpet is 75 years old,
with natural fibre and natural dye.

Comparison shopping iş essential. You are
unlikely to find a bargain at the Grand Bazaar,
but you do have one of the world's largest
selections to choose from. Take your time. Ask
questions about materials and designs. Don't

feel guilty about having the hundredth kilim
unfolded or accepting yet another glass of tea.
Unless you're qualified to make skilled
judgements on age, rarity, condition, artistic
quality, quality of workmanship and materials
and current international prices, rely on the one
judgement only you can make: do you like it? A
final tip: the best way to avoid finding a more
attractive carpet at a lower price once you get
home is to do your scouting before your holiday.

The following shops have English-speaking
staff, no bargaining policy and are outside of
the bazaar. They can be all be trusted to handle
overseas posting and they all allow exchange
of purchases.

Bread and Water

*Çorlulu Ali Paşa Medresi, Yeniçeriler Caddesi 1-
3, Çemberlitaş (0212 519 0990). Tram
Çemberlitaş.* **Open** 10am-midnight daily. **Credit**
AmEx, DC, MC, V. **Map** p302 L10.
Kilims, carpets, cicims and saddlebags from all
over Turkey displayed in an old Ottoman
medrese that doubles as a *nargile* café. Prices
start at $8 to $10 for handmade silk cushions
incorporating antique Turkmen textiles.

Ottoman Gallery

*Arasta Bazaar 139, Sultanahmet (0212 516
0063). Tram Sultanahmet.* **Open** 9.30am-8pm
daily. **Credit** AmEx, MC, V. **Map** p303 N11.
Bright designs, reasonable prices and a lesson
in geopolitics. Brothers Fahrettin and
Selahattin have licensed Afghani refugees in
Pakistani camps to weave Turkish double-knot
carpets in colourful Caucasian designs using

Eat, Drink, Shop

Asri Turşucu

Opposite the Firuzağa Mosque on Ağa Hamamı Sokak, off Siraselviler Caddesi, Cihangir (0212 244 4724). **Open** 8.30am-8pm Mon-Sat; 2pm-6pm Sun. **No credit cards. Map** p309 O4.
Has been pickling just about everything since 1938. Large jars of artistically arranged fruits and vegetables, as much decorative objects as edibles.

Diğer Lezzetler

Cevdet Paşa Caddesi 342, Bebek (0212 265 0333). **Open** 10am-9pm Mon-Sat; 11am-1.30pm, 6pm-8.30pm Sun. **Credit** MC, V.
The name means 'different tastes' and is especially apt in Istanbul. Bloody Mary mix, imported camembert, watermelon jam, squid-ink pasta and special teas are some of the rich pickings. Prices are reasonable, considering the luxury factor, with 113 grams (4oz) of Beluga caviar yours for about $45.

Kurukahveci Mehmet Efendi

Tahmis Caddesi 66, Eminönü (0212 511 4262). **Tram** *Eminönü.* **Open** 8.30am-6.45pm Mon-Sat; closed Sun. **Credit** MC, V. **Map** p302 L8.
Situated at the back of the **Egyptian Market** (*see p83*), this is a long-established business with a reputation for selling the best finely ground Turkish coffee in town. It also attracts quite a few customers for ground orchid root, used to flavour and thicken ice cream.

Manhattan Gourmet Shop

Güzelbahçe Sokak 14, Nişantaşı (0212 225 0047/www.gurmeonline.com). **Open** 10am-7pm Mon-Sat; closed Sun. **Credit** MC, V.
In addition to a large range of flavoured and premium filter coffee, the Manhattan Gourmet shop also stocks hard-to-find items such as rice vinegar and oyster sauce.

premier Afghani wool. The striking results sell for $200 a square metre. Less pricey items include $10 kilim cushion covers and fine, though machine-made, shawls smuggled by Iranians out of Pakistan and into Turkey; yours for $15.

Ortaasya ve Semertkan El Sanatlar

İç Cebeci Han 2nd floor, Yağlıkçılar Caddesi, Grand Bazaar, Sultanahmet (no phone). **Tram** *Çemberlitaş.* **Open** 8.30am-7pm Mon-Sat; closed Sun. **No credit cards. Map** p302 L9.
Heaped with Central Asian embroidered suzani fabrics, elaborate silver and silk bridal headdresses, cloaks, camelhair caftans and

antique leather shoes. Owner Aziz's English isn't quite up to explaining exactly what ikats and puttees are, but he'll provide you with tea and let you leaf through books that do. Prices start at $5 for a Kirghiz cushion cover.

Van Halıcılık

Arasta Bazaar 149, Sultanahmet (0212 516 3058). **Tram** *Sultanahmet.* **Open** 9am-8pm daily. **Credit** AmEx, DC, MC, V. **Map** p303 N11.
A diverse collection of kilims, carpets and cicims, mainly from East Turkey, some of them Kurdish. Patterns run from Kereke to animist, fabrics from silk to wool and prices from $60 to $1,000. No antiques or rare collector's items, just value for money.

Savoy
Sıraselviler Caddesi 181-3, Cihangir (0212 249 1818).
Open 6am-midnight daily. **Credit** MC, V.
Map p309 O3.
Don't let the tacky mirrors and displays of gaudy candy dishes mislead you. This is one of the finest cake shops in Istanbul, offering everything from brownies to raspberry tarts, and getting them right.

Sütte
Duduodaları Sokak 21, off Balık Pazarı, Beyoğlu (0212 293 9292). **Open** 9am-8pm Mon-Sat; closed Sun. **Credit** MC, V. **Map** p308 N3.
The Macedonian owners stock a wide range of pork products, including ham and bacon, plus an array of imported cheeses, sauces and condiments.

Health food

Bünsa
Duduodaları Sokak 26, off Balık Pazarı, Beyoğlu (0212 243 6265). **Open** 8am-8pm daily. **No credit cards.** **Map** p308 N3.
The wholesale distributor and retailer for Bünsa, Turkey's first producer of wholefoods. It stocks organic brown rice, herbal tea, royal jelly, spices, jams and grains.

Nuh'un Ambarı
Yeniçarşı Caddesi 54, Beyoğlu (0212 292 9272/ www.dhkd.org). **Open** 10.30am-7.30pm Mon-Sat; closed Sun. **Credit** AmEx, MC, V. **Map** p308 N3.
Rather slim pickings for a place called 'Noah's Larder', but high-quality olive oil, natural sun-dried

tomatoes, organic chickpea flower, beans and grains make a visit worthwhile. Café open until 7pm.

Supermarkets

The corner shop (*bakkal*) is fighting a losing battle against the spread of supermarkets, local and international. There are dozens of chains throughout the city, the largest being Migros and the most upmarket Makro.

Makro
Abdi İpekçi Caddesi 24, Nişantaşı (0212 248 9455). **Open** 8.30am-9pm daily. **Credit** AmEx, MC, V.
Makro stocks a wide selection of imported foods and alcohol, and also sells pork products.
Branches: Akmerkez Mall, Nispetiye Caddesi, Etiler (0212 282 0310); Muallim Naci Cadessi 170, Kuruçeşme (0212 257 1381).

Migros
19 Mayıs Caddesi 1, Şişli (0212 246 6480/ www.migros.com.tr). **Open** 9am-10pm Mon-Sat; 10am-10pm Sun. **Credit** DC, MC, V.
Extremely competitive prices, but no frills and few imported items. Shopping can be ordered via the Internet in some parts of the city.
Branches: Akasyah Sokak 53, B Blok, Yeni Levent (0212 282 3369); Damaga Sokak 23/15, Caferağa Mahallesi, Kadıköy (0216 418 1929).

Wine

International wines are hard to come by because of punishing import duties. Rumours are that

Sweet treats ready to eat at **Savoy**, Istanbul's best source of authentic raspberry tarts.

Sweet stuff

To the foreign palate, Turkish confectionery seems tooth-achingly sweet. Put that down to their Ottoman origins – a dynasty known for cloying excesses. The most famous confection of all, Turkish Delight, known locally as *lokum*, was invented by Hacı Bekir, who has been immortalised by the sweet shops bearing his name. Principal ingredients are sugar and cornstarch. Typical flavourings include rosewater, essence of lemon and orange, and arabic gum. It can then be rolled in coconut or powdered sugar, and studded with pistachios and hazelnuts. Freshness is crucial. Old delights deteriorate into stale chewy torture, so avoid buying at the Egyptian Market in favour of the two branches of Hacı Bekir listed below, both of which have a much brisker turnover.

Istanbul almond and pistachio pastes (*badem* and *şam fıstığı ezmesi*), plain or dipped in chocolate, bear no resemblance to their humble German cousin, marzipan. Regional specialities available in Istanbul include *pişmaniye*, from the Iznik region, which looks a bit like thick cotton candy and is made of spun butter and flour, and Anatolian *üzüm sucuğu*, made by repeatedly dipping stringed walnuts

into hot, concentrated grape juice. The brownish candle-like result is a chewy, nutty energy food. Turkish folklore has it that nuts and honey have aphrodisiacal powers, hence numerous variations of sticky nut balls lumped under the heading 'Turkish Viagra' and displayed next to postcards and statuettes of Priapus sporting an enormous erection.

Ali Muhiddin Hacı Bekir

Istiklal Caddesi 129, Beyoğlu (0212 244 2804). **Open** 8am-9pm daily. **Credit** AmEx, MC, V. **Map** p309 O3.

In the confection-making business since 1777. Turkish Delight, marzipan, biscuits, candied green figs and pastries. Gift-wrapped boxes available. Small café in the back.
Branch: Hamidiye Caddesi 81, Sirkeci (0212 522 0666).

Meşhur Bebek Badem Ezmesi

Cevdet Paşa Caddesi 238/1, Bebek (0212 263 5984). **Open** 8.30am-10.30pm daily. **Credit** AmEx, MC, V.

An old-fashioned sweet shop selling almond and pistachio marzipan, chocolates and classic Turkish sweets.

---

these will soon be dropped, meaning more foreign wines at cheaper prices and a kick up the backside to local producers. Meantime, drinkable local *şarap* is on sale at supermarkets, many corner markets and at licensed TEKEL (government tobacco and alcohol) shops.

La Cave

Sıraselviler Caddesi 207, Cihangir (0212 243 2405/ www.lacavesarap.com). **Open** 9am-9pm. **Credit** AmEx, DC, MC, V. **Map** p309 O3.

Turkey's largest wine shop. Some 45 firms provide La Cave with over 250 kinds of Turkish wine, ranging from $1.50 to $15. Also stocks French, Italian, Californian, Chilean and Argentine wines. Plans to add a 'cigar corner' and market Turkey's largest selection of imported and local cheeses.

Flowers

Some of the best and least expensive places for flowers are the stands run by Gypsies just off Taksim Square on Tarlabaşı Caddesi, and at the **Kadıköy**, **Karaköy** and **Beşiktaş** ferryboat docks. Prices drop dramatically at all itinerant flower stands as the day progresses. At other times, haggle. If you hand over the initial asking price, then you're paying too much.

Gold

When inflation was sky-high and possessing foreign currency illegal, Turkish women invested their money in gold coins and slave bangles, both of which could be bought and sold for a price that fluctuated according to the gold rate. Not many shops in the **Grand Bazaar** are patronised by locals, but the gold shops are an exception. Trade remains brisk in the street of jewellers (**Kuyumcular Caddesi**), which you enter through the Çarşıkapı Gate (to the right from Yeniçeriler Caddesi where the buses stop). Prices are by the gram and any piece you are interested in will be weighed in front of you and the price worked out using a calculator. Check the daily newspaper for the gold rate before you go. All gold is a minimum of 14 carat and goes up to 22 carat (nine carat is not considered gold in Turkey). Taxes on gold are less than in the UK, but prices are not hallmarked.

Hair & beauty salons

According to Islam, excessive body hair is unattractive and neglecting to remove it is considered unclean. Most women won't let more

Eat, Drink, Shop

La Cave – Turkey's largest wine shop stocks over 250 home-produced varieties. *See p171.*

than about 40 days elapse between waxings. This is usually done at beauty salons – legs, underarms, pubic area and any down on the face, it all goes. At the same time it's usual to have a manicure, pedicure and the thick skin on the soles of your feet removed, and maybe an all-over body massage too.

Gizem Beauty Centre
Dereboyu Caddesi 168, Ortaköy (0212 261 0094).
Open noon-9pm Mon-Sat; closed Sun. **Credit** MC, V.
Hairdressing, waxing, depilation, skincare, pedicure, manicure, make-up and massage. They also stock cosmetics and perfume.

MOS Kuaför
Akmerkez Mall, Nispetiye Cadessi, Etiler (0212 282 0554) Metro Levent. **Open** 9am-9pm daily. **Credit** MC, V.
One of the best known hairdressers in Istanbul, patronised by the rich and famous. A dye and cut will cost around $80. Unisex.

Barbers

Neighbourhood barber shops provide incredible pampering for the price. Nostril hairs are snipped away, ear hairs singed off, shoulders and forehead massaged, beard shaven twice and head thoroughly doused with colognes and balms. But while local barbers are usually experts in straight hair and all things moustache-related, they may find it a little more difficult to cope with any curls or frizz.

Cihangir Erkek Kuaförü
Akarsu Caddesi 49/1, Cihangir (0212 251 1660).
Open 8am-9pm Mon-Sat; noon-6.30pm Sun.
No credit cards. Map p309 O4.
Used to trimming foreigners; some English spoken.

Handicrafts

Carpets (*see page 168* **The rug trade**) are the obvious buy, but Istanbul boasts a wide range of other traditional – and more portable – handicrafts. Skill in ceramics dates back to the era of the Selçuk Turks and is particularly associated with the town of Iznik (*see page 255*). Original tiles are now museum pieces, but several companies do high-quality modern interpretations of old designs. Ebru is the Uzbek Turk variation on marbling, applied to papers, card and glass. Other Istanbul handicrafts include inlaid boxes, miniatures, book-binding, copperware, prayer beads, painted fabrics and carved meerschaum pipes. Most of this stuff can be found at the **Grand Bazaar**; *see page 167* **Shopping the Bazaar**. For glassware try **Paşabahçe** (*see page 174*).

Anadolu Sanat
Tünel Geçidi 15, Tünel, Beyoğlu (0212 249 2527).
Open 9am-7pm Mon-Sat; closed Sun. **Credit** MC, V.
Map p308 M4.
If you can't bear the haggling at the Bazaar, here's a good assortment of reasonably priced copperware, brassware and woodwork, patterned tiles and reproduction graveurs of Istanbul panoramas.

Arasta Bazaar

Kabasakal Caddesi 5, Sultanahmet. Tram Sultanahmet. **Open** 9am-8pm daily. **Map** p303 N11.
Old Ottoman bazaar behind Sultanahmet Mosque with two long rows of shops either side of a narrow lane selling all kinds of handicrafts, including carpets, silver, copper, calligraphy, ceramics and ebru. Salesmen tend to be a bit pushy.

Aznavur Pasajı

Istiklal Caddesi 212, Beyoğlu. **Open** 8.30am-9pm daily. **Map** p308 N3.
One of the elegant old Pera arcades, now given over to various small handicraft shops. Far less hassle than the bazaars over on the Sultanahmet side, and generally with more interesting pieces, particularly ceramics and silverwork. The shopowners tend to be pretty knowledgeable about their stock and the prices are reasonable.

Cafer Ağa Medresesi Applied Handicrafts Centre

Caferiye Sokak, Soğukkuyu Çikmazi, off Alemdar Caddesi, Sultanahmet (0212 513 3601). Tram Gülhane. **Open** 8am-7pm daily. **Credit** MC, V. **Map** p303 N10.
A courtyard at the end of an alley, just up from the entrance of Gülhane Park, belonging to a theological school built by Sinan in 1559. The former students' lodgings are now craft workshops with all products for sale, including silver, jewellery,

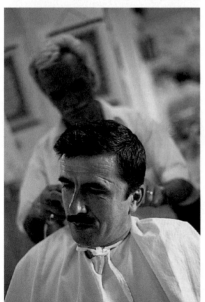

Cihangir Erkek Kuaförü. *See p172.*

calligraphy, miniatures, ebru and some ceramics. Good prices. There is also a very pleasant café-restaurant in the courtyard.

Deli Kızın Yeri

Francalacı Sokak 2, Arnavutköy (0212 287 1294). **Open** 10am-7pm Mon-Sat; noon-6pm Sun. **Credit** MC, V.
Linda Caldwell designs and makes a range of off-beat gifts in her workshop-cum-showroom. Stock includes handmade clothes and drapes that bring traditional block-print designs into the 21st century with bold and bright colours.

Dosim

Soğukçeşme Sokak, Sultanahmet (0212 526 5947). **Open** 8.30am-5pm Mon, Wed-Sun; closed Tue. **Credit** AmEx, MC, V. **Map** p303 N10.
Run by the Ministry of Culture, with a prime location opposite the Topkapı Palace. Silver, jewellery, textiles, hand-painted handkerchiefs and ceramics at fixed but fair prices and of reliable quality.

Ebristan Istanbul Ebru Evi

Hafız Mehmet Bey Sokak 8, Ihsaniye, Üsküdar (0216 334 5934/www.ebristan.com). **Open** 1pm-5pm Mon-Sat; closed Sun. **Credit** MC, V.
Specialises in Turkish marbled papers and books.

Golden Horn Handicrafts Centre

Zindan Han 54-56, Ragıp Gümüşpala Caddesi, Tahtakale (212 512 4270). Tram Eminönü. **Open** 9am-6.30pm daily. **Credit** AmEx, DC, MC, V. **Map** p302 L7.
This is a converted Genoese prison now known as the Zindan Han, just west of Rüstem Paşa Mosque, selling high-class but expensive jewellery, leather and other crafts. Group tours can be arranged.

Istanbul Handicrafts Centre

Kabasakal Caddesi 7, Sultanahmet (0212 517 6782). Tram Sultanahmet. **Open** 9.30am-6pm daily. **Credit** AmEx, MC, V. **Map** p303 N10.
Old *medrese* converted into a workshop and sales point for handicrafts, just to the right of the Yeşil Ev hotel. Fun place to shop, as you can watch artisans at work and the surroundings are beautiful.

Iznik Vakfı

Öksüz Çocuk Sokak 14, Kuruçeşme (0212 287 3243). **Open** 8.30am-6pm Mon-Fri; 10am-5pm Sat; closed Sun. **Credit** MC, V.
Modern reproductions of Ottoman ceramic plates, dishes and jugs, with patterning similar to the tiling you see in the old mosques around town. Not cheap and ill-suited to minimalist urban apartment living, but pretty classy if you have the right kind of pad to go with it.

Kevser

Muallim Naci Caddesi 72, Ortaköy (0212 327 0586). **Open** 10.30am-8.30pm daily. **Credit** AmEx, MC, V.
Ceramics shop displaying and selling the work of Sıtkı Olcar, one of the modern masters, who creates his own designs and has widely exhibited abroad.

Eat, Drink, Shop

Ottomania – furniture and fabrics.

Ortaköy Market

Near the quay in Ortaköy. **Open** 9am-midnight Sat, Sun; closed Mon-Fri. **No credit cards.**

A good place for quirky jewellery, plus bags, clothes, glass, silver and old copper work. A big weekend draw for people from all over Istanbul and not at all touristy.

Sırça Handicrafts Centre

Akbıyık Caddesi 2, Sultanahmet (0212 638 5184). Tram Sultanahmet. **Open** 9.30am-8pm daily. **Credit** AmEx, MC, V. **Map** p303 N11.

One of the best places for ceramics, pottery and porcelain, much of which originates in Cappodocia. A speciality is 'red earth' work, a modern update of Hittite pottery from 4,000 years ago. Pieces increase in quality and price as you move up through the building; ground floor is student work, second is Sırça house artists; third is museum pieces.

Sofa

Nuruosmaniye Caddesi 42 & 106/B, Cağaloğlu (0212 527 4142). Tram Sultanahmet. **Open** 9.30am-6.30pm Mon-Sat; closed Sun. **Credit** AmEx, MC, V. **Map** p303 M9.

Two small shops for connoisseurs selling highest quality Ottoman engravings, ceramics, miniatures, carpets, jewellery and calligraphy.

Household, furniture & gifts

Doğubank Işhanı

Hamidiye Caddesi 30, Sirkeci (0212 526 4313/ www.dogubank-ishani.gen.tr). Tram Sirkeci. **Open** 9am-6.30pm Mon-Sat; closed Sun. **Credit cards** accepted in some shops. **Map** p303 M8.

This was set up by a state-owned bank to profit from the customs-exempt status of migrant Turkish workers bringing TVs and irons back from Germany. Still the cheapest place for imported electronics and white goods, although with Turkey's entry to the European customs union, no one can figure out why. Three floors of tiny shops are heaped high with every conceivable item that runs on electricity. Cash up front and bargaining bring prices down fast. No receipts, no guarantees, no questions asked.

Ottomania

Mim Kemal Öke Caddesi 7, Nişantaşı (0212 233 5225). **Open** 10am-7pm Mon-Sat; closed Sun. **Credit** AmEx, MC, V.

Although originally carrying only Ottoman-style furniture and fabrics it now sells mainly top-line Italian linen, towels and candles. Tableware and bedding designs are frequently rotated. Only the lush fabrics at the back have an Ottoman theme.

Paşabahçe

Istiklal Caddesi 314, Beyoğlu (0212 244 0544/ www.pasabahce.com.tr). **Open** 9.30am-7pm Mon-Fri; 9.30am-8pm Sat; closed Sun. **Credit** AmEx, DC, MC, V. **Map** p308 M4.

Mainly Turkish-made, good quality dinnerware and glassware, vases and decorative objects displayed on three floors. There's a small household appliances section downstairs. As a nod to international clientele, frosted bowls and glasses with Hittite and Selçuk motifs are available to the right of the main entrance.

Branch: Bağdat Caddesi 392/7-8, Şaşkinbakkal, Asian Shore (0216 386 1689).

Key-cutting & locksmiths

There are hundreds of locksmiths around town, recognisable by their yellow key-shaped signs.

Gizem Ahahtar

Galip Sokak 1/A, Beyoğlu (0212 243 2445/ 24hr emergency service 0532 611 6978). **Open** 8am-7pm Mon-Sat; closed Sun. **No credit cards.** **Map** p309 O3.

As with most such shops, offers outservice for all kinds of locks, from safes to cars.

Markets

Once a week, a few streets in every neighbourhood are covered with awnings and jammed with stands selling fruit and veg, rice and beans, dairy products, clothes and the like.

A few markets have grown so large that they have begun to attract customers from all over Istanbul, and even other cities. Markets tend to get going in early morning and generally start to wind down by early afternoon.

Çarşamba

Darüşşafaka Caddesi, Fatih. **Open** Wed.
Map p305 F6.
A giant open-air village market in the heart of Istanbul's most traditional district. The perfect antidote to feeling conspicuous and foreign at the Grand Bazaar is to be swept along by the ruthless headscarves and bristling beards intent on a bargain. Not for claustrophobes or the faint of heart.

Salıpazarı

Kuşdili Sokak, Fenerbahçe. **Open** Tue, Sun.
Map p311 X7.
Draws a large and diverse crowd; middle-class matrons jostle with beetle-browed Anatolian mamas in search of the freshest figs and cheapest brassieres – 'hats for twins' in market talk. For antiques, furniture and jewellery, come on Sunday, when a European-style flea market is held on the same site.

Ulus Market

Nispetiye Caddesi, Etiler. **Open** Thur.
In posh Etiler and a more genteel version of what normally passes for a market. Donna Karan-clad,

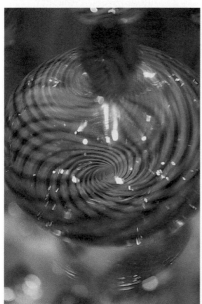

A touch of glass at **Paşabahçe**. *See p174.*

carefully coiffed types sort through tables of knock-off labels. Smoked Circassian cheese and cold-press olive oil are mixed in among the feta cheese and olives. Hand-painted wooden breakfast trays, well-designed cutlery and smart kitchen accessories sell for a fraction of those at the Akmerkez Mall across the street. Even the rich can't resist a bargain.

Music

CDs are no cheaper in Istanbul than in Europe and far more expensive than in the US. International releases are about $16 to $18. Local pressings of Turkish artists cost about $10 to $12. Pirate CDs and MP3 downloads of international artists go for $3 to $5 in the backstreets of Tahtakale (*see page 80*) and from street traders around Taksim.

Ada Music

Orhan Adli Apaydin Sokak 20, off Istiklal Caddesi, Tünel, Beyoğlu (0212 251 3878). **Open** 9am-10pm Mon-Thur, Sun; 9am-11pm Fri, Sat. **Credit** AmEx, V. **Map** p308 M4.
Opened by Turkish record company Ada, this is the first shop to offer a large collection of Turkish rock and protest music in a smart, airy setting. Some foreign CDs, international newspapers and magazines and some English-language books. Café, too.

Kod Music Shop

Atlas Pasajı 16, off Istiklal Caddesi 209, Beyoğlu (0212 244 2422/www.kodmuzik.com). **Open** noon-9pm Mon-Sat; closed Sun. **Credit** MC, V. **Map** p308 N3.
Groundbreaking music shop and a great place to find out what's going on. If the savvy staff at Kod don't know about something happening in the city then it's not worth knowing about.

Megavizyon

Istiklal Caddesi 79-81, Beyoğlu (0212 293 0759/www.megavizyononline.com). **Open** 10am-11pm daily. **Credit** AmEx, MC, V. **Map** p309 O2.
Biggest music store in Istanbul with widest range of genres in one place. Branches at the Carousel and Capitol shopping malls. Also sells computer equipment, videos, English-language books, Internet packages and a limited selection of magazines.

Raksotek

Istiklal Caddesi 162, Beyoğlu (0212 292 0208). **Open** 9.30am-11pm Mon-Sat; 10.30am-11pm Sun. **Credit** MC, V. **Map** p308 N3.
Three-storey shop opened to great fanfare as Turkey's answer to Virgin Records. International and Turkish artists, as well as Internet packages, CD racks, headsets, speakers and children's toys.

Zihni Music Center

Mühürdar Caddesi 70/13, Kadıköy (0216 349 2268/ www.zihnimusic.com). **Open** 11am-8pm daily. **Credit** MC, V. **Map** p311 W7.
Best place for CDs, music expertise and concert tickets on the Asian side.

Eat, Drink, Shop

Opticians

There is no in-house eye-testing in Turkey, so the procedure is to get your eyes tested by an eye doctor and take the prescription to the high street optician. Most opticians do repairs. An eye-popping amount of them can be found on Hamdiye Caddesi, just west of Sirkeci station.

Photography

Many high-street photographers have studios where you can have your portrait taken, get a passport photograph that actually resembles you and also buy and develop films.

Erol Fotoğrafçılık

Ortabahçe Caddesi 22/3, Beşiktaş (0212 259 6800). **Open** 8am-8.30pm Mon-Sat; closed Sun. **Credit** MC, V.
Offers printing from CD, diskette and digital camera as well as traditional film-processing services and portraits. Used by the professionals.

Yalçın Express

Ankara Caddesi 199-201, Sirkeci (0212 526 0686). Tram Sirkeci. **Open** 8am-8pm Mon-Sat; closed Sun. **Credit** MC, V. **Map** p303 M9.
Handy for tourists staying in Sultanahmet, Yalcın offers passport photographs, film and developing.

Repairs

Bicycle Repairs

Sales and repair shops are conveniently grouped together in Unkapanı and Sirkeci. In Sirkeci, head for Mimar Kemalettin Caddesi, near the Sirkeci tram stop.

Hasım

İşcan Alt Geçidi, Unkapanı. **Open** varies. **Credit** varies. **Map** p302 H8.
Beneath the arches of the aqueduct on Atatürk Bulvarı is a whole block of bicycle stores with a wide selection of Turkish and foreign brands, plus spares and repair services.

Watch & jewellery repairs

The gold shops in the Grand Bazaar repair items made of gold and buy scrap gold, which they use to manufacture new pieces. They don't repair items made of silver – and shops selling silver don't repair pieces made of gold.

Gün Şah

Kemankeş Caddesi 25, Karaköy (0212 249 3666). **Open** 8.30am-7.30pm Mon-Fri; 9am-7pm Sat; closed Sun. **Credit** AmEx, MC, V. **Map** p306 N6.
Repairs all brands of clocks and watches and can find spare parts for all makes.

Lider Mücevherat

11/12/13 İç Bedesten, Grand Bazaar (no phone). Tram Beyazıt or Çemberlitaş. **Open** *winter* 8.30am-7pm Mon-Sat. *Summer* 8.30am-8pm Mon-Sat; closed Sun. **No credit cards. Map** p302 L9.
In the Old Bedesten at the heart of the Grand Bazaar, Lider does repairs while you wait.

Shoe repairs

Barbaros Bulvarı Belediye Dükkanları

The square at the bottom of Barbaros Bulvarı, with the tall cylindrical monument in the middle, is lined with small wooden booths, many of them housing shoeshine and repair shops and key cutters. It's best to establish the price before getting any of the work done.

Jet Set

Ihlamuryolu 11, Nişantaşı (0212 241 7390). **Open** 9am-7pm Mon-Fri; 9am-6pm Sat; closed Sun. **No credit cards.**
Express shoe repairs in the heart of Nişantaşı.

Sporting goods

Galatasaray Başar Spor

Büyükparmakkapı Sokak 10/1, off İstiklal Caddesi, Beyoğlu (0212 252 2052). **Open** *summer* 9am-8pm daily. *Winter* 9.30am-7pm daily. **Credit** MC, V. **Map** pp309 O3.
Established eight years ago, the Galatasaray football club shop has been doing a booming business since the team's UEFA Cup win in 2000. Uniforms, scarves, hats and footballs in red and yellow.

Sportland

İstiklal Caddesi 189, Beyoğlu (0212 249 3108). **Open** 9.30am-9.30pm Mon-Sat; 10.30am-8pm Sun. **Credit** AmEx, MC, V. **Map** p309 O3.
Two well-stocked floors of international and local sportswear and shoes. But Sportsland does not sell any sports equipment.

Video rental

There used to be a video store on every corner, but the introduction of private television and cable put most of them out of business. Film buffs and DVD have meant a few have kept going. Foreign and indie/art films are nearly impossible to come by.

Şimşek Video

Aslıhan Pasajı 36-7, off Balık Pazarı, Galatasaray (0212 243 5385). **Open** 10am-8pm Mon-Sat; closed Sun. **Credit** MC, V. **Map** p308 N3.
A large collection of films of the Oscar-winning variety. Membership is $16 annually plus $2.50 per rental. Same rates for video and DVD. Videos must be returned within 48 hours.

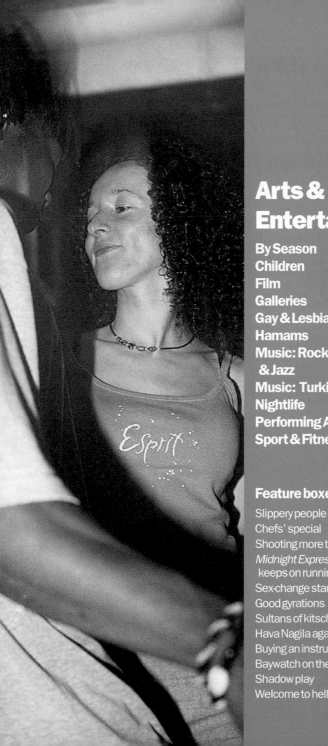

Arts &
Entertainment

Istanbul by Season

Between Atatürk's anniversary and oil-wrestling week, Istanbul's calendar fair sparkles with cultural events.

Except for winter, which sees Istanbul go into hibernation, the city hosts a decent array of cultural events and festivals, to which it manages to attract an impressive line-up of international names. But, other than the **Conquest Week Celebrations** – themselves a fairly recent phenomenon – surprisingly few of these affairs have any historical traditions.

This is ironic, because a love of pomp and splendour was a hallmark of imperial Istanbul right up until the 20th century. Grandiose celebrations were held on every possible occasion, with the sultan providing most of the excuses. The birth of an imperial child, circumcision of the sultan's son, setting off on campaign, returning from campaign – all of these were marked with incredible extravagance. For the circumcision of three of Süleyman's sons in 1530, tents sewn with tulips were erected on gold-plated poles at the Hippodrome, where crowds were entertained by tightrope walkers performing on a cord stretched from the Egyptian Obelisk. The public was fed on roast oxen, out of which fled live foxes as the meat was set down.

More than 400 years later, in the mid 19th century, visiting storyteller Hans Christian Andersen was in the city for the Prophet's Birthday and recorded seeing the Bosphorus filled with a vast fleet of small boats all burning lanterns so that 'Everything looked as if it were outlined in flame . . . Everything was enveloped in a magical light'.

That light was extinguished at the birth of the republic, which put an end both to imperial traditions and overt religious observance. In their place were inserted a dour bunch of annual excuses for flag-waving, such as Republic Day and Victory Day (*see page 283*). More tragic still is the recent infiltration, via the marketing people, of a slew of imports, novelties like Sevgililer Günü (Valentines Day), Mothers' Day and even Christmas, which naturally tends to get confused with New Year's Day, given that over 95 per cent of the population is Muslim. Istanbulites' inner partying beast only comes raging out when one of the three big football teams scores an international victory and thousands of supporters hit the streets to tread the thin line between glorious celebration and outright rioting (*see page 231* **Welcome to Hell!**).

International Istanbul Film Festival spells glitter and glamour. *See p179.*

To encounter truly Turkic off-the-wall traditions it's necessary to leave town. Olive-oil wrestling (*see page 181* **Slippery People**) should top anyone's list of reasons for getting on a bus, while the Mengen food festival (*see page 182* **Chefs' special**) is a wonderful celebration of gastronomic eccentricity. Camel wrestling, which takes place throughout Aegean Turkey every winter, lies beyond the geographical scope of this book. That's a pity, as the presence of one-and-a-half-ton, hairy, evil-tempered, four-legged combatants in Taksim Square could provide exactly the tonic for strait-laced festivals that Istanbul needs.

Information & tickets

In Turkish, by far the best resource is the monthly magazine *Kültür-Sanat*, put out by the Istanbul municipality and distributed free through bookstores, museums and cafés. *Istanbul*

Kültür Sanat Haritası (Istanbul Cultural & Arts Map) is similarly exhaustive, while *Aktüel*, *Tempo* and *Istanbul Life* all also carry cultural listings. Non-Turkish-speakers have to make do with the *Turkish Daily News*, which seems to miss more events than it covers. There's also *Istanbul: The Guide*, which is good but infrequent. Check its website instead at www.theguideturkey.com. And then there's always the tourist office (*see page 282*).

The following are major ticket outlets for festivals:

Atatürk Cultural Centre (AKM)

Taksim Square (0212 251 5600/251 1023). **Open** 10am-6pm daily. **No credit cards. Map** 307 P2.
The big ugly building on Taksim Square. Tickets for most festivals can be obtained here. Students receive discounts.

Vakkorama Store

Osmanlı Sokak 13, Taksim (0212 251 1571). **Open** 10am-8pm Mon-Sat; closed Sun. **Credit** AmEx, DC, MC, V. **Map** p309 p2.
On the left down the steep street to the right of the entrance to the Marmara Hotel.

Spring

Fujifilm World Music Days

Various venues (information 0212 252 5167/ www.pozitif-ist.com). **Dates** last weekend in Mar. **Tickets** Vakkorama stores **Admission** $15-$20.
Istanbul's own version of WOMAD. Dispersed across various live music venues around town, this two-day festival takes the form of themed 'parties' such as 'Africa Sounds', 'Brasil Nova', or 'New York Underground'. Transglobal Underground, Baaba Maal and Khaled have all appeared in recent years, as have a host of ethno-techno DJs.

Orthodox Easter

Patrikhane (Orthodox Patriarchate Building), Ali Paşa Caddesi 35, Fener (0212 531 9674). **Date** April. **Map** 305 G4.
The celebratory Easter Sunday mass is held in the venerable Patriarchate building in Fener (*see p86*) on the Golden Horn. In a church illuminated by hundreds of candles, the aura of ancient ritual is powerful enough to shake the scepticism of even the most ardent of atheists. Note, Orthodox Easter falls one week after Western Easter.

International Istanbul Film Festival

Uluslararası Istanbul Film Festivali
Various venues (information 0212 293 3133/ www.istfest.org). **Date** second half of April. **Admission** varies.
One of the biggest events on the cultural calendar, and eagerly anticipated by even non-film fans for the glamour and glitter of visiting celebrities. It is organised by the Istanbul Foundation of Culture and Arts (Istanbul Kültür ve Sanat Vakfı), whose

phone number is given here. For tickets, the best bet is to make pre-paid reservations one month before the festival starts. Tickets can also be booked over the Internet and, once the festival has started, are available from the various movie theatre box offices. *See also p191.*

International Istanbul Theatre Festival

Various venues (information 0212 293 3133/ www.istfest.org). **Date** May. **Admission** varies. **Credit** MC, V.
This event provides about the only opportunity to see international theatre in Istanbul. In past years draws have included Robert Wilson, Pina Bausch, the Berliner Ensemble, the Piccolo Teatro di Milano and Britain's Royal Shakespeare Company. The programme also features a selection of the year's best Turkish plays. Most performances are at the city theatres such as the Atatürk Cultural Centre, the Kenter Theatre (*see below* **International Istanbul Puppet Festival**) and the Aksanat Cultural Centre (*see p194*). A few take place at more unique venues, such as the Rumeli Hisarı fortress on the Bosphorus. *See p104.*

International Istanbul Puppet Festival

Kenter Theatre, Halaskargazi Caddesi 35, Harbiye (information Cengiz Özek 0212 246 3589/ www.tiyatronline.com). **Date** May. **Admission** $5-$6. **No credit cards.**

The Royal Shakespeare Company at the **International Istanbul Theatre Festival**.

Puppet, marionette and shadow theatre was strong in Ottoman times, but is rarely performed today (*see p227* **Shadow play**). The festival provides an opportunity to witness this almost forgotten art, with around a dozen shows by Turkish and international companies at the Atatürk Cultural Centre (AKM) and Kenter Theatre. Most of the plays are silent and suitable for children and adults. Tickets can be purchased at the AKM or over the Internet.

Conquest Week Celebrations

Fetih Haftası
Information 0212 227 3390/www.ibb.gov.tr.
Date end of May.

The city council celebrates the Ottoman conquest of Constantinople (29 May 1453) with exhibitions of traditional Turkish arts, concerts of popular songs from the Istanbul Metropolitan Municipality Cemal Reşit Rey Symphony Orchestra (*see p227*), parades by the 'Ottoman' Mehter band, plus conferences, lectures, screenings of worthy films and a few fireworks. Most fun of all, they also stage a re-enactment of the conquest, which in 2000 involved a fancy-dress procession carrying fancy 'boats' from Taksim down to Dolmabahçe, where they then chucked the whole lot into the Bosphorus.

Summer

H2000 Music Festival

Ömerli Dam (*information 0212 219 6193/ www.h2000musicfestival.com*). **Date** June. **Tickets** AKM, Vakkorama. **Admission** *3-day pass* $30-$45. **Credit** AmEX, DC, MC, V.

A stab at a Glastonbury-style event, with three days of music at a large open-air site next to the Ömerli Dam, about 40km (25 miles) outside the city. The first festival, in 2000, attracted the likes of Bush, Republica, Chumbawumba and about 40 other bands and DJs, foreign and local. Despite the absence of heavyweight names, some 25,000 came to hear. The festival has become an annual fixture, with provision for on-site camping and free shuttle transport back to town for those who prefer their own beds. Tickets go on sale in May or can be bought at the site for $45.

International Bosphorus Festival

Various venues (information 0212 232 9830/ www.ibb.gov.tr. **Dates** June. **Tickets** AKM, Vakkorama. **Admission** $8-$30.

Like May's Conquest Week Celebrations, this event is organised by Istanbul city council and features a similar sort of dartboard-and-blindfold approach to programming. The 2000 event had a typically bizarre line-up, with ageing big band meister Chuck Mangione and pensionable disco queen Gloria Gaynor rubbing shoulders with the likes of hip raï outfit Sawt El Atlas or the Chinese State Ballet. Performances, most of them open-air, take place in Istanbul's main venues, as well as various historical sites such as the Yıldız Palace (*see p100*) and the Emirgan White Pavilion.

Fête de la Musique

Avrupa Müzik Şenliği
Various venues (information 0212 245 4037/ www.geocities.com/fetedelamusique). **Date** around 21 June. **Admission** free.

Launched in France in 1982, the Fête has since spread across Europe, reaching Istanbul in 1998. Here it takes the form of a couple of days of live performances by local amateur bands and bottom-of-the-barrel foreign solo artists in various open-air locations, such as the garden of the French Cultural Centre (Istiklal Caddesi 8) and Taksim and Sultanahmet squares.

International Istanbul Music Festival

Various venues (information 0212 293 3133/ www.istfest.org). **Dates** June-July. **Tickets** AKM. **Admission** varies.

Launched in 1973 on the occasion of the 50th anniversary of the Turkish Republic, this may be the most prestigious event on the city's cultural calendar. It features around 30 concerts, including orchestra and chamber music, recitals, dance and ballet performances, some of them worth attending just for the venues alone – the festival is one of the few times, for example, that it's possible to get to see inside Haghia Irene (*see p72*). Big names in 2000

Any excuse for flags: **Victory Day**, 30 August.

Slippery people

In 1361, or so the story goes, two Ottoman soldiers entertained their fellow warriors by wrestling one another until they both simultaneously collapsed and died of exhaustion. The two were buried under a fig tree, around which 40 geysers then miraculously gurgled up.

To commemorate the fabled fight, every summer during the first week of July, the drum calls up the spirits of the fatally knackered duo to lend courage to some hundreds of wrestlers who converge on Kırkpınar ('40 springs'), just outside Edirne. Competing in 12 category levels, classed by height, they bare their chests, pull on their leather knickers and make their way to the *yağcı*, the oil man. His job is to baptise each wrestler with a shower of olive oil. Many consider him too stingy though, and lube up themselves, applying the salad sauce liberally so that opponents won't be able to get a good grip. Plenty of it goes down the breeches as a precaution against the *kepçe* – the move in which one wrestler puts his hand down the front of his opponent's pants, grabs a hold and flips him over.

As a warm-up before the bouts, 20 drummers beat the hell out of their *davuls*, accompanied by a row of *zurna* players, puffing into their horns and making a noise like an ancient kazoo. The wrestlers drop to one knee, slap the ground and then take off on a stylised lumbering walk that has them looking like extras in *Night of the Living Dead*. This is the *peşrev*, or salutation ceremony. Once over, the grappling begins.

Bouts can take anything from a few minutes to the best part of an hour, some mad-dash slapstick with opponents swatting and sliding off each other, some taking place in slo-mo. But then suddenly the hand goes down the breeches and – bam! – one unfortunate is flat on his back. We have a winner.

Kırkpınar Oil Wrestling & Cultural Activities Week

Kırkpınar Yağlı Güreş ve Kültür Etkinlikleri Haftası
Information 0284 2319208/0284 225 5260.
Dates last week of June or first week of July.
Admission *one day* $5-$8; *two-day pass* $15.
No credit cards.
Oil wrestling is the centrepiece of an annual festival on Kırkpınar island outside Edirne. Concerts, theatre shows, exhibitions, international folk dancing and beauty contests are all part of the fun, and free to all. There's no charge for watching the kids' wrestling contest on the first day. The main event takes place over the last two days.

included Kiri Te Kanawa, Phillip Glass, the Michael Nyman Ensemble and the Kronos Quartet.

International Istanbul Jazz Festival

Various venues (information 0212 293 3133/ www.istfest.org). **Date** July. **Admission** varies.
Past years have witnessed the likes of Keith Jarret, Wynton Marsalis and Dizzy Gillespie performing in the 4,000-seat Harbiye open-air theatre, along with those other well-known jazzers Björk, Lou Reed, Patti Smith and Roni Size's Reprazent. But then this two-week festival often goes far beyond the bounds of jazz, which might upset purists, but keeps the rest of the city ecstatically happy with what remains consistently the best programme of any Turkish music festival. Outside of the big gigs and jam sessions at Babylon (*see p207*) are the hottest tickets of the year and sell out within days of being announced.

Rumeli Hisarı Concerts

Rumeli Hisarı (information 0212 335 9335). **Date** July-Aug. **Admission** $12-40. **Credit** MC, V.
The appeal here is the venue – open green spaces within the walls of the Ottoman fortress of Rumeli Hisarı (*see p145*) complete with stunning views of the Bosphorus. Against this backdrop, concerts run throughout the summer with something happening almost every night. The varied programme mixes rock and pop and the odd international name – Ray Charles in 2000 – but the focus is largely on Arabesque and other forms of Turkish music. Regardless of who's playing, it's worth attending at least once for one of the best ways to pass a balmy August evening in Istanbul.

J&B Dance & Techno Festival

Contact: Hip Productions, Erzurumlu Şükrü Paşa Sokak 13/3, Arnavutköy (212 263 0819/ www.hippro.com). **Date** early Sept. **Admission** $25.
Credit MC, V.
Running since 1998, this is a 24-hour non-stop event featuring international artists and DJs playing hip hop, trip hop, house, techno, funk, trance, drum 'n' bass, Asian underground, ambient and UK garage. It's an open-air venue – the wooded Park Orman in the suburb of Maslak – with three arenas. The line-up in 2000 was impressive, with the Jungle Brothers, Basement Jaxx, Talvin Singh and Jimi Tenor keeping some 20,000 ravers on their feet around the clock.

International Istanbul Biennale

Information 0212 293 3133/www.istfest.org.
Dates 22 Sept-17 Nov 2001. **Admission** $2.50;
$1.50 per person for groups of 15 or more.
More than 50 artists from, at last count, 30 different
countries exhibit around a general theme set by a
guest curator every other year. As well as conventional hangings there are installations, video
screenings, walkabouts, films, panel discussions,
lectures and even daily guided tours (in English). It
is held in three venues, all of them wonderful:
Haghia Irene, the adjacent old Ottoman Mint building and the Yerebatan Sarayı (*see p 74*).

Intercontinental Istanbul Eurasia Marathon

Information 0212 234 4200/
www.istanbulmarathon.org. **Dates** mid Oct.
Beginning on the Asian Shore, the marathon route
passes over the Bosphorus Bridge to the European
side, loops through the city centre and across the
Atatürk Bridge, under the Valens Aqueduct then
back along the Sea of Marmara shore, over the
Galata Bridge and up the Bosphorus to finish 42km
(26 miles) later at İnönü Stadium, home ground of
Beşiktaş (*see p232*). In its 22nd year in 2000 the
marathon attracted over 2,000 runners, half of them
foreigners, with close on 200,000 participating in
the day's ten-kilometre (six-mile) fun run.

Akbank Jazz Festival

Various venues (information 0212 252 5167/
www.pozitif-ist.com/www.akbank.com.tr/sanat).
Dates Sept or Oct. **Tickets** AKM, Vakkorama.
Admission $2-$6.
Less about big names and more about jazz than
July's international affair, this is the real deal for the
true aficionado. Some ten bands perform every day
over the two weeks of the festival, with jam sessions
at venues including Babylon (*see p207*) and
Gramofon (*see p212*). There are also film screenings and workshops.

Istanbul Arts Fair

Istanbul Sanat Fuarı
Meşrutiyet Caddesi, Istanbul Sergi Saray, Tüyap,
Tepebaşı (0212 241 6535/www.tuyapfair.com).
Date Oct. **Admission** $3-$4. **No credit cards.**
Map p308 M3
Held at the Tüyap Centre, the eyesore of an exhibition complex just up from Beyoğlu's Pera Palas (*see
p62* **Bed, board & legends**), this is basically a
vast week-long sales fair. Some 50 Istanbul galleries take stands, as well as a handful of companies
from abroad, all aiming to offload as much as they
can in the way of paintings, sculpture and ceramics
on an increasingly receptive local market.

Chefs' special

Did your mother ever tell you not to play with
your food? Well, that's one imperative that you
don't hear around Mengen, a little town five
hours east of Istanbul set in the lush green
mountain meadows of Bolu. Around these
parts playing with food is something of a local
obsession, celebrated annually with a great
blow-out of a culinary festival that typically
culminates in the kind of meal that's more likely
to make it into the *Guinness Book of Records*
than a recipe book. Where else would you go for
a 100-metre (328-foot) kebab?

Mengen and cooking have a relationship that
locals would have you believe goes right back to
the time of Sultan Mehmet II 'the Conqueror',
when a chef working at the imperial palace was
charged with hiring a bunch of new kitchen
staff, pronto. Hailing from Mengen, he did what
anyone in a bind might do – he pulled in his
relatives and friends and hurriedly trained them
to prepare the sultan's dishes. If you're eating
at a top-class diner in Istanbul ask where the
chef comes from – if it's not Paris, it's Mengen.

Once a year, during the first or second
weekend in August, the chefs all head home for
a weekend to celebrate their town's prestigious
culinary history at the **Mengen Cooks' Festival**.
Dressed in the white garb and hat of the trade,
they judge the food creations of apprentice
chefs from the town's cooking college.

Forget the sprigs and sprinkles and dashes
of Modern British. In Mengen the fashion is for
mountains and heaps and lashings. In 2000
there was a whole Vesuvius of stuffed grape
leaves studded with lava-bright red peppers,
a garden of watermelon flowers, and an entire
cooked goat with olives for eyes, kneeling on
a platter like it was just taking time out from
munching on the grass. Centrepiece was a
massive vat of *keşkek çorbası*, a traditional
Mengen broth knocked up from a mere ton of
flour, 480 kilos (1,060lb) of beef, 30 kilos
(66lb) of tomato paste, ten huge tins of oil, 200
kilos (442lb) of onions, three kilos (6⅔lb) of
pepper and a veritable field full of carrots.
Festival-goers were invited to eat as much of
this as they possibly could.

Admittedly, five hours is a long way to travel
for a free feed, but you probably won't need to
eat for a week afterwards.

For the festival dates, check at any of the
Istanbul tourist offices (see page 282).

International Istanbul Biennale – Maurizio Nannucci installation at Yerebatan Sarayı. *See p182.*

Efes Pilsen Blues Festival

Hilton Convention & Exhibition Centre,
Cumhuriyet Caddesi, Harbiye (0212 252 5167/
www.efespilsen.com.tr). **Date** Last week of Oct.
Admission $15. **No credit cards.**
Istanbul and the blues don't exactly make obvious
bedfellows, but this two-day festival has been
going since 1990. Bands touring Europe are
persuaded to go a bit further and hit the Bosphorus
for a late-night blues marathon; three bands a night
kicking in at 7.30pm and jamming until past
midnight. The odd star musician makes it (such as
Bobby Rush or Long John Hunter), but it's also a
showcase for new generation talent. The biggest
drawback is the venue – the Hilton convention centre. 'Woke up this morning, got those little neatly-
wrapped complimentary mini-bars of soap blues.'

Anniversary of Atatürk's Death

Date 10 November.
Every 10 November at 9.05am, Mustafa Kemal
Atatürk's death is commemorated with a minute's
silence. Sirens blare out for one minute across the
country and everyone in the streets stops and
stands still for a minute or two. Buses and cars also
stop on the roads and highways.

IFSAK Istanbul Photograph Days

Various venues (information 0212 292 4201/
www.ifsak.org). **Date** Nov. **Admission** free.
A month devoted to photographic events including
slide shows, seminars, conferences, discussions
and exhibitions with both domestic and foreign
photographers. Amateur snappers are invited to
take part in a 'photomarathon': participants are

given three themes and 48 hours in which to shoot.
Prizes are awarded and all entries are exhibited.

Istanbul Book Fair

Istanbul Kitap Fuarı
Meşrutiyet Caddesi, Istanbul Sergi Saray, Tüyap,
Tepebaşı (0212 212 3100/www.tuyapfair.com).
Date Nov. **Admission** $1.50-$2. **No credit cards.**
Map p308 M3.
Almost all Turkish publishing houses – more than
200 – as well as a number from abroad, gather for
ten days at the Tüyap Centre. Discounts on new
publications are given and non-stop conferences,
panel and round-table discussions are held with
leading writers, academicians, journalists and
intellectuals. It's one of the most well attended of
any of Istanbul's cultural events. Avoid weekends,
when crowds and queues are at their worst.

All year

Yapı Kredi Arts Festival

Various venues (information 0212 252 4700 ext 501/
www.ykykultur.com.tr). **Dates** year-round.
Admission varies.
The Yapı Kredi bank is a big sponsor of the arts,
operating a major gallery-cum-cultural centre and
its own publishing house. The festival is a series of
12 concerts staggered throughout the year, taking
in anything from flamenco and jazz to classical
music and dance, usually performed by international artists. The usual venues are the Haghia
Irene, Cemal Reşit Rey Concert Hall and the Cemil
Topuklu open-air theatre. Tickets available from
the Yapi Kredi Cultural Centre (*see p194*).

Children

Turks go gaga over kids, but don't do much to keep them entertained.

Children are universally adored in Istanbul. It is not unusual for a group of teenagers or a businessman talking on a mobile phone to stop to smile at a cute child. You may even need to prevent the overzealous from kissing and hugging your baby.

Families are very close and it's natural that children should accompany their parents everywhere: shopping, to restaurants, even to a concert or opera. People generally tend to be very tolerant of other people's kids and unruly behaviour that in other countries would draw stern looks is here more likely to inspire indulgent cooing.

Despite all that, there isn't much that's geared to children's needs or entertainment. And where facilities are laid on, such as at the wonderful **Play Barn** (*see below*), few Turkish families make use of them. Family life does not take place in the public realm.

Even at home, wealthier parents often prefer to leave their kids in the care of nannies or maids. The less well-off stick them in front of the TV or leave them to play in the streets or, worse, in badly designed, run-down playgrounds that are as dangerous as they are diverting.

The risk of scrapes and bumps aside, Istanbul is mostly safe for children. There are few crimes against kids and few fear when their children are out of sight.

Sightseeing with children is difficult. Apart from cafés, there are few parks or other places to take a break from walking, and amenities such as washrooms and toilets are scarce. Pushing a pram is almost impossible because of high kerbs and the poor state of pavements.

As well as the parks and activity venues listed here, other good places to go include the fortresses of **Rumeli Hisarı** (*see page 104*) and **Yedikule** (*see page 89*), or anything that involves mucking about on boats, such as a **Bosphorus cruise** (*see page 240*).

Activities

Sports are a way of life in Istanbul, and many of the facilities available to children centre around them. Asphalt courts with facilities for tennis, basketball and football are everywhere, usually with cafés attached. Other than those, there are precious few playgrounds specifically for children's amusement.

Akademi Istanbul

Bahçelihamam Sokak 3, Beyoğlu (0212 251 7484). **Open** 9am-6pm daily. **Credit** MC, V. **Map** p307 P2.
Offers music, dancing, drama and art classes taught by professionals. Both ballet and music classes are held every Saturday and Sunday and cost around $70 a month for nine to 12 hours' tuition.

Bosphorus Zoo

Boğaziçi Hayvanat Bahçesi
Tuzla Caddesi 15, Bayramoğlu, Izmit (0262 653 8315). **Open** 8.30am-8pm daily. **Admission** $8 adults; $5 children; free under-6s. **Credit** MC, V.
Although way out in Darica, about 30 miles (45km) from the city centre, this zoo park is worth the trip. It has a wide range of exotic birds and animals, kept on over 70 hectares of tropical plant-filled gardens. Also a restaurant and playground.

Cosmic Bowling

Maslak Üç Yol Mevkii, Büyükdere Caddesi (0212 286 1276). **Open** 10am-midnight daily. **Admission** $2.50-$5 per person per game. **Credit** MC, V.
Bowling centre with pool tables and two restaurants.

Dance Akademik

Cevher Sokak 6, Etiler (0212 257 0154). **Open** 10am-8pm Mon-Fri; 10am-1.30pm Sat; closed Sun. **No credit cards.**
Workshops for children and adults in all types of dance, including salsa and rumba. Dozens of programmes with average prices about $70 per month.

Enka Sports Centre

Sadi Gül Spor Sitesi, Istinye (0212 276 5084). **Open** 7.30am-10pm daily. **No credit cards.**
Indoor facilities for swimming, tennis, basketball and volleyball, with regular classes for children.

Play Barn

Kirazlıbağ Sokak 4, Yeniköy (0212 299 4803). **Open** 10am-7pm Tue-Sun; closed Mon. **Admission** $8 1hr; $18 30hr. **Credit** DC, MC, V.
New to Turkey, an indoor playground with six different age-related rooms, featuring mazes, tube slides, spinners, rollers and more. Each room has a supervisor. Also a café with a children's menu.

Tatilya

Beylikdüzü Mevkii, Avcılar (0212 852 0505). **Open** 2-10pm Tue-Fri; 11am-10pm Sat, Sun. **Admission** $15. **Credit** MC, V.
A large, covered entertainment complex with fairground-type rides suitable for all ages, a simulation cinema, restaurants and shops. It also has a small theatre with hourly shows on the weekends.

Splash out! **Park Orman** has a pool, playgrounds and plenty of picnic areas.

Museums

Although there's no Istanbul museum devoted specifically to kids, several have displays and artefacts aimed at children.

The **Archaeology Museum** (*see page 112*) has an area, albeit a small one, set aside for children with displays at youngsters' eye level.

The **Military Museum** (*see page 113*) has tanks and soldiers' uniforms. Best is the **Rahmi M Koç Industrial Museum** (*see page 115*), which has a number of interactive displays and working models. Take the kids on a Saturday when all the buttons, bells and whistles are in action.

Air Force Museum

Havacılık Müzesi
Havalimanı Caddesi, opposite Yeşilköy station, Yesilköy (0212 574 3894). **Open** 9am-4.30pm Wed-Sun; closed Mon, Tue. **Admission** $0.50. **No credit cards.**
The Air Force Museum has displays covering the history of air travel and the Turkish Air Force, with loads of planes.

Parks & playgrounds

Just north of the city centre, **Yıldız Park** is beautiful and leafy and a fine place to let kids run free off the leash; *see page 100*. The summer-only, small fairground **Maçka Luna Park** is in a park north of Taksim.

Emirgan Park

Emirgan Korusu, Emirgan.
Large park beside the Bosphorus, with an ornamental lake, playground and some of the nicest landscaping to be found in Istanbul. There are also two old palaces restored as restaurants.

Park Orman

Maslak Caddesi, Fatih Çocuk Ormanı (0212 223 0759).
A woodland setting north of the city with sports facilities for families and children, including a large swimming pool, picnic areas, playgrounds and fast food outlets.

Restaurants

Although most Istanbul restaurants welcome children, beyond the fast-food chains (a blessing for parents with young kids), few restaurants offer amenities such as high chairs or children's menus. However, if asked, many places will serve children's portions and even cook special requests. In fact, having a child often ensures that you receive better service.

Hippopotamus

Park Plaza 22, Eski Büyükdere Caddesi, Maslak (0212 345 0830). **Open** noon-1am daily. **Children's menu** $9. **Credit** AmEx, MC, V.
This well-known French chain has a large outlet in Istanbul and features a set children's menu (starter, main, dessert and drink) served with crayons.

Arts & Entertainment

Princess Hotel Sports Bar

Büyükdere Caddesi 49, Maslak (0212 285 0900).
Open 10am-1am Mon-Fri; 10am-3am Sat, Sun.
Main courses $5-$10. **Credit** AmEx, MC, V.
Wide range of international food including a buffet
and a kids' menu. Also a games area with small
rides and video games.

TGI Fridays

Nispetiye Caddesi 19, Etiler (0212 257 7078). **Open**
noon-midnight daily. **Main courses** $5-$8. **Credit**
AmEx, DC, V.
This is a child-friendly place that serves up hotdogs,
burgers and fancy ice-cream desserts. It also has a
dedicated kids' menu.

Practicalities

Shopping

Kid's clothing and toy stores can be found in all
large shopping centres and malls (*see page 157*
Mall contents), usually along with some
entertainment for the children.

Pharmacists (*eczane*) are numerous and found
in most neighbourhoods. Most carry a range of
healthcare products for children. Packaged baby
food is relatively new to Turkey but a small
selection of locally produced jars can be found in
most *eczanes*. You can find Gerber and other
international products at **Ece Eczane**
(Güzelbahçe Sokak 37, Nişantaşi, 0212 240 4625).
Toys R Us and **Migros** supermarkets carry a
good selection of Hipp baby food.

Nappies, wipes and so on can be found at all
large grocery stores, including Migros and
Makro (*for both, see page 170*), and most small
markets. See *chapter* **Shopping & Services** for
information on supermarkets.

Bookworm's LC

Yaprak Sokak 11, Etiler (0212 287 5155). **Open**
9.30am-6pm Mon-Sat; closed Sun. **No credit cards.**
A child-friendly bookstore and lending library,
which carries a range of English language books as
well as a range of creative activity packs, puzzles
and art supplies.

Carrefour

*E5 Highway, Içerenköy junction, Asian Shore (0216
416 2322).* **Open** 10am-7pm daily. **Credit** MC, V.
Large French department store carrying a line of
inexpensive children's clothes, books, nappies and
toys. Located in a mall that also has a Kiddieland
with children's rides and restaurants.

Gelar

Birlik Sokak 9/20, 1 Levent (0212 280 8089). Metro 1
Levent. **Open** 9am-6pm Mon-Sat; closed Sun. **Credit**
MC, V.
Imported educational tools, wooden toys and play-
ground equipment of excellent quality. Prices are
high but the range is unique in Turkey.

It's wheely good! **Maçka Luna Park**. *See p185*.

Toys R Us

*Migros Building, Büyükdere Caddesi 61, Maslak,
(0212 286 0016).* **Open** 10am-7pm daily. **Credit**
AmEx, MC, V.
Carries the largest selection of children's toys in
Istanbul. Also small-size clothing, shoes, baby food
and nappies.

Malls

Akmerkez

Nispetiye Caddesi, Etiler (0212 282 0170).
Metro Levent. **Open** 10am-10pm daily. **Credit** varies.
The lower floor has a number of shops selling
children's clothes, including Benetton, Chicco, and
Oilily as well as four or five toy shops. The top floor
has numerous fast-food outlets and Kiddieland, a
small play area with rides.

Carousel

*Halit Ziya Uşaklıgil Sokak 1, Bakırköy (0212 570
8434).* **Open** 10am-10pm daily. **Credit** varies.
Clothing stores (Benetton, Chicco), a well-stocked
MotherCare and a large Toys R Us. There's also a
huge kiddies' roundabout in the atrium.

Babysitting

All of the high-end and deluxe hotels provide
babysitting services for guests. Smaller hotels
will usually make every effort to find someone.
Beyond that, you could try **Anglo Nannies
London** (0212 265 1878), which provides live-in
nannies from England.

Arts & Entertainment

Film

Turkish cinema thrives on all fronts, but *Midnight Express* still rankles.

Kutluğ Ataman's **Lola + Bilidikid** reached the international arthouse circuit.

▶ For other **films with an Istanbul connection** see page 287.

Too often consigned to the ghetto of Third World filmmaking, Turkish cinema has until recently been identified exclusively with the 1983 film *Yol* and its director, Yılmaz Güney (*see page 189* **Shooting more than films**). The attention garnered by the charismatic Güney served to obscure virtually the whole of the rest of Turkish cinema from the West. That is now changing.

A series of festival successes has brought growing international recognition with, in some cases, the reward of commercial distribution. Ferzan Özpetek's *Hamam* (Italian man repairs bathhouse, falls in love with local boy) and Kutluğ Ataman's *Lola + Bilidikid* (tortured Turkish gay life on the streets of Berlin) both reached the international arthouse circuit. Those films were co-productions with European companies, giving them advantages in financing, production and distribution. The home-grown Turkish box-office hits *Propaganda* by Sinan Çetin and *Byzantium the Perfidious* by Gani Müjde have also done the rounds in France and Germany.

At press time, *Journey to the Sun* by Yeşim Ustaoğlu was scooping festival awards around the world. It's the story of a young guy from the provinces struggling to make a life in Istanbul, only to be arrested and brutalised because he looks like a Kurd. Powerful and haunting, it benefits from luscious

Byzantium the Perfidious – good box office.

Nuri Bilge Ceylan's **Clouds of May**.

camerawork by Jacek Petrycki, a favourite of
Krzystof Kieslowski.

Also highly regarded was the recent *Clouds of
May* by Nuri Bilge Ceylan, about a director who
returns to his home village in Anatolia to shoot a
movie. It's being compared to the work of Iranian
auteur Abbas Kiarostami.

Such films, though lauded in critical circles,
don't hold much appeal for mainstream Turkish
audiences. The top home-grown box-office draws
are lightweight comedies, preferably starring
TV celebrities. Anything political, arty or
otherwise worthy receives only a limited
screening. You've as much chance of catching
such films on the international festival circuit
as you have in Istanbul.

Cinemas

Istanbul is surprisingly good when it comes
to movie-going, with over 200 screens and an
annual world-class festival. Between them
they offer a relatively balanced and substantial
cinematic diet, ranging from Hollywood
blockbuster junk food to indigenous local
flavours. As anywhere, US product
predominates, but at least five cinemas specialise
in independent European and Turkish film.
Several other institutes screen retrospectives
and themed weeks. In fact, it's surprising what
does turn up – one high street cinema recently
screened Gregg Araki's trashy, ultraviolent
The Doom Generation.

All films, bar animated ones, are shown in
their original language with Turkish subtitles.
Despite the prominence of Islamic parties in
municipal government, censorship is not a big
issue. Filmmakers are in the majority on the
board of censors and over the last ten years the
scene-snipping scissors have lain pretty much
untouched in the drawer. David Cronenberg's
Crash made it to Istanbul screens virtually
unscathed and Catherine Breillat's *Romance*
was shown in its full penetrative glory.

Multiplexes are proliferating in chi-chi
suburbs such as Etiler, adding reclining seats
and champagne to the big-screen experience. Or

you can take your movies straight with hard
seats and bare floorboards in the older cinemas
of Beyoğlu or Kadıköy.

Movie-going is cheap, with tickets costing
$3-$5, except up in Etiler, where everything is
more expensive. At most cinemas Wednesday is
'People's Day', when all ticket prices are reduced;
some cinemas also lower their prices on
Mondays. Matinée screenings are generally
cheaper than evening shows and students can
often get a discount at other times.

Reservations are accepted at the AFM
cinemas, but few take credit cards. Most
cinemas have reduced-price matinées, and a
student card gets you a discount. Seating is
usually assigned and ushers expect a tip; the
going rate is about $0.25. All screenings have
a ten-minute intermission so everyone can nip
out for a quick cig.

There is no source of English-language film
listings. For what's on, consult the Turkish press.
See pages 276-7.

Sultanahmet

Şafak

*Darüşşafaka Sitesi Pasajı, Yeniçeriler Caddesi,
Çemberlitaş (0212 516 2660). Tram Çemberlitaş.*
Tickets $5. **Credit** MC, V. **Map** p302 L10.
This grim concrete bunker is buried deep in the
sub-basement of a shopping mall, but it's the only
cinema in – or anywhere near – Sultanahmet. The
auditoria aren't bad at all and with seven screens
there's a reasonable choice of films, mixing current
US releases with local fare.

Beyoğlu

AFM Fitaş

*Fitaş Pasajı, İstiklal Caddesi 24-26 (0212 292 1111/
www.afm.com.tr).* **Tickets** $5. **No credit cards**.
Map p309 O2.
Just 200m (65ft) down from Taksim Square, a popular multiplex at the back of a short arcade that's also
a CD/book store. Hollywood blockbusters hog all
ten screens, the two newest of which offer the best
sound quality in town. Upstairs is one of the North
Shield chain of pubs (*see p152*), plus 35mm, a
decent, cinematically themed café (*see p143*).

Akademi İstanbul

*Bahçeli Hamam Sokak 3-5, off İstiklal Caddesi (0212
249 6897).* **Tickets** $3-$5. **No credit cards**.
Map p309 O3.
Run by the Academy of Performing Arts, located
just next door, this cinema specialises in Turkish
films, if not the kind most Turks want to watch.
This is where to see *Journey to the Sun* or *Clouds of
May*, for example. Sound quality is often poor and
the seats are uncomfortable – you've got to suffer
for your art movies.

Shooting more than films

Yılmaz Güney is a legend in Turkey and only a part of that is to do with his films. Of these, best known is *Yol*, which shared a Palme d'Or at Cannes (with Costa-Gavras's *Missing*) in 1983 and went on to do resoundingly good box office worldwide. Except, ironically, in Turkey, where, like his other works, it was banned on political grounds. It finally got a release in 1999, but with cuts.

Güney's talent as a writer (not just of screenplays), actor and director is without dispute. When he released his second film, *The Hope*, in 1970 it was acclaimed as the best Turkish film ever made. Over the course of a further nine films his reputation continued to grow. Aside from critics, the young directors he influenced and intimates of the film world, his work also struck a chord with ordinary Turkish people. His sympathetic treatment of the poor and downtrodden, and appealingly strong sense of social justice, honed by his humble origins on the cotton farms of the south, made him a figure of mass adulation. This remains true today; any journalist who dares disparage the myth of Güney in print is risking career suicide.

But this iconic status also glosses over some interesting bumps. Güney, a self-willed hypochondriac – he complained on set once of a leaking brain after being whacked on the head by a stone – also spent almost a quarter of his 47 years behind bars, and not always for the left-wing populist sympathies that season his heroic status.

His life off-screen seemed often to fuse with his gangster-style roles on-screen. In 1974 a judge who'd had a few too many made the mistake of insulting Güney's wife. Güney shot him dead. He was put back inside. But while incarcerated he wrote prolifically and even managed to do some vicarious directing, including much of *Yol* via proxy director Şerif Gören. With filming completed, in 1981 Güney unilaterally cut short his sentence, doing a runner while on day release then dramatically fleeing the country by boat. He escaped to Switzerland to edit a negative of his film, which had also been smuggled out of Turkey. He later moved to Paris, where he made one last film, *Duvar* (*The Wall*), before dying of cancer in 1984.

Alkazar

Istiklal Caddesi 179 (0212 293 2466). **Tickets** $3-$5. **No credit cards. Map** p308 N3.

A porn theatre until 1994, when it was renovated, restoring to respectability an attractive art nouveau interior with caryatids in the foyer and a pretty good café on the ground floor (*see p143*). Programming now leans toward European independents and art-house staples – Almodóvar, Von Trier, Wenders and their ilk.

Atlas

Atlas Pasajı, Istiklal Caddesi 209 (0212 252 8576). **Tickets** $3-$5. **No credit cards. Map** p308 N3.

Recently restored, comfortable cinema above a charmingly raffish arcade filled with costume jewellery, antique and second-hand stores. The most steeply raked auditorium in Istanbul. Gets bums on seats with a mix of star-driven Hollywood fare and crowd-pleasing Turkish comedies.

Beyoğlu

Halep Pasajı, Istiklal Caddesi 140 (0212 251 3240/ www.beyoglusinemasi.com.tr). **Tickets** $3-$5. **No credit cards. Map** p308 N3.

Directly across from the Atlas arcade, the Beyoğlu concentrates on European and Turkish independents. From July to September it screens a different film every day, under the banner of 'Best Foreign Films Festival'; the idea is that the films are the best of this year's crop as selected by the Association of Turkish Film Critics, but as the summer wears on the net is flung further afield and pretty much anything made in the last decade will suffice.

Emek

Yeşilçam Sokak 5, off Istaklal Caddesi (0212 293 8439). **Tickets** $5; $2.50 OAPs, handicapped. **No credit cards. Map** p308 N3.

During the 1960s, the 'golden age' of Turkish cinema, Yeşilçam Sokak was 'film alley', home to the big movie companies. No more. But Emek still remains one of Istanbul's oldest working cinemas, built in the 1920s with an impressive 875-seat hall beneath an ornate ceiling. If a film is worth watching, then try to catch it here. A main venue for the International Istanbul Film Festival (*see p191*) and host of the opening ceremony.

Sinepop

Yeşilçam Sokak 22, off Istiklal Caddesi (0212 251 1176/www.ozenfilm.com.tr). **Tickets** $5. **Credit** MC, V. **Map** p308 N3.

One of the newest city centre cinemas. Very comfortable seating, digital sound and the cleanest, classiest bathrooms in town. It's all usually given over to Hollywood pap, but the odd classy film does occasionally turn up. Decent café in the foyer.

Yeşilçam

Imam Adnan Sokak 10, off İstiklal Caddesi (0212 249 8006). **Tickets** $5. **Credit** MC, V. **Map** p309 O2.
Opened in 2000 by one of Turkey's new generation of film directors, this basement arthouse cinema concentrates on Turkish films old and new, as well as features and documentaries drawn from festivals around the world. In a first for Istanbul, the main programme is preceded by a short film.

Etiler

AFM Akmerkez

Akmerkez Mall, Nispetiye Caddesi (0212 282 0505/ www.afm.com.tr). Metro Levent. **Tickets** $6; $9 after 6pm. **No credit cards.**
Multiplex in Istanbul's largest mall (*see p157* **Mall contents**), out of the centre but on the new metro. Sound and screen quality are the best.

Ortaköy

Feriye

Çırağan Caddesi 124 (0212 236 2864/ www.umutsanat.com.tr). Bus 22, 25E, 40. **Tickets** $3-$5. **No credit cards.**

The cinema is part of a cultural complex on lawns beside the Bosphorus, along with an open-air restaurant, bar and large garden. Wonderful spot to catch a film and hang around later. Just a short walk from the bars and cafés of waterfront Ortaköy.

Asian Shore

Rexx

Sakız Gülü Sokak 20-22, off Bahariye Caddesi, Kadıköy (0216 336 0112/www.rexx_online.com). **Tickets** $5. **No credit cards. Map** p311 W8.
Big is not always best. A former theatre, the Rexx is a vast hangar seating 1,000. This can make for a lonely movie experience on a weekday night. A venue for the International Istanbul Film Festival.

Süreyya

Bahariye Caddesi 29, Kadıköy (0216 336 0682/ www.sureyya.com). **Tickets** $3-$5. **No credit cards. Map** p311 X7.
This late 19th-century opera house is the oldest surviving cinema in Istanbul. It's a real nostalgia-fest, still with the original opera boxes in its large, elaborately decorated auditorium. The films on show are standard Hollywood bubblegum.

Midnight Express keeps on running

Along with döner kebabs and Galatasaray supporters, Alan Parker's 1978 movie *Midnight Express* remains one of the West's key reference points for Istanbul and its inhabitants. That is unfortunate, as it also remains a deeply resented cause of offence to the average Turk. And justifiably so.

A terrifying story of a young American, Billy Hayes (played by Brad Davis), banged up in a Turkish jail for trying to smuggle hashish out of Istanbul, the movie is an endurance test for the squeamish. It focuses on the brutality and degradation of Turkish prison life and gained infamy for its tongue-biting scene, multiple rapes and beatings, plus a discomforting 'Turks are pigs' speech delivered by Hayes. Violent but powerful stuff – and markedly homoerotic – it won international fame for its director and a slew of Oscar nominations, including one for screenplay writer Oliver Stone.

Having admitted taking liberties with the source material – the book Hayes wrote of his experiences – Parker has allowed that, yes, he got some things wrong. Venerated US film critic Pauline Kael nailed it in one: 'The Americans, the Englishman and the Swede [Hayes and his fellow prisoners] are civilised and sensitive, and the Turks are bestial, sadistic, filthy.' So

the Turks sodomise and torture the Westerners at every opportunity. They don't wash. And their food is lousy and gives you the shits.

As a consequence, there has been a long, aggrieved fascination in Turkey with anything to do with the movie. National newspapers covered in detail Brad Davis's 1991 death from AIDS, which he had, rather ironically, contracted from an infected needle while shooting up heroin. As recently as March 2000 the film was invoked again when, following the stabbing of two Leeds United football fans, there were accusations in the local press that British TV was screening it in order to whip up anti-Turkish sentiment. In fact, it hadn't been screened at all.

Turks will also go out of their way to point up discrepancies between the book and the film, the film and real events, the book and real events, the screenplay and the film, the laundry list and... Other things that rankle are that it's not real Turkish that's spoken but made-up gibberish, and that the swarthy sadists on screen are not Turks at all, but played by a mixture of Italian, Greek, Armenian and even American actors. That may all be true, but it is somewhat irrelevant. Turkish actors or not, it is a great movie. It is also inexcusably racist.

Emek, Yeşilçam Sokak, once 'film alley' – key venue for the International Istanbul Film Festival.

Open-air cinemas

AFM Outdoor Cinema

AFM Açık Hava Sineması
Conrad Hotel, Yıldız Caddesi, off Barbaros Bulvarı, Beşiktaş (0212 227 3000/www.afm.com.tr).
Open *June-Aug. Sept-May* closed. **Tickets** $8.
No credit cards.
Movies take over the Conrad's tennis courts every evening from June to September. Films, mostly mainstream Hollywood, change every three or four days. There's an outdoor bar and Latin and Cuban music after the screening.

Other venues

Bilgi Cinema Centre

Bilgi'de Sinema
İnönü Caddesi 28, Kuştepe, Şişli (0212 216 2315/ www.bilgi.edu.tr/sinema). **Tickets** $3. **No credit cards. Map** p307 Q2.
A cine club run by Bilgi University, open to all. Screenings take place twice daily, on weekdays only, at 2pm and 8.30pm. The eclectic programme covers retrospectives, cinema history, world cinema – a real grab-bag, but with plenty of interest. All films have English subtitles, except the Turkish ones. Get there by taxi or take the free minibus departing one hour before screenings from in front of Bilgi University building off Taksim Square.

Kafika

Bolahenk Sokak 8, Cihangir (0212 244 5167/ www.kafika.com). **Tickets** $5.50. **Credit** MC, V.
Map p307 P2.
A café-cum-restaurant with three small (25-seat) auditoria for private screenings. Book one, then choose from a menu of more than 2,500 films on DVD or Laser Disc. Hire of the room and film is $5.50 per person, with a minimum charge of $20.

Festivals

International Istanbul Film Festival

Uluslararası Istanbul Film Festivali
0212 293 3133/www.istfest.org. **Date** late April.
From modest beginnings – only six films were shown in 1982 – the International Istanbul Film Festival has become one of the highlights of the Turkish cultural calendar. In recent years, the festival's 15 days have crammed in up to 150 films from around the world, as well as a selection of new Turkish films. Besides general international and national competitions, there are sections such as 'Arts and the Movies' or 'Tributes' (honouring, in 2000, Angelopoulos, Kitano and Loach). There are also other special events, such as silent classics accompanied by a local orchestra. Big names attending in recent years have included Antonioni, Elia Kazan, Peter Greenaway and Abbas Kiarostami. *See also p179.*

Galleries

There ain't no Turks at the Tate, but it's only a matter of time.

Istanbul has never been a name on the international art map, but that's more to do with history than with any lack of raw talent.

Although as early as the 15th century Sultan Mehmet II commissioned a portrait from the Italian artist Gentile Bellini, painting was never really an Ottoman thing. It remained a minor court art, subsidiary to more decorative pursuits, such as calligraphy, ceramics, metal, woodwork and textiles, which are favoured by Islam – the faith has traditionally tended to consider representations of human or animal forms idolatrous.

It wasn't until the latter part of the 19th century that the *paşas* (nobles) first took any notice of what had been going on in Europe since the Renaissance and pursued their new-found interests in art with studies abroad.

A lot of catching up has been done since then and, despite fits and starts over the last few decades, the scene is currently enjoying sustained growth. It has been buoyed by a slew of private collectors who grew rich on the proceeds of government privatisation policies in the mid-1980s.

In a society showy by nature, many wealthy Istanbulites now consider a piece of suitably expensive art a required acquisition to go along with the Merc, the Rolex and the Cartier. Visiting the annual **Istanbul Arts Fair** (*see page 182*) is a real eye-opener, with vacuous Sunday-school works going for inflated sums of money.

That's not to say there isn't any fine work around. There is. Just to browse in a handful of the 100-plus galleries around town is to see the diversity of the local scene and understand how

Installation by Anish Kapoor at the **International Istanbul Biennale**. *See p182.*

Salih Coşkun (left) and Omer Kaleşi at **Tem**, leading space for new figurative art. *See p195.*

aware Turkish artists are of what's going on elsewhere. Increasing numbers are spending time living, studying and working abroad, where some succeed in making names for themselves. Before he died, **Erol Akyavaş** established a following in the United States for his colourful abstracts incorporating 'Ottoman' elements such as tents and calligraphy. In Paris, **Ömer Kaleşi** has achieved notice for his oversize figures, which seem to have a direct link to a Byzantine heritage of icon painting, while in New York **Serdar Arat** has done for air vents, wash basins and toilets what Francis Bacon did for the human form. And there are numerous equally celebrated artists resident and working in Istanbul.

Coverage of exhibitions has also increased in the daily newspapers in recent years and art is no longer an item reserved for Sunday supplements and specialist magazines. Galleries have also been quick to see the benefits of the Internet in a city increasingly web-savvy.

WHERE ART'S AT

Most of the leading, upmarket commercial galleries are in the moneyed shopping districts of **Maçka**, **Teşvikiye** and **Nişantaşı**, north of Taksim Square. Less slick and possibly more exciting is what's going on in the small neighbourhood of **Asmalımescit**, just off Istiklal Caddesi in Beyoğlu. Since the late 1990s the area has been developing into a small quarter of artists' studios, galleries and cafés, particularly along Sofyalı Sokak. Along **Istiklal Caddesi** itself are several public galleries financed by banks and holding companies, which host regularly changing shows of work by prominent Turkish artists both living and dead.

In addition to the galleries listed below, the **Atatürk Cultural Centre** (*see page 226*) in Taksim Square hosts temporary exhibitions by leading Turkish artists, as well as visiting shows from abroad. Just north of the square on Cumhuriyet Caddesi the **Istanbul Büyük Şehir Sanat Galerisi** is one of several city council-run exhibition spaces (known as 'Belediye Sanat Galerisi'), funded by the local authorities. Artists and members of the public apply for exhibition slots and shows range from the downright appalling to the… well, admission is free anyway.

Also of note is the biggest event in the Istanbul art calendar, the **International Istanbul Biennale**, which attracts leading artists from around the world every second autumn,

> ► For art museums and permanent collections *see chapter* **Museums**.

alongside the Turkish contingent (*see page 182*). As a barometer of where the art scene is at, the private viewing that precedes the public opening has become a major society event. Note that most galleries close during July and August.

Beyoğlu

Aksanat Art Centre

Istiklal Caddesi 16-18, Beyoğlu (0212 252 3500/ www.akbank.com.tr/sanat). **Open** 9.30am-7.30pm Tue-Sat; closed Mon, Sun. **No credit cards.** **Map** p309 O2.

At the top end of Istiklal Caddesi close to Taksim Square, and part of the Aksanat Cultural Centre run by Akbank. The bank, which possesses a large art collection and annually takes a stand at the Istanbul Arts Fair (*see p182*), has other galleries around Istanbul, but this is the main show space. Exhibitors include big names such as Adnan Çoker, Utku Varlık, Tanju Demirci and the enchanting figurative painter Turan Erol. **Branch:** Cevdet Paşa Caddesi 56, Bebek (0212 263 5548).

Asmalımescit Art Gallery

Asmalımescit Sanat Galerisi
Sofyalı Sokak 5, Tünel, Beyoğlu (0212 249 6979/ www.asmalimescit.com). **Open** 10am-8pm daily. **No credit cards.** **Map** p308 M4.

Motto: 'We never close!' Except nightly at 8pm, no? Perhaps what owner Uğur Bekdemir means is that his excellent gallery is open all year round, with excellent and regularly changing exhibitions of work by both local artists and artists from abroad, such as Chicago-based Marianne Angersbach and acclaimed hard-edge German abstractionist Herbert Enz Enzer. The gallery occupies two floors with a snug cellar bar-café below.

Borusan Culture & Art Centre

Borusan Kültür ve Sanat Merkezi
Istiklal Caddesi 421, Beyoğlu (0212 292 0655). **Open** 10.30am-7pm Tue-Sat; closed Mon, Sun. **No credit cards.** **Map** p308 M4.

Sponsored by a car- and engine-manufacturer whose stated aim is to introduce and promote Turkish culture at home and abroad. The modern exhibition space is at street level and comprises one floor plus a mezzanine. Shows emphasise conceptual work and feature both established and young Turks as well as international names, living and dead, which have included Beuys, Man Ray and Warhol.

Galatea Art Gallery

Galatea Sanat Galerisi
Soyfalı Sokak 16, Asmalımescit (0212 292 5430/ konak@turk.net). **Open** 11am-7pm Tue-Sun; closed Mon. **Credit** MC, V. **Map** p308 M4.

Gaining a reputation as a showcase for nascent home-grown talent. Also shows well-established names, including Orhan Taylan, whose atmospheric nudes have become very collectable. Worth a

visit for the beautiful fresco on the ceiling of the entrance hall. There's an elegant bar and restaurant in the upstairs gallery.

Yapı Kredi Kazım Tashkent Art Gallery

Yapı Kredi Kazım Taşkent Sanat Galerisi
Istiklal Caddesi 285, Beyoğlu (0212 252 4700). **Open** 10am-7pm Mon-Fri; 10am-6pm Sat; closed Sun. **No credit cards.** **Map** p308 N3.

Next to the Galatasaray Lycée, a large space on one floor, plus mezzanine. Concentrates on retrospectives by important Turkish artists living and dead. Styles encompass figurative, abstract and installations; past exhibitions have been devoted to Fikret Mualla, Balkan Naci Islimyeli and Ibrahim Çallı.

Maçka, Teşvikiye, Nişantaşı

Gallery Baraz

Galeri Baraz
Kurtuluş Caddesi 191, Kurtuluş (0212 225 4702/ www.galeribaraz.com). **Open** 9am-7pm Mon-Sat; closed Sun. **Credit** AmEx, DC, MC, V.

Founded in 1975 by the intrepid Yahşi Baraz, this is one of the most venerable private galleries in the city. At the time he opened, says Baraz, there was no market value for art and he started off by selling work for as little as $100-$200. He now represents some 70-80 artists, including Güngör Taner, Adem Genç and Adnan Çoker. These days he only holds one or two exhibitions a year at the gallery and concentrates his efforts on organising large shows in such public venues as the Atatürk Cultural Centre (*see p226*). A second space, Galeri Baraz 2, was recently opened across town and is fast gaining a reputation as a showcase for new talent. **Branch:** Galeri Baraz 2, Eşrefefendi Sokak 21, Pangaaltı (0212 231 2788).

Gallery Nev

Galeri Nev
Maçka Caddesi 33/B, Maçka (0212 231 6763/ www.galerinev.com). Teşvikiye dolmuş from Taksim. **Open** 11am-6.30pm Tue-Sat; closed Mon, Sun. **Credit** MC, V.

Now in its fifteenth season, Gallery Nev handles internationally known Turkish artists such as Ergin Inan, Erol Akyavaş and Burhan Doğançay, as well as younger up-and-coming Turks such as New York-based Serdar Arat and Istanbul-based Inci Eviner. It generally holds eight one-person shows per year with a group show over summer.

Kaş Art Gallery

Kaş Sanat Galerisi
Abide-i Hürriyet Caddesi 151, Şişli (0212 247 1185). **Open** 9am-7pm Mon-Sat; closed Sun. **No credit cards.**

Big gallery a stone's throw from Şişli Mosque. It shows both 2-D and 3-D figurative Turkish art (including large-scale works) with eight one-person shows per season. Regular artists include Mustafa

Gallery Nev handles internationally known Turks as well as up-and-comers. *See p194.*

Ata, Mustafa Aslier and Ekrem Kahraman, a household name after completing Turkey's longest painting, exhibited in 1990.

Milli Insurance Art Gallery

Milli Reasürans Sanat Galerisi
Teşvikiye Caddesi 43/57, Teşvikiye (0212 231 4730/ www.mre.com). Teşvikiye dolmuş from Taksim. **Open** 9am-6.30pm Tue-Sat; closed Mon, Sun. **No credit cards.**

A large gallery beside the main Milli Reasürans building in Teşvikiye. In 2000 the gallery hosted one of the best exhibitions of recent years, a series of dress sculptures by Turkish multi-media artist Suzy Hug-Levy. Constructed from partially unravelled and re-woven painted wire mesh, these objects were like a post-industrial update on the marble *kore* that deck ancient Greek temples.

Tem Art Gallery

Tem Sanat Galerisi
Prof Dr Orhan Ersek Sokak 44/2, off Valikonağı Caddesi, Nişantaşı (0212 247 0899/www.temartgallery.com). Teşvikiye dolmuş from Taksim. **Open** 11am-7pm Mon-Sat; closed Sun. **Credit** MC, V.

Around since the mid-1980s, this is the leading Istanbul gallery for contemporary figurative art. Owner Besi Cecan's policy is to exhibit work of quality, regardless of commercial considerations. Her spacious gallery covers four floors; two for exhibitions, two for storage. The lower floor is reserved primarily for sculpture – if Salih Coşkun's wonderful wooden angels are still there, go and see them. Other Tem artists include Paris-based painter Ömer Kaleşi, Kemal Önsoy and Abidin Dino.

Teşvikiye Art Gallery

Teşvikiye Sanat Galerisi
Abdi İpekçi Caddesi 48/3, Teşvikiye (0212 241 0458/ tsanat@superonline.com). Teşvikiye dolmuş from Taksim. **Open** 10am-7pm Mon-Sat; closed Sun. **No credit cards.**

Airy gallery showing mainly smaller works by big-name Turkish figurative artists, including Ergin Inan, Komet, who paints on Turkish carpets, Doğan Paksoy and Mahir Güven. Six exhibitions per year divided between one-person and group shows. Most of the 2-D work is oil or mixed media on canvas. The gallery remains open during the summer months.

Urart Art Gallery

Urart Sanat Galerisi
Abdi İpekçi Caddesi 18/1, Nişantaşı (0212 241 2183). Teşvikiye dolmuş from Taksim. **Open** 9am-7pm Mon-Sat; closed Sun. **No credit cards.**

Offshoot of the classy Anatolian jewellery firm of the same name (*see page 166*), and upstairs from its plush showrooms. Exhibitions are a mixture of abstract and figurative with some conceptual work. Regular artists include painter Arzu Başaran and sculptor Dilek Hekimoğlu.

Asian Shore

Home & Abroad Art Gallery

Yurt ve Dünya Sanat Galerisi
Aylin apt. 270, Moda Caddesi, Moda (0216 349 2610/www.yurtvedunya.com). Moda dolmuş from Kadıköy ferry terminal. **Open** 10am-7pm Mon-Sat; 2pm-7pm Sun. **No credit cards. Map** p311 W8.

Owner Nevzat Metin has published more books on art than the Turkish government, with over 50 monographs on prominent Turkish artists to date. He also organises shows abroad, most recently in Paris, and attends international art fairs, including those in Stockholm and Tokyo. Turkish artists on show include Ekrem Kahraman, Tanju Demirci and Ibrahim Çiftçioğlu. The owner also shows artists from the UK, France and Germany. Its location south of the Asian suburb of Kadıköy makes getting to the gallery a nuisance, but more often than not it's worth the effort.

Arts & Entertainment

Gay & Lesbian

A history of Ottoman buggery, a transgender tradition and oodles of steamy hamam action.

All mouth and no trousers at transsexual dungeon **Güllüm**. *See p201.*

Things in Istanbul are ambiguous at best. Moustaches, snug jeans, leather bomber jackets, blow-dried hair, preening, hairy hand-holding, meaningful stares and crotch-rubbing – no, that's not a posse of Colt Studio poster boys sauntering towards you, just some lads on the way to the local teahouse.

Despite a glorious history of Ottoman buggery and male court favourites, resulting in some of literature's most passionate odes to boy, long gone is the openness in Karaköy's back streets described by Gustave Flaubert: 'We walked through (no more than that) the street of the male brothels. I saw bardashes buying sugared almonds, the anus thus about to provision the stomach instead of the other way around.'

Male sex has never disappeared, but only the passive partner has ever been considered homosexual. That said, social proscriptions kept anything like a Western gay scene from emerging until just over a decade ago.

The more enlightened approach to sexual roles is limited to a few venues, where the music and decor generally reflect the more Western attitude of the clientele. At the 'à la Turca' bars, a foreigner may have the feeling of being the only one unable to interpret a room full of invisible colour-coded back pocket hankies, but the lack of delicacy serves to make things clearer. A discreetly flashed 'OK' sign, thumb and forefinger clenched into a circle, is actually a come-hither representation of what your new friend finds most compelling about you. And don't expect attention to be paid to any other part of your anatomy.

In effect, the Istanbul gay community remains for the time being a subculture of the man-to-man sex scene, but the younger bar-going generation is gay, growing, informed and surprisingly unselfconscious.

Advice & information

KAOS GL

kaosgl@geocities.com

Turkey's first gay and lesbian magazine, published since 1994. Although the mainstream Turkish press runs gay-related stories almost daily, and it seems no weekly glossy or evening broadcast news is complete without a gay-oriented dose of something titillating, sensational or lurid, *KAOS GL* was established to provide both a gay readership and the media with a more balanced view. The *KAOS* monthly magazine can be bought from Mephisto Bookstore at Istıklal Caddesi 173.

LAMBDA Istanbul

PO Box ACL 222, Istanbul 80800 (0212 233 4966/ lamda@lambdaistanbul.org).

This umbrella group has links to international organisations, including the International Gay and Lesbian Association, which is led these days by Turkish activist Kürşad Kahramanoğlu. LAMBDA is involved in a wide range of legal, social, cultural, health and political issues of concern to the gay community. The group holds Sunday evening meetings every week at Bekar Sokak 14, just off Istıklal Caddesi, and has also organised four national conferences to date. The governor of Istanbul has issued several last-minute bans against LAMBDA-sponsored international conferences, on the grounds of their likelihood to 'incite public disorder', although actual police harassment is reserved for prostitution and public sex.

Sapphonun Kızları

sapphonunkizlari@hotmail.com.

The first organisation for lesbians, 'Daughters of Sappho' was established in May 1998. The group organises workshops and meetings dealing with issues ranging from female sexuality and literacy to wife-battering.

Websites

The largest, most comprehensive Turkish gay site is **www.eshcinsel.net**. There are regularly updated English-language links for the organisations above, with more under construction. The easiest way to enter a Turkish gay chat room is through the international floor of **www.gay.com**. English-speaking Turks are usually eager to strike up email friendships with foreigners.

Venues

The line dividing bars and clubs is slightly blurred, with the former closing an hour or two earlier and the latter charging admission on the weekends. **Neo** is the glaring exception, a bar that charges hefty admission. The only time you'll find a boisterous crowd is late on weekends; otherwise, Wednesday gets busy too. Early evening and weekday cruising and socialising is centred on Vatan Caddesi just off Taksim Square, also home to a brazen rent boy scene. Borsa Fast Food and Han Café, which flank McDonald's, usually trigger any finely tuned gaydar into overdrive, and are places to sip beer, lean back and people-watch.

Western-style venues are straight- and lesbian-friendly, but there are aren't yet any venues for women only. Still, the existence of lesbian-owned cafés, Sapphic organisations and websites and a well-known dyke DJ prove that lesbians do exist. They just have nowhere to congregate.

Underground dance music is abruptly replaced by Turkish pop and dance as closing time nears, so get there early or be prepared for some serious gyrating. Police sweeps are extremely rare at gay venues, occurring more frequently at mainstream clubs, bars and cafés unable to fork over bribes. In the event of one, just hand over your passport for inspection and remember that you've done nothing illegal.

Güllüm and **Hengame** (*for both, see page 201*), the first a bar, the second an after-hours club, draw a mixed bag of transgenders, their admirers and gay men.

Bars

Bar Bahçe

1st floor, Soğancı Sokak 7, off Sıraselviler Caddesi, Cihangir (0212 243 2879 ext 117). **Open** 9pm-2am Mon-Sat; closed Sun. **Admission** free Mon-Thur; $8 Fri, Sat. **No credit cards. Map** p309 O3.

In the most recent of Bar Bahçe's many incarnations, a young, energetic crowd does its best to out-glitter the postmodern decor. House and breakbeat aficionados bop away below silver cornices and dangling disco balls in the cramped back half of the bar that serves as a makeshift dancefloor.

Hans Bar

Tarlabaşı Bulvarı 248/1, Taksim (0212 297 2556). **Open** 9pm-4am daily. **Admission** free. **No credit cards. Map** p308 N2.

Those misled by the name into expecting a German leather bar will be disappointed, but the whiskered blokes hunkering up against the walls and occasionally breaking into a folkloric stamp after a hard day's work filling in potholes make up in authenticity what they lack in style. Vying for their attention are wriggling young midriffs and a sprinkling of transgenders. Best to come early to enjoy a cheap beer, Turkish pop and the garish surroundings before moving on.

Neo

Lamartin Caddesi 40, Taksim (212 254 4526/ neobar@hotmail.com). **Open** 10pm-2am Tue-Sun; closed Mon. **Admission** free Tue-Thur, Sun; $7 Fri, Sat. **No credit cards. Map** p307 O1.

'Bigger, Better, Batter' boasts Neo's slogan, perfectly summing up the two defining traits of Istanbul's hottest gay bar: snooty ambition paired with just not quite getting it. Scowling bodyguards turn away overtly Anatolian types, but a mixed stream of the upwardly mobile and moneyed pass through the 'chat room' (foyer to you and me) to present drink tickets to shirtless, strutting barmen. Elbow your way on to where the Western pop dance

Arts & Entertainment

Bar Bahçe – young, energetic. *See p197.*

tunes, black light and bottle cap-studded walls of the dance floor may just convince you that sometimes 'batter' can be gooder. Admission price includes a drink ticket.

Clubs

Club 14
Abdülhak Hamit Caddesi 63, Taksim (0212 256 2121). **Open** 11pm-4am Tue-Sun; closed Mon. **Admission** $15. **Credit** AmEx, MC, V. **Map** p307 O1.
Istanbul's oldest gay venue, established in 1988, is still going strong, drawing a mixed after-hours crowd and the occasional Turkish celebrity to a small metallic space for some frenetic last-chance cruising, thumping techno and thoroughly abandoned drinking and dancing.

Club Cubana 99
Meşrutiyet Caddesi 81A, below Dünya Hotel, Galatasaray (no phone). **Open** 11pm-4am daily. **Admission** free Mon-Thur, Sun; $5 Fri, Sat. **No credit cards. Map** p308 M4.
The dreary decor of this basement nightclub does nothing to dispel the initial feeling of descent into a dungeon. Depending on how much you're prepared to stomach, blaring Turkish pop and the decidedly down-at-heel gathering of bedraggled transgenders, rough rent boys and assorted hoodlums either add to the sense of torture or provide a bracing blast of something long absent from Western gay clubs: fear.

Prive
Tarlabaşı Bulvarı, 28/A, Taksim (0212 235 7999). **Open** midnight-4am daily. **Admission** free Mon-Thur, Sun; $8 Fri, Sat. **No credit cards. Map** p309 O2.
The relatively unpretentious stepsister of Club 14 still welcomes moustaches, but has been tarted up with a badly thought-out facelift that contrasts oddly with its clientele, the sort who prefer music with words. Prive peaks late, when half-hearted dancing to Latin and Western pop gives way to thumping Turkish tunes, uplifted arms and quivering bellies.

Hamams & saunas

None of Istanbul's hamams and saunas are officially gay, but the ones listed below cater almost exclusively to men unabashedly seeking a bit more than a good exfoliation. Remember that hamam owners and staff are usually straight, and tolerance of sexual activity is neither consistent nor wholehearted. Pointing out that a couple in the next room were moments ago having sex will not necessarily save you from rapid ejection if you're spotted doing the same. *See chapter* **Hamams** for details on washing and services, but be warned that the attendant who supplies your towel at gay hamams may try to inflate his tip by providing unsolicited groping. Hamams are most crowded early evenings and weekends and draw all types, from the middle-aged married to flamboyant eightysomethings and teens looking for a first experience. One of few places where class distinctions fade and rigid role-play relaxes.

Ağa Hamam
Turnacıbaşı Sokak 66, Beyoğlu (0212 249 5027). **Open** *Men* 6pm-6am daily; midnight Sat- Midnight Sun. *Women* 9am-6pm Mon-Sat; closed Sun. **Admission** *men* $11; *women* $8.00. **No credit cards.** **Map** p309 O3.
Beautifully restored historical hamam with a large sauna and cabins for two on the upper floors. Gets going well after midnight when the bars close. TV appearances by the owner disputing hamam workers' unsavoury reputation haven't prevented his staff from perpetuating it. *See also p204.*

Çeşme Hamam
Yeni Çeşme Sokak 9, off Perşembe Pazarı Caddesi, Karaköy (0212 252 3441). **Open** 8am-8pm daily. **Admission** $5. **No credit cards. Map** p306 M6.
Recent renovation has done little to brighten up this dingy hamam. Formerly relaxed, but staff have recently issued warnings that open sexual activity, the only real draw here, will no longer be tolerated.

Çukurcuma Hamam
Çukurcuma Caddesi 57, Beyoğlu (0212 243 2401). **Open** 9am-8pm daily. **Admission** $6. **No credit cards. Map** p308 N4.
Join the owner and his son for poetic flattery, a drink, and an account of their efforts to keep alive a centuries-old tradition of male sex. So gay that the main room is often not even heated and the sauna functions as a back room. Lounge, bar and exercise equipment are all part of the package. On the flip side, the hamam's reputation has spread well beyond its front doors, resulting in the sporadic harassment of departing clientele on the street outside.

Park Hamam
Dr Emin Paşa Sokak 10, off Divan Yolu, Sultanahmet (0212 513 7204). **Open** 7am-9.30pm daily. **Admission** $6; with scrub and massage $12. **No credit cards. Map** p303 M10.

Arts & Entertainment

The occasional uninformed tourist and unusually vigilant and rude staff keep the mainly gay clientele slightly inhibited. A pleasant place in terms of cleanliness and architectural details. Package deal a plus for those prone to being badgered into overtipping.

Yeşildirek Hamam

Tersane Caddesi 74, Azapkapı (0212 253 0289). **Open** 11am-9pm daily. **Admission** $4. **No credit cards. Map** p306 L5.

Run-down but friendly neighbourhood hamam across from the Azapkapı Mosque at the Taksim base of the Atatürk Bridge. Moss-covered ivy-draped toilet and drab cabins detract from the recent addition of a large, new sauna. The management seems willing to overlook a lot in exchange for a little custom.

Transsexuals

Islam is more often associated with strict separation of the sexes, but in Turkey the boundaries get a bit blurred when it comes to its high-profile transgender communities.

Turkey's fascination with transsexuals and transvestites dates back to Ottoman times when, during military campaigns, the reigning sultan would take along a large contingent of pretty boys for his own personal 'use'. Ordinary soldiers were left to their own devices, but had very little trouble rooting out their own effeminate nocturnal distractions from within the ranks.

Now, in a contemporary Turkish society that prizes masculinity like an international football trophy, and where the expression of female sexuality is also considered strictly taboo, the foothold of ostentatious transsexuals and transvestites in urban space is precarious. Often considered merely flashy upstarts by the gay community, transsexuals and transvestites evoke an almost voyeuristic curiosity from the general public. Trouble for the 2,000-strong gender-bending community started in the mid 1990s when the Islamic-oriented Welfare Party came to power in Beyoğlu, the Soho of Istanbul. Harassment and frequent raids by police brought protests from the International Gay & Lesbian Human Rights Commission and Amnesty International.

Despite the pitfalls, Istanbul's exuberant transsexual and transvestite community struts on. Small packs of scantily clad girls hang out in bars and on the streets, using their numbers for safety like flocks of migrating birds, creating a brilliant blaze of flamboyant colour amid the

Sex-change star shows the way

To grasp the phenomenon that is Turkish singer Bülent Ersoy is better to comprehend the bundle of contradictions that is Turkey. To follow her life, from middle-class son of conservative eastern parents, to glamorous gay divorcée about Istanbul, is to gain insight into the country that made her a star.

Extremely effeminate, but still decidedly male, Bülent took the 1970s Turkish music hall scene by storm, combining the flamboyant costumes of Liberace with the overwrought delivery of an *à la Turca* Ethel Merman. Savvy '70s audiences were familiar with gender-bending and glam, and the country was going through one of its periodic phases of rapid change, upheaval and experimentation. Scarcely an eyebrow was raised until Bülent bared a pair of perfectly formed breasts during a 1979 performance, followed not long after by a sex change operation in London. Things were spinning out of control.

General Kenan Evren seized power, putting an end to the activities of both Bülent and extremists on the left and right. Banned from the stage, Bülent joined the many artists and intellectuals exiled to Europe. While they secretly kept in touch with their comrades in Turkey through underground organisations, she maintained her popularity by starring in musicals shot in Germany and smuggled on to the Turkish black market. Audiences thrilled to leading lady Bülent's portrayals of a heart-of-gold wet nurse uncomplainingly supporting her shiftless, abusive husband and children, rags-to-riches singer casting her fur coat into a stream at film's end as she realises that true happiness comes from baking bread, and hapless mantrap ensnared by her dastardly manager into drug-smuggling. And that's the synopsis for just one of her films.

The triumphant appearance of Bülent Ersoy on state-run Turkish television on New Year's Eve 1989 signified that democracy was truly back on track, and pointed the way for previously banned political leaders to become prime minister and president several years later. As much a reflection of the times as a harbinger of things to come, Bülent responded to Turkey's first Islamist government by gaining 50 pounds, covering up and appearing for photo opportunities in front of the tombs of obscure holy men.

typically bland street fauna. Real girls gaze in envy at perfectly shaped breasts and cellulite-free thighs displayed in fluorescent pink hot-pants or tiny leather minis.

Club 34

Zambak Sokak 23/A, Beyoğlu (0212 249 2397). **Open** 11pm-4am daily. **Admission** free. **No credit cards. Map** p309 O2.

The only bar in Istanbul – or possibly the world – with a strict policy of no gays, no women and no transvestites. Transsexuals and straight men only, please. Seedy interior with circular dance floor strobed by disco lighting. Tasteless, but fun.

Cumba

Gezi Dükkanları 19, off Cumhuriyet Caddesi, Taksim (0212 244 4751). **Open** 10pm-2am daily. **Admission** free. **No credit cards. Map** p307 P2.

This dark, smoky bar serving overpriced drinks is filled with trannies, *magandas* (pot-bellied, hairy, country folk wearing gold chains) and loud, fizzy Turkish pop. The tiny tables are draped with sombre-looking middle-aged gender-benders sporting an undulating wave of impressive silicon breasts. Dressing to show it all off, they seriously look like they'd thrive on mud-wrestling and truck driving. Being ripped-off is a possibility.

Güllüm

Istiklal Caddesi 373, Beyoğlu (no phone). **Open** 10pm-2am daily. **Admission** free Mon-Thur; $1.50 Fri, Sat; free Sun. **No credit cards. Map** p308 M4.

This dingy underground dungeon caters to gays, lesbians, transvestites, transsexuals and straight men. Loud pumping pop gives the excuse for lots of pulsating would-be hedonists to rub up against each other. Definitely a meat-market. 'Güllüm' is gay slang derived from a dialect of Gypsy Turkish that means 'to let your hair down'. And they do. Over-zealous police raid the place from time to time.

Hengame

Sahne Sokak 6, Balık Pazarı, Beyoğlu (0212 249 1178). **Open** midnight-4am daily. **Admission** free Mon-Thur, Sun; $6 Fri, Sat. **No credit cards. Map** p308 N3.

A slick marble stairway leads up to three rooms filled with transvestite glamour. Champagne and sofas create a vaguely decadent air, hung heavy with mixing perfumes. The entry fee includes one drink.

Tequila

Gezi Dükkanları 18, off Cumhuriyet Caddesi, Taksim (0212 245 3954). **Open** 11pm-4am daily. **Admission** free. **No credit cards. Map** p307 P2.

Tiny drinking hole with impractically loud music. Conversation is impossible, but most are happy just to ogle the staff.

The ever-ebullient **Bülent Ersoy.**

Even her piety sparked controversy when she became the first woman to record the call to prayer, and her Islamic credentials were questioned when she got hitched to a 19-year-old. Three years ago Bülent filed for divorce, slimmed down and had her sphincter tightened. She is now back to flashing her breasts on the front of the daily papers, showing her country the way forward once more.

Hamams

Soak in some history and take a good pounding – bath night will never be the same again.

There's a Turkish saying, 'You enter a hamam, you sweat', meaning that in any task you undertake there's good and there's bad. In the case of a visit to the hamam, boy, do you sweat. And if you accept the attentions of a masseur there's the scraping, the pummelling and the pulling. The net effect is to leave you feeling that you've just gone 12 rounds with Mike Tyson at a venue in the Ninth Inferno. But – and it's a big, wonderful but – having gone through the ordeal, you emerge feeling so clean it borders on the virginal.

Which is as it should be. Hamams were intended to purify. Part of Islamic tradition is that its followers adhere to a strict set of rules for ablutions, washing hands, arms, face and feet with running water before praying. Another saying, '*Temizlik imandan gelir*', declares that cleanliness comes from faith.

The physical cleansing was not necessarily carried out in a hamam, but the link between mosque and hamam was always close and the courtyards of most mosques incorporated a public bathhouse.

In the earliest times, the hamam was for men only, but the privilege was later extended to women. No mixing, of course. Either the hamam would have two sections, one for each sex, or it would admit men and women at separate times of the day. This is still the case. In male-dominated Ottoman times women particularly valued their visits to the hamam as a rare freedom and a chance to socialise. If a husband denied his wife access to the hamam she had grounds for divorce.

Used by all on an almost daily basis, hamams became far more than just somewhere to get clean. They became the favoured places for arranging marriages, somewhere a mother could

The *hararet* (this picture) and *camekan* (right) of **Cağaloğlu Hamam**. *See p204.*

get a good eyeful of any prospective daughter-in-law. When the wedding came along, the equivalent of an Ottoman stag or hen night was spent getting steamed and lathered.

Even now, on occasion you still see brides and friends taking over a hamam the night before the big day and going through the rituals of washing, depilation, maybe even the hennaing of hair. In Ottoman times, a baby would be taken out of the family home for the first time 40 days after its birth for a visit to a hamam, an event also marking the end of housebound confinement for the mother. After a lifetime of hamam-going came to its inevitable end, a person's body would be carried in one last time to be washed before being taken to the mosque, where prayers would be said over it prior to burial. Be reassured, this tradition has definitely gone the way of the dodo and there is no chance that you might have to bathe with a corpse.

With the advent of internal plumbing, the tradition of the hamam has faded. Eighty years ago, there were more than 2,500 bathhouses in Istanbul alone; now there are only a few hundred. Many of these struggle to survive. Despite rising ticket prices, hamams barely break even. The few that flourish do so largely by courting the tourist dollar, and are thus accused of lacking authenticity. Don't let that put you off: whether in an Ottoman original or a tarty baroque showpiece, a long, slow steam laid flat on a marble slab beneath a star-studded dome is one of Istanbul's hedonistic highlights.

BARE ESSENTIALS

For the uninitiated, entering a hamam for the first time can be a baffling experience. Lengthy menus offer such treats as massage, depilation and pedicures. Outside tourist-frequented hamams such as **Çemberlitaş**, **Cağaloğlu** and **Galatasaray** this will all be in Turkish. You must first choose which services you want (the basic choice is between hamam, or hamam plus massage) then buy the according ticket. All hamams listed below accept major foreign currency.

Once you've paid, you'll be let through to the *camekan*, a kind of reception area, generally with a gurgling fountain in the middle. Some *camekan* are splendid affairs with several storeys of wooden cubicles, like boxes at an opera house. This is where you get changed. You will be given a colourful checked cloth, known as a *peştemal*, to be tied around the waist for modesty. Men keep this on – it's bad form to flash. Women are less concerned and often ditch the *peştemal* in the steam room, though many keep on their knickers. Both sexes also get *takunya*, wooden clogs that can be absolutely lethal on wet marble floors.

Before you reach the heat there is a section known as the *soğukluk*, which is for cooling off and has showers and toilets. But what you're really looking for is the *hararet*, or steam room. These can be plain or ornate, but are nearly always covered in marble and feature a great dome with little pieces of star-shaped coloured glass admitting a soft, diffuse half-light. Billowing clouds of water particles usually fog the air.

There are no pools, as Muslims traditionally consider still water unclean. Instead, at the centre is a great marble slab known as the 'navel stone' (*göbektaşı*), positioned directly over the furnaces, usually covered with prone bodies sizzling away.

It's on the navel stone that your massage is delivered. Normally the masseur (*keseci*) will rub you down with a *kese*, a cloth usually made of camel hair that feels like a Brillo pad. After a soaping and a rinse the massage begins. This is painful. Your joints will be manipulated in directions that you never thought they could move. There has been the odd occasion when something really has gone the way it shouldn't – in autumn 2000 there was a story in the local

Çemberlitaş Hamam – setting for centuries of naked indolence. *See p205.*

press about a massage victim who ended up with broken bones. The fact that this made the news shows what a freak happening it was. Resist the urge to fight back, and relax.

Afterwards, retire to one of the small semi-private rooms off the main chamber, in which you'll find basins with taps and water scoops. There's no limit on the amount of time you can spend inside, although an hour or two is usually sufficient. When you're done you'll be given a towel and you return to the *camekan*, where soft drinks, tea and coffee are usually served. Some *camekans* have benches or beds for anyone who's too shagged out to move. Drink lots of water to rehydrate.

The hamams

Anyone interested in the unique architecture of the hamams, but who fancies neither the heat nor the attentions of the masseur, can visit a few old places that have been restored and converted to other uses. Chief of these is the **Baths of Roxelana** (Haseki Hürrem Hamamı) on Sultanahmet Square opposite Haghia Sophia. It was built in the mid-16th century by Sinan (*see page 38* **Keeping up with the domes's**) and named in honour of the wife of Süleyman the Magnificent. It is now a state-owned carpet sales centre.

For gay-friendly hamams *see page 199.*

Ağa Hamam
Turnacıbaşı Sokak 66, Beyoğlu (0212 249 5027).
Open *men* 6pm-6am Mon-Sat; midnight Sat-midnight Sun. *Women* 9am-6pm Mon-Sat; closed Sun. **Admission** $11 men; $8 women. **No credit cards.** Map 309 O3.
Built in 1454, the year after the Ottomans took Constantinople, the Ağa Hamam was reputedly a favourite of Mehmet the Conqueror. Over the years it has undergone major restoration, so it's doubtful whether much of what remains is original, but it's still a beautiful place. In recent times, as Beyoğlu has developed into the city's entertainment district, the Ağa's patrons have tended to be men hitting the steam in the early hours of the morning to sweat out the excesses of the night before. A certain amount of gay activity goes on (*see p199*), so straights might be better advised to visit earlier in the evening. Entry fee includes a massage.

Cağaloğlu Hamam
Prof Kazim Ismail Gürkan Caddesi 34, Cağaloğlu (0212 522 2424/www.cagalogluhamami.com.tr).
Tram Sultanahmet. **Open** *for men* 8am-10pm daily; *for women* 8am-8.30pm daily. **Admission** $10; $15 assisted bathing; $20 bath & massage; $30 full service. **No credit cards.** Map 303 M9.
More or less unchanged since it was built on the orders of Sultan Mahmut I in the middle of the 18th century, this is the most famous of the city's hamams. It is beloved of makers of TV ads, who consider it essential in flogging soap products. The

camekan is a two-storey affair with a central fountain, while the vast *hararet* seems to have drawn its inspiration from the grand domed chamber of an imperial mosque. Celebrity bathers have supposedly included Franz Liszt, Florence Nightingale and Tony Curtis, though locals still make up the majority of its patrons. After steaming there's a pleasant bar-café within the complex. If you enjoyed your hamam experience, you can take one home – the owners advertise a hamam-building service, individually tailored to a client's wishes.

Çemberlitaş Hamam
Vezirhan Caddesi 8, Çemberlitaş. (0212 522 7974/ www.cemberlitashamami.com.tr). Tram Çemberlitaş. **Open** 6am-midnight daily. **Admission** $8; $15 with massage; students $6-$12. **Credit cards** MC, V. **Map** p303 M10.

The most atmospheric of all Istanbul's hamams, particularly when you're stretched out flat on the great round navel stone, dreamily watching the diffractions of shafts of daylight in the steam. The intensity of the experience is further enhanced by the sound of splashing water and muffled chatter echoing round the dome. These baths were built in 1584 by Sinan, commissioned by Nurbanu, wife of Sultan Selim the Sot, as a charitable foundation to raise money for the poor. They've been in continual use ever since. There are both men's and women's sections, which were originally identical until the next-door restaurant annexed part of the women's area. Being so close to the heavily-touristed bazaar area, these baths see a lot of foreigners. If you've never experienced a hamam before, then this is the place to begin.

Galatasaray Hamam
Turnacıbaşı Sokak 24, Galatasaray, Beyoğlu (men 0212 252 4242/women 0212 249 4342). **Open** *men* 8am-10pm daily; *women* 8am-8pm daily. **Admission** $23. **Credit** MC, V. **Map** 308 N3.

Built in 1481 during the reign of Beyazıt II, for almost 500 years this hamam was men-only. That changed only as recently as 1963 with the addition of a small women's section. That aside, little else has been altered. The *camekan* here is particularly wonderful, decked out with furniture to make an antiquarian froth. There's also some beautiful tilework at the entrance to the men's steam room. Unlike other hamams, the Galatasaray has marble slabs in the *soğukluk*, where bathers can have massages in semi-privacy rather than on the heated navel stone. To find the hamam, take the sidestreet beside Istiklal's Atlas Pasajı, just north of the Galatasaray Lycée. Admission buys the full works, including massage.

Gedikpaşa Hamam
Hamam Caddesi 65-67, off Gedikpaşa Caddesi, Beyazıt (0212 517 8956). Tram Beyazıt. **Open** *for men* 5am-midnight daily; *for women* 9am-midnight daily. **Admission** $6; $12 with massage. **No credit cards. Map** p302 L10.

Galatasaray Hamam – men-only for half a millennium; women allowed since 1963.

One of Istanbul's oldest hamams, Gedikpaşa was built in 1457 by one of Mehmet the Conqueror's viziers. Although not in the same league architecturally as marble palaces such as the **Çemberlitaş** or **Cağaloğlu**, it has suffered little in the way of renovations, a big plus for the connoisseur. It's split into men's and women's sections, both of which are a little rundown (but clean), which adds to the charm. Low prices mean it attracts a regular local clientele. The women's section may close early.

Köşk Hamam
Alay Köşkü Caddesi 17, Cağaloğlu (0212 512 7397). Tram Gülhane. **Open** 8am-8.30pm daily. **Admission** $5. **No credit cards. Map** p303 N9.

Just up the hill from Gülhane Park, the Köşk, which dates from the 15th century, is less grand than most other hamams, but is well looked after and has an extremely friendly staff. The clientele are predominantly foreigners, guests from nearby hotels. The Köşk is also worth noting because, although it's a men-only establishment, you can arrange for it to stay open after hours for families or parties (male masseurs only) at a price to be negotiated.

Arts & Entertainment

Music: Rock, World & Jazz

There's more of it than you'd think.

The amazing thing is that Istanbul has a rock, pop and jazz scene at all. Turkish traditional music, with all its folky, Arabic, Ottoman and religious influences, is so diverse and vibrant that you'd wonder why any Istanbulite would be interested in 4/4 beats or 12-bar. But, of course, they are. Apart from a few blips around the early 1970s and 1980s when military rule kept the West at arm's length – fatally stalling the advent of a Turkish Glam or New Romantic movement – global fashions have always had a strong influence in Istanbul. Back in the late 1960s, legends such as **Cem Karaca**, **Erkin Koray** and **Barış Manço** famously coupled the folk rhythms of Turkey's Anatolian heartland with guitar-driven rock and prog-rock, to create a sound like the Moody Blues meeting… well, a bunch of Turkish folkies. These days pop idol **Tarkan** has his sights on becoming the next Ricky Martin (*see page 210* **Good gyrations**).

TICKETS AND INFORMATION

The best way to find out what's going on is to walk down Istiklal Caddesi and check out the flyposters. Listings and programmes are also given in the offbeat monthly rag *Istanbull…. Magazine* (in English) and the weekly *Zip* (in Turkish). Both are free from venues and various bars and cafés round Beyoğlu (94.9) and **Radio Oxi-Gen** (95.9) are also good news sources, though in Turkish only.

Information can also be obtained from the online ticket sales organisation **Biletix** (0216 454 1555/www.biletix.com). In-person sales points can be found at the Atatürk Cultural Centre (*see page 226*), the Vakkorama store at Taksim, the Yapi Kredi Tashkent Kazım Art Gallery (*see page 194*) and music shops such as Kod Music Shop, Raksotek and Zihni Music Centre (for all three, *see page 175*).

Rock & world music

Appreciative, beer-swilling audiences all over central Istanbul may lap up live rock, metal, blues and punk, but too often it's a set of covers performed by a cut-rate local version of a Western band. Sometimes there's an interesting Turkish twist, but usually that's nothing more

than mangled pronunciation or an alarming affection for 1970s rock anthems.

But there are some original sounds among the duff notes. A boho experimental fringe led by art rockers **Baba Zula** and **Zen** peddle a very distinctive blend of traditional Turkish music and postmodern avant rock – think Frank Zappa in a fez. More popular are the **Istanbul Blues Kumpanyası**, who fuse blues and oriental music with occasional wacky forays into genres like surf. Similarly accessible is the transnational **Groove Alla Turka**, led by percussion genius **Burhan Öçal** and drawing on the talents of New York bass player Jamaaladeen Tacuma and London-based, sometime-TransGlobal Underground chanteuse Natacha Atlas.

Other groups to look out for include old-timers **Bulutsuzluk Özlemi**, purveyors of no-nonsense leftist rock, who play frequently at Hayal Kahvesi (*see page 207*), and virtuoso punks **The Replikas**. In a similar vein, the highly politicised **Radical Noise** brought old school hardcore punk and skate punk fashions to Turkey with a sound remarkably like Rage Against the Machine without the scratching. The skate punk thing has become big in Istanbul over the last couple of years, inspiring a clutch of angst-driven bands, such as **Crunch** and the more metallic **Rashit**. Catch them at **Kemancı** (*see page 208*), home of the perforated eardrum.

One positive development in recent years has been the influx of African immigrants, forming groups such as **Tegemeo** and introducing euphoric Tanzanian and Ghanaian rhythms to the Istanbul scene. Problems with residence visas and the police, however, drastically reduce the lifespan of such musical projects. Even more eclectic are **Dokuz Sekiz**, whose members are Irish, Russian, Iranian and Turkish. They've created a bizarre fusion of ethnic music that picks up on the foot-tapping popularity of all things Irish then flies off in all directions where Aer Lingus don't go. Homemade instruments add a further experimental edge. You can catch them at **Shaman** (*see page 208*).

Meanwhile, revivals are not just something limited to Saturday night UK TV programming. The Anatolian rockers that kicked the whole

Bare bricks, bar room, no frills – **Hayal Kahvesi**.

scene off in the 1960s are currently enjoying a bit of a renaissance. **Moğollar** ('the Mongols') who started in 1967 and disbanded in 1976, reformed in the early 1990s due to popular demand (so they say) and still play regularly at the **Jazz Stop** (*see below*). **Karaca** and **Koray** are also still active and continue to inspire a new generation of Turkish musicians, some with a wish to emulate them and some with revulsion.

Visitors may be taken aback by the cramped conditions and poor ventilation of Istanbul's venues – they are significantly less spacious than their western European counterparts. Due to the disproportionate number of males frequenting the venues, men may have trouble entering if not accompanied by women, although foreigners usually get the nod. It's one of the few perks of being an outsider. At most places, a free drink is included in the price of admission.

Beyoğlu

Babylon

Şehbender Sokak 3, Asmalımescit, Tünel (0212 292 7368/www.babylon-ist.com). **Open** *mid Sept-mid July* 9.30pm-2am Wed, Thur; 10.30pm-3am Fri, Sat; closed Mon, Tue, Sun. *Mid-July-mid Sept* closed. **Admission** $10-$15. **Credit** MC, V. **Map** 308 M4.

Babylon is currently Istanbul's most happening live music venue, with arguably the best sound system. Its stripped brickwork and minimalist ethnic decor has been the backdrop to sets from *Wired*-generation artists such as John Lurie & the Lounge Lizards, Mouse on Mars and Cheikh Lo performing for the city's cool sophisticated set. Staff are charming, but go easy on the drinks, as prices are steep. Current programmes can be picked up just inside the door.

Hayal Kahvesi

Büyükparmakkapı Sokak 19, off Istiklal Caddesi (0212 243 6823/www.hayalkahvesi.com). **Open** noon-2am daily. **Admission** free Mon-Thur, Sun; $9 Fri, Sat. **No credit cards. Map** p309 O3.

Live music after 11pm in a basic no-frills, bare-brick bar-room with a raised stage at the far end. Lots of jostling at weekends when the place fills to capacity with rock-loving twentysomethings. Old rockers Bulutsuzluk Özlemi have made this their home base; otherwise, expect lots of posturing as Aerosmith wannabes take to the boards and ransack the US MOR songbook. Bands take to the stage at 11pm.

Home Bass

Sadri Alışık Sokak 15, Beyoğlu (0212 251 0007). **Open** 10pm-4am Tue-Sun; closed Mon. **Admission** free. **No credit cards. Map** p309 O3.

Follow the zebra stripes down to the basement to discover Beyoğlu's newest global music club. The theme is primitive: indigenous murals and tribal paraphernalia. Home Bass appeals to the city's African/Rastafarian community and serious fans of alternative music who come to guzzle cheap beer and writhe on the spacious dancefloor. Live bands every night in winter; on weekends only in summer.

Jazz Stop

Tel Sokak 9, off Büyükparmakkapı Sokak (0212 252 9314/www.jazzstop.com). **Open** *Sept-June* 6pm-3am daily. *July-Aug* closed. **Admission** free Mon-Thur, Sun; $8 Fri, Sat. **Credit** MC, V. **Map** p309 O3.

Not actually a jazz venue at all, this place is run by Engin Yorukoğlu of the band Moğollar, and his bunch of near-pensionable rockers are one of the regular acts here. Other Turkish rock legends like Cem Karaca frequently sit in on impromptu jam sessions. There's a good-quality sound system and high tables give a great view of the stage. Beware: although admission is free, the first drink on Tuesday and Sunday nights costs $8, as a form of cover charge.

Arts & Entertainment

Pop, covers, death metal, Levent (right) – you get all sorts over three storeys at **Kemancı**.

Kemancı

Sıraselviler Caddesi 69/1, Taksim (0212 251 2723/ www.kemancirockbar.com). **Open** 9pm-4am daily. **Admission** $4 Mon-Thur, Sun; $9-11 Fri, Sat. **No credit cards. Map** p309 O3.

A three-storey rock emporium for those who still have a mane to toss and whose musical tastes linger in decades gone by. While the erotic sci-fi, cartoon art and rock graffiti decor runs throughout, musically each floor has a different flavour. At street level, bands cover old favourites by punk heroes – very grim if you're at all familiar with the originals. One floor down is pop and alternative rock. The searing guitars of death metal are confined to the lower basement. Slam-dancing occasionally erupts into outright violence, so watch your step. Watch your pint too, or it may get nicked.

Mojo

Büyükparmakkapi Sokak 26, off Istiklal Caddesi (0212 243 2927). **Open** 9pm-4am daily. **Admission** free Mon, Tue, Sun; $3 Wed, Thur; $9 Fri, Sat. **No credit cards. Map** p309 O3.

Basement space decorated with huge posters of the rock 'n' roll pantheon hosts conservative trad rock groups performing the back catalogues of the Doobies, Supertramp, The Eagles and worse. Better are the occasional blues acts that turn up. Live music starts at midnight.

Peyote

Imam Adnan Sokak 24, off Istiklal Caddesi (www.peyote.allhere.com). **Open** Sept-June 8pm-4am Mon-Sat; closed Sun. July-Aug closed. **Admission** free. **No credit cards. Map** p309 O2.

Poorly illuminated hole-in-the-wall place with a tiny stage and primitive sound system, but definitely worth a look for its bill of garage psychedelia, surf music, punk and out-there rock. Zen, Baba Zula and The Replikas have all done time here. Draws a diehard student crowd kept happy by cheap beer and staff with smiles.

Riddim

Büyükparmakkapı Sokak 8/1, off Istiklal Caddesi (0212 249 8333). **Open** 6pm-2am Tue-Sun; closed Mon. **Admission** free Tue-Thur, Sun; $8 Fri, Sat. **No credit cards. Map** p309 O3.

Latin, reggae and world music bar run by local Sudanese rastafarian celebrity DJ Osman. Tegemeo play here frequently. The crowd of African immigrants and students acts as a magnet for the police, who regularly target the place sniffing for illegal aliens and drugs. Otherwise, it's nothing but good vibes and cheap beer.

Roxy

Arslan Yatağı Sokak 3, off Sıraselviler, Taksim (0212 245 6539/www.roxy.com.tr). **Open** Oct-mid July 10pm-4am Tue-Sat; closed Mon, Sun. Mid July-Sept closed. **Admission** $6-$8 Mon-Thur, Sun; $10-$12 Fri, Sat. **Credit** MC, V. **Map** p309 O3.

Major live venue with industrial decor housed in a large basement. Has hosted an impressive array of visiting artists, including Ben Harper, John Zorn, TransGlobal Underground and Zydeco Twisters. Live events are irregular but well publicised on Roxy's website and through its efficient monthly events list that gets posted around the city. Staff are enthusiastic and friendly, drinks pricey.

Shaman

Kazancı Yokuşu 49, off Sıraselviler Caddesi, Taksim (0212 249 9606/shaman@dilson.com). **Open** 8.30pm-3am Tue; 8.30pm-6am Wed-Sat; closed Mon, Sun. **Admission** free Tue-Thur; $11 Fri, Sat. **Credit** MC, V. **Map** p309 P2.

Tucked beneath the Dilson Hotel (*see p59*) and with unappealing interior decor involving porthole windows and kitsch African masks. Low stage and confined space means the bands are right in your face. Dokuz Sekiz, the Turkish-Irish fusion specialists, peddle their ethno-folk experiments here. The Senegalese drum collective Djiembes Africains were also regulars in 2000. Live music starts at 11.30pm.

Arts & Entertainment

Latin, reggae, world music, good vibes and police raids at **Riddim**. *See p208.*

Good gyrations

Elvis had his pelvis. Ricky Martin has his hips. Turkish pop phenomenon **Tarkan** looks poised to capture the international spotlight with his belly. The 21-year-old Tarkan burst on to the Turkish music scene in 1993, with his debut album *Yine Sensiz* ('Without You Again'). Radio and television had recently been privatized, and Tarkan was one of the first artists to appear in a professionally made Turkish video on a private music channel. The two were made for each other, in the same way young Madonna and early MTV scratched backs – and bucks.

Tarkan sold over 700,000 copies of *Yine Sensiz* and the fledgling Turkish pop industry was established. Tarkan also pioneered the use of slangy lyrics and sexual innuendo that, just a few years earlier, would have been banned from state-run television. Mind you, the nation was also forced to endure lyrics along the lines of: 'Hey George, lend me money; can't Michael, I'm broke too.' In 1994, Tarkan cemented his popularity with his second album *Acayipsin* ('You're Awesome'). A record-breaking two million copies were snapped up in Turkey and a further 700,000 copies sold in Europe.

But it was Tarkan's video that had Turks of all ages glued to the screen. While gyrating men and over-the-top dancing were hardly new, never before had a fairly masculine type bared his hairy belly, gyrated while staring suggestively into the camera and demanded to know, using a standard street come-on line: 'Is It All Yours?' Even as his fame grew, the media did what it could to cut him down to size. His ex-manager claimed Tarkan was his old lover, photographs of Tarkan posed in a nude sprawl, a puppy concealing his private bits, were unearthed. Nothing worked. So the media blew up an incident that could only have had implications in Turkey.

When asked at a press conference how he was, Tarkan responded, 'Well, I have to pee'. It was nearly his undoing. Nothing fires up the Turkish public more than displays of bad breeding. Even hardcore headbangers know to mind their manners. While his image-makers worked overtime to win back the fickle public, Tarkan fled to New York to learn English. While there, he met the Istanbul-born co-founder of Atlantic Records, Ahmet Ertegun. The producer of acts from Aretha Franklin to Led Zeppelin, Ertegun liked what he saw and Tarkan's next album, *Ölürüm Sana* ('I'll Die For You') was prepared with an eye to the international market.

But there was still a snag. Tarkan's avoidance of compulsory military service had left Turks wondering whether he was willing to die for his country. The controversy dogged Tarkan for years, even as his album, released in June of

Ortaköy

Rock House

Dereboyu Caddesi 36/38 (0212 259 8911). **Open** noon-2.30am daily. **Admission** free Mon-Thur, Sun; $11 Fri, Sat. **Credit** AmEx, MC, V.

A misguided attempt to emulate the Hard Rock Café. Surly staff, bland surroundings and huge TV screens frame well-scrubbed Turkish groups doing Chuck Berry and Guns 'n' Roses covers. Good place to catch up on Eurosport, but as a live music venue you do not want to go there. The cover charge at weekends and for special events allows you to consume the equivalent in drinks at no further cost.

Asian shore

Buddha

Caferağa Mah. Kadife Sokak 14, Kadıköy (0216 349 7022). **Open** 3pm-2am daily. **Admission** $5. **No credit cards. Map** p311 W8.

A student hangout where low-grade bands play mostly run-of-the-mill blues and rock covers. But a good relaxed atmosphere and rarely crowded.

Shaft

Osmancık Sokak 13, off Serasker Caddesi, Kadıköy (0216 349 9956/www.shaftclub.com.tr). **Open** 11am-4am daily. **Admission** free Mon-Thur, Sun; $8 Fri, Sat. **No credit cards. Map** p311 W7.

For the source of the name think Blaxploitation and Richard Roundtree, rather than coal-mining and Arthur Scargill. Although chances are it would be Arthur who'd feel more at home here. Shaggy Anatolian rockers, ageing beatniks, students and expats make up the crowd, drawn by a mix of blues and rock, and jazz on Wednesday. Good ventilation and sound system. Probably the best rock bar on the Asian side of town, though that's not saying a whole hell of a lot. Live music starts after 9pm.

Jazz

It's not that long ago that in Istanbul the word 'jazz' didn't mean much to anybody. But then in 1988 a couple of Turkish enthusiasts returned to Istanbul from New York and set up a company, RH Pozitif, with the intention of promoting big jazz events at some of the many ancient amphitheatres scattered around Turkey. At that

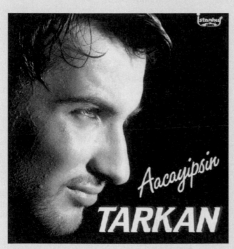

Aacayipsin

TARKAN

dancer crooning the 'Kiss Kiss Song' would single-handedly restore Turkey's tattered image. MPs even floated the idea of granting Tarkan honorary status as a Cultural Ambassador. Political leaders were asked for their opinions, with many promising to 'work for Tarkan'.

The military brass, however, were having none of it. Tarkan was warned he would either have to serve 18 months as a private, or be stripped of his Turkish citizenship. Tarkan once more disappeared abroad, giving sold-out concerts in London (Hippodrome) and Berlin (Arena). Finally, in October of 1999, the government hit upon a post-earthquake revenue-raising scheme of permitting conscripts to get away with just one month's service in exchange for $16,000. Tarkan came straight back and put on his camouflage gear.

1997, sold three million copies in Turkey and the single Şımarık ('Spoilt') reached the top three in France and number one spot in Belgium. Turks were delighted to see the likes of Prince Albert of Monaco and Claudia Schiffer singing along in Turkish as Tarkan collected his music awards. It was widely believed that a green-eyed male belly

In 2000, Tarkan was shuttling between studios in New York, Boston, Nice and Istanbul, putting the final touches on his latest album, due to be released in 45 countries sometime in 2001. The rumour mill has it that, for the first time, Tarkan will be wowing them in English. But definitely jiggling in Turkish.

time, just one small under-promoted, sparsely attended jazz festival existed. Now, brothers Ahmet and Mehmet Uluğ are responsible for the emergence of the **Akbank Jazz Festival** (*see page 182*), the **Efes Pilsen Blues Festival** (*see page 183*) and the **Fujifilm World Music Days** (*see page 179*), events that regularly bring in artists such as Courtney Pine, Andy Sheppard, James Blood Ulmer and Manu Dibango to introduce Istanbulites to the global groove. The brothers are also responsible for the city's best music venue, **Babylon** (*see page 207*), and their record label Doublemoon is not doing badly.

Local talent may soon find enough happening in Istanbul to consider sticking around. Traditionally, Turkish jazzers have always upped and left to swing their thing abroad. After Dizzy Gillespie discovered trumpet and piano player **Maffy Falay** in 1956, the Turkish jazzman moved to Germany and then to Sweden to bebop with the likes of Don Cherry and Lars Gullin. **Okay Temiz**, percussionist extraordinaire, also moved to Sweden in the 1960s to later play with **The Oriental Wind &**

Magnetic Band. Of the more recent generation, ace percussionist **Burhan Öçal** took off for European soil and now spends only half his time in Turkey (he returned recently to play an amazing gig with the Kronos Quartet). **Selahattin Can Kozlu**, a superb drummer, lived among African tribes to soak up their rhythms and now sometimes plays around town accompanied by pianist **Kerem Görsev**. Tenor sax player **Ilhan Erşahin** has made his name in the US and gigs around New York with his band **Sweet Basil**, but regularly exchanges the Hudson for the Bosphorus to play and record. Likewise, guitarist **Önder Focan** hangs out mostly in Finland, but comes back to Istanbul for festivals and concerts.

The lengthening list of young and upcoming Turkish jazz notables also includes **Aydın Esen**, a virtuoso pianist who has performed with the likes of Pat Metheny, and **Emir Işılay**, a newcomer who, when not here, tears up the piano for **Swamp Things** in Boston.

With the exception of Öçal and Temiz, all these names are jazz musicians who just happen to be

Turkish. Their styles are Chicago and New York. But Öçal is a traditional player who's gone jazz, while Temiz has long combined the two, and in doing so they're bringing about some significant changes. Most Turkish jazzers have long been disparaging of traditional music, but, encouraged perhaps by the interest shown by musicians from Europe and the US, there's now some really exciting fusion going on. In 1998 New York outfit **Brooklyn Funk Essentials** combined with **Laço Tayfa**, a folk outfit with an edge (band leader **Hüsnü Şenlendirici** is a killer clarinettist) to produce a sort of Gypsy jazz that has completely invigorated the whole Istanbul scene and left everybody eagerly waiting to see where this whole thing goes.

Jazz venues

City Lights Bar

Ceylan Inter-Continental Hotel, Asker Ocağı Caddesi 1, Taksim (0212 231 2121). **Open** 2pm-2am daily. **Admission** free. **Credit** AmEx, DC, MC, V.
A top-floor lounge bar with superb views over the Bosphorus, featuring slinky jazz, Latin and salsa house bands. Rarely on the cutting edge, the band are there for ambience, providing mood music to accompany cocktails, caviar and moonlit cityscapes. Subdued lighting ensures that it's not possible to make out the small type on the menu, perhaps so that patrons won't be frightened away by the prices. No live music on Sundays.

Gramofon

Tünel Square 3, Tünel, Beyoğlu (0212 293 0786). **Open** 9am-2am daily. **Admission** $8-$11; free if no live band. **Credit** MC, V. **Map** p308 M4.
Istanbul's most venerable jazz venue, with a prime location right next to the upper Tünel station. By day it's open as a café overlooking the small square, but there's live music from 10.30pm every night except Sunday and Monday. The intimate nature of the place means that it's mostly small local outfits performing, often vocal-led, but the crowd is usually appreciative and the atmosphere is especially lively at weekends. Food is served.

Harry's Jazz Bar

Hyatt Regency Hotel, Taşkışla Caddesi, Taksim, (0212 225 7000). **Open** 8pm-2am Tue-Thur; 9pm-3am Fri, Sat; closed Mon, Sun. **Admission** free Tue-Thur; $8 Fri, Sat. **Credit** AmEx, MC, V.
Local bands nightly from September through to May playing nothing too challenging – unlike the decor, which is strictly avant garde, sort of *Alice in Wonderland* meets *The Matrix*. Far more relaxing is the garden area, with plump sofas, low lighting, ivy-covered trellises and flaming oil lamps. In summer, canned music is played in the garden and winter sees live bands play inside. Musically speaking, the management haven't quite got it all together and the bands aren't always top quality.

Jazz Café

Hasnun Galip Sokak 20, off Büyükparmakkapi Sokak, Beyoğlu (0212 245 0516). **Open** noon-2am Mon-Sat; closed Sun. **Map** p309 O3.
Closed for renovations at the time of going to press but due to reopen sometime in late 2000. Hopefully there'll be no change in policy, which was to showcase a real mix of talent from outright jazzers to studio players to artists better known for their pop work, with very reasonable admission prices.

Kerem Görsev Jazz Bar

Abdi İpekçi Caddesi 61/1, Teşvikiye (0212 231 3950/ www.keremgorsev.com). **Open** Sept-mid May 9pm-1am Mon; 9pm-2am Tue-Thur; 9pm-2.30am Fri, Sat; closed Sun. *Mid May-Sept* closed. **Admission** $15-$19. **Credit** MC, V.
Music every night from 11pm onwards. Mostly local trios and quartets, but with the occasional visiting artists, particularly around festival time. Görsev, one of Turkey's best-known jazz musicians, often sits in. It's his bar, after all. It's worth going early to eat, as the American cuisine's not at all bad. Students get a 50% discount on admission weeknights, while Wednesday is 'Ladies' Night' with no cover charge for the fairer sex. No cover for anyone on Mondays, when there is no live music.

Q Jazz Club

Çırağan Palace Kempinski Hotel, Çırağan Caddesi 84, Beşiktaş (0212 236 2121/www.infoqjazzclub.com). **Open** 10am-4am daily. **Admission** $20 for live music. **Credit** AmEx, MC, V.
Insanely expensive, but then this is the Çırağan, Istanbul's most out-of-this-world hotel (*see p55*). And past artists here have included Natalie Cole and Ray Charles. Sometime hotel-guest Whitney Houston has apparently performed an impromptu set on more than one occasion. More usually, though, it's the likes of Keisa Brown and Imer Demirer, both classy acts, performing in the cellar bar during winter and in the garden in the summer. The cover may vary depending on who's in town, so call first to check.

Festivals

Istanbul has no problems attracting big names for one-off gigs. Major corporations frequently fund arena rock events that in recent times have featured Alanis Morrisette, Garbage, Metallica and the Rolling Stones. All sell-outs. But the best opportunity to catch the good bands, both local and international, is at July's **International Istanbul Jazz Festival** (*see page 181*). In addition, for indie bands there's June's **H2000 Music Festival** (*see page 180*); for dance acts there's September's **J&B Dance & Techno Festival** (*see page 182*); blues fans should check out October's **Efes Pilsen Blues Festival** (*see page 183*); and for more jazz try the **Akbank Jazz Festival** (*see page 182*).

Music: Turkish

Folk, *fasıl*, Ottoman, Sufi – a variety of Turkish traditions still obstinately survives and thrives in the face of globalised pop.

Turkish music – blasting from taxis, echoing out of kebab joints, wafting through markets – is one of the more startling sensual surprises for the visitor to Istanbul. This is a culture that was never overwhelmed by pop and rock to the point of losing a taste for its indigenous sound, and Turkey boasts a local music scene as diverse and deep as any found in world music centres such as Brazil, Ireland or Cuba.

In the days before electrified 'Arabesque' pop conquered Istanbul with its incessant electric dum-shikka-shikka, Turkish music was one of the most influential of the world's musics. Even Mozart parodied the sounds of Ottoman military *mehter* bands. The Ottoman courts melded their Central Asian tastes to the remnants of Byzantine and Persian court music, producing a deep and difficult classical music tradition. Elsewhere, provincial Arab princedoms copied and adapted the new musical styles of Istanbul. In time, this classical tradition lightened into the popular sound of *fasıl*. In the 19th century, when playing with instruments wasn't considered a proper profession for good Muslims, ethnic Armenians, Greeks, Gypsies and Jews supplied the musicians. The result was the inter-ethnic east Mediterranean urban contemporary pop of its time, the echoes of which are heard today in genres from Jewish Klezmer to Greek *bouzouki* to Romanian *lautar* music. And the roots are still here and growing.

SONGS OF OLD STAMBOUL

To get a sense of how this music courses through the blood of the city, spend an evening in a meyhane restaurant. As you nibble on plates of meze a quartet of musicians (usually Roma) starts by warming up the crowd with nostalgic songs from old Stamboul. By the time the main courses arrive – several hours and not a few drinks later – the rhythm has been upped a few notches and the whole place is swinging. Diners head back, giving it full voice, and the dancing has spilled out into the streets. Afterwards drop

▶ For **rock, world & jazz**, see page 206, for **classical music**, see page 225, for buying **Turkish musical instruments**, see page 219, and for a **discography of Turkish music**, see page 287.

into a 'folk music' bar, often the haunt of rural immigrants. The bar will be full of youngish folk seated on Anatolian rugs, singing along to the *bağlama* lute. As the atmosphere fills with 700-year-old hymns and goodwill rises, your fellow customers offer you fruit from their tables, cigarettes, even the ice from their drinks if yours has melted. You are dragged into a dance, hugged and sung to… all for the price of a glass of rakı.

One striking feature of Turkish music is the wide variety of rhythms. If you can't keep time clapping, that could well be because it's in 9/8 or 10/16 or some other bizarre signature. Turkish music, to the untrained western ear, may sound out of tune, due to the different kind of tuning system used in Turkish music theory. Turkish scales often employ notes between the notes, sometimes referred to as quarter tones – think of them as a new spice for your ears.

Traditional Turkish music can be divided into four basic styles: **folk**, which generally has a regional or rural flavour; **fasıl**, the frequently boisterous music found most often in meyhanes and restaurants; **Turkish Classical** (or Ottoman Music), a refined court music; and **Sufi Müziği**, the ethereal music often associated with the Whirling Dervishes. Crossover genres abound, as do forays into jazz and pop.

Folk

Halk müziği (folk music) forms an important part of the music scene in Turkey. Usually what gets labelled as folk are the slightly modernised *bağlama*-heavy songs that are played in bars. The *bağlama* is a long-necked lute, also called a *saz*, whose rural Anatolian connotations led it to be adopted by Atatürk's reformers as a national folk symbol of Turkey.

It's the instrument favoured by the Alevi and Bektaşi, sects of Islam that stress intersectarian tolerance and equality between men and women, and are frowned upon by the orthodox majority. Their folk poets, known as *aşıks*, have been wandering the Anatolian plains since at least the tenth century. Their vast repertoire includes ancient and beautiful folk poems, but they are folkies with a conscience; *aşık* music has a tradition of focusing on social injustices, which in the recent history of Turkey has often led to radio censorship and arrests. Most

Arts & Entertainment

Sultans of kitsch

Savvy travellers know to steer clear of venues promising one-stop 'traditional entertainment', with set menus and special discounts for tour groups. But those from the 'so bad it's good' school who actively seek out tourist kitsch, will find Istanbul's 'Turkish Nights' dinner clubs excruciatingly wonderful. The oldest such venue is **Kazablanka** (pictured). To enjoy the full effect, arrive at 8.30pm, half an hour before show time. Startled harem girls in gold lamé trousers will hastily stub out cigarettes to usher you into an empty, cavernous and dimly lit hall featuring a Medieval/Tex-Mex decoration scheme. By the time your waiter places a small flag indicating your country of origin on the table and you dig into your traditional Turkish potato salad and slice of bologna, several tour buses will have disgorged loads of elderly, blinking and bewildered fellow seekers of the exotic.

The show begins. Fasıl singers in fezzes get things going, then make way for a strange procession, half mehter marching band, half harem girl display, led by a Teletubby sultan. The parade works its way through the popping flashes to the stage, then the performers treat the crowd to ten minutes of clashing cymbals, synchronised aerobics and artful languishing on throw cushions. After an interval of belly-dancing, protesting members of the audience are dragged onstage to play bride and groom in a 'traditional wedding'. At Kazablanka this is followed by 'Turkey's greatest belly dancer', a wired Nancy Sinatra lookalike who tosses her hair and trembles maniacally, only to be upstaged by a Caucasian folk dance troupe featuring the now turban-less sultan in black spandex and leather boots throwing himself about the place. Most of the audience clears out at 11.30pm, missing 'international singer' Hakan and his multilingual medley beginning with 'Que Sera Sera'.

Kervansaray and Gar offer up further helpings of essentially the same fare.

Kazablanka

Kuytu Sokak 4, off Tarlabaşı Bulvarı, Beyoğlu (0212 293 6212). **Show** 9pm-midnight daily. **Cost** negotiable. Up to $75 per person inc. dinner and two drinks. Groups of ten or more $25 per person. **Credit** AmEx, MC, V. **Map** p308 M4.

Kervansaray

Cumhuriyet Caddesi 30, Elmadağ (0212 247 1630). **Show** 9pm-midnight daily. **Cost** $75 per person inc. dinner and unlimited drinks. Negotiable rates for groups. **Credit** AmEx, DC, MC, V.

Gar

M Kemal Paşa Caddesi 3, Yenikapı (0212 588 4045). **Show** 9pm-midnight daily. **Cost** $50 per person inc. dinner and two drinks. Lower rates for groups. **Credit** AmEx, MC, V.

brutally, in 1993 a get-together of Alevis at a hotel in Sivas in north-central Anatolia was attacked and the building set alight, resulting in the death of 37 prominent musicians and *aşıks*. However, a relaxing of the political climate in the past decade or so has seen the opening of many Alevi venues in Istanbul, catering mainly to Anatolian immigrants. At such places, songs – some even in Kurdish – are now openly sung that until very recently might have landed someone in jail.

Istanbul also hosts many immigrants from the Black Sea coast, whose characteristic instrument is the *kemençe*. The wonderfully chaotic music of this pear-shaped fiddle accompanies improvised song 'duels' between singers and players.

Folk venues

Bağlama bars, or 'Alevi Bars' with signs announcing 'Halk Müziği', are all over the place, but are especially thick in the sidestreets along

Istiklal Caddesi in Beyoğlu and across the water on the Asian Shore in Kadıköy. Cosy, with seating low to the ground and decorated with folk art and kilims, they exude nostalgic Anatolian homeliness. It's not unusual to see family groups out together late at night and men and women mingling more freely than is the norm for bars in Turkey.

Though it is not a loud instrument, the *bağlama* tends to be amplified all the way up to 11 so that the musicians can be heard over what more often than not will be a crowded room of singing revellers. Carrying earplugs is not as foolish as it sounds.

Beer, rakı and 'Amerikan' drinks (*cintonik*, *viski* and other spirits) are usually available alongside tea, fruit juices and soft drinks. Few Turks drink without eating, so mixed nuts and fruit are always on hand. Some bars can stretch to the odd grilled meat platter and salad, but these are not really eating places. Sharing a table is common and recommended – Turkish generosity is taken to extremes at a *bağlama* bar. There is sure to be dancing and you may well be dragged into the fray. Patrons often pass along requests written on napkins with a generous tip folded inside.

Bağlama bars are generally cheap and don't usually charge a cover, but you may want to check that, especially on weekends. Some famous players take the stage from time to time; look out for names such as **Ali Ekber Çiçek**, **Mehmet Erenler** and **Muzaffer Özdemir** posted at the

door. The only way to find out who's playing where is to take a stroll, especially along Büyükparmakkapı Sokak and neighbouring Hasnun Galip Sokak, the city's richest sources of folk music.

Jasmine Café Bar

Akarsu Sokak 10, Galatasaray, Beyoğlu (0212 252 8974). **Open** 3pm-2am daily. **No credit cards.** **Map** p308 N3.

Small, lively and popular with musicians, who hang out here to hear other musicians. The dancing has been known to spill out on to the cobblestoned street. Because the place is so tiny, reservations are recommended at weekends, especially during the winter months.

Şal

Büyükparmakkapı Sokak 18/A, off Istiklal Caddesi, Beyoğlu (0212 243 4196). **Open** 3pm-1.30am daily. **Credit** V. **Map** p309 O3.

A low-ceilinged room with bank seats around the edges and low 'coffee tables'. Feels very intimate. Musicians here often play the *zurna*, a kind of reed pipe that inspires *halays*, the Turkic form of line dancing. At such times spectating is simply not an option. The music starts early: 3pm on Fridays and Saturdays, 5pm the rest of the week.

Türkü Bar

Imam Adnan Sokak 9, off Istiklal Caddesi, Beyoğlu (0212 292 9281). **Open** 8pm-1.30pm daily. **Credit** V. **Map** p309 O2.

An attractive open-fronted establishment on one of the busiest bar streets in Beyoğlu. As at Jasmine

As soon as the dancing starts at **Şal**, remaining a mere spectator is no longer an option.

Arts & Entertainment

(*see above*), patrons have a habit of taking the dancing to the streets, forming conga lines round the potted trees and back into the bar.

Yol Café Bar

Akarsu Sokak 13/1, Galatasaray, Beyoğlu (0212 249 1465). **Open** 4pm-4am daily. **No credit cards. Map** p308 N3.
Slightly subterranean, Yol is also larger than most other *bağlama* bars, making it popular with groups. Noise levels are correspondingly greater than elsewhere and conversation is a definite non-starter. But then you don't come here to talk.

Fasıl

Defining *fasıl* is one for the musicologists. At times it sounds like Gypsy music, then again it's also quite classical, or maybe it's just folk. In truth, it's all three and then some. How about semi-classical urban folk? *Fasıl* is what Edith Piaf or Jacques Brel would have been singing if they'd been brought up in Kadıköy.

The word *fasıl* comes from Ottoman classical music and refers to a suite involving different types of vocal and instrumental works strung together on the basis of their *makam* (mode and melodic shape). Not that this has too much to do with the *fasıl* that you hear today, except for the tendency of musicians to organise their sets of tunes in a *makam*.

The standard modern *fasıl* band features any of the following instruments: *darbuka* (hourglass-shaped hand drum), violin, *ud* (fretless short-necked lute), clarinet, and *kanun* (plucked zither). The *cümbüş* (*see page 219* **Buying an instrument**), a louder, banjo-like cousin of the *ud*, sometimes makes its appearance in street bands.

Unlike folk/*bağlama*, which is bar music, *fasıl* is most commonly encountered in restaurants, particularly meyhanes, the traditional meat, meze and rakı places. The musicians tend to appear later in the evening, by which time most of the diners are already softened up by a few glasses of spirits.

The vast majority touring the restaurants are Roma, skilled in working their audience into a state of *keyif* – an ecstatic good mood. Not that anyone needs much help in losing their inhibitions; the Turks don't have any to start with. Every song is belted out by all present and tables are likely to be pushed aside to create an impromptu dance floor.

Most of the songs are standards written in the last 50 years and popularised by artists like **Zeki Müren**, **Müzeyeyen Senar** and **Münir Nurettin Selçuk**, the big names of the 1940s, '50s and '60s. Nostalgia is a big part of *fasıl*, and most meyhanes are decorated to evoke the old days of Beyoğlu, with photos and prints and

other memorabilia. Singing *fasıl* brings on the same wistful smiles and sunset glow in Turks as a quavery 'La vie en rose' does for a certain generation of Parisians.

Dining at a meyhane with *fasıl* accompaniment is an all-night affair. Most places offer fixed menus with drinks and music included, although it is customary to tip the musicians a dollar or two per person at the end of each set. Bring an appetite and try to go with a group of Turkish friends. And remember, a *fasıl* night is a participatory event.

Fasıl venues

A word of warning that applies to every venue on this list: if, for some reason, the meyhane isn't filling up, if it's a slow night with only one or two tables, the musicians may not play or the management may send them home early. This is more likely to occur early in the week and during summer.

Aynalı Meyhane

Tramvay Caddesi 104, Kuruçeşme (0212 265 9600). **Open** 8pm-1.30am Mon-Sat; closed Sun. **No credit cards.**
Near Ortaköy on a strip of the shoreline better known for its upmarket nightclubs. The clientele here tend to be a little more moneyed than their

Kallavi 20 – atmospheric. *See p217.*

Hava Nagila again

It's a quintessential Istanbul experience, dining alfresco in a narrow lane crammed with tables, fending off wandering vendors of tat, trying to catch the eye of a harassed waiter to point out that of the eight dishes of meze that have arrived you ordered only two. All of this to the backdrop of three sets of wandering musicians, all simultaneously within earshot.

Almost every one of the tightly packed scrum of restaurants has a house band hopping from table to table. The quality of the musicians varies, but who cares? They aren't there to impress with their virtuosity; they're there to provide the music for what is essentially

Turkish karaoke. Diners name the songs, the musicians oblige and everybody gets their spot. Out of tune, off key, it doesn't matter. The only real bum notes come when the musicians hit a table of foreigners. Confronted by non-Turkishness, nine times out of ten the performers smile broadly then launch into a fevered rendition of 'Hava Nagila'. It's what they think you want. If that doesn't elicit any response, the fallback is 'Kalinka'. Then 'Hava Nagila' again. Until you pay them to go away. To spare yourself, utter the magic words, '*Oyun havası,*' Turkish music. And may you never be Hava Nagila'd again.

downtown counterparts, but no less boisterous. In fact, the Aynalı can get positively raucous. Name musicians and singers have been known to step up and join the house band. *See also p131.*

Bekriya

1. Caddesi 90 Kat: 2, Arnavutköy (0212 257 0469). **Open** 7.30pm-1am Mon-Sat; closed Sun. **No credit cards**.
The music at this small meyhane in an old house beside the Bosphorus is usually provided by a lone *ud* player, who goes from table to table. It's all very low-key, but there's a nice buzz about the place. Flavour is enhanced by photographs, costumes and various other memorabilia from the owner's family collection.

Despina

Açıkyol Sokak 9, Kurtuluş (0212 232 6720). **Open** noon-midnight daily. **Credit** V.
Tucked away in the far from glamorous district of Kurtuluş, an area once home to a sizeable Greek community, Despina looks far from promising. Its fluorescent lights and plastic flowers are a long way from the nostalgia-inducing meyhanes of Beyoğlu. But some fine musicians frequent the place, drawing an appreciative and demonstrative audience, who submit requests for their favourite *oyun havaları* (dance songs). On the right night this can be the most fun spot in town.

Galata Restaurant

Orhan Apaydın Sokak 11-13, Tünel, Beyoğlu (0212 293 1139). **Open** 7.30pm-midnight Mon-Sat; closed Sun. **Credit** MC, V. **Map** p308 M4.
A meyhane popular with celebrating groups with a stage for the musicians, although unfortunately not every table has a clear view. *See also p131.*

Kallavi 20

Kallavi Sokak 20, off Istiklal Caddesi, Beyoğlu (0212 251 1010). **Open** 7pm-2am Mon-Sat; closed Sun. **No credit cards. Map** p308 M3.
A classic little meyhane with decent food and on most weekend nights a rousing atmosphere, expertly conducted by the resident trio or quartet of Roma musicians. It's not unknown for clientele to abandon food and tables and hit the streets to dance. Recommended. *See also p131.*

Süheyla

Kalyoncu Kulluk Caddesi 45, off Balık Pazarı, Beyoğlu (0212 251 8347). **Open** *Summer* 6pm-2am daily. *Winter* 6pm-2am Mon-Sat; closed Sun. **No credit cards. Map** p308 N3.
This is another prime *fasıl* venue, buried among the dozens of restaurants in the Nevizade Sokak area. It has two good-sized rooms and better than average musicians. On the minus side, it's become a little pricey in recent years; expect to pay upwards of $40 per head for the set menu, and for some reason you can't charge the set menu to your credit card. Gets packed at weekends, when reservations are recommended.

Turkish Classical

Real Turkish Classical music is not something that most casual visitors to Istanbul will get to hear. That's because relatively little of it is publicly performed nowadays. In the new Turkish republic of the 1920s, Ottoman classical music was considered elitist and backward and the state tried to bury it. In the last 20 years or so there has been a slow revival and now musicians such as **Göksel Baktagir** and **Ihsan Özgen**

Arts & Entertainment

are attempting to reinvigorate the genre by wedding Ottoman traditions to contemporary Western instrumentation. Still, many musicians find their efforts are better appreciated outside Turkey, where the public has not been numbed by decades of bland renditions by massive state choruses and the uninspired output of duty-bound radio performers. A pity, because the Ottomans managed to produce a high art form that rivals the classical traditions of India, Iran, the Arab world and the West.

Although definitely not easy listening, Turkish Classical (also known as Ottoman, Osmanlı or Court-Enderun music), is based on the principle of *makam*. Like the Indian *raga* system, the *makam* system is modal, whereas Western music is based on chord changes. Turkish Classical is subtle, the rhythms are gentle, sometimes quite slow, although towards the end of a programme you'll often hear lively numbers. The melodic lines are long and highly ornamented and singers must have great range and control. Traditional instruments employed are the *kanun*, *ud*, *tambur* (long-necked lute), *ney* (reed flute), and *kemençe*. For percussion there are various frame drums, such as the *daire* and *bendir*, and the *kudüm* (small kettle drums). Many ensembles include violins, too.

Istanbul-based **Bezmara** is the one ensemble that has tried to revive and play some of the older forms of the instruments. Other ensembles and performers of note include **Lalezar** and **Necdet Yaşar**.

Turkish Classical venues

This introspective and subtle art form is done no justice at all in Istanbul today. No single venue devotes itself exclusively to performances of Turkish Classical, though it does feature in the programmes of the **International Istanbul Music Festival** (*see page 180*) and in a specialist Akbank-sponsored event held each May.

For detailed information it's a good idea to swing by the venues listed below and pick up a programme.

Akbank Music Festival

Tophane-i Amire, Tophane. Information Aksanat Cultural Centre, Istiklal Caddesi 16, Beyoğlu (0212 270 0044/www.akbank.com.tr/sanat). **Dates** end of May.
Themes of this event vary, but it often explores the various musical legacies of the Ottoman period. The venue is an old cannon foundry in Tophane.

Atatürk Cultural Centre

Atatürk Kültür Merkezi/AKM
Taksim Square (0212 251 5600/251 1023). **Open** 10am-6pm daily. **No credit cards. Map** p307 P2.

This hall on Taksim Square is the most likely place in which to find Turkish Classical music. The Türk Müziği chorus performs here most Sundays from autumn through until late spring in the lower auditorium. These concerts tend to be surprisingly well attended.

Cemal Reşit Rey Concert Hall

Cemal Reşit Rey Konser Salonu
Darülbedai Caddesi 1, Harbiye (0212 248 5392/240 5012). **Open** 10am-7pm daily. **Credit** MC, V.
Hosts occasional Turkish Classical events.

Tarık Zafer Tunaya Salonu

*Tarık Zafer Tunaya Kültür Merkezi
Şahkulu Bostanı Sokak. 8, Tünel, Beyoğlu (0212 293 1270/293 1271/227 3390).* **Open** 9am-6pm daily. **No credit cards. Map** p308 M4.
A former wedding parlour, now cultural centre, this municipality-run venue host various music performances, often including Turkish Classical.

Sufi music

To a casual listener the music of the Muslim mystical Sufi sects and Turkish Classical sound very much alike. They do have much in common, being part of the same musical continuum. Many Turkish Classical composers, such as **Dede Efendi**, wrote both sacred and secular. Like Classical, *tasavvuf müziği* (Sufi music) is based on the *makam* system, and the two genres share similar instrumentation. The major differences lie in forms and rhythms and in the arrangement of instrumentation. Sufi music accords greater prominence to the *ney* flute and percussion – including frame drums of various types and the *kudüm* kettle drums – creating hypnotic, mind-numbing beats.

Sufis are one of a number of dervish sects that use music, dance and *zikr* (a form of rhythmic breathing) as a way of establishing an ecstatic connection with God. It's a practice frowned upon by orthodox Islam, which considers music at prayer improper and a distraction from pure thoughts.

It's something of an irony, then, that until recently, the form of Turkish music best known abroad was Sufi music, specifically, the music of the Mevlevi order, the 'Whirling Dervishes'. Sadly, as with Turkish Classical, Sufi music has suffered from the vicissitudes of Turkey's 20th-century political history. During the turbulent early years of the republic, *tekkes*, the places of Sufi worship, were outlawed. The influence of the Dervish leaders was seen as a threat by Turkey's struggling young leaders, and Sufiism was driven underground. Over time the laws relaxed and a few *tekkes* re-emerged. Best known is the Galata Mevlevihanesi in Tünel, which is sanitised as a Museum for Classical Literature

Buying an instrument

Whether you are a serious musician or an idle strummer looking for an interesting sound, Istanbul's music stores are a world musician's dream. Dozens of exotic strings, flutes, and strange fiddles hang from ceilings, and drums line the walls. For somebody with a recently acquired taste for Turkish music, taking home an instrument can lead to a deeper involvement with the culture – or at least a nice wall ornament.

The *bağlama*, or *saz*, is a reasonable choice. Deceptively easy for a novice guitarist, you can get a beginner's one (with bargaining) for $100 or less. Buy a book in English (such as *Bağlama Method* by Temel Karahasan), learn how to tune it and buy a selection of picks and a couple of extra sets of strings. A soft case should be included in your purchase. Avoid the really cheap ones – good only for wall ornaments. *Uds*, the fretless Middle Eastern lutes, are an excellent buy at around $100 and up, and Turkish ones are known for their bright sound and volume. Be sure to acquire a hard-shell case for stringed instruments.

The *cümbüş* was born a century ago when Abidin Cümbüş, music-lover and owner of the gigantic Cümbüş Aluminium salad bowl factory, decided to slap a fretless *ud* neck on a salad bowl and cover it with a banjo head. *Voila!* A loud and extremely adaptable instrument that aurally captures the spirit of Turkish modernification. They come in a number of sizes (*ud*, *bağlama*, mandolin, *tambur*) and are cheap (around $70 with case if you get it at the Cümbüş Store, Atatürk Bulvarı, as stamped on the metal of the banjo rim) and indestructible. Necks come in a variety of amusing Formica colours as well.

Small instruments may be easier to stick in your luggage: a Black Sea *kemençe* – whose music appeals to the more frenetic celtic fringe – can be had for under $50. The reed *shawm zurna* is both quite loud and

cheap – excellent for sadistic sax players who hate their neighbours. Make sure you have at least two extra reeds in good working order and protect them.

Drummers probably have it the easiest. The *darbuka* comes in a number of sizes – heavy is generally considered better. Frame drums, such as the *bendir* and *daire*, are fun and also not expensive; some are tuneable. Drums can be as little as $15 and go right on up.

The best instrument stores are found in Beyoğlu near the Tünel station along Istiklal Caddesi and Galip Dede Caddesi. Numerous lower priced wholesale dealers are found north of the Aksaray Viaduct in the Unkpanı district along Atatürk Bulvarı.

(Divan Edebiyat Müzesi), thus relegating Sufiism to the status of a colourful historical oddity, with monthly performances solely for the pleasure of tourists. When the real thing can be found, it is not always accessible to the outsider. One such place is in Fatih, where the Cerrahi brotherhood operates the Museum for the Study and Preservation of Tasavvuf Music, actually a fully functional mosque. Visitors are not necessarily welcome, as the place is obliged to keep a low profile. Apart from attending a staged

performance at the Galata Mevlevihanesi, the only other opportunity to hear Sufi music in Istanbul comes during the mystic music festival.

International Festival of Mystic Music

Uluslararası Mistik Müzik Festivali
Cemal Reşit Rey Concert Hall, Darülbedai Caddesi 1, Harbiye (information 0212 231 5497/0212 232 9830/www.ibb.gov.tr). **Date** Nov.
Always features at least one Turkish performance on the programme.

Nightlife

Just like its denizens, Istanbul's clubbing scene is young, vibrant and not yet ready to settle down.

Istanbul's club scene is not what you'd call venerable. It kicked off in 1994 when **Club 20** decided to stop playing top 40 hits and start doing something more interesting. It's been a slow build since, but the number of clubs is steadily growing, with one-offs and open-air parties adding welcome diversity to the scene. People tend to move around the clubbing circuit and dancefloor as individuals rather than in a clique. The positive side of this is that clubbers, and Turkish people in general, are open to meeting new faces.

To the outsider, the clubber crowd in Istanbul may appear somewhat 'cool'. Don't expect people to go wild on the dancefloor – mass passion is reserved for the city's football stadiums. For this reason, whistles are considered in bad taste and not appreciated.

House and techno predominate, and there's some trance. Hip hop and drum 'n' bass don't have much of a following; about the only place they feature – and then only on a very occasional basis – is at **Babylon**. Local DJs are regularly supplemented by top names from clubs abroad; Derrick May, Kenny Larkin, Mr C, Darren Emerson, MJ Cole, Dmitri, Paul Oakenfold, Talvin Singh and Roni Size have all recently guested in Istanbul.

Most clubs live short lives, as clubbers ruthlessly abandon them for the next new thing. Clubs open up, run for about a year, and disappear without trace. Ministry, Millennium, Airport, Taxim Night Park, High End and the legendary Hangar 2019 – all briefly seen then gone, gone, gone.

Istanbul clubbing flourishes from October to May, as most serious party-goers migrate south in summer to party in hot spots like Kemer, Bodrum, Antalya and Alanya. Should you find yourself in need of a summer techno injection, your best bet is to try **Switch**, **Scene** or **Club 20**, where the air-conditioning systems are fully functional. If money is no object, you can always join the jet-set in the summer clubs along the Bosphorus (*see page 222* **Baywatch on the Bosphorus**).

Before summer 1999, there were no restrictions on club closing hours, so it was possible to party through to breakfast time. However, in August of that year a new law was passed requiring all entertainment venues, including cafés and bars,

to close by 4am. Since then, after-hours events and parties just don't happen. Even so, Istanbul's clubs don't get full before 1am. Prior to hitting the dancefloor, people usually go to bars or so-called 'pre-clubs' like **Godet**, **Cantina** and **Dulcinea**. On a typical night, Istanbul clubbers take in two or more venues.

Bargaining may be accepted in the Grand Bazaar, but it won't endear you to the average doorman, who has limited patience when dealing with difficult customers. However, a telephone call made in advance may secure you a group reduction at the manager's discretion. As long as you are reasonably clean and presentable and smile sweetly, your chances of entering the bastions of electronica are pretty good. Keep your passport handy, as ID is routinely checked at the door. Only at the most exclusive clubs, such as **Scene**, **Laila** and **Havana**, is a tip expected to ensure smooth access.

Getting around Istanbul late at night is no problem. Taxis are plentiful, and around 2am there's more of them on the streets than there are people. Usually clubs have a string of them waiting outside at the kerb. Rates go up 50 per cent after midnight, but, as all clubs with the exception of **Cubuklu Hayal** are close to the city centre, you won't break the bank getting home to bed.

To keep up with what's happening, pick up a free copy of *Zip Istanbul* or *ISTANbull... Magazine* (*see page 278*) from bookshops and cafés around Beyoğlu, the district with the highest concentration of worthwhile clubs. These places also carry flyers and posters advertising upcoming events. Another option is simply to call the clubs for details – there will usually be someone who speaks English at the other end of the phone. Or try the club websites listed below.

Festivals & events

One-off parties and festivals are organised between April and November. They are widely publicised in all media, including the Internet. Useful sites to check out are:
www.hippro.com,
www.orientation.com,
www.pozitif-ist.com and
www.mydonose.com.tr.

Be seen at **Scene**. *See p224.*

The biggest dance event in the Istanbul calendar is September's J&B **Dance & Techno Festival**. Around 20,000 people attend this open-air 24-hour event. *See page 181*.

See page 181.

Venues

Babylon

Şehbender Sokak 3, Asmalımescit, Tünel (0212 292 7368/www.babylon-ist.com). **Open** 9.30pm-2am Wed, Thur; 10.30pm-3am Fri, Sat; closed Mon, Tue, Sun. **Admission** $10-15. **Credit** MC, V. **Map** p308 M4. Better known as a music venue *(see p207)*, Babylon also hosts club nights with hip hop, drum 'n' bass and house on the menu.

Cantina

Zambak Sokak 19, off Istiklal Caddesi, Beyoğlu (0212 252 4804). **Open** noon-2am Mon-Thur, Sun; noon-4am Fri, Sat. **Admission** free. **Credit** MC, V. **Map** p309 O2.

Cantina is a small pre-club with a long bar and a drop-level dancefloor that holds about 30 people. It is therefore a good choice for anyone prone to claustrophobia in more frantic, packed venues. Cantina's decor is icy-minimalist, but it's thawed by mild house during the week and hard house at the weekends.

Club 20

Belediye Dükkanlari 75, off Abdülhak Hamit Caddesi, Taksim (0212 235 6197). **Open** *Mid May-mid Sept* 11pm-4am Fri, Sat; closed Mon-Thur, Sun. *Mid Sept-mid May* 11pm-4am Wed, Fri, Sat; closed Mon, Tue, Thur, Sun. **Admission** $15. **Credit** AmEx, MC, V. **Map** p307 O1.

The oldest club in Istanbul maintains its reputation with a contingent of respected DJs – MET, Macit and Murat – who create an upward ambience with a mix of house and techno sounds. Club 20 is located in a converted warehouse where

Baywatch on the Bosphorus

Summer is dead season for Istanbul's clubs. Unless, that is, you have cash to spare and a desire to flaunt it at one of the exclusive summer clubs on the Bosphorus. Don't expect club music. Don't expect a club crowd. Don't even expect to get in.

Still, for a certain kind of person, **Laila** and **Havana** offered the biggest nights out in the summer of 2000. What makes people fork over $100 a head at restaurants where the thumping music renders conversation impossible, push through crowds of Armani and DKNY for a $6 beer or pay $30 admission to groove to uptempo flamenco? Perhaps the inflated prices themselves create an impression of elitism, the massive walls and massed security a feeling of privilege. It probably also has something to do with spectacular Bosphorus views, moonlight on the water, and refreshing offshore breezes.

The popularity of these venues certainly says something about aspirants to *sosyete*: fiercely upwardly mobile, keen to consume as conspicuously as possible and firm believers in fame by association. Where else can you toy with your sushi in front of an 'exclusive' audience of 5,000, glide directly off a boat and on to the dancefloor, or be elbowed aside by a television star desperate for a drink?

Above all else, it is undoubtedly the shrewd packaging and promotion that packs them in. Summer venues stage spectacular spring openings, invariably boasting a fresh *konsept*, an almost entirely new roster of watering holes

and eateries and photo opportunities for this year's crop of celebrities. Never mind that the venues are merely last year's hot spots under different names; last year's Pasha is this year's Laila, Havana's Café de Paris becomes Le Select, and people sip 'Votka Melon' instead of last season's 'Sex on the Beach'. Baywatch by the Bosphorus is a series set to run and run.

Cubuklu Hayal Kahvesi

Ağaçlik Mesire Yeri, A+B, Çubuklu, Asian Shore (0216 413 6880/www.hayal.kahvesi.com.tr). **Open** *Mid May-Sept* Club 11am-4am daily; bar 5pm-4am daily. *Oct-mid May* closed. **Admission** $20. **Credit** MC, V.

One of Istanbul's most pleasant locations, right on the waterfront in a leafy Asian suburb. Free service boats whisk you across the Bosphorus to the club's own jetty. (Boats bound for Hayal Kahvesi leave from the Istinye Motor Iskelesi every 30 minutes, from 5pm until closing time.) Once you get there, a varied programme of live music and DJs is on offer in the honey-coloured stone building. Such beauty does not come cheap, and the venue is popular with the smart young things of the city.

Havana

Muallim Naci Caddesi 120, Kuruçeşme (0212 259 5919). **Open** *Mid May-mid Sept* 6pm-4am daily. *Mid Sept-mid May* closed. **Admission** free Mon-Thur, Sun; $23 Fri, Sat. **Credit** AmEx, MC, V. A select nightclub on the waterfront with dancefloor arranged around a central swimming pool and with an upper gallery of restaurants.

Arts & Entertainment

five-star hotel land meets the underworld beyond. Alongside the new generation of clubbers are the veteran party-goers who have hired a babysitter for the night.

DIP

Nispetiye Caddesi 32, Etiler (0212 287 5785). **Open** *Sept-June* 11pm-4am Fri, Sat, sometimes Wed; closed Mon, Tue, Thur, Sun. *July-Aug* closed. **Admission** $10. **No credit cards.**

DIP's ultra-glossy black-mirrored interior for its ultra-posh clientele is located in one of the city's most exclusive neighbourhoods. Just ride the lift downwards for exceptionally good house and techno or occasional trance nights. Contrary to expectations generated by the surroundings, the drinks here are in fact reasonably priced. The club's reputation was dented by a mafia shoot-out in 1999, so there tends to be a little more space on the dancefloor these days.

Dulcinea

Meşelik Sokak 20, off Istiklal Caddesi, Beyoğlu (0212 245 1071/café@dulcinea.org). **Open** 10.30am-2am daily. **Admission** free. **Credit** MC, V. Map p309 O2.

The spacious interior at Dulcinea, fitted out with blonde Welsh-dresser style cladding, functions as a bar, café, restaurant and art gallery throughout the week. On Friday and Saturday club nights, however, the turntables are handed over to an amateur DJ group, deep eXperience, who spin uplifting trance and funky techno for the skint clubbers who come here.

Godet

Zambak Sokak 15, off Istiklal Caddesi, Beyoğlu (0212 244 3897/www.soapsystem.com). **Open** *Sept-June* 10.30pm-4am Mon-Sat; closed Sun. *July-Aug* closed. **Admission** free Mon-Thur, $20 Fri-Sat. **Credit** MC, V. Map p309 O2.

Music is top 40 with some of the big names in Turkish pop taking the microphone in the restaurants. A regular jet set haunt – the perfect place to be seen but not heard.

Laila

Muallim Naci Caddesi 141-142, Kuruçeşme (0212 227 1711). **Open** *June-Sept* 6.30pm-3am daily. *Oct-May* closed. **Admission** free Mon-Thur, Sun; $27 Fri, Sat. **Credit cards** AmEx, DC, MC, V.

An outdoor waterfront complex of bars and restaurants, although you may need to consider taking out a second mortgage to sample them. This club is the number one choice of the paparazzi. The music is strictly pop, Turkish and international, with occasional live performances by one-hit-wonders.

The heaving dancefloor at **Babylon**, live music venue with hip hop and house nights. *See p222.*

By day the club functions as a café and, more unusually, as a store for clubwear including T-shirts, strides and accessories. By night it serves as a pre-club, mainly for **Magma**-ites, with blaring techno beats and inflated prices that may deter all but the clubber with more money than taste. There seems to be enough of those, though, as Godet is always so packed it's hard to move around, let alone dance.

The Lab

1st floor, Cumhuriyet Caddesi 349, Harbiye (no phone). **Open** *Oct-June* 10pm-4am Wed-Sat; closed Mon, Tue, Sun. *July-Sept* closed. **Admission** $10. **No credit cards. Map** p307 P1.

A melting pot for promising new DJs during the week, featuring pink triangle night on Thursdays for enterprising lesbian DJs. Top Turkish DJs playing techno and house are hosted at the weekend. It's not really the ideal venue for drum 'n' bass, as the bass has to be turned down to pacify the grumpy retired general upstairs. Helpful chemical brothers abound to cater for the needs of the ecstatic crowd.

Magma

Akarsu Sokak 5, off Istiklal Caddesi, Beyoğlu (0212 292 1119). **Open** *Sept-June* 10pm-4am Fri, Sat; closed Mon-Thur, Sun. *July-Aug* closed. **Admission** $15. **No credit cards. Map** p308 N3.

Magma is located behind reinforced steel doors in one of the oldest buildings of the district in a side-street lined with lurid nightclubs. Resident DJ Baris Bergiten attracts a regular core of clubbers with his deep techno and trance sounds. DJ Emre spins hard house/hard techno once a month. Occasional guest nights with DJs from Germany and Switzerland are also featured. No attitude at the door please, as the doormen are famous for their own.

Roxy

Arslan Yatağı Sokak 3, off Sıraselviler Caddesi, Taksim (0212 245 6539/www.roxy.com.tr). **Open** *Oct-mid July* 10pm-4am Tue-Sat; closed Mon, Sun. *Mid July-Sept* closed. **Admission** $10 Tue-Thur, $25 Fri, Sat. **Credit** MC, V. **Map** p309 O3.

Roxy is an established club featuring sets by live commercial rock and pop bands. (For details of live performances, *see p208*). The highlight of the week is undoubtedly Wednesday night, when DJ Fuchs shakes the house.

Scene

Muallim Naci Caddesi 109, Ortaköy (0212 261 1988). **Open** midnight-5am Wed, Fri, Sat; closed Mon, Tue, Thur, Sun. **Admission** free Wed, $23 Fri, Sat. **Credit** MC, V.

Scene boasts a romantic location on the shore of the Bosphorus, directly beneath the thundering traffic of the suspension bridge. This is one of Istanbul's largest underground clubs, with a glowing Saharan sunset interior, pyramid-lined ceiling and chill-out garden with bar. The sounds are excellent: house/techno on Friday, trance on Saturday and garage/jazzy house on Wednesday. Posh clientele with prices to match. Arrive in Porsche and Prada jeans.

Spica

Duvardibi Sokak 4/6, off Yedi Kuyular Caddesi, Elmadağ (0212 231 1116). **Open** *Mid Sept-mid June* 9pm-4am Wed-Sat; closed Mon, Tue, Sun. *Mid June-mid Sept* closed. **Admission** $23. **Credit** MC, V.

Spica is a transitional club whose young clientele can indulge their taste for mainstream Turkish pop on the upper floor, then venture boldly to the futuristic lower floor, where lightweight underground sounds barely penetrate the cortex. Domestic beer, wine, and some basic food are included in the admission price. Thursdays are movie nights.

Switch

Muammer Karaca Çıkmazı 3, off Istiklal Caddesi, Beyoğlu (0212 292 7458/www.hippro.com). **Open** *Mid Oct-mid Aug* 11pm-4am daily. *Mid Aug-mid Oct* closed. **Admission** $15; before midnight $12. **Credit** AmEx, MC, V. **Map** p308 N4.

Owned by the alternative music promoter Hip Productions, Switch caters to just about every breed of electronica enthusiast. DJ Murat Uncuoğlu (deep trance) and DJ Turgay (uplifting trance) hypnotise the Friday night regulars, while on Saturday nights DJ UFUK subjects the building's ancient vaults to garage, house and techno. DJs from the Netherlands, UK, France and Israel are hosted every three weeks, and there are live electronic bands on Wednesdays.

Performing Arts

Western theatre and classical music remain alien art forms in Istanbul.

Despite the best efforts of the reformist Turkish state in the early years of the republic, Western performing arts have always failed to find large audiences. Theatre aside, they are still largely seen as alien impositions competing poorly with a rich heritage of indigenous art forms.

Classical Music, Opera & Ballet

European-style classical music is usually associated with a few overplayed selections such as Vivaldi's *Four Seasons*, which tend to be blasted out through speakers in the gardens of imperial Ottoman palaces like Beylerbeyi to lend 'ambience'. Opera and ballet remain the preserve of the upper classes or educated elite. Ordinary Istanbulites would rather listen to traditional folk music (*see page 231*) or *fasıl* (*see page 216*). And why not?

Turkey has no long tradition of Western performing arts. Rather it had its own imperial court music (*see page 217*) which, until it was actively supressed under the new republic, had been inspiring big-gun European composers, most notably Mozart. Traffic went both ways and Italian composer Gaetano Donizetti introduced opera to Turkey in the early 19th century when he was invited to the imperial court as General Instructor of the Ottoman State Bands.

Sidelining its imperial heritage, republican Turkey instead emphasised nationalism based on a Western model. The first Turkish operas were written by composers such as Cemal Reşit Rey and Adnan Saygun, both members of 'The Five', the first generation of Turkish opera composers. Hungarian composer Béla Bartók was brought in to advise on a new state conservatory founded in Ankara in 1936. Dame Ninette de Valois, founder of Britain's Royal Ballet, chaired its ballet department.

Despite the solid foundations, a lack of popular support and funding means that performance standards for classical music, opera and ballet are typically less than overwhelming. Turkey does produce some high-calibre performing artists, such as conductors **Gürer Aykal** and **Cem Mansur**, soprano **Leyla Gencer**, violinist **Suna Kan**, pianist **İdil Biret**, the **Pekinel**

Atatürk Cultural Centre. *See p226.*

sisters and, more recently, the young pianist **Fazıl Say**, but without exception they are forced to ply their trade abroad.

For anyone looking to attend classical concerts in Istanbul, the fare is limited. In the absence of any real public funding most orchestras are sponsored by private banks. Opera and ballet are represented solely by the Istanbul State Opera and Ballet company. The rare sparkle on the scene is supplied by the **International Istanbul Music Festival** and the **International Bosphorus Festival** (*for both, see page 180*), both of which feature performances by local orchestras supplemented by foreign guests.

Arts & Entertainment

Concert halls

Atatürk Cultural Centre

Atatürk Kültür Merkezi
Taksim Square (box office 0212 251 1023/251 5600/classical music enquiries 243 1068/opera & ballet enquiries 243 2011). **Box office** 10am-6pm daily. **Performances** *Classical music* 7pm Fri; 11am Sat. *Opera and ballet* 7pm Fri; 8pm Tue, Thur. **Tickets** $4-$10. **No credit cards. Map** 307 P2.
Istanbul's premier performing arts venue. Despite the brutalist 1960s design, the AKM is surprisingly vibrant inside. It has five halls, plus art gallery and movie theatre. The Grand Hall and Concert Hall are mainly for concerts, opera and ballet. The smaller Chamber Hall, Aziz Nesin Stage and Taksim Stage are mostly used for theatre. Ticket prices are kept low through heavy state subsidies; sales begin one month before performances but seats can usually be secured right up until the last minute.

Cemal Reşit Rey Concert Hall

Cemal Reşit Rey Konser Salonu
Darülbedai Caddesi 1, Harbiye (0212 232 9830/ www.ibb.gov.tr). **Performances** *Oct-May* 8pm daily. *June-Sept* closed. **Tickets** $5-$10. **No credit cards.**
Built in 1989 and run by the city, the 860-seater CRR provides a diverse programme, including concerts of Turkish religious and traditional music. This is also the home of the CRR Symphony Orchestra. Tickets can be purchased at the CRR Concert Hall and AKM (*see above*) box offices. The hall is a main venue for the International Bosphorus Festival

each June (*see p180*), as well as for December's International CRR Piano Festival and the International Youth Festival in May. It also hosts other cultural activities, particularly exhibitions, meetings and conferences.

Hacı Ömer Hall

Hacı Ömer Salonu
Sabancı Centre, 4th Levent (0212 264 2045/ www.akbank.com.tr/sanat). **Performances** *Nov-May* 8pm one Thur per month. *June-Oct* closed. **Tickets** $3-$9. **No credit cards.**
The Hacı Ömer Hall is the preserve of the Akbank Chamber Orchestra (*see below*). Concerts here are not exactly an entirely conventional experience: the Sabancı Centre is an impressive twin-tower skyscraper in 4th Levent, modern Istanbul's answer to Manhattan. A Taksim-Sarıyer minibus (which departs from behind the Atatürk Cultural Centre; *see above*) or taxi will get you here. Tickets can be purchased at Akbank offices in Nişantaşı, Beşiktaş and Bahariye, as well as at the Aksanat Arts Centre in Beyoğlu (*see p194*) and at various branches of Vakkorama (*see p179*).

Ensembles

Akbank Chamber Orchestra

Akbank Oda Orkestrası
Sponsored by a private bank and active since 1992, this orchestra offers a broad selection of classical music from baroque to contemporary and sometimes performs with top soloists such as pianist Idil

Arts & Entertainment

Mozart at the Topkapı Palace during the **International Istanbul Music Festival**. *See p225.*

Shadow play

In Karagöz, Turkish shadow theatre, audiences watch and hear characters represented by shadows on a two-dimensional screen. The name comes from the main character, 'Black Eye', who is usually accompanied by his foil, Hacivat. There's no real plot, just a succession of short scenes comprising jokes, dances and comic impersonations during which, most of time, Karagöz and Hacivat fight with each other or meet (and fight) with other characters. These are drawn from a wide array of stock types representing various peoples of the Ottoman empire, all depicted as caricatures.

Karagöz shows were traditionally characterised by obscenity and extreme licentiousness, sometimes showing Karagöz rigged with a huge phallus, even if the audience – as it is nowadays – was mainly made up of children. Political and social satire was its basis until the late 19th century. In the face of rigid censorship, Karagöz was a political weapon – no one was spared its sarcasm, except perhaps the sultan – and used as agitprop by subject peoples of the Ottoman empire. Many Karagöz shows were banned by the authorities.

The introduction of Western culture and European drama in the 19th century destroyed both traditional folk and popular art, including Karagöz. Nowadays, only a few puppetmasters are still active in Istanbul and performances are rare. During Ramazan, Karagöz shows can be seen on TV and at the 'Ramazan Nights', a series of cultural events on Sultanahmet Square. Karagöz also features at the **International Istanbul Puppet Festival** (see page 179), organised every year by Cengiz Özek of the Kenter Theatre (see page 228).

Biret. Conductor Cem Mansur is a former conductor of the Istanbul State Opera. The Akbank gives regular Thursday evening performances at the Hacı Ömer Hall (*see p226*). It's also worth checking the programmes of such events as the International Istanbul Music Festival (*see p180*) or December's International Cemal Reşit Rey Piano Festival at the Cemal Reşit Rey Concert Hall (*see p226*).

Borusan Istanbul Philharmonic Orchestra

Borusan Istanbul Filarmoni Orkestrası
Information: Borusan Cultural and Art Centre 421 Istiklal Caddesi, Tünel (212 292 0655/ www.borusansanat.com). Map p308 M4.
Founded in 1993 as a chamber orchestra, the Borusan became Turkey's largest private orchestra after evolving into a philharmonic in 1999. Under Gürer Aykal, one of Turkey's leading conductors, it performs two concerts every month, on a Tuesday and Wednesday of the same week at 7.30pm. Venues are on both the European and Asian sides and the season lasts from September to June. Tickets and programme information are available from the Borusan Cultural and Arts Centre, which also houses a library boasting the richest music and CD archive in Turkey.

Istanbul Metropolitan Municipality Cemal Reşit Rey Symphony Orchestra

Istanbul Büyükşehir Belediyesi Cemal Reşit Rey Senfoni Orkestrası
Active since 1995, this is Turkey's only municipally funded orchestra and performs a mixed repertoire that includes works by Turkish composers in almost every concert. The 90 musicians are also sometimes joined by national and international conductors and artists such as José Carreras or celebrated Turkish pianists Idil Biret and Fazıl Say. It generally performs once or twice a month at the Cemal Reşit Rey Concert Hall (*see p226*).

Istanbul State Opera & Ballet

Istanbul Devlet Opera ve Balesi
Founded in 1960, the Istanbul State Opera and Ballet is still the only company to provide a regular and varied programme. With an impressive 25 performances a month from October to May, the state company performs a broad repertoire of works (baroque, classical, modern) to world standards. European classics from the likes of Mozart, Bizet, Offenbach and Orff combine with Turkish works. All performances are given at the Atatürk Cultural Centre (*see p226*).

Istanbul State Symphony Orchestra

Istanbul Devlet Senfoni Orkestrası
Founded in 1945 by Turkish composer, pianist and conductor Cemal Reşit Rey as the Municipality Symphony Orchestra, this institution has always played an important role in the musical life of Istanbul. In 1972, the orchestra was taken over by the Ministry of Cultural Affairs and given its current name. Today, it offers an extensive programme and its 105 musicians have occasionally been supplemented by renowned soloists such as Yehudi Menuhin, Luciano Pavarotti and Jean-Pierre Rampal. The orchestra has premiered many works by Turkish composers and has also toured overseas on several occasions. It performs twice a week at the Atatürk Cultural Centre (*see p226*).

Arts & Entertainment

Theatre

Theatre in Istanbul is far more vital and varied than the classical music, opera or ballet scenes. More than 30 stages are scattered across the city, even in the most remote districts.

Istanbul's theatres are grouped into three main categories: Istanbul Devlet Tiyatroları (state theatres), Istanbul Büyükşehir Belediyesi Tiyatroları (metropolitan municipality theatres) and Özel Tiyatrolar (private theatres).

The Istanbul State Theatre company offers a broad programme of classic and contemporary productions, including Turkish works, which are performed regularly in five theatres. About 15-20 different plays are staged every month, including plays for children and musicals, at the **Atatürk Cultural Centre** (*see page 226*).

The city also owns six theatres in Harbiye, Fatih, Gaziosmanpaşa and the Asian districts of Üsküdar and Kadıköy. Plays are often penned by Turkish writers and they're performed by the municipality theatre company. The same plays rotate through different theatres, so even if you miss a performance at one, the chances are you can catch it at another.

A more eclectic programme is on offer from various private or independent companies. For a different taste of classic and contemporary productions, take in the **Kent Oyuncuları** (City Players) starring Yıldız Kenter at the Kenter Theatre (*see below*); the **Tiyatro Stüdyosu** (Theatre Studio) directed by Ahmet Levendoğlu; or the **Aksanat Production Theatre** (Aksanat Prodüksiyon Tiyatrosu), which is run in collaboration with director Işıl Kasapoğlu. All three companies stage productions of contemporary theatre, most of them premiering in Turkey.

During summer, from June to October, most theatres close. All performances are in Turkish. Foreign theatre tours to Istanbul are virtually unknown. May's **International Istanbul Theatre Festival** is the principal cultural event of the season. *See page 179.*

Venues

Aksanat Production Theatre

Aksanat Prodüksiyon Tiyatrosu
Aksanat Arts Centre, Istiklal Caddesi 16-18, Beyoğlu (0212 252 3500/www.akbank.com.tr/sanat).
Box office 9.30am-7.30pm Tue-Sat; closed Mon, Sun. **Performances** 7pm Fri, Sat. **Tickets** $2.50-$5. **No credit cards. Map** p309 O2.
The Aksanat Production Theatre in the Aksanat Arts Centre annually stages a new production by Işıl Kasapoğlu, a leading name in Turkish theatre. The repertoire consists of classical plays, including

both foreign and Turkish. The performances may seem like low-budget productions, with only a handful of actors, minimalist decor and lighting, but director and performers utilise the facilities masterfully and the hall with its narrow stage creates an intimate atmosphere.

Bilsak Theatre Workshop

Bilsak Tiyatro Atölyesi
7 Soğancı Sokak, off Sıraselviler Caddesi, Cihangir (0212 243 2879). **Box office** 9am-5pm Mon-Sat; closed Sun. **Performances** *Nov-May* 8pm Fri. *June-Oct* closed. **Tickets** $5-$8. **No credit cards. Map** p309 O3.
Founded in 1984, Bilsak was an association of more than 150 artists, writers, intellectuals and journalists at a time when almost any kind of association or meeting was banned. Today, the Bilsak building houses many activities including ceramics, photography and theatre workshops. There is also a lively gay bar on the ground floor (Bar Bahçe; *see p197*) and a great post-theatre bar up on the fifth floor (*see p143*), with a fine view over the Bosphorus. Staging relatively uncommon plays, such as works by Edward Bond or Sevim Burak, and using a self-taught method, Bilsak can claim to be one of the most original independent companies in Turkish theatre. It mounts one new production every year.

Istanbul Arts Centre

Istanbul Sanat Merkezi
Sakızağacı Caddesi, 12 Eskiçeşme Sokak, Tarlabaşı (0212 235 5457). **Box office** 8am-8pm Mon, Fri, Sat. *June-Oct* closed. **Tickets** $3-$8. **No credit cards. Map** p308 N2.
This venue on the main street of the lively and popular Tarlabaşı district opened to the public in 1989. It was built in 1843 as an Armenian Catholic convent and school. The complex includes two small theatres, several artists' workshops and a top-floor open-air restaurant with a fine view. It hosts three different independent companies that concentrate on mostly experimental contemporary dance or theatre. Most notable of the three is Kumpanya (Troupe), which has gained a reputation for its ambitious mix of absurd theatre, traditional musicals and design research.

Kenter Theatre

Kenter Tiyatrosu
35 Halaskargazi Caddesi, Harbiye (0212 246 3589/ 247 3634). **Box office** 11am-6pm daily.
Performances 9pm Thur-Sat; 3pm Sun.
Tickets $5-$10. **Credit** MC, V.
A private, 450-seat theatre founded in 1968 by Yıldız Kenter, one of Turkish theatre's leading actresses. The City Players (Kent Oyuncuları) perform two or three plays a year, usually standards by the likes of Shakespeare and Chekhov. Although the company claims to favour the Stanislavsky method, performances have a flavour very different from that of the Actor's Studio. They usually star Yıldız Kenter, are staged by her brother Müşfik

Kumpanya mix absurd theatre and traditional musicals at **Istanbul Arts Centre**. *See p228.*

Kenter, and can feel a bit academic, old-world, even dusty. The Kenter also hosts performances of Karagöz, the Turkish shadow theatre (*see p227* **Shadow play**). Shows are put on by theatre manager Cengiz Özek, one of Turkey's leading Karagöz performers, around four times a month, usually on Saturday and Sunday mornings.

Muhsin Ertuğrul Stage

Muhsin Ertuğrul Sahnesi
Darülbedai Caddesi 3, Harbiye (0212 240 7720/246 0628/www.ibb.gov.tr). **Box office** 8am-4.30pm Mon-Fri; closed Sat, Sun. **Performances** 3pm, 8.30pm Tue-Fri; 3pm, 8.30pm Sat, Sun. **Tickets** $1-$3. **No credit cards.**

Founded in 1914 as a conservatory, then renamed the Istanbul Municipal Theatre in 1931, this venue had significant influence on the development of Turkish theatre under the directorship of Muhsin Ertuğrul, who was appointed to the post in 1927. Ertuğrul is regarded as the founder of modern Turkish theatre, thanks to his staging of the great western classics, his encouragement of Turkish playwrights and his outstanding abilities as a director and teacher. Nowadays, the Muhsin Ertuğrul theatre (558 seats) and the 'Pocket' Theatre (62 seats) host regular performances by the Istanbul Municipality Company. Of the classic and contemporary plays performed here, half are by Turkish writers and include musicals and children's plays. The Istanbul Municipal Theatre attempts to create popular theatre, less elitist than the state theatre. The season begins in October and continues until the end of April. Houses are usually packed, due to low ticket prices and student reductions. It's recommended to book at weekends.

Ses-1885. Ortaoyuncular Theatre

Ses-1885. Ortaoyuncular Tiyatrosu
Istiklal Caddesi 140/90, Beyoğlu (0212 251 1865/ www.ortaoyuncular.com). **Box office** 11am-8pm. **Performances** *Oct-May* 8pm Mon, Thur, Fri; 3pm, 8pm Sat; 3pm, 6pm Sun. *June-Sept* closed. **Tickets** $8-$15. **No credit cards. Map** p308 N3.
Istanbul's oldest functioning theatre and one of its most beautiful. The wooden 550-seat hall, made up of two floors, boxes and a balcony, creates a nostalgic atmosphere. The Ses-1885. usually hosts performances by the Ortaoyuncular Company under Ferhan Şensoy, who trained in France in the famous Magic Circus band of Jérome Savary. All of the plays are comedies – usually written by Şensoy himself – and most are based on improvisation, wordplay and slang, using a contemporary version of traditional Turkish storytelling techniques. The company's productions are extremely popular and some run into hundreds of performances. *Ferhangi Şeyler*, a solo act by Şensoy and their biggest hit, has been performed more than 1,500 times. Around seven plays are staged every season.

Taksim Stage

Taksim Sahnesi
Sıraselviler Caddesi 39, Taksim (0212 249 6944/ www.istdt.gov.tr). **Box office** 10am-8pm Tue-Sat; 10am-6pm Mon, Sun. **Performances** 8pm Tue-Fri; 3pm, 8pm Sat; 3pm Sun. **Tickets** $3-$5. **Credit** MC, V. **Map** p309 P2.
Intimate 520-seat hall owned by the Ministry of Cultural Affairs and home to the Istanbul State Theatre. Around four different plays are put on every month, each for one week (no performances on Mondays). Productions are rather academic.

Sport & Fitness

Football rules, and rouses infamously fierce passions, leaving Turks little energy for anything else.

Turkey has had precious little success in international sport, with the exceptions of Greco-Roman wrestling, weightlifting and, in 2000, football. Schools lack the facilities and funds to encourage children to take an interest in sport. Although infrastructure, especially on the municipal level, has improved in recent years, affordable sports centres and training opportunities remain few and far between. Turkey's unsuccessful bid for the 2000 Olympics and its bid to host the 2008 event indicate that government officials, at least, are beginning to take sports more seriously.

The media have begun to devote more space to the rare Turk who manages against all odds to achieve glory, with recent examples in swimming and diving. As in so many other areas, Turkey looks set for rapid improvement, starting from a low base.

Spectator sports

A glance through the sports pages of the national press tells the story: football rules. Maybe 90 per cent of media sports coverage is concerned with soccer, even in close season. Running a distant second is basketball, which takes up most of the remaining ten per cent. And very occasionally, when it isn't too busy floating transfer rumours or putting the boot into Fenerbahçe's manager, the press spares the odd column for one of the other few national sporting diversions. Traditional oil-wrestling (*see page 181* **Slippery People**) has a small but devoted following, as does the modern Greco-Roman version seen in the Olympics. Weightlifting is another Olympic sport where Turks have excelled in recent years; Naim Süleymanoğlu carried off gold in 1988, 1992 and 1996. Athletics is less popular, but there is the occasional track and field meeting. Istanbul recently hosted the European Swimming Championships and this could be a sign that officials are interested in diversifying the country's sporting interests. It's a nice idea, but it might take a successful Olympic bid if football's grip is to be weakened.

Fixtures for all sporting events are listed in all the local press. If you don't read Turkish, ask any male and chances are you'll get not just the where and when but also the team list and a rundown on form.

Football

Football has always been by far the most popular sport in Turkey, and a big match remains one of the few occasions when the streets of Istanbul fall silent – at least until the final whistle. And if the result is right the streets quickly fill with flag-waving, horn-honking fans (*see page 231* **Welcome to hell!**).

Istanbul dominates Turkey's footballing life, hosting its three biggest clubs: Galatasaray, Beşiktaş and Fenerbahçe (the Black Sea side Trabzonspor supposedly completes a 'big four', but has struggled to keep up in recent years). This may not be healthy for Turkish football, but it's good news for the visitor hoping to catch a game.

Istanbul's clubs are increasingly looking to Europe as the measure of success or failure. They know that this means spending serious money, and more and more high-profile foreign stars have begun arriving. The Turkish press delights in fantasy transfer stories, linking the world's superstars to Istanbul clubs; in reality, it tends to be those in the twilight of their careers who opt for a final payday on the shores of the Bosphorus. But there have been success stories: the brilliant Romanian Gheorghe Hagi probably played the best club football of his career at Galatasaray.

Sadly, spending on transfers and salaries has not yet been matched by upgrading of club facilities. None of Istanbul's stadiums holds much more than 30,000 people – and none scores highly in terms of amenities, though this may change if Turkey makes a serious bid for an international tournament.

There are two daily newspapers devoted solely to football, *Fanatik* and *Fotomaç*, both of which notch sales in the hundreds of thousands. Each boasts several columnists devoted to the three big Istanbul clubs. With news thin on the ground, their stock in trade is speculation. Coverage of other Turkish teams is weak – as are the teams themselves.

Domestic competition focuses on the league championship, which runs from August to May and has a lopsided feel, as little clubs line up for a battering from the Istanbul heavyweights. For a really intense atmosphere, try to catch one of the Istanbul derbies. To satisfy the TV companies,

Welcome to hell!

It's not only the growing strength of Turkish football clubs on the field that makes them an unwanted draw in European competitions. Opposing teams also rarely relish a tie in Istanbul because of the intimidating cauldron that Turkish fans specialise in brewing up for their foreign visitors.

Visiting sides are usually welcomed with a cheery 'Welcome to Hell!' banner at the airport, and team buses are often attacked on their way into town. Fans have been known to serenade visiting teams outside their hotel rooms in an effort to keep them awake all night. And they are versatile linguists: 'Fuck you, Chelsea,' roared 25,000 voices in a 1999 Champions League encounter.

Such intimidation spilled over into violence in April 2000, when two Leeds supporters were stabbed to death before a UEFA cup tie against Galatasaray. This incident, which followed reports of drunken and provocative behaviour from English fans, had the inevitable effect of souring footballing relations between the countries. In the final, Galatasaray faced Arsenal, another English team, and the two sets of fans were involved in running battles through the centre of Copenhagen.

After a 1997 derby, Galatasaray fans (pictured) stabbed a Fenerbahçe player in the street and Turkish fans have even been known to attack their own players after a particularly useless performance.

But aside from the violence, what Turkish fans specialise in is noise. Football stadiums around the world are hardly places of quiet contemplation, but Turkish fans create a special intensity. At Euro 96 in England, the Turks were among the loudest of all – although it failed to have the desired effect and the Turks lost all three of their games, failing to score even a single goal.

It takes a lot to discourage a Turkish crowd. When a team surrenders a two-goal lead, or falls behind early in a game, many European stadiums tend to fall silent. The normal reaction of a Turkish crowd is the opposite: shout louder. In their European adventures over the last couple of years, Galatasaray sometimes seem to have been willed to victory by the sheer burning desire of their fans to be part of the continent's elite.

After a major victory, the immediate reaction of an Istanbul football fan is to grab his flag, jump in his car (or on top of somebody else's) and head for Taksim Square. More dangerous is the tradition of firing celebratory shots in the air – many Turks own guns and don't think twice about using them in narrow city streets.

So if you're wondering what all that noise is outside, don't lean over the balcony to find out. Two people died during the celebrations that followed Turkey's victory over Hungary to qualify for Euro 96.

Arts & Entertainment

league fixtures are staggered over a whole weekend, from Friday evening to Sunday evening. The fixture list is normally organised so that matches involving Istanbul teams don't clash with each other.

Tickets go on sale two or three days prior to a match, although for all but the biggest games it is surprisingly easy to pick them up at the stadium on the day. For Beşiktaş and Fenerbahçe (though not for Galatasaray), tickets can be bought in advance through:

Biletix

0216 454 1555/www.biletix.com. **Credit** DC, MC, V.
Tickets for Beşiktaş and Fenerbahçe can be booked on the phone or through their website as well as at one of the many branches found in selected outlets of clothing retailer Vakkorama, music retailer Raksotek and supermarket Migros. When booking on the phone by credit card, an extra $3 will buy delivery to your address.

Beşiktaş

Inönü Stadium, Dolmabahçe Caddesi, Beşiktaş (0212 236 7202). **Tickets** *league matches* $8.50-$110. **No credit cards. Map** p307 R2.
Istanbul's third team, though don't say it to their face. Some Beşiktaş fans like to see the team as representative of the traditional working class; it also seems to be the favourite of the leftish intelligentsia. Beşiktaş teams tend to play solid, unflamboyant football, though they have been at the forefront of the tendency to import foreign coaches – Gordon Milne and Christoph Daum have been among the most successful. The Inönü Stadium is the finest in Istanbul, superbly located opposite Dolmabahçe Palace (*see* p99).

Fenerbahçe

Rüştü Saraçoğlu Stadium, Kadıköy (reservations 0216 369 0784/stadium 0216 330 8996/ www.fenerbahce.org). **Tickets** *league matches* $6-$25. **No credit cards. Map** p311 Y8.
Once indisputably the biggest club in Turkey, Fener has had to watch from the sidelines with a forced smile in recent years, as arch-rival Galatasaray grabbed European glory. Despite winning a record number of Turkish league championships, Fener's own European record is patchy, though in 1996 it inflicted Manchester United's first ever home defeat in European competition. Fenerbahçe was Atatürk's team and has historic links with the Turkish army, despite its most unmilitary nickname, 'the Canaries'. Its stadium is in the wealthy suburb of Fenerbahçe, on Istanbul's Asian side. From the European side, you can take a boat from Eminönü to Bostancı or Kadıköy, and then a bus or taxi. Two or three days before a match, tickets are available at the club office behind the stadium, and can be reserved on the phone (though not by credit card) or can be obtained through **Biletix** (*see above*). On match days, tickets can be purchased at the stadium itself.

Galatasaray

Ali Sami Yen Stadium, Mecidiyeköy (0212 251 5707/www.galatasary.org.tr). **Tickets** *league matches* $8-110. **No credit cards.**
A string of European successes, crowned by victory over Arsenal in the UEFA Cup final in 2000, has lifted Galatasaray to the position of unchallenged monarch of Turkish football. Known to its fans as 'Cim Bom Bom' for reasons nobody can explain, Galatasaray has dominated the league since the mid-1990s. With its historic links to the old Galata Lycée, where a large chunk of Turkey's ruling class was educated, Galatasaray sees itself as the aristocracy of Turkish football. The Ali Sami Yen stadium is somewhat decrepit, in the rather drab commercial district of Mecidiyeköy. It's a transport hub, with frequent bus connections to all parts of town, although the simplest way to get there is by taxi from Taksim, which shouldn't cost more than around $3. Tickets go on sale two days before match days, and can only be bought in person at the stadium.

Basketball

The affair isn't nearly as passionate as the one between Istanbulites and football, but basketball has an increasingly large fan base and Turkish clubs are getting better at it. Nowadays both men's and women's teams are regularly found in the last stages of European competitions, and it's only a matter of time before they bring home a major trophy.

The basketball season lasts roughly from October to June, when clubs play at least twice a week, usually in the afternoon or early evening. Istanbul's three football giants also have basketball teams, but the top performers have been Efes Pilsen and Ülkerspor, run by a brewer and biscuit maker respectively.

All clubs have men's and women's teams; tickets for all but the biggest matches are easily available on match days, but can also be bought two or three days earlier, though it is not possible to make telephone reservations. Information on games and fixtures can be found at the **Turkish Basketball Federation** website: www.tbf.org.tr.

Beşiktaş

Süleyman Seba Spor Salonu
Çitlembik Durağı Arkası, off Emirhan Caddesi, Dikilitaş (0212 261 6319). **Tickets** $4-$8. **No credit cards.**
Even further behind the others in basketball than they are in football. The only time Beşiktaş won the basketball championship was in 1975.

Efes Pilsen

Ayhan Şahenk Spor Salonu
Darüşşafaka Lisesi, Büyükdere Caddesi, Derbent Mevkii, Maslak (0212 642 9100/

http://basket.efespilsen.com.tr). **Tickets** $2-$8.
No credit cards.
Founded in 1976, Efes Pilsen have since won the
Turkish title eight times and in 1996 (a year they
won every competition they entered) bagged the
European Korac Cup – the first Turkish team to win
any kind of European cup whatsoever.

Fenerbahçe
Haldun Alagaş Spor Salonu
*Alemdağ Caddesi, Ümraniye (0216 347 4762/
www.fenerbahce.org).* **Tickets** $2-$5. **No credit
cards.**
Galatasaray's deadly rivals last won the national
championship in 1991.

Galatasaray
Abdi Ipekçi Spor Salonu
*Onuncu Yıl Caddesi, Zeytinburnu (0212 574 2916/
www.galatasaray.org.tr).* **Tickets** $2-$3. **No credit
cards.**
The club with the most glorious history – both the
men's and women's have at different times won the
Istanbul league in ten consecutive seasons – has
waned somewhat in recent years.

Ülker
Ahmet Cömert Spor Salonu
*9. Kısım Olympiyat Evi Arkasi, Ataköy (0212 576
0739/ulker@attglobal.net).* **Tickets** from $2-$3.
No credit cards.
Ülker won the Turkish championship in 1997-8,
and got to the last eight of the Korac Cup the season
before. Tickets are also available from Ülker Spor
Klubü, Davut Paşa Caddesi 10, Topkapı.

Wrestling
The major annual event is the Republic Cup
(Cumhuriyet Kupası), an international
competition held on 27-29 September. For
information on this and other wrestling events
and facilities, contact the following:

Gençlik ve Spor Müdürlügü
Sıraselviler Caddesi 57, Taksim (0212 251 7340).
Open 8am-5pm Mon-Fri. **Map** p309 O3.

Active sports
With so few Turks able to work up the energy to
follow spectator sports, it's not surprising that an
even smaller group actively participate in sport.
A large chunk of the rural labour force exercises
by toiling in the fields, and urban dwellers
generally work ten-hour days between long
commutes.
   Leisure activities, for men at least, are
traditionally centred on the thousands of
neighbourhood *kiraathane,* where they sip tea,
watch television and play cards, backgammon
and other sedentary games. Even for those who
can find the time, exercise in Istanbul is an

expensive habit limited to the well-heeled.
Walking, jogging and fishing are free, of
course, and popular along the sea coast
walkways stretching from Kuruçeşme to Bebek
(*see chapter* **Ortaköy to Rumeli Hisarı**).
   The Kadıköy and Bakırköy municipalities
have established bicycle paths along the sea
coast roads, which are usually filled with joggers.
In-line skating and skateboarding are not
specifically catered for, but seaside parks and
Beşiktaş Square have been taken over by
whizzing teens.

Adventure sports
The Ministry of Tourism's efforts to pitch
Turkey as the ideal spot for sports lovers has at
least succeeded in interesting more Turks in
sport. University clubs and organisations
catering to the recent demand for sport on the
wild side have mushroomed.

Adrenalin
*Büyük Beşiktaş Carşısı 19, off Ortabahçe
Caddesi, Beşiktaş (0212 260 6002/
adrenalin@adrenalin.com.tr).* **Open** 10am-8pm
Mon-Sat; closed Sun. **Credit** MC, V.
This equipment shop sometimes organises rock
climbing in Gebze, about one hour from Istanbul,
and mountain-climbing in Çınarcık and Bursa
provinces, which are located two and three hours
out of town respectively. The $150 fee for each
activity includes transport, meals and equipment
hire. However, these are group tours only. Adrenalin
also operates a training centre in Beşiktaş for
mountain and rock-climbing.

Arnika
*Mis Sokak 6/5, off Istiklal Caddesi, Taksim (0212
245 1593/www.arnika.com.tr).* **Open** Mon-Sat
9am-7pm; closed Sun. **Credit** AmEx, MC, V.
Map 309 O2.
Organises trekking tours in Adapazarı, a rapidly
developing province one and a half hours east of
central Istanbul. Minimal English spoken.

Debitur
*Iba Blokları 12/9, off Barbaros Bulvarı, Balmumcu
(0212 211 5271/www.debitur.com).* **Open** 9am-6pm
Mon-Sat; closed Sun. **Credit** MC, V.
Debitur organises rafting, horse riding, trekking
and mountaineering tours. English spoken.

DSM Doga
*Rüstiye Sokak 27/8, Kızıltoprak (0216 414 2590/
www.dsm.com.tr).* **Open** 9am-7pm Mon-Fri; 9am-1pm
Sat; closed Sun. **Credit** MC, V.
Adventure sports centre organising activities that
include rafting, mountain climbing, caving, camping, trekking and paragliding, often under the
guidance of expert trainers. Also sells related
sports equipment conforming to CE, UIAA and
TUV standards. English spoken.

Arts & Entertainment

Top cueing action at the **Ağa Bilardo Salonu**.

Gezici YAK
Selçuk Apt, Recep Paşa Caddesi 14/7, off Cumhuriyet Caddesi, Taksim (0212 238 5107/ www.geziciyak.com). **Open** 8.30am-8.30pm Mon-Sat; closed Sun. **Credit** MC, V.

Organises rafting and trekking trips to Köprüçay, Antalya (a mountainous region on the Mediterranean), as well as diving expeditions to Saros and Çanakkale (Gallipoli), on the northern Aegean. The two-day rafting expedition costs $60, including meals and camping accommodation, but not transport. Also offerred is basic training in rafting in co-operation with Antalya-based Med-raft. The fee for scuba diving is $200, which includes meals and camping accommodation, and the use of all equipment, but not transport costs. A doctor's certificate is required for scuba diving. English spoken.

Ogzala
Bekar Sokak 16/4, off Istaklal Caddesi, Beyoğlu (0212 252 3039/www.ogzala.com). **Open** 9.30am-6.30pm Mon-Sat; closed Sun. **Credit** MC, V. **Map** 309 O2.

Organises walking tours near lakes, mountains and waterfalls in Yalova, Izmit, Adapazarı and Bolu provinces, all of which are within three hours of Istanbul. The $20 fee includes lunch, transport and a guide.

Billiards

Sleazy snooker saloons, long a staple of the Beyoğlu scene, have recently been joined by smart American-style pool halls. While the former remain smoke-filled, men-only affairs, the latter are popular with a mix of young male and female students.

Ağa Bilardo Salonu
Ağa Hamamı Caddesi 17, Beyoğlu (0212 251 7469). **Open** 8.30am-midnight daily. **Rates** $2.50-$3 per hr. **No credit cards**. **Map** p309 O3.

A spacious hall with nine tables, three 'Amerikan' – pool tables, in other words – and six snooker tables. There are also two ping-pong tables in the musty basement, as well as areas for playing cards and board games and a café. Children under 18 must be accompanied by a parent.

Omayra Billiards & Internet Café
Aznavur Pasajı, Istiklal Caddesi 212, Beyoğlu (0212 244 3002). **Open** 8am-1am daily. **Rates** $3 per hr. **Credit** MC, V. **Map** p308 N3.

Spacious room with seven billiard tables, Internet access and fast-food café.

Bowling

Istanbul's first bowling alley opened just nine years ago, but there are now at least seven, with more opening all the time.

Bab Bowling Café
Yeşilçam Sokak 24, off Istaklal Caddesi, Beyoğlu (0212 251 1595). **Open** 10am-midnight daily. **Credit** MC, V. **Map** 308 N3.

Only six lanes – reserve ahead evenings and weekends. Fast-food bar and café attached. Rates vary from $2.50 per game on a weekday morning to $5 per game on weekends and holidays.

Time Out Bowling Centre
7th floor, Profilo Shopping Mall, Cemal Sahir Sokak 26/28, Mecidiyeköy (0212 217 0992). **Open** 10am-2am daily. **Credit** MC, V.

The largest bowling alley in Istanbul, with 16 lanes. Billiard tables, pro shop for sports equipment and an Internet café. Rates vary widely depending on day, time and season. Special discounts for purchases made at shop and for higher than average bowling scores.

Horse riding

Believe it or not, you can ride a horse within city limits, although there are better facilities and superior scenery out on the **Princes' Islands** (*see page 243*).

Bahçeşehir Atlı Spor Kulübü
Hoşdere köyü (village), Isparta klub, merkii, Bahçeşehir (0212 669 6762). **Open** 9am-midnight Tue-Sun; closed Mon. **Rates** *Tue-Fri* $15 for 30 min. *Sat, Sun* $23 for 30 min. **Credit** AmEx, MC, V.

This little ranch in the village of Hoşdere köyü offers indoor and outdoor riding facilities.

Ferhat Bey Binicilik Kulübü
Turgut Özal Caddesi 140, Alemdaı (0212 669 6761). **Open** 9.30am-5.30pm Tue-Sun; closed Mon. **Rates** *Daily* $18. *Monthly membership* $180. **No credit cards**.

Small outdoor riding track in wooded land.

Istanbul Riding Club
Istanbul Atlů Spor Kulübü
Istinye Yolu, Istinye (0212 276 2056). **Open** 9am-5.30pm Tue-Sun; closed Mon. **Rates** $30 per hr. **No credit cards**.

The most centrally located club, in what used to be countryside but is now hemmed in by skyscrapers, offering a large track for riding. Horses for hire and instruction available. Some English spoken.

Ice skating

Pushing 35°C outside? How about some ice – a rink full. Skating is more a summer escape from the heat than a sport, and as such very popular.

Galleria Ice Skating

Galleria Shopping Mall, Bakırköy Sahil Yolu, Ataköy (0212 560 8550/turenturiam@hotmail.com). **Open** 10am-11pm daily. **Rates** $6 per 45 mins. **Credit** AmEx, MC, V.

The only rink open to the public. Should be called the Elvis Costello skating rink – full of skaters that can't stand up for falling down. But very relaxed and fun. Evening ice-skating classes are available.

Skiing

There are two major ski resorts within a four-hour drive of Istanbul: Uludağ, above Bursa (*see page 251*) and Kartalkaya, halfway to Ankara. Uludağ has easy and intermediate runs but is less good than most local tour operators would have you believe. Kartalkaya is better.

Sporting

Gürsoylu Sokak 40A, off Bayar Caddesi, Kozasker (0216 410 4054/www.sporting.com.tr). **Open** Nov-Mar 9am-7pm daily. Apr-Oct 9am-7pm Mon-Sat; closed Sun. **Credit** AmEx, MC, V.

This shop sells skiing and general sports equipment, and organises ski trips on a regular basis.

Swimming

The city's few Olympic-size pools are part of university campuses or expensive members-only sports complexes. Guests at both must be accompanied by a member. One luxurious option is to take advantage of the special day passes and seasonal memberships available at some of the five-star hotels (*see below*). It's always best to call in advance before showing up with swimming togs and towel, as terms change frequently. None of the hotel pools has lanes – it's pretty much a swim-for-all.

Although Istanbul is surrounded by water, swimming near the city is likely to result in an appointment with a dermatologist. The lower Bosphorus has become so polluted that swimming is banned. The upper Bosphorus, near Sarıyer is cleaner, but certainly not clean, and is also subject to treacherous currents.

The closest beach to Istanbul with anything aproaching clean sand and clear, unpolluted water is on Marmara Island, near the eastern shore of the Sea of Marmara (*see page 249*). It takes two and a half hours to get there and the round trip costs approximately $30, but the island is completely unspoiled and makes for a worthwhile day out of town.

Ceylan Inter-Continental

Asker Ocağı Caddesi 1, Takism (0212 231 2121/ www.interconti.com). **Open** 5.30am-9pm daily. **Rates** *Day pass* $15 Mon-Fri, $25 Sat, $30 Sun. **Credit** AmEx, DC, MC, V.

Outdoor 20m (66ft) pool. Fee includes use of the health club, hamam and sauna.

Çırağan Palace Hotel Kempinski

Çırağan Caddesi 84, Beşiktaş (0212 258 3377/ ciraginpalace.com.tr). **Open** *Indoor pool* 7am-10pm daily. *Outdoor pool* 8am-7pm daily. **Rates** *Day pass* $35 Mon-Fri; $40 Sat, Sun; 40% discount for 6-12s; free under-6s. **Credit** AmEx, DC, MC, V.

Wedged between the Çırağan Palace and the Bosphorus, this is the pool with the most spectacular setting in Istanbul. At 33m (108ft) long, it is also one of the largest pools in downtown Istanbul.

Conrad International

Yıldız Caddesi, off Barbaros Bulvarı, Beşiktaş (0212 227 3000/www.conradinternational.com). **Open** *Indoor pool* 6.30am-10pm daily. *Outdoor pool* 8am-8pm daily. **Rates** *Day pass* $25 Mon-Fri; $35 Sat, Sun; free under 10s. **Credit** AmEx, MC.

Outdoor pool 23.5m (77ft) long. Fee includes use of locker and towel.

Hyatt Regency

Taşkışla Caddesi, Taksim (0212 225 7000/ www.istanbulhyatt.com). **Open** 10am-7pm daily. **Rates** *Day pass* $25 Mon-Fri; $50 Sat, Sun. **Credit** AmEx, DC, MC, V. **Map** p307 Q2.

Outdoor 23m (75ft) pool. Fee includes use of tennis court, sauna and hamam. Even brunch is included in weekend admission fee.

Korukent Gym & Hobby Club

Korul Sokak, Korukent Sitesi, A Blok, Levent (0212 274 0668/www.korukent.com). **Open** 9am-10pm Mon-Fri; 9am-8pm Sat, Sun. **Rates** *Day pass* pool $15 Mon-Fri; $18 Sat, Sun; pool & gym $20 Mon-Fri; $25 Sat, Sun. **Credit** MC, V.

Fee includes use of all fitness centre facilities (*see below* **Fitness**).

Fitness

Weight-lifting and bodybuilding are beloved of Turkish men across all income brackets and social groups (check the number of magazines on the newsstands devoted to ballooning musculature). Cheaper gyms and fitness centres tend to be dominated by men, and women will certainly not feel comfortable. Women should find the places listed below hassle-free, largely because they're expensive enough to keep out the oglers.

Akatlar Sports Complex

5.Gazeteciler Sitesi, Mayodrom Yanı, Levent (0212 283 6600). **Open** 9am-10pm daily. **Rates** *Monthly pass* $38. *Tennis* $12 per 45 mins. **No credit cards.**

Vakkorama Gym – good equipment, choice of classes and a department store upstairs.

Fitness centre, martial arts courses, basketball and tennis courts. Monthly memberships available for non-residents.

Flash Gym

Aznavur Pasajı, 4th floor, Istiklal Caddesi 212, Beyoğlu (0212 249 5347). **Open** 10am-10pm Mon-Fri; 10am-9pm Sat; closed Sun. **Rates** *Day pass* $6; *monthly membership* $30-$50. **No credit cards. Map** p308 N3.
One of the few moderately priced gyms where women are not completely outnumbered and testosterone levels are kept tame. Equipment is adequate, if dated. Evening step classes also available. Some English spoken.

Korukent Gym & Hobby Club

A Blok, Koru Sokak, Korukent Sitesi, Levent (0212 274 0668/www.korukent.com). **Open** 9am-10pm Mon-Fri; 9am-8pm Sat, Sun. **Rates** *Day pass* gym $15 Mon-Fri; $18 Sat, Sun; gym & pool $20 Mon-Fri; $25 Sat, Sun. **Credit** MC, V.
Facilities include indoor and outdoor swimming pools, jacuzzi, jet stream, sauna, fitness, bodybuilding, aerobics and step. There are tennis and basketball courts and bowling lanes. Instruction is offered in kung-fu, tai-chi, whu shu and kick boxing.

Kuzey Yıldızı Kültür ve Spor Merkezi

Havyar Sokak 30-2, off Sıraselviler Caddesi, Cihangir (0212 252 6716). **Open** 8am-10pm Mon-Fri; 9am-7.30pm Sat; 10am-2.30pm Sun.

Rates *Day pass* $12; *monthly membership* $50-$100. **Credit** MC, V. **Map** 309 O4.
In addition to a weight room the centre has a range of martial arts and dance courses. There's a café upstairs, while downstairs a counter sells hokey New Age gifts and books with titles like *Buddhism and Sex*. Some English spoken.

Marmara Gym

Marmara Hotel, Taksim Square (0212 251 4696 ext 374/www.themarmara.com.tr). **Open** 7.30am-10pm daily. **Rates** *Day pass* $22. **Credit** AmEx, MC, V. **Map** p309 O2.
A high-tech fitness centre offering the latest equipment and a spectacular view of Istanbul. Fitness, sauna, Turkish bath, steam room, solarium, massage, jacuzzi and swimming pool. Step, aerobic, yoga and dance classes. English spoken.

Vakkorama Gym

Osmanlı Sokak 13, Taksim (0212 251 1571/ www.vakkorama.com.tr). **Open** 7.30am-10pm Mon-Fri; 10am-6pm Sat, Sun. **Rates** *Day pass* $25; *monthly membership* $100-$150. **Credit** AmEx, DC, MC, V. **Map** p309 P2.
A spotless and sleek set-up in the basement of the Vakkorama department store targeting the young, affluent and fashion-conscious. Equipment is the best of any gym of similar cost. Also offers aerobic, step, spinning and Haikkido classes. Hands-on instruction. Some English spoken.

Trips Out of
Town

Feature boxes

Getting Started

Easy getaways from Istanbul offer Greek temples, skiing, spas, seasides and, yes, more mosques.

Istanbul is surrounded by a diverse and interesting region, so when the 'Queen of Cities' starts to lose its sparkle or the traffic and fumes begin to get on top, it's time to venture beyond the city limits. The **Princes' Islands** (*see page 243*) are the city's most celebrated escape, car-free havens that'll make you feel like you've stepped back in time. Similarly, the suburbs overlooking the **Upper Bosphorus** (*see page 240*) with their graceful wooden waterside mansions (*yalıs*), fish restaurants and sea breezes are a perfect antidote for the urban blues. If it's sea and sand you're after, the resorts of Kilyos, Şile and Avşa have some of the best beaches on the Black Sea coast.

For those whose architectural appetite hasn't been sated by the historic buildings of Istanbul, the pleasant provincial town of **Edirne** (*see page 245*), once the centre of the Ottoman empire, has more of Sinan's creations, including what critics consider to be his finest work, the Selimiye Camii. **Bursa** (*see page 251*), the first Ottoman capital, also has a wealth of mosques, seminaries and bazaars to discover. Its nearby suburb Çekirge is renowned for its therapeutic hot baths, perfect for relaxing the muscles after a day on the ski slopes of Uludağ, winter playground of the rich and famous. There's also a spa at **Termal** (*see page 255*) in the hills above Yalova, which has been used since Roman times.

Further afield, **Çanakkale** (*see page 259*) stands beside the dark waters of the Dardanelles, across which the battlefields and memorials of Gallipoli stand in a poignantly beautiful rural setting. A short drive south there's **Troy** (*see page 263*), fabled city of Homer and Paris, which dates back at least 3,000 years. And across the unspoilt Troad, the ancient ruins of **Assos** (*see page 263*) stand guard over a pretty fishing harbour – the perfect weekend getaway.

The Ministry of Tourism has a number of offices across the city, but they are of little help beyond handing out glossy brochures. More useful are the local information offices in the towns covered here.

By car

Istanbul, like many large cities, can be hard to escape. Physically, it sprawls for miles in every direction, with congested roads meaning that at the wrong time of day it can literally be hours

before you finally put the city behind you. If you are driving or on a bus, the secret is in the timing: avoid the morning and evening rush hours at all costs. Excellent new highways stretch out of the city towards Edirne and Ankara; other roads are generally two-lane affairs and frequently pretty rough. Extra care should also be taken of other road users with the emphasis very much on defensive driving.

Car ferries to Yalova are the fastest way to begin a trip to Bursa and Iznik. A car ferry to Bandırma is an alternative to the overland route to Çanakkale.

By bus

Relatively fast, reliable and cheap, buses are the way most Turkish people get around, though with the Sea of Marmara between you and places such as Çanakkale and Bursa, distances and journey times are long. Much better, therefore to take to the water if possible (*see page 239* **By ferry**). There are, however, some places you just can't get to by boat – or maybe you missed the last ferry – in which case you'll need to catch a bus from one of the city's two *otogars*.

Bus stations

Esenler bus station

Büyük İstanbul Otogarı, Bayrampaşa (0212 658 0505). **Open** 24hrs daily.

By far the bigger of the two bus stations, Esenler is a virtual city in its own right, about ten kilometres (six miles) northwest of Sultanahmet and accessible by metro. It can be a daunting place for the first-timer: an enormous concrete bull-ring with well over 150 bus company offices around its central courtyard. Each company has a numbered gate (*peron*) leading to bays from which their buses depart. In fact, all you have to do is stroll around looking for your destination on the signs displayed out front. You'll be approached by any number of touts eager to sell you a ticket; if they don't sell tickets to the destination you want, they'll point you to somebody who does.

Most bus companies also have offices in town and provide free transportation to Esenler for ticket holders. Because services are so frequent, if you turn up without a booking the most you'll have to wait is an hour – except during public holidays, when the whole Turkish nation is on the move.

Boats – Istanbul's best means of escape.

Harem bus station
Harem Sahil Yolu, Harem (0216 333 3763).
Open 24hrs daily.
The city's second bus station is a much smaller affair on the Asian side of the Bosphorus. It doesn't take a genius to figure out that if you're heading to destinations in Asiatic Turkey, including Bursa, getting on a bus here will save you sitting through the crosstown traffic. The bus company offices above can reserve you a seat from Harem, but the best way to get there is the car ferry from Eminönü.

Bus companies

It's best to stick with the larger, more reputable names, which have a better record when it comes to service and safety. Among them are:

Kamil Koç
35/B Inönü Caddesi, Taksim (0212 252 7223).
Open 24 hrs daily. **Map** p307 P2.

Pamukkale
16 Mete Caddesi, Taksim (0212 249 2791).
Open 8am-12.30am daily. **Map** p307 P2.

Radar
Inönü Caddesi 57/1, Taksim (0212 293 9203).
Open 24 hrs daily. **Map** p307 P2.

By ferry

With so much water surrounding the city, ferries are an important means of escape. State-owned Turkish Maritime Lines (TML) operate regular ferries to the Princes' Islands, although services up the Bosphorus are restricted to a few sightseeing (*see page 240*) and commuter (*see page 101*) services each day from Eminönü and Beşiktaş. Much larger TML ferries also depart for the Marmara Islands. Information about these long-haul TML services and tickets can be obtained from their headquarters at Karaköy, just east of the Galata Bridge.

These traditional craft have been joined by a new generation of high-speed *deniz otobüsleri* ('sea buses'), usually catamarans but sometimes hydrofoils) run by the city's municipal government. These jet out to the Princes' Islands from Kabataş, just south of Dolmabahçe Palace, and from Sarayburnu pier at Eminönü, just east of Sirkeci station. Further on, towards Seraglio Point, hulking TML ferries depart for the Marmara Islands. Much larger *hızlı feribotlar* (speed ferries), capable of carrying vehicles, shuttle across the Sea of Marmara to Yalova and Bandırma from Yenikapı, south of Aksaray on the coast road heading out to the airport. With or without a car, these beasts are by far the fastest and least stressful way of beginning your journey to Bursa, Iznik, Çanakkale or Assos.

Istanbul Denizotobüsleri
Yenikapı Iskele (information 0212 516 1212/ reservations 0212 517 9696/www.ido.com.tr).
Open 6.30am-9.30pm daily.

Turkish Maritime Lines
Türkiye Denizcilik Işletmeleri Rıhtım Caddesi, Karaköy, (information 0212 249 1896/reservations 0212 249 9222). **Open** Mon-Fri, 9am-6pm; closed Sat, Sun.

By train

Though atmospheric and scenic, train journeys in Turkey are ponderously slow and long-winded. The story goes that the lines were laid by a German company who got paid per kilometre. A more fundamental problem is that, Edirne aside, none of the destinations covered in this guide are anywhere near a railway line.

So for the rail enthusiast the only option is the less than salubrious Edirne Ekspresi, which crawls out of Sirkeci station at 3.25pm each day and takes six hours to trundle across the empty Thracian landscape to Edirne (the bus does the trip in 21 / 2 hours).

Sirkeci Station
Istasyon Caddesi 24/2, Sirkeci (0212 527 0051). Tram Sirkeci. **Open** 5am-1am daily. **Map** p303 N8.

The Upper Bosphorus

Boat trips, Byzantine castles and lucky wires for wannabe brides.

The shores of the long, slow upper twist of the Bosphorus are where Istanbul escapes to relax. Yachts bob at anchor in over a dozen natural harbours, while beautiful old Ottoman *yalıs* (waterfront mansions) slowly age in the company of a myriad excellent fish restaurants.

Walking the narrow, built-up streets of Istanbul it's easy to forget that it was born, grew up and grew old on the sea. It's a maritime city, with the Bosphorus as its main drag, a watery highway through the heart of town. Under the Ottomans the water was as busy, if not more so, than the roads.

In more recent times Istanbul has turned its back on the water but on a boat trip it's evident that historically the city has always presented its best face to the Bosphorus.

Bosphorus cruise

It's one of Istanbul's must-dos: a boat trip up the Bosphorus. Daily cruises lasting five hours depart from piers at Beşiktaş and Eminönü. On the way, the boat tacks back and forth from Europe to Asia, stopping briefly at some dozen Bosphorus-side halts.

After passing between the twin fortresses of Rumeli and Anadolu Hisarı, and under the second of the soaring Bosphorus suspension bridges, the first halt is **Kanlıca**. Since the 17th century the place has been famed for its rich yoghurt and crates are brought on board for sale. Next stop is **Yeniköy** over on the European side. As the Ottoman empire deteriorated in the early 19th century, increasingly desperate rulers used lavish gifts of land as a way of securing the support of foreign embassies in Istanbul. Yeniköy was the real estate of choice and the waterfront is lined with the greatest concentration of restored Bosphorus mansions, several of which remain the summer residences of the city's consulates.

North of Yeniköy on the European shore are Tarabya and Büyükdere, neither of which are stops on the cruise. Büyükdere is usually visited as part of a trip out to the **Belgrad Forest** (*see page 242*). Instead, the ferry carries straight on up to **Sarıyer**, largest village on the upper Bosphorus. It is also one of Greater Istanbul's most conservative suburbs, where in 1995 a local woman was stoned to death on suspicion of being a prostitute. It is worth getting off the boat

here though for the excellent **Sadberk Hanım Museum**. There's also a bunch of decent seafood restaurants a short walk north of the ferry landing in the historic fish market (Balıkçılar Çarşısı).

From Sular Caddesi in Sarıyer it's possible to catch a dolmuş for the next waterside village up, **Rumeli Kavağı**, which if you were staying on the ferry would be the next stop. Travelling by dolmuş, en route you pass a sign for **Telli Baba**, the burial place of a revered mystic Muslim saint and now the focus of a surviving bit of regional folklore. Wannabe brides come here to pray at the saint's tomb and take away a charmed piece of golden wire, guaranteed to secure them a husband.

Newly-weds traditionally return on their wedding day to reattach the wire to the grill of saint's tomb and pay homage to the power of Telli Baba's magic. Saturday and Sunday afternoons can see major traffic snarl-ups as convoys of husband-seekers pile up along the narrow Bosphorus-side road.

Rumeli Kavağı itself is a sleepy little place that gets its excitement from the arrival of the ferry. It's no more than a string of houses and restaurants along the shore road, which cluster more densely around the ferry landing. From here the road runs north on up the Bosphorus, along the way passing dozens more restaurants set into the cliff face, plus a few small sandy beaches. These are private and usually charge entrance of around $1.50.

The coast road finishes up at the gates of an army base, but just before this is Altınkum, the best of the area's beaches, accessed down a narrow path through the trees. There you'll find a restaurant serving mezes and cold beer. The water is marked off about 20 metres (64 feet) out by a line of buoys – worth sticking within if you're swimming, as the Bosphorus is swept by some strong currents further out.

Last stop for the ferry is **Anadolu Kavağı** on the Asian Shore almost opposite Rumeli Kavağı. The boat halts here giving passengers enough time to stroll through a village that thrives purely on serving up fish dinners to the passing trade. There's little to choose between any of them and in fact time might be better spent clambering up to the Byzantine Yoros castle, which looms on the headland north of the village, commanding the Black Sea approaches.

Stop at **Anadolu Kavağı** on the Asian shore for friendly moggies and fish suppers. *See p240.*

It's a stiff walk up the hill, taking 20-30 minutes. Originally the site of a temple to Zeus, where early Greek sailors would stop to make a sacrifice to ensure safe passage through the straits, the present fortress was built by the Byzantines, occupied by the Genoese in the mid-14th century, then by the Turks, who strengthened the battlements. It lay abandoned and out of bounds until the 1980s, when it was opened to the public. Heading back down from the castle, take the steeply descending path across the heath. This gives out into scrub where you'll find a teahouse with half a dozen rickety tables and a great view.

From Anadolu Kavağı the ferry sails straight back down to Beşiktaş and Eminönü with no stops on the way.

Sadberk Hanım Museum

Sadberk Hanım Müzesi
Piyasa Caddesi 25-29, Büyükdere (0212 242 3813).
Open 10.30am-6pm Mon, Tue, Thur-Sun; closed Wed.
Admission $1.50. **No credit cards.**
Collection of Ottoman costumes, worth a look for the luscious colours and intricate embroidery. Also archaeological and ethnographic artefacts, including Iznik and later Kütahya tilework.

Getting there

Bosphorus boat trip

Boats depart from a landing stage at Eminönü 200m east of the Galata bridge three times a day Mon-Sat, four times on Sunday. Times vary through the year but first departure is never earlier than 10am and the last no later than 3pm. You can also board at the ferry landing at Beşiktaş. The round-trip takes about five hours and costs $5.

Where to eat

Emek Manti Evi

Köybaşı Caddesi 218, Yeniköy (0212 262 6981). **Open** 9am-11.30pm daily. **Main courses** $4. **Credit** MC, V.
Tiny *manti* (Turkish ravioli) house with a dozen tables on two levels. Always crammed but justly so.

Deniz Park Restaurant

Daire Sokak 9, Yeniköy (0212 262 0415).
Open noon-midnight daily. **Main courses** $12. **Credit** DC, MC, V.
Restored Ottoman *yalı* on the lip of the Bosphorus. House special is fish *buğlama*: catch of the day in a tomato, kasseri cheese, parsley, mushroom, green pepper and shrimp sauce.

Trips Out of Town

Tribeca

Kapalı Bakkal Sokak 5, Yeniköy (0212 223 9919).
Open 7.15am-11pm Mon-Sat; 7.15am-10pm Sun.
Main courses $1. **Credit** MC, V.
Istanbul's best bagels. Eat out on the garden deck.

Yeniköy Iskele

*Iskele Sokak 15-17, off Köybaşı Caddesi, Yeniköy
(0212 262 3549).* **Open** 11am-1am daily.
Main courses $10. **Credit** AmEx, DC, MC, V.
Excellent waterside fish restaurant on two levels
with an open-air deck.

Belgrad Forest

A popular haunt for summer picnickers and
health freaks, cyclists and joggers, the Belgrad
Forest (Belgrad Ormanı) is Istanbul's nearest
swath of woodland.

It takes its name from the Serbs who
historically inhabited the area, entrusted by
Süleyman the Magnificent with guarding the
city's water supplies. With its leafy glades and
tree-covered hills, populated with oaks, pines,
plane trees and beeches, it also has a distinctly
Balkan feel. Walking the forest today you'll
come across the remains of the reservoirs and
aqueducts that supplied Istanbul with most of
its fresh water under both Byzantines and
Ottomans. The Serbs were got rid of in the 1890s
when the fruitcake sultan Abdül Hamit II fell
prey to suspicions that they might be poisoning
the water and had them removed.

The forest was also long popular with European
residents of Istanbul and its most wealthy
Christians, who would retreat to Belgrad village
come summer to escape the heat and bouts of
pestilence. In 1771, Lady Mary Montague Wortley
described the summer scene at the village in
her diaries as a kind of Arcadian rural idyll, the
inhabitants of which would meet every night 'to
sing and dance, the beauty and dress of the women
exactly resembling the ancient nymphs'.

Following Mahmut II's purge of the Janissary
corps in 1826 (*see page 14* **Swords of misrule**),
the few Janissaries who escaped the massacre
fled to the forest, where they took up traditional
woodland pursuits such as shooting the sultan's
deer and ambushing local traders. The sultan's
radical response was to set the forest on fire,
a scorched-earth policy that succeeded in
barbecuing the rogue Janissaries.

Visiting Belgrad village now, it's obvious that
they had a lot more fun back then, as the place is
nothing but a few bumps in the forest floor, hidden
off the road near one of the largest picnic areas at
the Büyük Bend reservoir. This is one of the oldest
parts of the water system, originally Byzantine,
though restored by a string of subsequent rulers.

Also worth visiting is the **Long Aqueduct**, on
the road to Kısırmandıra. This is another work by

Mimar Sinan (*see page 38* **Keeping up with the
domes's**), built for Süleyman the Magnificent in
1563. The stream it crosses is the Kağıthane Suyu,
which eventually flows into the Golden Horn.

Getting there

From the Taksim Square area in central Istanbul, take
a dolmuş from beside the Atatürk library on Miralay
Şefik Bey Sokak for Sarıyer, getting off at Büyükdere
($0.75). From there, take another dolmuş from
Sırmacılar Sokak to Bahçeköy, which lies on the east
side of the forest; from here it's a walk of around a mile
(1.5km) to Büyük Bend.

Kilyos & Şile

North of the twin points of Rumeli Kavağı and
Anadolu Kavağı, the mouth of the Bosphorus
widens out on both sides to meet the Black Sea
(Karadeniz). On its European shore is the beach
resort of Kilyos; across on the Asian side is the
holiday town of Şile.

While Kilyos possesses an extensive sandy
beach, it has also been hung, drawn and
quartered by development, leaving it an ultra-
tacky hangout of dodgy bars and disappointed-
looking Russian package tourists. From here you
can also look up the coast to see that this formula
is being used as a model for the rest of the Black
Sea seaboard, the environment not so much
damaged as devoured.

Şile is a more attractive choice, although far
more difficult to reach. With a 14th-century
Genoese castle on a tiny island in the bay, this
cliff-top resort gets pretty crowded in summer,
understandably given its long sandy beaches.
The trip here is do-able in a day, but there's no
shortage of pensions and hotels if you fancy
staying longer.

Getting there

Kilyos

Kilyos is 15km (10 miles) north of Sarıyer. From the
Taksim Square area in central Istanbul take a dolmuş
from beside the Atatürk library on Miralay Şefik Bey
Sokak for Sarıyer. From there walk up Sular Caddesi
to the Kilyos dolmuş stop on the right-hand side of the
road. The journey takes around half an hour and costs
$0.50. Last dolmuş back to Sarıyer from Kilyos is
around 8pm.

Şile

Catch the city bus from Üsküdar's Doğancılar Caddesi
($1.50) for the hour-and-a-half journey. These leave on
the hour from 9am to 4pm.

Where to stay

In Şile try the **Değirmen Hotel** (Plaj Yolu 24, 0216 711
5048, rates $30/$45, credit MC, V) by the main beach.

The Princes' Islands

Monasteries, donkey rides, barefoot hill climbs – island life at its best.

For centuries a place of exile for the victims of Byzantine and Ottoman court intrigues, the four visitable islands just off Bostancı are now some of the last around the city where you can catch a glimpse of the old ethnic mix of Istanbul. Greeks, Armenians and Jews still rub shoulders with Turks in the local squares, and churches are more numerous than mosques. The streets are also car-free, and echo to the clop of horse-drawn phaetons cantering past fine old wooden mansions, often set in some of the country's best-tended gardens.

The overall effect is of a 19th-century ambience – strongest in winter, when the hordes of summer day-trippers are far away. The islands also provide a glimpse of what the city was once like, with wooded slopes carpeting the hinterlands and hills, an instant refresher after the city smog. If you travel to the west coast of Büyükada or Burgazada, Istanbul itself also disappears from view, to be replaced by the sparkling Marmara and a view more reminiscent of Ionia than Istanbul. There are nine islands in total. Of the four that can be visited, Büyükada is the largest and most popular.

Getting there

By ferry
Regular ferries to the islands leave from Sirkeci (the quay nearest the railway station) and Bostancı, with hydrofoils to Büyükada from Kabataş. Ferries visit all the islands in turn. The departure times on show at the ferry stops change with the seasons.

Tourist information

There are no tourist information offices on any of the islands.

Büyükada

The biggest of the Princes' Islands, as the name Büyükada ('Large island') implies. It was previously known as Prinkipo in Greek – possibly for similar reasons, or else a reference to the number of nobles that ended up banished or in hiding here. The Byzantine empress Zoe was a regular at the convent, now long gone. The Ottomans captured the island before they took Constantinople, though its Christian identity persists to this day.

Mansion on **Büyükada** – the 'large island'.

More recently, from 1929-33, it was the home of Leon Trotsky, who bashed out his *History of the Russian Revolution* in exile at the Izzet Paşa Köskü, a now-restored wooden mansion at 55 Çankaya Caddesi. This was rather ironic, as at the time Istanbul was home to some 34,000 White Russians, living in exile after being defeated by Trotsky's Red Army. Trotsky lived in the house surrounded by armed 'secretaries', though, according to Turkish police reports, he did make one trip into Istanbul, to see Charlie Chaplin's *City Lights*. This was also the house where, in 1933, his daughter committed suicide.

In the town itself, you'll find the transport pool, a corral of horse-drawn phaetons just up from the ferry dock. Here you can take the big or small tour ($10 or $7). Both tours are well worth it, as you'll be rattled and rolled around the island and end up at the foot of the hill on which stands **St George's Monastery**. You have to walk the steep slope to the top, unless you fancy hiring a donkey for $2 a ride. Along the way you'll see hundreds of pieces of thread, cloth and even paper tied to the branches of the trees and shrubs lining the path. Each one is a prayer tied by the faithful of all religions, Muslim included. In times gone by, most of the prayers were from women desiring babies; the infertile still ascend barefoot.

At the top, be prepared for a fine view, and an excellent restaurant next to the monastery. Open lunchtimes and afternoons, it serves food in a traditional Turkish style, with a view far out over the Marmara. The monastery has no fixed opening hours. The chapel is usually open to visitors – though in winter you'll need to find the attendant for the key. Inside you'll find a number of icons to the old dragon-slayer himself, and a collection of bone fragments from a variety of other saints.

From here the islands of Yassıada and Sivriada are visible, the former distinguished by a fort-like prison. Neither has a particularly wholesome history. It was in the Yassıada jail that former prime minister Adnan Menderes and two of his ministers were hanged in 1961 following a military coup, while Sivriada is famous for an incident in 1911 when Istanbul's stray dogs were rounded up and taken there to be left to starve. Neither island can be visited.

Where to stay

There's no accommodation in winter. In summer try the **Hotel Princess** (Iskele Meydanı, 0216 382 1162, rates $60-$90), or the **Hotel Splendid Palas** (23 Nisan Caddesi, 0216 382 6950, rates $60-$80) which has a pool and a fine restaurant. Booking essential.

Where to eat & drink

The **Hamdi Baba** (18 Gulistan Caddesi, 0216 382 3733; main course $10) near the ferry stop on Büyükada, is particularly worth a visit. The **St George's Monastery Restaurant** (no phone, main course $10), is a restful stop at the top of the hill.

Heybeliada, Burgazada & Kınalada

Over on **Heybeliada**, there's an interesting juxtaposition of the Turkish Naval High School with the 19th-century Greek Orthodox School of Theology at the **Haghia Triada Monastery**. The latter is a point of international contention, with the recent Greek-Turkish rapprochement leading to calls for its reopening from world leaders, including President Bill Clinton. The extensively wooded 'saddlebag island' Heybeliada is a summer favourite for picnickers. The means of transport is the phaeton, available from Ayyildiz Caddesi near the ferry dock, but it's small enough for walking or cycling. Bicycles can be rented from shops on the quayside ($10). There are also some beaches, but tales abound of swimmers contracting diseases from its waters.

Burgazada is even smaller, but still popular, particularly for the **Sait Faik Restaurant**, named after one its more famous inhabitants, on its western shore, accessed by a 15-minute walk from the ferry dock or by phaeton. A statue to Sait Faik, sometimes known as the Turkish Mark Twain, stares out to sea over restaurant terraces down the hill to a hooked headland and a wooded beach. Back in town, a small **Sait Faik Museum** is dedicated to him. There's also a fine **Armenian church**, still in service, and the Greek Orthodox **Church of St John the Baptist**. The latter was believed haunted, as local residents claimed to hear a deathly howling from within. With the priest gearing up for an exorcism, imagine the disappointment when it turned out to be a trapped owl inside its dome.

Kınalada is probably the least impressive of the four islands, as it is covered by houses. It's also a favourite for swimming, with its south side beaches allegedly sheltered from the worst of Istanbul's outpourings. Historically, it was the home of exile Romanus IV, who led the Byzantines to a decisive defeat by the Selçuks at the Battle of Manzikert in 1071.

Sait Faik Museum
15 Burgaz Çayiri Sokak. **Open** 10am-noon, 2-5pm Tue-Fri, Sun; closed Mon, Sat. **Admission** free.

Armenian church,
Burgaz Cayıri Sokak 55. **Open** 9am-9pm Sun; closed Mon-Sat.

Church of St Jonn the Baptist
Takimaga Meydanı **Services** 9am Sun; closed Mon-Sat.
The caretakers, who live on the grounds, may let you in during daylight if you ask them nicely.

Where to stay

In winter, all the islands' hotels and pensions close. In summer try the seafront **Panorama Hotel** (Ayyıldız Caddesi, 0216 351 8543, rates $30). Booking essential.

Where to eat & drink

The **Merit Halki Palace** (88 Refah Sehitleri Caddesi, 0216 351 0025, main course $30) serves full meals on Heybeliada. On Burgazada, the **Sait Faik Restaurant** (Kalpazan Kaya Yolu, 122 Gönüllü Caddesi, 0216 381 1504, main course $15) is popular for its fine sea view.

Edirne

Sinan's finest mosque is only one of the attractions in this city of two rivers.

Frontier city, one-time capital of the Ottoman empire and the subject of a tussle for control between just about anyone who has ever been anyone in the Balkans, Edirne today can be a welcome scaling-down from Istanbul. Moving at a much slower pace, with fresher air and countryside, it's also the site of the annual Kırkpınar oil-wrestling competition (*see page 181* **Slippery People**) and two major Roma meetings, making the early summer Edirne's most lively months.

CONQUESTS AND CATASTROPHES

First a Thracian settlement called Uscudama, then a Hellenistic city known as Oresteia, the town shot to fame as Hadrianople after the

Edirne moves at a slower pace.

Roman emperor Hadrian turned it into a provincial capital. It was also the scene of one of the greatest catastrophes of Roman military history, when the emperor Valens (of Istanbul's aqueduct fame) got a bad pasting from the Goths in 378 AD. After that it was all downhill, with Krum Khan and his Bulgars taking the city in the ninth century, the Crusaders sacking it on numerous occasions in the tenth and 11th centuries, and the city finally falling to the Ottomans after a siege in 1361.

Murat I transferred the Ottoman capital here from Bursa after the siege to give his still fledgling empire a solid European base. It also demonstrated which direction he was looking in for further expansion. Mehmet the Conqueror, however, decided to head south first, and set out to embark on the siege of Constantinople from Edirne. The Ottoman court followed him to Istanbul in 1458.

In the centuries of Ottoman expansion that followed, Edirne flourished, also remaining a favourite among the sultans for its hunting. Strategically located as a river crossing, it retained a sense of being the Ottoman capital in Europe, at least until the 19th century, when the city entered another period of turmoil.

Two Russo-Turkish wars, in 1829 and 1878-9, led to the city's occupation by the Tsar's troops, and although it was later returned to Ottoman control, the First Balkan War of 1913 saw a five-month siege by the Bulgarians that ended in Ottoman defeat and some appalling massacres. However, under the command of Enver Paşa, the Ottomans retook the city when the Second Balkan War broke out a few months later. The Greeks then occupied Edirne in 1920, following the Ottoman collapse after World War I. With victory in the Independence War, however, the Turks reoccupied the place on 25 November 1923, still celebrated as the city's Liberation Day.

FRONTIER FEEL

Looking at Edirne's location, it's easy to see why it's had so much trouble over the years, and its present position, with the Greek border a few miles to the west and the Bulgarians on the edge of town to the north, still gives it a frontier feel, particularly out of season when the only other visitors you're likely to meet are traders and truck drivers traversing Euroroute 5, the continent's longest motorway.

Trips Out of Town

Selimiye Camii – Edirne's focal point, Sinan's finest mosque.

Give it some sun, though, and things get
decidedly pleasant, with some fine architecture
and two rivers – the Tunca and Meriç – offering
good strolls along their banks.

Edirne's focal point and symbol is the
Selimiye Camii, widely seen as the most
accomplished mosque in Turkey and a late *pièce
de résistance* by Mimar Sinan (*see page 38*
Keeping up with the domes's), who was an
octogenarian during its design and construction.
Built in 1569 for Selim II, its four minarets are
the second highest in the world at 71 metres (248
feet), beaten only by Mecca. The dome is also a
final triumph over that of Istanbul's Haghia
Sophia (*see page 69*), topping its diameter by a
few centimetres at 31.5 metres (103 feet). From
the outside, the massive flying buttresses, the top
ends of eight huge supporting pillars within,
are concealed with decorative turrets as you
approach through the central park, Dilaver
Bey. This contains a statue of Sinan, and leads
through the Cobbler's Arcade (Kavaflar Arasta)
to the entrance. Inside, Sinan has produced
another astonishingly light-flooded structure,
the dome some 44 metres (144 feet) above
the floor and spiralled with late Ottoman
calligraphy. There's also some fine marble
work on the *mihrab* and *mimber* (pulpit), and
Iznik tiles beside them.

The mosque has an astrological theme, with
the dome representing the heavens, and a sun
disc surrounded by stars carved into the marble
mimber. The front door sports two bosses
representing sun and moon, also surrounded by
heavenly bodies, a reminder that astronomy was
once central to the Muslim world.

In the *medrese* south-east of the mosque is the
city's **Museum of Turkish and Islamic Arts**.
It has a passable collection of local work, but is
better known for its collection of mementoes from
the oil-wrestling competitions, including a pair of
wrestler's trousers. Just east of the mosque is the
Archaeology and Ethnographic Museum,
which does have something of a routine feel to it,
with Roman and Hellenistic exhibits and local
carpet weaving, in detail.

Down the hill through the park from the
Selimiye stands the **Eski Cami**, the city's oldest
mosque, begun under Beyazıt I in 1403, but not
completed until 1414 by Mehmet I, on account of
Beyazıt's defeat by Tamerlane and a subsequent
bloody power struggle. Known as the first
cousin of the Ulu Cami in Bursa (*see page 251*),
it resembles a clunky series of boxes slotted
together, which is largely what it is, with
nine domed square units fitted into a larger
square. Each represents the heavens above a
four-cornered earth, a design repeated frequently

in Ottoman architecture. The Eski Cami is well fortified, unlike the Selimiye, reflecting the changing fortunes of the empire in the century and a half between them.

Outside you'll see two large Arabic inscriptions painted beside the doorway, one the name of Allah, the other that of Mohammed. Inside, the massive calligraphy continues, though restoration work, due to finish in early 2001, restricts access. Ask an attendant and you might get lucky.

COMMON MARKETS

Outside the Eski Cami, you'll be well placed for the **Bedesten**, another Mehmet I brainwave, which used to fund the mosque's upkeep and was the city's first covered market. This was the city bank vault, too, in Ottoman days, and Bedesten traders were known for their gold and silverware. Lady Montague Wortley described it in her diary as 'glittering everywhere with gold, rich embroidery and jewels'. Though this isn't the case today, it remains an impressive structure of 14 vaulted chambers, recently restored.

Close by is the city's other covered market, the **Semiz Ali Paşa Çarşısı**, begun by Sinan in 1568, Semiz Ali Paşa being the Grand Vizier of the time. Regrettably, a major fire gutted the place in 1992, but it's now up and running again under its multi-domed ceiling. Exiting from the north entrance, you'll see the **Kule Kapısı**, a lone remnant of the original city defences, now with a Byzantine-era base and a late Ottoman top. Used variously after the city's capture as a prison, a school, an armoury, a clock tower and a fire tower, it was once a noted part of the city skyline before an earthquake and urban development did their best to conceal it.

The third of the city's major mosques and attractions is the **Üç Şerefeli Cami**, the 'Three-balconied mosque', north of Hürriyet Meydanı. Contrast this with the Selimiye's elegance and the Eski Cami's boxiness and it fits well as an intermediary stage, full of experiment and deviation, its massive dome, at 24.1 metres (80 feet), a triumph for architects who at the time had not seen Haghia Sophia up close – the mosque was built under Murat II in 1447. The three-balconied minaret contrasts with the mosque's other minarets, known as the Spiralled, Diamond and Ribbed. Some of the mosque's smaller semi-domes are circular, others elliptical, adding to the impression that this is a kind of mosque designer's training course, a composite of 15th-century end-of-term architecture projects.

TRAILS ON THE RIVERBANK

Out of the city centre is one of Edirne's other attractions – walking the river banks. This will bring you to the city's many fine Ottoman

bridges and secondary mosques and medreses, and to **Kırkpınar**, where the annual oil wrestling takes place. Head up Mimar Sinan Caddesi to the banks of the Tunca and you'll find the **Muradiye Camii**, dedicated by Murat II in 1435. He was somewhat into the mystical and had this building first constructed as a Dervish *tekke* (lodge*)* after receiving instructions in a dream from the Mevlana, founder of the order. He later had it turned into a mosque and put the Whirling Dervishes in another lodge in the gardens. Access is tricky, but possible at prayer times, when you can catch an eyeful of some excellent Iznik tilework covering the walls and mihrab.

Going back west from here, following the river and crossing the Kanuni Köprüsü, built by Sinan in 1554 for Süleyman the Magnificent, you come to the islet of **Sarayiçi**, or Kırkpınar, on which sits the stadium for the oil wrestling, usually held in early July. It's also here that the Roma spring festival is held in early May, and a Roma music festival takes off in late June. Sarayiçi is the site of the one-time Ottoman Imperial Palace, the only remains of which are a single tower and a few piles of rubble. This is partly due to the fact that what remained of it by 1877 was comprehensively blown up by the Turks to prevent it falling into Russian hands. The far bank of the island has another Ottoman bridge, the **Fatih Köprüsü**, built in Mehmet II's time. Cross this and you'll find a memorial to the struggle for the city in the Balkan Wars.

Continuing, you'll come to another island in the Tunca on which stands the **Ikinci Beyazıt Külliye** mosque complex. It can be accessed from the city by the 17th-century bridge known as the Yalnızgöz Köprüsü or, more colourfully, the Tek Göz Köprüsü – the 'One-eyed bridge', a reference to its single hump. From the far bank, you cross the Yeni Imaret Köprüsü, which dates from the same time as the külliye.

The complex was built between 1484 and 1488 for Beyazıt II, and included the mosque, schools, a hospital, a soup kitchen, food stores and a lunatic asylum. Nowadays it's a sad old place, closed to visitors, but still worth a stroll round its cracked pavement courtyards and weed-infested terraces.

Evliya Celebi visited here in 1652, to find the külliye's physicians battling with an epidemic of ennui. 'In springtime,' he wrote, 'which is the season of madness, the numbers of patients in the hospital increased because melancholic sufferers from Edirne who had fallen into the depths of the sea of love were admitted.' Here they received treatment that included being forced to wolf down the likes of roasted partridge, pheasant, duck and, more poignantly, nightingale. If found to be faking it just for the free nosh, then, according to the charter of the charitable foundation running the place, 'may they become diseased and may the curse of the Pharaoh and of Croesus be upon them'.

Pondering the spectacle of rooms full of lovesick and soon-to-be overweight Ottomans, heading on round along the dikes and water-meadows you'll hit the Gazi Mihal bridge, the oldest of the lot, as it's an Ottoman respray of a Byzantine original. Making a left here, you'll head back into town, most likely to one of the shady tea gardens around the central square.

Archaeology & Ethnographic Museum

Kadir Paşa Mektebi Sokak 17, behind the Selimiye Camii, (0284 225 1120). **Open** *May-Oct* 8.30am-noon, 1.30pm-5.30pm Tue-Sun; closed Mon. *Nov-Apr* 8am-noon, 1pm-5pm Tue-Sun; closed Mon. **Admission** $1.50.

Bedesten

Bedesten Çarşısı (no phone). **Open** 8am-midnight daily.

Eski Camii

Eski Camii Meydanı (no phone). **Open** hours vary due to restoration work. **Admission** free.
The mosque is always open at prayer times, despite restoration work.

Muradiye Camii

Muradiye Bey Sokak (no phone). **Open** prayer times only. **Admission** free.

Museum of Turkish & Islamic Arts

Kadir Paşa Mektebi Sokak 1, in the Selimiye Camii garden (0284 225 1120). **Open** *May-Oct* 8.30am-noon, 1.30pm-5.30pm Tue-Sun; closed Mon. *Nov-Apr* 8am-noon, 1pm-5pm Tue-Sun; closed Mon. **Admission** $1.50.

Selimiye Camii

Selimiye Camii Meydanı (no phone). **Open** 9am-9pm daily. **Admission** free.

Semiz Ali Paşa Carşısı

Bedesten Çarşısı (no phone). **Open** 8am-midnight daily.

Üç Şerefeli Camii

Hükümet Caddesi, Erdoğan Park (no phone). **Open** 9am-9pm daily. **Admission** free.

Where to eat & drink

Eating out isn't something Edirne is famous for, though there are a number of passable restaurants, such as the **Balkan Piliç** (14 Saraçlar Caddesi, 0284 213 5288, main course $10), but the best is by the river, where the **Lalezar** (Kara Ağaç, near Söğütlük Orman Parkı, 0284 212 2489, main course $15), 11 kilometres (seven miles) south of town, serves riverfront Turkish cuisine, and the **Doruk**, (Karaç Yolu Üzeri Iki Köprü Arası, 0284 224 2844,

main course $15) a meyhane between the Yeni and Meriç bridges on the same route but closer in, serves more of the same.

Where to stay

Top of the range is the **Rüstem Paşa Kervansaray** (57 Iki Kapılıhan Caddesi, 0284 215 2489, rates $60), located in a Mimar Sinan caravanserai with courtyards and cell-like rooms that have a water problem, which is hardly in keeping with the price. It has a superb location, bang in the centre, plus a bar and internet café. There's also the **Otel Şaban Açıkgöz** (9 Çilingirler Caddesi, 0284 213 1404, rates $30-$45), which has better service, or the **Efe Otel** (Maarif Caddesi, 0284 213 6166, rates $30-$40), a new, good-quality arrival in a street full of iffy joints.

Getting there

By coach

Coaches leave hourly from Esenler in Istanbul, the trip taking around three hours. The coach puts you down at the otogar, which is none too convenient, but a short taxi ride will take you to the centre.

By car

Head for the E5, going north, which is a motorway and a clear road, but be ready for toll booths.

By train

The Edirne Ekspresi leaves Sirkeci station at 3.25pm daily, and takes six hours to make the journey. Edirne station is around 3km (2 miles) south-east of the centre, so you'll need to take a taxi.

Getting around

The city is well served with dolmuşes. The one to Kırkpınar leaves from Mimar Sinan Caddesi opposite the Selimiye Camii. It's only about 20 minutes to walk it, though.

Tourist information

There are two tourist information offices, but neither has much information and both are liable to be thrown into confusion by the arrival of tourists. Both stay open until 8pm during oil-wrestling week.

Tourist Information office

Turizm Danışma Müdürlüğü
Talat Paşa Caddesi, near Hürriyet Meydanı (0284 213 9208). **Open** *May-Sept* 8.30am-5.30pm daily. *Oct-Apr* 8am-5pm daily.

Edirne Tourist Department

Edirne Turizm il Müdürlüğü
Talat Paşa Caddesi 76/A (0284 225 5260). **Open** *May-Sept* 8.30am-5.30pm daily. *Oct-Apr* 8am-5pm daily.

The Marmara Islands

Sand, sun, secluded swimming and lots of working-class Turks on holiday.

On the map, this cluster of islands off an improbably shaped peninsula in the western Sea of Marmara appears to have all the makings of a perfect escape from the city. Not too far away, but distant enough to feel like you've actually gone somewhere. What the map doesn't show is that the rocky archipelago is also gifted with beaches of white(ish) sand, and although the Marmara Islands have historically been ignored by visitors from abroad, they've been popular with working-class Turkish holiday-makers for decades. Herein lies the main snag, as the islands' settlements have slowly been submerged beneath a wave of unplanned concrete development. So don't expect quaint fishing villages. But if you're only after a couple of unpretentious days on the beach and are happy staying in a simple pension, then the Marmara Islands could fit the bill.

Avoid July and August unless you want to satisfy an anthropological interest in the holidaying habits of Turkish families. Most of the rest of the year, many guest houses and restaurants are closed and ferry crossings are liable to be cancelled because of bad weather. June and September are the best times to visit. Marmara and Avşa are the two most popular islands. There isn't a whole lot to see or do, and hardly anywhere at all to stay or eat, on the other five in the archipelago.

Getting there

By ferry

From a pier just east of Istanbul's Sirkeci train station, a ferry sets off on the 5-6 hour journey to Marmara and Avşa daily at 8.30am from late June to mid-September. The rest of the year it goes out only on Wednesday and Friday and returns on Thursday and Sunday. Tickets are bought from the TML office (see p239) and cost $5 one-way.

A better option from mid-September to June is to take the regular high-speed ferry from Yenikapı to Bandırma (see p239) and from there a bus to Erdek. From Erdek there are year-round ferries to Marmara Island at 11am (3.15pm Tuesday) and 8pm (10.30pm Friday and Sunday, no service Tuesday).

By deniz otobüsleri

The deniz otobüsleri hydrofoil (see p239) leaves from Bostancı and Yenikapı every morning from the end of June to mid-September, cutting the travel time to just over two hours. A one-way ticket costs $13 and should be reserved well in advance.

Marmara Island – gifted with beaches.

Marmara

Largest and most mountainous of the seven islands, Marmara earnt its name from the marble quarries along its northern coast, source of the celebrated grey and blue streaked Proconnesian used in great buildings such as Haghia Sophia. Clustered beneath the rugged slopes of Ilyas Dağı on the south side of the island, the main settlement, Marmara, certainly wouldn't win any prizes for its native architecture. It's pleasant enough, though, with a small fishing fleet and a row of shore-front cafés where local menfolk sit chatting and playing cards. The short strip of beach is five minutes' walk around the point to the west, past a pair of old buildings saved from the bulldozer by a preservation order, but now left forlorn and unwanted.

When you've exhausted the pleasures in town, take a 15-minute dolmuş ride to Çınarlı on the west coast. Set in a verdant valley, it must have been an idyllic place before all the white-washed concrete. It still retains some charm with a long beach backed by small holiday homes and dotted with fishing boats. Shading the village green are the magnificent plane trees (çınar) from which the village takes its name. One is said to be over 1,000 years old. Several local families rent out rooms and there is a simple eatery on the front.

East from Marmara the road soon turns into a dusty track which winds over the scrubby mountains to the north coast. This side of the island has been carved away by centuries of quarrying. Huge piles of slag pour down the mountainsides and everything is covered in a thick layer of dust. Once exposed, the marble is cut into immense blocks that are trucked off to the harbour at Saraylar.

Marmara's main settlement – no architectural prize-winner, but pleasant enough. *See p249.*

Populated mainly by migrant quarry workers from the Black Sea coast, the only attraction in **Saraylar**, apart from cheap marble, is the so-called **Open Air Museum**. Actually it's more of an archaeological dumping-ground, a small field filled with Roman and Byzantine stonework uncovered in the surrounding area, open to the elements and the public. Nearby, several Roman sarcophagi lie partially buried.

Where to eat

The Marmara Islands are not known for fine dining, but have plenty of cheap and fairly good restaurants. Accommodation usually includes cooking facilities, so if you stay for any length of time you may prefer self-catering.

The height of culinary excellence in Marmara town is the **Melis Restaurant** (Sahil Yolu, Marmara, main courses $3-$6) where you can enjoy meze followed by grilled meat or fish at shady outside tables. Also on the front but nearer the ferry station, the simpler **Birsen Restaurant** (Sahil Yolu, Marmara, main courses $3) serves tasty soups and stews.

Where to stay

Accommodation is basic and many family-run guesthouses and pensions open only for the brief holiday season. When summer starts things fill up fast, so booking is essential. Local families also rent out rooms and small apartments. Ask around in local shops if that's what you're after.

In Marmara, the **Marmara Hotel** (Kole Plaj Yolu, 0266 885 6140, $16-$20) to the west of town near the beach, has simple, clean rooms with huge expanses of local marble, although the toilet cubicles don't afford much privacy. The rooms at the **Şato Motel** (Kole Mevki, 0266 885 5003, $16-$20) are also plain but have sea views from the balcony and more conventional bathrooms.

If you want to stay in Saraylar, there's a simple guesthouse on the square.

Avşa

South of Marmara, Avşa is gifted with the archipelago's best beaches and is thus the most developed of the islands. The main centre, **Türkeli**, is a scrappy affair stretching for several kilometres along the west coast. The beach has clean sand and clear water, but pensions and apartments crowd right up to it. At night the focus shifts to the promenade and the hangar-like cafés by the jetty where families sit drinking *çai* and playing cards.

Across the island, the village of **Yiğitler** is fairly unpromising but has a good stretch of sandy beach, less encroached on by building than Turkeli's. For more secluded swimming you'll need to head off on foot or by bicycle around the southern coast of the island, where numerous small coves await discovery. Another option is the tractor-pulled 'train' that conveys people north of Türkeli to another stretch of beach and yet more holiday homes at Maviköy.

Where to eat

The **Yarar** (Plaj Yolu, Türkeli, main courses $3-$6) in Avşa has been serving decent meze, seafood and meat dishes for 30 years. It's on the beach south of the jetty, so you can enjoy a meal next to the water. On the other side of the quay, the **Köfteci Tarzan** (Türkeli Rıhtım, main courses $2.50) is also deservedly popular.

Where to stay

The **Geçim Pansiyon** (Türkeli, 0266 896 1493, rates $13-$40) has a good choice of rooms and compact, fully equipped apartments. It's set back from the front about 500 metres (550 yards) north of the ferry jetty. South of the jetty on the beach front you could try the **Yalı Pansiyon** (Plaj Yolu, Türkeli, 0266 896 2085, rates $12-$16), a small family-run place with a dozen or so simple rooms overlooking the water.

Bursa

Ottoman historical monuments, a refreshingly hassle-free bazaar, and excellent skiing for beginners.

A view that demonstrates why the Turks call this city Yeşil Bursa – 'Green Bursa'.

Draped along a wide valley with the soaring slopes of Mount Uludağ for a backdrop, the city of Bursa, 250 kilometres (155 miles) south-east of Istanbul, has a wonderful location. As Turkish provincial centres go, it's prosperous and modern with a population of over a million people – and growing fast. Known to the Turks as Yeşil (Green) Bursa, much of the city's green space has been gobbled up in the last 30 years by urban and industrial development, as workers flock to jobs in the textile mills, car factories and canning plants that ring the city.

It's not all new, though. Established in 183 BC by Prusa I of Bithynia, the city prospered in Roman times as an important spa town. The Byzantines, who also had a penchant for wallowing in hot water, graced the city with palaces and fancy bathhouses, and introduced silk production – an industry that thrived until the modern era of mechanisation and international trade. The most celebrated period in Bursan history began in 1326, when it was captured by Orhan Gazi and soon became the first capital of the nascent Ottoman empire. Despite losing its pre-eminent status to Edirne

less than 50 years later, Bursa remained an important provincial town and was graced with many fine buildings by the Ottoman elite.

Today, this architectural legacy, along with the famous hot baths and bazaars, are the attraction for most visitors, but a couple of days wandering around reveals a civilised and, after Istanbul, laid-back city. It's also on a more manageable scale than Istanbul, with most of the sights within walking distance, or at most a ten-minute dolmuş ride of one another.

MOSQUES, BURSA-STYLE

One of the city's largest mosques, the **Ulu Mosque** (Ulu Cami) is slap-bang in the middle of things, making it a convenient place to begin your wanderings. Built from 1396 to 1399 at the behest of Sultan Beyazıt I, it exemplifies the 'Bursa style' of early Ottoman architecture. Inside, the spacious feeling attained in later mosques is absent, with the interior divided by rows of thick columns supporting the multi-domed roof. An unusual feature is the indoor ablution fountain, which fills the mosque with the relaxing sound of running water.

From the mosque's courtyard, steps lead down into the **Emir Han** and the city's retail district: a maze of courtyards, covered streets and bazaars. Historically, hans provided merchants with a secure place to store their wares, while they received food and lodgings and conducted business in the chambers upstairs. The courtyard of the Emir Han, centred on a pretty fountain, is now a busy café where you can rest your legs before delving deeper into the bazaar.

Bursa's covered bazaar is geared for the local population rather than tourists, so you'll find it refreshingly hassle-free after the Grand Bazaar in Istanbul. Bargains to look out for include silk and cotton goods, as well as towels and clothes, all made locally. The bustling main drag, Kapalı Çarşı Caddesi, is lined with gold merchants and shoe shops. Across from the Emir Han, the **Bedesten** harbours more glittering jewellery shops beneath its vaulted ceiling. This, the oldest part of the bazaar, dates from the 14th century, although what you see today has been reconstructed several times, most recently in 1955 after a devastating fire.

Nearby is the **Eski Aynalı Market**, originally a bathhouse. Its vaulted chambers are filled with shops, including Karagöz (*see page 227* **Shadow play**), the modern home of Turkish shadow puppetry. To the east, the 14th-century **Koza Han** is the city's most handsome caravansarai, or old merchants' hostel, restored in 1985 with funds from the Aga Khan Foundation. A two-storey stone affair topped by a veritable forest of peaked chimneys, its shady courtyard, now a popular tea garden, has a dainty prayer hall built over a fountain in the centre. This was traditionally the focus of the city's silk industry and breeders would gather annually in the courtyard to sell sacks of tiny white silk cocoons. Unfortunately, this event is now a thing of the past, though the shops of the han are still devoted to selling silk, these days imported mostly from the Far East and woven into colourful scarves, shirts and ties.

Exiting the Koza Han by its front gate brings you out into a pedestrianised area flanked to the east by the **Orhan Gazi Mosque** (Orhan Gazi Camii). Originally a hostel for wandering dervishes, the mosque was built in 1336 soon after Orhan Gazi, the second Ottoman leader, wrested the city from the Byzantines.

To the south of the Ulu Mosque and the Koza Han, Atatürk Caddesi leads east through the administrative heart of the city and up the smart shopping street of Namazgah Caddesi. Beyond the Setbaşı Bridge, spanning one of the streams that tumble down from the heights of Uludağ, it's a short walk up Yeşil Cadde to the city's most beautiful imperial mosque, the **Green Mosque** (Yeşil Camii). Commissioned by Mehmet I in 1413

after he'd emerged victorious from a bloody ten-year civil war with his two brothers, the mosque was never actually finished. The most conspicuous omission is the lack of a portico on the front of the mosque, although this doesn't detract from the overall harmony of the building. The real action is inside, where a dizzying display of polychrome tiles covers the walls.

Up a flight of steps behind the mosque, the striking **Yeşil Türbe** (Green Tomb) was originally revetted in, you guessed it, green tiles. But following damage in an 1855 earthquake they were replaced with the turquoise tiles from Kütahya that you see today. Inside, the decor is original, with colourful faïence covering the *mihrab* (pulpit) and a verse from the Koran above each window. Naturally, the largest tomb is that of Mehmet I, who financed the construction.

Back on Yeşil Cadde, the **Museum of Turkish & Islamic Art** is housed in the *medrese* of the Yeşil Mosque. Though nowhere near as extensive as its namesake in Istanbul, the museum has some interesting artefacts, such as pre-Ottoman and Iznik ceramics, metalwork and exquisitely decorated Korans.

OTTOMANS ON THE RAMPARTS

At the western end of Atatürk Caddesi rises the rampart-topped Hisar. This is the oldest quarter of town, still home to a few Ottoman timber-frame houses. In a small park at the top the tombs of Osman and Orhan Gazi reside in a pair of nondescript late-Ottoman buildings. There's also a 19th-century clock tower and cafés, favoured by locals in the summer for the cool breeze and the stunning views of the city.

To the west of Hisar, the area of Muradiye takes its name from the Muradiye Külliyesi, an extensive religious complex built for Murat II in 1424. Apart from the mosque, there are a number of interesting imperial tombs, several lavishly decorated with Iznik tiles. The best day to visit is Tuesday, when there's a colourful street market in the surrounding streets, stopping for a bite at the **Darüzziyafe Restaurant** in the mosque's *imaret* (soup kitchens) afterwards.

Another good reason to visit Muradiye is to call in at the **Hüsnü Züber Evi**, an early 19th-century Ottoman residence lovingly restored in 1992 by local artist Hüsnü Züber and dubbed the 'Living Museum'. Hüsnü makes a charming host, showing guests around his immaculate home. Displays include his incredible collection of handmade spoons, collected from across Anatolia or carved personally and decorated using a technique known as 'pyrogravure'.

A short distance north of Muradiye is the **Kültür Park**, where Bursalı go to stroll and drink tea in cafés. Within the park is the city's **Archaeology Museum**, with exhibits dating

Yeşil Türbe (Green Tomb) – damaged in an 1855 earthquake, but the interior decor is original.

back to Roman times, although it can hardly compare with Istanbul's extensive collection.

Several kilometres to the west of the centre, the suburb of **Çekirge** has been famous since Roman times for its thermal baths. Today, the hot, supposedly therapeutic waters attract tourists from across the Middle East. The **Eski Kaplıcalar** (Old Baths) is said to date back to the time of the Byzantine ruler Justinian; the present multi-domed structure was built during the reign of Murat I (1362-89). Recently restored, it now offers a fairly upmarket hamam experience, with a bar and loungers to relax in after cooking yourself in the grand marble pool.

To the west of the Kültür Park the **Yeni Kaplıcalar** (New Baths) has a more down-to-earth clientele. Despite the name, they were constructed nearly 500 years ago at the behest of Süleyman the Magnificent after the mineral waters cured his gout. Next door in the Karamustafa Çamur Banyosu you can subject yourself to a warm, sticky mud bath, said to cure everything from rheumatism to skin complaints.

Archaeology Museum

Arkeoloji Müzesi
Kültür Parkı (0224 234 4918). **Open** 8.30am-noon, 1pm-5pm Tue-Sun; closed Mon. **Admission** $1.50. **No credit cards.**

Eski Kaplıcalar

Çekirge Meydanı, Çekirge (0224 233 9300). **Open** 8am-10.30pm daily. **Admission** $7 men; $6 women; *massage* $5; *scrub* $5. **Credit.** MC, V.

Hüsnü Züber Evi

3 Uzunyolu Sokak, Muradiye (0224 221 3542). **Open** 10am-noon, 1pm-5pm Tue-Sun; closed Mon. **Admission** $1.50. **No credit cards.**

Karagöz

Eski Aynalı Çarşı, Kapalı Çarşı (0224 221 8727). **Open** 9am-5.30pm Mon-Sat; closed Sun. **Credit** AmEx, MC, V.

Museum of Turkish & Islamic Art

Türk ve Islam Eserleri Müzesi
Yeşil Cadde, Yeşil (0224 327 7679). **Open** 8.30am-noon, 1pm-5pm Tue-Sun; closed Mon. **Admission** $1.50. **No credit cards.**

Yeni Kaplıcaları/Karamustafa Çamur Banyosu

Mudanya Caddesi 10, Osmangazi (0224 236 6968). **Open** *men* 5am-11pm; *women & families* 7am-11pm daily. **Admission** $5men; $4 women; *mud bath* $4; *massage* $4; *scrub* $2. **No credit cards.**

Yeşil Türbe

Yeşil Cami
Yeşil Cami yanı (no phone). **Open** 8.30am-noon daily. **Admission** free.

Where to eat

Bursa is the home of the döner kebab, invented by an ingenious cook named Iskender Usta in 1867, now a popular fast food across the world. Bursalı claim that their 'iskender kebabs', sliced döner meat on a *pide* soaked in tomato sauce, yoghurt and butter, are without compare. Judge for yourself at **Hacıbey Iskender** (4 Taşkapı Sokak, main course $3), which bills itself as the original *dönerci* in town, and therefore the world. It's a bustling little place with loads of atmosphere, just off Atatürk Caddesi opposite the town hall.

For something a little more refined try the **Darüzziyafe** (36 Ikinci Murat Caddesi, Muradiye, 0224 224 6439, main course $6-$8), in the arching halls of the Muradiye mosque's *imaret*. The meat-based menu reflects the historic location, with Ottoman-style dishes you won't find anywhere else in town. In keeping with the Ottoman theme, no alcohol is served; instead there's a choice of fruity *şerbet* drinks.

For seafood, seek out **Hasır Izgara** (15 Sakarya Caddesi, Kuruçeşme Mahallesi, main course $4-$7) a lively and informal place in the city's fish market. Many of Bursa's best bars are also found on this street.

Where to stay

Although theoretically it's possible to whistle around Bursa in a very long day trip from Istanbul, the city deserves at the very least an overnight stay. There are plenty of hotels to choose from and prices are generally a bit lower than in Istanbul.

Pamper yourself at the five-star **Hotel Kervansaray Termal** in Çekirge (Çekirge Meydanı, 0224 233 9300, rate $170), which has internal access to the adjacent Eski Kaplıcalar (*see page 253*), as well as a health and fitness centre and a swimming pool.

The **Safran Hotel** (Kale Sokak, Hisar, 0224 224 7216, rates $50-$80) has well-appointed rooms with TV and air-conditioning in a handsomely renovated Ottoman house. What's more, it's in a great location up on the Hisar.

For a cheaper option in the centre of town try the **Hotel Çamlı Bel** (Ulucami Karşısı, Inebey Caddesi 71, 0224 221 2565, rates $19-$30), up a side street opposite the Ulu Mosque.

Getting there

By car

Catch the high-speed ferry from Istanbul's Yenikapı to Yalova (see below for departure times). From there, the city is a 69km (43mile) drive across the mountains.

By bus

Regular buses from the Esenler and Harem bus stations cost $10 and take about three hours. Take one marked 'feribot ile', which uses the ferries across the bay of Iznik to Yalova. The overland bus takes four hours. Kamil Koç (*see p239*) runs buses to Bursa from stands 12-18. Buses operated by Pamukkale (*see p239*) depart from stand 58. It's faster to get a catamaran (*deniz otobüsü*) to Yalova, then a bus to Bursa. From the Kabataş docks south of the Dolmabahçe Palace cats run three times daily weekdays and four times at weekends. They go every two hours from Yenikapı. The one-hour trip costs $6.50. At Yalova dock, buses wait for ferry passengers. To Bursa takes 70 minutes.

Tourist information

Tourist Information Office

Ulu Cami Parkı, Atatürk Caddesi (0224 220 1848). **Open** *Summer* 8.30am-noon, 1pm-5.30pm Mon-Fri; closed Sat, Sun. *Winter* 8am-noon, 1pm-5pm.

Uludağ

High above the city on the flanks of 2,543-metre (8,343-foot) Mount Uludağ stands the ski resort of **Uludağ**. A purpose-built cluster of hotels, each with its own lift, it offers good skiing for beginners, with gentle runs down through the pine trees. It's also a popular winter haunt for the Istanbul *glitterazzi*, who spend more time posing in their pristine ski gear than on the pistes. In summer things are much quieter, with some good walking trails on the mountain.

Where to stay

The **Hotel Kervansaray** (0224 285 2187, rates $85 weeknights, $135 weekends) is at the bottom of the nursery slopes with its own ski hire shop and chairlift. Other facilities include a restaurant, café, bar, pool and sauna to relax those muscles after a day on the slopes. The **Hotel Beceren** (0224 285 2111, rates $80 weeknights, $260 weekends) is a smaller Alpine-style hotel.

Getting there

By car

Uludağ is accessible via a winding 32km (20mile) road from the Bursa suburb Çekirge. *See above* for how to get to Bursa.

By bus

Dolmuşes depart from Orhangazi Caddesi in Bursa. It's $4 one-way for the one-hour trip. Alternatively, cable cars run up the mountain every 30 minutes from 8am to 10pm, weather permitting, from the suburb of Teleferik, accessible by dolmuşes leaving from behind Heykel. From the top of the cable car dolmuşes take you the last six km (3.5 miles) to the resort. The whole trip costs $5 one-way. *See above* for how to get to Bursa.

Iznik & Termal

A history of theological and military clashes underpins beautiful tilework and soothing baths.

From Istanbul, the chance to shift down several gears for the weekend is just a short hydrofoil ride away. With the hot springs of Termal ideal for a pampering winter break, nearby Iznik offers laid-back strolls by the lake, combined with a miniaturised version of Istanbul's massive historical sweep. Both are south of the city in rolling countryside, the trip alone being a useful eye-opener for the way of life lived outside Turkey's main conurbations.

Iznik

Nestled by the side of a lake and surrounded by thick Byzantine walls, the town of Iznik, some 130 kilometres (80 miles) south of Istanbul, was not only once the home of the Ottoman empire's most skilled tilemakers, but also the site of many defining moments in the history of Christianity.

These days the town is a relaxed backwater surrounded by olive groves, still largely contained within the grid plan of the original Hellenistic city. Behind the town rises a range of hills, complete with Roman and early Christian tombs. In front, Lake Iznik provides the townsfolk with one of their principal occupations – the evening stroll along the waterfront, ambling past cafés, teahouses and restaurants.

Originally named Nikaia after the wife of one of Alexander the Great's generals, the town became Nicaea following conquest by the king of Bithynia in the second century BC. Under the Romans, it was a provincial capital that rivalled neighbouring Nicomedia – present day Izmit – and was also known for its wild annual sex and drugs festival, held in honour of its mythical founder, Dionysus.

CHRISTIAN CONTROVERSY

Nicaea hit the headlines when Constantine the Great decided to hold the first Ecumenical Council in the palace (now submerged under the lake opposite the **Çamlık Motel**). This was a crucial moment in the history of Christianity and established a tradition of such meetings to nail down the ground rules of the faith.

In AD 327, the big controversy at Nicaea was over something that later became known as the Arian heresy. The idea, put about by a rabble-rousing Alexandrine, Arius, was that Jesus was not made of the same stuff as God, but was a 'perfect man' created by the Lord to do his work down on Earth.

Nowadays it's hard to understand why this caused riots and massacres throughout the Near East, but, back then, it was explosive stuff. Constantine called the Ecumenical Council to sort it out and, he hoped, restore the peace of his largely Christian empire. After four weeks of debate and, most likely, coercion, the result was a victory for the anti-Arians, Jesus being found to be of 'one substance' with God, and Arius was condemned. Constantine himself took part, and produced the final declaration, still known as the Nicaean Creed.

The town's role in shaping Christianity didn't end there. In the eighth century the Seventh Ecumenical Council rolled in, this time at the Empress Irene's behest, to ditch the policy of iconoclasm, under which icons had been banned from the empire's churches. The council ruled that these pictures weren't so bad after all, as long as people were worshipping what they symbolised rather than the icons themselves.

Byzantine rule over the town ebbed and flowed from then on – it fell to the Selçuk Turks in 1081, then to the Crusaders, then back to the Byzantines, then finally to the Ottomans in 1331. Thus it stayed until 1920, when it was held for two years by the Greek army during its disastrous Anatolian campaign. The town celebrates its liberation by Atatürk's army on 28 November.

WALLS WITHIN WALLS

The road into town from Yalova passes straight by the Istanbul gate built by Roman Emperor Hadrian, a classic of ancient defensive architecture. The double walling leads through to a looped inner courtyard, where any enemy breaking through the outer wall could be contained in a free fire zone in front of the main, inner gate.

The walls stretch round the entire town and take some three hours to walk. Outside Istanbul, they're the most complete Byzantine walls in Turkey. The northern, Lefke gate – also built by Hadrian – is still in use as a road entrance. Outside that, you'll find a low Roman aqueduct and a track that leads on past a Muslim cemetery and into the hills. This is a great walk, leading you past a number of ancient tombs cut into rock

Iznik's **Haghia Sophia** – turbulent history, masterly Byzantine mosaics.

and winding through fields and orchards before finishing at a small mosque on a crest above the town. The mosque has a tea garden, plus a fantastic view of Iznik and the lake.

Back in town, the cross plan of the streets leads to the centre and **Haghia Sophia** on Atatürk Caddesi, formerly the church that hosted the Seventh Ecumenical Council, now a museum. The current, rather wasted, structure is the remains of the Justinian original, adapted and rebuilt after an earthquake in 1065, converted into a mosque in 1331, then burnt down by Tamerlane the Great in 1402. Rebuilt by Mimar Sinan (*see page 38* **Keeping up with the domes's**) in the 16th century, it was reconsecrated as a church during the 1920 Greek occupation, then finally blasted in the fighting over the town that accompanied its

recapture by the Turks. A turbulent history. Its mosaic pavement is a fine example from the Byzantine era.

Heading north up Kılıçaslan Caddesi, you'll see the distinctive minaret of the **Yeşil Camii**, or Green Mosque. Built by Murat I's grand vizier towards the end of the 14th century, the minaret was originally covered with Iznik tiles, though it is now clad in less artful work from Kütahya. Back across the small park is the Nilüfer Hatun Imaret, now the home of the **Archaeological Museum**. Before you go in, pause to see the hooped stump of a minaret to the left of the museum. This is all that remains of the Şeyh Kubettin Camii, blown to bits by the Greeks on their retreat from the city in 1922.

The museum is pretty much lacking in actual Iznik tiles – the best examples of these are in

Istanbul and abroad – but there's a dancing Pan, some interesting gold Roman and Byzantine jewellery and some Selçuk ceramics that suggest some of the artistic roots of later Iznik ware.

It's at the museum that you have to ask for the keys to one of Iznik's most interesting out-of-town sites. Some five kilometres (three miles) back up the Istanbul/Yalova road lies the **underground painted tomb** (*yeraltı mezarı*) of a fourth-century Byzantine trader's family. Its frescoes are splendidly preserved, including two large painted peacocks, early symbols of the Christian faith.

Back in town, Iznik tiles have recently been making a comeback. The golden era for these exquisite ceramics was the 16th century, when captured Persian tilemakers were settled here and began producing the distinctive colours and patterns that came to cover the Ottomans' finest mosques and public buildings.

Since 1995, the **Iznik Foundation**, on Iznik Sahil Yolu, has been trying to recreate this work. Using traditional methods, they have begun turning out new Iznik tiles, which are often finely crafted, but highly pricey. Expect to pay $100-$150 for one of their pieces.

The lake is fine for swimming, though the best places are away from town. Try walking south, where the built-up area vanishes and there are plenty of shady spots along the waterfront.

Archaeological Museum

Müze Sokak, Yeşil Camii Meydanı, Nilüfer Hatun Imareti (0224 757 1027). **Open** *May-Oct* 8.30am-noon, 1pm-5pm daily. *Nov-Apr* 8am-noon, 1pm-5pm Mon-Fri; closed Sat, Sun. **Admission** $1.50. **No credit cards**.

Haghia Sophia

Atatürk Caddesi (information 0224 757 1027). **Open** *Apr-Nov* 9am-noon, 1pm-4pm daily. *Dec-Mar* closed. **Admission** $1.50. **No credit cards**.

Iznik Foundation

Vakıf Sokak 13 (0224 757 6025/www.iznik.com). **Open** 8am-6pm daily. **Credit** MC, V.

Yeşil Camii

Yeşil Camii Meydanı, Kılıçaslan Caddesi (no phone). **Open** prayer times. **Admission** free.

Where to eat & stay

It's possible to do the trip in a day, but more pleasant to stay over, with plenty of choices in accommodation.

The lakeside **Çamlık Motel** (11 Göl Sahili Caddesi, 0224 757 1362, rates $23) has simple, clean rooms and a restaurant with the finest fish kebabs in Anatolia. A dining alternative is the **Barbaros Restaurant**, (22 Göl Sahili Caddesi, 0224 757 5203, main courses $10).

Getting there

By hydrofoil & bus

See p254 for information on ferries to Yalova. For Iznik, turn right out of the sea bus port at Yalova and walk 100 metres (328ft) for the bus station. Minibuses leave here for Iznik regularly, the one-hour trip costing $2.50. The last one back to Yalova leaves at 8pm, in time for the 10.30pm hydrofoil to Yenikapi.

By bus

There are few buses direct to Iznik from Istanbul, but more frequent ones to Yalova from the Asian side bus station at Harem. From Yalova take the dolmuş, which goes frequently from opposite the ferry dock for the 15-minute, $0.50 trip. Dolmuşes also return frequently, but die out around 10.30pm in summer, 8pm in winter. *See p254* for how to get to Yalova.

By car

Take the Boğaziçi Köprüsü, the first bridge from the European side, and follow signs for Izmit. Once there, turn right, then follow signs for Gölcük and Yalova. At Yalova, head south for Orhangazi, then double back along the lakeside for Iznik.

Tourist information

Iznik Tourist Information

Belediye İş Hanı, behind Haghia Sophia (0224 757 1933). **Open** *May-Oct* 8.30am-noon, 1pm-5pm daily. *Nov-Apr* 8am-noon, 1pm-5pm Mon-Fri; closed Sat, Sun.

Termal

Folded into a tree-covered valley, the hot springs of Termal are a boon during the cold and rainy months. With ancient baths set among botanical gardens, the surrounding hills are excellent for trekking, the trees and shrubs laced with a brilliant pattern of reds and golds come autumn.

In Roman times this was Therma Pythia, a health spa said to provide miraculous cures for every ailment. Much the same was true when the resort was revived in the 19th century as part of the European health spa trend, and it still has a medicinal 'purpose, with many long-term residents 'taking the cure' and shorter term day-trippers drinking the mineral-saturated waters.

A highlight is the **Kurşunlu Hamam**, or Great Bath, a small, shallow indoor pool of near-scalding water, built on Byzantine foundations and restored over the centuries by Ottoman and Republican rulers. Get a towel and leave your valuables with the doorman, change into swimming gear and head on into its steamy, atmospheric interior. It also houses steam and massage rooms and is completely mixed, male and female.

Trips Out of Town

Outside, there's the hot water open-air pool, surrounded by changing rooms. It creates a bizarre sight amid winter snow as the steam rises to drift down the narrow valley, hauntingly lingering amongst the dark pines on freezing December evenings.

Further back towards the **Sayav Tesisleri Termal Kaplıcaları Hotel**, but still within the same complex, are separate hamams for men and women, as well as private baths. The latter are great marble tanks with enormous Ottoman faucets that can be rented by the hour for individual use. No one seems to mind if couples or even groups troop in to the same bathroom.

The area around Termal is also good for walking. The 19th-century gardens surrounding the baths feature a number of shorter strolls, or you can head off into the hills for longer trips. Take the road up to Üvespınar, a neighbouring village, from where it's possible to loop back through the woods following signs for Termal, on the way getting some fine views of the surrounding hills. To the west looms the snow-capped peak of Mount Uludağ, Turkey's premier ski resort, with the forests spreading on down to Bursa, capital of the Marmara region (*see page 251*).

Kurşunlu Hamam

Termal Hamam Sokak, 1 (0226 675 7400). **Open** 8.30am-10pm daily. **Admission** *hamam* $5; *outdoor hot pool* $2; *indoor hot pool* $2.

Where to eat & stay

Best option is the **Sayav Tesisleri Termal Kaplıcaları** (5 Termal Hamam Sokak, 0226 675 7400, rates $45), a state-run institution with a useful restaurant.

Getting there

By bus

From Yalova to Termal, take the Termal dolmuş, which goes frequently from opposite the ferry dock for the 15-minute trip costing $0.50. The dolmuşes also return frequently, but die out around 10.30pm in summer, 8pm in winter. A taxi back to Yalova should cost around $10. *See p254* for how to get to Yalova.

By car

Take the Boğaziçi Köprüsü, the first bridge from the European side, and follow signs for Izmit. Once there, turn right, then follow signs for Gölcük and Yalova. At Yalova, keep straight on through the town, and follow signs for Cınarcık and Termal.

Tourist information

There's no information office in Termal, though the staff at the **Sayav Tesisleri Termal Kaplıcaları** (*see above*) are pretty helpful.

Iznik tiles – making a comeback, though not at the local Archaeological Museum.

Çanakkale & Gallipoli

What were once scenes of carnage are now serene sites for remembrance.

Anzac Cove – nothing here now but the cemeteries.

For many visitors, especially those from Australia and New Zealand, no trip to Turkey would be complete without a pilgrimage to the battlefields of the 1915 Gallipoli Campaign, one of World War I's most ambitious and tragic chapters. For Turks, too, the region holds an almost mystic significance, as the campaign made famous a hitherto little-known officer, Mustafa Kemal, later Atatürk. The best base for exploring is the town of Çanakkale, which has a developed tourist industry, offering restaurants and places to stay.

Born out of a need to assist an ailing Russia, the original plan behind the Gallipoli Campaign was for a fleet of British and French battleships to force their way through the Dardanelles Strait, the southern outlet for the Black Sea into the Aegean, and then move on to Istanbul to threaten the city with destruction. It was believed this would cause the surrender of the Ottoman empire, knocking it out of the war. However, after the fleet was repulsed with heavy losses on 18 March 1915, it was decided to land troops on the Gallipoli Peninsula to capture the guns that provided the major threat to the warships.

The initial landings took place on 25 April at Seddülbahir, on the toe of the peninsula, and at Arıburnu, 20 kilometres (12 miles) north. Thanks to poor planning and the stubborn defence of the Ottoman forces, both attacks ended in bloody failure, as did subsequent offensives, such as the August landings at Suvla Bay. Turkish efforts to dislodge the invaders also resulted in massive losses, but no victory. After seven months of deadlocked trench fighting, the Allies admitted defeat and, in the only truly successful operations of the campaign, slipped away from Arıburnu and Suvla in late December 1915 and from the southern front the following January. Though a great victory for the Ottoman empire, it was to be its last: the Allies returned in 1918 to occupy Istanbul and dismember Turkey, giving rise to Mustafa Kemal's revolt.

More than 52,000 Allied soldiers died during the campaign, with Ottoman losses estimated at anything between 57,000 and 200,000. There are 31 Allied cemeteries scattered across the peninsula, with the greatest concentration, and the most visited, around ANZAC Cove, landing place of the Australian and New Zealand forces. Others lie at the south of the peninsula, including a memorial containing the remains of the 15,000 or so men of France and its colonies who died during the campaign. Though slower to commemorate its dead than the Allies, Turkey has also constructed a number of monuments, most notably the Şehitler Anıtı, or Martyrs' Memorial, near Seddülbahir. Most Turkish memorials and cemeteries are of more recent construction, coinciding with an upsurge of interest in the campaign in the past 20 years.

ANZAC COVE AND SUVLA BAY

If you are touring the battlefields and using the town of Eceabat on the European shore of the Dardanelles as your starting point, you travel five kilometres (three miles) back up the highway towards Istanbul before turning left on to the well-signposted road leading to **ANZAC Cove**. After six kilometres (3½ miles), you reach the **Kabatepe Museum and Information Centre** (admission $2), which has a decent display of artefacts from the battle, though it also displays a grisly range of human bones, to 'show the horror of war'.

Most guided tours start at Arıburnu, a small headland at the southern end of ANZAC Cove four kilometres (2½ miles) from the museum, where the first Australians landed at dawn on 25 April (the New Zealanders would come ashore later). The cemetery at Arıburnu is the last resting place of some of those who fell on that first day, many never making it any further than the beach. There is also a memorial to Atatürk, quoting his words of reconciliation that told mothers of the Allied fallen not to weep, as their sons are also now sons of Turkey.

South past Arıburnu and the new site for the 25 April Dawn Service are a series of small cemeteries – **Canterbury**, **Number 2 Outpost**, **New Zealand Number 2 Outpost**, **Embarkation Pier** and **7th Field Ambulance**. The first three mainly contain graves of New Zealand servicemen, as this area was the main sector in which they operated.

Beyond these cemeteries lies the **Suvla Bay** front, rarely visited by tour groups. Following the signs, you can make your way north to **Hill 60 Cemetery**, right on the old front line after the August landings, and the four mainly British cemeteries in the region – **Green Hill**, **Azmak**, **Hill 10** and **Lala Baba**. All four are well marked by road signs in English and Turkish, though the road to Lala Baba on the coast is a rough dirt track almost inaccessible after rain.

Back along ANZAC Cove to its northern arm is **Beach Cemetery**, where lies one of the most famous of the campaign's casualties, the Australian stretcher-bearer John Simpson Kirkpatrick. Known as the Man with the Donkey, for the first four weeks of the battle Simpson, as his headstone names him, carried the wounded down from the front lines to the beach on a stolen donkey, until he was himself killed on 19 May.

Off the coast road, 90 metres (295 feet) past Beach Cemetery, is the opening to **Shrapnel Gully**, which leads up into the hills to what were the Allied front lines. Heavily overgrown, it's a stiff hike, but worth it. This was the supply route for the trenches, with everything from water to ammunition hauled up. At the mouth of the valley is **Shrapnel Gully Cemetery**, one of the larger in the area and lovely in spring when the Judas trees are in flower. On the hill is **Plugge's Plateau Cemetery**, reached by a steep path behind Shrapnel Gully Cemetery.

The tour route then takes you back towards the museum, turning left just before it on the signposted road up to the front-line cemeteries. This leads to the main Australian memorial at **Lone Pine**, scene of some of the heaviest fighting of the campaign. Below the Lone Pine Cemetery, reached by a dirt track, is the little-visited **Shell Green Cemetery**, one of the quietest and most beautiful in the area.

Just off the road south from Lone Pine towards **Johnston's Jolly** (named after an artillery officer who liked to 'jolly the Turks up' with his guns) are many of the trenches and tunnels from the campaign. Some are separated by only a few metres. There are also Allied cemeteries and Turkish memorials such as **Courtney's and Steel's**, **Quinn's**, a monument to Mehmetçik (the nickname for Turkey's soldiers) and the Turkish **57th Regiment** memorial – this is a recent construction with no burials within its walls, despite what some guides will tell you.

Further along the road are the Turkish and Allied memorials at the **Nek**, scene of Peter Weir's 1980 film *Gallipoli*. The road forks and climbs up to **Baby 700 Cemetery**, the high-water mark of the Allied advance on 25 April, past an old Turkish cannon placed here after the campaign and **Chunuk Bair** (Conkbayırı), crowned by both Turkish and New Zealand memorials. It was here that the New Zealand Wellington Battalion reached the final objective of the April landings. Of the 670 men who started the battle, only 69 left the hill four days later. Most of the dead are buried in unmarked graves in the nearby Chunuk Bair Cemetery. The Allied advance was swept away by a counter attack led by Mustafa Kemal, saving the campaign and his country. Though there is another graveyard, **Farm Cemetery**, below Chunuk Bair, it is here that most of the guided tours end before turning back to Eceabat.

ANZAC Day

The region's biggest day of the year, for tourists at least, is 25 April. While Çanakkale has other ceremonies to mark the Gallipoli campaign, notably on 18 March to commemorate the defeat of the Allied fleet, ANZAC Day is the one that draws the crowds.

In the days leading up to the 25th, visitors start drifting into Çanakkale, turning the region into an Antipodean colony. Where their forefathers failed in 1915, latter-day ANZACs annually succeed in their now welcome invasion, a yearly boost for the local economy. Many arrive early, but thousands of others come down the night before on tours organised from Istanbul, run by the many travel agencies in Sultanahmet. Companies in Çanakkale and Eceabat also run special ANZAC Day tours, taking in most of the commemorative ceremonies, as well as providing transport, guides and breakfast.

The day itself begins with the Dawn Service at 5.30am, now held at a purpose-built site near where the first boatload of Australians landed on 25 April 1915. To get a good vantage point, it is advisable to arrive early. The local police

close some of the roads on the peninsula after about 3am, citing security, and parking is limited, so you might want to camp overnight.

Until recent years, the service was a rather friendly *ad hoc* affair, with no official speeches, and few officials or prayers. However, the 75th anniversary of the battle in 1990 changed that. With thousands instead of hundreds now attending, proceedings have become more formal. The days of some New Zealand or Australian tourist lugging a bugle on his travels to play the 'Last Post' as the sun rises over ANZAC Cove are gone.

Following the 45-minute Dawn Service there is a breakfast break before ceremonies resume later in the morning. Wreath-laying services are held at the British, French and Turkish memorials at Seddülbahir on the toe of the peninsula, followed by services at the Australian memorial at Lone Pine and the New Zealand monument at Chunuk Bair. As most of the visitors are Australians or New Zealanders, not all tours cover the ceremonies at Seddülbahir. If you wish to attend these, check before booking.

Trips Out of Town

THE SOUTHERN BATTLEFIELDS

To reach the Franco-British sector of the Gallipoli battlefields, either head down the well-signposted coast road along the Dardenelles from Eceabat, or, if coming from the ANZAC Cove region, turn south on the road just before the Kabatepe Museum. There is an occasional minibus from Eceabat to the village of Seddülbahir, otherwise your own transport is required, as no tours visit these areas except by special arrangement. Most of the area has returned to being the farmland it was before the campaign, unlike the more rugged ANZAC region, which remains largely as it was in 1915.

Clustered around the west of Seddülbahir is the **Cape Helles Memorial**, commemorating those of the British empire forces who died but have no known grave, and the **V Beach Cemetery**, which contains the remains of many who died on 25 April when British forces attempted to land on the nearby beach. One and a half kilometres (one mile) to the west is **Lancashire Cemetery**, while three kilometres (two miles) to the north is **Pink Farm Cemetery**, with **Twelve Tree Copse Cemetery** and a memorial to New Zealand soldiers who fell in this sector.

Again starting at Seddülbahir, travelling inland on the northern road is **Skew Bridge Cemetery** and **Redoubt Cemetery**, four kilometres (2½ miles) further on. Just before Skew Bridge, the road forks to the right, leading to the French memorial and a vast, table-like monument to the Ottoman soldiers. There is also a small museum at the base of the Turkish monument (admission $2), with much the same displays as at Kabatepe.

Where to stay, eat & drink

If planning a visit to coincide with ANZAC Day, take a tour of the battlefields the day before or the day after. ANZAC Day itself, 25 April, attracts crowds and tour buses racing from one commemorative service to the next (*see page 261* **ANZAC Day**).

Another consideration if planning an ANZAC Day pilgrimage is that, although accommodation in Çanakkale and Eceabat proves sufficient for most of the year, come late April the 'House full' signs go up, as tour companies reserve most beds months in advance. However, **TJ's Hotel** in Eceabat (*see below*) has a good record of housing latecomers.

Eceabat

TJ's Hotel, also known as TJ's Place (Cumhuriyet Caddesi 5a, 0286 814 2940, rates $6), is just 100 metres to the right of the ferry dock. It offers 54 beds in mixed double, twin share and five-person rooms for approximately $6 per person. All 22 rooms have

en suite bathrooms. TJ's also operates daily tours for $20 including packed lunch.

Apart from the usual Turkish fare served up in Eceabat's various family-run eateries, the **Liman Restaurant** by the wharfside offers fresh seafood and cold beer.

Çanakkale

The main crossing point over the Dardanelles and with an active tourist industry, Çanakkale has a wide range of accommodation, and bookings are rarely needed except for ANZAC Day. Top of the range is the four-star **Akol** (Kordonboyu, 0286 217 9456, rates $60-$90). This waterfront hotel has bars, a restaurant and pool. A favourite with backpackers is the **Yellow Rose Pension** (5 Yeni Sokak, 0286 217 3343, rates $7-$15). It has singles and doubles with a bathroom, or dorm beds for $4 per night. Battlefield tours and other travel arrangements can also be made.

Getting there

By bus

Buses to Çanakkale depart hourly from Istanbul's Esenler bus station (*see p238*). Either **Radar** (0212 658 0552) or **Çanakkale Truva** (0212 658 3640) will get you to Eceabat in about five and a half hours for around $10. From there, it's a 25-minute ferry trip to Çanakkale. For the less adventurous, **Pasifik Tours** (Divan Yolu 34, Sultanahmet, 0212 512 3050, pasifiktours@turk.net) can provide travel, a one-day tour of the various battlefields and a night's accommodation. Call for prices.

By car

Take the E5 motorway out of Istanbul, turning left onto the E25 some 80 kilometres (50 miles) out of the city. Follow the road through Tekidağ and Keşan then bypass the town of Gelibolu to Eceabat. The 320km (200mile) trip takes four hours if the traffic is not heavy, as it often is on summer weekends.

Getting around

Tours to the ANZAC battlefields can be arranged through either **TJ's Hotel** (*see above* **Where to eat, drink & stay**) or **Troy-ANZAC Tours** in Çanakkale (Yalı Caddesi 6, 0286 217 5847). A six-hour tour of the peninsula costs $20 and includes entrance to the museum and a packed lunch.

For the keen walker, minibuses marked for Kabatepe leave from Eceabat's main square and can drop you at the museum south of the ANZAC battlefield area. From there it is a further five-kilometre (three-mile) hike to ANZAC Cove. The buses are frequent in summer. To reach the southern sector, take a minibus to Seddülbahir. There are occasional buses from Eceabat, with more regular services from Kilitbahir, a village five kilometres (three miles) down the Dardanelles. Kilitbahir is also served by a frequent ferry to and from Çanakkale.

Troy & Assos

A day in a fabled city, a night by a picturesque harbour.

South of Çanakkale stretches a gently undulating region of unspoilt rural scenery known in ancient times as the Troad. Bounded by the forested mountains of the Kaz Dağı in the east and lapped by the Aegean to the west, it's an area that receives scant attention from tourists, but for two notable exceptions: the remains of the legendary city of **Troy**, and the village of **Assos** to the south, picturesquely sited on the Gulf of Edremit.

Troy

Inhabited almost continuously for over 4,000 years, Troy was a strategic juncture on ancient trade routes. It both prospered and grew, was conquered and sacked. It was occupied by Mycenaeans, later by Greeks, then Alexander the Great popped by. Some 600 years later Emperor Constantine nearly picked the city instead of Byzantium as his New Rome.

Troy is best known, however, for its role in Homer's *Iliad*, the Bronze-Age epic of how the Greek army of Agamemnon lays siege to the city, eventually outwitting the defences with the help of a wooden horse.

Troy's past was of little concern to the Ottomans and from the 14th century it slipped into obscurity, buried and forgotten except as myth. So it remained until an obsessive amateur archaeologist, Heinrich Schliemann, dug a trench through the mound at Hisarlık in 1871 and struck gold, quite literally, uncovering the remnants of the lost city.

Despite its fabled past, visiting Troy can be unsatisfactory. It takes a lively imagination to envisage the ancient city from the scant visible remains. It's also a complex site, involving layer upon layer of ruins from successive civilisations. But a new signage system has improved things and the *Sightseeing Plan for Troy* (available from the gift shop) is useful.

The first thing that greets you is a replica of the wooden horse. A scale model based on images from ancient coins found at the site, it's now a compulsory photo-stop, filled with European tourists rather than Achaean warriors. Nearby is the visitor's centre, offering some interesting displays. From there a path strikes off in an anti-clockwise direction around the site, passing between the perimeter walls of Troy VI (1800-1275 BC) and the Roman city. The circuit takes at least an hour; highlights include a scenic

Troy's wooden horse. A replica, of course.

terrace, once part of the Temple of Athena; a stone ramp that gave access to Troy II; and a well-preserved Roman odeon.

Ruins of Troy

Open *Summer* 8am-7.30pm daily. *Winter* 8am-5pm daily. **Admission** $1.50. **No credit cards**.

Where to eat

At Troy food is limited to snacks on sale at the site shop or you can get a meal at the **Hotel Hisarlık** (main course $5; *see below*).

Where to stay

There are several simple hotels in the sleepy village of Tevfikiye, near the ruins of Troy. Try **Hotel Hisarlık** (Ana Yol, 0286 283 1126, rates $20-$30). But it's better to stay 32 kilometres (20 miles) away at **Çanakkale** (*see page 259*) with its wider choice of food and accommodation.

The remnants of Assos's Byzantine citadel.

Getting there

By car

Troy is a 20-minute drive south along the E87 from Çanakkale. Follow signposts for Ayvacık and Izmir, turning right after about 30 kilometres (19 miles). For how to get to Çanakkale, *see p262*.

By bus

Dolmuşes to Troy depart from a garage on Atatürk Caddesi in Çanakkale hourly during the day at a fare of $1.50. Finding the dolmuş station is the hard part: walk inland from the docks on Cumhuriyet Bulvarı and eventually turn right on Atatürk Caddesi. Departure point is 300 metres (985 feet) up on the right-hand side before a bridge. For how to get to Çanakkale, *see p262*.

Assos

From Troy, on the E87, it's about 50 kilometres (30 miles) south to Ayvacık, and a further 17 kilometres (11 miles) down a twisting country lane to the village of Behramkale, as Assos is officially known.

Or, with a decent road map you could head off the E87 at Ezine, wind east to the ruins of Alexandria Troas, then go south along the coast to **Gülpınar**, home of a Greek temple to Apollo Lord of the Mice.

Built on to a hill among the ruins of ancient Assos, the village of **Behramkale** is a tonic. An ancient sarcophagus by the road as you approach sets the tone for what has remained a pretty village of stone houses, thanks to a well enforced preservation order. The sinuous main street leads up through a small square to the ruins of a 14th-century mosque and the remnants of Assos's Byzantine citadel. Crowning the hill and enjoying a stupendous view across the Gulf of Edremit to the island of Lesbos is a temple dedicated to Athena.

The rest of the ancient city, established in the seventh century BC and home to a school of philosophy established by Aristotle, is scattered across the steep, seaward side of the acropolis.

Below the village is a tiny fishing harbour, brightly painted boats tied up along its stone wharf. Clustered at the waterside are hotels and restaurants, and there's a long stretch of beach at Kadırga, four kilometres (two and a half miles) to the east. Things can get claustrophobic in peak season; time your visit to avoid August crowds.

Where to eat

All hotels below have restaurants with tables outside, most by the waterside. Try the **Assos Hotel** (main courses $4-$6; *see below*).

Where to stay

Most Assos hotels are in solid stone buildings at the harbourside. It's a 20-minute walk from the main village, and there's an hourly dolmuş in summer. Best positioned is the **Assos Hotel** (Assos Iskele, 0286 721 7017, rates $45-$75) which has small but comfortable rooms with en suite bathrooms and lovely sea views.

The newer **Assos Kervansaray** (Assos Iskele, 0286 721 7093, rates $50-$85) has similar rooms and better facilities, including pool, sauna and games room.

Slightly simpler is the **Yıldız Saray** (Assos Iskele, 0286 721 7025, rates $45-$60) on the right before you reach the harbour, which also has a sister hotel overlooking the beach at Kadırga. The cheaper **Dolunay Pansiyon** (Behramkale Köyü, 0286 721 7172, rates $15-$20) is up in the main village.

Getting there

By car

From Troy, south along the E87 until Ayvacık, 51 kilometres (32 miles) south of Çanakkale. From there follow signs to Assos (Behramkale).

By bus

Take any southbound bus, for example to Izmir, from the docks in Çanakkale and get off in Ayvacık. From Ayvacık there are hourly dolmuş in summer between 8am-5pm, they run less frequently in winter between 8am-4pm. For how to get to Çannakale, *see p262*.

Directory

Directory

Getting Around

Arriving by air

Istanbul's international air gateway is Atatürk Airport, approximately 25 kilometres (15 miles) west of the city centre in Yeşilköy. Its new international terminal (*dış hatlar*) has all the usual stuff, including shops, restaurants, bars, cafés, post office, 24-hour banking, exchange bureaux, car hire outlets, a tourist information office and a hotel reservation desk. It's also very compact and easily navigated. From landing to clearing customs usually takes no more than about 20 minutes. Beware when departing though, as security checks prior to check-in can take up to 30 minutes. Turn up a good hour and a half before your flight.

Construction of a new domestic terminal (*iç hatlar*) is underway and is expected to be completed by mid 2001.

Construction has also begun on a second international airport in Kurtköy on the fast-growing Asian side of the city. Sabiha Gökçen International Airport is expected to be completed some time in 2001, with an international terminal capable of handling three million travellers annually.

Atatürk International Airport

Atatürk Hava Limanı Yolu (24-hour English language airport and flight information 0212 663 6400 ext 4155 or 4157).

Major airlines

In addition to the following, Istanbul is served by many international carriers, including Air France, KLM, Lufthansa, SAS and Swissair.

British Airways

Istanbul 0212 234 1300 UK 0845 773 3377/ www.britishairways.com

Istanbul Airlines

Istanbul 0212 423 7000 UK 020 8688 7555

Turkish Airlines

Istanbul 0212 252 1106 (ticket prices) 0212 6636363 (bookings) UK 020 7766 9300/ www.turkishairlines.com.

Connections to the city

There are two options from the airport: bus or taxi. The choice depends to some extent on where you're staying. A company called Havaş operates the express airport bus, which departs half-hourly between 6am and 11pm from a signposted halt outside the arrivals hall. It makes one stop in Aksaray *en route* to its terminus in Taksim Square – which is fine if you're staying in Beyoğlu, around Taksim or at one of the five-stars in Harbiye, but not much use otherwise. The fare is around $3, collected by an attendant once the bus is moving.

If you're heading for the hotels in and around Sultanahmet, take a taxi. There's a large taxi rank right outside the arrivals hall. Fares are metered, and to the area around the Hippodrome and Haghia Sophia should be around $10-$12. The ride takes about 20 minutes, but can stretch to as much as 45 minutes if the traffic's bad.

Car rental desks can be found in the arrivals hall. They all operate 24 hours daily (*see page 270*).

Arriving by train

The days of the Orient Express are long gone; rail travel from Europe to Istanbul is now the preserve of backpackers and the lower-income end of Turkey's Balkan diaspora. From Greece, the only direct route to Istanbul is from Thessalonika, with a daily 7am departure taking anything from 10 to 16 hours to cover the 850 kilometres (510 miles). The only other international services are the daily Balkan Express between Budapest and Istanbul (31 hours) and a service between Bucharest and Istanbul (17 hours).

Trains from Europe pull in at Sirkeci Station (*gar*), beside the Golden Horn in Eminönü. From here a taxi to Taksim or Sultanahmet costs less than $2. Trains from the east and south terminate at Haydarpaşa Station on the Asian side. The two stations are connected by ferries, though there's a tunnel link on the drawing board. A 24-hour info line (0216 348 8020) serves both stations but in Turkish only. Call 0216 336 4470 for reservations.

Sirkeci Station

Ankara Caddesi, Eminönü (0212 527 0051).

Haydarpaşa Station

Haydarpaşa Istasyon Caddesi, Kadıköy (0216 336 0470).

Arriving by coach

Turkish coach companies (such as Ulusoy and Varan) run regular direct services from many European cities. Be prepared for lengthy waits at the border – particularly with Bulgaria, where it can take up to three hours to clear customs procedures. Travellers arriving by coach disembark at the vast main international and intercity bus terminal (*otogar*) in the western district of Esenler, approximately ten kilometres (six miles) from the city centre. There are courtesy minibuses to Taksim and Sultanahmet. There's also an underground line known as the 'light metro' that connects the terminal to Aksaray, but, given that this is a district far from where most visitors want to be, the service is of little use.

Esenler bus terminal
Uluslararası Istanbul Otogarı
Büyük Istanbul Otogari, Bayrampaşa (0212 658 0505). **Open** 24hrs daily.

Ulusoy
Inönü Caddesi 59, Gümüşsuyu (domestic routes 0212 252 3787/ international 0212 658 3000/ www.ulusoy.com.tr). **Open** 24hrs daily. Tickets sold 7.30am-1.30am. **Credit** AmEx, MC, V.
Buses to and from Greece twice weekly (Thessalonika, 12hrs, $40; Athens 22hrs, $60), and once a week to Germany via Greece and Italy (two days, $100). Bookings can be made through the website.

Varan
Inönü Caddesi 29, Gumussuyu (0212 251 7474/www.varan.com.tr). **Open** 24hrs daily. **Credit** AmEx, DC, MC, V.
Weekly buses to and from Thessalonika, Athens and Vienna (44 hours, $75, plus $20 for ferry). Bookings through the website.

Public transport

Public transport, though cheap, isn't often the best way to get around. The system is designed to get residents between the centre and the suburbs, and it doesn't serve the needs of visitors very well.

Fortunately there are just two main areas in which you're likely to spend the majority of your time, the sightseeing districts around Sultanahmet and the entertainment centre of Beyoğlu over the other side of the Golden Horn. Both of these are easily explored on foot. In

Beyoğlu walking is the only option, as, apart from a 'historic' tram, the area isn't served by public transport south of Taksim Square.

Getting between Sultanahmet and Beyoğlu is less than straightforward and involves a tram down to Eminönü and then either a bus to Taksim Square or a walk across Galata Bridge and the funicular up the hill.

Listings in this guide frequently don't include any public transport information, simply because there is often no convenient bus or tram. For further information on getting around, *see page 62.*

Despite new landfill roads along the coasts, demolition of historical neighbourhoods to widen existing roads and constant tinkering by the municipality to create new routes, Istanbul endures permanent gridlock along major arteries. To combat congestion the city began constructing modern tram and metro systems in the 1990s, but as yet there is still no true city-wide transport network. Instead there is a variety of different modes from light railways to ferries, but these tend to be localised, serving only a small portion of the city. It is thus often difficult to work out the best way to get from A to B. The usual answer is to simply grab a cab.

However, there are journeys that are best undertaken by public transport. Moving around the Sultanahmet area is definitely easier by tram, while the fastest, most convenient way to get to shopping and business districts in Nişantaşı, Şişli, Mecidiyeköy, Etiler and Levent is via the new metro line. Buses are useful for heading up the Bosphorus coast to Ortaköy, Arnavutköy, Bebek and beyond, while trips to the districts of Üsküdar and Kadıköy on the Asian side are best undertaken by ferry.

Akbil

Akbil is an electronic travel pass that can be used for all forms of public transport except dolmuşes, minibuses and sea buses. It's a little silver metal stud fixed into a plastic grip, for which you pay a small refundable deposit. Booths at all main bus stations, including those in Eminönü, Taksim and Beşiktaş, sell Akbils and electronically charge them up with units. To use, firmly press the circular metal bit into the socket on the orange machine located next to the driver on buses or to the left of special turnstiles at all metro, light rail, tram and ferry boat stations. Recharge at automatic Akbil machines located at large bus stations and ferry terminals or at specially designated Akbil booths around town.

Buses

Most city buses (*belediye otobüsü*) are operated by the municipality, but there are also privately run versions (*halk otobüsü*). Municipal buses are red or green, private ones orange or blue. Tickets for municipal buses must be bought before boarding (they won't take money on the bus), whereas on private buses you pay a conductor seated just inside the doorway (he won't take municipal tickets). Tickets for municipal buses are sold from booths at main stops and stations; you can also buy them from newsstands for a 30 per cent premium. When boarding, deposit your ticket in the metal box near the driver. Rather than empty the full boxes, drivers just torch the contents, so don't be alarmed by spirals of smoke coming out of the slot where your ticket goes.

Newer buses display electronic signboards with route information. Bus stands

The Traffic Monster

As your taxi suddenly veers across four lanes of traffic to make an unsignalled exit and you nearly puncture the upholstery attempting to cling on, relax in the knowledge that you have at least enjoyed an authentic Istanbul experience: an encounter with the dreaded Traffic Monster.

Istanbulites are notoriously bad drivers. It's a macho thing. Once upon a time, a Turk's pride rested on his horsemanship, now it's about asserting superiority on four wheels. It's about speed and aggression, with no quarter given, like *Ben Hur*, but with Fiats instead of chariots. Pity the woman driver, as no Turkish man worth his swagger can tolerate a woman ahead of him. Worst of all are the taxi drivers, who relish their status as cocks of the road, hurtling around with one hand on the wheel, oblivious to other road users as they turn to you to vent their feelings about last night's Galatasaray game or some other compelling matter.

No surprise then to learn that more than twice as many people have died on Turkey's roads over the last decade than in the army's entire 16-year campaign against Kurdish separatism. This does at least worry the authorities. Consistently high road mortality rates have resulted in a lot of hand-wringing, but not much effective legislation.

That's all right, though, because now the real culprit has been found: it's the *Trafik Canavarı*, or 'Traffic Monster'. Twelve people killed in a multi-vehicle pile up? The work of the Traffic Monster! In an amazing abdication of responsibility, this voracious beastie – pictured on road signs at accident black spots – has been blamed for road carnage in much the same way as a force of nature.

Slaying the monster is a big issue of the moment. Imams delivering Friday sermons at the mosque have recently been given to cautioning vigilance. More direct action has been taken by the traffic police, whose low salaries have traditionally meant that a little sweetener offered by stopped motorists was enough to let the monster get away. They recently instituted a scheme in which any drivers hauled over for speeding were fined and subjected to a compulsory eye test to see if they could even read the signed limits that they were breaking. It's an initiative that's gone down a storm with many of those caught, as the fine works out at far less than the bill at an optician's. The Traffic Monster looks set to rage on.

---

also have route maps. Still, the sheer number of routes and the fact that there are no set timetables can make bus travel a bewildering experience. If you're having problems then fellow passengers are always a good source of help; scribble your destination on a scrap of paper and someone is bound to be able to point you in the right direction. Bus services run from 6am to 11pm.

Dolmuşes & minibuses

Dolmuş means 'full', a hangover from the days when passengers crammed into vintage American cars, sputtering out the last years of their lives as community taxis – drivers only set off when every seat was taken. The municipality ordered that the old cars be replaced by more spacious yellow diesel minibuses, but the name has stuck. Dolmuşes run fixed routes (points of origin and final destination are displayed in the front window), but with no set stops. Passengers flag the driver down to get on (if there's room) and holler out to be let off. There's just one fixed fare, no matter how far you go. Ask a fellow passenger how much or just watch what everybody else is paying. Dolmuşes run later than buses, often as late as 2am.

Minibuses are the crowded, less comfortable cousins of dolmuşes. Fares are lower, but chances are you'll make your journey standing while being blasted by tinny Turko-pop. Pay and get on/off as you would a dolmuş. The main minibus route is from Taksim/Beşiktaş to the upper Bosphorus districts. They are also prevalent over on the Asian Shore.

Metro & trams

New metro and tram systems provide a comfortable, efficient alternative to clogged roads and overcrowded buses. However, coverage remains scant. At present the metro, opened in autumn 2000, runs only from Taksim north to the district of 4th Levent, stopping at Osmanbey, Şişli and Levent. Given that these are largely business and wealthy residential districts, few of Istanbul's visitors benefit. There's also the 'light metro', connecting the district of Aksaray (west of the Grand Bazaar) to the Esenler bus terminal beyond the city walls. Few visitors will ever have cause to use it.

The city's single tramway runs from Zeytinburnu (out toward the airport) via Aksaray to Sultanahmet and on to terminate at Eminönü beside the Galata Bridge. This is a genuinely useful service for visitors, linking tourist spots such as the Grand Bazaar, Haghia Sophia and Sultanahmet Mosque, Topkapı Palace and the Egyptian Bazaar and Golden Horn area. You can also use the tram to visit the city walls. Where relevant, tram stops are given in the listings throughout this book. Tokens are bought in advance from kiosks at the tram stops, which are fed into the automatic barriers to allow you on to the platform. A single trip costs about 30 cents.

Extensions to link up the two metro lines and tram are expected to be completed by 2004.

Tünel & tram

A 125-year-old funicular, known as the tünel, ascends from Karaköy, near the north end of the Galata Bridge, up to Tünel Square at the southern end of Istiklal Caddesi. It's only a very short run, but it saves an extremely tiring climb up steeply sloping streets (or an equally tiring descent). It connects with a reproduction 19th-century tram that shuttles up Istiklal Caddesi to Taksim Square and back. Given that it's a mile-and-a-half-long drag the idea has merit, but why then make the lone tram so small and twee? Akbil (*see page 267*) can be used for either, but regular bus tickets can not. You need to buy a token for the funicular at the entrance, and a ticket for the tram from the Tünel Square funicular station or from a vendor in Taksim Square.

Ferries

There's a range of boats and ships of all sizes shuttling back and forth between the European and Asian shores. The main services are between Eminönü and Karaköy on the European side and Üsküdar and Kadıköy on the Asian. These are large, once-white state-run ferries capable of carrying hundreds. Departures are every 20 minutes or so. *See page 105.*

Less frequent are the services that go up the European Bosphorus coast, starting at Eminönü and calling at Karaköy, Kabataş, Beşiktaş, Ortaköy and Bebek. Again, these *vapur* are big, state-run boats, but they run only at peak commuter times. *See page 101.*

In addition to the big ferries, there are sleek modern catamarans (called *deniz otobüsleri* or 'sea buses'), faster but considerably more expensive. They run from Yenikapı and Kabataş, with a few services from Eminönü and Karaköy, crossing over to the Asian shore terminals of Bostancı and Kartal. These are not routes many visitors use, but are a real time-saver when travelling to suburban districts farther out along the Asian and European shores of the Sea of Marmara.

There's an extremely popular Bosphorus tour that departs three times daily and lasts three or five hours depending on the sailing. *See also page 241.*

Şehir Hatları İşletmesi

(0212 522 0045). **Departures** *June-Sept* 10.30am, noon, 1.30pm daily. *Oct-May* 10.30am daily. **Tickets** $2.75. **No credit cards.** Boats depart from the Eminönü quay. Look for Bosphorus line 3 (3 Nolu Boğaz Hatti Iskelesi). The boats call at Beşiktaş, Kanlica, Yeniköy, Sariyer, Rumeli Kavaği and Anadolu Kavaği, where they stop for two hours before returning. Total trip time is five hours.

Bicycling

One look at the traffic in Istanbul will explain why there are hardly any cyclists on the road. In addition, the streets themselves are unfriendly, with slippery cobbles, hazardous tyre-trapping tram lines and more potholes than surface. There are exceptions. The Bosphorus shore road north of Ortaköy is great for biking; a wide, well surfaced road with fine views and sea breezes. The Princes' Islands are also fun on two wheels, and in fact a bike is one of the few options for getting around, as cars are banned. Bicycles can be hired on the islands. For bicycle repair facilities *see page 176.*

Walking

Given that public transport often doesn't go where you want to go, walking is absolutely the best way of getting around Istanbul. The main vistors' areas of Sultanahmet, the Bazaar Quarter and Beyoğlu are all relatively compact and perfect for exploring on foot. Main roads are few, while backstreets tend to be narrow and sloping and better suited to pedestrians than cars, though the city's many hills mean that calves will ache at the end of a day's exploring.

Taxis

Taxis are numerous and there's never a problem finding one whatever the time, day or night. Just stand at the kerb and hail them. Licensed taxis are bright yellow, with a roof-mounted *taksi* sign and plate-number stencilled on the door. They are all metered. If the meter isn't running, get out and grab another cab. During the day the meter displays the word *gündüz* (day rate) and starts off with the equivalent

Directory

of 60 cents on the clock. From midnight to 6am it shows *gece* (night rate) and kicks in at $1. Running rate during the day is about 60 cents per kilometre (about $1 per mile); depending on the route and traffic, a trip between Sultanahmet and Taksim Square costs $3-4. There's no room for cheating or haggling and even tips are not required. However, like New York, where taxi driving is the expedient option for new immigrants, plenty of Istanbul taxi drivers (*taksi şoförü*) don't know the streets outside their own neighbourhoods. It's not unusual to have your driver ask directions of other cars and passers-by. If you cross the Bosphorus bridges then the toll is added to the fare.

There is no city-wide dispatching system. Hotels, restaurants, bars, clubs and so on will call the nearest taxi stand, although taxis usually wait in front of such venues.

Driving

In most big cities, if you don't know the place then driving is not recommended. That goes double in Istanbul, where heavy congestion is dealt with by flooring the accelerator whenever the slightest opening allows it – the limit in urban areas is 50kmh (30mph), rising to 120kmh (75mph) on motorways. Although Turkish road signs conform to international protocol and drivers and passengers must wear seat belts, observance of traffic regulations seems to be optional (*see page 268* **The Traffic Monster**).

On the positive side, petrol prices are lower than in most European countries. Filling stations are dispersed throughout the city. Unleaded is *kurşunsuz*.

Street parking is difficult. Avoid the hassle by using car parks, which are plentiful. At most open-air car parks it is

standard practice to leave keys so cars can be moved around. Upscale clubs, bars and restaurants usually have valet parking; you are expected to tip around $3 for the service.

Paperwork

If you plan to take your own car to Turkey, prepare to be enmeshed in red tape and bowed under a weight of paperwork. Drivers are asked to provide registration documents and a valid driving licence at the point of entry. Cars, minibuses, caravans, towed sea craft and motorcycles can be taken into Turkey for up to three months without a Carnet de Passage or triptyque. Your vehicle is registered in your passport and you are issued a certificate that should be carried at all times, along with your driving licence and passport. If you stay in Turkey for more than three months, you either have to leave and re-enter the country, or apply to the **Turkish Touring & Automobile Association** (*below*) for a triptyque. You will not be allowed to visit another country without taking your vehicle unless you first visit the nearest Customs Office to cancel the registration of the car in your passport. Drivers from Europe also need a Green Card (available from your insurance company). There is a rarely enforced law requiring cars to be equipped with a fire extinguisher, first-aid kit and two warning triangles. You must also have an international driving licence.

Turkish Touring & Automobile Association

Türkiye Turing ve Otomobile Kurumu
Oto Sanayi Sitesi Yanı, Seyrantepe, 4 Levent (0212 282 8140/fax 282 8042).
Turkey's equivalent of the AA.

Breakdown services

Gökşenler
Atatürk Oto Sarayi Sitesi, 2. Kisim, Gökşenler Plaza 213, Maslak (0212 276 3640/). **Open** 8.30am-6pm Mon-Fri; 8.30 am-2.30pm Sat; closed Sun. **Credit** MC, V.
Provides 24-hour emergency service.

Istanbul Traffic Foundation
0212 282 4232/0212 279 5803/0212 278 8869
Provides 24-hour towing services.

Mazda auto helpline
0800 211 4092

Renault auto helpline
0800 211 4100

Car hire

Rental rates generally include insurance and unlimited mileage, but they're still high compared with Europe because of steep excise tax on new cars. Most companies also have rental offices at the airport (*see page 266*). Rates do not include VAT and insurance, which add about 35 per cent to the cost.

Avis
Hilton Hotel, Cumhuriyet Caddesi, Elmadağ (0212 241 2917). **Open** 9am-7pm daily. **Rates** $70-150 per day. **Credit** AmEx, DC, MC, V. **Branch**: Atatürk International Airport (0212 663 0646/663 0647).

Budget
Cumhuriyet Caddesi 13, Taksim (0212 253 9200). **Open** 8.30am-7.30pm daily. **Rates** $50-130 per day. **Credit** AmEx, DC, MC, V. **Branch**: Atatürk International Airport (0212 663 0858).

Europcar
Topçu Caddesi 1, off Cumhuriyet Caddesi, Taksim (0212 256 7788; airport 0212 663 0746). **Open** 8.30am-7.30pm daily. **Rates** $70-150 per day. **Credit** AmEx, DC, MC, V. **Map** p307 O1. **Branch**: Atatürk International Airport (0212 663 0746/663 0747).

Hertz
Cumhuriyet Caddesi 295, Harbiye (0212 233 1020). **Open** 9am-7pm daily. **Rates** $60-195 per day. **Credit** AmEx, MC, V. **Branches**: Atatürk International Airport (0212 663 0807).

Resources A-Z

Business services

Istanbul is by far the largest city in Turkey, with the largest market and the best communications, the country's centre for business and manufacturing. But though alive with opportunity, the city is also fraught with difficulties.

The Turkish economy, while registering steady growth, is reliant on a few sectors that are sensitive to changes of fortune. The immense textile sector, for example, was badly affected by the Far East economic crisis of 1997, which saw prices plummet in Asia and left Turkey unable to shift stock that had all of a sudden become too expensive. Thousands of companies have ceased trading as a result. Another big national earner, tourism, was hobbled in 1999 by threatened terrorist activity from the Kurdish PKK. In the event, trouble was minimal, but visitors stayed anyway.

For foreign investors, the traditional view of Turkey as a high-risk market has been replaced by the perception that it's a market well worth courting. Demographics speak for themselves: a quarter of the country's 63 million population is under 25; some 70 per cent live in cities, compared with 15 per cent 50 years ago; levels of education and literacy have shown similar leaps. But, of the many foreign companies that have successfully entered the Turkish market, few have done so alone. Foreign concerns have either looked to buy controlling interests in local businesses, or to work with Turkish partners. Corruption and interminable bureaucracy make it essential to have good local representation, preferably with plenty of *torpil* – 'influence'.

Practicalities

Attitudes to doing business are slowly changing, but it's going to be a while before Istanbul experiences the phenomenon of the power breakfast. It's not that Turkish employees don't work long hours – they do, and they take few holidays – but they seem to have inherited their administrative methods directly from the Byzantines. Official paperwork takes forever, and then some, while the vocabulary of the average civil servant seems to consist entirely of negatives. Most foreign companies farm out tasks such as getting work permits and residence permits to local lawyers or accountants. Dealings with private-sector business are somewhat less fraught.

Accountants

Arthur Anderson
Beytem Plaza, Büyükdere Caddesi, Şişli (0212 232 1210).

PriceWaterhouse-Coopers
Ninth floor, B Blok, BJK Plaza, Spor Caddesi 92, Akaretler, Beşiktaş (0212 251 7454).

Deloitte & Touche
5th floor, B Blok, Yapı Kredi Plaza, Büyükdere Caddesi, Levent (0212 283 1585).

Foreign banks

American Express Bank
Suite 23, 15th floor, Maya Akar Centre 23, Büyükdere Caddesi, Esentepe (0212 275 9526). Open 9am-5pm Mon-Fri; closed Sat, Sun. Representative office only.

Chase Manhattan Bank
11th floor, A Blok, Emirhan Caddesi 145, Dikilitaş (0212 326 8300). Open 9am-6pm Mon-Fri; closed Sat, Sun. Corporate banking services, import-export credit. No personal banking.

Citibank
Büyükdere Caddesi 100, Esentepe (0212 288 7700). Open 9am-5pm Mon-Fri; closed Sat, Sun.

Dresdner Bank
İnönü Caddesi 70 K5, Gümüşsuyu (0212 252 6684). Open 9am-5.30pm Mon-Fri; closed Sat, Sun. Representative office only.

Turkish banks

Akbank
Sabancı Center, 4th Levent (0212 270 0044). Open 9am-6pm Mon-Fri; closed Sat, Sun.

Garanti Bankası
Büyükdere Caddesi 65, Maslak (0212 335 3535). Open 9am-6pm Mon-Fri; closed Sat, Sun.

Türk Ticaret Bankası/Türkbank
Yıldız Posta Caddesi 2, Gayreteppe (0212 288 5900). Open 9am-6pm Mon-Fri; closed Sat, Sun.

Yapı ve Kredi Bankası
D Blok, Yapı Kredi Plaza, Büyükdere Caddesi, Levent (0212 339 7000). Open 9am-6pm Mon-Fri; closed Sat, Sun.

Business organisations

Banks Association
Türkiye Bankalar Birliği *Akmerkez B3 Blok K 13-14, Nispetiye Caddesi, Etiler (0212 282 0973).* Open 9am-5.30pm Mon-Fri; closed Sat, Sun.

Foreign Economic Relations Board
Dış Ekonomik İlişkiler Kurulu *9th floor, Odakule İş Merkezi, İstiklal Caddesi 286, Beyoğlu (0212 243 4180).* Open 9am-6pm Mon-Fri; closed Sat, Sun. Map p308 N3. This body organises joint business councils between Turkey and 56 other countries throughout the world. There is also a small library and resource centre.

Istanbul Convention & Visitors Bureau
Istanbul Kongre ve Ziyaretçi Bürosu *Meşrutiyet Caddesi 57/4, Beyoğlu (0212 293 3950/istanbul@icvb.org).* Open 8.30am-5pm Mon-Fri; closed Sat, Sun. Map p308 M3.

Directory

Nonprofit organisation that offers information and service related to conventions and meetings planned for Istanbul.

Istanbul Stock Exchange

Istanbul Menkul Kıymetler Borsası *Maslak Caddesi Itü Kampüsü yanı, Istinye (0212 298 2100).* **Open** 8.30am-5.30pm Mon-Fri; closed Sat, Sun.
Open to the public by prior appointment only.

Chamber of Commerce

Istanbul Ticaret Odası
Şeyh Mehmet Geylani Mahallesi Yalı Köşkü Sokak, off Reşadiye Caddesi, Sirkeci (0212 455 6000). **Open** 9am-5.30pm Mon-Fri; closed Sat, Sun. **Map** p303 M8.
Has a good business library with indexed clippings from local press and a good selection of international publications.

Legal & consulting services

AB Consultancy and Investment Services

Seher Yıldızı Sokak 33/15, Etiler (0212 287 2870/ www.abconsult.com.tr). **Open** 9am-6pm Mon-Fri; closed Sat, Sun.

Denton Güner Fox and Gibbons

9th floor, B BLok, Yapı Kredi Plaza, Büyükdere Caddesi Levent (0212 282 4385/ www.dentonwildesapte.com). **Open** 9am-6.30pm Mon-Fri; closed Sat, Sun.

Ertan & Oran

3rd floor, Cumhuriyet Caddesi 173, Elmadağ (0212 225 0952/ ayhanoran@superonline.com). **Open** 9am-6pm Mon-Fri; closed Sat, Sun.
Consultancy and law firm specialising in commercial, corporate, international trade and maritime.

IBS

Abdi Ipekçi Caddesi 59/6, Nişantaşı, Maçka (0212 231 0480/ www.ibsresearch.com). **Open** 9am-6pm Mon-Fri; closed Sat, Sun.
English-owned and run. Producers of the enormous *Doing Business in Turkey* guide.

Wordsmith

Beyazgül Sokak 58, Arnavutköy (0212 287 3970/ wordsmith@netone.com.tr). **Open** 9am-6pm Mon-Fri; closed Sat, Sun.
Advertising, promotional films and translation.

Courier services

Aktif Dağıtım

Perpa Ticaret Merkezi 1742K 11, Okmeydanı (0212 222 7272). **Open** 8.30am-6pm Mon-Sat; closed Sun.
Deliveries within Istanbul only.

DHL

Kasap Sokak 17B, Esentepe (0212 275 0800). **Open** 9am-6pm Mon-Sat; closed Sun.
International service only. Customer services provided 24 hours daily.

Express Cargo

Turgüt Özal Caddesi 102, Ikitelli Organize Sanayi Bölgesi (0212 549 0565). **Open** 8.30am-6pm Mon-Fri; 8.30am-1.30pm Sat; closed Sun.
Deliveries within Turkey.

Federal Express

Ikitelli Organize Sanayi Bölgesi, Türgüt Özal Caddesi 102, Ikitelli (0212 549 0404/ www.fedex.com). **Open** 8.30am-5.45pm Mon-Sat; closed Sun.
International service only.

TNT

Ertürk Sokak Uska Iş Merkezi 9, off Ekinciler Caddesi, Kavacık (0216 425 1730/www.tnt.com). **Open** 8.30am-6.30pm Mon-Fri; 8.30am-2.30pm Sat; closed Sun.
International service only.

UPS

A Blok, Ambarlar Caddesi 6, Zeytinburnu (0212 547 1220/ www.ups.com). **Open** 8.30am-7.45pm Mon-Fri; 8.30am-5pm Sat; closed Sun.
International and national deliveries.

Estate agents

Agents listed here conduct business in English and cater for the top end of the market. For a local realtor it's best to visit the neighbourhood you intend to settle in. Look for signs saying *emlakcı*. Expect to pay a standard commission of ten per cent of annual rent. Landlords generally ask for a month's deposit and two months' advance rent. Most are open to bargaining. A cheaper alternative is to do what the Turks do: wander through the streets searching for *kiralık* (for rent) signs posted in windows of vacant flats and jot down the phone numbers. Sometimes the number turns out to belong

to an estate agent. Unfurnished flats often lack even light fixtures and water heaters, and are almost invariably without refrigerators. Foreigners without residence permits may rent flats, but are unlikely to get a legal contract.

Evren

Küçükbebek Caddesi 3/1, Bebek (0212 257 7184/www.evrenint. com.tr). **Open** 9am-7pm Mon-Sat; closed Sun.

Mavi Ay

Istinye Caddesi 110/1, Istinye (0212 323 0763/maviayemlak @superonline.com). **Open** 9am-6pm Mon-Sat; closed Sun.

Premier

Cevdetpaşa Caddesi 374, Bebek (0212 287 2797/www. premieremlak.com). **Open** 9am-6.30pm Mon-Fri; 9.30am-2pm Sat; closed Sun.

Translation agencies

Çitlembik

Şehbender Sokak 18/4, Asmalımescit, Beyoğlu (0212 292 3032/www.citlembik.com.tr). **Open** 9am-6pm Mon-Fri; closed Sat, Sun. **Map** p308 M4.
Long-established American-owned bureau.

Lin.go Communication Services

Abidei Hürriyet Caddesi 282/2, Şişli (0212 225 7066). **Open** 9am-6pm Mon-Fri; closed Sat, Sun.

Consulates

Foreign embassies are in Ankara, although many countries also have a consulate in Istanbul. Some countries have representation in Istanbul at honorary consul level only.

Australian Consulate

Tepecik Yolu 58, Etiler (0212 257 70 50). **Open** 8.30am-12.30pm, 1pm-4.30pm Mon-Fri; closed Sat, Sun. *Visa section* 10am-noon Mon-Fri; closed Sat, Sun.

Canadian Honorary Consulate

Istaklal Caddesi 373, Beyoğlu (0212 217 6227). **Open** 9am-5pm Mon-Thur; 9am-1pm Fri; closed Sat, Sun. **Map** p308 M4.

Republic of Ireland Honorary Consulate

Cumhuriyet Caddesi 26/A, Harbiye (0212 246 6025). **Open** 9.30am-noon, 1.30-5pm Mon-Fri; closed Sat, Sun. *Visa section* 9.30am-noon Mon-Fri; closed Sat, Sun.

New Zealand Consulate

Yeşilçimen Sokak 75, Ihlamur, Beşiktaş (0212 327 2211). **Open** 9.30am-12.30pm, 1.30pm-4.30pm Mon-Thur; 9.30am-1.30pm Fri; closed Sat, Sun.

UK Consulate

Meşrutiyet Caddesi 34, Tepebaşı, Beyoğlu (0212 293 7546/ emergencies 0532 322 9945). **Open** 8.30am-1pm, 2-4.30pm Mon-Fri; closed Sat, Sun. *Visa section* 8.30-11.30am Mon-Fri; closed Sat, Sun. **Map** p308 M3.

US Consulate

Meşrutiyet Caddesi 104/108, Tepebaşı, Beyoğlu (0212 251 3602). **Open** 8am-4.30pm Mon-Fri; closed Sat, Sun. **Map** p308 M4.

Customs

Turkish customs regulations allow foreign visitors to import the following free of duty charges: one litre of alcohol, 200 cigarettes, 50 cigars and five litres of wine. You may be asked to register electronic equipment to ensure that it leaves Turkey with you.

For further information on customs, ring the airport information line on 0212 663 6400 ext 3298. Otherwise, customs advise you to contact the airline or shipping agency bringing you to Istanbul for a full list of items that may be problematic. Note that it is illegal to possess or take any antiquities out of the country. Proof of purchase may be requested when exiting the country with a carpet.

Disabled access

Istanbul is tough on anyone with a mobility problem. The city is spread over several hills, roads and pavements are narrow, pitted and often paved with cobblestones, kerbs are high and flights of steps are frequent. Public transport is basically inaccessible. Outside of some top hotels, no buildings make any provision or offer any facilities for the handicapped.

Drugs

Turkey is a major transit point for heroin and the use of locally grown marijuana and ecstasy smuggled in from abroad is increasing. Enforcement is uneven but heavy-handed, with police conducting periodic sweeps of bars and nightclubs in the Taksim and Beyoğlu areas. You may be physically searched and have the insides of your forearms checked for needle tracks. Sentencing for drug offences is mild by American standards, but harsh by European ones.

Electricity & gas

Electricity in Turkey runs on 220 volts. Plugs have two round pins. Adaptors for UK appliances are readily available at hardware shops and electricians. Transformers are required for US 110-volt appliances, but these are also easily found. There are frequent, brief power cuts, and it's not a bad idea to have a torch in your baggage.

Although much of Istanbul has switched over to natural gas for heating, most people still rely on liquid propane gas canisters for cooking, and many water heaters use canisters. If you stay in rented accommodation, you may need to change the canister. Fleets of small trucks cruise the streets all day playing their company's jingle over loudspeakers. You'll quickly become familiar with the names Aygaz, Ipragaz and Likidgaz. Shout from the window the name of whatever company you want as the appropriate truck passes by. Alternatively, you can call and order a *büyük tüp* (large canister) by phone:

Aygaz
0212 293 8361.

Ipragaz
0212 2490408.

Likidgaz
0212 252 2730.

Health

Turkey doesn't have reciprocal health care agreements with any other countries, so taking out your own medical insurance is advisable. No vaccinations are required for Istanbul, although cases of rabies contracted from stray dogs have been reported as recently as 1999. Some travellers complain of stomach upsets, but this is more often due to the change in diet rather than food poisoning. Play safe by avoiding tap water; inexpensive bottled water is available at all restaurants and cafés.

Hospitals

State hospitals all have emergency services, but they are understaffed and overcrowded. In the case of anything going wrong, private hospitals are better. They are more expensive, though not prohibitively so, and they offer care on a par with western Europe and the US. Doctors, dentists, pharmacists and opticians nearly always have at least some degree of fluency in English; the same is not necessarily true of nurses and emergency services personnel.

American Hospital

Amerikan Hastanesi *Güzelbahçe Sokak 20, Nişantaşı (0212 311 2000/www. amerikanhastanesi.com.tr).* **Credit** AmEx, DC, MC, V.
One of the city's best – well equipped and staffed, under US management. Also has a dental clinic.

Directory

European Hospital

Avrupa Hastanesi
Fulya Sağlık Tesisleri, Cahit Yalçım Sokak 1, off Mehmetçik Caddesi, Mecidiyeköy (0212 212 8811/ www.florence.com.tr). **Credit** AmEx, MC, V.
Modern, well equipped and more female-friendly than most.
Specialises in treating children.

Istanbul Surgical Hospital

Istanbul Cerrahi Hastanesi
Ferah Sokak 18, Nişantaşı (0212 296 9450/www.istanbulcerrahi.com). **Credit** V.
Ophthalmology, ear, nose and throat, neurology, orthopaedics, gynecology, radiology and laboratory.

Taksim State Emergency Hospital

Taksim Ilkyardım Hastanesi
Sıralselviler Caddesi 112, Taksim (0212 252 4300). **No credit cards**.
Map p307 O3
State-run, deals with emergencies only, often sends patients afterwards to other state hospitals around town.

Florence Nightingale Hospital

Abidei Hürriyet Caddesi 290, Çağlayan (0212 224 4950/ www.florence.com.tr). **Credit** AmEx, MC, V.
Specialises in heart problems.

Dentists

As with hospitals, there are state clinics and private practices; the latter are more expensive, but standards are higher and waiting times shorter. All the following have staff that speak some English:

Bural Cankat

Inönü Caddesi 11/1, Taksim (at American Hospital 0212 231 4050; office 0212 252 1568/www. amerikanhastanesi.com.tr). **Open** 9am-noon, 2pm-6pm Mon, Tue, Thur, Fri; 9am-noon Wed; closed Sat, Sun. **Credit** *Hospital* AmEx, DC, MC, V. *Office* **no credit cards**.
Map p307 Q2.
Dr. Cankat is one of several dentists associated with the American Hospital.

Catherine Feyzioglu

Abdi Ipekçi Caddesi 12/5, Nişantaşı (0212 233 0627). **Open** 10am-5pm Mon, Wed, Fri; closed Tue, Thur, Sat, Sun. **No credit cards**.
Phone ahead for appointments outside normal opening hours.

German Hospital Dental Clinic

Sıraselviler Caddesi 119, Taksim (0212 293 7979). **Open** 24hrs daily. **Credit** AmEx, MC. V. **Map** p307 O3.
Has special children's and orthodontics sections.

Doctors

Making appointments is generally pretty easy with private physicians, as most have their own clinics, though some also operate through hospitals – both private and (unofficially) state. However, don't expect to find the Turkish equivalent of a general practitioner. Private doctors specialise. Expect to pay after treatment unless covered by an international health insurance scheme.

For recommendations of reputable English-speaking doctors consult your consulate, or try the following:

Azmi Hamzaoğlu

Florence Nightingale Hospital, Abdi Ipekçi Caddesi 79/1, Maçka (hospital 0212 224 4950; office 0212 231 2837). **Open** varies Mon-Sat; closed Sun. **Credit** AmEx, MC, V.
An orthodontist associated with the Florence Nightingale Hospital. Contact Cenghizhan Bey at the hospital number for appointments.

Doğan Şenocak

Biyikli Mehmet Paşa Sokak 1/7, Çamlık, Etiler (hospital 0212 586 1519; office 0212 263 1388). **Open** *Hospital* 10am-noon Mon-Fri; closed Sat, Sun. *Office* 3pm-6.30 pm Mon-Fri; closed Sat, Sun.
No credit cards.
An ear, nose and throat specialist, who is especially good with children.

Beyoğlu Emgen Optik

Istiklal Caddesi 65, Beyoğlu (0212 245 4425). **Open** 9am-7.30pm Mon-Sat; closed Sun. **Credit** AmEx, DC, MC, V. **Map** p308 N3.

Pharmacies

Pharmacies (*eczane*) are plentiful and easily found in most neighbourhoods. Otherwise, they tend to be clustered around hospitals. In addition to dispensing medicine, pharmacists are licensed to measure blood pressure, give injections, clean and bandage minor injuries and suggest medication for minor ailments. Opening hours are typically 9am to 7pm Monday to Saturday. Each neighbourhood also has a *nöbetçi* pharmacy open all night and on Sundays. Any closed pharmacy will have a sign indicating the nearest open pharmacy.

Vets

Household pets are still largely a preserve of the wealthy, so most vets are found in the expensive parts of town.

Ju-En Veterinary Clinic

Ergin Sokak 13, Garanti Mahallesi, Etiler (0212 263 3110/ www.juenvet.com). **Open** 9.30am-7.30pm Mon-Sat; 10am-7pm Sun. **Credit** MC, V.

Moda Veterinary Clinic

Evren Apt, Moda Caddesi 225, Moda, Asian Shore (0216 346 6174/friends@prizma.net.tr). **Open** 24hrs daily. **Credit** MC, V. **Map** p311 W8.

Women's clinics

There is just one specialist women's clinic in Istanbul, although some of the private hospitals are equipped to handle most situations.

Jinepol Women's Illness & Maternity Center

Ground floor, Kervan Apt, Nispetiye Caddesi 17, Etiler (0212 351 4571/351 4572). **Open** noon-7pm Mon-Fri; 9am-2pm Sat; closed Sun. **Credit** MC, V.
The doctors here, Dr Figen Ateşal and Dr Başak Direm, speak English.

Women & Children's Health, Education & Research Unit

Kadın ve Çocuk Sağliği Eğitim ve Araştırma Birimi
Cerrahi Monoblok Karşisi, Millet Caddesi, Çapa (0212 631 9831/ womanchild@superonline.com). **Open** 8.30am-4pm Mon-Fri; closed Sat, Sun.
Best place for smear tests, pregnancy and abortion and HIV testing.

Helplines

Alcoholics Anonymous

Union Han Building, 3rd floor, Istiklal Caddesi 485-7 (0212 249 2191). Map p308 M4.
Sessions for English-speakers are held Monday and Wednesday at the above address. Meetings are also held in Kadıköy at 7pm Fridays and noon Wednesdays. Contact Michael (0532 761 6466).

Insurance

Turkey is not covered by EU mutual health insurance schemes, which means both EU and non-EU citizens are advised to get a comprehensive private insurance policy before they leave, covering medical as well as personal loss. Turkish state hospitals will take in emergency cases who plead absolute penury, but as a tourist this will be difficult to prove. Those with residence in Turkey are entitled to state health care once they have a full residence permit.

Internet

Istanbul's Internet sector is booming. There are more websites ending in Turkey's .tr than in China's .cn. From an estimated 100,000 dial-up users in 1997, the number had swollen to over a million by the end of 1999. Cybercafés have mushroomed as well, although outside of Beyoğlu, proper cybercafés, where patrons sip coffee while paying to surf the net, are rare in Istanbul. What you get instead, particularly around Sultanahmet, are hybrids such as travel agents with a couple of online terminals out back, or a telephone/fax office with an Internet terminal. Many hotels have a computer for guests to access and send email.

In summer 2000 several Internet cafés in Beyoğlu were threatened with closure after complaints from parents that their kids were using such

Waiting for the big one

Izmıt, some 80 kilometres (50 miles) south of Istanbul: 'Four fifths [of the city] was demolished and as many as 4,000 people were killed under the ruins. Six mosques collapsed and 600 were killed inside. Aqueducts which bring water to the city collapsed and a 25m-long channel "migrated" 10 paces.'

This is the scene as described by the Ottoman chronicler Silhahdar in May 1719, the aftermath of a devastating earthquake. Then, 280 years later, on 17 August 1999, the Izmıt region was again the epicentre of a catastrophic quake, which this time killed more than 18,500 and left over 100,000 homeless.

With the exception of the western district of Avcılar, most of Istanbul was physically undamaged by the 1999 trembler. But the force with which the quake was felt throughout the city filled local parks and wastelands for weeks afterwards with residents afraid to return to their homes. The psychological aftershocks have also been profound, as many Istanbulites lost relatives and friends.

The quake was a big reminder that the city occupies a highly precarious seismological position. Northern Turkey has a subterranean crack going all the way from Erzurum in the east to some indeterminate point in the Aegean to the west. Known as the North Anatolian Fault, this fracture is under constant pressure from the African tectonic plate to the south, which is going north, and the Asian plate to the north, which is going south. The result is that much of Turkey is like a bar of wet soap, being squished out sideways.

History reveals a rather alarming pattern to all this tectonic activity. Roughly every 250 years, the pressure builds up to a devastating eruption in the Izmıt area, then, between ten and 25 years later, the big one goes off right next to Istanbul itself. The regional quake of 1999 was thus a notice served on the city.

Quake fears are not eased by the total lack of preparedness exhibited by the state emergency services in 1999, nor by their Keystone Cop efforts since. In June 2000 there was an earthquake drill in the central city district of Beşiktaş, but nobody thought to inform the police or many of the local residents. The result was mass panic and at least one death by heart attack.

As for warning systems, these seem to focus on one man, greying 58-year-old professor Ahmet Mete Işikara, director of Istanbul's Kandilli Earthquake Observatory. His efforts to get the city ready for the next big quake have won him massive popularity to the extent that in 1999 readers of a leading daily voted him Turkey's sexiest man. It's said that the quake of that year was only acknowledged to be over when Işikara finally shut his office and took himself off to watch a football match. Residents of Istanbul are hoping he felt confident enough this year to buy a season ticket.

places to access hardcore porn. The places we list below have been open for some time.

You will need some patience: ISPs tend to be oversubscribed and download times are often frustratingly slow. Frequent power failures are an additional nuisance.

If travelling with your own laptop, for both Compuserve and AOL the dial-in number is 0212 234 6100. Both services levy a $6 per hour surcharge.

Modern phone sockets take the US-style RJ11 plug, although older hotels and apartments use a Turkish model for which there don't seem to be any adaptors.

Internet access kits are sold at most large music/media and computer shops (*see pages 161 and 175*). There is a bewilderingly large range of options and increasingly ISPs require a credit-card number. Be sure to bring a Turkish-speaker with you, find a shopkeeper fluent in English or telephone one of the major providers in advance to learn details and the nearest stockist of the Internet package you want. The following are reputable providers with English-language technical and back up services.

Superonline
0212 473 7475.

Turknet
0212 444 0077.

Netone
0212 213 2035.

Internet cafés

Anatolia Internet Café
Yerebatan Caddesi 17/2, Sultanahmet (0212 511 8349). Tram Sultanahmet. **Open** 9am-10pm daily. **Rates** $2 per hour. **No credit cards.** Map p303 N10.
Twenty computers in a spacious, first-floor café over the road from Haghia Sophia. Incongruous 'Anatolian' décor (carpets and kilims lining the walls) makes for a 'rustic high-tech' effect. Separate smoking area off to the side.

Internet C@fé Chat
Zambak Sokak 7, off Istiklal Caddesi, Beyoğlu (0212 243 3428). **Open** 8am-1am daily. **Rates** $1.20 per hour. **No credit cards.** Map p309 O2.
Twenty terminals spread over the second and fourth floors of the building. One of few places offering scanning and printing at reasonable rates. Smoking, drinking and eating permitted. Some English spoken.

Internet Sinera Café
Mis Sokak 6, off Istiklal Caddesi, Beyoğlu (0212 244 2343/ sinera1@superonline.com). **Open** 9am-midnight daily. **Rates** $1.20 per hour **No credit cards.** Map p309 O2.
Frequented by studious types, so no distracting whoops and groans from game players or porn downloaders. No smoking, but there is tea and coffee. Some English spoken.

Otantik Internet Café
Alayköşkü Caddesi, Yerebatan Sokak 2/B, Çağaloğlu (0212 511 2433). Tram Gülhane. **Open** 10am-2am daily. **Rates** $1.20 per hour. **No credit cards.** Map 303 N9.
Ten computers, also with Japanese and Chinese-language keyboards. Just down the hill from Sultanahmet.

Taxim Internet Café
Sıraselviler Caddesi 45, Taksim (0212 252 3557). **Open** 9am-1am daily. **Rates** $1.20 per hour. **No credit cards.** Map p309 O2.
Twelve computers and a small juice and coffee bar. Often spoiled by distractingly loud pop music.

Yağmur Cybercafé
Şehbender Sokak 18/2, Asmalımescit, Beyoğlu (0212 292 3020). **Open** 10am-11pm daily. **Rates** $1.50 per hour. **No credit cards.** Map p308 M4.
One of the oldest internet cafés in town. Ten computers, smart decor, all staff speak English. Also a great café (*see p152*).

Libraries

Istanbul lacks the library culture of western cities. Such libraries as exist are generally specialist places open to researchers and students only.

British Council Library
Istiklal Caddesi 251/3, Beyoğlu (0212 249 0574). **Open** 10.30am-8.30pm Mon, Tue; 10.30am-6.30pm Wed; 10.30am-5.30pm Thur, Fri; 9.30am-2.30pm Sat; closed Sun. Map p308 N4.

Like a local British town library transplanted to Istanbul, has fiction and non-fiction, as well as music tapes and CDs and a selection of VHS videos. Also offers Internet facilities and a café, along with an educational advice centre for studying in the UK.

Istanbul Library/Çelik Gülersoy Foundation
Ayasofya Pansiyonları, Soğukçeşme Sokak, Sultanahmet (0212 512 5730). **Open** 10am-noon, 1.30-4.30pm Mon, Fri; closed Tue-Thur, Sat, Sun. Map p303 N10.
A collection of antique and modern books on Istanbul in a host of languages lodged in a restored Ottoman house beside the Topkapı Palace. Used mainly by academics and specialists.

American Information and Resource
US Consulate, Meşrutiyet Caddesi 104-8, Beyoğlu (0212 251 2675). **Open** 10am-4.30pm Mon-Fri; closed Sat, Sun. Map p308 M4.
This former library is now only a research centre for academics, business people, and journalists. Access by appointment only.

Lost property

To report a crime or loss of belongings, file a report at the local police station (*karakol*). For more complicated situations, it may be a good idea to report to the Tourist Police Station (0212 528 5369) opposite **Yerebatan Sarayı** in Sultanahmet (*see page 75*). Most officers here speak English or German. Consulates require that you first fill out a police report in the event of a lost or stolen passport.

Media

Ten years ago, print journalism was in the doldrums, there were only two TV channels, both state-owned, and just a handful of radio stations, also state-owned. Then along came Star TV, beamed in from Germany to flout the regulations on private ownership and given a helping hand in deference to the station owner, brother of the then-Turkish president.

Directory

Subsequent de facto private ownership of other TV and radio stations forced a ministerial rethink and a loosening up of restrictive media laws. The ensuing scramble to get in on the money saw the emergence of several huge and obscenely influential media combines. Among the most ubiquitous is that run by mogul Aydın Doğan. He has stakes in three of Turkey's four bestselling newspapers and its biggest magazine group, as well as six TV channels, a bank and an Internet portal. Monopolies commission? Pah. In theory, yes, there are laws preventing such excessive concentrations of power, but in practice such restrictions can be evaded through complicated networks of cross holdings.

Newspapers

National newspapers fall into two broad categories, secular and pro-Islamic. The secular press is dominated by two companies, both of which publish several titles. Between them they account for almost 60 per cent of the market. What remains is split between a handful of smaller media companies and the smaller media interests of a few giants. Circulation figures are unverified but all-important, as papers employ every gimmick to boost sales. All major dailies distribute gifts – everything from Internet directories to toothpaste – and publish coupons redeemable against yet more giveaway goodies.

The most serious of the secular papers is *Cumhuriyet* (Republic). You can tell it's serious because it's the only paper not to publish in full colour. Once the official organ of the republic, but now left of centre, it's struggling to maintain its readership. Competition comes from three big hitters: *Hürriyet*, *Sabah*

and *Milliyet*, serious but indistinguishable popular dailies that occupy the political centre ground. Journalistic standards are undermined by low pay and the real news comes from the columnists, of whom there's practically one per page. Every worthwhile columnist has his 'sources' – in other words they're all on someone's payroll.

The main pro-Islamic daily is *Zaman*, distinguished by surprisingly good coverage of international film and literature. More radical is *Yeni Şafak*, which lines up behind the main Islamic Party, Fazilet. Worst by far is the hate-mongering *Akit*, with its habit of insinuating that successful secular business leaders are secretly Jews or Christians.

The Turkish newspaper business can be dangerous. Many small-circulation left-wing newspapers suffer continual official harassment. In 1995 a photographer from the weekly *Evrensel* was beaten to death by police. Turkey is repeatedly cited by Amnesty International as one of the countries with the most jailed journalists.

In Istanbul, tabloid journalism is known as '*asparagas*' news – which is nothing to do with stylish vegetables, it's just a term that refers to schlock horror stories of dubious origin. Worst offender is *Star*. Due to a dispute with the main media groups this is sold only on street corners by a fleet of the unemployed – a bit like *The Big Issue* but without the worthy credentials. Rival publication *Sabah* took print journalism to new lows in 1999 with the English-language headline 'Shit Heads' leading an article on anti-Turkish bias in the European press.

Numerous weekly satirical comics also sell in high numbers, offering a mix of sex, politics and surreal humour.

One of the longest running is *Gir Gir*, reckoned to be the third biggest-selling magazine in Europe in the late 1980s. Current biggest seller is *LeMan*, something like a cross between *Private Eye* and *Viz*. No subject is taboo, but the humour, while crude, is usually right on the mark.

Magazines

It's boom time in magazine publishing, with new titles appearing almost weekly. Established leaders of the pack are *Tempo* and *Aktüel*, mixing photo-led news, fashion and scandal, often with a free cover-mounted CD or VCD. Competition comes mainly from Turkish editions of titles such as *Cosmopolitan*, *Esquire*, *FHM*, *Marie Claire*, *Harper's Bazaar* and *Elle*.

Other sectors show more local initiative with *Ekonomist* (no relation) and *Paraborsa* being the pick of general business and economics titles. Production values are high and design, if not groundbreaking, is more than competent.

Where the magazines fail badly is in coverage of what's on. The weekly free magazine *Zip Istanbul* is the only publication offering anything like comprehensive listings.

English-language media

For a city with such a cosmopolitan heritage, Istanbul boasts little in the way of foreign-language publications. The only English-language newspaper is the *Turkish Daily News*, which offers reasonable coverage of domestic politics, but pads it with indigestible features and soapbox columnists. The monthly *Turkish Business World* covers exactly what it says, but a lot of its features read suspiciously like advertorial. For more objective business reporting, Turkey's leading business daily *Dünya* offers English-language summaries of its main stories at: www.dunya-gazete.com.tr.

Istanbul: The Guide is about the closest the city gets to an English-language listings paper, but its usefulness is hamstrung by the fact that it only appears once every two months. The city also boasts an English-language fanzine, *ISTANbull.... Magazine*, whose editor Roni Askey-Doran suffers a love-hate relationship with the place. Formerly known as *Istanbullshit*, it's opinionated and honest and a good way of keeping up with the ever-changing nightlife scene. Pick it up free at bars and cafés.

Foreign press

Foreign newspapers are easy to find, but are a day old. You can usually get today's *Guardian Europe* by late afternoon. Otherwise, a hunt around will turn up everything from *Sight & Sound* to *Wallpaper*. Best places to look are the small news-shacks just along from the Marmara Hotel on Taksim Square or any of at least a dozen book and CD shops along Istiklal Caddesi (*see page 158*).

Radio

The airwaves over Istanbul are so crammed with broadcasts that it's practically impossible to pick up any station without overlapping interference from another. Stations generally offer either Turkish music or foreign music, but rarely both. One exception is **Açık Radyo** (94.9). Among those offering western dance and pop music are **Kiss FM** (90.3), **Metro FM** (97.2), **Capital FM** (99.5), **Energy FM** (102) and **Number One FM** (102.5). **Radio Blue** (94.5) specialises in Latin and jazz. For Turkish

music try **Kral FM** (92.0), **Lokum FM** (89.0) and **Show Radyo** (89.9). Many of these stations are available online at www.creatonic.com/tronline/.

Television

Amazingly for a country which had no private TV until 1991, Turkey now has over 260 registered channels, although some 230 of these are regional. Not surprisingly, production values are low and programme quality is dire. Cable TV is available in many areas, offering improved reception of terrestrial channels, plus BBC Prime, CNN, Discovery, Eurosport and others. For areas without cable, satellite TV is cheap and offers further imports. Digital TV is represented by the new **Digiturk** platform, which carries programming from Europe and the US, plus the biggest Turkish TV and radio stations. **Cine5** is a good film and concert channel, **Kanal E** also has films in English and original-language American series such as *Saturday Night Live*, *Seinfeld* and *Married With Children*.

Money

Currency

Local currency is the Turkish Lira, abbreviated TL. However, inflation of around 50 per cent means that any attempt to quote liras in this guide would make it out of date long before it goes to print. Inflation has resulted in ever larger notes, requiring Turks to deal with absurdly long rows of zeros for even the smallest of transactions. A pack of cigarettes that cost TL 80,000 on 1 Jan 1997 is four years later TL 750,000.

Coins in circulation come in denominations of 5,000, 10,000, 25,000, 50,000 and 100,000 lira, but this kind of small change is

so worthless that it is common for shopkeepers to give customers chewing gum or sweets in lieu of coins. Banknotes come in denominations of 100,000, 250,000, 500,000, 1,000,000, 5,000,000 and 10,000,000 lira. All are in similar colours and feature Atatürk. For the visitor it's a nightmare trying to total the zeros to match what's on the bill. The government has launched a deflationary programme intended to lower inflation to single digits by end 2001. If this is successful, the Treasury plans to knock six zeroes off the currency in 2002.

ATMs

Automated Teller Machines (ATMs) or cashpoints are quite common, particularly on and around Istiklal Caddesi in Beyoğlu. Most machines will accept UK cashcards linked into the Cirrus or Plus networks and will supply Turkish lira to order. They'll also give cash advances on major credit cards, providing you know your PIN number.

Banks

Non-residents can open savings accounts at Turkish banks, but must provide a passport and confirmation of local address. Even those without an account can pay telephone and utility bills at all branches of Demirbank, Egebank, Emlakbank, Esbank, Finansbank and Pamukbank.

Money transfer

Most banks will not accept transfers unless you have an account. An exception is Koçbank, in partnership with Moneygram. They will take a $30 commission on a $500 transfer. Call Koçbank (0212 274 7777) to find out the nearest branch. One central branch is:

Koçbank Beyoğlu Branch
Istiklal Caddesi 417, Beyoğlu (0212 274 7777). **Open** 9am-5:30pm. **Map** p308 M4.

Bureaux de change

Many shops and restaurants accept payment in US dollars or sterling, but there are dozens of exchange bureaux (*döviz*) in the main tourist and shopping districts. These are easier to deal with than banks, where transactions can take forever. Rates vary – they are worst around Sultanahmet, and significantly better around Taksim. Exchange bureaux are open long hours, generally 9am-7:30pm, Mon-Sat.

Klas Döviz
Sıraselviler Caddesi 39, Taksim (0212 249 3550). **Open** 8.30am-8.30pm Mon-Sat; 10am-7pm Sun. **Map** p309 O2.

Nizam Döviz
Istiklal Caddesi 23, Taksim (0212 245 0808). **Open** 9am-7pm Mon-Sat; closed Sun. **Map** p309 O2.

Çetin Döviz
Istiklal Caddesi 39, Taksim (0212 252 6428). **Open** 9am-7pm Mon-Sat; closed Sun. **Map** p309 O2.

Credit cards

Istanbul is far from being a fully plastic city, but major credit cards are becoming ever more widely accepted in hotels, shops, restaurants and petrol stations. Just make sure that you carry cash as back-up. You can also use your card for cash advances. In case of credit card loss or theft call the following 24-hour services; all have English-speaking staff:

American Express
Akbank TAS Sabancı Center, Kule 1 Kat 31, 4th Levent (0212 283 2201). **Open** 24hrs daily.

Diners Club
C Blok, Morbasan Sokak, Kozaiş Merkezi, Balmumcu (0212 274 7777/24hr hotline 0212 212 1035/444-0555) **Open** 9am-6pm Mon-Fri; closed Sat, Sun.

Mastercard
Global service centre 0800 13 887 0903.

Visa International Information Center
If you lose your Visa card in Turkey, dial 001410581 3836. This is a US number, but you can make a collect call through the international operator.

Travellers' cheques

Travellers' cheques can be cashed in banks or post offices, though not usually at exchange bureaux. You will need to provide a passport. Individual banks charge different rates of commission, and some none at all, but the post office offers the best exchange rates.

Opening hours

Opening hours are extremely variable, but here are some general guidelines:

Banks 9am-noon and 1.30-6pm Mon-Fri; closed Sat, Sun. **Bars** 11am or noon-2am daily. **Businesses** 9am-6pm Mon-Fri; closed Sat, Sun. **Municipal offices** 9am-noon and 1.30-4pm Mon-Fri; closed Sat, Sun. **Museums** generally closed Mondays and open 8.30am-5.30pm Tue-Sun. **Petrol stations** 24 hours daily. **Post offices** 8am-8pm Mon-Sat; 9am-7pm Sun. **Shops** 10am-8pm Mon-Sat, although in main shopping areas places open as late as 10pm and on Sun. Grocery stores (*bakals*) and hypermarkets are open 9am-10pm daily.

Police & security

Istanbul is a safe city. Crime against visitors is still low, although on the rise. Physical violence (football supporters aside) is almost unheard of, but you should beware of purse- and bag-snatching, especially around Sultanahmet and Beyoğlu. Hassle of single women (*see page 32*) can be a real nuisance, and women going home late at night in the Beyoğlu/Taksim area should probably make sure they're accompanied. Avoid Tarlabaşı altogether.

The police are often more trouble than help, except in tourist-heavy areas, where they are on their best behaviour. The main force is known as the Security Police (*Emniyet Polisi*), who come kitted out in dark blue uniforms and caps, with pale blue shirts. Rapid-reaction police (*Yunus*, or 'Dolphins') wear black uniforms with a red stripe and dolphin insignia and patrol on motorcycles.

It's illegal to be out without some form of photo ID, so carry your passport with you at all times. Police occasionally conduct drugs-sweeps of bars and clubs in the Beyoğlu and Taksim and ID is checked.

Post

Post offices can be recognised by their yellow-and-black PTT (Posta, Telefon, Telegraf) signs – even though they no longer operate the telephone network. Main post offices are beside the McDonald's just north of Taksim Square, midway along Istiklal Caddesi in Galatasaray, on Şehinşah Pehlevi Caddesi near Sirkeci Station in Eminönü and in the north-west corner of the Grand Bazaar. Stamps (*pul*) are available from post offices and PTT kiosks.

Mail can be kept poste restante at the central post office in Sirkeci (*see below*). Address letters to: recipient's name, poste restante, Büyük Postane, Büyük Postane Caddesi, Sirkeci, Istanbul.

To collect mail you'll need to produce your passport and pay a small fee.

When sending packages, remember that the contents will be inspected at the post office, so it's a good idea not to seal them completely, and to bring tape with you. Also bear in mind the fact that packages often go missing.

Directory

Rates

Postcards are $0.50 to Europe, $0.70 to US.

For **packages**, rates start at $1.00 to Europe overland. Packages of up to 2 kilograms (4.4 pounds) are accepted.

You can also send post by an express service called APS, although this only performs well for deliveries within Turkey. This costs extra (for under 500g, $1.50 in Turkey, $12 to the UK, $16 to the US) and you'll have to fill out a form, available from the APS counter at the post office. For anything larger than a normal letter it is cheaper to use a normal courier. *See page 272.*

Major post offices

Sirkeci
Büyük Postane, Büyük Postane Caddesi, Sirkeci (0212 513 3407). **Open** 8.30am-4.30pm Mon-Fri; closed Sat, Sun. **Map** p303 N9. Letters sent poste restante can be collected here. Open 24 hours for telephone, post and telegrams.

Beyoğlu
Yeniçarşı Caddesi 20, Galatasaray, Beyoğlu (0212 252 0140). **Open** 8.30am-5pm daily. **Map** p308 N3.

Taksim
Cumhuriyet Caddesi 2, Taksim (0212 292 4085). **Open** 8.30am-5pm Mon-Fri; 8.30am-1pm Sat; closed Sun. **Map** p309 P2.

Religion

A former centre of Christianity – still the home of the Greek and Armenian Orthodox Patriarchates – and a city with a strong Jewish tradition (*see page 16*), Istanbul has a multitude of places of worship besides mosques. Churches and synagogues open only for services and security is especially tight at synagogues. These are mostly Sephardic and Conservative, with congregations segregated between the sexes. Services are in Ladino, Hebrew and Turkish. For general

information on synagogues and services call the Rabbinate (0212 293 8794). They'll probably require a photocopy of your passport.

Christian

Christ Church (Anglican)
Serdari Ekrem Sokak 82, Tünel, Beyoğlu (0212 251 5616). **Services** 9am, 6pm Mon-Sat; 10am Sun. **Map** p308 N5.

Union Church of Istanbul (Protestant)
Postacılar Sokak, Beyoğlu (0212 244 5212). **Services** 9.30am, 11am, 1pm Sun. **Map** p308 N4. In the garden of the Dutch consulate.

St Anthony's (Catholic)
İstiklal Caddesi 325, Beyoğlu (0212 244 0935). **Services** English & Italian 8am Mon-Fri. Turkish 11.30am Tue, 7pm Sun. Italian 7am, 7pm Sat, 11.30am Sun. Polish 9am Sun. English 10am Sun. **Map** p308 N3.

Haghia Triada (Greek Orthodox)
Meşelik Sokak 11/1, Taksim (0212 244 1358). **Services** 9am-11am Sun. **Map** p309 O2.

Uç Horon (Gregorian Armenian)
Balık Pazarı, Sahne Sokak 24, Beyoğlu (0212 244 1382). **Services** 10am-noon Tue, Sun. **Map** p308 N3.

Jewish

Those wishing to visit Istanbul synagogues or to attend services must first obtain permission. To do this, you will be asked to fax a copy of your identity papers or relevant passport pages.

Ashkenazi Synagogue
Banker Sokak 10, Yüksek Kaldırım, Karaköy (0212 243 5166/fax 0212 244 2972). **Services** sunset Fri; 8am Sat. **Map** p306 M6.

Bet Israel Synagogue (Sephardic)
Efe Sokak 4, off Rumeli Caddesi, Şişli (0212 243 5166/fax 292 0305). **Services** 7am daily. Sunset prayer daily. Provides information on all Istanbul synagogues.

The cheapest way to move a few articles of furniture is to make an arrangement with a local grocer (*manav*). You will be expected to pay according to the height of the floor you are moving to or from. You can also hire a removal agent for as little as $10, although the lorry may cost up to $50.

Akyüz Nakliyat
0212 293 6396.

Sumerman International
0212 223 5818.

Smoking

Laws to restrict smoking on public transport have been passed, but otherwise Istanbul is firmly in thrall to nicotine. Non-smokers are outcasts and few cafés or restaurants recognise the concept of a clean-air environment. So why buck the trend? If you don't smoke, then Istanbul is the place to start. Foreign cigarette brands cost less than $1.50 for 20, while the best of the domestic product, Tekel 2000, goes for less than a dollar a packet. Voluntary smoking or passive, it's your choice, but Bill's way just won't work – you've got to inhale sometime.

Street names

When writing an address, the house number comes after the street name with a slash separating the flat number. If it's on a side street (*sokak*), the custom is to include the nearest main street (*caddesi*) usually written first. So in the following case, Mehmet Aksoy lives at flat 7 at 14 Matar Sokak, which is off Sıraselviler Street in the Cihangir district:

Mehmet Aksoy
Sıraselviler Cad.
Matar Sokak No. 14/7
Cihangir
Istanbul

Directory

Student discounts

Museums, travel agents and sports centres recognise International Student Identity Cards (ISIC), but some cinemas and theatres offer discounts only to foreigners studying at Turkish educational institutes.

Study

Language courses

Turkish at all levels is taught at a variety of private schools and colleges, or you could find a private tutor via small ads in the *Turkish Daily News*.

Boğaziçi University

Mail to Boğaziçi University, 80815 Bebek, Istanbul (0212 263 1500/ www.boun.edu.tr).
$275 courses last seven weeks, with three two-hour lessons per week.

Tömer/Dilmer Turkish Language Centre

Tarik Zafer Tunaya Sokak 18, off Inönü Caddesi, Taksim (0212 292 9696/www.taksimdilmer.com).
Open 9am-8pm Mon-Fri; 9am-5pm Sat, Sun. **Map** p307 Q2.
The cost of an eight-week course in Turkish varies as follows: 8 hours per week $224; 10 hours $280; 12 hours $336; 20 hours $560.

Universities

A couple of the city's universities use English as the language of instruction for undergraduate and postgraduate studies.

Boğaziçi University

Zincirlikuyu-Bebek Caddesi, Rumeli Hisarüstü, Bebek (0212 263 1500).
Costs are lower than in the UK or US (for example, $800 per annum for a two-year MA course) and standards are high. Once the American College and maintaining strong US links. Address correspondence to: 80815 Bebek, Istanbul.

Bilgi University

Inönü Caddesi 28, Kuştepe, Şişli (0212 216 2222/www.ibun.edu.tr).
Map p307 Q2.
One of the city's newer private universities, with a variety of courses in arts and social sciences. Has a good reputation for its international relations and politics departments.

Telephones

Istanbul's Asian and European sides have different area codes: 0212 for Europe; 0216 for Asia. You must use the code when calling the opposite shore. When dialling from abroad omit the zero. The country code for Turkey is 90.

Public phones

A few old-style public phones operated by tokens (*jeton*) still exist, but have been largely replaced by card phones. Cards (*telefon kartı*) are bought at post offices or from street vendors and kiosks. Metered calls (*kontörlü*) can also be placed at post offices or the private phone and fax offices (*telefon ofisi*) dotted all over town, although these places usually charge over the odds. Standard public phone rates are around $1.50 a minute to the UK, $2 to the US. Reduced rates are in effect 6pm to 8am weeknights, weekends and national holidays.

Directories are no longer issued by the national telephone authority Türk Telekom, but a few private ventures have attempted to fill the gap; their phone books can be purchased at book shops.

Mobile phones

Turkey has two mobile networks, Turkcell and Telsim, with two more due by the end of 2000. If you bring your UK phone with you, you'll have no problem logging on to one of these if you've set up a roaming facility with your provider beforehand.

Mobiles can be hired from most big hotels. Longer-term residents have two options to get one of their own, provided they have a residence permit. With a permit it's possible to get a 'Hazır Kart' phone with a line in your own name. This is a counter system, using PIN-numbered cards available in units of 100 ($6.50), 250 ($12.50) and 500 ($25). When the card is used up, you recharge with a new one from mobile-phone shops displaying the orange 'Hazır Kart' sign. You can't send data on this system or use it overseas.

For a normal line, in addition to a residence permit you need a Turkish guarantor prepared to swear they'll stump up $400 if you don't pay your bills. Your Turkish friend must also have a mobile line with the same company.

Because the Turkish system currently operates on 900 MHz mobile phones bought in the US are useless here.

Rent-a-phone

Lamartin Caddesi 16/4, Taksim (0212 235 9359/9360). **Credit** AmEx, MC, V. **Map** p307 O1.
Rental is $30 a day, with calls charged at $2 per minute local, $3 per minute international.

Time

Turkey is two hours ahead of Greenwich Mean Time (GMT) and seven hours ahead of New York. There is no Turkish equivalent of am and pm, so the 24-hour clock is used: 1pm is 13.00 and midnight is 24.00. Daylight saving time runs from the last Sunday in March to the last Sunday in September. This creates a three-hour time difference between Turkey and the UK for one month each year, as British summer time doesn't end until the last Sunday in October.

Tipping

A rule of thumb is to leave around 10 per cent. If service has already been factored in, this will be indicated at the foot of the bill: *servis dahil*. If in doubt ask: 'Servis dahil mi?' Doormen, porters, guides, hairdressers and hamam attendants expect a tip of $1 or so. Do not tip drivers.

Toilets

Public toilets are plentiful, especially in tourist areas. They are usually indicated with a big 'WC', but when asking, use the term *tuvalet*. The gents' is *Bay*; the ladies' is *Bayan*. Usually they're the squat type – basically a hole in the floor, uncomfortable if you're not used to them, but hygienic. There's often no paper, so get used to carrying around a small pack of tissues (*kağıt mendil*), sold by street-corner vendors. City plumbing cannot cope with toilet paper; use the wastepaper bin. Most bars and restaurants have western-style toilets.

Public toilets are usually well looked after. In some cases they're objects of great pride, as in Beşiktaş, where the public toilet beside the PTT is adorned with flowers and fairy lights and there's a handout detailing its history.

Tourist information

There is no central tourist office; instead there are several small places dotted about the city. Staff speak English.

Atatürk Airport
International arrivals hall (0212 573 4136). **Open** 24 hrs daily. Will help book hotel rooms.

Istanbul Hilton
Cumhuriyet Caddesi, Harbiye (0212-233 0592). **Open** 9am-5pm Mon-Sat; closed Sun.

Karaköy sea port
Kemankeş Caddesi (0212 249 5776). **Open** 9am-5pm daily. **Map** p306 N6.

Sirkeci Station
Istasyon Caddesi 24/2, Sirkeci (0212-511 5888). Tram Sirkeci. **Open** 9am-5pm daily. **Map** p303 N8.

Sultanahmet Square
In the park between Haghia Sophia and Sultanahmet Mosque, Sultanahmet (0212 518 1802). Tram Sultanahmet. **Open** 9am-5pm daily. **Map** p308 N10.

Tourist police
Yerebatan Caddesi 6, Sultanahmet (0212 528 5369). Tram Sultanahmet. **Open** 24 hrs daily. **Map** p308 N10.
Where to report thefts, losses, scams and other woes. Officers speak English and are helpful.

Visas

Visas are required by most nationalities and are issued at the airport on arrival. At press time rates were: for citizens of the UK £10; USA and Canada $45; Australia $20; Ireland £5. Visas are good for up to three months. Citizens of New Zealand don't need a visa, just a valid passport. Fees must be paid in foreign currency; no Turkish lira, credit cards or travellers' cheques.

When to go

December through March Istanbul is cold and blustery. Temperatures average 5°C (42°F), though they rarely fall below zero and snow is uncommon. Summers can be oppressive; temperatures

average 25-30°C (78-88°F) June through August, occasionally pushing up beyond 35°C (104°F). The heat and humidity drain energy and there's a limit to how much you can expect to get done during the day. Yet for those who can cope with the heat this is the best time. However hot the days, it cools at sundown and the city moves down to the Bosphorus to while away languid pink-skied evenings at waterfront cafés.

For the best weather, aim for spring and autumn. Not every day is perfect – *poyraz*, a chill Balkan wind, and *lodos*, hot humid air arriving from the south, can both have a dramatic effect, resulting in a kind of 'four seasons in a day' syndrome. But generally days are temperate and evenings mild. Both are busy festival seasons and early autumn is when the bar, club and cultural scenes start to pick up, loaded with energy and enthusiasm after the dormant summer.

Public & religious holidays

Turkey's five secular public holidays occupy a single day each. Banks, offices and post offices close, but many shops stay open and public transport runs as usual.

Religious holidays are different. For a start, they last three or four days, and if these happen to fall midweek, then the government commonly extends the holiday to cover the whole working week. With weekends either side, it effectively becomes a nine-day holiday. The whole city shuts down as Istanbulites flock out to the country. Coaches and flights are jammed, so book well ahead if your own travel plans happen to coincide.

Observance of Ramazan, the Islamic month of fasting, is widespread. Many Istanbulites abstain from food, drink and cigarettes between sunrise and

---

Useful numbers

Police 155
Fire 110
Ambulance 112
Directory enquiries 118
International operator 115
International access code 00; **country codes** UK 44; US and Canada 1; Australia 61; Ireland 353; New Zealand 64

Directory

sunset. This has little impact on visitors, as most all bars and restaurants remain open, but it's bad form to flaunt your non-participation by smoking or eating in the street, especially in the more religious parts of the city, such as Fatih and Üsküdar. In areas like these, Ramazan nights are some of the busiest of the year, as, come sundown, eateries are packed with large groups communally breaking their fast with *iftar* ('breakfast'). The end of Ramazan is marked by the three-day Şeker Bayramı, or 'Sugar Holiday', named after the traditional practice of giving chocolates or sweets to friends and family.

Islamic religious holidays are based on a lunar calendar, approximately 11 days shorter than the Gregorian (western) calendar. This means Islamic holidays shift forward by ten or 12 days each year.

New Year's Day (Yılbaşı Günü), 1 January.
Feast of the Sacrifice (Kurban Bayramı), 5-8 March (2001); 6-9 March (2002).
National Sovereignty & Children's Day (Ulusal Egemenlik ve Çocuk Bayramı), 23 April.
Youth & Sports Day (Gençlik ve Spor Bayramı), 19 May.
Victory Day (Zafer Bayramı), 30 August.
Republic Day (Cumhuriyet Bayramı), 29 October.
Sugar Holiday (Şeker Bayramı), 17-19 December (2001); 7-9 December (2002).

Women

Though Istanbul is Islamic, few special rules apply. With some provisos, you needn't dress any differently here than at home, certainly not in the more European areas such as Beyoğlu and points north. But if you've a liking for minis and micros, leave those home. Shorts are out too. To avoid being stared at, wear trousers or dresses and skirts that reach the knee. In more conservative areas, such as the Asian Shore

or anywhere west of the Grand Bazaar, and especially at mosques and churches, keep your shoulders covered.

In touristy areas like Sultanahmet, you may get hit on. It's usually harmless and nothing more than you might experience in Italy or Greece, but all the same can be annoying. It's also generally easy to shrug off. Avoid eye contact. Don't beam wide smiles. Don't respond to invitations, come-ons or obnoxious comments. If a man is persistent and in your face, try saying 'Ayıp' – literally 'Shame on you'. Raise your voice so others around know you're being bothered. Chances are someone will intervene on your behalf. It seldom extends beyond that, but, should you need help, the word is 'İmdat'.

For more information on women in Istanbul *see page 32*. For women's medical resources *see page 274*.

Istanbul Women's Association (ISKADE)

www.iskade.org
One of a world-wide network of affiliated clubs, this non-political, non-profit and non-religious organisation is aimed simply at bringing women together. You can fill in a membership form online.

Women's Library

Kadın Eserleri Kütüphanesi
Fener Mahallesi, Abdul Ezel Paşa Caddesi, Haliç (0212 534 9550). Open 10.30am-6.30pm Mon-Fri; closed Sat, Sun.

Working in Istanbul

Finding a job is not difficult, especially for native English-speakers with a degree. There's a large market for teachers of English – although schools often require a recognised English-language teaching qualification. Other foreigners end up working as journalists with local English-language publications or managing bars and clubs.

Many work on tourist visas, hopping to North Cyprus or Greece and back every three months to obtain a new visa. Strictly speaking, this is illegal, but people get away with it for years.

Work permits

To be legal, you need a work permit, which can be obtained only by a sponsoring employer. The application must be made at a Turkish consulate abroad, so if you're already here you'll have to leave Turkey to submit the paperwork. Closest consulates are in Lefkosa, North Cyprus, or Thessalonika in Greece.

Residence permits

Anyone with a work permit should also have a residence permit. As with work permits, the application has to be made at a Turkish consulate abroad. It then goes to the police department in Ankara, and is forwarded to the Emniyet Müdürlüğü (police HQ) in Istanbul (on Vatan Caddesi, Aksaray). You will need copies of your passport and degree certificate, six photos, an application form, a letter from your local *muhtar* (district councillor – ask your landlord how to find him) stating your address, plus stacks of million-lira bills and lots of time. Queues are lengthy and the whole process is tedious. Take a book, and if you can, a local who knows the ropes.

Work and residence permits are usually valid for two years, but you can also apply for five. There are private agencies that will obtain permits for you:

Persona Eğitim ve Danişmanlık

Başa Sokak 18/6, Nişpetliye Caddesi, Levent (0212 284 7400/ www.personatr.com). **Open** 9am-6pm Mon-Fri; closed Sat, Sun. **Cost** $1,500 per permit. **No credit cards**. Work and residence permits arranged within two weeks.

Vocabulary

Istanbulites living and working in tourist areas usually have at least some knowledge of English and generally welcome the opportunity to practise it with foreigners. However, a bit of Turkish goes a long way and making the effort to use even a few phrases and expressions will be greatly appreciated.

Pronunciation

All words are written phonetically and, save for ğ, there are no silent letters; so for example the word for museum, *müze*, is pronounced 'moo-zeh'. Syllables are articulated clearly and generally evenly. *See page 281* for information on language courses and *page 136* for Turkish menu terms.

The key to learning basic Turkish is to master the pronunciation of the few letters and vowels that differ from English:

c – like the 'j' in jam, so *caddesi* (street) is pronounced 'jaddessy'
ç – like the 'ch' in chip, so *çiçek* (flower) is pronounced 'chi-check'
ğ – silent, but indicates lengthened preceding vowel
ı – an 'uh', like the 'a' in cinema
ö – like the 'ir' in girdle
ş – like the 'sh' in shop, so *şiş* (as in kebab) is pronounced 'shish'
ü – as in the French tu

General expressions

hello *merhaba*
good morning *günaydın*
good afternoon *iyi günler*
good evening *iyi akşamlar*
good night *iyi geceler*
OK *tamam*
yes *evet*
no *hayır*
How are you? *nasılsınız?*
How's it going? *nasıl gidiyor?*
Sir/Mr *Bay/Bey* (with first name)
Madam/Mrs *Bayan/Hanım* (with first name)
please *lütfen*
thanks *teşekkürler/sağol* (informal)

thank you very much *çok teşekkür ederim*
sorry *pardon*
excuse me *affedersiniz*
Do you speak English? *İngilizce biliyor musunuz?*
I don't speak Turkish *Türkçe bilmiyorum*
I don't understand *Anlayamıyorum*
Speak more slowly, please *Daha yavaş konuşun, lütfen*
Leave me alone (quite forceful) *Beni rahat bırakın*
Have you got change? *Bozuk paranız var mı?*
There is/there are... *...var*
There isn't/there aren't... *...yok*
good/well *iyi*
bad/badly *kötü*
small *küçük*
big *büyük*
beautiful *güzel*
a bit *biraz*
a lot/very *çok*
with *-ile* (usually suffix)
without *-sız,-siz* (suffix)
this *bu*
that *şu*
and *ve*
or *veya*
because *ama/fakat*
if *eğer*
Who? *Kim?*
When? *Ne zaman?*
Which? *Hangi?*
Where? *Nerede?*
Where to? *Nereye?*
Where from? *Nereden?*
Where are you from? *Nerelisiniz?*
I am English *İngilizim*
Irish *İrlandalıyım*
American *Amerikalıyım*
Canadian *Kanadalıyım*
Australian *Avustralyalıyım*
a New Zealander *Yeni Zelandalıyım*
Why? *Niye/Niçin/Neden?*
How? *Nasıl?*
At what time/when? *Saat kaçta?*
forbidden *yasak*
out of order *arızalı*

Emergencies

Help! *İmdat!*
I'm sick *Hastayım*
I want a doctor/policeman *Doktor/Polis istiyorum*
hospital *hastane*
There's a fire! *Yangın var!*

On the phone

hello (telephone) *alo*
Who's calling? *Kim arıyor?*
Hold the line *Hatta kalın/hattan ayrılmayın*

Getting around

train *tren*
ticket *bilet*
station *gar*
platform *peron*
bus/coach station *otogar*
entrance *giriş*
exit *çıkış*
left *sol*
right *sağ*
straight on *düz/doğru*
street *sokak*
street map *sokak haritası*
road map *yol haritası*
bank *banka*
post office *postane*
stamp *pul*
no parking *park yapılmaz*
toll *paralı geçiş*
speed limit 40 *hız limiti 40*
petrol *benzin*
unleaded *kurşunsuz*
speed *hız*

Sightseeing

museum *müze*
church *kilise*
exhibition *sergi*
ticket *bilet*
open *açık*
closed *kapalı*
free *bedava*
reduced price *indirimli*
except Sunday *pazar günü hariç*

Accommodation

hotel *otel*
bed & breakfast *pansiyon*
Do you have a room (for this evening/for two people)? *(Bu akşam için/iki kişilik) odanız var mı?*
no vacancy *yer yok*
vacancy *yer var*
room *oda*
bed *yatak*
double bed *çift kişilik yatak*
a room with twin beds *iki yataklı bir oda*
a room with a bathroom/shower *banyolu/duşlu bir oda*
breakfast *kahvaltı*
included *dahil*
lift *asansör*
air-conditioned *klimalı*

Shopping

I would like... *...istiyorum*
Is there a/are there any...? *...var mı?*
How much/how many? *Ne kadar/kaç?*
expensive *pahalı*
cheap *ucuz*

Eating out

restaurant *restoran/lokanta*
menu *mönü/yemek listesi*
I'd like to book a table (for three/at 7pm) *Saat 19:00 için üç kişilik bir rezervasyon yaptırmak istiyorum*
lunch *öğlen yemeği*
dinner *akşam yemeği*
coffee (instant) *neskafe*
coffee (filter) *filtre kahve*
coffee (white) *sütlü*
coffee (black) *sütsüz*
no sugar *şekersiz*
Turkish coffee *Türk kahvesi*
very/somewhat/a bit sweet *çok/orta/az şekerli*
tea *çay*
wine *şarap*
beer *bira*
water *su*

mineral water (sparkling) *maden suyu*
mineral water (still) *şişe suyu*
The bill, please *Hesap, lütfen*

Numbers

0 *sıfır*; 1 *bir*; 2 *iki*; 3 *üç*; 4 *dört*; 5 *beş*; 6 *altı*; 7 *yedi*; 8 *sekiz*; 9 *dokuz*; 10 *on*; 11 *onbir*; 12 *oniki*; 20 *yirmi*; 21 *yirmibir*; 22 *yirmiiki*; 30 *otuz*; 40 *kırk*; 50 *elli*; 60 *altmış*; 70 *yetmiş*; 80 *seksen*; 90 *doksan*; 100 *yüz*; 1,000 *bin*; 1,000,000 *milyon*; 1,000,000,000 *milyar*

Days of the week

Monday *Pazartesi*
Tuesday *Salı*
Wednesday *Çarşamba*
Thursday *Perşembe*

Friday *Cuma*
Saturday *Cumartesi*
Sunday *Pazar*

Months & seasons

January *Ocak*
February *Şubat*
March *Mart*
April *Nisan*
May *Mayıs*
June *Haziran*
July *Temmuz*
August *Ağustos*
September *Eylül*
October *Ekim*
November *Kasım*
December *Aralık*
Spring *İlkbahar*
Summer *Yaz*
Autumn *Son bahar*
Winter *Kış*

Bored, or just having regular sex?

Turkish is what's known as an agglutinative language. This means that words are built up by adding suffixes on to the end of shorter words. For example, by adding suffixes you can turn the word for student (*öğrenci*) into 'Are you a student?' (*öğrencimisin*?) or the word swim (*yüz-*) into 'I can't swim' (*yüzemiyorum*) or 'Shall we swim?' (*yüzelimmi*?).

Which is all very nice, except as suffixes pile up, words get out of hand. For example, *Çekoslovakyalılaştıramadıklarımızdanmısınız*? which is more a short story than a single word. Literally translated, it means 'Aren't you one of those whom we were unable to turn into a Czech?' This isn't a word that liberally peppers day-to-day conversations, and in fact it may never have been used at all except to frighten students just beginning their Turkish lessons.

But don't be put off: Turkish is in many ways an easy language to learn. It's strictly logical, with no irregular verbs, and words are always pronounced exactly as they are written. Anybody who knows some French will recognise hundreds of borrowings, from *otogar* (bus station) to *mersi* (probably heard more frequently in strictly courteous Istanbul than it is in Paris).

Like other languages, Turkish contains plenty of traps for the unwary beginner. Just a single vowel sound separates 'Excuse me, waiter' (*bakar mısınız*?) from 'Are you single?' (*bekar mısınız*?), or 'I'm bored' (*sıkılıyorum*) from 'I'm having regular sex' (*sikiliyorum*).

Anyone wrestling with beginners' Turkish should spare a thought for the generation of Turks who had to learn their own language again, after the shift from the Arabic to the Latin alphabet in the 1920s. This move was accompanied by a massive vocabulary cleansing as nationalists, headed by Atatürk, were determined to replace Arabic and Persian words with 'pure' Turkish equivalents. This reforming zeal (Atatürk even went around teaching language classes himself) frequently made their speeches incomprehensible to their contemporaries.

Late in his life, Atatürk even adopted the bizarre Sun Language Theory, which claimed that of all languages Turkish was closest to the sounds made by primitive man. This meant Turkish was the root of all other languages, and the theory's advocates delighted in finding Turkish derivations for foreign words. One of the silliest examples is the river Amazon, which supposedly earned its name when a Turkish speaker exclaimed, *ama uzun* ('But it's so long!')

Fortunately, though, the reformers failed to achieve their rather sinister dream of a pure language. Today's Turkish is still full of Arabic and Persian words, and has added a new layer of French and English ones for a new generation of purists to worry about. They shouldn't worry too much. Turkish is spoken in various dialects by hundreds of millions of people, from the Balkans to western China, and is better placed than most languages to resist the dominance of English.

Directory

Further Reference

Books

Turkey has a vibrant literary scene, although you wouldn't know it from a browse around Waterstone's or Borders. Little has surfaced in translation. Ignoring the present, Western publishers seem fixated on Istanbul's imperial past – admittedly a source of the kind of stories any writer of fiction would find it hard to beat. Most titles here are available in Istanbul; try the **Pandora** or **Robinson Crusoe** bookshops (*see pages 158-9*).

Fiction

Ali, Tariq: *The Stone Woman*
Historical novel by the former Trotskyist activist in which the family of an Ottoman noble observes the decay of the empire. The third of his 'Islam Quartet'.
Christie, Agatha: *Murder on the Orient Express*
Christie fans rate it as one of her best, set on the famed train stuck in a snowdrift on the Turkish border with one of the passengers dead of multiple stab wounds.
de Souza, Daniel: *Under A Crescent Moon*
True-life tale of a guy banged up in Istanbul for drug smuggling. Comparisons with *Midnight Express* end there; this is thoughtful, even compassionate, and dedicated 'To the Turks, the most misunderstood people in the world'.
Greene, Graham: *Stamboul Train*
Lesser yarn about a bunch of characters crossing central Europe on the Orient Express. Greene's advance wouldn't pay for him to go beyond Cologne, so all the detail east was cribbed from Baedeker's.
Hikmet, Nazim: *Poems of Nazim Hikmet*
Currently undergoing a long-overdue bout of global recognition, Hikmet, a communist who died in exile in 1963, is considered the finest Turkish poet of the 20th century.
Kemal, Yashar: *Memed, My Hawk*
The book that established Kemal as Turkey's premier contemporary writer is a gritty insight into the kind of rural life only recently left behind by many Istanbulites.
Pamuk, Orha: *The New Life*
Turkey's other great literary sensation and an Istanbul bestseller,

Pamuk spins postmodernist tales that need unravelling. Try also *The White Castle* and *The Black Book*.
Unsworth, Barry: *The Rage of the Vulture*
Booker Prize-winner Unsworth once taught English in Istanbul and his precise geographical details enrich a complex political intrigue set as the 'vultures of Europe' circle the dying Ottoman empire.

History & politics

Freely, John: *Istanbul: The Imperial City*
Freely is Istanbul's premier English-language chronicler, with dozens of books on the subject . This is a dry, straightforward historical trawl, good on Byzantines and Ottomans, light on the Republic and after.
Goodwin, Jason: *Lords of the Horizons*
Portrait of the Ottoman empire covering all the pomp, madness and decadence in sometimes excruciatingly florid prose.
Hutchings, Roger & Rugman, Jonathan: *Atatürk's Children: Turkey and the Kurds*
One of the best books on an explosive national issue – the conflict in the country's South-east, a shadowland for a great many of Istanbul's youth.
Mango, Andrew: *Atatürk*
Latest in a long line of Atatürk bios benefits from earlier works, but adds a strong narrative drive that makes the book read almost like a novel.
Mansell, Philip: *Constantinople: City of the World's Desire*
Grand discourse on the world of the Ottomans, thematically structured, but enough chronology to provide a good overview of the rise and long decline of the imperial capital.
Pope, Hugh & Nicole: *Turkey Unveiled*
Best available primer for a stay in Turkey – a balanced and detailed tour of the contemporary political and cultural landscape by two long-term Istanbul journalists.
Procopius: *The Secret History*
The first-century Byzantine historian wrote the official history of Justinian, then wrote what he really thought of the tyrannical emperor and his ex-prostitute wife in these scandalous and salacious diaries.
Rubin, Barry: *Istanbul Intrigues*
Subtitled 'A true-life Casablanca', this is history as a black-and-white classic with a screenplay of plots, counterplots and narrow escapes set in wartime Istanbul, a neutral city enmeshed in German, Italian and Allied intrigues. Sadly, out of print.

Art & architecture

Barillari, Diana & Godoli, Ezio: *Istanbul 1900: Art Nouveau Architecture and Interiors*
Gorgeous coffee-table book on a lesser-known aspect of Istanbul's urban heritage. Costs nearly £100 in English, half that in Turkish.
Beck, Christa & Fausting, Christiane: *Istanbul: An Architectural Guide*
Excellent little gazetteer of nearly 100 of the city's most significant buildings. Obvious candidates like Justinian and Sinan are in there, but the focus is on more obscure 19th- and 20th-century contributions.
Hellier, Chris & Venturi, Franscesco: *Splendours of Istanbul: Houses and Palaces along the Bosphorus*
Glossy photos of the interiors of impossibly lavish waterside mansions you'll never see the inside of any other way. Good text, too.
Hull, Alastair & Luczyc-Wyhowska, Jose: *Kilims: The Complete Guide*
Lavish but practical large format paperback; not the sort of thing to consult at the bazaar, but a definite good read before and after.
Sozen, Metin: *The Evolution of Turkish Art and Architecture*
A bit academic with some stodgy language, but a profusely illustrated good primary work.

Travel

Goodwin, Jason: *On Foot to the Golden Horn: A Walk to Istanbul*
Istanbul only makes a cameo right at the end of the book, the bulk of which deals with the author's walk from Poland following the path of a Byzantine pilgrim. Fascinating on Ottoman influence in the Balkans.
Kelly, Laurence (ed): *Istanbul: A Traveller's Companion*
A mass of historical writings and travellers' tales (largely 18th- and 19th-century) covering places, people, court life and social diversions. Lacks context but fun nonetheless.
Montagu, Mary Wortley: *Turkish Embassy Letters*
London socialite Lady Montagu was a diplomatic wife in Istanbul from 1716-8 and an amusing correspondent equally at home with court politics and harem gossip.
Seal, Jeremy: *A Fez of the Heart*
A cone-shaped hat as the key to understanding modern Turkey? Why not? Certainly the most fun read on the country.

Film

Istanbul has yet to be properly immortalised on celluloid for an international audience as Berlin has been by Wim Wenders, Rome by Fellini or New York by Woody Allen. Instead, it's been limited to a few brief cameos, employed to add a dash of Oriental spice to some otherwise bland cinematic fare. For Turkish films *see page 187*.

Journey to Fear (*Norman Foster, 1942*)
Wonderful murky World War II spy thriller written by, produced by and starring Orson Welles. As intelligence officer Colonel Haki he gets to deliver lines in Turkish. The lead is Joseph Cotton who paired again with Welles seven years later for *The Third Man*. Though much less known, this is every bit as good.
Istanbul (*Joseph Pevney, 1957*)
Suspected diamond smuggler (Errol Flynn), returns to Istanbul to find his old flame, who he thought dead, still alive. Nat King Cole cameos with 'When I Fall in Love'.
From Russia with Love (*Terence Young, 1962*)
'He seems fit enough. Have him report to me in Istanbul in 24 hours.' Lotte Lenya as Rosa Klebb in the best Bond movie of all. 007 casually dispatches East Bloc assailants in a variety of popular tourist spots and gets to shag two wrestling Gypsies.
America, America (*Elia Kazan, 1963*)
Autobiographical film (Kazan was born in Istanbul) picturing the working-class neighbourhoods of Istanbul through the eyes of the director's uncle as he journeys from Anatolia to the New World.
Topkapi (*Jules Dassin, 1964*)
Caper movie in which a small-time con-man (Peter Ustinov) gets mixed up in a bigtime jewellery heist. Good fun, and Istanbul looks stunning. Supposedly the inspiration for *Mission Impossible*.
Murder on the Orient Express (*Sidney Lumet, 1974*)
Albert Finney, Lauren Bacall, Ingrid Bergman, Sean Connery and John Gielgud ham it up something rotten.
Pascali's Island (*James Dearden, 1988*)
British film based on a novel by Barry Unsworth in which Pascali (Ben Kingsley) is a spy for the Ottoman sultanate. Shot solely in Greece, but has a good feel for the period. Charles Dance and Helen Mirren raise the quality level.

The World Is Not Enough (*Michael Apted, 1999*)
Bond is back. In Istanbul. Except he wasn't. Brosnan and co stayed away because of PKK activity. The scenes where he swims in the Bosphorus against distinctive spiky mosque backdrops were all computer-matted.

Music

Rock and pop releases are on local labels and are unlikely to be available outside of Turkey. Traditional Turkish releases may find their way into the World Music sections of larger and specialist stores in major western cities. One of the best labels with the widest selection of recordings is **Kalan Music**, which has a superb sales website (www.kalan.com) with RealPlayer sound downloads. Also good is the roots label **Traditional Crossroads** (www.rootsworld.com), which is strong on Turkey and the Middle East. New label Golden Horn, based in California, is getting together a decent catalogue of Turkish traditional and Turkish jazz. Their website (www.goldenhorn.com) acts as a discussion forum as well as selling their CDs. For background on Turkish music *see pages 212*; for places to buy CDs and tapes in Istanbul *see page 175*.

Fasıl

For such a popular genre there's surprisingly little out on the market. Two names to ask for are **Müzeyyen Senar** and **Zeki Müren**. Generally, the older the recording, the better. Also look for reissues of recordings by **Hamiyet Yüceses** and **Safiye Ayla**, who epitomise the nostalgic feel many contemporary fasıl artists strive for. In recent years a young singer, **Muazzez Ersoy**, has built a following on interpretations of old standards and film songs, and her CDs are easy to find.

Folk music

Bosphorus *Balkan Dusleri* (Ada Muzik)
Turkish classical musicians revive Istanbul Greek repertoire with funk influenced bass clarinet.
Ali Ekber Çiçek *Klasikleri* (Mega Müzik)
One of the most respected exponents of the saz, whose deceptively simple sound comes both from the heart and from mastery of the instrument.
Mehmet Erenler *Mehmet Erenler ve Bozlakları* (Folk Müzik Center)
One of the few non-Alevi saz players to make an impact, anything you can find by Erenler is worth picking up; this is his most recent recording.
Neşet Ertaş (Kalan)
Now living in Germany, Ertaş is a hugely influential musician and a cult figure on the Turkish folk music scene. The Kalan label has issued an eight-CD series of his stuff.
Fuat Saka *Lazutlar II* (Kalan)
Multi-ethnic mix of Black Sea folks (Laz, Turk, Greek and Georgian) meld hyperkinetic kemanche music into melodious jazz/pop.
Muhabbet *Volumes 1-7* (Kalan)
Fantastic aşık – Alevi songs of mystical quest – performed by top names such as Arif Sağ, Yavuz Top and Musa Eroğlu.

Ottoman, classical & court music

Erol Deran *Solo Kanun* (Mega)
A welcome re-release, this is what Turkish classical music should be: introspective, subtle and virtuosic.
Emirgan Assemble *Klasik Osmanlı Müziği* (Kalan)
Ottoman-period instrumental works, some quite lively, featuring kemençe, ud, kanun, ney and percussion. Good introduction to the genre.
Kani Karaca *Kani Karaca* (Kalan)
He's a hafız, someone who can recite the Koran from memory. His voice has the power to cause goosebumps and he's something of a living national treasure.
Münip Utandı *Münip Utandı* (Kalan)
Fine singer whose repertoire straddles both Ottoman and later periods. Tasteful performer with a classical sensibility.
Various *Gazeller 1&2* (Kalan)
Amazing archival recordings of traditional vocal improvisations, rescued from ancient 78rpm vinyl.
Various *Lalezar* (Istanbul Büyük Belediye)
Four-CD set featuring different aspects of the Ottoman musical world, including compositions by sultans and a suite of Köçek – imperial dance music.

Directory

Rock & pop

Istanbul Blues Kumpanyası *Şair Zamanlar* (Doublemoon)
Quirky, high-spirited Turkish take on various rock styles. Popular with both Istanbul expats and Turkish hipsters.
Cem Karaca *Best of* (Yavuz ve Burç Plakçilik)
Turkey's answer to Scott Walker has been around since the 1960s. This provides a good overview of a brilliant musical career.
Erkin Koray *Şaşkın* (Kalite Ticaret)
Great introduction to the legend of Turkish psychedelia and key member of the Anatolian rock scene.
Barış Manco *Mançoloği* (Stereo)
Former leading proponent of Anatolian rock turned TV celeb whose recent death inspired a general resurgence of interest in old Turkish rockers.
Moğollar *Moğollar* (Emre Muzik)
Released in 2000, this is a long overdue collection of tracks from the seminal Anatolian prog-rock group that just won't go away.
Bulutsuzluk Özlemi *Yol* (Ada)
Not the soundtrack to the film, but back-to-basics, big-hearted, guitar-driven rock by a well respected trad-rock outfit.
Sultana *Çerkez Kızı* (Doublemoon)
Phat beats and New York attitude. Sultana proves that it is possible to rap in Turkish. (In case you'd ever wondered.)
Tarkan *Aacayipsin* (Istanbul Plak)
Love or hate him. Actually, just hate him. However, there are those would argue that this represents the hottest Turkish pop of the 1990s.
Zen *Zenistanbul* (Kodmuzik)
Dadaistic sound collages from the original oriental rock DIY experimenters who gave birth to Baba Zula (*see below*). Demanding and outlandish, but there are fans.
Baba Zula *Üç Oyundan Onyedi Müzik* (Doublemoon)
Sophisticated percussion, electric saz, wacky lyrics and studied sampladelia; these guys are the veteran avant savants of Istanbul. A must for anyone interested in Turkish art rock.

Roma (Gypsy)

Kemanı Cemal & others *Sulukule: Rom Music of Istanbul* (Traditional Crossroads)
An Istanbul district famed for its Roma musicians, Sulukule is also the closest the city has to a no-go area. Go for this exhilarating CD instead.
Ciguli *Ciguli* (Dost)
Accordion-led recording that was hugely popular when released in the late 1990s, catapulting Ahmet Ciguli from street musician to stardom.

Roman Oyun Havaları *Volumes 1 & 2* (EMI-Kent)
These two polished collections feature Istanbul's top Roma session musicians thumping out a selection of much-loved dance tunes.
Mustafa Kandırali *Caz Roman* (World Network)
The so-called 'Benny Goodman of Turkey', a wild Gypsy clarinettist who toured the US in the 1960s as a band leader. This recording also includes some of Turkey's other best-known fasıl musicians.
Selim Sesler & Grup Trakya *The Road to Keşan* (Traditional Crossroads)
Collection of songs and dances from Keşan, a town on the Turkish-Greek border and centre of a Roma musical community. Excellent sleeve notes.

Sufi-religious

Asitane *Simurg* (Istanbul Ajans)
Very good new recording by a young ensemble featuring tanbur, kemençe, ney and bendir (frame drum).
Doğan Ergin *Sufi Music of Turkey Vol 2* (Mega)
Taksim – improvisations – on the ney flute. Ephemeral and meditative.
Music of the Whirling Dervishes *Sufi Music of Turkey* (Mega)
Music to twirl by. Do try it at home.
Various *Mevlana Dede Efendi* (Kalan)
A recording made in 1963 featuring some of the finest performers of the genre, including Kani Karaca.

Websites

Atatürk.com
www.ataturk.com
Evangelistic site aiming both to educate the world about Atatürk and let it know what a bad lot the PKK are with gruesome photos to prove it.
Compagnie des Wagons-Lits
www.wagons-lits-paris.com
Founders of the original *Orient Express*. Historic photos, merchandise, notice of special train-related events and a stern warning to others to stop nicking the name.
Daughters of Atatürk
www.dofa.org
Not literally but spiritually. Devoted to the great Turk and Turkish women with a strange mixture of ideology and recipes. Sincere and fascinating.
Earthquake News
www.earthquakenews.com
Find out where the earth moves with global news and reviews of all the big shakers. Turkey features heavily.
Galatasaray SK
www.galatasaray.org.tr
Official club site with text in Turkish and English.

Galatasaray SK
www.nommaz.com
Fansite with club history, news and downloadable anthem.
The Grand Bazaar
www.kapali-carsi.com
Istanbul's bazaar online. Bizarre. Limited at present by the number of merchants who have web access. Also lacking a little in atmosphere. We suggest improving authenticity with a pop-up message every 30 seconds, 'Hello friend, wanna buy a carpet'.
Great Buildings Online
www.greatbuildings.com
Download then virtually explore a digital 3D model of the Haghia Sophia or investigate Sinan and his wonderful architectural creations.
HiTiT Turkey
www.hitit.co.uk
Subtitled 'An Alternative Guide'. Destination coverage is thin and text sophomoric but some interesting articles in the background section.
Istanbul Foundation for Culture & Arts
www.istfest.org
Information, programmes and ticket sales for Istanbul's international film, jazz, music and theatre festivals.
Istanbul City Guide
www.istanbulcityguide.com
Closest it gets locally in English to a *Time Out*-style service. Daily updated what's-on listings plus mini-features and news snippets.
Istanbul: The Guide
www.theguideistanbul.com
Online version of print magazine with tons of information plus what's on, the contents of the current issue and archived back issue highlights.
Municipality of Metropolitan Istanbul
www.ibb.gov.tr
Happy bulletins on how great things are going plus fascinating news items like 'the city council made 689 decisions during the 1999 period'.
Skylife
www.turkishairlines.com/skylife
Archive of back issues of Turkish Airlines' inflight magazine. Honestly, there's some good stuff in there.
Turkey: Crossroads of Civilisations
www.turkey.org
Beautifully designed with animated graphics and an encyclopedic amount of info on politics, business and culture. Put together by the Turkish embassy in Washington.
The Turkish Daily News
www.turkishdailynews.com
Livelier than its print counterpart with frontpage news, comment, business and sport.
Turkish Music Club
www.turkishmusic.com
Slick Amazon.com-style presentation devoted to selling Turkish music in its many forms. Also the place to purchase your Atatürk CD-ROM.

Directory

Index

Advertisers' Index

Please refer to the relevant pages for
addresses and telephone numbers.

Place of Interest and/or Entertainment	
Railway Station	
Park	
College/Hospital	
Pedestrian Streets	
Steps	
Area Name	**GALATA**
Church	✚
Mosque	☾★
Post Office	✉
Tram Stops	●

Maps

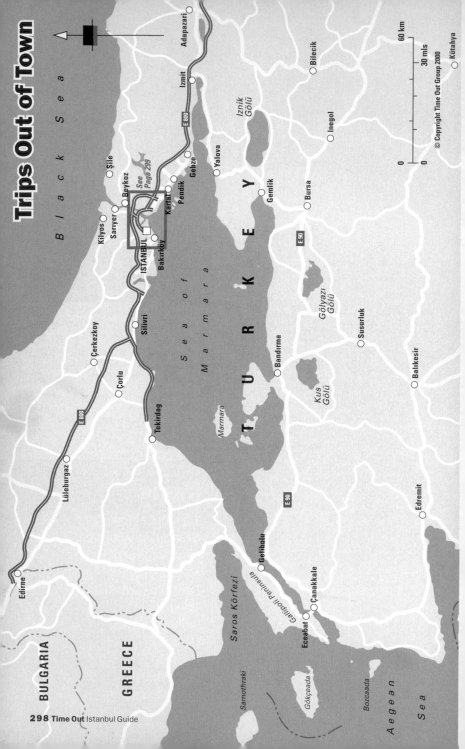

Trips Out of Town

Greater Istanbul

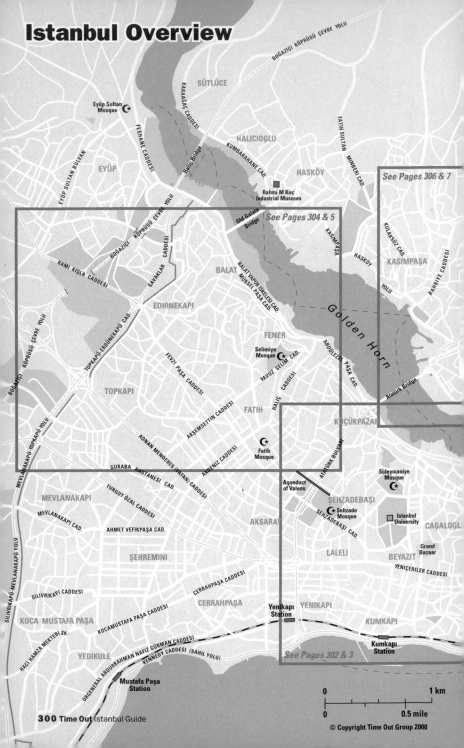

Istanbul Overview

SÜTLÜCE

BOĞAZİÇİ KÖPRÜSÜ ÇEVRE YOLU

KARAAĞAÇ CADDESİ

Eyüp Sultan
Mosque ☪

FESHANE CADDESİ

HALICIOĞLU

KUMBARAHANE CAD.

FATİH SULTAN

MİNBERİ CAD.

HASKÖY

EYÜP

EYÜP SULTAN BULVARI

Haliç Bridge

Rahmi M Koç
Industrial Museum ■

See Pages 306 & 7

KULAKSIZ CAD.

BOĞAZİÇİ KÖPRÜSÜ ÇEVRE YOLU

SAVAKLAR CADDESİ

Old Galata
Bridge

See Pages 304 & 5

KASIMPAŞA

KASİMPAŞA

BAHRİYE CADDESİ

RAMİ KIŞLA CADDESİ

BALAT

BALAT VAPUR İSKELESİ CAD.

MÜRSEL PAŞA CAD.

HASKÖY
YOLU

HASKÖY

EDİRNEKAPI

TOPKAPU-EDİRNEKAPU CAD.

FENER

Selimiye
Mosque ☪

YAVUZ SELİM CAD.

ABDÜLEZEL PAŞA CAD.

Golden Horn

BOĞAZİÇİ KÖPRÜSÜ ÇEVRE YOLU

FEVZİ PAŞA CADDESİ

HALİÇ CADDESİ

Atatürk Bridge

TOPKAPI

FATİH

AKŞEMSETTİN CADDESİ

KÜÇÜKPAZAR

MEVLANAKAPU-TOPKAPU YOLU

ADNAN MENDERES (VATAN) CADDESİ

AKDENİZ CADDESİ

Fatih
Mosque ☪

ATATÜRK BULVARI

Süleymaniye
Mosque ☪

GURABA HASTANESİ CAD.

Aqueduct
of Valens

ŞEHZADEBAŞI

MEVLANAKAPI

TURGUT ÖZAL CADDESİ

Şehzade
Mosque ☪

ŞEHZADEBAŞI CAD.

Istanbul
University ■

CAĞALOĞL

MEVLANAKAPI CAD.

AHMET VEFİKPAŞA CAD.

AKSARAY

ŞEHREMİNİ

LALELİ

BEYAZIT

Grand
Bazaar

SİLİVRİKAPI CADDESİ

CERRAHPAŞA CADDESİ

YENİÇERİLER CADDESİ

SİLİVRİKAPU-MEVLANAKAPU YOLU

CERRAHPAŞA

Yenikapı
Station ▦

YENİKAPI

KOCA MUSTAFA PAŞA

KOCAMUSTAFA PAŞA CADDESİ

KUMKAPI

HACI HAMZA MEKTEBİ SK.

Kumkapı
Station ▦

YEDİKULE

ORGENERAL ABDURRAHMAN NAFİZ GÜRMAN CADDESİ

KENNEDY CADDESİ (SAHİL YOLU)

See Pages 302 & 3

Mustafa Paşa
Station ▦

| 0 | | 1 km |
| 0 | | 0.5 mile |

300 Time Out Istanbul Guide

© Copyright Time Out Group 2000

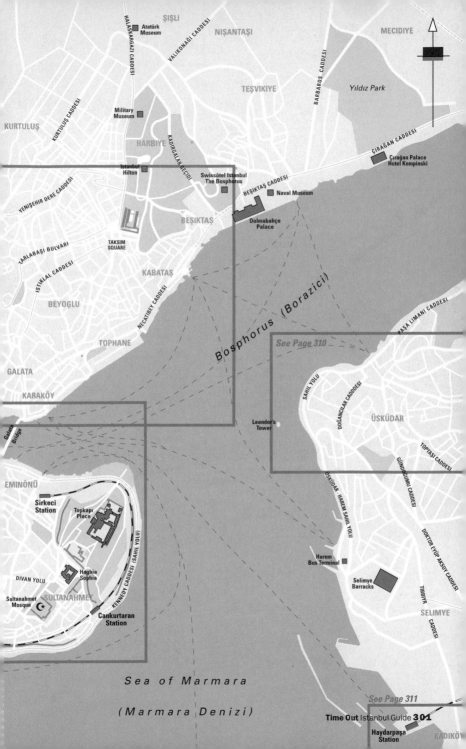

SİŞLİ

Atatürk
Museum

HALASKARGAZI CADDESİ

VALİKONAĞI CADDESİ

NİŞANTAŞI

MECİDİYE

BARBAROS CADDESİ

Yıldız Park

TEŞVİKİYE

Military
Museum

KADIRGALAR BEÇİDİ

HARBİYE

KURTULUŞ

KURTULUŞ CADDESİ

ÇIRAĞAN CADDESİ

Çırağan Palace
Hotel Kempinski

İstanbul
Hilton

Swissôtel Istanbul
The Bosphorus

BEŞİKTAŞ CADDESİ

Naval Museum

YENİŞEHİR DERE CADDESİ

BEŞİKTAŞ

Dolmabahçe
Palace

TARLABAŞI BULVARI

TAKSİM
SQUARE

İSTİKLAL CADDESİ

KABATAŞ

BEYOĞLU

NECATİBEY CADDESİ

Bosphorus (Borazici)

PAŞA LİMANI CADDESİ

TOPHANE

See Page 310

SAHİL YOLU

DOĞANCILAR CADDESİ

ÜSKÜDAR

GALATA

KARAKÖY

Galata
Bridge

Leander's
Tower

TOPTAŞI CADDESİ

GÜNDOĞUMU CADDESİ

EMİNÖNÜ

Sirkeci
Station

Topkapı
Place

ÜSKÜDAR - HAREM SAHİL YOLU

DOKTOR EYÜP AKSOY CADDESİ

KENNEDY CADDESİ (SAHİL YOLU)

Harem
Bus Terminal

DİVAN YOLU

Haghia
Sophia

Selimye
Barracks

SELİMYE

TIBBİYR CADDESİ

Sultanahmet
Mosque

SULTANAHMET

Cankurtaran
Station

Sea of Marmara

(Marmara Denizi)

See Page 311

Haydarpaşa
Station

KADIKÖY

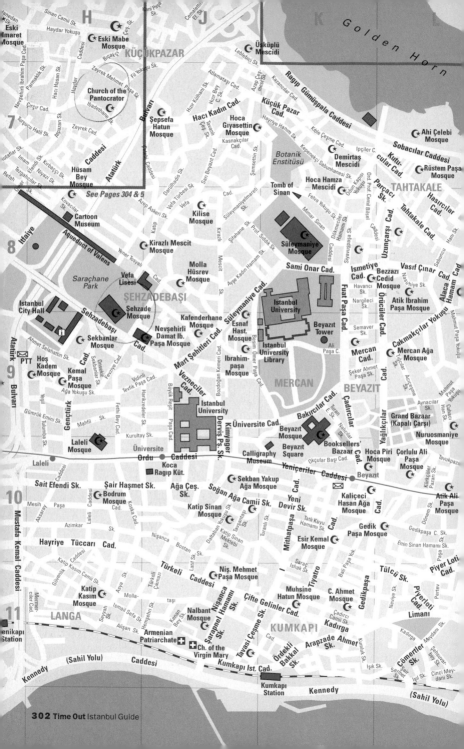

Golden Horn

H   **J**   **K**   **L**

Eski
Imaret
Mosque

★ Eski Mabe
Mosque

KÜÇÜKPAZAR

Sinan Camii Sk.
Haydar Yokuşu

Üsküplü
Mescidi

Ragıp Gümüşpala Caddesi

Leblebici Sk.

Atatürk Bulvarı

Church of the
Pantocrator

7

★ Şepsefa
Hatun
Mosque

Hacı Kadın Cad.

Küçük Pazar
Cad.

Hoca
Gıyasettin
Mosque

★ Ahi Çelebi
Mosque

Sobacılar Caddesi

★ Rüstem Paşa
Mosque

TAHTAKALE

Hüsam
Bey
Mosque

Atatürk   Caddesi

Botanik
Enstitüsü

Demirtaş
Mescidi

Hoca Hamza
Mescidi

Hasırcılar Cad.

Tahtakale Cad.

See Pages 304 & 5

Cartoon
Museum

★ Kilise
Mosque

Tomb of
Sinan

★ Süleymaniye
Mosque

Ismetiye
Cad.

Bezzazi
Cedid
Mosque

Vasıf Çınar

★ Kirazlı Mescit
Mosque

Sami Onar Cad.

Atik Ibrahim
Paşa Mosque

8 Itfaiye

Aqueduct of Valens

Molla
Hüsrev
Mosque

★ Süleymaniye Cad.

İstanbul
University

Çakmakçılar Yokuşu

Saraçhane
Park

Vefa
Lisesi

ŞEHZADEBAŞI

Kafenderhane
Mosque

Esnaf
Hast.
Mosque

Beyazıt
Tower

Mercan
Cad.

Mercan Ağa
Mosque

İstanbul
City Hall

★ Şehzade
Mosque

Şehzadebaşı

★ Nevşehirli
Damat İb.
Paşa Mosque

İstanbul
University
Library

MERCAN

BEYAZIT

9 ⓘ

PTT
Atatürk Bulvarı

★ Hoş
Kadem
Mosque

★ Sekbanlar
Mosque

★ Kemal
Paşa
Mosque

Mart Şehitleri Cad.

Vezneciler Cad.

İbrahim-
paşa
Mosque

Bakırcılar Cad.

Çadırcılar

Grand Bazaar
(Kapalı Çarşı)

Gençtürk

İstanbul
University

Üniverste Cad.

Beyazıt
Mosque

Beyazıt
Square

Nuruosmaniye
Mosque

★ Laleli
Mosque

Üniverste

Ordu Caddesi

Calligraphy
Museum

Booksellers'
Bazaar

Hoca Piri
Mosque

Çorlulu Ali
Paşa
Mosque

Laleli

Yeniçeriler   Caddesi

Beyazıt

Koca
Ragıp Küt.

10

Sait Efendi Sk.

Şair Haşmet Sk.

★ Bodrum
Mosque

Ağa Çeş.
Sk.

Soğan Ağa Camii Sk.

★ Sekban Yakup
Ağa Mosque

Yeni
Devir Sk.

Kaliçeci
Hasan Ağa
Mosque

★ Atik Ali
Paşa
Mosque

Mesih
Paşa

Katip Sinan
Mosque

Esir Kemal
Mosque

Gedik
Paşa Mosque

Piyer Loti
Cad.

Hayriye   Tüccarı   Cad.

Mustafa Kemal Caddesi

Türkeli
Caddesi

Niş. Mehmet
Paşa Mosque

Çifte Gelinler Cad.

Muhsine
Hatun Mosque

C. Ahmet
Mosque

Tülcü Sk.

Piyerloti
Cad.

★ Katip
Kasım
Mosque

KUMKAPI

Limanı

LANGA

Nalbant
Mosque

Nişanca
Sarapnel Hamamı Sk.

Armenian
Patriarchate

Kadırga

Arapzade Ahmet
Sk.

Cömertler
Sk.

11 enikapı
Station

✚ Ch. of the
Virgin Mary

Kumkapı İst. Cad.

Kennedy

(Sahil Yolu)   Caddesi

Kennedy

Kumkapı
Station

Kennedy

(Sahil Yolu)

Sultanahmet

See Pages 306 & 7

M
N
Θ
P

7

Yeraltı Mosque

✉ M

Rıhtım Caddesi

Karaköy Square

Karaköy-Haydarpaşa-Kadıköy
Eminönü-Beşiktaş
Karaköy-Bakırköy

Sirkeci-Harem (Araba Vapurları) (Ferry Boat)

İstanbul-Marmara-Akdeniz Hattı

Seraglio Point

Atatürk Statue

Bus Station

Bus Station

Eminönü Maydanı

Tahmis Cad.

Eminönü

Reşadiye Caddesi

Kennedy Caddesi

New Mosque

Meydan Sk.

Egyptian Market

Arpacılar Mosque

EMINÖNÜ

SIRKECI

8

Çiçek Pazarı Sk.

Bankacılar Sk.

Hamidiye Cad.

Mimar Kemalettin Cad.

Sirkeci

Sirkeci İstasyon Caddesi

Saka Sk.

Vakıf Cad.

S. Hamid Türbesi

Şehin Şah Pehlevi Cad.

Ankara Cad.

Sirkeci Station

Mehmet Sk. Hanı Sk.

İstasyon Arkası Sk.

Hoca

Aşir Efendi Cad.

Muradiye Cad.

Nöbethane Cad.

Hüdavendigar Cad.

Taya Hatun Sk.

Karaki Hüs. Çelebi Mosque

Gülhane Zoo

Gülhane Park

See Page 71

Goths Column

Aacuncu Sk.

Hani

Aşir Ef. Cad.

Ebussuut Cad.

İbni Kemal

Orhaniye Cad.

Gülhane

Tanzimat Museum

CAĞALOĞLU

Bab-ı-Ali Mosque

İstanbul Erek Lisesi

İstanbul Vilayet

Bab-ı-Ali

Tiled Kiosk

Topkapı Palace

9

Türkocağı Cad.

Ankara

Hükümet Konağı Sk.

Cağaloğlu Hamam

Alay Köşkü

Archaeology Museum

Topkapı Palace Ticket Office

Konstantin Suru

Kennedy (Sahil Yolu) Caddesi

Mahmut Paşa Mosque

Prof. K. İsmail Gürkan Cad.

Ağa Mosque

Alay Köşkü Cad.

Zeynep Sultan Mosque

Haghia Eirene

Nuruosmaniye Cad.

Molla Fenari Mosque

Yerebatan Cad.

Yerebatan Mosque

Çeşme Sk.

Soğukçeşme Sk.

Burnt Column

Çemberlitaş Hamam

Babıali Caddesi

SULTANAHMET

Çatal

Atemdar Cad.

Haghia Sophia

Imperial Gate

10

emberlitaş

Köprülü Meh. Paşa Mosque

Divan Yolu

Sultanahmet

İncili Çavuş Sk.

Yerebatan Sarayı

Babıhümayun Cad.

Fountain of Ahmet III

Peykhane Sk.

Binbirdirek Cistern

Klodfarer Cad.

Museum of Turkish & Islamic Art

Mimar

Sultanahment Square

Baths of Roxelana

Kabasakal Cad.

Four Seasons Hotel

Ishak Paşa Cad.

Cankurtaran Station

11

Katip Sinan Cad.

Üçler Sk.

Dizdariye Yok.

At Meydanı

Hippodrome

Tomb of Sultan Ahmet I

Sultanahmet Mosque

Vakfilar Carpet Museum

Dalbastı Sk.

Sokollu Mehmet Paşa Mosque

Şehit Çeş. Sk.

Örme Sütun

Tavukhane Sk.

Şifa Hamamı Sk.

Mosaic Museum

Sea of Marmara
(Marmara Denizi)

İzbekler Sk.

Kaleci Sk.

Nakilbent Sk.

Ayasofya Cad.

Nakilbent Mosque

400 m

400 yds

Küçük Haghia Sophia Mosque

Küçük

Aksakal Sk.

Aksakal Sk.

Oyuncu

© Copyright Time Out Group 2000

Caddesi

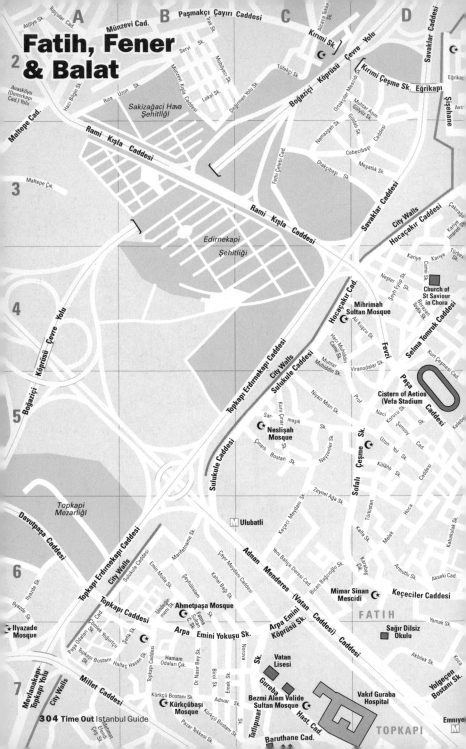

Fatih, Fener & Balat

2

A Topçular Cad. Atölye Sk. Münzevi Cad. B Paşmakçı Çayırı Caddesi Ntara Tekke C Kırımi Sk. D Savaklar Caddesi

Avasköyu (Demirkapı Cad.) Yolu

Servi Sk. Trak Sk. Boğaziçi Köprüsü Çevre Yolu Kırımi Çeşme Sk. Eğrikapı Şişehane

Hacı Bilgin Sk. Münzevi Kışla Sk. Mobilyacı Sk. Deİşmen Yolu Sk. Lokal Sk. Tülekçi Sk. Ortaçılar Mescidi Muhtar Asım Güya Sk. Gülali Sk.

Maltepe Cad.

Ruza Uzun Sk. Sakizağaci Hava Şehitliği Namazgah Sk. Cebecibaşı

3

Maltepe Çık. **Rami Kışla Caddesi** Fethi Çelebi Cad. Otakçıbaşı Sk. Meşatlık Sk.

Rami Kışla Caddesi **Savaklar Caddesi** City Walls Hocaçakır Caddesi

Edirnekapi Şehitliği Kariye İmaret Sk. Kariye Camii Sk. Kariye Kariye Türbes Sk.

4

Boğaziçi Köprüsü Çevre Yolu Neşter Sk. Seyh Eyüp Sk. Church of St Saviour in Chora

Hocaçakır Cad. **Mihrimah Sultan Mosque** Ali Kuşçu Sk. Bıçakçı Sk. Beşir Sk.

Hacı Muhiddin Camii Sk. Fevzi Selma Tomruk Caddesi

Muhtar Muhiddin Sk. Viranodalar Sk. Kürt Çeşmesi Cad. Paşa

Topkapı Erdırmekapı Caddesi City Walls **Sulukule Caddesi** Kuru Çınar Sk. Niyazi Mısrı Sk. Prof. Naci Cistern of Aetios (Vefa Stadium Caddesi

5

Boğaziçi Köprüsü Çevre Yolu Sar. maşık Sk. Korucu Sk. Şemsoy Uzun Yol Sk. Cad. Kalebe

Neslişah Mosque Çınarlı Bostan Sk. Neyzenler Sk. Sofalı Çeşme Sk. Külahlı Sk. Caddesi

Topkapi Mezarlığı Zeynel Ağa Sk. Türkistan Hoca Sk. Kabakulak Sk.

6

Davutpaşa Caddesi Keçeci Meydanı Sk. **M** Ulubatlı Melek Kalfa Sk.

İlyade Sk. **Topkapı Erdırmekapı Caddesi** City Walls Sulukule Caddesi Emin Molla Sk. Marifenname Sk. Çayır Meydanı Caddesi Kahal Bağı Sk. Yeni Bahçe Deresi Cad. Bican Bağcıoğlu Sk. Koralbaş Çık. Armutlu Sk. Akseki Cad.

İlyazide Sk. **Topkapı Caddesi** Şehpilüslam Sk. **Adnan Menderes (Vatan Caddesi)** **Mimar Sinan Mescidi** **Keçeciler Caddesi** Yamak Sk.

★ **İlyazade Mosque** Ündağlı-men Sk. **Ahmetpaşa Mosque** Fatma Sultan Camii Sk. **FATİH**

Paşa Odaları Sk. Çömlek Yoğurtçu Sk. **Arpa Emini Yokuşu Sk.** **Arpa Emini Köprüsü Sk.** **Sağır Dilsiz Okulu** Akbilek Sk. Koca

7

Mevlanakapı-Topkapı Yolu City Walls **Millet Caddesi** Topkapı Bostan Sk. Hallaç Hasan Sk. Hamam Odaları Çık. Dr. Nasır Bey Sk. Birol Sk. Emek Sk. Adıvar Sk. Norova Sk. **Vatan Lisesi** **Bezmi Alem Valide Sultan Mosque** **Vakıf Guraba Hospital** Yolgeçen Bostanı Sk.

Kürkçü Bostanı Sk. ★ **Kürkçübaşı Mosque** Kürkçü Bostan Sk. Pazar Tekkesi Sk. Mehmet Efendi Çeş Sk. **Gureba Sk.** Tatlıpınar Sk. **Baruthane Cad.** Hast. Cad. **TOPKAPI** Emniye **M**

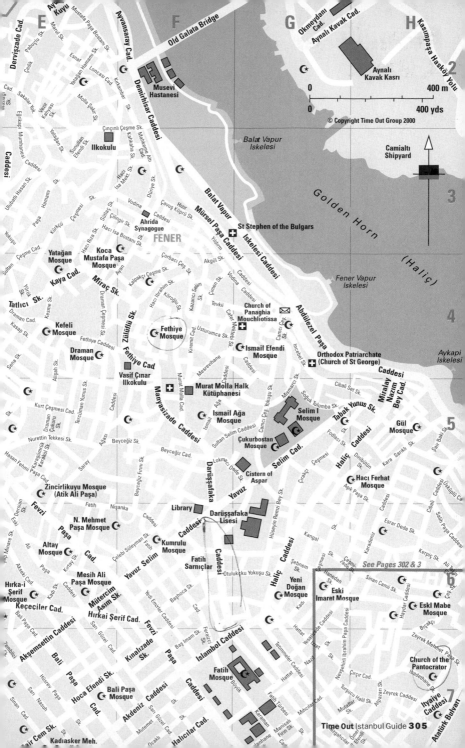

Beyoğlu

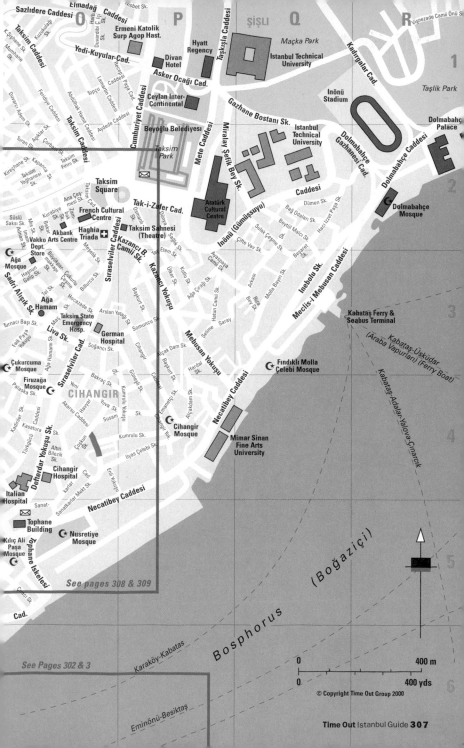

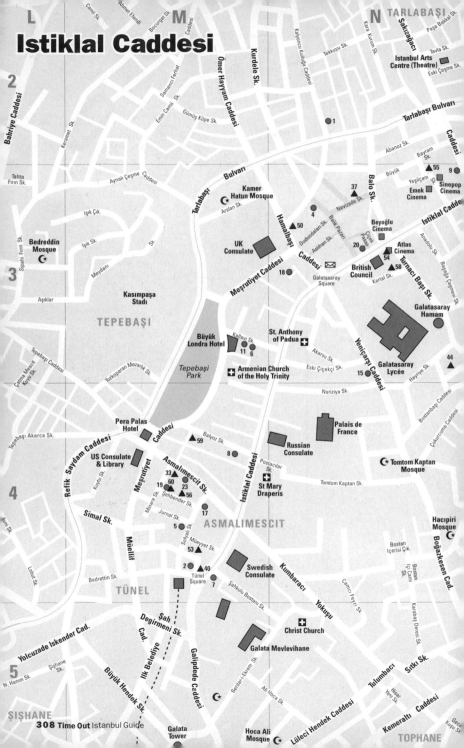

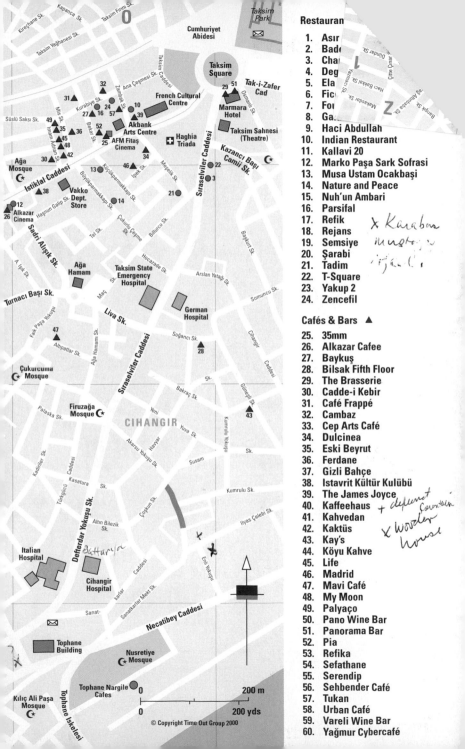

Restauran

1. Asır
2. Bade
3. Cha
4. Deg
5. Ela
6. Fic
7. Fo
8. Ga
9. Haci Abdullah
10. Indian Restaurant
11. Kallavi 20
12. Marko Paşa Sark Sofrasi
13. Musa Ustam Ocakbaşi
14. Nature and Peace
15. Nuh'un Ambari
16. Parsifal
17. Refik
18. Rejans
19. Semsiye
20. Şarabi
21. Tadim
22. T-Square
23. Yakup 2
24. Zencefil

Cafés & Bars ▲

25. 35mm
26. Alkazar Cafee
27. Baykuş
28. Bilsak Fifth Floor
29. The Brasserie
30. Cadde-i Kebir
31. Café Frappé
32. Cambaz
33. Cep Arts Café
34. Dulcinea
35. Eski Beyrut
36. Ferdane
37. Gizli Bahçe
38. Istavrit Kültür Kulübü
39. The James Joyce
40. Kaffeehaus
41. Kahvedan
42. Kaktüs
43. Kay's
44. Köyu Kahve
45. Life
46. Madrid
47. Mavi Café
48. My Moon
49. Palyaço
50. Pano Wine Bar
51. Panorama Bar
52. Pia
53. Refika
54. Sefathane
55. Serendip
56. Sehbender Café
57. Tukan
58. Urban Café
59. Vareli Wine Bar
60. Yağmur Cybercafé

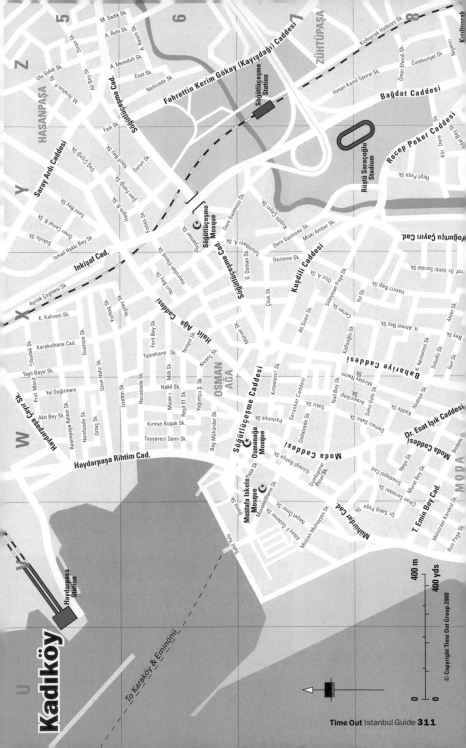

Kadıköy

5 / 6 / 7 / 8

Z

M. Sadık Sk.
A. Ruhi Sk.
A. Rasim Sk.
A. Memduh Sk.
Esat Sk.
Nebizade Sk.

Ulu Suluk Sk.
Ali Bey Sk.
M. İbrahim P.
Sınan Sk.

HASANPAŞA

Söğütlüçeşme Cad.

Fahrettin Kerim Gökay (Kayışdağı) Caddesi

ZÜHTÜPAŞA

Söğütlüçeşme Station

Kıvıtoprak Hatboyu Sk.
Ömer Efendi Sk.
Cumhuriyet Sk.
Kızıltoprak
Nişancı Sk.
Hasan Kamil Sporel Sk.

Bağdat Caddesi

Y

Saray Ardı Caddesi

Dağ Çiçeği Sk.
Nazif Bey Sk.
Şen Talip Sk.
Surun Sk.

Faik Sk.

Sami Bey Sk.
Ömer Cemal B. Sk.

Sokullu Sk.
İsmail Hakkı Bey Sk.

Haşim B. Sk.
Fıstıklı Sk.

Recep Peker Caddesi

Rüştü Saraçoğlu Stadium

Beşir Paşa Sk.
Kör Dere
Bağ Bey Sk.

Söğütlüçeşme Mosque

Dilpesler Sk.
Söğütlüçeşme Cad.
Dere Gazinosu Sk.
Miski Amber Sk.
Kuşdili Çayırı Sk.

Söğütlüçeşme Cad. A. Sk.
Tulumbacı A. Sk.
G. Osman Sk.
Gezinme Sk.

Dere Gazinosu Sk.

Oğurtçu Çayırı Cad.

İnkişaf Cad.

Haydullah Efendi Sk.
Nurr Bey Sk.

Ayrılık Çeşmesi Sk.

Kuşdili Caddesi

Çilek Sk.

Çenan Sk.
Otuz A. Sk.
Süleyman Paşa Sk.
Yol Sk.

Prof. Dr. Vehbi Sandal Sk.
Hasırcı Başı Sk.

X

K. Kahvesi Sk.

Yurtara Sk.
Keşler Sk.
Yeniyol Sk.

Halit Ağa Caddesi

Mürver Sk.

Ali Suavi Sk.

Kaftanoğlu Sk.
H. Ahmet Bey Sk.

Alter Sk.
Bey Sk.

Erbudak Sk.
Karakolhane Cad.
Taşlı Bayır Sk.
Prof. Macit

Duatepe Sk.
Ferit Bey Sk.
Talimhane Sk.

OSMAN AĞA

Kırtasiyeci Sk.

Bahariye Caddesi

Mısak-ı
Nakil Sk.
Milli Sk.

Serasker Caddesi
Nail Bey Sk.
Şakız Sk.

Sokullu Sk.
Nüshat Sk.
İlen Sk.

Yel Değirmeni
Uzun Hafız Sk.
İzzettin Sk.
Reşit Ef. Sk.
Yoğurtçu Ş. Sk.

Dellalzade Sk.

Arzıvebaşı Sk.
Miralay Nazım Sk.
Sakız Gülü Sk.
Damacı Sakız Sk.

Kadife Sk.

Akit Bey Sk.
Rasimpaşa Rihtım Sk.
Nemlizade Sk.
Ortaç Sk.
Recaizade Sk.

Kırmızı Kuşak Sk.
Tayyareci Sami Sk.

Baş Mühürdar Sk.

Söğütlüçeşme Caddesi

Osmanağa Mosque

Pavlonya Sk.

Moda Caddesi

Alege Sk.
Murat Bey Sk.

Dr. Esat Işık Caddesi

Moda Cad.
Bedem

Haydarpaşa Çayırı Sk.

Haydarpaşa Rihtim Cad.

Güneşli Bahçe Sk.

Dumpunar Pınar Sk.

Sıvastopol Cad.

MODA

Mustafa İskele Mosque

Sahil Yolu

Dilan Sk.

Muvakkahane Sk.
Neşet Ömer Sk.
Albay F. Özdemir Sk.

Cihan Serasker Sk.
Dr. Şakir Paşa

Mühürdar Cad.

Dumlupınar Pınar Sk.

Rıza Paşa Sk.

T. Emin Bey Cad.

Mühürdür Karako Sk.

Haydarpaşa Station

Kadıköy

To Karaköy & Eminönü

400 m
400 yds
0

© Copyright Time Out Group 2000

Street Index

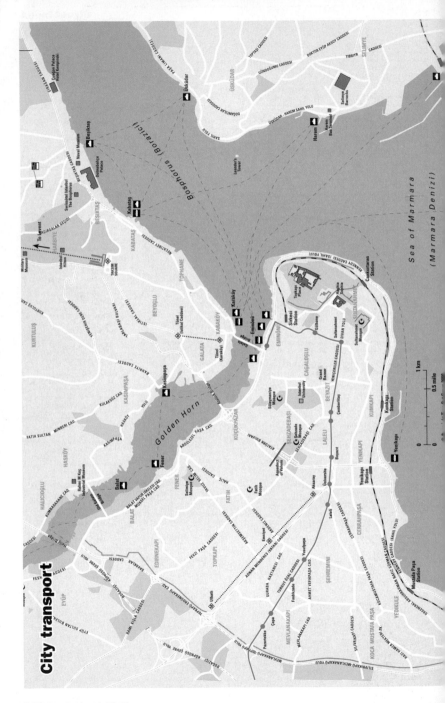

City transport